Lial/Miller/Greenwell

Instructor's Guide and Solution Manual
to accompany
Calculus with Applications, Fifth Edition,
and Calculus with Applications,
Brief Version, Fifth Edition

Prepared with the assistance of

Jane Brandsma
Suffolk County Community College

Kathleen Pellissiere

August Zarcone
College of DuPage

Richard Zylstra

📖 *HarperCollinsCollegePublishers*

Instructor's Guide and Solution Manual to accompany *Lial /Miller/Greenwell: CALCULUS WITH APPLICATIONS, FIFTH EDITION, and CALCULUS WITH APPLICATIONS, BRIEF VERSION FIFTH EDITION*

Copyright © 1993 by HarperCollins*CollegePublishers*

ISBN 0-673-55073-7

92 93 94 95 9 8 7 6 5 4 3 2 1

PREFACE

This book provides several resources for instructors using <u>Calculus</u> <u>with</u> <u>Applications</u>, fifth edition, by Margaret L. Lial, Charles D. Miller, and Raymond N. Greenwell.

- One open–response form and one multiple–choice form of a pretest are provided. These tests are an aid to instructors in identifying students who may need assistance.

- Test items are included for each chapter. These exercises are grouped by chapter and section and can be used as a source of problems for tests, quizzes, and additional practice.

- One open–response form and one multiple–choice form of a final examination are provided.

- Solutions for nearly all of the even–numbered exercises in the textbook are included. Solutions are not provided for exercises with open–response answers or for those that require the use of a computer.

- A list of the conceptual, writing, and challenging exercises that are in the textbook follows this preface.

- Hints for teaching <u>Calculus</u> <u>with</u> <u>Applications</u> are provided as a resource for faculty.

- A chart which correlates textbook topics with <u>The</u> <u>Electronic</u> <u>Spreadsheet</u> <u>and</u> <u>Elementary</u> <u>Calculus</u> (ISBN: 0–673–46595–0) by Samuel W. Spero is included for faculty who want to use the spreadsheet as a pedagogical tool. Your college bookstore either has this supplement or can order it for you.

The following people have made valuable contributions to the production of this <u>Instructor's</u> <u>Guide</u> <u>and</u> <u>Solution</u> <u>Manual</u>: Marjorie Seachrist, editor; Judy Martinez and Sheri Minkner, typists; Therese Brown and Charles Sullivan, artists; David Eldersveld, John Sullivan, and August Zarcone, answer checkers; and Carmen Eldersveld and Norma Foust, proofreaders.

List of Conceptual, Writing, and Challenging Exercises

SECTION	CONCEPTUAL	WRITING	CHALLENGING
1.1	87d, 88i, 88j, 89h, 89i	88k, 88l, 89f, 89j	
1.2	59-61, 65g, 65h	69c, 70c	55-61
1.4		26e	23, 39, 40
1.5	29b, 33d	29c, 50, 57	24, 33, 34
1.6	25-32, 33a, 33b	33b	33
Review		1-4	
2.1	9, 37, 38, 56e	7, 8	
2.2	19, 20d, 21d, 21e, 26d, 27d, 29c, 29d	18, 20e, 31e	
2.3	19-21, 36-39	49c, 50	38, 39, 47, 49, 50
2.4	22, 38	31, 39	
2.5	31, 32	36e	34
2.6	43, 44	15, 22, 46f	43, 44
Review	40, 41, 73	1, 2, 40, 41, 72, 83l	
3.1	29, 30		
3.4	47, 52	47c, 69	51
3.5	31-34		
Review		1-4	
4.1	43d	28b	28
4.2	2, 21, 22		9, 11
4.3	37		
Review		1-4, 19, 26, 27, 47c, 48	47, 48

SECTION	CONCEPTUAL	WRITING	CHALLENGING
5.1	17, 34-36	37	
5.2	25, 39-44	26	64, 65
5.3	13, 14, 16-18, 40d	13, 15	37
5.4	41, 42, 45c, 46d, 50c	25	
5.5	45, 46		
Review	89-91	1, 2, 83c, 85d, 86c, 87e, 88c, 91	
6.3	9b, 10b		
6.4	49-51, 55c, 58c		
Review	37	1-4, 56	
7.1		43c	
7.3			23
7.4			13, 14
7.5	39	40	37-40
Review	36, 47, 65e	1-4	
8.1	22		34-36
8.2		54b	
8.3	21-28	19, 20	
8.4		15, 16	
8.5	2, 7c, 13c, 14c, 17c	1-2, 17c	
8.7	39, 40	67	

SECTION	CONCEPTUAL	WRITING	CHALLENGING
9.1	33, 34		31, 32, 50
9.2	29		
9.3		25c	
Review		1-4, 29, 34, 47d	46
10.1	17	18-20	
10.2	9, 10	9, 10	
10.3		15-17	20
Review	1, 3, 12, 13	2	44
11.1			76b
11.2			34, 35
11.4		36	
Review	4, 42	1-3, 35, 89-91, 95c	

Hints for Teaching Calculus with Applications

Algebra Reference
Some instructors get best results by going through this chapter carefully at the beginning of the semester. Others find it better to refer to it as needed throughout the course. Use whichever method works best for your students. In this edition, we refer to the chapter as a "Reference" rather than a "Review," and the regular page numbers don't begin until Chapter 1. We hope this will make your students less anxious if you don't cover this material.

Chapter 1
Instructors sometimes go to either of two extremes in this chapter. Some feel that their students have already covered enough precalculus in high school or in previous courses, and consequently begin with Chapter 2. Unfortunately, if they are wrong, their students may do poorly. Other instructors spend at least half a semester on this chapter and the algebra reference chapter, and subsequently have little time for calculus. Such a course should not be labeled as calculus. We recommend trying to strike a balance, which may still not make all your students happy. A few may complain that the review of algebra, functions, and graphs is too quick; such students should be sent to a more basic course. Those students who are familiar with this material may become lazy and develop habits that will hurt them later in the course. You may wish to assign a few challenging exercises to keep these students on their toes.

Sec. 1.1
Much research recently has been devoted to students' misunderstandings of the function concept. Such misunderstandings are among the major impediments to learning calculus. We have no easy fix; unless sufficient time is devoted to this section, the results will become apparent later when students don't understand the derivative. One device that helps students distinguish $f(x + h)$ from $f(x) + h$ is to use a box in place of the letter x, as we do in this section just before discussing graphs.

Sec. 1.2
This section may seem fairly basic to students who covered linear functions in high school. Nevertheless, many students who have graphed hundreds of lines in their lifetime still lack a thorough understanding of slope, which hampers their understanding of the derivative. Such students could benefit from doing dozens of exercises similar to 15-18.

Perpendicular lines are not used in future chapters and could be skipped if you're in a hurry.

Sec. 1.3
This section is a continuation of ideas described in the previous section. Although you may be tempted to skip it, this section offers vital reinforcement on linear functions and word problems and introduces basic business and economic applications that are referred to throughout the text.

Sec. 1.4
This section has been revised from the previous edition, in which quadratic functions were graphed by completing the square. In this edition, completing the square has been moved to Sec. 1.6. Our experience is that students graph quadratics most easily by first finding the y-intercept, then finding the x-intercepts when they exist (using factoring or the quadratic formula), and finding the vertex last by locating the point midway between the x-intercepts or, if the quadratic formula was used, by letting $x = -b/(2a)$.

Quadratics are among a small group of functions that can be analyzed completely with ease, so they are used throughout the text. On the other hand, the advent of graphing calculators has made ease of graphing less important, so we rely on quadratics less than in previous editions.

Sec. 1.5
Graphing calculators have made point plotting of functions less important than before. Plotting points by hand should not be entirely neglected, however, because a small amount is helpful when using the derivative to graph functions.

The two main goals of this section are to have an understanding of what an n-th degree polynomial looks like, and to be able to find the asymptotes of a rational function. Students who master these ideas will be better prepared for the chapter on curve sketching.

Sec. 1.6

This new section on translations and reflections of functions has been added to give further help to students in curve sketching. Some instructors pressed for time may choose to skip this. But we have found that students who understand that the graph of $f(x) = 5 - 2e^{-3x}$ is essentially the same as the graph of $f(x) = e^x$, just moved and stretched a bit, will have an easier time when using the derivative to graph functions.

Before continuing with the next chapter, some instructors may wish to cover the first three sections of the chapter on exponentials and logarithms. We don't necessarily recommend this approach, but for those who prefer it, we reorganized the chapter on exponentials and logarithms to make it possible.

Sec. 2.1

This is the first section on calculus, and perhaps the most important, since limits are what really distinguish calculus from algebra. Students will have the best understanding of limits if they have studied them graphically (as in Exercises 1-6), numerically (as in Exercises 10-14), and analytically (as in Exercises 25-36).

In the previous edition, continuity was in the section with differentiability; now it is in this section on limits. The presentation flows more smoothly this way, and still covers the topics in sufficient depth for students at this level. To make room for continuity, limits at infinity were moved to a new section in the chapter on curve sketching.

Sec. 2.2

This section introduces the derivative, even though that term doesn't appear until the next section. In a class full of business and social science majors, an instructor may wish to place less emphasis on velocity, an approach more suited to physics majors. But we have found velocity to be the manifestation of the derivative that is most intuitive to all students, regardless of their major.

Sec. 2.3

Students who have learned differentiation formulas in high school usually want (and deserve) some explanation of why they need to learn to take derivatives using the definition. You might try explaining to your students that getting the right formula is not the only goal; there are calculators that can take derivatives. The most important thing for students to learn is the concept of the derivative, which they don't learn if they only memorize differentiation formulas.

One way to get students to focus on the concept of the derivative is to emphasize graphical differentiation, which we have covered briefly in Exercises 49 and 50. This is difficult for almost anyone to learn, because there are no formulas to rely on. A student must thoroughly understand what's going on to do anything.

After students have learned the differentiation formulas, they may forget about the definition of derivative. We have found that if we want them to use the definition on a test, it is important to say so clearly, or they will simply use the shortcut formulas.

Sec. 2.4

Students tend to learn these differentiation formulas fairly quickly. These and the formulas in the next section are included in a summary at the end of the chapter.

Sec. 2.5

The product and quotient rules are more difficult for students to keep straight than those of the previous section. People seem to remember these rules better if they use an incantation such as "The first times the derivative of the second, plus the second times the derivative of the first." Some instructors have argued that this formulation of the product rule doesn't generalize well to products of three or more functions, but that's not important at this level. Some instructors allow their students to bring cards with formulas to the tests. This does not eliminate the need for students to understand the use of the formulas, but it does eliminate the anxiety students may have about forgetting a key formula under the pressure of an exam.

Sec. 2.6

No matter how many times an instructor cries out to his or her students, "Remember the chain rule!", many will still forget this rule at some time later in the course. But if a few more students remember the rule because the instructor reminds them so often, such reminders are worthwhile.

Chapter 3

This chapter and the next were previously in a single chapter. With the addition of the new section on limits at infinity and curve sketching, this chapter seemed unbearably long, so it was split. Separating curve sketching from other applications of the derivative also seems to help students focus better on each separate application.

Sec. 3.1 and 3.2

If students have understood Chapter 2, then the connection between the derivative, increasing and decreasing functions, and relative extrema should be obvious, and these sections should go quickly and smoothly.

The instructions for the Computer/Graphing Calculator exercises in this chapter and the next are deliberately vague because the details depend upon what hardware and software the students use. Some reviewers wanted the instructions to be more specific and the calculator or computer examples more thoroughly integrated with the text, but this didn't seem possible without alienating those users who use different hardware or software or who skip the Computer/Graphing Calculator exercises entirely. One method we recommend for the exercises is the software Graph Explorer, which is available for both IBM and Macintosh computers at no cost to schools that adopt the text. The zoom feature allows the solution of any equation or the relative extrema of any function to be quickly found. Most graphing calculators have a similar feature.

Sec. 3.3

This section should not be conceptually difficult, but students need constant reminders to check the endpoints of an interval when finding the absolute maxima and minima.

Sec. 3.4

Students often confuse concave downward and upward with increasing and decreasing; carefully go over Figure 34 or the equivalent with your class.

Sec. 3.5

This section combines material on limits at infinity that was in the previous chapter in the last edition, and material on curve sketching that was previously in the section on the second derivative. Curve sketching is now dealt with more thoroughly, receiving the coverage it deserves. Graphing calculators have made this material less essential, but curve sketching is still one of the best ways to unify the various concepts introduced in this chapter.

Because this section is the culmination of many ideas, students often find it difficult and start to forget things they previously knew. For example, a student might state that a function is increasing on an interval and then draw it decreasing. The best solution seems to be lots of practice with immediate help and feedback from the instructor.

Sec. 4.1

This section is one of the high points of the course. Some of the best applications of calculus involve maxima and minima. One change in this section from the previous edition is that more problems have a maximum or minimum at the endpoint of an interval, so students cannot ignore checking endpoints.

Almost everyone finds this material difficult because most people are not skilled at word problems. Remind your students that if they ever wonder whether mathematics is of any use, this section will tell them.

Why are word problems so difficult? One theory is that word problems require the use of two different modes of thinking, which students are using simultaneously for the first time. People use words in daily life without difficulty, but when they study mathematics, they often turn off that part of their brain and begin thinking in a very formal, mechanical way. In word problems, both modes of thinking must be active. If and when the NCTM Standards become widely accepted in the schools, children will get more practice at an early age in such ways of thinking. Meanwhile, the steps for solving applied problems given in this book might make the process a little more straightforward, and hence achievable by the average student.

Sec. 4.2

This section continues the ideas of the previous one. In the last edition, all of the exercises on inventory involved applying Equation (3), and students found they could safely ignore the derivation. In this edition, we have added exercises in which we vary the assumptions, so Equation (3) does not necessarily apply. The point of this section should not be applying Equation (3), but how to apply calculus to solve problems of economic lot size and order quantity.

The material on elasticity can safely be skipped, but it is an important application that should interest students who have studied even a little economics.

Sec. 4.3

There are two main reasons for covering implicit differentiation. First, it reinforces the chain rule. Second, it is needed for doing related rate problems. If you skip related rates due to lack of time, it is not essential to cover implicit differentiation either.

Sec. 4.4

Related rate applications are less important than applied extrema problems, but they use some of the same skills in setting up word problems, and for that reason are worth covering. The best application exercises are under the heading "Physical Sciences," because those are the exercises where the student has no formula to begin with, but must construct one from the words. The geometrical formulas needed are kept to a minimum: the Pythagorean theorem, the area of a circle, the volume of a sphere, the volume of a cone, and the volume of a cylinder with a triangular cross section. Some instructors allow their students to use a card with such formulas on the exam.

Sec. 4.5

Differentials may safely be skipped by instructors in a hurry. You need not fear that this omission will hamper your students in the chapter on integration. The differentials used there are not the same as those used here, and the required techniques are easily picked up when integration by substitution is covered. The exception is for instructors who intend to cover Sec. 9.3 on Euler's Method, since differentials are used to motivate and derive that method.

Chapter 5

The material on exponential and logarithmic functions has been arranged so the first three sections require no knowledge of calculus, except that a limit is used in the definition of e. These sections can therefore be covered with the other functions in Chapter 1.

Previous editions of the text referred to tables of exponentials and logarithms in the back. Those tables are now gone; we assume the student has a calculator that can compute exponentials and logarithms. You may need to spend some time with individual students showing them how to use these functions on their calculators, since calculators vary greatly.

Sec. 5.1

Students typically have no problem with $f(x) = 2^x$, but the number e often remains a mystery. Like π, e is a transcendental number, but students have had years of schooling to get used to π. Have your students approximate e with a calculator, as the textbook does before the definition of e. The motivation using compound interest also seems to help them get a handle on this number.

Sec. 5.2

Logarithms are a very difficult topic for many students. It's easy to say that a logarithm is just an exponent, but the fact that it is the exponent to which one must raise the base to get the number whose logarithm we are calculating is a rather obtuse concept. Therefore, spend lots of time going over examples that can be done without a calculator, such as $\log_2 8$. Students will also tend to come up with many incorrect pseudoproperties of logarithms, similar in form to the properties of logarithms given in this section. Take as much time and patience as necessary in gently correcting the many errors students inevitably will make at first.

Even after receiving a thorough treatment of logarithms, some students will still be stumped when solving a problem such as Example 8. Some of these students can get the correct answer using trial-and-error. The instructor should take consolation in the fact that at least such a student understands exponentials better than the one who uses logarithms incorrectly to solve Example 8 and comes up with the nonsensical answer $t = -7.51$ without questioning whether this makes sense. Be sure to teach your students to question the reasonableness of their answers; this will help them catch their errors.

Sec. 5.3
This section gives students much needed practice with exponentials and logarithms, and the applications keep the students interested and motivated. Instructors should keep this in mind and not worry about having students memorize formulas such as the one for present value.

Sec. 5.4 and 5.5
In going through these sections, you may need to frequently refer back to the first two sections of the chapter, as well as to the rules of differentiation in the previous chapter.

Sec. 6.1
Students sometimes start to get differentiation and antidifferentiation confused when they reach this section. Some believe the antiderivative of x^{-2} is $(-1/3)x^{-3}$; after all, if n is -2, isn't $n + 1 = -3$? Carefully clarify this point.

Sec. 6.2
The main difficulty here is teaching students what to choose as u. The advice given before Example 3 should be helpful.

Sec. 6.3
Some instructors who are pressed for time go lightly over the topic of the area as the limit of the sum of rectangular areas. This is possible, but care should be taken that students don't lose track of what the definite integral represents. Also, a light treatment here lessens the excitement of the Fundamental Theorem of Calculus.

Sec. 6.4
The Fundamental Theorem of Calculus should be one of the high points of the course. Make a big deal about how the theorem unifies these two separate topics of area as a limit of sums and the antiderivative.

When using substitution on a definite integral, the text recommends changing the limits and the variable of integration. (See Example 4 and the Caution following.) Some instructors prefer instead to have their students solve an indefinite integral, and then to evaluate the integral using the limits on x. One advantage of this method is that students don't have to remember to change the limits. This method also has two disadvantages. The first is that it takes slightly longer, since it requires changing the integral to u and then back to x. Second, it prevents students at this stage from solving problems such as $\int_0^{1/2} x\sqrt{1 - 16x^4}\, dx$, which can be solved using the substitution $u = 4x^2$ and the fact that the integral $\int_0^1 \sqrt{1 - u^2}\, du$ represents the area of a quarter circle.

Sec. 6.5
This section gives more motivation to the topic of integration. Consumer's and producer's surplus are important, realistic applications. In this edition, we have downplayed sketching the curves that bound the area under consideration. Such sketches take time and are not necessary in solving these problems. But they clarify what is happening and make it possible to avoid memorizing formulas.

Sec. 7.1
Students usually find column integration simpler than integration by parts. We would have emphasized

column integration more in the text except that some reviewers criticized it as too mechanical. Actually, the method is no more mechanical than integration by parts; the two methods are equivalent. Column integration just makes organizing the details easier. At Hofstra University, students even use this method when neither the teacher nor the book discuss it. They find out about it from other students, and so it has become an underground method. Some instructors feel that students will lose any theoretical understanding of what they are doing if they use this method. Our experience is that almost no students at this level have a theoretical understanding of what integration by parts is about, but the better students can at least master the mechanics. With column integration, almost all of the students master the mechanics.

Sec. 7.2

The ubiquity of computers and programmable calculators has made numerical integration more important. Rather than computing a definite integral by an integration technique, one can just as easily enter the function into a calculator and press the integration key. This issue is discussed in the paragraph at the end of the section. Some instructors may choose to skip the previous section for this same reason.

Simpson's rule is the most accurate of the simple integration formulas. To achieve greater accuracy, a more complicated method must be used. This is why, unlike the trapezoidal rule, Simpson's rule is actually used by mathematicians and engineers.

Sec. 7.3 and 7.4

These two sections give more applications of integration. Coverage of either section is optional.

Sec. 7.5

Improper integration is not really an application of integration, but it makes further applications of integration possible.

Many mathematicians use shorthand notation such as the following: $\int_0^\infty e^{-x}\,dx = -e^{-x}\big|_0^\infty = 0-(-1) = 1$. For students at this level, it may be best to avoid the shorthand notation.

Sec. 8.1

The major difficulty students have with this section, and indeed with this entire chapter, is that they cannot visualize surfaces in 3-dimensional space, even though they live there. Fortunately, such visualization is not really necessary for doing the exercises in this chapter. A student who wants to explore what various surfaces look like can use any of the commercial or public domain computer programs available.

Sec. 8.2

Students who have mastered the differentiation techniques should have no difficulty with this section.

Sec. 8.3

This section corresponds to the section on applied extrema problems in the chapter on applications of the derivative, but with less emphasis on word problems.

Sec. 8.4

Lagrange multipliers are an important application of calculus to economics. In some colleges, the school of business is very insistent that the mathematics department cover this material.

Sec. 8.5

Many students have seen the least squares line in a statistics course, so the concept is not new. In their statistics course, they were probably just given the formulas for m and b; now they can see where these formulas come from. To be honest, we should mention that these formulas can also be derived without calculus, using the fact that the sum of the squares is a quadratic function of m and b.

You can easily come up with real data for test problems by looking in newspapers and magazines. We have more problems with real data in this section than anywhere else in the text. Instructors who read Exercise 15 may be disturbed; the data comes from a professor at Hofstra University, who concluded that at least one of these two widely-used tests was useless.

Sec. 8.6

This section corresponds to the section on differentials in the chapter on applications of the derivative. It is less important than the other sections in this chapter.

Sec. 8.7

Students who have trouble visualizing surfaces in 3-dimensional space are sometimes bothered by double integrals over variable regions. Instructors should assure such students that all they need to do is draw a good sketch of the region in the xy-plane, and not try to draw the volume in three dimensions.

Sec. 9.1

Differential equations of the form $dy/dx = f(x)$ are treated lightly in this section because they were already covered in the chapter on integration, although the terminology and notation was different then. Remind students that solving such differential equations is the same as antidifferentiation. The reduced treatment of this topic allows separable differential equations to be included in this section, resulting in more concise coverage of differential equations.

Sec. 9.2

If you get this far, your students have covered most of the techniques for solving first-order differential equations. You can find further techniques in differential equations texts, but most first-order equations that come up in real applications are either separable, linear, or not solvable by any exact method.

Sec. 9.3

This and Sec. 7.2 are the two most calculator/computer-intensive sections of the book. In practice, more accurate methods than Euler's method are almost always used, but Euler's method introduces students to a way of solving problems that would otherwise be beyond their grasp.

Sec. 9.4

This is a fun section of assorted applications, showing students that the techniques they have learned were not in vain. You can pick and choose those applications of greatest interest to yourself and your students. You can also supplement the text with applications from other sources, such as those published by the Consortium for Mathematics and Its Applications Project (COMAP).

Chapter 10

Probability is one of the best applications of calculus around. In fact, statistics instructors often feel the temptation to start discussing the definite integral even when their students know no calculus. This chapter is just a brief introduction, but it covers some of the most important concepts, such as mean, variance, standard deviation, expected value, and probability as the area under the curve. The third section covers three of the most important continuous probability distributions: uniform, exponential, and normal.

Chapter 11

This chapter is a brief introduction to trigonometry and its uses in calculus. Students who need a more thorough treatment of this subject would be better served by a calculus book designed for mathematics majors. In this edition, we have added more application exercises, making the chapter more consistent in flavor with the rest of the book. To keep the chapter from becoming too large, examples in the text similar to the new applied exercises have not been added. As a result, students may find some of these exercises challenging. Therefore, tread carefully through this chapter.

Correlation between Lial/Miller/Greenwell *Calculus with Applications*, Fifth Edition, and Samuel W. Spero *The Electronic Spreadsheet and Elementary Calculus*.

Lial/Miller/Greenwell	Spero
Ch. 1 Functions and Graphs	Part I
Ch. 2 The Derivative	Part II
Ch. 3 Curve Sketching	Part II
Ch. 4 Applications of the Derivative	Part II
Ch. 5 Exponential and Logarithmic Functions	Part II
Ch. 7 Further Techniques and Applications of Integration	Part III
Ch. 8 Multivariable Calculus	Part III
Ch. 9 Differential Equations	Part III
Ch. 10 Probability and Calculus	Part III

Chapters 9 and 10 are not included in the Brief Version of *Calculus with Applications*, Fifth Edition.

CONTENTS

PRETESTS
AND
ANSWERS

PRETEST, FORM A
FINITE MATHEMATICS

NAME_____

HOUR_____

Find the value of each of the following expressions.

1. $(.5)^3 \cdot (.2)^2$

1._____

2. $\sqrt{27\left(\frac{1}{3}\right)\left(1 + \frac{1}{3}\right)}$

2._____

3. $2000\left(1 - \frac{1}{2}\right)^4$

3._____

4. $\dfrac{8 \cdot 7 \cdot 6 \cdot 5 \cdot 4 \cdot 3 \cdot 2 \cdot 1}{4 \cdot 3 \cdot 2 \cdot 1}$

4._____

5. $\dfrac{.5(.7)}{.5(.7) + 2(.35)}$

5._____

6. Find the value of $\dfrac{3(a + 2b - 1)}{a(b + 1)}$ if $a = 6$ and $b = -2$.

6._____

Solve each of the following equations.

7. $\frac{5}{8}y = 30$

7._____

8. $6t - 13 = 21$

8._____

9. $3x - (4x + 8) = 25$

9._____

10. $4(2z - 3) + 5 = -2(z + 6)$

10._____

11. $.03x + .05(200 - x) = 9$

11._____

PRETEST, FORM A, PAGE 2

12. Solve the equation 4x − 5y = 8 for y.

12. _____

13. Find the point where the line
    6x − 5y = 10 crosses the x-axis.

13. _____

14. Suppose C = 35x − 250. Find x when
    C is 450.

14. _____

15. A coat that sells for $125 is put on
    sale for $80. Find the percent of
    markdown.

15. _____

16. 66 is 120% of what number?

16. _____

17. Margaret can travel 216 mi on 9 gal
    of gas. How many gallons will she
    need to travel 336 mi?

17. _____

18. Solve the inequality −5x + 6 > 41.

18. _____

19. Graph the equation 5x − 2y = 10.

19.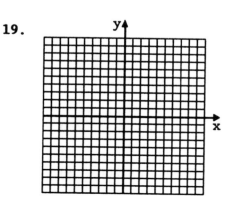

20. Find the slope of the line through $(4, 7)$ and $(-3, 5)$.

20. _____

21. Write an equation in the form $ax + by = c$ for the line through $(2, -3)$ and $(5, 6)$.

21. _____

22. Solve the following system of equations.
$$3x + 4y = 14$$
$$-2x + 5y = 29$$

22. _____

23. Which of the following describes the graph of the equation $x = -4$?

    (a) A line with slope -4

    (b) A line with slope 4

    (c) A horizontal line

    (d) A vertical line

23. _____

24. Find the slope of the line with equation $4x - 5y = 10$.

24. _____

25. Graph the inequality $3x + 5y \geq 15$.

25.

4

NAME_____

HOUR_____

Choose the best answer.

Find the value of each of the following expressions.

1. $(.3)^2 \cdot (.7)^1$

    (a) 2.1   (b) .63   (c) .21   (d) .063   1. _____

2. $\sqrt{16\left(\frac{1}{2}\right)\left(1 - \frac{1}{2}\right)}$

    (a) 8   (b) 4   (c) 2   (d) $4\sqrt{2}$ 2. _____

3. $4000\left(1 + \frac{1}{2}\right)^3$

    (a) 13,500   (b) 9000   (c) 6000   (d) 3000   3. _____

4. $\dfrac{9 \cdot 8 \cdot 7 \cdot 6 \cdot 5 \cdot 4 \cdot 3 \cdot 2 \cdot 1}{5 \cdot 4 \cdot 3 \cdot 2 \cdot 1}$

    (a) 9876   (b) 6789   (c) 3024   (d) 120   4. _____

5. $\dfrac{.6(.3)}{.6(.3) + .4(.9)}$

    (a) 2   (b) $\frac{1}{2}$ (c) $\frac{1}{3}$ (d) .54   5. _____

6. Find the value of $\dfrac{2(a + 1 - b)}{a(a + 1)}$ if $a = 10$ and $b = 5$.

    (a) 1   (b) $\frac{6}{55}$ (c) $\frac{1}{11}$ (d) $-\frac{4}{15}$ 6. _____

PRETEST, FORM B, PAGE 2

Solve each of the following equations.

7. $\frac{3}{5}x = 6$

    (a) 10   (b) $\frac{18}{5}$ (c) $\frac{5}{3}$ (d) $\frac{1}{10}$ 7. _____

8. $8x - 3 = 15$

    (a) $\frac{4}{9}$ (b) $\frac{9}{4}$ (c) $\frac{3}{2}$ (d) $-\frac{9}{4}$ 8. _____

9. $2x - (3x + 7) = 18$

    (a) 11   (b) -11 (c) 25   (d) -25 9. _____

10. $-2(k - 1) + 8 = -2(k + 3)$

    (a) 4   (b) 10   (c) -6 (d) No solution   10. _____

11. $.04x + .07(900 - x) = 51$

    (a) 4000   (b) 400   (c) 317   (d) 2083   11. _____

12. Solve the equation $3x + 6y = 7$ for y.

    (a) $y = -\frac{1}{2}x + 7$ (b) $y = \frac{1}{2}x + \frac{7}{6}$

    (c) $y = -2x + \frac{7}{3}$ (d) $y = -\frac{1}{2}x + \frac{7}{6}$ 12. _____

13. Find the point where the line 7x − 4y = 8 crosses the y-axis.

    (a) (0, 7)   (b) (0, 4)

    (c) (−2, 0)   (d) (0, −2)   13. _____

14. Suppose C = 20x + 500. Find x when C is 650.

    (a) 13,500   (b) 1150   (c) 7.5   (d) 3   14. _____

15. A boat that sells for $5000 is marked up to $8000. What is the percent increase?

    (a) 80%   (b) 60%   (c) 62.5%   (d) 37.5%   15. _____

16. 68 is 85% of what number?

    (a) 125   (b) 80   (c) 57.8   (d) 54.4   16. _____

17. Bob can travel 160 mi on 8 gal of gas. How many gallons will he need to travel 400 mi?

    (a) 80   (b) 30   (c) 20   (d) 16   17. _____

18. Solve the inequality −3x + 8 ≤ 32.

    (a) x ≥ −8   (b) x ≤ −8

    (c) x ≥ 8   (d) x ≤ 8   18. _____

19. Graph the equation 4x − 3y = 12.   19. _____

(a)   (b)   (c)   (d)

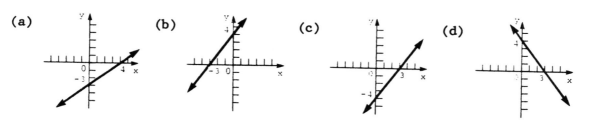

20. Find the slope of the line through (3, 8) and (−2, 4).

    (a) 6   (b) $\frac{5}{4}$ (c) $\frac{4}{5}$ (d) $-\frac{4}{5}$ 20. _____

21. Write an equation in the form ax + by = c for the line through (5, 8) and (6, 4).

    (a) 4x − y = 12   (b) 4x + y = 12

    (c) x + 4y = 37   (d) 4x + y = 28   21. _____

22. Solve the following system of equations.

    $$x + 2y = 5$$
    $$x - 20 = 3y$$

    (a) (−50, 25)   (b) (11, −3)

    (c) (−5, 5)   (d) (5, −5)   22. _____

23. Which of the following describes the graph of the equation y = 7?

    (a) A vertical line   (b) A parabola

    (c) A line with slope 7   (d) A horizontal line   23. _____

24. Which of the following lines does *not* have slope 4?

    (a) y = 4x − 8   (b) 2y − 8x = 7

    (c) x = 4   (d) 4x − y = 19   24. _____

25. Graph the inequality 6x + 4y > 12.   25. _____

(a) 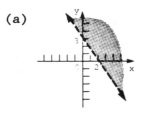   (b) 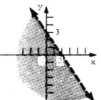   (c) 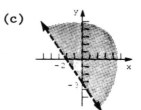   (d)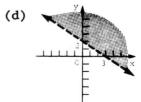

PRETEST FORM A

1. .005

2. $2\sqrt{3}$

3. 125

4. 1680

5. 1/3

6. −1/2

7. 48

8. 17/3

9. −33

10. −1/2

11. 50

12. $y = \frac{4}{5}x + \frac{8}{5}$

13. (5/3, 0)

14. 20

15. 36%

16. 55

17. 14

18. $x < -7$

19.
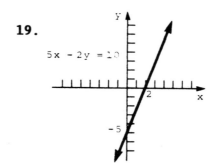

20. 2/7

21. $3x - y = 9$

22. (−2, 5)

23. (d)

24. 4/5

25.
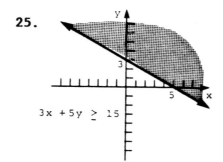

PRETEST, FORM B

1. (d)

2. (c)

3. (a)

4. (c)

5. (c)

6. (b)

7. (a)

8. (b)

9. (d)

10. (d)

11. (b)

12. (d)

13. (d)

14. (c)

15. (b)

16. (b)

17. (c)

18. (a)

19. (c)

20. (c)

21. (d)

22. (b)

23. (d)

24. (c)

25. (a)

TEST ITEMS

CHAPTER 1   FUNCTIONS AND GRAPHS

Section 1.1

List the ordered pairs obtained from each of the following if the domain of x for each exercise is {−3, −2, −1, 0, 1, 2, 3}. Give the range.

1. $y = 5x + 7$

2. $3x + 4y = 24$

3. $y = (x + 5)(x − 3)$

4. $2x − y = 5$

5. $y = (2x + 3)(x − 1)$

6. $y = (x + 1)(2x + 5)$

7. $y = 3 − x^2$

8. $y = 2x^2 + 5$

9. $y = -|x|$

10. $y = \dfrac{2}{x + 5}$

11. $y = \dfrac{-1}{x^2 - 5}$

12. $y = \dfrac{5 + x}{x - 5}$

13. $y = -5$

14. $2y + 1 = 0$

15. $y = |x - 1|$

16. Which of the following rules define y as a function of x?

(a)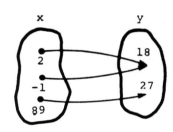

(b)

x	y
−3	0
2	7
2	15
1	−5

(c) $y = \sqrt{x - 2}$

(d) $|y| = x$

(e) $x = y^2$

17. Decide whether or not each graph represents a function.

(a)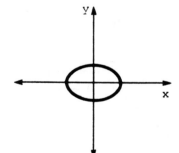

(b)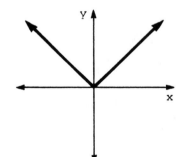

(c)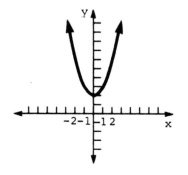

(d)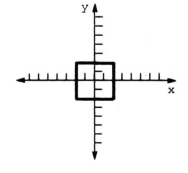

In each of the following exercises, find

      (a) f(5)   **(b)** f(0)   **(c)** f(-1/2)   **(d)** f(2a + 1).

18. $f(x) = 2x + 5$ 19. $f(x) = 4x - 3$

20. $f(x) = x^2 - 5x - 6$ 21. $f(x) = 9 - x - 4x^2$

22. $f(x) = \dfrac{2x + 5}{2x - 3}$ 23. $f(x) = \dfrac{5 - x}{6x - 1}$

24. $f(x) = (3x + 1)(x - 6)$ 25. $f(x) = 3$

In each of the following exercises, find

    (a) f(6)   **(b)** g(1)   **(c)** f(-4)   **(d)** g(-2)

    (e) f(-a)   **(f)** g(-2a)   **(g)** f(r - 2)   **(h)** g(r + 1)

    (i) f(3/y)   **(j)** g(-4/z)   **(k)** f(x + h)   **(l)** g(x + h)

    (m) $\dfrac{f(x + h) - f(x)}{h}$ **(n)** $\dfrac{g(x + h) - g(x)}{h}$.

26. Let $f(x) = 3x - 5$ and $g(x) = 2x^2 - 7x + 9$

27. Let $f(x) = 2x - 3$ and $g(x) = -x^2 - 3x + 10$

Give the domain and range of the functions graphed. Use interval notation.

28.

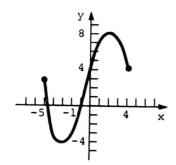

29.

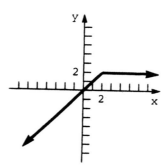

Give the domain of each of the following. Use interval notation.

30. $f(x) = \sqrt{x^2 - 36}$ 31. $f(x) = \sqrt{25 - x^2}$

32. $f(x) = \sqrt{\dfrac{3}{x^2 - 4x - 5}}$ 33. $f(x) = \dfrac{x}{x^2 - 9}$

34. $f(x) = |x + 4|$ 35. $f(x) = \dfrac{1}{x - 1}$

36. Rental of a compact car from one agency costs $24 per day or fraction of a day. Let C(x) represent the cost of renting the car for x days. Find each of the following.

    (a) C(1/2)   **(b)** C(3)   **(c)** C(2 1/2)   **(d)** C(1 5/24)

    (e) Give the range of C(x).

Section 1.2

Graph each of the following.

37. $y = -3$

38. $x - 2 = 0$

39. $y = x + 1$

40. $y = 2x - 4$

41. $2x + y = 6$

42. $3x - 2y = 12$

43. $2x + 3 = y$

44. $5y - 2x = 0$

45. $7x + 3y = 21$

46. $y = -10 + 5x$

47. $y = \frac{1}{2}x$

48. $2y = x - 2$

49. The line through $(1, -2)$, $m = 1/2$

50. The line through $(4, 0)$, $m = -2$

In Exercises 51–52, let p represent the price for a supply or demand, respectively, of q units. Find the supply and the demand when the price is

    (a) 5   **(b)** 10   **(c)** 15.

    (d) Graph both the supply and the demand functions on the same axes.

    (e) Find the equilibrium price.

    (f) Find the equilibrium quantity.

51. Let the supply and demand functions for a certain commodity be given by the following equations.

    Supply: $p = 3q + 2$ Demand: $p = 20 - \frac{3}{5}q$

52. Let the supply and demand functions for a certain commodity be given by the following equations.

    Supply: $p = \frac{7}{5}q - \frac{11}{5}$ Demand: $p = -\frac{3}{5}q + \frac{89}{5}$

53. For a particular product, 84 units will be supplied at a price of 7, while 54 units will be supplied at a price of 9. Write a supply function for this product.

In each of the following exercises, find the slope for each line that has a slope.

54. Through $(9, -6)$ and $(-3, 4)$

55. Through $(0, 8)$ and $(-2, 5)$

56. Through the origin and $(-11, -7)$

57. Through $(7.54, 2.38)$ and $(-1.12, 5.69)$

58. $2x - 5y = 15$

59. The y-axis

60. $x = 12$

61. $y = 1$

62. $y = 6x + 7$

63. $14x - 12y = 28$

64. The line parallel to $3x + 4y = 10$

65. The line perpendicular to $y = 4x - 1$

Find the slope of each of the lines shown.

66.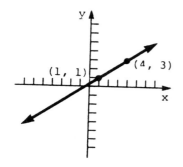

67.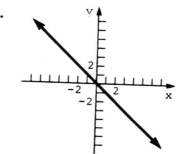

In each of the following exercises, write an equation in the form $ax + by = c$ for each line.

68. Through $(-2, 3)$, slope $5/6$

69. Through $(-5, 4)$, slope $-2/3$

70. Through $(6, 2)$, slope $1/2$

71. Through $(4, -1)$ and $(2, 7)$

72. Through $(1, -3)$ and $(-1, -2)$

73. Through $(2, 4)$ and $(0, 1)$

74. Through $(3, 0)$, undefined slope

75. Through $(1, 3)$, slope 0

76. Through $(3, 7/2)$, horizontal

77. Through $(-8, 6)$, vertical

78. x-intercept -2, y-intercept 2

79. x-intercept $-6/5$, y-intercept $3/2$

80. Through $(0, -4)$, parallel to $x - 3y = 7$

81. Through $(2, 3)$, parallel to $x + y = 6$

82. Through $(-3, -1)$, perpendicular to $3y + 5x = -4$

83. Through $(-1, 7)$, perpendicular to $-4x + 10y = 20$

84. Through $(6, 1)$, parallel to $x = 5$

85. Through $(-1, -5)$, parallel to $y = 6$

86. Through $(-4, -5)$, perpendicular to $2x = 4$

87. Through $(0, 3)$, perpendicular to $2y = 1$

88. Through $(2.728, -1.344)$, $m = 5.872$

89. Through $(0, 0)$, undefined slope

90. The x-axis

91. Through $(-4.035, 5.112)$, $m = -9.274$

Section 1.3

Assume that each situation can be expressed as a linear cost function, and write the appropriate cost function.

92. Fixed cost, $550; 11 units cost $770.

93. Fixed cost, $750; 50 items cost $5250.

94. Twenty-five units cost $1050; thirty units cost $1175.

95. Twenty units cost $260; fifty units cost $500.

96. Marginal cost $70; 150 items cost $15,700.

97. Marginal cost $55; 10 items cost $1200.

Solve each problem.

98. The cost of producing x units of a product is $C(x)$. The revenue from selling x units is $R(x)$, where

$$C(x) = 75x + 900$$

and $$R(x) = 150x.$$

   (a) Find the break-even point.

   (b) Find the average cost per item.

99. Suppose the number of restaurants in a particular fast-food chain satisfies the relationship

$$N(x) = 100x + 200,$$

where $N(x)$ represents the number of restaurants in the chain in year x, with $x = 0$ corresponding to 1990. Find the number of restaurants in each of the following years.

(a) 1991   **(b)** 1994   **(c)** 2000   **(d)** 1990

(e) Find the annual rate of change of the number of restaurants.

100. Management has determined that a reasonable function for the total cost of producing x items at plant A is

$$C(x) = 40,000 + 2.5x.$$

Find

(a) the total cost to produce 800 items

(b) the fixed cost of production

(c) the marginal cost

(d) the average cost per item to produce 1000 items.

101. The cost to produce x units of a certain item is

$$C(x) = 75x + 4000,$$

while the revenue is $R(x) = 125x$.

(a) Find the break-even point.

(b) If no more than 50 units can be sold, is it wise to produce? Why or why not?

Section 1.4

Graph each of the following parabolas. Give the vertex, axis, x-intercept(s) (if any), and y-intercept.

102. $y = x^2 + 2$ 103. $y = -x^2 - 4$

104. $y = x^2 - 6x + 10$ 105. $y = -3x^2 - 6x - 1$

106. $y = -\frac{1}{2}x^2 + 5x - \frac{13}{2}$ 107. $y = 2x^2 + 3x - 5$

108. $y = x^2 - 5x - 1$ 109. $y = -3x^2 - 15x - 9$

110. $y = \frac{1}{3}x^2 - \frac{1}{3}x + \frac{1}{4}$ 111. $y = \frac{3}{4}x^2 - \frac{3}{2}x - \frac{1}{4}$

Solve each problem.

112. Find two numbers whose sum is 50 and whose product is a maximum.

113. Mr. Smith wants to enclose a rectangular area for grazing. He has 100 ft of fencing available to fence off three sides and will use an existing fence for the fourth side. What should the dimensions be if the enclosed area is to be a maximum?

114. If an object is thrown upward with an initial velocity of 48 ft/sec, then its height after t seconds is given by

$$h = 48t - 16t^2.$$

   (a) Find the maximum height attained by the object.

   (b) Find the number of seconds it takes the object to hit the ground.

115. The demand for product A is given by

$$p = 400 - x,$$

where p is the price in dollars when x units are demanded.

   (a) Find the revenue R(x) that would be obtained at a price p.

   (b) What price will produce the maximum revenue?

   (c) What is the maximum revenue?

Section 1.5

Make an intelligent guess about the shape of each polynomial function. Then sketch the graph of the function by point plotting or by using a graphing calculator and compare the graph with what you expected it to look like.

116. $y = x^3 - 1$

117. $y = (x - 1)^3$

118. $y = x^3 + x^2 + x + 1$

119. $y = x^4 - 1$

120. $y = x^4 - 5x^3 + 5x^2 + 5x - 6$

Find the horizontal and vertical asymptotes of each of the rational functions in the following exercises. Graph each function, including any x- or y-intercepts.

121. $f(x) = \dfrac{5}{x + 1}$

122. $f(x) = \dfrac{3}{4x - 3}$

123. $f(x) = \dfrac{1}{2x - 5}$

124. $f(x) = \dfrac{2x - 3}{4x + 12}$

125. $f(x) = \dfrac{x + 1}{3 - 2x}$

126. $f(x) = \dfrac{4x}{(x + 3)(x - 3)}$

127. Suppose a cost—benefit model is given by

$$y = \frac{25x}{104 - x},$$

where y is the cost in thousands of dollars of removing x percent of a certain pollutant. Find the cost of removing each of the following percents of pollutants.

(a) 0%   (b) 20%   (c) 50%   (d) 95%   (e) 99%   (f) 100%

Section 1.6

Use the ideas of horizontal and vertical translations and reflections to graph the following. For Exercise 131, begin by completing the square.

128. $f(x) = -3x^3 + 1$

129. $f(x) = \sqrt{x - 5} - 2$

130. $f(x) = \dfrac{2}{x - 1}$

131. $f(x) = x^2 - 10x + 21$

CHAPTER 2   THE DERIVATIVE

Section 2.1

Find each of the following limits, if it exists.

1. $\lim\limits_{x \to 2} f(x)$

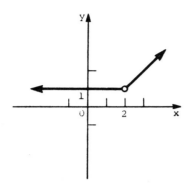

2. $\lim\limits_{x \to 2} f(x)$

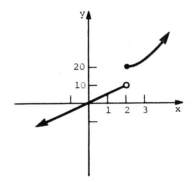

3. $\lim\limits_{x \to 1} f(x)$

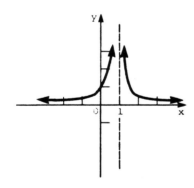

4. $\lim\limits_{x \to -2} f(x)$

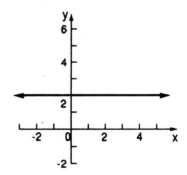

5. $\lim\limits_{x \to 1/2} f(x)$

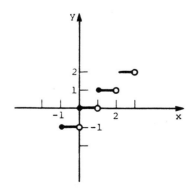

Complete the tables and use the results to find the indicated limits. Use a calculator.

6. If $f(x) = 3x^3 - 2x^2 + 7$, find $\lim_{x \to 1} f(x)$.

x	.9	.99	.999	1.001	1.01	1.1
f(x)						

7. If $h(x) = \dfrac{\sqrt{x} + 3}{x - 2}$, find $\lim_{x \to 2} f(x)$.

x	1.9	1.99	1.999	2.001	2.01	2.1
h(x)						

Let $\lim_{x \to 3} f(x) = 7$ and $\lim_{x \to 3} g(x) = -2$. Use the limit rules to find the following limits.

8. $\lim_{x \to 3} [-4 \cdot f(x)]$

9. $\lim_{x \to 3} \dfrac{[g(x)]^2}{f(x)}$

10. $\lim_{x \to 3} \left[\dfrac{2 \cdot g(x) - f(x)}{1 + f(x)} \right]$

Evaluate each limit that exists.

11. $\lim_{x \to 3} \dfrac{5x - 1}{2x + 1}$

12. $\lim_{x \to -2} (-x^2 + 5x - 1)$

13. $\lim_{x \to 3} (x + 1)^2 (2x + 3)$

14. $\lim_{x \to 3} \dfrac{x^2 - 9}{x + 3}$

15. $\lim_{x \to 5} \sqrt{x^2 - 16}$

16. $\lim_{x \to 3} \dfrac{x^2 - x - 6}{x + 2}$

17. $\lim_{x \to 1} \dfrac{x^2 + x + 1}{x - 1}$

18. $\lim_{x \to -2} \dfrac{x^2 - 4}{x + 2}$

19. $\lim_{x \to -5} \dfrac{x^2 - x - 30}{x + 5}$

20. $\lim_{x \to 2} \dfrac{x^2 + 2x - 8}{x^2 - 2x}$

21. $\lim_{x \to 0} \dfrac{\dfrac{1}{x + 4} - \dfrac{1}{4}}{x}$

Find all points x = a where the function is discontinuous. For each point of discontinuity, give f(a) and $\lim\limits_{x \to a} f(x)$.

22.

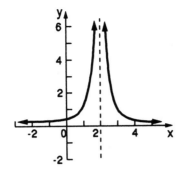

23.

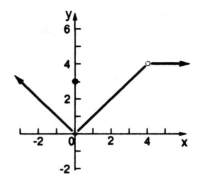

24.

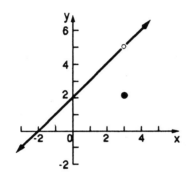

In the following exercises, is the function continuous at each of the given values of x?

25. $f(x) = \dfrac{3x + 1}{5x - 2}$ **(a)** x = -1/3   **(b)** x = 2/5   **(c)** x = 3

26. $g(x) = \dfrac{3}{x^2(x^2 - 4)}$ **(a)** x = 0   **(b)** x = -2   **(c)** x = 3

27. $h(x) = \dfrac{-1}{x^2 + 9}$ **(a)** x = 3   **(b)** x = -3   **(c)** x = 0

28. $f(x) = \dfrac{x^2 - 16}{x + 4}$ **(a)** x = 1   **(b)** x = 4   **(c)** x = -4

29. $f(x) = 3x^2 + 2x + 4$ **(a)** x = 0   **(b)** x = -1/2   **(c)** x = 2

30. $f(x) = \dfrac{4 - x}{x(2x - 1)(x + 1)}$ **(a)** x = 0   **(b)** x = 1/2   **(c)** x = -1
                 (d) x = 4

31. $f(x) = \dfrac{|x - 3|}{3 - x}$ **(a)** x = -3   **(b)** x = 0   **(c)** x = 3

32. A hotel in New Orleans charges guests $70 per day or portion of a day for a period of 1 to 4 days. The charge for days 5 through 9 is $65 per day. Let A(t) represent the average cost per day to stay at the hotel for t days, where $0 < t \leq 8$. Find the average cost for a stay of each of the following number of days.

   (a) 4   (b) 5   (c) 6

   (d) Find $\lim_{t \to 4^-} A(t)$.   (e) Find $\lim_{t \to 4^+} A(t)$.

   (f) Where is A discontinuous on the given interval?

Section 2.2

In each of the following exercises, find the average rate of change for the function on the given interval.

33. $y = 3x^2 + 2x + 5$ between $x = 1$ and $x = 3$

34. $y = -x^3 + x^2 - 5$ between $x = -1$ and $x = 4$

35. $y = \dfrac{2 - x}{x - 1}$ between $x = 5$ and $x = 8$ 36. $y = \dfrac{3}{2x + 5}$ between $x = 5$ and $x = 8$

Use the properties of limits to find the following limits.

37. $\lim_{h \to 0} \dfrac{s(5 + h) - s(5)}{h}$, if $s(t) = t^2 + 3t - 4$

38. $\lim_{h \to 0} \dfrac{s(3 + h) - s(3)}{h}$, if $s(t) = t^3 - t + 7$

39. Find the instantaneous rate of change for $f(x) = 9x - x^2$ at

   (a) $x = 3$ (b) $x = -2$.

Section 2.3

Use the definition of the derivative to find the derivative of each of the functions in the following exercises.

40. $f(x) = 3$ 41. $f(x) = 2x - 5$ 42. $f(x) = 4x - x^2$

43. $f(x) = x^3 + x^2 - 5$ 44. $f(x) = 2x^2 - x^3$ 45. $f(x) = \dfrac{1}{x - 2}$

46. $f(x) = 2\sqrt{x}$

Find **(a)** the slope and **(b)** the equation of the tangent line to each curve when x has the given value.

47. $f(x) = 4x - x^2$ (see Exercise 42) at $x = 1/2$

48. $f(x) = x^3 + x^2 - 5$ (see Exercise 43) at $x = -1$

49. $f(x) = 2x^2 - x^3$ (see Exercise 44) at $x = 0$

50. $f(x) = 2\sqrt{x}$ (see Exercise 46) at $x = 9$

Estimate the slope of the tangent line to each curve at the given point (x, y).

51.
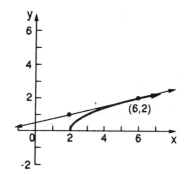

52.
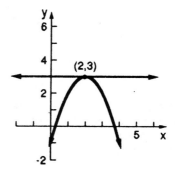

Find $f'(-2)$, $f'(0)$, and $f'(1/2)$ for each of the given functions.

53. $f(x) = -2$ **54.** $f(x) = 3x^2 - 4x + 2$ **55.** $f(x) = \dfrac{1}{x - 3}$

Find the x-values where the following do not have derivatives.

56.
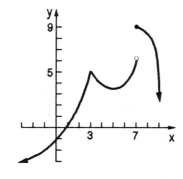

57.
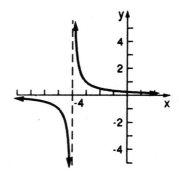

58.

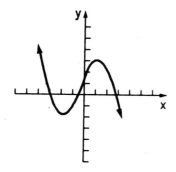

Solve each problem.

59. Suppose that the cost function is $C(x) = 4x^2 + 10x + 36$.

   (a) Find the marginal cost.

   (b) Find and interpret $C'(100)$.

   (c) Find the exact cost to produce the 101st item.

60. The management of the Better Widget Company has determined that each unit of widgets should be sold for \$20 and the cost of producing each unit of widgets is given by $C(x) = x - 8$ where x is the number of units of widgets produced.

   (a) Find the profit function.

   (b) Find the average change in profit when production goes from x = 3 to x = 5.

Section 2.4

In Exercises 61 and 62, find the slope of the tangent line to the curve at the given value of x. Then find the equation of the tangent line.

61. $y = 2x^2 + x - 3$ at $x = 2$

62. $y = 2 - 3x^2$ at $x = 1$

Find the derivatives in the following.

63. If $y = 10x^2 - 8x + 7$, find y'.

64. If $y = x^5 + 3x^4$, find $\frac{dy}{dx}$.

65. Find $\frac{d}{dx}(3x^{2/3})$.

66. Find $D_x(-2x^{-4})$.

67. If $f(x) = 2x^{-3} + \sqrt{x}$, find $f'(x)$.

68. If $f(x) = 3x^{-2} - 3\sqrt[3]{x}$, find $f'(x)$.

69. If $f(x) = -3x^{-1} + 2x^{1/2}$, find $f'(x)$.

70. If $y = \frac{1}{x} - 2x^2 + \sqrt{x}$, find $\frac{dy}{dx}$.

Solve each problem.

71. Suppose the profit in cents from selling x apples is given by
$$P(x) = 12x + 30x^2.$$
Find the marginal profit when

    (a) x = 5   **(b)** x = 10   **(c)** x = 20.

72. In Exercise 71, find the average profit function and the marginal average profit function.

73. If p is the price of x items, the demand function for this product is
$$p = 300 - .02x.$$
The cost of producing x items is
$$C = 250x + 10,000.$$
Find the marginal profit of production of each of the following number of units.

    (a) 100   **(b)** 1200   **(c)** 1250   **(d)** 1300

    (e) Interpret the results of **(a)**–**(d)**.

74. Given the position function
$$s(t) = -2t^3 + 6t^2 - 6t + 5,$$
find the velocity when

    (a) t = 0   **(b)** t = 1   **(c)** t = 5.

75. If an object is dropped from the top of a building that is 100 ft tall, its position (in feet above the ground) is given by
$$s(t) = -16t^2 + 100,$$
where t is the time in seconds since it was dropped.

    (a) What is its velocity 2 sec after being dropped?

    (b) When will it hit the ground?

    (c) What is its velocity upon impact?

76. A ball is thrown vertically with an initial velocity of 96 ft/sec. Its position (in feet above the ground) is given by
$$s(t) = -16t^2 + 96t.$$
What is the maximum height reached by the ball?

Section 2.5

In each of the following exercises, find the slope of the tangent line to the curve at the given value of x. Find the equation of the tangent line.

77. $y = \dfrac{2}{x - 4}$ at $x = 2$

78. $y = \dfrac{-2}{x^2 + 1}$ at $x = -1$

79. $y = (3x^2 - 1)(x^2 + 2)$ at $x = 3$

80. $y = \dfrac{3}{6 - x}$ at $x = 9$

Find the derivative of each of the functions in the following exercises.

81. $y = 8(4 - 3x)\sqrt{x}$

82. $y = (-4x + 3)(2x^3 - 5x)$

83. $g(t) = -2t^{2/3}(5t^2 - 8)$

84. $y = \dfrac{4x}{x - 1}$

85. $y = \dfrac{-3}{5 - 2x}$

86. $y = \dfrac{\sqrt{x} + 3}{2x + 3}$

87. $y = \dfrac{3x^2 - 2}{1 - x}$

88. $y = \dfrac{x^2 - x + 1}{x - 2}$

89. $y = \dfrac{x^3 - 3x}{x^2 - 4}$

90. $y = \dfrac{2 + x^{1/3}}{x^{1/3}}$

91. $y = \dfrac{1}{4x^2 - 4x + 1}$

Find each of the following.

92. $D_x\left(\dfrac{1 - \sqrt{x}}{1 + \sqrt{x}}\right)$

93. $D_x\left(\dfrac{x - \sqrt{x}}{x - 1}\right)$

94. $f'(2)$ if $f(x) = \left(x^2 - \dfrac{1}{x}\right)(x^2 + 2)$

95. $f'(4)$ if $f(x) = \sqrt{x}(2x^2 + 1)$

Solve each of the following.

96. The sales of a company are related to expenditures by
$$S(x) = 500 + 10\sqrt{x} + 5x$$
where $S(x)$ gives sales in millions of dollars when x thousand dollars are spent. Find dS/dx when

(a) $x = 9$ (b) $x = 25$ (c) $x = 36$.

97.   Suppose the profit in hundreds of dollars from selling x units of a product is given by P(x) where

$$P(x) = \frac{x^3}{x^2 + 2}.$$

Find the marginal profit when

   (a) x = 2   **(b)** x = 4   **(c)** x = 10.

98.   The "Round It Off" Widget Company has found that its profits are related to expense account expenditures by the function

$$P(x) = 4000 + 8x - 4x^2$$

Where P(x) is the profit when x hundred dollars are spent on expenses.

   (a) Find the marginal profit function.

   (b) At an expenditure of $200 (x = 2), is the profit increasing or decreasing?

   (c) For what expenditures does the marginal profit begin to decrease?

Section 2.6

Let $f(x) = 3x^2 - 4$ and $g(x) = 4x - 1$. Find each of the following.

   99. f[g(2)]   **100.** g[f(-1)]   **101.** f[g(0)]   **102.** g[f(3k)]

103.   If $f(x) = \frac{3}{x^3}$ and $g(x) = 3 - x$, find each of the following.

   (a) f[g(x)]   **(b)** g[f(x)]

In each of the following exercises, find the slope of the tangent line to the curve at the given value of x. Find the equation of the tangent line.

104. $y = \sqrt{6x - 3}$ at x = 2   **105.** $y = \sqrt{x + 5}$ at x = 4

Find the derivative of each of the functions in the following exercises.

106. $y = -2\sqrt{7 - 5x}$ **107.** $y = 2x(2x^2 + 1)^5$

108. $f(x) = (6x + 4)^4$ **109.** $y = \frac{-5}{(8x - 3)^2}$

110. $y = (2x + 5)^{25}$ **111.** $f(x) = \frac{5}{(6x - 5)^4}$

112. $y = (4 - 2x)^{1/2}$

113. $y = \left(\dfrac{1}{x^{-2} + 3x^{-1}}\right)^{10}$

114. $y = \dfrac{(3x - 5)^3}{(2x^2 + 1)^4}$

115. $y = \sqrt[3]{2x^3 + 1}\ (x^3 - 4)^2$

116. $f(x) = 3x\sqrt{x + 6}$

Find the indicated value of the derivative in each of the following exercises.

117. $f'(2)$ if $f(x) = \dfrac{\sqrt{2x - 1}}{1 - x}$

118. $f'(1)$ if $f(x) = \sqrt{2 - x}$

119. $f'(1)$ if $f(t) = \dfrac{2t + 5}{\sqrt{t - 1}}$

120. A certain boat depreciates in value according to the formula

$$V = \dfrac{10,000}{(.2t + 1)^2}$$

where t is the time (in years) since its purchase. At what rate is the value of the boat depreciating 1 yr after its purchase.

CHAPTER 3   CURVE SKETCHING

Section 3.1

Find the largest open intervals where the functions graphed as follows are increasing or decreasing.

1.
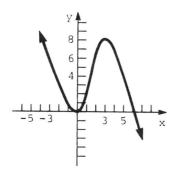

2.
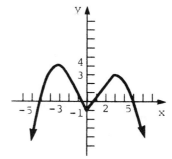

3.
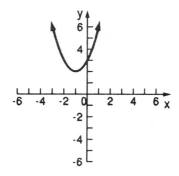

4.
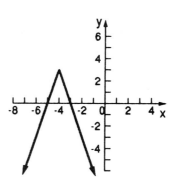

In each of the following exercises, find the largest open intervals where the function is increasing or decreasing.

5. $f(x) = -3x^2 + 18x + 4$

6. $f(x) = \frac{1}{3}x^3 + 3x^2 + 5x - 8$

7. $f(x) = -2x^3 + 7x^2 - 4x + 2$

8. $f(x) = \frac{x - 1}{x - 2}$

9. $f(x) = x + \frac{4}{x}$

10. $f(x) = \frac{4}{3x - 1}$

11. $f(x) = |x - 3|$

12. $f(x) = \sqrt{2 - x}$

13. $f(x) = \sqrt{4 + x^2}$

14. $f(x) = -(x - 2)^{2/5}$

Solve each problem.

15. The total cost to manufacture x units of a product is given by
$$C(x) = x^3 - 15x^2 + 72x + 300.$$
Over what interval(s) is the total cost increasing and over what interval(s) is the total cost decreasing?

16. Suppose that the total cost function is
$$C(x) = .002x^3 - 1.2x^2 + 24.0x + 400.$$
Over what interval(s) is the marginal cost increasing?

17. The concentration of a certain drug in the bloodstream t hr after being administered is given by
$$c(t) = \frac{10t}{16 + t^3}.$$
Find the open intervals of t in which the concentration is

(a) increasing   (b) decreasing.

Section 3.2

Find the locations and values of all relative extrema for the functions with graphs as follows.

18.

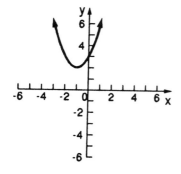

19.

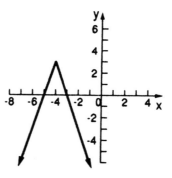

20.

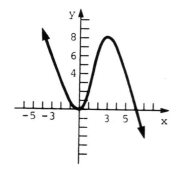

21.

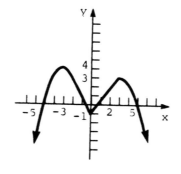

In the following exercises, find the locations and values of all relative extrema.

22. $f(x) = 3x^2 - 2x + 5$

23. $f(x) = -2x^2 + 4x - 9$

24. $f(x) = -6x^2 + 12x + 5$

25. $f(x) = 5x^2 - 9x$

26. $f(x) = 2x^3 - 5x^2 - 4x + 1$

27. $f(x) = 4x^3 - 27x^2 - 30x - 4$

28. $f(x) = -2x^3 - \frac{1}{2}x^2 + 2x + 1$

29. $f(x) = 4x^3 + 15x^2 - 18x + 1$

30. $f(x) = 5 - .2x - .3x^2$

31. $f(x) = \dfrac{x^2 - 4x + 4}{x + 1}$

32. $f(x) = -x^4 + 8x^2 + 7$

33. $f(x) = x^3 - 3x^2 + 3x - 1$

34. $f(x) = \dfrac{2x - 2}{3x - 1}$

35. $f(x) = \dfrac{1 - 2x}{x^2}$

36. $f(x) = (2 - 3x)^{2/3}$

37. $f(x) = \dfrac{x^2}{x^2 + 9}$

Solve each problem.

38. A costume jewelry store sells ceramic earrings for $5 a pair. The daily cost function is given by

$$C(x) = .0006x^3 - .03x^2 + 3.5x + 40,$$

where x is the number of pairs of earrings sold on a particular day.

   (a) How many pairs of earrings should be sold to maximize the profit?

   (b) What is the maximum daily profit on these earrings?

39. Suppose the cost of manufacturing an item is $C(x) = x^2 - 4x + 14$ where x is the number of items produced.

   (a) What number of items will minimize the cost?

   (b) What is the minimum cost?

40. The total profit in dollars from the sale of x thousand crates of apples is given by

$$P(x) = -\frac{10}{3}x^3 + 10x^2 + 30x + 500.$$

   (a) Find the number of crates of apples that should be sold to maximize profit.

   (b) Find the maximum profit.

Section 3.3

Find the locations of any absolute extrema for the functions with graphs as follows.

41.

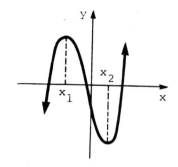

42.

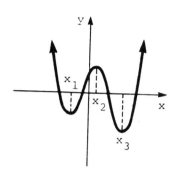

43.

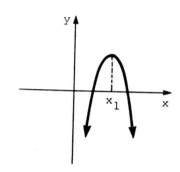

44.

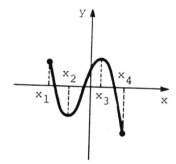

Find the locations and values of all absolute extrema for the functions defined as follows with the specified domains.

45. $f(x) = -x^2 + 4x - 8$; $[-4, 4]$

46. $f(x) = 2x^2 - 6x + 6$; $[0, 5]$

47. $f(x) = 2x^3 - 3x^2$; $[-3, 2]$

48. $f(x) = x^3 + 3x^2 - 9x - 7$; $[-4, 2]$

49. $f(x) = \dfrac{1}{x + 3}$; $[-2, 1]$

50. $f(x) = \dfrac{x}{x^2 + 4}$; $[1, 3]$

51. $f(x) = x + \dfrac{16}{x}$; $[2, 5]$

52. $f(x) = x^4 - 4x^2 + 2$; $[-1, 2]$

53. $f(x) = (x^2 + 10)^{2/3}$; $[-3, 3]$

54. $f(x) = \dfrac{1}{\sqrt{x^2 + 3}}$; $[-2, 1]$

Solve each problem.

55. A company has found that its weekly profit, in hundreds of dollars, from the sale of x thousand calculators is given by

$$P(x) = x^3 - 12x.$$

A union contract requires that at least 1000 but no more than 10,000 calculators be produced weekly. Find the maximum weekly profit that this company can make.

56. The revenue equation for a certain product is

$$R(x) = .25x^3 - 30x^2 + 900x, \quad 0 \le x \le 60.$$

Find the value of x that maximizes revenue.

Section 3.4

Find the second derivative of the function in each of the following exercises. Then find $f''(-1)$ and $f''(2)$.

57. $f(x) = 4x^4 - 5x^2 - 2x + 6$

58. $f(x) = 7x^3 - \dfrac{2}{x}$

59. $f(x) = \dfrac{3x + 2}{6x - 5}$

60. $f(x) = \dfrac{2 - 3x}{1 - x}$

61. $f(t) = \sqrt{3t^2 - 2}$

62. $f(t) = \dfrac{-2t}{t^2 + 5}$

63. $f(t) = \sqrt{22 - 5t^2}$

64. $f(t) = (2t - 3)^3$

65. $f(t) = 4t^{3/4}$

Find $f'''(x)$, the third derivative of f, and $f^{(4)}(x)$, the fourth derivative of f, for each of the following.

66. $f(x) = -3x^5 + 4x^3 - 2$

67. $f(x) = \dfrac{5x}{x - 2}$

68. $f(x) = 4x^3 + 2x^2 - x + 1$

In Exercises 69–77, find the largest open interval where the functions are concave upward or concave downward. Find any points of inflection.

69. $f(x) = x^3 - \dfrac{3}{2}x^2 + 1$

70. $f(x) = -\dfrac{1}{6}x^3 + \dfrac{1}{2}x^2 + 2x + 2$

71. $f(x) = x^4 + 1$

72. $f(x) = 3x^3 - \dfrac{3}{4}x^4$

73. $f(x) = x + \dfrac{3}{x}$

74. $f(x) = \dfrac{3x}{4 - x}$

75.

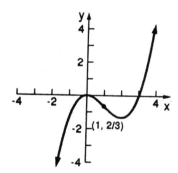

76.

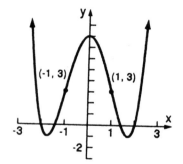

77.

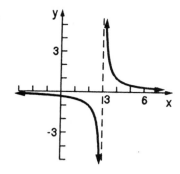

Each of the following functions gives the displacement at time t of a particle moving along a line. Find the velocity and acceleration functions. Then find the velocity and acceleration at t = 0 and t = 2. In this problem, velocity is measured in centimeters per second and acceleration, in centimeters per second per second.

78. $s(t) = -4t^2 + 8t + 4$

79. $s(t) = 2t^3 - 6t^2 + 5t - 8$

Solve each problem.

80. A manufacturer estimates that the total cost in dollars to produce x thousand widgets is given by

$$C(x) = .5x^3 - 18x^2 + 250x + 500.$$

At what level of production will the marginal cost be minimized?

81. Suppose the number of electric frying pans assembled by a worker t hr after arriving at the plant is given by

$$N(t) = -t^3 + 3t^2 + 5t + 1, \text{ for } 0 \le t \le 4.$$

What is the point of diminishing returns?

Section 3.5

Decide whether the following limits exist. If a limit exists, find its value.

82. $\lim\limits_{x \to \infty} f(x)$

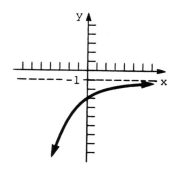

83. $\lim\limits_{x \to -\infty} g(x)$

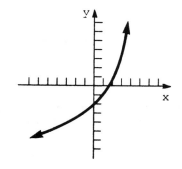

84. $\lim\limits_{x \to \infty} \dfrac{4x - 3}{7x + 2}$

85. $\lim\limits_{x \to -\infty} \dfrac{2x}{x - 1}$

86. $\lim\limits_{x \to \infty} \dfrac{3x^2 + 5x}{2x^2 - 8x + 1}$

87. $\lim\limits_{x \to -\infty} \dfrac{x^2 - 5x + 1}{x^4 + 7}$

88. $\lim\limits_{x \to \infty} \left(x - \sqrt{x^2 + 5} \right)$

Graph each of the following functions. List critical points, regions where the function is increasing or decreasing, points of inflection, regions where the function is concave up or concave down, intercepts where possible, and asymptotes where applicable.

89. $f(x) = x^3 - 7x^2 - 5x + 3$

90. $f(x) = 6x^4 - 4x^2 + 1$

91. $f(x) = x^5 - 4x^3$

92. $f(x) = x + \dfrac{1}{x}$

93. $f(x) = \dfrac{3x}{x - 2}$

94. $f(x) = \dfrac{1}{x^2 + 2}$

CHAPTER 4   APPLICATIONS OF THE DERIVATIVE

Section 4.1

Solve each of the following problems.

1. Find two numbers whose sum is 40 and whose product is a maximum. Give the maximum product.

2. Find two nonnegative numbers whose sum is 60 such that the sum of the squares of the two numbers is minimized. Give the minimum sum of the squares.

3. Find x and y such that $x + y = 3$ and x^2y is maximized. Give the maximum value of x^2y.

4. A farmer wishes to enclose a rectangular grazing region with one side along a river. If no fence is needed along the river, find the dimensions of the region of maximum area that can be made with 1200 m of fencing.

5. A farmer has 1200 m of fencing from which he wishes to construct two adjacent rectangular pens, as shown below in Figure 1. Find the maximum total area of the pens.

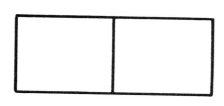

Figure 1

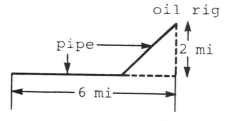

Figure 2

6. Oil that is drilled at an offshore rig 2 mi from the shore is pumped to a location on the shore 6 mi west of the oil rig, as shown above in Figure 2. The cost of constructing a pipe in the ocean is 1.5 times the cost of construction on land. How should the pipe be laid to minimize cost?

7. Find the production level x for which the average cost per item is a minimum if the total cost function is

$$C(x) = x^2 + 4x + 16.$$

8. The Cheap Motel can rent 500 rooms if it charges $30 per room. For each $1 increase in room rate, 10 fewer rooms will be rented. What room rate will maximize revenue?

9. An excursion boat offers a trip for a group of 200 people at $9 per person. The owner of the boat offers a fare reduction to all passengers of 2¢ per person for each additional person over 200 taking the cruise. What number of passengers will maximize the income?

10. A truck burns fuel at the rate of G(x) gal/mi, where

    $$G(x) = \frac{1}{24}\left(\frac{72}{x} + \frac{x}{15}\right),$$

    while traveling x mph.

    (a) If fuel cost $1.20/gal, find the speed that will produce a minimum total cost for a 300-mi trip.

    (b) Find the minimum total cost.

11. A closed cylindrical tin can is to have a volume of 54π in^3. What radius and height should the can have to minimize the cost of material? (Hint: The volume of a circular cylinder is $\pi r^2 h$ where r is the radius of the circular base and h is the height; the surface area of a closed cylinder is $2\pi rh + 2\pi r^2$.)

12. A box manufacturer wishes to construct a rectangular box with a bottom but no top. The length of the box is to be three times its width. The surface area of the box must be 144 in^2. What should be the dimensions of the box in order to maximize the volume of the box?

13. A rectangular field is to be enclosed on all four sides with a fence. Fencing material costs $8/m for two opposite sides and $4/m for the other two sides. Find the maximum area that can be enclosed for $6400.

14. Suppose water in a small pond is treated to control the growth of bacteria. The concentration of bacteria per cubic centimeter over an 8-day period is found to be

    $$k(t) = 30t^2 - 240t + 680.$$

    How many days after treatment will the bacteria concentration be lowest? What is the lowest concentration?

Section 4.2

Solve each problem.

15. Each year a drug store sells 400 cases of a solution for cleaning contact lenses. It costs $32 to store one case for one year. The fixed cost of placing the order is $25. Find the number of cases that should be ordered each time.

16. A paint manufacturer produces 500,000 gal of paint annually. It costs $.10 to store 1 gal of paint for one year, and it costs $250 to set up the factory to produce each batch. Find the number of batches of paint that should be produced each year.

17. A large pet store sells 50,000 bags of dog food annually. It costs $.20 to store one bag for one year and $2 to place a reorder. Find the number of times each year that the pet store should order dog food.

18. A local drive-in restaurant sells 100,000 frozen tacos a year. It costs $4 to store one taco for one year and $20 to place a reorder. Find the number of orders that should be placed annually.

19. Given the demand function $q = 500 - \frac{1}{2}p$, $0 \leq p \leq 1000$, find

    (a) E   **(b)** the value of q for which the total revenue is maximized.

20. The demand function for a product is $q = 200 - p$ for prices p between 10 and 200. For which prices is the demand

    (a) elastic   **(b)** inelastic?

21. Refer to Exercise 20. Does the total revenue increase or decrease if the price increases from 20 to 21? Why?

Section 4.3

Find dy/dx by implicit differentiation in each of the following exercises.

22. $2x^2 - 5y^2 = 8$ 23. $x^2y^2 = 4$

24. $3xy^2 + 5xy = 6$ 25. $xy^3 - xy + 6 = 0$

26. $\frac{3x}{5y} - x = y$ 27. $4\sqrt{x} + 5y^4 = \frac{3}{x^2}$

28. $5\sqrt{2y + 3} = x^{5/3}$ 29. $2\sqrt{x} - 4\sqrt{y} = 7$

30. $\frac{2}{3x} - \frac{4}{5y} = 3$

31. $\frac{3x + 2}{2y - 5} = \frac{1}{2x}$

32. $\sqrt{3xy} - 1 = 2y^2$

33. $\frac{3x - 2y}{x + 3y} = 2y^{3/2}$

34. $(6y^2 + 2x)^{3/2} = 4x$

35. $(x + 2y^{1/2})^4 = 6y^4$

Find the equation of the tangent line at the given point on each curve.

36. $x^2 + y^2 = 5$ at $(1, 2)$

37. $x + xy + 2y^2 = 6$ at $(2, 1)$

38. $y^2 = 8 - \sqrt{x}$ at $(16, 2)$

39. $y^2 - xy - 6 = 0$ at $(1, 3)$

Solve each problem.

40. The graph of $x^2 + y^2 = 16$ is a circle of radius 4 with center at the origin. Find the equations of the tangent lines at $x = -2$. Graph the circle and the tangent lines.

41. The graph of $xy = -2$ is a hyperbola. Find the equations of the tangent lines at $x = 1$ and $x = -1$. Graph the hyperbola and the tangent lines.

Section 4.4

Find dy/dt in each of the following exercises.

42. $y = 4x^3 + 6x^2;$ $\frac{dx}{dt} = 3$, $x = 3$

43. $y = \frac{6 - 3x}{4 + 5x};$ $\frac{dx}{dt} = -2$, $x = -1$

44. $y = \frac{\sqrt{x} + 5}{3 - \sqrt{x}};$ $\frac{dx}{dt} = -2$, $x = 4$

45. $\frac{3x^2 + y}{x + y} = 5;$ $\frac{dx}{dt} = 5$, $x = 1$

46. $x^2y^3 = 432;$ $\frac{dx}{dt} = 2$, $x = 4$

Solve each problem.

47. A stone is thrown into a pool. Ripples spread out in a circle with the radius of the circle increasing at the rate of 6 in/sec. Find the rate of change of the area of the circle when the radius is 3 in.

48. A math teacher is standing on the top rung of a 10-ft ladder that is leaning against a building. A student pulls the bottom of the ladder away from the wall at the rate of 3 ft/sec. Find the rate at which the teacher is descending when the base of the ladder is 6 ft from the wall.

49. A snowball is melting at the rate of 2.5 ft³/min. Find the rate of change of the radius when the radius is 1.1 ft.

50. The volume of a cube is increasing at 8 cm³/min. How fast is the total surface area changing when the surface area of the cube is 96 cm²?

51. A manufacturer has determined that the revenue from the sale of x units of his product per month is $R(x) = 400x - 6x^{2/3}$ dollars. If the production level x is increasing at the rate of 5 units per month, at what rate is revenue changing at a production level of 1000 units per month?

52. Suppose the profit of Better Widget Company is given by $P = 200 + 20x - .5x^2$ hundred dollars when x hundred dollars is spent on advertising per month. At what rate is profit changing when the advertising budget is $1500 and is decreasing by $20 per month?

Section 4.5

Find dy in each of the following exercises.

53. $y = 3x^3 + 3x$

54. $y = 3(2x^3 - 4)^5$

55. $y = \dfrac{3x - 2}{4 - x}$

56. $y = \sqrt{8 - x^2}$

57. $y = \left(3 + \dfrac{2}{x}\right)\left(2 - \dfrac{1}{x^2}\right)$

58. $y = \sqrt{\dfrac{2x}{x^2 - 1}}$

Find the value of dy in each of the following exercises.

59. $y = 6 + 2x^2 + 4x^5$; $x = -1$, $\Delta x = .03$

60. $y = \dfrac{2x + 5}{3x - 1}$; $x = 2$, $\Delta x = .002$

61. $y = \sqrt{3x + 1}$; $x = 5$, $\Delta x = .02$

62. $y = \dfrac{3 - x}{2\sqrt{x}}$; $x = 4$, $\Delta x = -.01$

63. $y = x^2$ as x changes from 3 to 3.001

Solve each problem.

64. Approximate the volume of a coating on a sphere of radius 2 cm if the coating is .01 cm thick.

65. The radius of a sphere is claimed to be 4 cm with a possible error of .02 cm. Estimate the possible error in the volume of the sphere.

66. The side of a cube is measured as 3 cm with an error .01 cm. Estimate the possible error in the volume of the cube.

67. Suppose that t days after an injection of a chemical into the bloodstream the amount A of that chemical remaining in the blood is $A = 2t^{-3/2}$ for $t \geq .5$. Use differentials to estimate the change in the amount of calcium remaining between 4 days and 4.5 days.

68. The profit in thousands of dollars for a certain company is given by

$$P = 200 + 20s - \frac{1}{2}s^2$$

where s is the amount in hundreds of dollars spent on advertising. Estimate the change in profit if there is

(a) an increase in spending for advertising from $1100 to $1175

(b) a decrease in spending from $2500 to $2450.

CHAPTER 5   EXPONENTIAL AND LOGARITHMIC FUNCTIONS

Section 5.1

Solve each of the following equations.

1. $2^x = \dfrac{1}{8}$

2. $e^x = \dfrac{1}{e^{10}}$

3. $9^x = 27$

4. $\left(\dfrac{2}{3}\right)^x = \dfrac{27}{8}$

5. $3^{6x} = \dfrac{1}{27}$

6. $\left(\dfrac{64}{125}\right)^x = \dfrac{4}{5}$

7. $16^{y-5} = 64^y$

8. $\dfrac{1}{3} = \left(\dfrac{b}{27}\right)^{1/5}$

9. $32^{-x} = \left(\dfrac{1}{8}\right)^{3x-5}$

10. $e^{-3x} = (e^2)^{2x+7}$

11. $2^{x^2-3x} = \dfrac{1}{4}$

12. $3^{-|2x|} = \dfrac{1}{27}$

Graph each of the following functions.

13. $y = 3^{-x}$

14. $y = \left(\dfrac{1}{4}\right)^x - 1$

15. $y = \left(\dfrac{1}{3}\right)^{x+1}$

16. $y = 4 + e^{x-1}$

Find the compound amount in each of the following exercises.

17. $4000 at 5% compounded annually for 10 yr

18. $678.52 at 12% compounded semiannually for 5 yr

19. $9000 at 9% compounded quarterly for 12 yr

20. $14,326.48 at 15% compounded monthly for 8 yr

Find the amount of interest earned by the deposits given in the following exercises.

21. $8305 at 10% compounded semiannually for 6 yr

22. $3124.53 at 7% compounded quarterly for 12 yr

23. Under certain conditions the number of individuals $y = P(t)$ of a species that is newly introduced into an area is given by the equation

$$y = 100(2^{.5t})$$

where t represents the number of years since the species was introduced into the area. Find each of the following.

(a) The number of individuals originally introduced into the area

(b) $P(2)$ (c) $P(3)$ (d) $P(4)$

24. The number of items produced by a worker is given by

$$p(x) = 150 - 150e^{-.3x}$$

where x is the number of days on the job. Find the number of items produced by a worker when she had been on the job the following number of days.

(a) 7 days   **(b)** 28 days

Section 5.2

For each of the following exercises, write the exponential equation in logarithmic form.

25. $5^3 = 125$

26. $7^{1/2} = \sqrt{7}$

27. $e^{.03} = 1.03045$

28. $10^{1.25527} = 18$

For each of the following exercises, write the logarithmic equation in exponential form.

29. $\log_3 81 = 4$

30. $\log_{10} \frac{1}{100} = -2$

31. $\ln 56.3 = 4.03069$

32. $\log 23.12 = 1.36399$

Evaluate the expression in each of the following exercises.

33. $\log_4 64$

34. $\log_5 \frac{1}{125}$

35. $\log_{81} 27$

36. $\log_{64} 4096$

37. $\log_{1/3} 27$

38. $\log_{1/4} \frac{1}{64}$

39. $\log_{100} 10$

40. $\ln e^{3/4}$

Graph each of the following.

41. $y = \log_3 x$

42. $y = 2 + \log x$

43. $y = \ln (x^2)$

44. $y = \log_{1/4} (x - 2)$

Use the properties of logarithms to write each expression as a sum, difference, or product.

45. $\log_7 5k$

46. $\log_3 \dfrac{2m}{n}$

47. $\log_4 \dfrac{3\sqrt{5}}{\sqrt[5]{7}}$

Use natural logarithms to evaluate each logarithm to the nearest hundredth.

48. $\log_3 20$

49. $\log_{12} 480$

Solve each of the following equations. Round decimal answers to the nearest thousandth.

50. $\log_x 16 = 2$

51. $\log_x 27 = -3$

52. $\log_{27} 9 = x$

53. $\log_x 6 = \dfrac{1}{2}$

54. $\log_3 (8x + 1) = 4$

55. $\log_3 (x - 1) - \log_3 (x - 5) = 2$

56. $7^x = 18$

57. $9^z = 14$

58. $3^{-p} = 7$

59. $17^{-t} = 5$

60. $e^{4+3x} = 7$

61. $e^{2x+1} = 10$

62. $\left(1 + \dfrac{p}{2}\right)^4 = 9$

63. $\left(1 + \dfrac{3p}{4}\right)^3 = 5$

Solve each problem.

64. Recall that if the threshold sound is assigned an intensity, I_0, the decibel rating of a sound of intensity I is

$$10 \cdot \log \frac{I}{I_0}.$$

Find the decibel rating of a dishwasher that has an intensity of $2{,}450{,}000\, I_0$.

65. In chemistry, pH is defined by

$$pH = -\log [H^+],$$

where $[H^+]$ is the hydrogen ion concentration in moles per liter. Find the pH for

(a) $[H^+] = 1.6 \times 10^{-8}$

(b) $[H^+] = 3.8 \times 10^{-4}.$

Section 5.3

Find the compound amount for the deposits in the following exercises if the interest is compounded continuously.

66. $1800 at 8% for 7 yr

67. $9000 at 11% for 5 yr

68. $52,100 at 6% for 3 yr

69. $6823 at 14% for 6 yr

Find the present value of each of the following deposits.

70. $3000 at 5% interest compounded annually for 6 yr

71. $12,000 at 9% interest compounded semiannually for 5 yr

72. $31,400 at 9% interest compounded quarterly for 3 yr

73. $8760 at 13% interest compounded monthly for 4 yr

Solve each problem.

74. Mr. and Mrs. Jones invested their savings in an account paying 7.5% interest compounded quarterly. What effective rate did they earn?

75. What effective rate would Mr. and Mrs. Jones earn if their money was invested in an account paying 7.2% compounded monthly?

76. A couple wants to have $20,000 in 5 yr for a down payment on a new house. How much must they deposit now at 7.8% compounded daily (assume 365 days in a year) so that they will have the required amount?

77. How long will it take for $1 to quadruple at an average inflation rate of 6% compounded continuously?

78. How long will it take for $2000 to double if it is invested at 10% compounded continuously?

79. Sales of a new food processor are approximated by
$$S(t) = 2000 - 400e^{-t}$$
where t represents the number of years that the processor has been on the market and S(t) represents sales in thousands. Find each of the following.

   (a) S(0)   (b) S(5)

   (c) The number of years it takes for sales to reach 1,960,000

80. In 1970, the population of the world was 3.6 billion. At that time it was estimated that the population P (in billions) was growing exponentially and could be approximated by

$$P(t) = 3.6e^{.02t}.$$

Based on this model, in what year would the population be triple what it was in 1970?

81. The production of eggs at a chicken farm has decreased exponentially from 125,000 eggs per week 2 yr ago to 95,000 eggs per week at present. Letting t = 0 represent the present time, find the following.

    (a) An exponential equation for production y in terms of time t in years

    (b) The time it will take for the egg production to fall to 60,000 eggs per week

82. Strontium 90 decays exponentially. A sample which contained 100 g 5 yr ago (t = 0) has decreased to 29 g at present.

    (a) Write an exponential equation to express the amount y present after t yr.

    (b) What is the half-life of this substance?

83. A population of 20,000 cattle on a ranch has grown exponentially to 35,000 in 6 yr.

    (a) Write an exponential equation to express the population growth y in terms of time, t, in years.

    (b) At this rate, how long will it take for the population to reach 80,000?

Section 5.4

Find the derivative of the function in each of the following exercises.

84. $y = \ln |-3x|$

85. $y = \ln |3 + 4x|$

86. $y = \ln |3 - x^3|$

87. $y = \ln |2x^2 - 5|$

88. $y = \dfrac{\ln |2x|}{4 - x}$

89. $y = \dfrac{2x - 5}{\ln |3x + 1|}$

90. $y = \ln (3x + 1)^{2/3}$

91. $y = x^2 \ln |3x + 1|$

92. $y = (\ln |2x + 1|)^3$

93. $y = x \ln \sqrt{x^2 + 1}$

94. $y = \sqrt{\ln |x|}$

95. $y = \log |x^2 - 1|$

96. $y = \log_5 |3x - 5|$

97. $y = \log_3 \sqrt{2x + 5}$

Find all relative extrema for the function in each of the following exercises.
Graph each function.

98. $y = 2x - \ln x^2$, $x > 0$ 99. $y = x^2 \ln x$

100. $y = \dfrac{\ln |4x|}{5x}$ 101. $y = \dfrac{x}{\ln |x|}$, $x > 1$

102. If the cost function is $C(x) = 2x + 5$ and the revenue function is $R(x) = 8x - x^2$, where x is the number of units produced (in thousands) and R and C are measured in millions of dollars, find the following.

(a) The marginal revenue

(b) The approximate revenue from one more unit when 3 units are sold

(c) The profit function

(d) The maximum profit

Section 5.5

Find the derivative of the function in each of the following exercises.

103. $y = -3e^{5x}$ 104. $y = 7e^{.3x}$

105. $y = e^{-4x^2}$ 106. $y = -3e^{5x^3}$

107. $y = 3xe^{3b}$ (b a constant)   108. $y = -4x^2e^{-2x}$

109. $y = e^{x^2+3x}$ 110. $y = \dfrac{e^x + e^{-x}}{2}$

111. $y = \dfrac{100}{1 + 99e^{-x}}$ 112. $y = (3x^2 + e^x)^3$

113. $y = (e^{3x-2} + 5)^5$ 114. $y = \dfrac{\ln |x^2 + 1|}{e^x}$

115. $y = 4 \cdot 3^{\sqrt{x}}$ 116. $y = 4^{5x}$

Find all relative extrema for the function in each of the following exercises.
Graph each function.

117. $y = 3xe^{3x}$ 118. $y = -xe^{-x}$

119. $y = \dfrac{e^x}{x + 2}$ 120. $y = (1 - x)e^x$

CHAPTER 6   INTEGRATION

Section 6.1

Find each indefinite integral.

1. $\displaystyle\int 7\ dx$

2. $\displaystyle\int (3 + 5x)\,dx$

3. $\displaystyle\int (4 - x^3)\,dx$

4. $\displaystyle\int (2x^3 + 3x^4 + 4x^5)\,dx$

5. $\displaystyle\int t^{-4}\,dt$

6. $\displaystyle\int (3x - 1)(5x + 1)\,dx$

7. $\displaystyle\int 4\sqrt[3]{x}\ dx$

8. $\displaystyle\int \frac{4}{x^3}\ dx$

9. $\displaystyle\int \frac{2}{\sqrt{x}}\ dx$

10. $\displaystyle\int e^{-.4x}\,dx$

11. $\displaystyle\int 3e^{4x}\,dx$

12. $\displaystyle\int \frac{x^2 + 4x - \sqrt{x}}{x^2}\ dx$

13. $\displaystyle\int \frac{e^{5x} + e^{-3x}}{e^{2x}}\ dx$

14. $\displaystyle\int (9x^{7/5} - 2x^{1/3} + 4)\,dx$

15. $\displaystyle\int (2x + 3)^2\,dx$

16. $\displaystyle\int x(x^2 + 2x - 1)\,dx$

17. $\displaystyle\int (2x^2\sqrt{x} + 3x\sqrt{x})\,dx$

18. $\displaystyle\int \left(e^{3u} - \frac{2}{u}\right)du$

19. $\displaystyle\int \left(\frac{x^2 - x + 2}{\sqrt{x}}\right)dx$

20. Find the equation of the curve whose tangent line has a slope of $f'(x) = x^2 + 1$ if the point $(3, 8)$ is on the curve.

Find the cost function for each of the following marginal cost functions.

21. $C'(x) = 7 - .4x$, 5 units cost \$50

22. $C'(x) = 5x + 3x^2$, 1 unit costs \$20

23. $C'(x) = 3x - x^{3/2}$, fixed cost is \$3000

24. $C'(x) = 3 + 2x^{-1/5}$, fixed cost is \$17,000

25. $C'(x) = 310 + 4x^{-1/4}$, where the first 16 units cost \$160,000

26. $C'(x) = 200 + 100e^{-x/100}$, fixed cost is \$17,000

27. $C'(x) = 150 + 10e^{-x/50}$, 50 units cost \$12,217

Solve each problem.

28. The marginal profit of a factory is given by $P'(x) = (3/25)x^2 - 2x + 120$ where x is given in thousands of items and the profit on 0 items is $-\$300$. Find the profit function.

29. A particle is moving along a straight line with a constant acceleration of 5 m/sec² and an initial velocity of 7 m/sec. Find $v(t)$, the velocity of the particle after t sec.

30. A ball falls from a window sill that is 17 m above the ground, that is, $s(0) = 17$. Assume that $v(0) = 0$ and $a(t) = -9.8$ m/sec². How long will it take the ball to hit the ground?

31. A ball is thrown directly upward from a window that is 42 m above the ground. Since the ball's initial velocity is 20 m/sec upward, $v(0) = 20$. Assume that $a(t) = -9.8$ m/sec². How long will it take the ball to hit the ground?

32. A cyst is observed to grow at the rate of .18t g per week. How much will the cyst grow from the third to the fourth week?

Section 6.2

Use substitution to find the following indefinite integrals.

33. $\displaystyle\int 5x^2(3x^3 - 1)^7 dx$

34. $\displaystyle\int 2x^3(3x^4 + 2)^3 dx$

35. $\displaystyle\int (3x^2 - 1)(x^3 - x)dx$

36. $\displaystyle\int \frac{x}{x^2 + 1}\, dx$

37. $\displaystyle\int \frac{1}{x + 1}\, dx$

38. $\displaystyle\int \frac{x + 1}{x^2 + 2x + 1}\, dx$

39. $\displaystyle\int \frac{2x + 1}{x^2 + x - 7}\, dx$

40. $\displaystyle\int \frac{3x^2 - 2}{x^3 - 2x + 1}\, dx$

41. $\displaystyle\int \sqrt{x^2 - 8x}(x - 4)dx$

42. $\displaystyle\int \sqrt[4]{2x^3 - 6x}(x^2 - 1)dx$

43. $\displaystyle\int \frac{8}{3v - 1}\, dv$

44. $\displaystyle\int \frac{3x^2 - 2}{(x^3 - 2x - 7)^5}\, dx$

45. $\displaystyle\int \frac{3x^2 + 4}{\sqrt{x^3 + 4x - 5}}\, dx$

46. $\displaystyle\int \frac{4x + 3}{\sqrt[3]{2x^2 + 3x + 4}}\, dx$

47. $\int 4e^{-.2m}dm$

48. $\int 4x^3 e^{x^4}dx$

49. $\int 5e^{2x-1}dx$

50. $\int 2xe^{x^2-1}dx$

51. $\int x^2 e^{2x^3+1}dx$

52. $\int x^2 e^{x^3}dx$

53. $\int \frac{x}{e^{x^2-1}} dx$

54. $\int x^2 e^{-x^3}dx$

55. $\int \frac{2x-1}{e^{3+x-x^2}} dx$

56. $\int \frac{e^x}{e^x+1} dx$

57. $\int p(p-1)^4 dp$

58. $\int (x+1)(x-1)^{20}dx$

59. $\int (x-1)(2x-1)^{21}dx$

60. $\int (x+2)(2x+1)^{10}dx$

Find the cost function for each of the following marginal cost functions.

61. $C'(x) = 25\sqrt{x+7}$, 9 units cost \$1200

62. $C'(x) = 30 + \frac{18}{x+1}$, fixed cost is \$8000

63. $C'(x) = 40 + \frac{2}{2x+1}$, 6 units cost \$700

Solve each problem.

64. A particle is moving along a straight line with velocity $v(t) = 1/(3t+5)$ m/sec and initial position 0. Find $s(t)$, the distance of the particle from the starting point after t sec.

65. A particle moves along the x-axis in such a way that at time t sec its acceleration is
$$a(t) = 12(2t+1)^{-3/2}.$$
If the particle starts from rest ($v(0) = 0$) at $x = 2$, where will it be 12 sec later?

66. The marginal cost for a certain product is $C'(x) = 2/\sqrt{4x+1}$. Find the cost function if 6 units cost \$15.

67. A manufacturer finds that the marginal cost for producing x units of a certain product is

$$C'(x) = 20 + \frac{10x}{1 + 2x^2}.$$

Find the cost function if $C(0) = 400$.

Section 6.3

Evaluate each sum.

68. $\displaystyle\sum_{i=1}^{4} (1 - 3i)$ 69. $\displaystyle\sum_{i=1}^{6} 7$

70. Let $x_1 = 2$, $x_2 = -1$, $x_3 = 3$, $x_4 = 6$, and $x_5 = 0$. Find $\displaystyle\sum_{i=1}^{5} x_i$.

In the following exercises, find $\displaystyle\sum_{i=1}^{5} f(x_i)$ for the given values of x and f(x).

71. $f(x) = 2x + 1$; $x_1 = 1$, $x_2 = 2$, $x_3 = 4$, $x_4 = 8$, $x_5 = 16$

72. $f(x) = x^2$; $x_1 = -2$, $x_2 = -1$, $x_3 = 0$, $x_4 = -1$, $x_5 = 2$

73. $f(x) = 3x^2 - x$; $x_i = i$

Approximate the area under the given curve and above the x-axis by using four rectangles. Let the height of each rectangle be the value of the function on the left side of the rectangle.

74. $f(x) = 5x + 3$, between $x = 1$ and $x = 5$

75. $f(x) = x^2 + 3x + 4$, between $x = -2$ and $x = 0$

76. $f(x) = x^{1/3}$, between $x = 0$ and $x = 8$

77. $f(x) = 1/x$, between $x = 1$ and $x = 3$

78. $f(x) = e^{-x^2}$, between $x = 0$ and $x = 2$

Find the exact value of each of the following using formulas from geometry.

79. $\displaystyle\int_0^2 4x \, dx$ 80. $\displaystyle\int_3^6 5 \, dx$ 81. $\displaystyle\int_{-5}^0 \sqrt{25 - x^2} \, dx$

82. The graph shows the rate of use of electrical energy (in kilowatt hours) in a certain city on a summer day. Estimate the total usage of electricity on that day (the area under the curve) by adding the areas of rectangles. Let the width of each rectangle be 3 hr, and let the function value at the left side of each rectangle give its height.

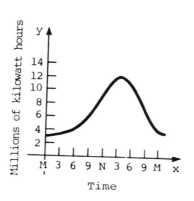

Section 6.4

Evaluate the following definite integrals.

83. $\displaystyle\int_2^4 -6 \ dx$

84. $\displaystyle\int_{-3}^1 4x \ dx$

85. $\displaystyle\int_2^3 (x + 7)\,dx$

86. $\displaystyle\int_1^5 (3x^2 - 2x)\,dx$

87. $\displaystyle\int_1^4 (3x^{-4} + x^{-2})\,dx$

88. $\displaystyle\int_2^3 \left(\frac{3}{x^3} + \frac{4}{x}\right)dx$

89. $\displaystyle\int_1^3 \left(\frac{2}{A} - e^{.2A}\right)da$

90. $\displaystyle\int_0^4 \frac{3}{2x + 1} \ dx$

91. $\displaystyle\int_1^5 \sqrt{2r - 1} \ dr$

92. $\displaystyle\int_1^4 \left(4y\sqrt{y} - 2\sqrt{y}\right)dy$

93. $\displaystyle\int_{-1}^1 \frac{2}{(2x - 3)^2} \ dx$

94. $\displaystyle\int_{-1}^2 x(2x^2 - 5)^4 dx$

95. $\displaystyle\int_0^2 3e^{2x}dx$

96. $\displaystyle\int_{-1}^1 7xe^{x^2+1}dx$

97. $\displaystyle\int_1^2 \frac{2}{x(11 + \ln x)} \ dx$

98. $\displaystyle\int_0^8 (3x^3 - x^{-1/3} + x^{1/3})\,dx$

99. $\displaystyle\int_2^3 \frac{e^{2t}}{e^{2t} - 3} \ dt$

For Exercises 100–108, find the area between the x-axis and f(x) over the indicated interval. Check first to see if the graph crosses the x-axis in the given interval.

100. $f(x) = 3x + 2$, $[2, 5]$

101. $f(x) = 3x^2 - 1$, $[1, 4]$

102. $f(x) = \sqrt{2x + 1}$, $[0, 4]$

103. $f(x) = \sqrt[3]{x - 1}$, $[2, 9]$

104. $f(x) = 1/x$, $[1, 9]$

105. $f(x) = e^{x+1}$, $[-1, 2]$

106. $f(x) = 3 - 2x^2$, $[3, 4]$

107. $f(x) = x^3 - x$, $[-1, 1]$

108. $f(x) = 2x^4 + x^3 - x^2$, $[-2, 2]$

109. Find the area of the shaded region.

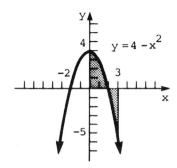

Solve each problem.

110. The rate at which a worker can install automobile engines in new cars in an eight-hour shift is given by

$$I'(t) = t^{1/2} - \frac{e^{t/8}}{4},$$

where t is time in hours from beginning of shift. How many engines can the worker install in one eight-hour shift?

111. The population of a city is decreasing at a rate given by

$$P'(t) = -10{,}500e^{-.1t},$$

where t is time in years, and t = 0 corresponds to the year 1993. In 1993 the population of the city was 105,000.

(a) How many people will leave the city from 1993 (t = 0) to 1995 (t = 2)?

(b) What is the population of the city expected to be in 2000?

112. The rate of growth of Sting Specialties, Inc., is given by
$$R'(t) = 7\sqrt{t + 4} - 10$$
thousands of dollars per month, where t is the time in months since the operation began. What is the total revenue for Sting during its first year of operation?

113. The rate of growth of a particular bacteria is given by
$$P'(t) = 7e^{.1t}$$
grams per day. If there are .3 g of bacteria when t = 0 days, how many grams of bacteria will there be when t = 4 days?

114. The rate of decay of a particular sample of a radioactive isotope is given by
$$P'(t) = -4e^{-.004t}$$
grams per year. At t = 0 there are 1000 g of the isotope.

   (a) When will there be 500 g of the isotope left?
   (b) When will there be 250 g of the isotope left?
   (c) When will all of the isotope be gone?

Section 6.5

Find the area of the region enclosed by the curves given in each of the following exercises.

115. $f(x) = x$, $g(x) = 2x$, $x = 0$, $x = 1$
116. $f(x) = 2x + 1$, $g(x) = 3x^2$

117. $f(x) = x^2 + 2$, $g(x) = x^4$
118. $f(x) = x^2 - 1$, $g(x) = 2x^2 - 3x + 1$

119. $f(x) = 2x^2$, $g(x) = \dfrac{x^2}{4} + 7$
120. $f(x) = x^3 + 4x^2 - 2x$,
     $g(x) = x^3 + 5x - 3$

121. $f(x) = 4 - 2x$, $g(x) = \dfrac{6}{x + 2}$
122. $f(x) = 9x + 10$, $g(x) = -\dfrac{1}{x}$

123. $f(x) = e^{-x}$, $g(x) = e^x$, $x = 2$
124. $f(x) = \sqrt{x}$, $g(x) = -x^2$, $x = 0$, $x = 4$

Solve each problem.

125. Suppose that the supply function of a particular calculator is
$$S(q) = .1q^2 + .2q + 25$$
and the demand function is
$$D(q) = 400 + .2q - .05q^2.$$

    (a) Find the producers' surplus.

    (b) Find the consumers' surplus.

126. Suppose that the supply function of a particular computer is
$$S(q) = 1200e^{.02q}$$
and the demand function is
$$D(q) = 2400e^{-.03q}.$$

    (a) Find the producers' surplus.

    (b) Find the consumers' surplus.

CHAPTER 7   FURTHER TECHNIQUES AND APPLICATIONS OF INTEGRATION

Section 7.1

Find the integrals using integration by parts, column integration, or techniques discussed earlier.

1. $\displaystyle\int 2x \ln x \, dx$ for $x > 0$

2. $\displaystyle\int \ln |3x + 1| \, dx$

3. $\displaystyle\int xe^{4x} dx$

4. $\displaystyle\int x(3 - 2x)^{3/2} dx$

5. $\displaystyle\int (x + 2)e^{2x} dx$

6. $\displaystyle\int (x + 3)^2 e^{3x} dx$

7. $\displaystyle\int (4x^2 - 2x + 1)e^{2x+1} dx$

8. $\displaystyle\int \frac{2x}{\sqrt{x + 4}} \, dx$

9. $\displaystyle\int_0^5 x\sqrt{x + 4} \, dx$

10. $\displaystyle\int_{1/2}^{e/2} \ln 2x \, dx$

11. $\displaystyle\int (4x + 1) \ln |2x + 1| \, dx$

12. $\displaystyle\int \frac{x + 2}{5e^x} \, dx$

13. $\displaystyle\int \ln x^2 \, dx$

14. $\displaystyle\int (x^2 + 3x + 4) \ln |2x| \, dx$

Solve each problem.

15. Find the area between the x-axis and the graph of $f(x) = 3xe^x$ from $x = 1$ to $x = 2$.

16. Find the area between the x-axis and the graph of $f(x) = x \ln x$ from $x = 1$ to $x = 4$.

17. Find the area between the x-axis and the graph of $f(x) = (x + 2)e^{-x}$ from $x = -3$ to $x = 0$.

Use the table of integrals to find each indefinite integral.

18. $\displaystyle\int \ln |7x| \, dx$

19. $\displaystyle\int \frac{1}{x^2 - 36} \, dx$

20. $\displaystyle\int \frac{-10}{\sqrt{x^2 - 49}} \, dx$

21. $\displaystyle\int \frac{1}{2x\sqrt{9 - x^2}} \, dx$

22. $\displaystyle\int \frac{1}{x(3x + 2)} \, dx$

23. $\displaystyle\int \sqrt{17 + x^2} \, dx$

24. $\displaystyle\int \frac{3x}{5 - 2x} \, dx$

25. $\displaystyle\int \frac{-2x}{(4x - 3)^2} \, dx$

Solve each problem.

26. Given that the marginal revenue in dollars from the sale of x computer printers is
$$R'(x) = xe^{-.0001x},$$
find the total revenue from the sale of the first 1000 printers.

27. Given that the marginal revenue in dollars from the sale of x cameras is
$$R'(x) = (x - 10)(x + 13)^{2/3},$$
find the total revenue from the sale of the 14th to the 51st camera.

28. Given that the marginal cost in dollars of manufacturing x time machines is
$$C'(x) = 10^8 x^2 e^{-.01x},$$
find the total cost of manufacturing 10 time machines.

29. Given that the marginal cost of building x m of a bridge is
$$C'(x) = x(2x + 1)^{.2}$$
thousands of dollars per meter, find the cost of a 5000-m bridge.

30. Given that the marginal profit in dollars earned by the Apricot Computer Company's new computer is
$$P'(x) = (x + 1)e^{.002x} - 300,$$
where x is the number of computers sold, find the total earnings from the sale of the first 200 computers. Find the earnings from the sale of the first 1000 computers.

31. Given that the marginal profit from selling x motors is
$$P'(x) = (x + 7)\sqrt{3x + 1}$$
dollars per motor, what is the profit from selling the first 100 motors?

Section 7.2

In Exercises 32–37, use n = 4 to approximate the value of each of the given integrals by (a) the trapezoidal rule and (b) Simpson's rule. (c) Find the exact value using integration.

32. $\int_1^3 \frac{5}{x}\, dx$

33. $\int_0^4 \frac{dx}{\sqrt{1 + x^2}}$

34. $\int_2^6 x \ln x\, dx$

35. $\int_2^6 \frac{x}{2x - 3}$

36. $\int_1^3 xe^x dx$

37. $\int_0^1 \frac{dx}{4 - x^2}$

Solve each problem.

38. Find the area between the curve $y = \sqrt{x^2 + 4}$ and the x-axis from $x = 0$ to $x = 3$ by using the trapezoidal rule with $n = 6$.

39. Find the area between the curve $y = 2^x \ln x$ and the x-axis from $x = 1$ to $x = 5$ by using Simpson's rule with $n = 4$.

40. Find the area between the curve $y = \dfrac{x + 1}{x^2 + 1}$ and the x-axis from $x = 0$ to $x = 4$ by using Simpson's rule with $n = 4$.

41. In a car with no odometer but a working speedometer, a passenger notes the following speeds at the given times.

Time	2:00	2:15	2:30	2:45	3:00	3:15	3:30	3:45	4:00
Speed (kph)	85	95	93	86	105	75	95	90	60

Use the trapezoidal rule to estimate the distance traveled during this time.

42. Use Simpson's rule to estimate the distance traveled by using the data in Exercise 41.

43. Find the area under the semicircle $y = \sqrt{9 - x^2}$ and above the x-axis by using $n = 6$ with **(a)** the trapezoidal rule and **(b)** Simpson's rule. **(c)** Find the area of the semicircle by using the geometric formula. Compare this result with the results in (a) and (b). Which of the two approximation techniques is more accurate?

Section 7.3

Find the volume of the solid of revolution formed by rotating about the x-axis each region bounded by the given curves.

44. $f(x) = 3x + 2$, $y = 0$, $x = 0$, $x = 2$

45. $f(x) = \dfrac{1}{2}x + 2$, $y = 0$, $x = 1$, $x = 4$

46. $f(x) = 4x - 1$, $y = 0$, $x = 1$, $x = 3$

47. $f(x) = \dfrac{1}{\sqrt{x + 1}}$, $y = 0$, $x = 0$, $x = 3$

48. $f(x) = \sqrt{x + 3}$, $y = 0$, $x = 1$, $x = 6$

49. $f(x) = \sqrt[3]{x + 4}$, $y = 0$, $x = -3$, $x = 4$

50. $f(x) = x\sqrt[3]{x^3 + 2}$, $y = 0$, $x = 1$, $x = 2$

51. $f(x) = x^{1/2}e^{x^2}$, $y = 0$, $x = 0$, $x = 2$

52. $f(x) = \dfrac{2}{\sqrt{x}}$, $y = 0$, $x = 1$, $x = 4$

53. $f(x) = x^{1/2}e^x$, $y = 0$, $x = 0$, $x = 2$

54. $f(x) = 4 - x^2$, $y = 0$

55. $f(x) = \sqrt{4 - x^2}$, $y = 0$

Solve each problem.

56. Find the volume of the solid of revolution formed by rotating about the x–axis the region bounded by $y = \sqrt{x^2 + 4}$, $y = 0$, $x = 0$, and $x = 3$.

57. Use the methods of Section 7.3 to find the volume of a sphere of radius 4.

Find the average value of each of the following functions f(x) on the given interval.

58. $f(x) = 4$; $[3, 6]$

59. $f(x) = 3x^2 - 1$; $[-2, 1]$

60. $f(x) = \sqrt{2x - 3}$; $[2, 6]$

61. $f(x) = e^x$; $[-1, 4]$

62. $f(x) = x(3x^2 + 1)^{1/2}$; $[0, 4]$

63. $f(x) = xe^{-x}$; $[-1, 1]$

64. $f(x) = xe^{-x}$; $[0, 1]$

65. $f(x) = \dfrac{e^{\sqrt{x}}}{2\sqrt{x}}$; $[1, 5]$

66. $f(x) = \dfrac{x}{x^2 + 1}$; $[-2, 2]$

67. $f(x) = \dfrac{\ln x}{x}$; $[1, 4]$

Solve each problem.

68. The temperature in degrees Celsius in a building is given by

$$x = 21 + t - \frac{t^2}{24},$$

where t is time in hours from the start of a 12–hr workday. Find the average temperature over the day.

69. The concentration of a drug in milligrams per milliliter in the bloodstream is given by

$$c(t) = 8e^{-.3t},$$

where t is measured in hours after injection. What is the average concentration during the first 4 hr?

Section 7.4

Each of the functions given in the following exercises represents the rate of flow of money in dollars per year over the given number of years, compounded continuously at the given annual interest rate. Find the present value in each case.

70. $f(x) = 6000$; 9 yr; 11%

71. $f(x) = 100,000$; 6 yr; 13%

72. $f(x) = 16,000e^{.2x}$; 10 yr; 10%

73. $f(x) = 1700e^{-.07x}$; 12 yr, 15%

74. $f(x) = 50x + 25x^2$; 10 yr; 12%   **75.** $f(x) = 1700x$; 7 yr; 13%

76. $f(x) = 10,000x$; 5 yr; 8%

Assume that the following functions give the rate of flow of money in dollars per year, with continuous compounding at the given rate. Find the amount at the end of the given time period.

77. $f(x) = 400e^{-.2x}$; 5 yr; 8%   **78.** $f(x) = 10x$; 4 yr; 12%

79. $f(x) = 500 - 50x$; 10 yr; 12%

Solve each problem.

80. Money is flowing continuously at a constant rate of $5000 a year for 10 yr. Assuming an interest rate of 12% compounded continuously, find each of the following.

    (a) The accumulated value (final amount) of this money

    (b) The present value of this money

81. A continuous flow of money starts at $4000 and decreases exponentially at 2% per year for 5 yr. Find the present value and the final amount at an interest rate of 15% compounded continuously.

Section 7.5

Find the value of each integral which converges. If an integral diverges, say that it does.

82. $\displaystyle\int_3^\infty -\frac{7}{x}\, dx$

83. $\displaystyle\int_{-\infty}^5 \frac{3}{x}\, dx$

84. $\displaystyle\int_{-\infty}^{-8} x^{-5/3} dx$

85. $\displaystyle\int_1^\infty \frac{3}{\sqrt{x}}\, dx$

86. $\displaystyle\int_2^\infty \frac{dx}{(4x-1)^2}$

87. $\displaystyle\int_{-\infty}^{-1} \frac{4}{(3x+1)^3}\, dx$

88. $\displaystyle\int_3^\infty \frac{dx}{x^3}$

89. $\displaystyle\int_2^\infty \frac{dx}{\sqrt{x+1}}$

90. $\displaystyle\int_5^\infty \frac{dx}{3x-1}$

91. $\displaystyle\int_0^\infty \frac{dx}{\sqrt{2x+1}}$

92. $\displaystyle\int_5^\infty \sqrt{x}\, dx$

93. $\displaystyle\int_{-\infty}^5 \frac{x^2\, dx}{x^3+3}$

94. $\displaystyle\int_0^\infty e^{-2x} dx$

95. $\displaystyle\int_0^\infty e^{-x} dx$

96. $\displaystyle\int_{-\infty}^{-1} \frac{x^2+1}{(x^3+3x)^2}\, dx$

97. $\displaystyle\int_2^\infty \frac{3}{x(\ln x)^3}\, dx$

98. $\displaystyle\int_{-\infty}^0 12e^{4x} dx$

Find the area between the graph of each function and the x-axis over the given interval, if possible.

99. $f(x) = 4e^{-2x}$ for $[0, \infty)$

100. $f(x) = \dfrac{1}{x}$ for $[1, \infty)$

101. $f(x) = \dfrac{1}{x^2}$ for $[1, \infty)$

102. $f(x) = \dfrac{1}{\sqrt{x + 1}}$ for $[0, \infty)$

103. $f(x) = \dfrac{1}{(x + 1)^2}$ for $[0, \infty)$

104. $f(x) = \dfrac{1}{(x - 2)^2}$ for $(-\infty, 1]$

105. $f(x) = \sqrt[3]{x}$ for $[1/8, \infty)$

106. $f(x) = \dfrac{1}{x + 1}$ for $[1, \infty)$

107. $f(x) = \dfrac{1}{(x - 1)^2}$ for $(-\infty, 0]$

Solve each problem.

108. Find the capitalized value of the site of an office building if the annual rent is $6000 paid in perpetuity with an interest rate of 12% compounded continuously.

109. Find the capitalized value of a small island in the Pacific rented by the U.S. from Japan if the annual rent is $1,500,000 to be paid in perpetuity, with an interest rate of 15% compounded continuously.

CHAPTER 8   MULTIVARIABLE CALCULUS

Section 8.1

1. Find $f(2, -3)$ if $f(x, y) = -2x^2 + 3xy - 7$.

2. Find $f(1, 0)$ if $f(x, y) = 3x^2y^2 - 2x^2 + 3xy - 3$.

3. Find $f(2, 3)$ if $f(x, y) = \dfrac{1}{x^2 + y^2}$.

4. Find $f(-2, 3)$ if $f(x, y) = \dfrac{1}{x^2 + y^2}$.

5. Find $f(e, e)$ if $f(x, y) = \dfrac{\sqrt{x^2 + y^2}}{\ln x}$.

6. Find $f(e^2, e^2)$ if $f(x, y) = \dfrac{\sqrt{x^2 + y^2}}{\ln x}$.

7. Find $f(100, 4)$ if $f(x, y) = \dfrac{\log x}{y^2 - \sqrt{x}}$

Complete the ordered triples $(0, 0, \quad)$, $(0, \quad, 0)$, and $(\quad, 0, 0)$ for the following planes.

8. $2x - 3y + 4z = 6$

9. $2x + 3y + 4z = 6$

10. $-2x - 3y + 4z = 6$

11. $-2x + 3y - 4z = 6$

12. Graph the level curves in the first octant at heights of $z = 1$ and $z = 3$ for $2x + y + 3z = 11$.

Graph the first-octant portion of each of the following planes.

13. $z = 2$

14. $x = 1$

15. $x + y = 3$

16. $x + z = 2$

17. $x + 8y + 8z = 8$

18. $2x + 3y + 6z = 6$

19. $2x + 2y + z = 2$

20. $x + y + z = 1$

21. If P dollars are deposited at the end of each year for n yr at an annual interest rate r, then the total value A of the account after n yr is given by

$$A = f(P, n, r) = P\left[\frac{(1 + r)^n - 1}{r}\right].$$

   Find

   (a) $f(1000, 10, .075)$ **(b)** $f(2000, 5, .08)$.

22. It has been determined that the effect of a dosage of x units of a certain drug on a patient t hr after it is administered is given by the function

$$E(x, t) = 30x^{3/2}e^{-.04t}.$$

Find E(4, 10).

23. The profit in dollars from the sale of x units of product A and y units of product B is given by

$$P(x, y) = 14x + 5y - 500.$$

Find P(100, 50).

Section 8.2

24. Let $z = f(x, y) = x^3y^2 + x^2y^3$. Find

   (a) $\dfrac{\partial z}{\partial x}$ (b) $\dfrac{\partial z}{\partial y}(-1, 2)$ (c) $f_{xy}(1, -1)$.

25. Let $z = f(x, y) = \dfrac{x + y}{x - y}$. Find

   (a) $\dfrac{\partial z}{\partial y}$ (b) $\dfrac{\partial z}{\partial x}$ (c) $\dfrac{\partial z}{\partial x}(1, 2)$.

For each of the following funcitons, find (a) f_x and f_y and (b) $f_x(1, 1)$ and $f_y(1, 1)$.

26. $f(x, y) = x^2 + 3y^2$ 27. $f(x, y) = x^2y^2 + x$

28. $f(x, y) = \dfrac{x}{x^2 + y^2}$ 29. $f(x, y) = \sqrt{x^2 + y^2}$

30. $f(x, y) = y^2e^{-x}$ 31. $f(x, y) = \ln(x^2 + y^2)$

32. $f(x, y) = \ln\dfrac{x}{y}$ 33. $f(x, y) = \ln xy$

34. $f(x, y) = \dfrac{\ln x}{y}$ 35. $f(x, y) = e^{x^2y^3}$

Find all second order partial derivatives for the following functions.

36. $f(x, y) = 6x^2 - 8xy + 9y^2$ 37. $f(x, y) = \ln|x^3 + y^2|$

38. $f(x, y) = e^{3x+2y}$

39. Find values of x and y such that both $f_x(x, y) = 0$ and $f_y(x, y) = 0$ for $f(x, y) = x^2 + xy + y^2 - 6x + 6$.

40. Find f_x, f_y, f_z, and f_{xz} for $f(x, y, z) = 2xyz^2 + \ln(x^2 + 3y^2)$.

41. A manufacturer has determined that its production function is given by

$$P(x, y) = 400x + 700y + 2x^2y - x^3 - \frac{y^2}{2}$$

where x is the size of the labor force in worker–hours per week and y is the amount of capital invested in thousands of dollars. Find the marginal productivity of labor and capital when $x = 40$ and $y = 60$.

42. Consider the production function $f(K, L) = 20K^{1/3}L^{2/3}$, where K is the amount of capital and L is the amount of labor. Find the following.

   (a) The marginal productivity of capital when $K = 27$ and $L = 8$

   (b) The marginal productivity of labor when $K = 27$ and $L = 8$

43. The amount of interest in dollars earned by a deposit of $1000 in a savings account paying r interest compounded continuously for t yr is

$$A(r, t) = 1000(e^{rt} - 1).$$

Find $\frac{\partial A}{\partial t}(.08, 5)$. What is the approximate increase in the earned interest from $t = 5$ to $t = 6$ if the interest rate remains fixed at 8%?

44. The resistance R (in ohms) of an electrical circuit whose current (in amperes) is I and whose voltage, or electromotive force (in volts) is E, is given by

$$R = \frac{E}{I}.$$

Find $\partial R/\partial E$ and $\partial R/\partial I$ when $I = 12$ amperes and $E = 150$ volts.

Section 8.3

In each of the following, find the critical points; that is, find the points (a, b) for which $f_x(a, b) = f_y(a, b) = 0$.

45. $f(x, y) = x^2 - xy + y$

46. $f(x, y) = \dfrac{1}{x^2 + y^2 + 1}$

47. $f(x, y) = 3xy^2 + x^3 - 3x$

48. $f(x, y) = 4xy - x^4 - y^4$

49. $f(x, y) = 6y - 8x - 2x^2 - y^2 + 4$

50. $f(x, y) = x^2 + y^2 - 2x + 4y$

51. $f(x, y) = e^{x^2+y^2}$

52. $f(x, y) = \ln(x^2 + y^2 + 1)$

Find all points where the functions have any relative extrema. Also identify any saddle points.

53. $f(x, y) = 4 - x^2 - y^2$ 54. $f(x, y) = x^3 - 6xy + 2y^3$

55. $f(x, y) = 9xy - x^3 - y^3 + 7$

56. Find all relative extrema for the function z graphed below.

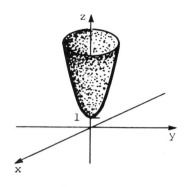

57. The cost of manufacturing x units of item A and y units of item B is given by
$$C(x, y) = 5x^2 + y^2 - 10x - 6y + 15.$$
Find the number of each item that should be produced to minimize costs.

Section 8.4

Use Lagrange multipliers to find extrema of the functions defined as follows, subject to the given constraints.

58. Maximum of $f(x, y) = 3xy$, subject to $x + 2y = 4$

59. Minimum of $f(x, y) = x^2 + y^2$, subject to $y - x = 4$

60. Maximum of $f(x, y) = 2x^2 - 3y^2$, subject to $y = x + 1$

61. Maximum of $f(x, y) = x^2y$, subject to $y + 4x = 84$

62. Minimum of $f(x, y, z) = x^2 + y^2 + z^2$, subject to $x + y + z = 1$

63. Find two numbers x and y such that $x - y = -5$ and $-x^2 + 6x - y^2 - 4y$ is maximized.

64. Find three positive numbers whose sum is 120 and whose product is a maximum.

65. A manufacturer produces two types of ceiling fans, A and B. Suppose x thousand units of fan A and y thousand units of fan B are produced. If the revenue function in dollars is

$$R(x, y) = 4x + 5y + xy - x^2 - y^2,$$

find the quantities of fans A and B that should be produced to maximize revenue.

66. A box with a square base and no top is to have a volume of 500 in³. Find the dimensions of such a box that has minimum surface area.

Section 8.5

67. Sales (in thousands of dollars) of a certain company are given in the table below.

Year, x	1	2	3	4	5	6	7
Sales, y	78	75	65	54	51	50	43

   (a) Plot the points on a scatter diagram and find the equation for the least squares line for this data. Graph this line on the same axes.

   (b) What sales amount would you predict for year 9 based on this equation?

68. The data below relate the score x on a pretest to the score y on a posttest.

x	52	46	69	54	61	48
y	74	66	94	91	84	80

   (a) Plot the points on a scatter diagram. Then find the equation of the least squares line and graph it on the same set of axes.

   (b) Using the equation of Part (a), predict the posttest score for someone whose pretest score is 60.

69. A meteorologist gives the following temperature readings in his weather updates.

Time (P.M.)	1	2	4	5
Temperature (°F)	82	87	95	98

   (a) Find the least squares equation for this data.

   (b) Estimate the temperature at 3 P.M.

Section 8.6

Find dz or dw, as appropriate, for each of the following.

70. $z = 3x^3 - 4y^2$

71. $z = 6x^2y - 3y^3$

72. $z = \dfrac{2x + y}{2x - y}$

73. $z = e^{xy}$

74. $z = 2x^2 - \sqrt{x - y}$

75. $z = xy^2e^{x+y}$

76. $z = \ln(x^2 + y^2) + x^2 \ln y$

77. $w = x^3 - 4y^2 + z$

78. $w = -5x^4y^3z^{10}$

In the following exercises, evaluate dz using the given functions and values.

79. $z = x^2 + y^2 - 4xy$, $x = -1$, $y = 2$, $dx = -.02$, $dy = .05$

80. $z = \ln(x + y)$, $x = 3$, $y = 2$, $dx = .02$, $dy = -.03$

In the following exercises, evaluate dw using the given functions and values.

81. $w = x^2y^2z^2$, $x = 1$, $y = 2$, $z = 3$, $dx = .01$, $dy = .02$, $dz = .03$

82. $w = \dfrac{\ln(x^2 + y^2)}{z^2}$, $x = 0$, $y = -2$, $z = 1$, $dx = .1$, $dy = .2$, $dz = -.1$

83. $w = x^2y + y^2z + z^2x$, $x = 1$, $y = 2$, $z = -1$, $dx = .2$, $dy = .1$, $dz = .2$

84. The manufacturing cost of a coffeemaker is approximated by
$$m(x, y) = x^2 + y^2$$
where x is the cost of materials and y is the cost of labor. The company presently spends \$1 on materials and \$3 on labor. Use differentials to approximate the change in cost if the company spends \$1.10 on materials and \$3.20 on labor.

85. A box with a square base has four rectangular sides. Approximate the change in volume if each edge of the base is increased from 10 cm to 10.1 cm and the height of the box is increased from 20 cm to 20.2 cm.

86. The production function for a small country is
$$z = x^{.7}y^{.3}$$
where x represents units of labor and y represents units of capital. At present 35 units of labor and 28 units of capital are available. Use differentials to estimate the change in production if the number of units of labor is increased to 40 units and capital is decreased to 24 units.

87. A cylindrical tank of radius 2 ft and height 10 ft is to receive an industrial coating 1/8 inch thick.

  (a) Approximate the volume of the coating needed.

  (b) If the coating costs $100 per cubic foot, how much will it cost to coat this tank?

Section 8.7

Evaluate each of the following integrals.

88. $\int_2^5 (3x^2 + y)\,dx$

89. $\int_{-2}^2 (x^2 + yx^3 + 1)\,dy$

90. $\int_0^1 (10x^2y^4 - 3xy^2 + 2y)\,dy$

91. $\int_2^4 xy\sqrt{x^2 + y}\,dx$

92. $\int_1^2 \frac{x^2}{y}\,dx$

93. $\int_1^4 (3x^2 + y)\,dy$

94. $\int_{-1}^0 xye^{x^2+y^2}\,dx$

95. $\int_{-1}^2 (8x^2y - 6xy^2)\,dy$

Evaluate each of the following iterated integrals.

96. $\int_0^1 \left[\int_0^2 (x^3y + 4xy^2)\,dx \right] dy$

97. $\int_2^4 \left[\int_1^3 \left(\frac{1}{x^2} + \frac{1}{y^2} \right) dx \right] dy$

98. $\int_1^e \left[\int_{-1}^1 \frac{y^2}{x}\,dy \right] dx$

99. $\int_0^2 \left[\int_0^1 xe^{xy}\,dy \right] dx$

100. $\int_0^1 \left[\int_{-2}^4 (4xy^3 - 3x^2y)\,dy \right] dx$

Evaluate each of the following double integrals.

101. $\int_0^2 \int_{\frac{1}{2}x}^x (x^2 + y^2)\,dy\,dx$

102. $\int_0^4 \int_{\sqrt{y}}^2 2xy\,dx\,dy$

103. $\int_0^4 \int_0^x e^{-x^2}\,dy\,dx$

104. $\int_1^2 \int_0^{\ln x} x^2e^y\,dy\,dx$

105. $\int_3^4 \int_1^2 \frac{1}{y}\,dx\,dy$

106. $\int_1^4 \int_0^2 (3x^2 + y)\,dx\,dy$

Find each double integral over the region R with boundaries as indicated.

107. $\iint\limits_{R} (2x + 3y)\,dx\ dy;\ 0 \le x \le 1,\ 0 \le y \le 2$

108. $\iint\limits_{R} (x^2 + y^2)\,dx\ dy;\ -1 \le x \le 1,\ 0 \le y \le 2$

109. $\iint\limits_{R} e^{x+y}\,dy\ dx;\ 0 \le y \le 1,\ 0 \le x \le 2$

110. $\iint\limits_{R} (x^2 y)\,dx\ dy;\ 1 \le x \le 3,\ 0 \le y \le 4$

111. $\iint\limits_{R} \sqrt{xy}\ dy\ dx;\ 1 \le y \le 4,\ 4 \le x \le 9$

112. $\iint\limits_{R} (2ye^x)\,dx\ dy;\ 0 \le x \le 1,\ -1 \le y \le 2$

CHAPTER 9   DIFFERENTIAL EQUATIONS

Section 9.1

Find general solutions for the following differential equations.

1. $\dfrac{dy}{dx} = 8x + 1$

2. $\dfrac{dy}{dx} + 3 = 3x^2 - 5x$

3. $\dfrac{dy}{dx} = \dfrac{x^2}{y}$

4. $\dfrac{dy}{dx} = \dfrac{x + 1}{y}$

5. $\dfrac{dy}{dx} = 3\sqrt{x} - 2x$

6. $\dfrac{dy}{dx} = e^{3x}$

7. $\dfrac{dy}{dx} = 2e^{-3x}$

8. $e^x \dfrac{dy}{dx} = e^y$

9. $\dfrac{dy}{dx} = \dfrac{3}{x + 2}$

10. $\dfrac{dy}{dx} = \dfrac{\ln |x|}{x}$

11. $\dfrac{dy}{dx} = x\sqrt{3x^2 + 1}$

12. $\dfrac{dy}{dx} = \dfrac{2 - 3x}{1 + 2y}$

13. $\dfrac{dy}{dx} = x\sqrt{3x + 1}$

14. $4x^2 + 7\dfrac{dy}{dx} = 0$

15. $\dfrac{dy}{dx} = xe^{3x}$

16. $\dfrac{dy}{dx} = e^{x+1}$

17. $\dfrac{dy}{dx} = y + 7$

18. $\dfrac{dy}{dx} = \dfrac{e^{-x}}{y}$

19. $\dfrac{dy}{dx} = (4 - 3x)y$

Find particular solutions for the following differential equations.

20. $\dfrac{dy}{dx} = 5x^4 + 2$; $y = 3$ when $x = 0$

21. $\dfrac{dy}{dx} = \dfrac{1}{xy}$; $y = 1$ when $x = 1$

Find particular solutions for the following differential equations.

22. $\dfrac{dy}{dx} = 2x^3 - 3x^2 + 2$; $y = 0$ when $x = 2$

23. $\dfrac{dy}{dx} = \dfrac{2x + 3}{y + 1}$; $y = 4$ when $x = 2$

24. $\dfrac{dy}{dx} = 2(e^{-x} - 4)$; $y = 3$ when $x = 0$

25. $\dfrac{dy}{dx} = \dfrac{1}{4x + 1}$; $y = 3$ when $x = 0$

26. $\dfrac{dy}{dx} = 4e^{-2x} + 2x$; $y = 0$ when $x = 0$

27. $\dfrac{dy}{dx} = e^{.2x-1}$; $y = 2$ when $x = 5$

28. $2x \dfrac{dy}{dx} - 4y\sqrt{x} = 0$; $y = 1$ when $x = 4$

29. $\dfrac{dy}{dx} = \dfrac{4x}{4x^2 + 3}$; $y = 2$ when $x = 0$

30. $\dfrac{dy}{dx} = \dfrac{2xy}{x^2 + 1}$; $y = 10$ when $x = 2$

31. $\dfrac{dy}{dx} = 4x^3 e^{-y}$; $y = 0$ when $x = 1$

32. $\dfrac{dy}{dx} = \sqrt[3]{x^2 y}$; $y = 8$ when $x = 1$

33. $\dfrac{dy}{dx} = \dfrac{e^{x+1}}{y}$; $y = 1$ when $x = 0$

34. The marginal profit of a certain company is given by

$$\frac{dy}{dx} = \frac{50}{18 - 2x}$$

where x represents the amount in thousands of dollars spent on advertising. If the profit is $1500 when nothing is spent on advertising, find the profit if $2000 is spent on advertising.

35. A company has found that the rate of change of sales during an advertising campaign is

$$\frac{dy}{dx} = 20e^{.02x},$$

where y is the sales in thousands of dollars at time x in months. If the sales are $100,000 when x = 0, find the sales at the end of 5 months.

36. If inflation grows continuously at 5%/yr, in how many years will $1 be worth $.25?

37. Assume that agriculture in the United States has the capacity this year to grow enough food to maintain 300 million people and that food output increases at 1%/yr. Also assume that the U.S. population is 230 million and growing at 3%/yr. Assume exponential growth in both cases. Based on these assumptions, in how many years will the U.S. population be equal to the food supply?

38. A fruit fly population grows in proportion to the number of fruit flies alive. Suppose the growth constant is 10% and there are 30 fruit flies initially, or when t = 0 days.

    (a) Find the number of fruit flies after 2 wk.

    (b) How many days are required for the population to reach 1000 fruit flies?

    (c) How long does it take for the population to double?

    (d) How many days are required for the population to go from 12,000 to 24,000 fruit flies?

39. A small fishing lake has been stocked with 100 trout. It is estimated that the lake can support a maximum of 5000 trout and that the growth constant for the trout is 40%/yr. If fishing will be permitted when the trout population reaches 1800, when will fishing be allowed?

40. (a) The Biff Beer Company had daily sales of 3,000,000 liters of beer on the day it decided to stop all of its advertising. Four months later its sales had been reduced by 50%. If the sales decline was exponential, what were the expected sales 1 yr after the advertising campaign was stopped?

    (b) After 6 mo of no advertising, the folks at Biff Beer returned to advertising on Smasher's football games. Their sales then began to increase by 5%/mo. How many months were necessary to achieve daily sales of 3,000,000 liters again?

41. It is determined that the rate of growth of the population of a certain town is given by

$$\frac{dP}{dt} = k\sqrt{P}.$$

If the population grew from 8000 in 1978 (t = 0) to 18,000 in 1988 (t = 10), in what year will the population reach 32,000?

Section 9.2

Find the general solution for each differential equation.   (Assume y′ = dy/dx.)

42. y′ − 4y = 2

43. y′ + 3y = 5

44. y′ + 4xy = 11x

45. y′ + 2xy = 5x

46. y′ + x²y = 5x²

47. $\frac{dy}{dx}$ = y − e⁻ˣ

48. eˣy′ + eˣy = x

Solve each differential equation subject to the given condition.

49. y′ + xy = x; y = 3 when x = 0

50. y′ = x²(1 − y); y = 4 when x = 0

51. y′ + 5y = eˣ; y = 1 when x = 0

52. y′ + 2x = 4xy; y = 2 when x = 0

53. xy′ + y = xeˣ²; y = e when x = 1

54. xy′ + 2y − 5 = 0; y = 0 when x = 1

55. x² $\frac{dy}{dx}$ + 5xy − x = 0; y = 16/5 when x = 1

56. A roast at a temperature of 50°F is put into a 300°F oven. After 1 hr the roast has reached a tmperature of 150°F. Newton's law of cooling states that

$$\frac{dT}{dt} = -k(T - T_F),$$

where T is the temperature of the object, T_F is the temperature of the surrounding medium at time t, and k is a constant. Use Newton's law to find the temperature of the roast after 2 hr.

57. A cooked roast is placed in the refrigerator when its temperature is 200°F. The temperature inside the refrigerator is 40°F. One half hour later, the temperature of the roast is 140°F.

   (a) Find an equation for the temperature of the roast in terms of the number of hours it has been in the refrigerator.

   (b) Find the temperature of the roast after 1 hr.

   (c) Find the temprature of the roast after 3 hr.

Section 9.3

Use Euler's method to approximate the indicated function value for $y = f(x)$ to three decimal places using $h = .2$.

58. $y' = x^2 + 1$; $f(0) = 1$; find $f(1)$ 59. $y' = x + y$; $f(0) = 1$; find $f(.4)$

60. $y' = \dfrac{2y}{x} + \dfrac{1}{x}$; $f(1) = 0$; find $f(1.6)$ 61. $y' = e^{-x} + 1$; $f(0) = 2$; find $(.6)$

Use Euler's method to approximate the indicated function value for $y = f(x)$ to three decimal places using $h = .1$.

62. $y' = 2x + 3$; $f(1) = 2$; find $f(1.4)$ 63. $y' = x^{-1} + y$; $f(1) = 1$; find $f(1.5)$

64. $y' = -xy + x$; $f(0) = 2$; find $f(.5)$ 65. $y' = \sqrt{xy}$; $f(1) = 1$; find $f(1.6)$

For each of the following exercises, solve the differential equation and find the indicated function value to three decimal places.

66. $y' = x^2 + 1$; $f(0) = 1$; find $f(1)$ 67. $y' = 2x + 3$; $f(1) = 2$; find $f(1.4)$

68. $y' = x + y$; $f(0) = 1$; find $f(.4)$ 69. $y' = e^{-x} + 1$; $f(0) = 2$; find $f(.6)$

70. $y' = x^{-1} + 1$; $f(1) = 1$; find $f(1.5)$ 71. $y' = \dfrac{2y}{x} + \dfrac{1}{x}$; $f(1) = 0$; find $f(1.6)$

72. $y' = -xy + x$; $f(0) = 2$; find $f(.5)$ 73. $y' = \ = \sqrt{xy}$; $f(1) = 1$; find $f(1.6)$

74. Let $y = f(x)$ and $y' = 2x^2 - 1$ with $f(0) = 0$. Use Euler's method with $h = .1$ to approximate $f(.3)$ to three decimal places. Then solve the differential equation and find $f(.3)$ to three decimal places. Also, find $y_3 - f(x_3)$.

75. Let $y = f(x)$ and $y' = 2 + y$, with $f(0) = 0$. Construct a table like the ones in Example 2 of this section for $[0, 1]$, with $h = .2$. Then graph the polygonal approximation of the graph of $y = f(x)$.

Section 9.4

76. Mr. Gordon deposits $1500 in an IRA at 8% interest compounded continuously. He makes continuous deposits at the rate of $1500/yr until his retirement in 15 yr. How much will he have accumulated at this time?

77. To provide for retirement, Mr. Gordon plans to make continuous deposits into a savings account at the rate of $2000/yr, with no initial deposit. How long will it take him to accumulate $74,800 if the money earns interest at 8% annually compounded continuously?

78. Suppose Mr. Gordon makes an initial deposit of $5000 into a savings account and then makes continuous deposits at the rate of $2000/yr. How long will it take him to accumulate $74,600 if the money earns interest at 8% annually compounded continuously?

In each of the following exercises, find an equation relating x to y, given the indicated equations which describes the interactions of two competing species and their growth rates. Find the value of x and y for which both growth rates are zero.

79. $\dfrac{dx}{dt} = 2x - 5xy$

$\dfrac{dy}{dt} = -3y + 4xy$

80. $\dfrac{dx}{dt} = 3xy - 2x$

$\dfrac{dy}{dt} = 4xy - y$

81. $\dfrac{dx}{dt} = y - 1$

$\dfrac{dy}{dt} = ye^{x-1} - y$

82. An influenza epidemic spreads at a rate proportional to the product of the number of people infected and the number not infected; that is, in a population of size N, when y people have been infected,

$$\frac{dy}{dt} = a(N - y)y$$

for a constant a.

(a) If 20 people in a community of 4000 people are infected at the beginning of an epidemic, and 100 people are infected 10 days later, write an equation for the number y of people infected after t days.

(b) When will half the community be infected?

83. The equation

$$\frac{dy}{dt} = a(N - y)y$$

can be used to describe the diffusion of information where N is the size of the population, y is the number of people who have heard a particular piece of information and a is a positive constant.

(a) If 4 people in an office with 100 employees heard the rumor initially and if 10 people have heard it 4 days later, write an equation for the number y that have heard the rumor in t days.

(b) When will 85 employees have heard the rumor?

84. Suppose a tank contains 100 gal of a solution of dissolved salt and water, which is kept uniform by stirring. If pure water is now allowed to flow into the tank at the rate of 4 gal/min, and the mixture flows out at the rate of 2 gal/min, how much salt will remain in the tank after t min, if 20 lb of salt are in the mixture initially?

85. A tank holds 100 gal of water which contains 20 lb of dissolved salt. A brine (salt) solution is flowing into the tank at the rate of 4 gal/min while the solution flows out of the tank at a rate of 4 gal/min. The brine solution entering the tank has a salt concentration of 1 lb/gal.

(a) Find an expression for the amount of salt in the tank at any time t.

(b) How much salt is present after 2 hr?

CHAPTER 10   PROBABILITY AND CALCULUS

Section 10.1

In the following exercises, decide whether or not the functions are probability density functions on the given intervals. If a function is not a probability density function, tell why not.

1. $f(x) = \frac{1}{4}(x - 3)$; [4, 6]

2. $f(x) = x^{3/2}$; [1, 4]

3. $f(x) = \frac{1}{5}x + \frac{2}{5}$; [0, 10]

4. $f(x) = \frac{1}{8}$; [2, 10]

5. $f(x) = 1 - x$; [0, 5]

6. $f(x) = e^{-2x}$; [0, ∞)

7. $f(x) = 4x^3$; [0, 1]

8. $f(x) = \sqrt{x}$; [3, 4]

9. $f(x) = \frac{1}{4}e^{-x/4}$; [0, ∞)

10. $f(x) = \frac{1}{3}x^{-2/3}$; [1, 8]

In each of the following exercises, find a value of k that will make f(x) a probability density function.

11. $f(x) = kx^{3/2}$; [1, 4]

12. $f(x) = 8k$; [2, 10]

13. $f(x) = k(1 + x)$; [0, 5]

14. $f(x) = ke^{-2x}$; [0, ∞)

15. $f(x) = -kx$; [1, 7]

16. $f(x) = kx^{1/2}$; [4, 9]

17. **(a)** Show that f(x) = .1 is a probability density function on [2, 12]. Then find the following probabilities.

   (b) P(x ≥ 10)   **(c)** P(4 ≤ x ≤ 7)   **(d)** P(x ≤ 6)

18. The probability density function of a random variable x is defined by

$$f(x) = \frac{1}{8}x \text{ for } [0, 4].$$

Find the following probabilities.

   (a) P(x ≤ 1)   **(b)** P(2 ≤ x ≤ 3)   **(c)** P(x ≤ 3)

19. The probability density function of a random variable x is defined by

$$f(x) = 1 - \frac{1}{\sqrt{x - 2}} \text{ for } [3, 6].$$

Find the following probabilities.

   (a) P(x ≥ 3)   **(b)** P(x ≤ 4)

20. The life (in months) of a cassette has a probability density function defined by

$$f(x) = .1e^{-.1x} \text{ for } [0, \infty).$$

Find the probability that a randomly selected cassette will last each of the following lengths of time.

(a) At most 10 mo

(b) More than 5 mo

(c) Between 2 mo and 10 mo

21. The length (in minutes) of a storm in a tropical rain forest is a continuous random variable with probability density function defined by

$$f(x) = 2x^{-3} \text{ for } [1, \infty).$$

Find the probability that a storm lasts less than 20 min.

22. The time in years until a particular radioactive particle decays is a random variable with probability density function defined by

$$f(t) = .05e^{-.05t} \text{ for } [0, \infty).$$

Find the probability that a certain such particle decays in less than 80 yr.

23. The number of arrivals per hour of customers at a ticket window is a random variable with probability density function defined by

$$f(x) = \frac{1}{120}(x - 3) \text{ for } [10, 20].$$

Find the probability that at least 15 customers will arrive within a particular hour.

24. Suppose that at Saul's Discount Stores the amount of time one must wait in a checkout lane is a random variable with probability density function defined by

$$f(x) = \frac{12}{5}(x + 2)^{-2} \text{ for } [0, 10].$$

Find the probability of having to wait more than 4 min to check out.

Section 10.2

For the probability density function defined in each of the following exercises, find the expected value, the variance, and the standard deviation. Round answers to the nearest hundredth.

25. $f(x) = \frac{1}{8}$ for $[2, 10]$

26. $f(x) = \frac{1}{4}(x - 3)$ for $[4, 6]$

27. $f(x) = 6x - 6x^2$ for $[0, 1]$

28. $f(x) = 24x^{-4}$ for $[2, \infty)$

29. $f(x) = 12x^2 - 12x^3$ for [0, 1]   30. $f(x) = \dfrac{1}{2\sqrt{x}}$ for [1, 4]

31. $f(x) = \dfrac{3\sqrt{x}}{16}$ for [0, 4]   32. $f(x) = \dfrac{1}{3}(1 - x^{-1/2})$ for [4, 9]

33. The lifetime in days of a certain plant species is a random variable with probability density function defined by

$$f(x) = \frac{x}{3200} \text{ for } [0, 80].$$

Find the expected lifetime, the variance, and the standard deviation.

34. The length of life in hours of a certain kind of battery is a random variable with probability density function defined by

$$f(x) = \frac{1}{18\sqrt{x}} \text{ for } [1, 100].$$

(a) What is the expected life of such a battery?

(b) Find σ.

(c) Find the probability that one of these bulbs lasts longer than one standard deviation above the mean.

35. The height in centimeters of a particular type of mushroom is a continuous random variable with probability density function defined by

$$f(x) = 4x^{-3} \text{ for } [1, \infty).$$

What is the expected height of a mushroom?

For the probability density function defined in each of the following exercises, **(a)** find the probability that the value of the random variable will be greater than the mean and **(b)** find the probability that the value of the random variable will be within one standard deviation of the mean. Round answers to the nearest thousandth.

36. $f(x) = .125$ for [2, 10]   37. $f(x) = .25(x - 3)$ for [4, 6]

38. $f(x) = 6x - 6x^2$ for [0, 1]   39. $f(x) = 24x^{-4}$ for [2, ∞)

40. $f(x) = 12x^2 - 12x^3$ for [0, 1]   41. $f(x) = \dfrac{1}{2\sqrt{x}}$ for [1, 4]

42. $f(x) = \dfrac{3\sqrt{x}}{16}$ for [0, 4]   43. $f(x) = \dfrac{1}{3}(1 - x^{-1/2})$ for [4, 9]

For the probability density function defined in each of the following exercises, (a) find the mean, (b) find the median, and (c) find the probability that the value of the random variable will be between the mean and the median.

44. $f(x) = \frac{1}{18}x$ for [0, 6]

45. $f(x) = 2(x - 1)$ for [1, 2]

Section 10.3

For the probability density function defined in each of the following exercises, find (a) the expected value, (b) the variance, and (c) the standard deviation.

46. $f(x) = .1e^{-.1x}$ for [0, ∞)

47. $f(x) = .05e^{-.05x}$ for [0, ∞)

For the probability density function defined in each of the following exercises, (a) find the probability that the value of the random variable will be greater than the mean and (b) find the probability that the value of the random variable will be within one standard deviation of the mean.

48. $f(x) = .1e^{-.1x}$ for [0, ∞)

49. $f(x) = .05e^{-.05x}$ for [0, ∞)

50. The number of bills per day sent out by a small business is uniformly distributed over the interval [2, 10].

   (a) Find the probability density function for this distribution.

   (b) What is the expected number of bills the business will send out on a particular day?

   (c) What is the probability that no more than 4 bills will be sent on a given day?

51. The rainfall in inches in a certain region is uniformly distributed over the interval [28, 50].

   (a) Find the mean.

   (b) Find the standard deviation.

   (c) Find the probability that the number of inches of rainfall will be greater than the mean.

52. The time in years that a seedling pine tree survives is exponentially distributed with an expected value of 2 yr.

   (a) Find the probability density function for this distribution.

   (b) Find the probability that a seedling survives at least 5 yr.

53. Suppose the useful life of an electronic component is exponentially distributed with an expected value of 100 days.

    (a) Find the probability density function for this distribution.

    (b) Find the probability that a component lasts between 70 and 80 days.

    (c) Find the probability that the component lasts more than 120 days.

Find the percent of area under a normal curve for each of the following.

54. The region to the left of $z = 2.10$

55. The region to the left of $z = -1.43$

56. The region to the right of $z = 1.87$

57. The region to the right of $z = -.72$

58. The region between $z = 2.31$ and $z = .48$

59. The region between $z = -.23$ and $z = -1.47$

60. The region between $z = 1.04$ and $z = -1.04$

61. The region between $z = 1.93$ and $z = -.75$

Find a z-score satisfying the condition given for a normal curve in each of the following.

62. 18% of the area is to the left of z.

63. 43% of the area is to the right of z.

64. The middle 50% of the area is between z and -z.

Assume a normal distribution in each of the following exercises.

65. The average inventory for a part in a certain stockroom is 23 with a standard deviation of 8.2. Find the probability that no more than 15 items are on hand.

66. The useful life in hundreds of hours of a certain transistor has a mean of 38.3 with a standard deviation of 19.2. Find the probability that a particular transistor would last for at least 5000 hr (or 50 hundred hr).

67. The average number of scales in hundreds on a particular species of fish is 7.1 with a standard deviation of 2.5. What is the probability that one such fish would have at least 500 scales?

CHAPTER 11   THE TRIGONOMETRIC FUNCTIONS

Section 11.1

Convert each of the following degree measures to radians. Leave each answer as a multiple of π.

1. 120°

2. 300°

3. −600°

4. −240°

5. 18°

6. 36°

7. 1.5°

8. 2.4°

9. 500°

10. 900°

Convert each of the following radian measures to degrees.

11. $\frac{7\pi}{3}$

12. $\frac{5\pi}{2}$

13. 8π

14. 3π

15. $-\frac{2\pi}{3}$

16. $-\frac{4\pi}{5}$

17. $\frac{11\pi}{20}$

18. $\frac{3\pi}{5}$

Find the values of the six trigonometric functions for angle α, in standard position, having the following points on its terminal side.

19. (9, 12)

20. (−4, 3)

21. (7, −24)

22. (−9, −40)

23. (−11, 60)

24. (6, −8)

25. (−8, −15)

Evaluate the following function values without using a calculator or a table.

26. $\sin\left(-\frac{\pi}{6}\right)$

27. $\sec\frac{2\pi}{3}$

28. $\tan\frac{7\pi}{4}$

29. $\csc\left(-\frac{\pi}{4}\right)$

30. $\cos\frac{\pi}{6}$

31. $\cot\frac{5\pi}{4}$

32. $\sin\left(-\frac{5\pi}{6}\right)$

33. $\tan\frac{5\pi}{6}$

34. $\cos\frac{7\pi}{3}$

35. $\csc 10\pi$

36. $\sec(-5\pi)$

37. $\cot\frac{3\pi}{2}$

38. $\cot\left(-\frac{2\pi}{3}\right)$

39. $\sin 4\pi$

40. $\tan\frac{8\pi}{3}$

41. $\sec\left(-\frac{5\pi}{3}\right)$

42. $\cos\frac{3\pi}{4}$

43. $\cot\left(-\frac{3\pi}{4}\right)$

44. $\csc\frac{7\pi}{6}$

45. $\sin\left(-\frac{8\pi}{3}\right)$

46. $\sin(-120°)$

47. $\tan 240°$

48. $\cos 150°$

49. $\csc 330°$

Use a calculator to find the following function values.

50. sin 67°   **51.** tan 123°   **52.** cos (−63°)

53. sec 85°   **54.** sin 2.314   **55.** cos .4974

56. tan 3.046   **57.** sin (−.6341)

Graph each function defined as follows over a two-period interval.

58. $y = -\frac{1}{2} \sin x$ **59.** $y = -2 \cos x$ **60.** $y = 3 \tan x$

61. $y = 5 \sin x$ **62.** $y = -2 \tan x$ **63.** $y = \cos 2x$

64. Without graphing, guess the minimum and maximum values for

$$f(x) = 4 + \sin x.$$

65. At a department store, swimsuit sales can be approximated by

$$S(t) = 500 + 400 \sin \frac{\pi}{12}t,$$

where t is time in months, with t = 0 corresponding to December. Find the sales for each of the following months.

(a) December   **(b)** February   **(c)** April

(d) June   **(e)** August   **(f)** October

66. The temperature (in degrees Fahrenheit) of a small lake on a summer day can be approximated by

$$T(x) = 78 + 3 \cos \left[\frac{\pi}{12}(t - 15)\right],$$

where t is time in hours and t = 0 corresponds to midnight, t = 1 corresponds to 1 A.M., and so on. Find the water temperature at the following times.

(a) Midnight   **(b)** 6 A.M.   **(c)** 3 P.M.   **(d)** 6 P.M.

Section 11.2

Find the derivative of each of the following functions.

67. $y = \cos 3x$ **68.** $y = \sin 5x$

69. $y = 3 \sin^5 x$ **70.** $y = 2 \tan 7x^2$

71. $y = \tan(4 - x^2)$

72. $y = 3\cos^3 3x^2$

73. $y = \tan^3 x$

74. $y = \sin e^x$

75. $y = \sin x \cos x$

76. $y = \dfrac{\sin x}{\tan x}$

77. $y = e^{-\cos x}$

78. $y = \dfrac{\sin x^4}{x^4}$

79. $y = (\sin x)(\tan x - 1)$

80. $y = x^2 \sin x$

81. $y = x \cos x^2$

82. $y = x^2 \sin 4x$

83. $y = \dfrac{x + 1}{\sin x}$

84. $y = \dfrac{\cos x - 1}{\cos x + 1}$

85. $y = \ln|\tan x|$

86. $y = \dfrac{\sin^2 x}{1 - \sin x}$

87. $y = e^{2x} \cos x$

88. $y = \cos(\ln x)$

89. $y = \left(\dfrac{\cos 2x}{\cos x}\right)^{1/3}$

90. $y = \dfrac{\sin x}{x - 4}$

91. $y = \dfrac{x \cos x}{\sin 2x}$

92. $y = \sin 3x \tan 3x$

93. $y = \sin x \sec^3 x$

94. A particle moves along a straight line. The distance of the particle from the origin at time t is given by
$$s(t) = 4 \sin t.$$
   (a) Find the velocity at $t = 0$ and at $t = \pi/2$.
   (b) Find the acceleration at $t = 3\pi/2$.

95. Find the equation of the line tangent to the graph of $y = 3\cos(x - \pi)$ at $x = \pi/4$.

96. Find the **(a)** velocity and **(b)** acceleration at time $t = \pi/4$, of the particle whose distance from the origin is described by
$$y = 3\sin 2t - \cos t.$$

Section 11.3

Find the following integrals.

97. $\displaystyle\int \sin 4x\, dx$

98. $\displaystyle\int (2 \sin x - \cos x)\, dx$

99. $\displaystyle\int \tan 6x\, dx$

100. $\displaystyle\int 4 \sec^2 3x\, dx$

101. $\displaystyle\int 2 \csc^2 5x\, dx$

102. $\displaystyle\int e^x \cos e^x\, dx$

103. $\displaystyle\int 2x \tan x^2\, dx$

104. $\displaystyle\int \frac{\cos x}{3 - 2 \sin x}\, dx$

105. $\displaystyle\int \sqrt{\sin x}\, \cos x\, dx$

106. $\displaystyle\int (\cos x)^{-3/4} \sin x\, dx$

107. $\displaystyle\int 4x^2 \sin 2x\, dx$

108. $\displaystyle -\int (x + 1) \sin (x + 1)^2\, dx$

Evaluate each definite integral.

109. $\displaystyle\int_0^{\pi/3} \sin 3x\, dx$

110. $\displaystyle\int_{\pi/2}^{5\pi/6} \cos x\, dx$

111. $\displaystyle\int_{\pi/6}^{\pi/3} (2 + 2 \sin x)\, dx$

112. $\displaystyle\int_0^{\pi/6} \sin x \cos x\, dx$

113. $\displaystyle\int_0^{\pi/4} x \sin 2x^2\, dx$

114. $\displaystyle\int_{\pi/3}^{\pi/2} \frac{\cos \sqrt{x}}{2\sqrt{x}}\, dx$

115. $\displaystyle\int_{\pi/6}^{\pi/3} \sec^2 x\, dx$

Find each improper integral by using the table of integrals.

116. $\displaystyle\int_{-\infty}^{0} e^x \sin 3x\, dx$

117. $\displaystyle\int_{0}^{\infty} e^{-x} \cos 2x\, dx$

Section 11.4

Give the value of y in radians.

118. $y = \sin^{-1} \dfrac{\sqrt{2}}{2}$

119. $y = \tan^{-1}\left(-\dfrac{\sqrt{3}}{3}\right)$

120. $y = \cos^{-1} \dfrac{1}{2}$

121. $y = \cos^{-1}\left(-\dfrac{\sqrt{3}}{2}\right)$

122. $y = \cos^{-1} 0$

123. $y = \tan^{-1} 0$

Use a calculator to give each value in degrees.

124. $\cos^{-1}(-.6428)$

125. $\sin^{-1} .5592$

126. $\tan^{-1}(-2.2671)$

Find the derivative of each of the following.

127. $y = \sin^{-1} 5x$

128. $y = \cos^{-1}(2 + x)$

129. $y = \tan^{-1} 3x^2$

130. $y = \cos^{-1}(-x)$

131. $y = \sin^{-1} x + \cos^{-1} x$

132. $y = \sin^{-1} x - \cos^{-1} x$

133. $y = \tan^{-1} \sqrt{x + 1}$

134. $y = \tan^{-1} e^x$

135. $y = \tan^{-1}(\ln |2x|)$

136. $y = \cos^{-1}\left(\dfrac{1}{x}\right)$

Find each of the following integrals.

137. $\displaystyle\int \dfrac{-2}{\sqrt{1 - x^2}}\, dx$

138. $\displaystyle\int \dfrac{5}{1 + x^2}\, dx$

139. $\displaystyle\int \dfrac{1}{\sqrt{1 - 9x^2}}\, dx$

140. $\displaystyle\int \dfrac{x^4}{1 + x^{10}}\, dx$

141. $\displaystyle\int \dfrac{-5}{\sqrt{1 - 25x^2}}\, dx$

142. $\displaystyle\int \dfrac{\sec^2 x}{1 + \tan^2 x}\, dx$

143. $\displaystyle\int \dfrac{3e^{3x}}{\sqrt{1 - e^{6x}}}\, dx$

144. $\displaystyle\int \dfrac{1}{x\sqrt{1 - (\ln x)^2}}\, dx$

145. $\displaystyle\int \frac{\ln x}{x\sqrt{1 - (\ln x)^4}}\, dx$ **146.** $\displaystyle\int_0^{1.5} \frac{1}{\sqrt{9 - x^2}}\, dx$

147. $\displaystyle\int_0^1 \frac{x^{1/2}}{1 + x^3}\, dx$ **148.** $\displaystyle\int_0^\infty \frac{1}{4x^2 + 1}\, dx$

Section 11.5

Find the slope of the tangent line to the graph of each equation at the given point.

149. $y = \sin x,\ x = \dfrac{\pi}{3}$ **150.** $y = \tan x,\ x = \dfrac{\pi}{4}$

151. $y = \cos x,\ x = \dfrac{\pi}{2}$ **152.** $y = \sin x,\ x = \dfrac{5\pi}{6}$

153. Verify that $s(t) = 4 \cos (\pi - t)$ satisfies the differential equation for simple harmonic motion; or, in this case, that $s''(t) = -4 \cos (\pi - t)$. Then find the maximum and minimum value of $s(t)$.

ANSWERS
TO
TEST ITEMS

CHAPTER 1   FUNCTIONS AND GRAPHS

Section 1.1

1. (-3, -8), (-2, -3), (-1, 2), (0, 7), (1, 12), (2, 17), (3, 22); range: {-8, -3, 2, 7, 12, 17, 22}   **2.** (-3, 33/4), (-2, 15/2), (-1, 27/4), (0, 6), (1, 21/4), (2, 9/2), (3, 15/4); range: {15/4, 9/2, 21/4, 6, 27/4, 15/2, 33/4}

3. (-3, -12), (-2, -15), (-1, -16), (0, -15), (1, -12), (2, -7), (3, 0); range: {-16, -15, -12, -7, 0}   **4.** (-3, -11), (-2, -9), (-1, -7), (0, -5), (1, -3), (2, -1), (3, 1); range: {-11, -9, -7, -5, -3, -1, 1}   **5.** (-3, 12), (-2, 3), (-1, -2), (0, -3), (1, 0), (2, 7), (3, 18); range: {-3, -2, 0, 3, 7, 12, 18}

6. (-3, 2), (-2, -1), (-1, 0), (0, 5), (1, 14), (2, 27), (3, 44); range: {-1, 0, 2, 5, 14, 27, 44}   **7.** (-3, -6), (-2, -1), (-1, 2), (0, 3), (1, 2), (2, -1), (3, -6); range: {-6, -1, 2, 3}   **8.** (-3, 23), (-2, 13), (-1, 7), (0, 5), (1, 7), (2, 13), (3, 23); range: {5, 7, 13, 23}   **9.** (-3, -3), (-2, -2), (-1, -1), (0, 0), (1, -1), (2, -2), (3, -3); range: {-3, -2, -1, 0}

10. (-3, 1), (-2, 2/3), (-1, 1/2), (0, 2/5), (1, 1/3), (2, 2/7), (3, 1/4); range: {1/4, 2/7, 1/3, 2/5, 1/2, 2/3, 1}   **11.** (-3, -1/4), (-2, 1), (-1, 1/4), (0, 1/5), (1, 1/4), (2, 1), (3, -1/4); range: {-1/4, 1/5, 1/4, 1}

12. (-3, -1/4), (-2, -3/7), (-1, -2/3), (0, -1), (1, -3/2), (2, -7/3), (3, -4); range: {-4, -7/3, -3/2, -1, -2/3, -3/7, -1/4}   **13.** (-3, -5), (-2, -5), (-1, -5), (0, -5), (1, -5), (2, -5), (3, -5); range: {-5}   **14.** (-3, -1/2), (-2, -1/2), (-1, -1/2), (0, -1/2), (1, -1/2), (2, -1/2), (3, -1/2); range: {-1/2}   **15.** (-3, 4), (-2, 3), (-1, 2), (0, 1), (1, 0), (2, 1), (3, 2); range: {0, 1, 2, 3, 4}   **16.** (a), (c)   **17.** (a) Not a function

(b) Function   **(c)** Function   **(d)** Not a function   **18.** (a) 15   (b) 5   (c) 4   (d) 4a + 7   **19.** (a) 17   (b) -3   (c) -5   (d) 8a + 1

20. (a) -6   (b) -6   (c) -13/4   (d) 4a² - 6a - 10   **21.** (a) -96   (b) 9   (c) 17/2   (d) -16a² - 18a + 4   **22.** (a) 15/7   (b) -5/3   (c) -1   (d) (4a + 7)/(4a - 1)   **23.** (a) 0   (b) -5   (c) -11/8

(d) $(4 - 2a)/(12a + 5)$ **24.** **(a)** -16 **(b)** -6 **(c)** $13/4$

(d) $12a^2 - 22a - 20$ **25.** **(a)** 3   **(b)** 3   **(c)** 3   **(d)** 3

26. **(a)** 13   **(b)** 4   **(c)** -17 **(d)** 31   **(e)** $-3a - 5$ **(f)** $8a^2 + 14a + 9$

(g) $3r - 11$ **(h)** $2r^2 - 3r + 4$ **(i)** $9/y - 5$ or $(9 - 5y)/y$ **(j)** $32/z^2 +$

$28/z + 9$ or $(32 + 28z + 9z^2)/z^2$ **(k)** $3x + 3h - 5$ **(l)** $2x^2 + 4xh + 2h^2 -$

$7x - 7h + 9$ **(m)** 3   **(n)** $4x + 2h - 7$ **27.** **(a)** 9   **(b)** 6   **(c)** -11

(d) 12   **(e)** $-2a - 3$ **(f)** $-4a^2 + 6a + 10$ **(g)** $2r - 7$ **(h)** $-r^2 - 5r + 6$

(i) $6/y - 3$ or $(6 - 3y)/y$ **(j)** $-16/z^2 + 12/z + 10$ or $(-16 + 12z + 10z^2)/z^2$

(k) $2x + 2h - 3$ **(l)** $-x^2 - 2xh - h^2 - 3x - 3h + 10$ **(m)** 2   **(n)** $-2x - h - 3$

28. Domain: $[-5, 4]$; range: $[-4, 8]$ **29.** Domain: $(-\infty, \infty)$; range: $(-\infty, 2]$

30. $(-\infty, -6] \cup [6, \infty)$ **31.** $[-5, 5]$ **32.** $(-\infty, -1) \cup (5, \infty)$

33. $(-\infty, -3) \cup (-3, 3) \cup (3, \infty)$ **34.** $(-\infty, \infty)$ **35.** $(-\infty, 1) \cup (1, \infty)$

36. **(a)** \$24   **(b)** \$72   **(c)** \$72   **(d)** \$48   **(e)** $\{24, 48, 72, 96, \ldots\}$

Section 1.2

37.

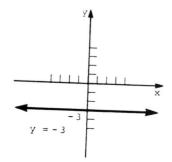

$y = -3$

38.

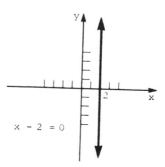

$x - 2 = 0$

39.

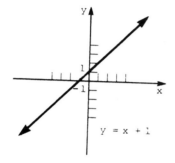

$y = x + 1$

40.

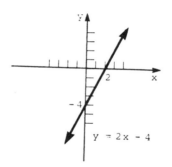

$y = 2x - 4$

41.

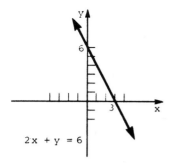

$2x + y = 6$

42.

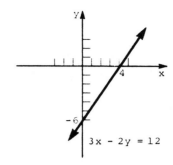

$3x - 2y = 12$

43.

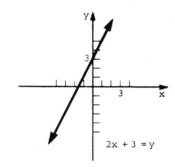

$2x + 3 = y$

44.

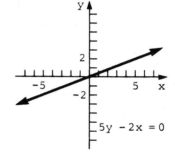

$5y - 2x = 0$

45.

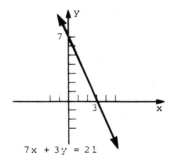

$7x + 3y = 21$

46.

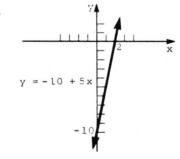

$y = -10 + 5x$

47.

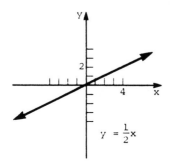

$y = \frac{1}{2}x$

48.

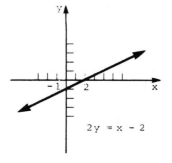

$2y = x - 2$

49.

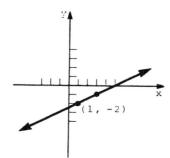

50.

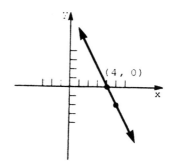

51. (a) Supply is 1, demand is 25.

    (b) Supply is 8/3, demand is 50/3.

    (c) Supply is 13/3, demand is 25/3.

    (d)

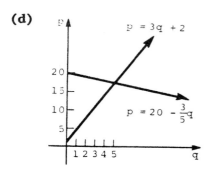

    (e) 17

    (f) 5

52. (a) Supply is 36/7, demand is 64/3.

    (b) Supply is 61/7, demand is 13.

    (c) Supply is 86/7, demand is 14/3.

    (d)

    (e) 59/5

    (f) 10

53. $p = (-1/15)q + 63/5$ **54.** $-5/6$ **55.** $3/2$ **56.** $7/11$

57. $-.3822$ **58.** $2/5$ **59.** Not defined   **60.** Not defined   **61.** 0

62. 6   **63.** $7/6$ **64.** $-3/4$ **65.** $-1/4$ **66.** $2/3$ **67.** -1

68. $5x - 6y = -28$ **69.** $2x + 3y = 2$ **70.** $x - 2y = 2$ **71.** $4x + y = 15$

72. $x + 2y = -5$ **73.** $3x - 2y = -2$ **74.** $x = 3$ **75.** $y = 3$

76. $2y = 7$ **77.** $x = -8$ **78.** $x - y = -2$ **79.** $5x - 4y = -6$

80. $x - 3y = 12$ **81.** $x + y = 5$ **82.** $3x - 5y = -4$ **83.** $5x + 2y = 9$

84. $x = 6$ **85.** $y = -5$ **86.** $y = -5$ **87.** $x = 0$ **88.** $5.872x - y = 17.363$ **89.** $x = 0$ **90.** $y = 0$ **91.** $9.274x + y = -32.309$

Section 1.3

92. C(x) = 20x + 550   **93.** C(x) = 90x + 750   **94.** C(x) = 25x + 425

95. C(x) = 8x + 100   **96.** C(x) = 70x + 5200   **97.** C(x) = 55x + 650

98. (a) 12 units   **(b)** C(x)/x = 75 + 900/x   **99. (a)** 300   **(b)** 600

(c) 1200   **(d)** 200   **(e)** 100   **100. (a)** $42,000   **(b)** $40,000

(c) $2.50 per unit   **(d)** $42.50   **101. (a)** 80 units   **(b)** No; cost will

be greater than revenue.

Section 1.4

102. Vertex is (0, 2); axis is
x = 0; no x-intercepts;
y-intercept = 2.

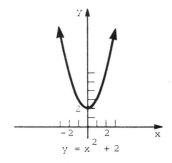

$$y = x^2 + 2$$

103. Vertex is (0, −4); axis is
x = 0; no x-intercepts;
y-intercept = −4.

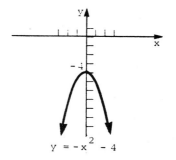

$$y = -x^2 - 4$$

104. Vertex is (3, 1); axis is
x = 3; no x-intercepts;
y-intercept = 10.

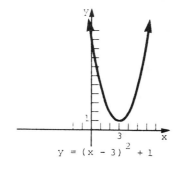

$$y = (x - 3)^2 + 1$$

105. Vertex is (−1, 2); axis is x = −1;
x-intercepts are $\dfrac{-3 \pm \sqrt{6}}{3} \approx -.184$
and −1.82; y-intercept = −1.

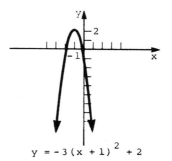

$$y = -3(x + 1)^2 + 2$$

106. Vertex is (5, 6); axis is x = 5; x-intercepts are $5 \pm 2\sqrt{3} \approx 8.46$ and 1.54; y-intercept = $-13/2$.

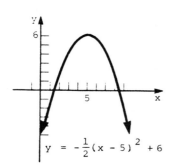

$$y = -\frac{1}{2}(x - 5)^2 + 6$$

107. Vertex is $(-3/4, -49/8)$; axis is x = $-3/4$; x-intercepts are $-5/2$ and 1; y-intercept = -5.

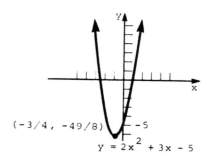

$$y = 2x^2 + 3x - 5$$

108. Vertex is $(5/2, -29/4)$; axis is x = $5/2$; x-intercepts are $\frac{5 \pm \sqrt{29}}{2} \approx 5.19$ and 2.31; y-intercept = -1.

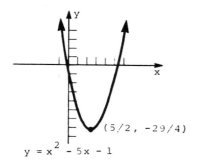

$$y = x^2 - 5x - 1$$

109. Vertex is $(-5/2, 39/4)$; axis is x = $-5/2$; x-intercepts are $\frac{-5 \pm \sqrt{13}}{2} \approx -.697$ and -4.30; y-intercept = -9.

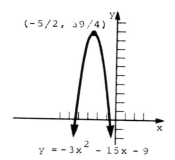

$$y = -3x^2 - 15x - 9$$

110. Vertex is $(1/2, 1/6)$; axis is x = $1/2$; no x-intercept; y-intercept = $1/4$.

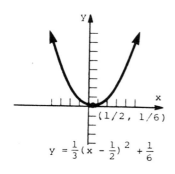

$$y = \frac{1}{3}\left(x - \frac{1}{2}\right)^2 + \frac{1}{6}$$

111. Vertex is (1, -1), axis is is x = 1; x-intercepts are $\frac{3 \pm 2\sqrt{3}}{3} \approx 2.15$ and $-.155$; y-intercept = $-1/4$.

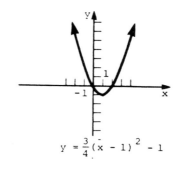

$$y = \frac{3}{4}(x - 1)^2 - 1$$

112. 25, 25   **113.** 50 ft by 25 ft   **114.** **(a)** 36 ft   **(b)** 3 sec

115. **(a)** $R(x) = 400x - x^2$ **(b)** $200   **(c)** $40,000

Section 1.5

116.

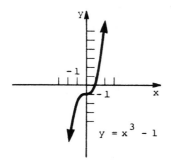

$y = x^3 - 1$

117.

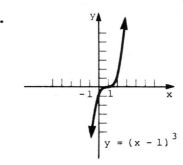

$y = (x - 1)^3$

118.

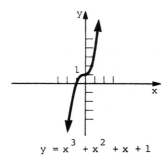

$y = x^3 + x^2 + x + 1$

119.

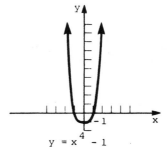

$y = x^4 - 1$

120.

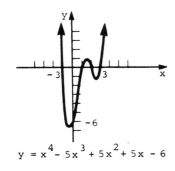

$y = x^4 - 5x^3 + 5x^2 + 5x - 6$

121. $y = 0$; $x = -1$; no x-intercept;
y-intercept = 5

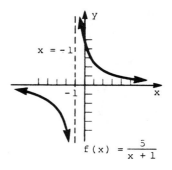

$f(x) = \dfrac{5}{x + 1}$

122. y = 0; x = 3/4; no x-intercept;
y-intercept = -1

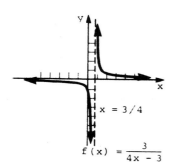

$$f(x) = \frac{3}{4x - 3}$$

123. y = 0; x = 5/2; no x-intercept;
y-intercept = -1/5

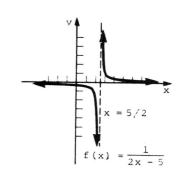

$$f(x) = \frac{1}{2x - 5}$$

124. y = 1/2; x = -3;
x-intercept = 3/2;
y-intercept = -1/4

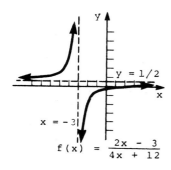

$$f(x) = \frac{2x - 3}{4x + 12}$$

125. y = -1/2; x = 3/2;
x-intercept = -1;
y-intercept = 1/3

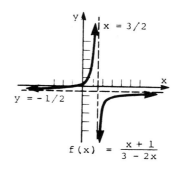

$$f(x) = \frac{x + 1}{3 - 2x}$$

126. y = 0; x = 3, x = -3;
x-intercept = 0;
y-intercept = 0

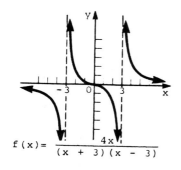

$$f(x) = \frac{4x}{(x + 3)(x - 3)}$$

127. **(a)** $0   **(b)** About $6000

(c) About $23,000

(d) About $264,000

(e) $495,000

(f) $625,000

Section 1.6

128.

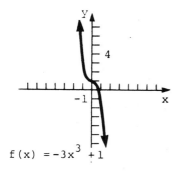

$f(x) = -3x^3 + 1$

129.

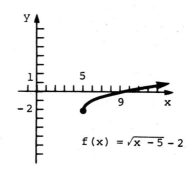

$f(x) = \sqrt{x-5} - 2$

130.

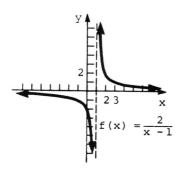

$f(x) = \dfrac{2}{x-1}$

131.

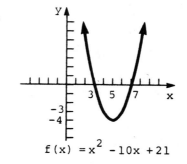

$f(x) = x^2 - 10x + 21$

CHAPTER 2   THE DERIVATIVE

Section 2.1

1. 1   2. Does not exist   3. Does not exist   4. 2   5. 0

6. 8   7. Does not exist   8. -28 9. $4/7$ 10. $-11/8$ 11. 2

12. -15 13. 144   14. 0   15. 3   16. 0   17. Does not exist

18. -4 19. -11 20. 3   21. $-1/16$ 22. Discontinuous

at $x = 2$; $f(2)$ does not exist; $\lim\limits_{x \to 2} f(x) = \infty$ 23. Discontinuous at

$x = 0$, $x = 4$; $f(0) = 3$, $f(4)$ does not exist; $\lim\limits_{x \to 0} f(x) = 0$, $\lim\limits_{x \to 4} f(x) = 4$

24. Discontinuous at $x = 3$; $f(3) = 2$, $\lim\limits_{x \to 3} f(x) = 5$ 25. (a) Yes   (b) No

(c) Yes   26. (a) No   (b) No   (c) Yes   27. (a) Yes   (b) Yes

(c) Yes   28. (a) Yes   (b) Yes   (a) No   29. (a) Yes   (b) Yes

(c) Yes   30. (a) No   (b) No   (c) No   (d) Yes   31. (a) Yes

(b) Yes   (c) No   32. (a) $70   (b) $69   (c) $68.33   (d) $70

(e) $69   (f) At $t = 4$, $t = 5$, $t = 6$, and so on

Section 2.2

33. 14   34. -10 35. $-1/28$ 36. $-2/105$ 37. 13   38. 26

39. (a) 3   (b) 13

Section 2.3

40. 0   41. 2   42. $4 - 2x$ 43. $3x^2 + 2x$ 44. $4x - 3x^2$

45. $-1/(x - 2)^2$ 46. $1/\sqrt{x}$ 47. (a) 3   (b) $12x - 4y = -1$

48. (a) 1   (b) $x - y = 4$ 49. (a) 0   (b) $y = 0$ 50. (a) $1/3$

(b) $x - 3y = -9$ 51. $1/4$ 52. 0   53. 0; 0; 0   54. -16; -4; -1

55. $-1/25$; $-1/9$; $-4/25$ 56. 3, 7   57. -4 58. Has derivatives for

all x 59. (a) $C'(x) = 8x + 10$ (b) 810; the cost of producing the 101st

item is approximately 810.   (c) 814   60. (a) $P(x) = 28x - x^2$ (b) $20

Section 2.4

61. 9; $9x - y = 11$ **62.** -6; $y + 6x = 5$ **63.** $y' = 20x - 8$

64. $\dfrac{dy}{dx} = 5x^4 + 12x^3$ **65.** $2x^{-1/3}$ **66.** $8x^{-5}$ **67.** $f'(x) = -6x^{-4} + \dfrac{1}{2}x^{-1/2}$

68. $f'(x) = -6x^{-3} - x^{-2/3}$ **69.** $f'(x) = 3x^{-2} + x^{-1/2}$ **70.** $\dfrac{dy}{dx} = -\dfrac{1}{x^2} - 4x + \dfrac{1}{2}x^{-1/2}$

71. **(a)** 312 cents, or $3.12   **(b)** 612 cents, or $6.12   **(c)** 1212 cents, or

$12.12   **72.** Average profit, $12 + 30x$; marginal average profit, 30 cents

73. **(a)** 46   **(b)** 2   **(c)** 0   **(d)** -2 **(e)** Profit increases as production

increases to 1250 items; when more than 1250 items are produced, the profit

decreases.   **74.** **(a)** -6 **(b)** 0   **(c)** -96 **75.** **(a)** -64 ft/sec

(b) 2.5 sec after being dropped   **(c)** -80 ft/sec   **76.** 144 ft

Section 2.5

77. $-1/2$; $2y + x = 0$ **78.** -1; $y + x = -2$ **79.** 354; $354x - y = 776$

80. $1/3$; $x - 3y = 12$ **81.** $y' = 16x^{-1/2} - 36x^{1/2}$ **82.** $y' = -32x^3 +$

$18x^2 + 40x - 15$ **83.** $g'(t) = -\dfrac{80}{3}t^{5/3} + \dfrac{32}{3}t^{-1/3}$ **84.** $y' = \dfrac{-4}{(x - 1)^2}$

85. $y' = \dfrac{-6}{(5 - 2x)^2}$ **86.** $y' = \dfrac{-x^{1/2} + (3/2)x^{-1/2} - 6}{(2x + 3)^2}$ or $y' = \dfrac{-2x + 3 - 12x^{1/2}}{2x^{1/2}(2x + 3)^2}$

87. $y' = \dfrac{-3x^2 + 6x - 2}{(1 - x)^2}$ **88.** $y' = \dfrac{x^2 - 4x + 1}{(x - 2)^2}$ **89.** $y' = \dfrac{x^4 - 9x^2 + 12}{(x^2 - 4)^2}$

90. $y' = \dfrac{-2}{3x^{4/3}}$ **91.** $y' = \dfrac{-4(2x - 1)}{(4x^2 - 4x + 1)^2}$ **92.** $\dfrac{-1}{\sqrt{x}(1 + \sqrt{x})^2}$

93. $\dfrac{(1/2)x^{1/2} + (1/2)x^{-1/2} - 1}{(x - 1)^2}$ or $\dfrac{x + 1 - 2x^{1/2}}{2x^{1/2}(x - 1)^2}$ **94.** 39.5   **95.** 40.25

96. **(a)** 20/3 million dollars   **(b)** 6 million dollars   **(c)** 35/6 million

dollars   **97.** **(a)** $111.11   **(b)** $108.64   **(c)** $101.88

98. **(a)** $P'(x) = 8 - 8x$ **(b)** Decreasing   **(c)** $100

Section 2.6

99. 143   **100.** -5 **101.** -1 **102.** $108k^2 - 17$ **103.** **(a)** $\dfrac{3}{(3 - x)^3}$

(b) $\dfrac{3x^3 - 3}{x^3}$ **104.** 1; $x - y = -1$ **105.** $1/6$; $x - 6y = -14$

106. $y' = 5(7 - 5x)^{-1/2}$ **107.** $y' = 2(2x^2 + 1)^5 + 40(x^2)(2x^2 + 1)^4$ or

$2(22x^2 + 1)(2x^2 + 1)^4$ **108.** $f'(x) = 24(6x + 4)^3$ **109.** $y' = \dfrac{80}{(8x - 3)^3}$

110. $y' = 50(2x + 5)^{24}$ **111.** $f'(x) = \dfrac{-120}{(6x - 5)^5}$ **112.** $y' = \dfrac{-1}{\sqrt{4 - 2x}}$

113. $\dfrac{10(2x^{-3} + 3x^{-2})}{(x^{-2} + 3x^{-1})^{11}}$ **114.** $y' = \dfrac{(3x - 5)^2(-30x^2 + 80x + 9)}{(2x^2 + 1)^5}$

115. $y' = \dfrac{2x^2(x^3 - 4)(7x^3 - 1)}{(2x^3 + 1)^{2/3}}$ **116.** $f'(x) = (x + 6)^{-1/2}(9x + 36)/2$

117. $2/\sqrt{3}$ **118.** $-1/2$ **119.** Does not exist   **120.** \$2315 per year

CHAPTER 3   CURVE SKETCHING

Section 3.1

1. Increasing on $(-1, \infty)$; decreasing on $(-\infty, -1)$ 2. Increasing on $(-\infty, -4)$; decreasing on $(-4, \infty)$ 3. Increasing on $(0, 3)$; decreasing on $(-\infty, 0)$ and $(3, \infty)$ 4. Increasing on $(-\infty, -3)$ and $(0, 3)$; decreasing on $(-3, 0)$ and $(3, \infty)$ 5. Increasing on $(-\infty, 3)$; decreasing on $(3, \infty)$

6. Increasing on $(-\infty, -5)$ and $(-1, \infty)$; decreasing on $(-5, -1)$

7. Increasing on $(1/3, 2)$; decreasing on $(-\infty, 1/3)$ and $(2, \infty)$

8. Increasing nowhere; decreasing on $(-\infty, 2)$ and $(2, \infty)$ 9. Increasing on $(-\infty, -2)$ and $(2, \infty)$; decreasing on $(-2, 0)$ and $(0, 2)$ 10. Increasing nowhere; decreasing on $(-\infty, 1/3)$ and $(1/3, \infty)$ 11. Increasing on $(3, \infty)$; decreasing on $(-\infty, 3)$ 12. Increasing nowhere; decreasing on $(-\infty, 2)$

13. Increasing on $(0, \infty)$; decreasing on $(-\infty, 0)$ 14. Increasing nowhere; decreasing on $(2, \infty)$ 15. Increasing on $(0, 4)$ and $(6, \infty)$; decreasing on $(4, 6)$ 16. $(200, \infty)$ 17. **(a)** $(0, 2)$ **(b)** $(2, \infty)$

Section 3.2

18. Relative minimum of 2 at -1 19. Relative maximum of 3 at -4

20. Relative maximum of 8 at 3; relative minimum of 0 at 0

21. Relative maxima of 4 at -3 and 3 at 3; relative minimum of -1 at 0

22. Relative minimum of 14/3 at 1/3   23. Relative maximum of -7 at 1

24. Relative maximum of 11 at 1   25. Relative minimum of $-81/20$ at 9/10

26. Relative maximum of 46/27 at $-1/3$; relative minimum of -11 at 2

27. Relative maximum of 15/4 at $-1/2$; relative minimum of -329 at 5

28. Relative maximum of 13/8 at 1/2; relative minimum of 1/27 at $-2/3$

29. Relative maximum of 82 at -3; relative minimum of $-15/4$ at 1/2

30. Relative maximum of 5.03 at $-.33$; relative minimum of 0 at 2   31. Relative maximum of -12 at -4;   32. Relative maximum of 23 at -2; relative minimum of 7 at 0   33. None   34. None   35. Relative minimum of -1 at 1   36. Relative minimum of 0 at 2/3   37. Relative minimum of 0 at 0   38. (a) 50 (b) \$35   39. (a) 2 (b) $C(2) = \$10$ 40. (a) 3000 (b) \$590

Section 3.3

41. No absolute extrema   42. Absolute minimum at x_3; no absolute maximum   43. Absolute maximum at x_1; no absolute minimum   44. Absolute maximum at x_3; absolute minimum at x_4 45. Absolute maximum of -4 at 2; absolute minimum of -40 at -4 46. Absolute maximum of 26 at 5; absolute minimum of 3/2 at 3/2   47. Absolute maximum of 4 at 2; absolute minimum of -81 at -3

48. Absolute maximum of 20 at -3; absolute minimum of -12 at 1

49. Absolute maximum of 1 at -2; absolute minimum of 1/4 at 1

50. Absolute maximum of 1/4 at 2; absolute minimum of 1/5 at 1

51. Absolute maximum of 10 at 2; absolute minimum of 8 at 4

52. Absolute maximum of 2 at 0 and 2; absolute minimum of -2 at $\sqrt{2}$

53. Absolute maximum of $19^{2/3}$ at -3 and 3; absolute minimum of $10^{2/3}$ at 0

54. Absolute maximum of $\sqrt{3}/3$ at 0; absolute minimum of $\sqrt{7}/7$ at -2

55. \$88,000   56. 20

Section 3.4

57. $f''(x) = 48x^2 - 10$; 38; 182   58. $f''(x) = 42x - 4/x^3$; -38; 167/2

59. $f''(x) = \dfrac{324}{(6x - 5)^3}$; $\dfrac{-324}{1331}$; $\dfrac{324}{343}$ 60. $f''(x) = \dfrac{-2}{(1 - x)^3}$; $-\dfrac{1}{4}$; 2

61. $f''(t) = \dfrac{-6}{(3t^2 - 2)^{3/2}}$; -6; $\dfrac{-3}{5\sqrt{10}}$ or $\dfrac{-3\sqrt{10}}{50}$ 62. $f''(t) = \dfrac{4t(-t^2 + 15)}{(t^2 + 5)^3}$;

$-\dfrac{7}{27}$; $\dfrac{88}{729}$ 63. $f''(t) = \dfrac{-110}{(22 - 5t^2)^{3/2}}$; $\dfrac{-110}{17\sqrt{17}} = \dfrac{-110\sqrt{17}}{289}$; $\dfrac{-110}{2\sqrt{2}} = -\dfrac{55\sqrt{2}}{2}$

64. $f''(t) = 48t - 72$; -120; 24 65. $f''(t) = \dfrac{-3}{4t^{5/4}}$; not a real number;

$\dfrac{-3}{8\sqrt[4]{2}} = \dfrac{-3\sqrt[4]{8}}{16}$ 66. $f'''(x) = -180x^2 + 24$; $f^{(4)}(x) = -360x$

67. $f'''(x) = \dfrac{-60}{(x-2)^4}$; $f^{(4)}(x) = \dfrac{240}{(x-2)^5}$ 68. $f'''(x) = 24$; $f^{(4)}(x) = 0$

69. Concave upward on $(1/2, \infty)$; concave downward on $(-\infty, 1/2)$; point of inflection at $(1/2, 3/4)$ 70. Concave upward on $(-\infty, 1)$; concave downward on $(1, \infty)$; point of inflection at $(1, 13/3)$ 71. Concave upward on $(-\infty, \infty)$; concave downward nowhere; no point of inflection   72. Concave upward on $(0, 2)$; concave downward on $(-\infty, 0)$ and $(2, \infty)$; points of inflection at $(0, 0)$ and $(2, 12)$ 73. Concave upward on $(0, \infty)$; concave downward on $(-\infty, 0)$; no point of inflection   74. Concave upward on $(-\infty, 4)$; concave downward on $(4, \infty)$; no point of inflection   75. Concave upward on $(1, \infty)$; concave downward on $(-\infty, 1)$; point of inflection at $(1, 2/3)$ 76. Concave upward on $(-\infty, -1)$ and $(1, \infty)$; concave downward on $(-1, 1)$; points of inflection at $(-1, 3)$ and $(1, 3)$ 77. Concave upward on $(3, \infty)$; concave downward on $(-\infty, 3)$; no point of inflection   78. $v(t) = -8t + 8$; $a(t) = -8$; $v(0) = 8$ cm/sec, $v(2) = -8$ cm/sec; $a(0) = -8$ cm/sec²; $a(2) = -8$ cm/sec²

79. $v(t) = 6t^2 - 12t + 5$; $a(t) = 12t - 12$; $v(0) = 5$ cm/sec; $v(2) = 5$ cm/sec; $a(0) = -12$ cm/sec²; $a(2) = 12$ cm/sec²   80. 12,000 widgets   81. At 1 hr

Section 3.5

82. -1 83. Does not exist   84. $4/7$ 85. 2   86. $3/2$ 87. 0

88. 0

89. Critical points at $(-1/3, 104/27)$ and $(5, -72)$; increasing on $(-\infty, -1/3)$ and $(5, \infty)$; decreasing on $(-1/3, 5)$; point of inflection at $(7/3, -920/27)$; concave down on $(-\infty, 7/3)$; concave up on $(7/3, \infty)$; intercepts at $(-1, 0)$, $(.4, 0)$, $(7.61, 0)$, and $(0, 3)$; no asymptotes

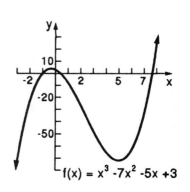

$f(x) = x^3 - 7x^2 - 5x + 3$

90. Critical points at $(0, 1)$, $(-\sqrt{1/3}, 1/3)$, $(\sqrt{1/3}, 1/3)$; increasing on $(-\sqrt{1/3}, 0)$ and $(\sqrt{1/3}, \infty)$; decreasing on $(-\infty, -\sqrt{1/3})$ and $(0, \sqrt{1/3})$; points of inflection at $(-1/3, 51/81)$ and $(1/3, 51/81)$; concave up on $(-\infty, -1/3)$ and $(1/3, \infty)$; concave down on $(-1/3, 1/3)$; intercept at $(0, 1)$

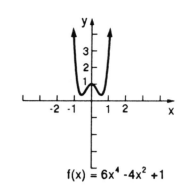

$f(x) = 6x^4 - 4x^2 + 1$

91. Critical points at $(-\sqrt{12/5}, -192\sqrt{15}/125)$, $(0, 0)$, and $(\sqrt{12/5}, 192\sqrt{15}/125)$; increasing on $(-\infty, -\sqrt{12/5})$ and $(\sqrt{12/5}, \infty)$; decreasing on $(-\sqrt{12/5}, \sqrt{12/5})$; points of inflection at $(-\sqrt{6/5}, 84\sqrt{30}/125)$, $(0, 0)$, and $(\sqrt{6/5}, -84\sqrt{30}/125)$; concave up on $(-\sqrt{6/5}, 0)$ and $(\sqrt{6/5}, \infty)$; concave down on $(-\infty, -\sqrt{6/5})$ and $(0, \sqrt{6/5})$; intercepts at $(-2, 0)$, $(0, 0)$, and $(2, 0)$

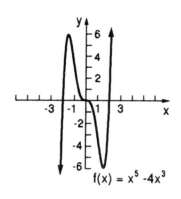

$f(x) = x^5 - 4x^3$

92. Critical points at $(-1, -2)$, $(1, 2)$; increasing on $(-\infty, -1)$ and $(1, \infty)$; decreasing on $(-1, 0)$ and $(0, 1)$; no point of inflection; concave up on $(0, \infty)$; concave down on $(-\infty, 0)$; no intercepts; vertical asymptote is $x = 0$; oblique asymptote is $y = x$.

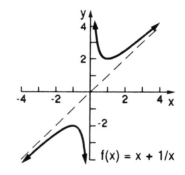

$f(x) = x + 1/x$

93. Increasing nowhere; decreasing on $(-\infty, 2)$ and $(2, \infty)$; no point of inflection; concave up on $(2, \infty)$; concave down on $(-\infty, 2)$; intercept at $(0, 0)$; horizontal asymptote is $y = 3$; vertical asymptote is $x = 2$.

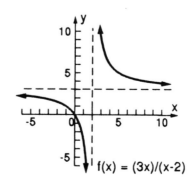

$f(x) = (3x)/(x-2)$

94. Critical point at (0, 1/2); in-
     creasing on (−∞, 0); decreasing
     on (0, ∞); points of inflection
     at $(-\sqrt{2/3}, 3/8)$ and $(\sqrt{2/3}, 3/8)$;
     concave up on $(-\infty, -\sqrt{2/3})$ and
     $(\sqrt{2/3}, \infty)$; concave down on
     $(-\sqrt{2/3}, \sqrt{2/3})$; intercept at (0, 1/2)

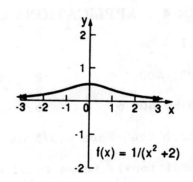

$f(x) = 1/(x^2 + 2)$

CHAPTER 4   APPLICATIONS OF THE DERIVATIVE

Section 4.1

1. 20; 20; 400

2. 30; 30; 1800

3. $x = 2$ and $y = 1$; 4

4. 300 m by 600 m

5. 60,000 m²

6. The pipe from the rig should reach the shore $4\sqrt{5}/5$ mi west of the rig.

7. 4 items

8. $40

9. 125 additional, for a total of 325

10. (a) 32.9 mph   (b) $65.73

11. Radius, 3 in; height, 6 in

12. Length, 12 in; width, 4 in; depth, 3 in

13. 80,000 m²

14. 4 days after treatment; 200 bacteria/cm³

Section 4.2

15. 25

16. 10

17. 50

18. 100

19. (a) $\dfrac{p}{1000 - p}$ (b) 250

20. (a) $100 < p \le 200$ (b) $10 \le p < 100$

21. Total revenue increases since demand is inelastic on [10, 100).

Section 4.3

22. $\dfrac{dy}{dx} = \dfrac{2x}{5y}$

23. $\dfrac{dy}{dx} = \dfrac{-y}{x}$

24. $\dfrac{dy}{dx} = \dfrac{-5y - 3y^2}{6xy + 5x}$

25. $\dfrac{dy}{dx} = \dfrac{y - y^3}{3xy^2 - x}$

26. $\dfrac{dy}{dx} = \dfrac{3y - 5y^2}{5y^2 + 3x}$

27. $\dfrac{dy}{dx} = \dfrac{-3 - x^{5/2}}{10x^3y^3}$

28. $\dfrac{dy}{dx} = \dfrac{x^{2/3}(2y + 3)^{1/2}}{3}$

29. $\dfrac{dy}{dx} = \dfrac{y^{1/2}}{2x^{1/2}}$

30. $\dfrac{dy}{dx} = \dfrac{5y^2}{6x^2}$

31. $\dfrac{dy}{dx} = \dfrac{12x^2y - 30x^2 + 4y^2 - 20y + 25}{2x^2(6x + 4)}$

32. $\dfrac{dy}{dx} = \dfrac{3y}{8y(3xy)^{1/2} - 3x}$

33. $\dfrac{dy}{dx} = \dfrac{11y}{3y^{1/2}(x + 3y)^2 + 11x}$

34. $\dfrac{dy}{dx} = \dfrac{4 - 3(6y^2 + 2x)^{1/2}}{18y(6y^2 + 2x)^{1/2}}$

35. $\dfrac{dy}{dx} = \dfrac{4y^{1/2}(x + 2y^{1/2})^3}{24y^{7/2} - 4(x + 2y^{1/2})^3}$ or $\dfrac{y^{1/2}(x + 2y^{1/2})^3}{6y^{7/2} - (x + 2y^{1/2})^3}$

36. $x + 2y = 5$

37. $x + 3y = 5$

38. $x + 32y = 80$

39. $3x - 5y = -12$

40. $x\sqrt{3} - 3y = -8\sqrt{3}$; $x\sqrt{3} + 3y = -8\sqrt{3}$

41. $2x - y = 4$; $2x - y = -4$

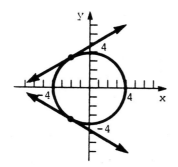

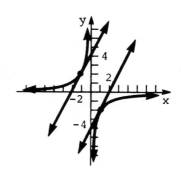

Section 4.4

42. 432   **43.** 84   **44.** −4   **45.** 5/4   **46.** −1   **47.** 36π in²/sec

48. Descending at 2.25 ft/sec   **49.** −.164 ft/min   **50.** 8 cm²/min

51. $1998/mo   **52.** Decreasing at $100/mo

Section 4.5

53. $(9x^2 + 3)dx$ **54.** $90x^2(2x^3 - 4)^4 dx$ **55.** $\dfrac{10\ dx}{(4 - x)^2}$ **56.** $\dfrac{-x\ dx}{\sqrt{8 - x^2}}$

57. $\left(\dfrac{6}{x^3} - \dfrac{4}{x^2} + \dfrac{6}{x^4}\right)dx$ **58.** $\dfrac{(-x^2 - 1)\,dx}{\sqrt{2x(x^2 - 1)^3}}$ **59.** .48   **60.** −.00136

61. .0075   **62.** .0022   **63.** .006   **64.** .503 cm³   **65.** 4.02 cm³

66. .27 cm³   **67.** A decrease of .047 units of calcium

68. (a) Increase of $6750   (b) Increase of $2500

CHAPTER 5   EXPONENTIAL AND LOGARITHMIC FUNCTIONS

Section 5.1

1. -3 2. -10 3. $3/2$ 4. -3 5. $-1/2$ 6. $1/3$ 7. -10

8. $1/9$ 9. $15/4$ 10. -2 11. $1, 2$ 12. $-3/2, 3/2$

13.
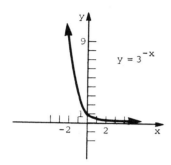
$y = 3^{-x}$

14.
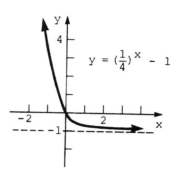
$y = (\frac{1}{4})^{x} - 1$

15.
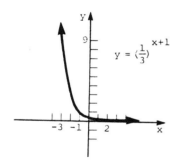
$y = (\frac{1}{3})^{x+1}$

16.
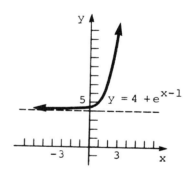
$y = 4 + e^{x-1}$

17. $6515.58   18. $1215.13   19. $26,186.76   20. $47,213.10

21. $6609.59   22. $4060.64   23. (a) 100   (b) 200   (c) 283

(d) 400   24. (a) 132 items   (b) 150 items

Section 5.2

25. $\log_5 125 = 3$ 26. $\log_7 \sqrt{7} = 1/2$ 27. $\ln 1.03045 = .03$

28. $\log 18 = 1.25527$ 29. $3^4 = 81$ 30. $10^{-2} = 1/100$

31. $e^{4.03069} = 56.3$ 32. $10^{1.36399} = 23.12$ 33. 3   34. -3

35. $3/4$ 36. 2   37. -3 38. 3   39. $1/2$ 40. $3/4$

41.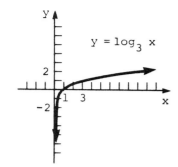

42.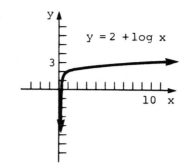

43.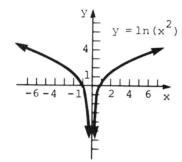

44.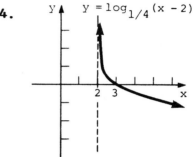

45. $\log_7 5 + \log_7 k$ **46.** $\log_3 2 + \log_3 m - \log_3 n$

47. $\log_4 3 + (1/2) \log_4 5 - (1/5) \log_4 7$ **48.** 2.73   **49.** 2.48

50. 4   **51.** 1/3   **52.** 2/3   **53.** 36   **54.** 10   **55.** 11/2

56. 1.485   **57.** 1.201   **58.** -1.771   **59.** -.568   **60.** -.685

61. .651   **62.** 1.464   **63.** .947   **64.** About 64 decibels

65. (a) 7.8   **(b)** 3.4

Section 5.3

66. $3151.21   **67.** $15,599.28   **68.** $62,375.02   **69.** $15,804.57

70. $2238.65   **71.** $7727.13   **72.** $24,041.96   **73.** $5222.58

74. 7.71%   **75.** 7.44%   **76.** $13,541.70   **77.** 23.1 yr   **78.** About
6.9 yr   **79. (a)** 1600   **(b)** About 1997   **(c)** About 2.3   **80.** 2025

81. (a) $y = 95,000e^{-.137t}$ **(b)** About 3.35 yr   **82. (a)** $y = 100e^{-.2476t}$

(b) About 2.8 yr   **83. (a)** $y = 20,000e^{.09327t}$ **(b)** 14.86 yr

Section 5.4

84. $y' = 1/x$ **85.** $y' = \dfrac{4}{3 + 4x}$ **86.** $y' = \dfrac{-3x^2}{3 - x^3}$ **87.** $y' = \dfrac{4x}{2x^2 - 5}$

88. $y' = \dfrac{4 - x + x \ln |2x|}{x(4 - x)^2}$ **89.** $y' = \dfrac{2(3x + 1) \ln |3x + 1| - 3(2x - 5)}{(3x + 1)[\ln |3x + 1|]^2}$

90. $y' = \dfrac{2}{3x + 1}$ **91.** $y' = \dfrac{3x^2}{3x + 1} + 2x \ln |3x + 1|$

92. $y' = \dfrac{6(\ln |2x + 1|)^2}{2x + 1}$ **93.** $y' = \dfrac{x^2}{x^2 + 1} + \dfrac{1}{2} \ln (x^2 + 1)$

94. $y' = \dfrac{1}{2x\sqrt{\ln |x|}}$ **95.** $y' = \dfrac{2x}{(\ln 10)(x^2 - 1)}$ **96.** $y' = \dfrac{3}{(\ln 5)(3x - 5)}$

97. $y' = \dfrac{1}{(\ln 3)(2x + 5)}$

98. Relative minimum of 2 at $x = 1$

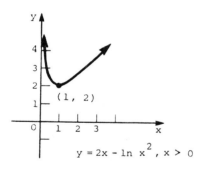

$y = 2x - \ln x^2, \; x > 0$

99. Relative minimum of $-1/(2e)$ at $x = 1/\sqrt{e}$

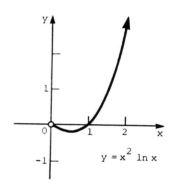

$y = x^2 \ln x$

100. Relative minimum of $-4/(5e) \approx -.29$ at $x = -e/4$; relative maximum of $4/(5e) \approx .29$ at $x = e/4$

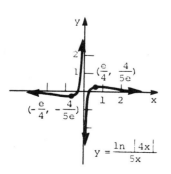

$y = \dfrac{\ln |4x|}{5x}$

101. Relative minimum of e at $x = e$

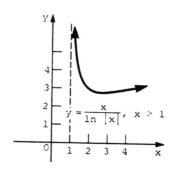

$y = \dfrac{x}{\ln |x|}, \; x > 1$

102. **(a)** $R'(x) = 8 - 2x$ **(b)** \$2 million   **(c)** $P(x) = -x^2 + 6x - 5$

(d) \$4 million

Section 5.5

103. $y' = -15e^{5x}$ **104.** $y' = 2.1e^{.3x}$ **105.** $y' = -8xe^{-4x^2}$

106. $y' = -45x^2e^{5x^3}$ **107.** $y' = 3e^{3b}$ **108.** $y' = -8xe^{-2x} + 8x^2e^{-2x}$

109. $y' = (2x + 3)e^{x^2+3x}$ **110.** $y' = \dfrac{e^x - e^{-x}}{2}$ **111.** $y' = \dfrac{9900}{e^x(1 + 99e^{-x})^2}$

112. $y' = 3(6x + e^x)(3x^2 + e^x)^2$ **113.** $y' = 15e^{3x-2}(e^{3x-2} + 5)^4$

114. $y' = \dfrac{2x - (x^2 + 1)\ln|x^2 + 1|}{e^x(x^2 + 1)}$ **115.** $y' = (2\ln 3) \cdot \dfrac{3\sqrt{x}}{\sqrt{x}}$

116. $y' = (5\ln 4) \cdot 4^{5x}$

117. Relative minimum of $-1/e \approx$ $-.37$ at $x = -1/3$

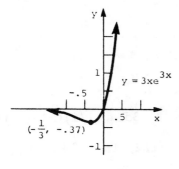

118. Relative minimum of $-1/e \approx$ $-.37$ at $x = 1$

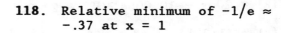
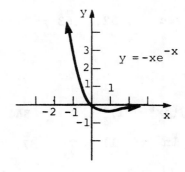

119. Relative minimum of $1/e \approx .37$ at $x = -1$

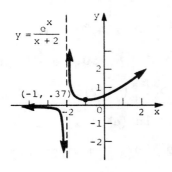

120. Relative maximum of 1 at $x = 0$

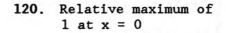
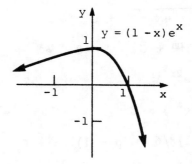

CHAPTER 6   INTEGRATION

Section 6.1

1. $7x + C$

2. $3x + (5/2)x^2 + C$

3. $4x - x^4/4 + C$

4. $(1/2)x^4 + (3/5)x^5 + (2/3)x^6 + C$

5. $-1/(3t^3) + C$

6. $5x^3 - x^2 - x + C$

7. $3x^{4/3} + C$

8. $-2/x^2 + C$

9. $4\sqrt{x} + C$

10. $-2.5e^{-.4x} + C$

11. $(3/4)e^{4x} + C$

12. $x + 4 \ln |x| + 2/\sqrt{x} + C$

13. $(1/3)e^{3x} - (1/5)e^{-5x} + C$

14. $(15/4)x^{12/5} - (3/2)x^{4/3} + 4x + C$

15. $(4/3)x^3 + 6x^2 + 9x + C$

16. $(1/4)x^4 + (2/3)x^3 - (1/2)x^2 + C$

17. $(4/7)x^{7/2} + (6/5)x^{5/2} + C$

18. $(1/3)e^{3u} - 2 \ln |u| + C$

19. $(2/5)x^{5/2} - (2/3)x^{3/2} + 4x^{1/2} + C$

20. $f(x) = (1/3)x^3 + x - 4$

21. $C(x) = 20 + 7x - .2x^2$

22. $C(x) = (5/2)x^2 + x^3 + 33/2$

23. $C(x) = (3/2)x^2 - (2/5)x^{5/2} + 3000$

24. $C(x) = 3x + (5/2)x^{4/5} + 17,000$

25. $C(x) = 310x + (16/3)x^{3/4} + 154,997.33$

26. $C(x) = 200x - 10,000e^{-x/100} + 27,000$

27. $C(x) = 150x - 500e^{-x/50} + 4900.94$

28. $P(x) = (1/25)x^3 - x^2 + 120x - 300$

29. $v(t) = 5t + 7$

30. 1.86 sec

31. 5.61 sec

32. $.63$ g

Section 6.2

33. $(5/72)(3x^3 - 1)^8 + C$

34. $(1/24)(3x^4 + 2)^4 + C$

35. $(1/2)(x^3 - x)^2 + C$

36. $(1/2) \ln (x^2 + 1) + C$

37. $\ln |x + 1| + C$

38. $(1/2) \ln |x^2 + 2x + 1| + C$ or $\ln |x + 1| + C$

39. $\ln |x^2 + x - 7| + C$

40. $\ln |x^3 - 2x + 1| + C$

41. $(1/3)(x^2 - 8x)^{3/2} + C$

42. $(2/15)(2x^3 - 6x)^{5/4} + C$

43. $(8/3) \ln |3v - 1| + C$

44. $(-1/4)(x^3 - 2x - 7)^{-4} + C$

45. $2\sqrt{x^3 + 4x - 5} + C$

46. $(3/2)(2x^2 + 3x + 4)^{2/3} + C$

47. $-20e^{-.2m} + C$

48. $e^{x^4} + C$

49. $(5/2)e^{2x-1} + C$

50. $e^{x^2-1} + C$

51. $(1/6)e^{2x^3+1} + C$

52. $(1/3)e^{x^3} + C$

53. $(-1/2)e^{1-x^2} + C$

54. $-1/(3e^{x^3}) + C$

55. $e^{x^2-x-3} + C$

56. $\ln (e^x + 1) + C$

57. $(p - 1)^6/6 + (p - 1)^5/5 + C$

58. $(x - 1)^{22}/22 + 2(x - 1)^{21}/21 + C$

59. $(2x - 1)^{23}/92 - (2x - 1)^{22}/88 + C$

60. $(1/48)(2x + 1)^{12} + (3/44)(2x + 1)^{11} + C$

61. $C(x) = (50/3)(x + 7)^{3/2} + 400/3$ **62.** $C(x) = 30x + 18 \ln |x + 1| + 8000$

63. $C(x) = 40x + \ln |2x + 1| + 457.44$ **64.** $s(t) = (1/3) \ln (3t + 5) -$
$(1/3)(\ln 5)$ **65.** At $x = 98$ **66.** $C(x) = \sqrt{4x + 1} + 10$

67. $C(x) = 20x + 2.5 \ln |1 + 2x^2| + 400$

Section 6.3

68. -26 **69.** 42   **70.** 10   **71.** 67   **72.** 10   **73.** 150   **74.** 62

75. 4.25   **76.** 9.33   **77.** 1.28   **78.** 1.13   **79.** 8   **80.** 15

81. $25\pi/4$ **82.** 165,000,000 kilowatt hours

Section 6.4

83. -12 **84.** -16 **85.** 9.5   **86.** 100   **87.** $111/64 \approx 1.73$

88. 1.83   **89.** $-.81$ **90.** $\ln 27$ or 3.30   **91.** 26/3   **92.** 40.27

93. .8   **94.** 24.3   **95.** 80.40   **96.** 0   **97.** .122   **98.** 3078

99. 1.025   **100.** 37.5   **101.** 60   **102.** 26/3   **103.** 45/4

104. $\ln 9 \approx 2.20$ **105.** 19.09   **106.** 21.67   **107.** 1/2   **108.** 20.66

109. 23/3   **110.** 11.65   **111.** **(a)** 19,033   **(b)** 52,141

112. \$141,333.33   **113.** 34.73   **114.** **(a)** In about 173 yr   **(b)** In about
347 yr   **(c)** Never

Section 6.5

115. 1/2   **116.** 1.19   **117.** 5.28   **118.** 1/6   **119.** 56/3   **120.** .0104

121. $8 - 6 \ln 3 \approx 1.41$ **122.** 2.25   **123.** 5.52   **124.** 80/3

125. **(a)** \$8583.33   **(b)** \$3916.67   **126.** **(a)** \$2780.24   **(b)** \$5268.97

CHAPTER 7   FURTHER TECHNIQUES AND APPLICATIONS OF INTEGRATION

Section 7.1

1. $x^2 \ln x - (1/2)x^2 + C$ 2. $(1/3)(3x + 1)(\ln |3x + 1| - 1) + C$

3. $(1/4)xe^{4x} - (1/16)e^{4x} + C$ 4. $(-1/5)x(3 - 2x)^{5/2} - (1/35)(3 - 2x)^{7/2} + C$

5. $(1/2)(x + 2)e^{2x} - (1/4)e^{2x} + C$ 6. $(1/3)(x + 3)^2 e^{3x} - (2/9)(x + 3)e^{3x} + (2/27)e^{3x} + C$ 7. $(1/2)(4x^2 - 2x + 1)e^{2x+1} - (1/2)(4x - 1)e^{2x+1} + e^{2x+1} + C$

8. $4x(x + 4)^{1/2} - (8/3)(x + 4)^{3/2} + C$ 9. $506/15$ 10. $1/2$

11. $(2x^2 + x) \ln |2x + 1| - x^2 + C$ 12. $\dfrac{-(x + 3)}{5e^x} + C$ 13. $x \ln x^2 - 2x + C$

14. $(x^3/3 + 3x^2/2 + 4x) \ln 2x - x^3/9 - 3x^2/4 - 4x + C$ 15. $3e^2$ or 22.17

16. $8 \ln 4 - 15/4$ or 7.34 17. $2e^2 - 3$ or 11.78 18. $x(\ln |7x| - 1) + C$

19. $(1/12) \ln \left| \dfrac{x - 6}{x + 6} \right| + C$ 20. $-10 \ln |x + \sqrt{x^2 - 49}| + C$

21. $(-1/6) \ln \left| \dfrac{3 + \sqrt{9 - x^2}}{x} \right| + C$ 22. $(1/2) \ln \left| \dfrac{x}{3x + 2} \right| + C$

23. $x\sqrt{x^2 + 17}/2 + (17/2) \ln |x + \sqrt{x^2 + 17}| + C$ 24. $-3x/2 - (15/4) \ln |5 - 2x| + C$

25. $3/[8(4x - 3)] - (1/8) \ln |4x - 3| + C$ 26. $\$467,884.02$

27. $\$11,337.83$ 28. $\$3.09 \times 10^{10}$ 29. About $\$71,702,000$

30. Loss of $\$33,527.79$; gain of $\$1,800,458.55$ 31. $\$77,595.83$

Section 7.2

32. (a) 5.583 (b) 5.500 (c) 5.493   33. (a) 2.092 (b) 2.077

(c) 2.095   34. (a) 22.96 (b) 22.87 (c) 22.87   35. (a) 3.848

(b) 3.708 (c) 3.648   36. (a) 41.72 (b) 40.21 (c) 40.17

37. (a) .2758 (b) .2747 (c) .2747   38. 7.82   39. 56.3

40. 2.70   41. 178 km   42. 176 km   43. (a) 13.13 (b) 13.73

(c) $9\pi/2$ or 14.14; Simpson's rule

Section 7.3

44. 56π or 175.9   **45.** $129\pi/4$ or 101.3   **46.** $326\pi/3$ or 341.4

47. 4.36   **48.** $65\pi/2$ or 102.1   **49.** $93\pi/5$ or 58.4   **50.** 25.2

51. 2340.5   **52.** $4\pi \ln 4 \approx 17.42$ **53.** 129.4   **54.** 107.23

55. $32\pi/3$ or 33.51   **56.** 21π or 66.0   **57.** $256\pi/3$ or 268.1   **58.** 4

59. 2   **60.** 13/6   **61.** 10.8   **62.** 9.5   **63.** $-1/e$ or $-.37$

64. $1 - 2/e$ or .26   **65.** 1.66   **66.** 0   **67.** .32   **68.** 25°C

69. 4.7 mg/ml

Section 7.4

70. \$34,277.64   **71.** \$416,610.76   **72.** \$274,925.09   **73.** \$7175.84

74. \$4658.50   **75.** \$23,254.67   **76.** \$96,174.90   **77.** \$1605.64

78. \$94.50   **79.** \$5777.86   **80.** (a) \$96,671.54   (b) \$29,116.91

81. \$13,472.59; \$28,521.47

Section 7.5

82. Divergent   **83.** Divergent   **84.** $-3/8$ **85.** Divergent

86. 1/28   **87.** $-1/6$ **88.** 1/18   **89.** Divergent   **90.** Divergent

91. Divergent   **92.** Divergent   **93.** Divergent   **94.** 1/2   **95.** 1

96. 1/12   **97.** $\dfrac{3}{2(\ln 2)^2} \approx 3.122$ **98.** 3   **99.** 2   **100.** Divergent

101. 1   **102.** Divergent   **103.** 1   **104.** 1   **105.** Divergent

106. Divergent   **107.** 1   **108.** \$50,000   **109.** \$10 million

CHAPTER 8   MULTIVARIABLE CALCULUS

Section 8.1

1. -33 2. -5 3. $1/13$ 4. $1/13$ 5. $e\sqrt{2}$ 6. $e^2\sqrt{2}/2$

7. $1/3$ 8. $(0, 0, 3/2)$, $(0, -2, 0)$, $(3, 0, 0)$ 9. $(0, 0, 3/2)$, $(0, 2, 0)$, $(3, 0, 0)$ 10. $(0, 0, 3/2)$, $(0, -2, 0)$, $(-3, 0, 0)$

11. $(0, 0, -3/2)$, $(0, 2, 0)$, $(-3, 0, 0)$

12.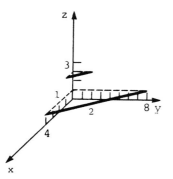

13.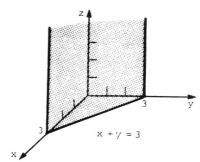

14.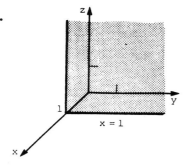

15.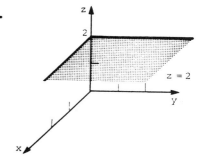

16.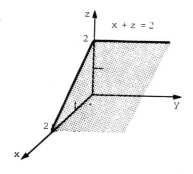

17.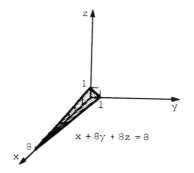

18.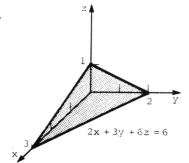

$2x + 3y + 6z = 6$

19.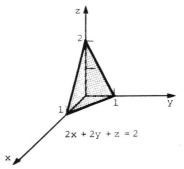

$2x + 2y + z = 2$

20.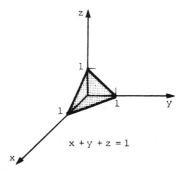

$x + y + z = 1$

21. (a) \$14,147.09 **(b)** \$11,733.20 **22.** 160.88 **23.** \$1150

Section 8.2

24. (a) $3x^2y^2 + 2xy^3$ **(b)** 8 **(c)** 0 **25. (a)** $\dfrac{2x}{(x-y)^2}$ **(b)** $\dfrac{-2y}{(x-y)^2}$

(c) -4 **26. (a)** $f_x = 2x$; $f_y = 6y$ **(b)** $f_x(1, 1) = 2$; $f_y(1, 1) = 6$

27. (a) $f_x = 2xy^2 + 1$; $f_y = 2x^2y$ **(b)** $f_x(1, 1) = 3$; $f_y(1, 1) = 2$

28. (a) $f_x = (y^2 - x^2)/(x^2 + y^2)^2$; $f_y = -2xy/(x^2 + y^2)^2$ **(b)** $f_x(1, 1) = 0$;

$f_y(1, 1) = -1/2$ **29. (a)** $f_x = x/\sqrt{x^2 + y^2}$; $f_y = y/\sqrt{x^2 + y^2}$ **(b)** $f_x(1, 1) =$

$\sqrt{2}/2$; $f_y(1, 1) = \sqrt{2}/2$ **30. (a)** $f_x = -y^2e^{-x}$; $f_y = 2ye^{-x}$ **(b)** $f_x(1, 1) =$

$-1/e$; $f_y(1, 1) = 2/e$ **31. (a)** $f_x = 2x/(x^2 + y^2)$; $f_y = 2y/(x^2 + y^2)$

(b) $f_x(1, 1) = 1$; $f_y(1, 1) = 1$ **32. (a)** $f_x = 1/x$; $f_y = -1/y$

(b) $f_x(1, 1) = 1$; $f_y(1, 1) = -1$ **33. (a)** $f_x = 1/x$; $f_y = 1/y$

(b) $f_x(1, 1) = 1$; $f_y(1, 1) = 1$ **34. (a)** $f_x = 1/(xy)$; $f_y = -(\ln x)/y^2$

(b) $f_x(1, 1) = 1$; $f_y(1, 1) = 0$ **35. (a)** $f_x = 2xy^3e^{x^2y^3}$; $f_y = 3x^2y^2e^{x^2y^3}$

(b) $f_x(1, 1) = 2e$; $f_y(1, 1) = 3e$ **36.** $f_{xx} = 12$; $f_{yy} = 18$; $f_{xy} = f_{yx} = -8$

37. $f_{xx} = 3x(2y^2 - x^3)/(x^3 + y^2)^2$; $f_{yy} = 2(x^3 - y^2)/(x^3 + y^2)^2$; $f_{xy} = f_{yx} =$

$-6x^2y/(x^3 + y^2)^2$ **38.** $f_{xx} = 9e^{3x+2y}$; $f_{yy} = 4e^{3x+2y}$; $f_{xy} = f_{yx} = 6e^{3x+2y}$

39. $x = 4$, $y = -2$ **40.** $f_x = 2yz^2 + \dfrac{2x}{x^2 + 3y^2}$; $f_y = 2xz^2 + \dfrac{6y}{x^2 + 3y^2}$; $f_z = 4xyz$;

$f_{xz} = 4yz$ **41.** 5200; 3840 **42. (a)** 2.96 **(b)** 20 **43.** \$119.35,

about \$119 **44.** $\partial R/\partial E = 1/12$ ohm/volt; $\partial R/\partial I = -25/24$ ohms/ampere

Section 8.3

45. (1, 2)   **46.** (0, 0)   **47.** (0, 1), (0, −1), (−1, 0), (1, 0)

48. (0, 0), (1, 1), (−1, −1)   **49.** (−2, 3)   **50.** (1, −2)   **51.** (0, 0)

52. (0, 0)   **53.** Relative maximum of 4 at (0, 0)   **54.** Relative minimum of −4 at $(2^{2/3}, 2^{1/3})$; saddle point at (0, 0)   **55.** Relative maximum of 34 at (3, 3); saddle point at (0, 0)   **56.** Relative minimum of 1 at (0, 0)

57. 1 unit of item A and 3 units of item B

Section 8.4

58. f(2, 1) = 6   **59.** f(−2, 2) = 8   **60.** f(−3, −2) = 6

61. f(14, 28) = 5488   **62.** f(1/3, 1/3, 1/3) = 1/3   **63.** (−2, 3)

64. 40, 40, and 40   **65.** 4333 type A fans and 4667 type B fans

66. 10 in by 10 in by 5 in

Section 8.5

67. **(a)** y = −6.04x + 83.6   **68.** **(a)** y = .949x + 29.31

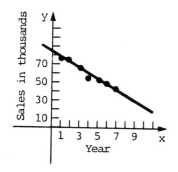

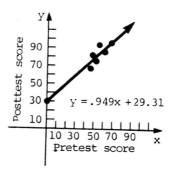

(b) $29,240   **(b)** 86

69. **(a)** y = 4x + 78.5   **(b)** 90.5°

Section 8.6

70. $dz = 9x^2 dx - 8y\,dy$

71. $dz = 12xy\,dx + (6x^2 - 9y^2)dy$

72. $dz = \dfrac{-4y}{(2x - y)^2}\,dx + \dfrac{4x}{(2x - y)^2}\,dy$

73. $dz = ye^{xy}dx + xe^{xy}dy$

74. $dz = \left(4x - \dfrac{1}{2\sqrt{x - y}}\right)dx + \dfrac{1}{2\sqrt{x - y}}\,dy$

75. $dz = (xy^2e^{x+y} + y^2e^{x+y})dx +$

$(2xye^{x+y} + xy^2e^{x+y})dy$

76. $dz = \left(\dfrac{2x}{x^2 + y^2} + 2x\ln y\right)dx + \left(\dfrac{2y}{x^2 + y^2} + \dfrac{x^2}{y}\right)dy$

77. $dw = 3x^2 dx - 8y\,dy + dz$

78. $dw = -20x^3y^3z^{10}dx - 15x^4y^2z^{10}dy - 50x^4y^3z^9dz$

79. .6   **80.** −.002   **81.** 2.16   **82.** .0773   **83.** 1.1   **84.** \$1.40

85. About 60 cm³   **86.** 1.87 units   **87.** (a) $\pi/2$ ft³   (b) About \$157

Section 8.7

88. $117 + 3y$ **89.** $4x^2 + 4$ **90.** $2x^2 - x + 1$ **91.** $y(16 + y)^{3/2}/3 -$
$y(4 + y)^{3/2}/3$ **92.** $7/(3y)$ **93.** $9x^2 + 15/2$ **94.** $ye^{y^2}/2 - ye^{1+y^2}/2$

95. $12x^2 - 18x$ **96.** $14/3$ **97.** $11/6$ **98.** $2/3$ **99.** $e^2 - 3$

100. 114   **101.** $19/6$ **102.** $32/3$ **103.** $(1 - e^{-16})/2$ **104.** $17/12$

105. $\ln(4/3) \approx .2877$ **106.** 39   **107.** 8   **108.** $20/3$

109. $e^3 - e^2 - e + 1$ **110.** $208/3$ **111.** $532/9$ **112.** $3e - 3$

CHAPTER 9   DIFFERENTIAL EQUATIONS

Section 9.1

1. $y = 4x^2 + x + C$

2. $y = x^3 - \frac{5}{2}x^2 - 3x + C$

3. $y^2 = \frac{2x^3}{3} + C$

4. $y^2 = (x + 1)^2 + C$

5. $y = 2x^{3/2} - x^2 + C$

6. $y = e^{3x}/3 + C$

7. $y = -\frac{2}{3}e^{-3x} + C$

8. $y = -\ln|e^{-x} + C|$

9. $y = 3\ln|x + 2| + C$

10. $y = (\ln|x|)^2/2 + C$

11. $y = (1/9)(3x^2 + 1)^{3/2} + C$

12. $y + y^2 = 2x - \frac{3x^2}{2} + C$

13. $y = (2/9)x(3x + 1)^{3/2} - (4/135)(3x + 1)^{5/2} + C$

14. $y = -\frac{4}{21}x^3 + C$

15. $(1/3)xe^{3x} - (1/9)e^{3x} + C$

16. $y = e^{x+1} + C$

17. $y = Me^x - 7$

18. $y^2 = -2e^{-x} + C$

19. $y = Ae^{4x-(3x^2/2)}$

20. $y = x^5 + 2x + 3$

21. $y^2 = 2\ln|x| + 1$

22. $y = \frac{x^4}{2} - x^3 + 2x - 4$

23. $y^2 + 2y = 2x^2 + 6x + 4$

24. $y = -2e^{-x} - 8x + 5$

25. $y = (1/4)\ln|4x + 1| + 3$

26. $y = x^2 - 2e^{-2x} + 2$

27. $y = 5e^{.2x-1} - 3$

28. $y = \frac{1}{e^8}e^{4\sqrt{x}}$

29. $y = (1/2)\ln(4x^2 + 3) + 1.45$

30. $y = 2(x^2 + 1)$

31. $y = 4\ln x$

32. $y^{2/3} = \frac{2}{5}x^{5/3} + \frac{18}{5}$

33. $y^2 = 2e^{x+1} + 1 - 2e$

34. \$1365.02

35. \$205,171

36. In about 27.7 yr

37. In about 13.3 yr

38. (a) About 122   (b) 35 days   (c) About 7 days   (d) About 7 days

39. 1.1 yr or about 13 mo   40. (a) 375,000 liters   (b) About 21 mo

41. 1998

Section 9.2

42. $y = Ce^{4x} - 1/2$

43. $y = Ce^{-3x} + 5/3$

44. $y = Ce^{-2x^2} + 11/4$

45. $y = 5/2 + Ce^{-x^2}$

46. $y = Ce^{-x^3/3} + 5$

47. $y = \left(\frac{1}{2}\right)e^{-x} + Ce^x$

48. $y = \frac{x^2}{2}e^{-x} + Ce^{-x}$

49. $y = 1 + 2e^{-x^2/2}$

50. $y = 1 + 3e^{-x^3/3}$

51. $y = \frac{1}{6}e^x + \frac{5}{6}e^{-5x}$

52. $y = \frac{1}{2} + \frac{3}{2}e^{2x^2}$

53. $y = \frac{1}{2x}(e^{x^2} + e)$

54. $y = \frac{5}{2} - \frac{5}{2x^2}$

55. $y = \frac{1}{5} + \frac{3}{x^5}$

56. 210°F

57. (a) $T = 160e^{-.94t} + 40$ (b) 102.5°F   (c) 49.5°F

Section 9.3

58. 2.240   **59.** 1.480   **60.** .700   **61.** 3.098   **62.** 4.120

63. 2.134   **64.** 1.903   **65.** 1.760   **66.** $y = \frac{x^3}{3} + x + 1$; $f(1) = 2.333$

67. $y = x^2 + 3x - 2$; $f(1.4) = 4.160$ **68.** $y = -x - 1 + 2e^x$; $f(.4) = 1.584$

69. $y = -e^{-x} + x + 3$; $f(.6) = 3.051$ **70.** $y = \ln|x| + x$; $f(1.5) = 1.905$

71. $y = \frac{-1 + x^2}{2}$; $f(1.6) = .780$ **72.** $y = 1 + e^{-x^2/2}$; $f(.5) = 1.882$

73. $y = \frac{(x^{3/2} + 2)^2}{9}$; $f(1.6) = 1.799$ **74.** $-.290$; $y = \frac{2}{3}x^3 - x$; $-.282$; $-.008$

75.

	Euler's Method	Actual Solution*	Difference
x_i	y_i	$f(x_i)$	$y_i - f(x_i)$
0	0	0	0
.2	.4	.442806	−.042806
.4	.88	.983649	−.103649
.6	1.456	1.644238	−.188238
.8	2.1472	2.451082	−.303882
1	2.97664	3.436564	−.459924

*to 6 decimal places

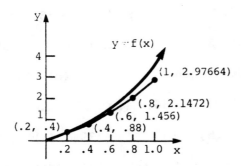

Section 9.4

76. $48,482.37   **77.** 17.3 yr   **78.** About 15 yr   **79.** $2 \ln y - 5y = -3 \ln x + 4x + C$; $x = 3/4$, $y = 2/5$ **80.** $3y - 2 \ln y = 4x - \ln x + C$; $x = 1/4$, $y = 2/3$ **81.** $y - \ln y = e^{x-1} - x + C$; $x = 1$, $y = 1$

82. (a) $y = \frac{4000}{1 + 199e^{-.163t}}$ (b) 32.5 days   **83.** (a) $y = \frac{100}{1 + 24e^{-.2452t}}$

(b) 20 days   **84.** $y = \frac{1000}{t + 50}$ **85.** (a) $y = 100 - 80e^{-.04t}$ (b) 99 lb

CHAPTER 10   PROBABILITY AND CALCULUS

Section 10.1

1. Yes   2. No; $\int_1^4 x^{3/2}\,dx \neq 1$ 3. No; $\int_0^{10} \left(\frac{1}{5}x + \frac{2}{5}\right)dx \neq 1$ 4. Yes

5. No; $\int_0^5 (1 - x)\,dx \neq 1$; also $1 - x < 0$ for x in (1, 5]

6. No; $\int_0^\infty e^{-2x}\,dx \neq 1$ 7. Yes   8. No; $\int_3^4 \sqrt{x}\,dx \neq 1$ 9. Yes

10. Yes   11. 5/62   12. 1/64   13. 2/35   14. 2   15. −1/24

16. 3/38   17. (a) $\int_2^{12} .1\,dx = .1x\Big|_2^{12} = 1$; f(x) = .1 ≥ 0 on [2, 12].

(b) .2   (c) .3   (d) .4   18. (a) .0625   (b) .3125   (c) .5625

19. (a) 1   (b) $3 - 2\sqrt{2} \approx .172$ 20. (a) .632   (b) .607   (c) .451

21. .9975   22. .982   23. .604   24. .2

Section 10.2

25. 6; 5.33; 2.31   26. 5.17; .31; .55   27. .5; .05; .22   28. 3; 3; 1.73   29. .6; .04; .2   30. 2.33; .76; .87   31. 2.4; 1.10; 1.05

32. 6.61; 2.05; 1.43   33. 53.33; 355.56; 18.86   34. (a) 37 hr

(b) 29.21   (c) .207   35. 4 cm   36. (a) .5   (b) .578

37. (a) .538   (b) .599   38. (a) .5   (b) .617   39. (a) .296

(b) .924   40. (a) .525   (b) .64   41. (a) .474   (b) .581

42. (a) .535   (b) .605   43. (a) .511   (b) .580   44. (a) 4

(b) 4.243   (c) .056   45. (a) 1.667   (b) 1.707   (c) .055

Section 10.3

46. (a) 10   (b) 100   (c) 10   47. (a) 20   (b) 400   (c) 20

48. (a) .368   (b) .865   49. (a) .368   (b) .865

50. (a) f(x) = 1/8 for [2, 10]   (b) 6   (c) .25   51. (a) 39

(b) 6.35   (c) .5   52. (a) $f(x) = .5e^{-.5x}$ for [0, ∞)   (b) .082

53.   (a) $f(x) = .01e^{-.01x}$ for $[0, \infty)$ (b)   .047   (c)   .301   54.   98.21%

55.   7.64%   56.   3.07%   57.   76.42%   58.   30.52%   59.   33.82%

60.   70.16%   61.   74.66%   62.   −.92   63.   .18   64.   .67

65.   .1635   66.   .2709   67.   .7995

CHAPTER 11   THE TRIGONOMETRIC FUNCTIONS

Section 11.1

1. $2\pi/3$ 2. $5\pi/3$ 3. $-10\pi/3$ 4. $-4\pi/3$ 5. $\pi/10$ 6. $\pi/5$

7. $\pi/120$ 8. $\pi/75$ 9. $25\pi/9$ 10. 5π 11. $420°$ 12. $450°$

13. $1440°$ 14. $540°$ 15. $-120°$ 16. $-144°$ 17. $99°$

18. $108°$

In Exercises 19–25, function values are given in the order $\sin \alpha$, $\cos \alpha$, $\tan \alpha$, $\cot \alpha$, $\sec \alpha$, $\csc \alpha$.

19. $4/5$, $3/5$, $4/3$, $3/4$, $5/3$, $5/4$ 20. $3/5$, $-4/5$, $-3/4$, $-4/3$, $-5/4$, $5/3$

21. $-24/25$, $7/25$, $-24/7$, $-7/24$, $25/7$, $-25/24$ 22. $-40/41$, $-9/41$, $40/9$, $9/40$, $-41/9$, $-41/40$ 23. $60/61$, $-11/61$, $-60/11$, $-11/60$, $-61/11$, $61/60$

24. $-4/5$, $3/5$, $-4/3$, $-3/4$, $5/3$, $-5/4$ 25. $-15/17$, $-8/17$, $15/8$, $8/15$, $-17/8$, $-17/15$ 26. $-1/2$ 27. -2 28. -1 29. $-\sqrt{2}$ 30. $\sqrt{3}/2$

31. 1 32. $-1/2$ 33. $-\sqrt{3}/3$ 34. $1/2$ 35. Undefined   36. -1

37. 0 38. $\sqrt{3}/3$ 39. 0 40. $-\sqrt{3}$ 41. 2 42. $-\sqrt{2}/2$

43. 1 44. -2 45. $-\sqrt{3}/2$ 46. $-\sqrt{3}/2$ 47. $\sqrt{3}$ 48. $-\sqrt{3}/2$

49. -2 50. $.9205$ 51. -1.540 52. $.4540$ 53. 11.474

54. $.7363$ 55. $.8788$ 56. $-.0959$ 57. $-.5925$

58.

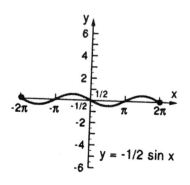

$y = -1/2 \sin x$

59.

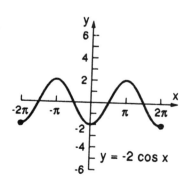

$y = -2 \cos x$

60.

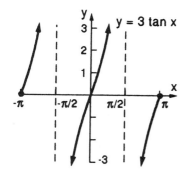

61.

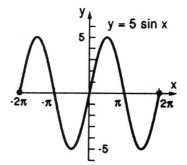

62.

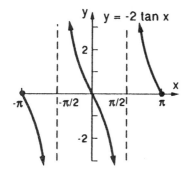

63.

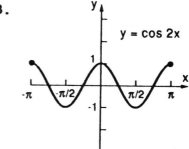

64. Minimum value is 3; maximum value is 5.

65. **(a)** 500 **(b)** 700 **(c)** About 850 **(d)** 900 **(e)** About 850 **(f)** 700

66. **(a)** 75.9°F **(b)** 75.9°F **(c)** 81°F **(d)** 80.1°F

Section 11.2

67. $y' = -3 \sin 3x$ **68.** $y' = 5 \cos 5x$ **69.** $y' = 15 \sin^4 x \cos x$

70. $y' = 28x \sec^2 7x^2$ **71.** $y' = -2x \sec^2 (4 - x^2)$

72. $y' = -54x \cos^2 3x^2 \sin 3x^2$ **73.** $y' = 3 \tan^2 x \sec^2 x$

74. $y' = e^x \cos e^x$ **75.** $y' = \cos^2 x - \sin^2 x$ **76.** $y' = -\sin x$

77. $y' = (\sin x) e^{-\cos x}$ **78.** $y' = 4(x^4 \cos x^4 - \sin x^4)/x^5$

79. $y' = \sin x \sec^2 x + \sin x - \cos x$ **80.** $y' = x^2 \cos x + 2x \sin x$

81. $y' = -2x^2 \sin x^2 + \cos x^2$ **82.** $y' = 2x \sin 4x + 4x^2 \cos 4x$

83. $y' = (\sin x - x \cos x - \cos x)/\sin^2 x$ **84.** $y' = -2 \sin x/(\cos x + 1)^2$

85. $y' = \sec^2 x/\tan x$ **86.** $y' = (2 \sin x \cos x - \sin^2 x \cos x)/(1 - \sin x)^2$

87. $y' = 2e^{2x} \cos x - e^{2x} \sin x$ **88.** $y' = (-1/x) \sin (\ln x)$

89. $y' = (\sin x \cos 2x - 2 \sin 2x \cos x)/[3(\cos x)^{4/3}(\cos 2x)^{2/3}]$

90. $y' = [(x - 4)(\cos x) - \sin x]/(x - 4)^2$

91. $y' = [\sin 2x(\cos x - x \sin x) - 2x \cos x \cos 2x]/(\sin 2x)^2$

92. $y' = 3 \sin 3x \sec^2 3x + 3 \tan 3x \cos 3x$ or $3 \sin 3x(1 + \sec^2 3x)$

93. $y' = 3 \sin x \tan x \sec^3 x + \cos x \sec^3 x$ or $\sec^2 x(1 + 3 \sin^2 x \sec^2 x)$

94. **(a)** 4; 0   **(b)** 4   **95.** $y - (3\sqrt{2}/2)x = (-3\sqrt{2}/2)(\pi/4 + 1)$

96. **(a)** $\sqrt{2}/2$ **(b)** $-12 + \sqrt{2}/2$

Section 11.3

97. $(-1/4) \cos 4x + C$ **98.** $-2 \cos x - \sin x + C$

99. $(-1/6) \ln |\cos 6x| + C$ **100.** $(4/3) \tan 3x + C$

101. $(-2/5) \cot 5x + C$ **102.** $\sin e^x + C$ **103.** $\ln |\sec x^2| + C$

104. $-\frac{1}{2} \ln |3 - 2 \sin x| + C$ **105.** $(2/3)\sqrt{\sin^3 x} + C$

106. $-4(\cos x)^{1/4} + C$ **107.** $-2x^2 \cos 2x + 2x \sin 2x + \cos 2x + C$

108. $(1/2) \cos (x + 1)^2 + C$ **109.** 2/3   **110.** $-1/2$

111. $\pi/3 - 1 + \sqrt{3} \approx 1.779$ **112.** 1/8   **113.** .167   **114.** .096

115. $2\sqrt{3}/3$ or 1.155   **116.** $-.3$ **117.** .2

Section 11.4

118. $\pi/4$ **119.** $-\pi/6$ **120.** $\pi/3$ **121.** $5\pi/6$ **122.** $\pi/2$ **123.** 0

124. 130°   **125.** 34°   **126.** $-66°$ **127.** $5/\sqrt{1 - 25x^2}$

128. $-1/\sqrt{1 - (2 + x)^2}$ **129.** $6x/(1 + 9x^4)$ **130.** $1/\sqrt{1 - x^2}$ **131.** 0

132. $2/\sqrt{1 - x^2}$ **133.** $1/[2(x + 2)\sqrt{x + 1}]$ **134.** $e^x/(1 + e^{2x})$

135. $1/[x(1 + (\ln |2x|)^2)]$ **136.** $1/(|x|\sqrt{x^2 - 1})$ **137.** $2 \cos^{-1} x + C$

138. $5 \tan^{-1} x + C$ 139. $(1/3) \sin^{-1} 3x + C$ 140. $(1/5) \tan^{-1} x^5 + C$

141. $\cos^{-1} 5x + C$ 142. $x + C$ 143. $\sin^{-1} (e^{3x}) + C$

144. $\sin^{-1} (\ln x) + C$ 145. $(1/2) \sin^{-1} (\ln x)^2 + C$

146. $\sin^{-1} .5 = \pi/6 \approx .5236$ 147. $\pi/6 \approx .5236$ 148. $\pi/4 \approx .7854$

Section 11.5

149. $1/2$ 150. 2 151. -1 152. $-\sqrt{3}/2$ 153. $4; -4$

FINAL EXAMINATIONS
AND
ANSWERS

FINAL EXAMINATION, FORM A
CALCULUS WITH APPLICATIONS

NAME_____

HOUR_____

1. Find the location(s) and value(s) of all absolute extrema for the function

$$g(x) = x^3 - 6x^2$$

   on the interval $[-1, 2]$.

   1. _____

2. Find the largest open intervals where the function

$$f(x) = x^4 - 4x^3 - 5$$

   is concave upward or downward. Find any points of inflection.

   2. _____

3. Find dy/dx, given $3\sqrt{x} - 5y^3 = 7/x$.

   3. _____

4. Find dy, given $y = -3(2 + x^2)^3$.

   4. _____

5. Approximate the volume of coating on a sphere of radius 5 inches, if the coating is .03 inch thick.

   5. _____

6. Solve $\dfrac{25}{49} = \left(\dfrac{7}{5}\right)^{2x}$.

   6. _____

7. Find the cost function for the marginal cost function

$$C'(x) = 8x - 9x^2,$$

   if the fixed cost is $20.

   7. _____

8. Find the average value of the function

$$f(x) = x(x^2 + 1)^3$$

   over the interval $[0, 2]$.

   8. _____

9. Let $z = f(x, y) = 3x^2 - 4xy + y^3$. Find $f_{xy}(1, -3)$.

   9. _____

FINAL EXAMINATION, FORM A, PAGE 2

10. The production function z for an auto-
    mobile factory is

    $$z = x^{.3}y^{.7},$$

    where x represents the amount of labor
    and y the amount of capital. Find the
    marginal productivity of the following.

    (a) Labor   (b) Capital

    10. (a)_____

        (b)_____

11. Find the general solution for the dif-
    ferential equation

    $$\frac{dy}{dx} = \frac{1 + e^x}{2y}.$$

    11. _____

12. Find the general solution for the dif-
    ferential equation

    $$\frac{dy}{dx} = 5.$$

    12. _____

13. The probability density function of a
    random variable is defined by

    $$f(x) = \frac{1}{4} \text{ for } [12, 16].$$

    Find the following probabilities.

    (a) $P(x \leq 14)$ (b) $P(x \geq 15)$

    13. (a)_____

        (b)_____

14. Graph one period of the function
    $y = -2 \cos x$.

    14.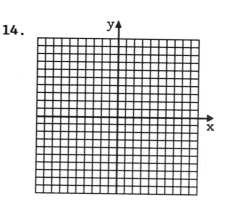

FINAL EXAMINATION, FORM A, PAGE 3

15. Find the location(s) and value(s) of all relative extrema for the function

$$f(x) = \frac{x^2 + 5x + 3}{x - 1}.$$

15. _____

16. A marketing research firm determines that the daily profit from a new product is given by

$$P(x) = -2x^2 + 30x + 45,$$

where x is the price (in dollars) of the product.

   (a) At what price will the maximum daily profit occur?

   (b) What is the maximum daily profit?

16. (a)_____

    (b)_____

17. Evaluate dy, given $y = x^2 - 8x + 20$; $x = -1$; $\Delta x = .01$.

17. _____

18. Graph the function $y = 5 + \ln(x + 2)$.

18.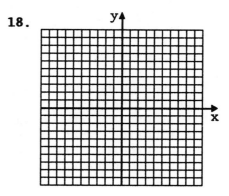

19. Write the equation $(1/5)^{-1/2} = \sqrt{5}$, using logarithms.

19. _____

20. Solve $e^{2x-5} = 10$, rounding your answer to the nearest thousandth.

20. _____

FINAL EXAMINATION, FORM A, PAGE 4

21. Find the area of the region enclosed
    by the curves $f(x) = x^2 - 4$ and
    $g(x) = 1 - x^2$.

    21. _____

22. Maximize $f(x, y) = x^2y$ subject to the
    constraint $y + 4x = 84$.

    22. _____

23. Find dz, given $z = 3x^2 - 4xy + y^2$,
    where $x = 0$, $y = 2$, $dx = .02$, and
    $dy = .01$.

    23. _____

Find particular solutions for the differential
equations in Problems 24 and 25.

24. $\dfrac{dy}{dx} = 3x^2 - 7x + 2$; $y = 4$ when $x = 0$.

    24. _____

25. $y' + 4x^3y = x^3$; $y = 3$ when $x = 0$.

    25. _____

26. Find the expected value, the variance,
    and the standard deviation for the
    probability density function defined
    by $f(x) = 3x^{-4}$ on $[1, \infty)$.

    26. _____

27. The average height of a particular
    type of tree is 20 ft, with a standard
    deviation of 2 ft. Assuming a normal
    distribution, what is the probability
    that a tree of this kind will be
    shorter than 17 ft?

    27. _____

28. The total cost to manufacture x units
    of a product is given by

    $$C(x) = \frac{x^3}{3} - 4x^2 + 12x.$$

    Over what interval(s) is the total
    cost

    (a) increasing   (b) decreasing?

    28. (a)_____

        (b)_____

29. Evaluate $\log_{1/3} 27$.

29. _____

30. Find the volume of the solid of revolution formed by rotating the region bounded by $f(x) = \sqrt{x + 4}$, $y = 0$, and $x = 12$ about the x-axis.

30. _____

31. Find an equation for the tangent line to the curve $y = e^x$ at the point $(0, 1)$.

31. _____

32. Evaluate $\tan^{-1} (-1)$.

32. _____

Find the derivative of each function in Problems 33–37.

33. $y = 7x^2 e^{3x}$

33. _____

34. $y = \dfrac{x}{3 \ln (9x + 5)}$

34. _____

35. $f(x) = \tan (3x^2 - 4)$

35. _____

36. $y = x^3 \sin^2 x$

36. _____

37. $f(x) = \cos^{-1} (2x^2)$

37. _____

Evaluate each integral in Problems 38–50. Use the table of integrals as necessary. Note any integrals that diverge.

38. $\displaystyle\int (3x^2 - 7x + 2)\, dx$

38. _____

39. $\displaystyle\int \dfrac{5}{x + 1}\, dx$

39. _____

40. $\displaystyle\int \frac{2x}{e^{2x^2}}\, dx$

40. _____

41. $\displaystyle\int_0^2 x\sqrt{3x^2 + 4}\, dx$

41. _____

42. $\displaystyle\int \frac{1}{(25 - 16x^2)}\, dx$

42. _____

43. $\displaystyle\int x^2 e^x dx$

43. _____

44. $\displaystyle\int_1^{e^2} 3x \ln x\, dx$

44. _____

45. $\displaystyle\int_4^\infty \ln (3x)\, dx$

45. _____

46. $\displaystyle\int_{-\infty}^{-1} x^{-2} dx$

46. _____

47. $\displaystyle\int_1^4 \sqrt{4x - 3y}\, dy$

47. _____

48. $\displaystyle\int_1^2 \left(\int_0^3 e^{2x} dy\right) dx$

48. _____

49. $\displaystyle\int \frac{9}{1 + x^2}\, dx$

49. _____

50. $\displaystyle\int_0^{\pi/6} \sin^3 x \cos x\, dx$

50. _____

FINAL EXAMINATION, FORM B
CALCULUS WITH APPLICATIONS

NAME_____

HOUR_____

Choose the best answer.

1. Find dy/dx, given $4x^2 - 7 = 3\sqrt{y} + 2/x^3$.

   (a) $\dfrac{4\sqrt{y}(4x^5 - 3)}{3x^4}$

   (b) $\dfrac{4\sqrt{y}(4x^5 + 3)}{3x^4}$

   (c) $\dfrac{4\sqrt{y}(4x^3 - 3)}{3x^2}$

   (d) $\dfrac{4\sqrt{y}(4x^3 + 3)}{3x^2}$

   1. _____

2. Botanists, Inc., a consulting firm, monitors the monthly growth of an unusual plant. They determine that the growth (in inches) is given by

   $$g(x) = 4x - x^2,$$

   where x represents the average daily number of ounces of water the plant receives. Find the maximum monthly growth of the plant.

   (a) 2 inches

   (b) 8 inches

   (c) 4 inches

   (d) 6 inches

   2. _____

3. Solve $\dfrac{1}{3} = 27^{4x}$.

   (a) $-\dfrac{3}{4}$ (b) $\dfrac{1}{108}$ (c) $-\dfrac{1}{108}$ (d) $-\dfrac{1}{12}$

   3. _____

4. Write the equation $\left(\dfrac{1}{6}\right)^{-1/2} = \sqrt{6}$ using logarithms.

   (a) $\log_{1/6} -\dfrac{1}{2} = \sqrt{6}$

   (b) $\log_{1/6} \sqrt{6} = -\dfrac{1}{2}$

   (c) $\log_{\sqrt{6}} \dfrac{1}{6} = -\dfrac{1}{2}$

   (d) $\log_{\sqrt{6}} -\dfrac{1}{2} = \dfrac{1}{6}$

   4. _____

5. Find the area of the region enclosed by the curves $f(x) = 9 - x^2$ and $g(x) = x^2 - 9$.

   (a) -36 (b) 36   (c) 0   (d) 72

   5. _____

FINAL EXAMINATION, FORM B, PAGE 2

6. Find the cost function for the marginal cost function
$$C'(x) = 10x - 7x^2,$$
if the fixed cost is $200.

    (a) $C(x) = 200 + 5x^2 - 14x$ (b) $C(x) = 5x^2 - 14x$

    (c) $C(x) = 5x^2 - \dfrac{7x^3}{3} + 200$ (d) $C(x) = 10 - 14x$

6. _____

7. Find the average value of the function $f(x) = \sqrt{3x + 1}$ over the interval $[0, 8]$.

    (a) $\dfrac{31}{3}$ (b) $\dfrac{248}{9}$ (c) $\dfrac{31}{9}$ (d) $\dfrac{248}{3}$

7. _____

8. Maximize $f(x, y) = x^2y$ subject to the constraint $y + 4x = 84$.

    (a) 0   (b) 14   (c) 5488   (d) 3642

8. _____

9. Given $z = f(x, y) = x^2 - 3xy + 2y^3$, find $f_{yx}(0, -2)$.

    (a) -16 (b) 2   (c) -24 (d) -3

9. _____

10. Evaluate dy, given $y = 45 - 2x - 3x^2$, with $x = 3$ and $\Delta x = .02$.

    (a) $-.4$ (b) $.4$ (c) $.32$ (d) $-.32$

10. _____

11. Approximate the volume of the coating on a cube with 3-cm sides, if the coating is .02 cm thick. Use calculus to arrive at the approximation.

    (a) $.54$ cm^3 (b) 27.54 cm^3

    (c) 26.46 cm^3 (d) 81.54 cm^3

11. _____

12. Solve $\left(\dfrac{1}{e}\right)^{2x} = 14$. (Round to nearest thousandth.)

    (a) -1.320 (b) 2.639 (c) -2.639 (d) 1.320

12. _____

13. Graph $y = 3^{-x}$.   13. _____

(a) 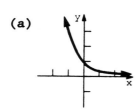   (b) 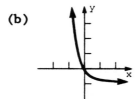   (c) 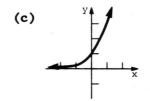   (d)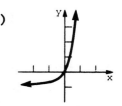

14. The total cost to manufacture x units of a product is given by
$$C(x) = \frac{x^3}{3} - 4x^2 + 12x.$$

Over what interval(s) is the total cost increasing?

(a) [2, 6]   (b) $(-\infty, 2]$

(c) $(-\infty, 2]$ and $[6, \infty)$ (d) $(-\infty, 6]$ 14. _____

15. Is the function $g(x) = x^3 - 6x^2$ concave up or down or neither at (0, 0)?

(a) Concave up   (b) Concave down   (c) Neither   15. _____

16. Find the absolute minimum of $f(x) = x^4 - 4x^3 - 5$ on the interval $[-1, 2]$.

(a) −30   (b) 0

(c) −21   (d) No absolute minimum   16. _____

17. The average height of a particular type of tree is 20 ft, with a standard deviation of 2 ft. Assuming a normal distribution, what is the probability that a tree of this kind would be taller than 17 ft?

(a) .0668   (b) .9332   (c) .8023   (d) .1977   17. _____

18. The probability density function of a random variable is defined by
$$f(x) = \frac{1}{5} \text{ for } [20, 25].$$

Find $P(x \le 22)$.

(a) .2   (b) .8   (c) .4   (d) .6   18. _____

FINAL EXAMINATION, FORM B, PAGE 4

19. Find the standard deviation for the probability density function $f(x) = 3x^{-4}$ on $[1, \infty)$.

    (a) 1.5   (b) .866   (c) .75   (d) .67   19. _____

20. Find the volume of the solid of revolution formed by rotating the region bounded by $f(x) = \sqrt{x-1}$, $y = 0$, and $x = 10$ about the x-axis.

    (a) 40.5   (b) $\dfrac{81\pi}{2}$ (c) 18π (d) 40π 20. _____

21. Find dz, given $z = \sqrt{x^2 + y^2}$, with $x = 3$, $y = 4$, $dx = -.01$, and $dy = .02$.

    (a) .022   (b) .01   (c) .001   (d) .05   21. _____

22. The production function z for a major manufacturing company is $z = x^{.4}y^{.6}$, where x represents the amount of labor and y the amount of capital. Find the marginal productivity of labor.

    (a) $.4x^{-.6}y^{.6}$ (b) $.4x^{.4}y^{.6}$

    (c) $.6x^{.4}y^{.6}$ (d) $.6x^{.4}y^{-.4}$ 22. _____

Find general solutions for the differential equations in Problems 23 and 24.

23. $\dfrac{dy}{dx} = 3$

    (a) $y = 3x^2$ (b) $y = 3x$

    (c) $y = 3x^2 + C$ (d) $y = 3x + C$ 23. _____

24. $\dfrac{dy}{dx} = \dfrac{e^{2x} - 4}{y^2}$

    (a) $y = \left(\dfrac{3}{2}e^{2x} - 12x + C\right)^{1/3}$ (b) $y = \dfrac{1}{2}e^{2x} - 4x + C$

    (c) $y = \left(\dfrac{1}{2}e^{2x} - 4x + C\right)^{1/3}$ (d) $y^2 = e^{2x} - 4$ 24. _____

FINAL EXAMINATION, FORM B, PAGE 5

Find particular solutions for the differential equations in Problems 25 and 26.

25. $y' - 3x^2y = 12x^2$; $y = 8$ when $x = 0$.

    (a) $y = 4e^{x^3}$ (b) $y = -4 + C$

    (c) $y = -4 + 12e^{x^3}$ (d) $y = 4e^{x^3} + C$ 25. _____

26. $\dfrac{dy}{dx} = 7 - 2x + 3x^2$; $y = -2$ when $x = 0$.

    (a) $y = 7x - x^2 + x^3 + C$ (b) $y = 7x - x^2 + x^3 - 2$

    (c) $y = -x^2 + x^3 + C$ (d) $y = 7x - x^2 + x^3 + 2 + C$ 26. _____

27. Find dy, given $y = 4 + 7(1 - x^3)^4$.

    (a) $[4 + 84x^2(1 - x^3)^3]\ dx$ (b) $-84x^2(1 - x^3)^3 dx$

    (c) $28(1 - x^3)^3 dx$ (d) $84x^2(1 - x^3)\ dx$ 27. _____

28. Evaluate dy, given $y = 45 - 2x - 3x^2$, with $x = 3$ and $\Delta x = .02$.

    (a) $-.4$ (b) $.4$ (c) $.32$ (d) $-.32$ 28. _____

29. Graph one period of $y = -2 \sin x$.   29. _____

  (a) 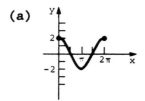   (b) 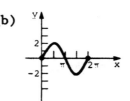   (c) 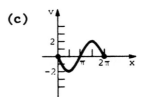   (d)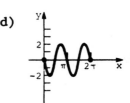

30. Evaluate $\sin^{-1}\left(-\dfrac{\sqrt{3}}{2}\right)$.

    (a) $\dfrac{4\pi}{3}$ (b) $\dfrac{5\pi}{3}$ (c) $-\dfrac{\pi}{3}$ (d) $\dfrac{\pi}{3}$ 30. _____

FINAL EXAMINATION, FORM B, PAGE 6

31. Find the equation of the tangent line to the curve $f(x) = -\dfrac{1}{x + 2}$ at the point $(2, -\dfrac{1}{4})$.

   (a) $x - 16y = 6$

   (b) $x - 4y = 3$

   (c) $f'(x) = \dfrac{1}{16}$

   (d) $y = \dfrac{1}{(x + 2)^2}$

31. _____

32. Find the location(s) and value(s) of all relative extrema for the function

   $$f(x) = \frac{x^2 + 5x + 3}{x - 1}.$$

   (a) Relative minimum of 1 at -2;
       relative maximum of 13 at 4

   (b) Relative maximum of 1 at -2;
       relative minimum of 13 at 4

   (c) No relative extrema

32. _____

33. Choose the expression that is equivalent to

   $$2 \log_a x^2 y + 3 \log_a y - \frac{1}{2} \log_a x.$$

   (a) $\dfrac{\log_a (x^4 y^5)}{\log_a \sqrt{x}}$

   (b) $\log_a (x^{7/2} y^5)$

   (c) $\log_a (x^{3/2} y^5)$

   (d) $\dfrac{\log_a (x^2 y^5)}{\log_a \sqrt{x}}$

33. _____

For Problems 34–38, find the derivative for each function.

34. $y = -3x^3 e^{2x}$

   (a) $-27x^2 e^{2x} - 6x^3 e^{2x}$

   (b) $-18x^2 e^{3x}$

   (c) $-9x^2 e^{2x} - 6x^3 e^{2x}$

   (d) $-6x^2 e^{2x} - 6x^3 e^{2x}$

34. _____

35. $y = \dfrac{x^2}{\ln 3x}$

    (a) $\dfrac{2x^2}{(\ln 3x)^2}$ (b) $\dfrac{6x \ln 3x - x}{3(\ln 3x)^2}$

    (c) $\dfrac{2x \ln 3x - x}{(\ln 3x)^2}$ (d) $\dfrac{6x \ln 3x + x}{3(\ln 3x)^2}$ 35. _____

36. $f(x) = x^2 \cos^3 x$

    (a) $x \cos^2 x \,(2 \cos x + 3x)$ (b) $x \cos^2 x \,(2 \cos x - 3x \sin x)$

    (c) $x \cos^2 x \,(2 \cos x - 3x)$ (d) $x \cos^2 x \,(2 \cos x + 3x \sin x)$

        36. _____

37. $y = \sin^{-1}(3x^4)$

    (a) $\dfrac{1}{\sqrt{1 - 9x^8}}$ (b) $\dfrac{12x^3}{1 - 9x^8}$

    (c) $\dfrac{12x^3}{\sqrt{1 - 9x^8}}$ (d) $\dfrac{72x^7}{\sqrt{1 - 9x^8}}$ 37. _____

38. $f(x) = \tan \sqrt{2x + 1}$

    (a) $\dfrac{\sec^2 \sqrt{2x + 1}}{\sqrt{2x + 1}}$ (b) $\dfrac{\sec^2 \sqrt{2x + 1}}{2}$

    (c) $x \sec^2 \sqrt{2x + 1}$ (d) $2x \sec^2 \sqrt{2x + 1}$ 38. _____

For Problems 39–50, evaluate each definite or indefinite integral, using the table of integrals as necessary.

39. $\displaystyle\int (4x^2 + 3x - 5)\, dx$

    (a) $\dfrac{4}{3}x^3 + \dfrac{3}{2}x^2 - 5 + C$ (b) $\dfrac{4}{3}x^3 + \dfrac{3}{2}x^2 - 5x$

    (c) $\dfrac{4}{3}x^3 + \dfrac{3}{2}x^2 - 5x + C$ (d) $8x + 3$ 39. _____

40. $\int \dfrac{-3}{(2x + 5)}\ dx$

    (a) $-\dfrac{3}{2}\ \ln\ |2x + 5| + C$ (b) $-3\ \ln\ |2x + 5| + C$

    (c) $-\dfrac{1}{6}\ \ln\ |2x + 5| + C$ (d) $\dfrac{1}{2}\ \ln\ |2x + 5| + C$ 40. _____

41. $\int \dfrac{4x}{e^{x^2}}\ dx$

    (a) $\dfrac{-2}{e^{x^2}} + C$ (b) $\dfrac{2}{e^{x^2}} + C$

    (c) $2e^{x^2} + C$ (d) $4x\ \ln\ (e^{x^2}) + C$ 41. _____

42. $\int_0^1 2x\sqrt{4x^2 + 5}\ dx$

    (a) $\dfrac{3}{8}$ (b) $\dfrac{27 - 5\sqrt{5}}{6}$

    (c) $\dfrac{27 - 5\sqrt{5}}{8}$ (d) $\dfrac{27 - 5\sqrt{5}}{4}$ 42. _____

43. $\int_1^4 9x^2\ \ln\ x\ dx$

    (a) $192\ \ln\ 4 - 45$ (b) $192\ \ln\ 4 - 65$
    (c) $192\ \ln\ 4 - 51$ (d) $192\ \ln\ 4 - 63$ 43. _____

44. $\int \dfrac{1}{(49 - 25x^2)}\ dx$

    (a) $\dfrac{1}{70}\ \ln\ \left|\dfrac{7 + 5x}{7 - 5x}\right| + C$ (b) $\dfrac{1}{14}\ \ln\ \left|\dfrac{7 + 5x}{7 - 5x}\right| + C$

    (c) $\dfrac{1}{14}\ \ln\ \left|\dfrac{5x - 7}{5x + 7}\right| + C$ (d) $\dfrac{1}{70}\ \ln\ \left|\dfrac{5x - 7}{5x + 7}\right| + C$ 44. _____

45. $\int 3x^2 e^{2x} dx$

    (a) $3e^{x^2} + C$ (b) $\frac{3}{2}x^2 e^{2x} - \frac{3}{2}xe^{2x} + \frac{3}{4}e^{2x} + C$

    (c) $x^3 e^{2x} + C$ (d) $3x^2 e^{2x} - 6xe^{2x} + 6e^{2x} + C$ 45. _____

46. Find $\int_2^\infty \ln(2x)\, dx$

    (a) $x \ln(2x) - x + C$ (b) $2\ln 4 + 4$

    (c) Diverges   (d) $\frac{1}{4}$ 46. _____

47. $\int_2^3 \sqrt{2x + y}\, dy$

    (a) $\sqrt{7}$ (b) $2\sqrt{2}$

    (c) 1 (d) $\frac{2}{3}[(2x + 3)^{3/2} - (2x + 2)^{3/2}]$ 47. _____

48. $\int_{-\infty}^{-2} \frac{1}{x^3}\, dx$

    (a) $-\frac{1}{8}$ (b) Diverges   (c) $\frac{1}{64}$ (d) $-\frac{1}{64}$ 48. _____

49. $\int \frac{25}{1 + x^2}\, dx$

    (a) $25 \sin^{-1}(1 + x^2) + C$ (b) $25 \tan^{-1}(1 + x^2) + C$

    (c) $25 \tan^{-1} x + C$ (d) $5 \sin^{-1} x + C$ 49. _____

50. $\int_0^{\pi/2} (10 - 10\sin^2 x \cos x)\, dx$

    (a) $\frac{20}{3}$ (b) $5\pi - 10$

    (c) $\frac{30\pi - 10}{3}$ (d) $\frac{15\pi - 10}{3}$ 50. _____

FINAL EXAMINATION, FORM A

1. Absolute minimum of -16 at 2; absolute maximum of 0 at 0

2. Concave up on $(-\infty, 0)$ and $(2, \infty)$; concave down on $(0, 2)$; points of inflection are $(0, -5)$ and $(2, -21)$.

3. $\dfrac{dy}{dx} = \dfrac{3x^{3/2} + 14}{30x^2y^2}$

4. $dy = -18x(2 + x^2)^2dx$

5. 3π in^3

6. -1

7. $C(x) = 4x^2 - 3x^3 + 20$

8. 39

9. -4

10. (a) $.3x^{-.7}y^{.7}$
    (b) $.7x^{.3}y^{-.3}$

11. $y^2 = x + e^x + C$

12. $y = 5x + C$

13. (a) .5
    (b) .25

14.

$y = -2\cos x$

15. Relative maximum of 1 at -2; relative minimum of 13 at 4

16. (a) \$7.50
    (b) \$157.50

17. $dy = -.1$

18.

$y = 5 + \ln(x + 2)$

19. $\log_{1/5} \sqrt{5} = -1/2$

20. 3.651

21. $10\sqrt{10}/3 \approx 10.54$

22. 5488

23. $dz = -.12$

24. $y = x^3 - \dfrac{7}{2}x^2 + 2x + 4$

25. $y = \dfrac{1}{4} + \dfrac{11}{4}e^{-x^4}$

26. $\mu = 3/2$; $\text{Var}(x) = .75$; $\sigma = .866$

27. .0668

28. (a) Increasing on $(-\infty, 2)$ and $(6, \infty)$
    (b) Decreasing on $(2, 6)$

29. -3

30. 128π

FINAL EXAMINATION, FORM A

31. $y = x + 1$

32. $-\pi/4$

33. $y' = 14xe^{3x} + 21x^2e^{3x}$ or
     $7xe^{3x}(2 + 3x)$

34. $y' = \dfrac{3(9x + 5) \ln (9x + 5) - 27x}{9(9x + 5)[\ln (9x + 5)]^2}$

35. $f'(x) = 6x \sec^2 (3x^2 - 4)$

36. $y' = 3x^2 \sin^2 x + 2x^3 \sin x \cos x$
     or $x^2 \sin x (3 \sin x + 2x \cos x)$

37. $f'(x) = -4x/\sqrt{1 - 4x^4}$

38. $x^3 - \dfrac{7}{2}x^2 + 2x + C$

39. $5 \ln |x + 1| + C$

40. $-\dfrac{1}{2}e^{-2x^2} + C$

41. $56/9$

42. $\dfrac{1}{40} \ln \left|\dfrac{5 + 4x}{5 - 4x}\right| + C$

43. $x^2e^x - 2xe^x + 2e^x + C$

44. $\dfrac{9}{4}e^4 + \dfrac{3}{4} \approx 123.596$

45. Diverges

46. 1

47. $-\dfrac{2}{9}(4x - 12)^{3/2} + \dfrac{2}{9}(4x - 3)^{3/2}$

48. $\dfrac{3}{2}e^4 - \dfrac{3}{2}e^2 \approx 70.81$

49. $9 \tan^{-1} x + C$

50. $1/64$

FINAL EXAMINATION, FORM B

1.	(b)		26.	(b)
2.	(c)		27.	(b)
3.	(d)		28.	(a)
4.	(b)		29.	(c)
5.	(d)		30.	(c)
6.	(c)		31.	(a)
7.	(c)		32.	(b)
8.	(c)		33.	(b)
9.	(d)		34.	(c)
10.	(a)		35.	(c)
11.	(a)		36.	(b)
12.	(a)		37.	(c)
13.	(a)		38.	(a)
14.	(c)		39.	(c)
15.	(b)		40.	(a)
16.	(c)		41.	(a)
17.	(b)		42.	(b)
18.	(c)		43.	(d)
19.	(b)		44.	(a)
20.	(b)		45.	(b)
21.	(b)		46.	(c)
22.	(a)		47.	(d)
23.	(d)		48.	(a)
24.	(a)		49.	(c)
25.	(c)		50.	(d)

SOLUTIONS

TO

EVEN–NUMBERED EXERCISES

ALGEBRA REFERENCE

Section R.1

2. $(-4y^2 - 3y + 8) - (2y^2 - 6y - 2)$

$= (-4y^2 - 3y + 8) + (-2y^2 + 6y + 2)$

$= -4y^2 - 3y + 8 - 2y^2 + 6y + 2$

$= (-4y^2 - 2y^2) + (-3y + 6y)$

$\quad + (8 + 2)$

$= -6y^2 + 3y + 10$

4. $2(3r^2 + 4r + 2) - 3(-r^2 + 4r - 5)$

$= (6r^2 + 8r + 4) + (3r^2 - 12r + 15)$

$= (6r^2 + 3r^2) + (8r - 12r)$

$\quad + (4 + 15)$

$= 9r^2 - 4r + 19$

6. $.83(5r^2 - 2r + 7) - (7.12r^2 + 6.423r - 2)$

$= (4.15r^2 - 1.66r + 5.81)$

$\quad + (-7.12r^2 - 6.423r + 2)$

$= (4.15r^2 - 7.12r^2)$

$\quad + (-1.66r - 6.423r) + (5.81 + 2)$

$= -2.97r^2 - 8.083r + 7.81$

8. Use the FOIL method to find

$(6k - 1)(2k - 3)$

$= (6k)(2k) + (6k)(-3) + (-1)(2k)$

$\quad + (-1)(-3)$

$= 12k^2 - 18k - 2k + 3$

$= 12k^2 - 20k + 3.$

10. $(9k + q)(2k - q)$

$= (9k)(2k) + (9k)(-q) + (q)(2k)$

$\quad + (q)(-q)$

$= 18k^2 - 9kq + 2kq - q^2$

$= 18k^2 - 7kq - q^2$

12. $\left(\frac{3}{4}r - \frac{2}{3}s\right)\left(\frac{5}{4}r + \frac{1}{3}s\right)$

$= \left(\frac{3}{4}r\right)\left(\frac{5}{4}r\right) + \left(\frac{3}{4}r\right)\left(\frac{1}{3}s\right) + \left(-\frac{2}{3}s\right)\left(\frac{5}{4}r\right)$

$\quad + \left(-\frac{2}{3}s\right)\left(\frac{1}{3}s\right)$

$= \frac{15}{16}r^2 + \frac{1}{4}rs - \frac{5}{6}rs - \frac{2}{9}s^2$

$= \frac{15}{16}r^2 - \frac{7}{12}rs - \frac{2}{9}s^2$

14. $(6m + 5)(6m - 5)$

$= (6m)(6m) + (6m)(-5) + (5)(6m)$

$\quad + (5)(-5)$

$= 36m^2 - 30m + 30m - 25$

$= 36m^2 - 25$

16. $(2p - 1)(3p^2 - 4p + 5)$

$= (2p)(3p^2) + (2p)(-4p) + (2p)(5)$

$\quad + (-1)(3p^2) + (-1)(-4p) + (-1)(5)$

$= 6p^3 - 8p^2 + 10p - 3p^2 + 4p - 5$

$= 6p^3 - 11p^2 + 14p - 5$

18. $(k + 2)(12k^3 - 3k^2 + k + 1)$

$= k(12k^3) + k(-3k^2) + k(k) + k(1)$

$\quad + 2(12k^3) + 2(-3k^2) + 2(k) + 2(1)$

$= 12k^4 - 3k^3 + k^2 + k + 24k^3 - 6k^2$

$\quad + 2k + 2$

$= 12k^4 + 21k^3 - 5k^2 + 3k + 2$

20. $(r - 3s + t)(2r - s + t)$

$= r(2r) + r(-s) + r(t) - 3s(2r)$

$\quad - 3s(-s) - 3s(t) + t(2r) + t(-s)$

$\quad + t(t)$

$= 2r^2 - rs + rt - 6rs + 3s^2 - 3st$

$\quad + 2rt - st + t^2$

$= 2r^2 - 7rs + 3s^2 + 3rt - 4st + t^2$

Section R.2

2. $3y^3 + 24y^2 + 9y$

$= 3y \cdot y^2 + 3y \cdot 8y + 3y \cdot 3$

$= 3y(y^2 + 8y + 3)$

4. $60m^4 - 120m^3n + 50m^2n^2$

$= 10m^2 \cdot 6m^2 - 10m^2 \cdot 12mn$
$+ 10m^2 \cdot 5n^2$

$= 10m^2(6m^2 - 12mn + 5n^2)$

6. $x^2 + 4x - 5 = (x + 5)(x - 1)$ since $5(-1) = -5$ and $5 + (-1) = 4$.

8. $b^2 - 8b + 7 = (b - 7)(b - 1)$ since $(-7)(-1) = 7$ and $-7 + (-1) = -8$.

10. $s^2 + 2st - 35t^2 = (s - 5t)(s + 7t)$ since $(-5t)(7t) = -35t^2$ and $-5t + 7t = 2t$.

12. $6a^2 - 48a - 120$

$= 6(a^2 - 8a - 20)$

$= 6(a - 10)(a + 2)$

14. $2x^2 - 5x - 3$

The possible factors of $2x^2$ are $2x$ and x and the possible factors of -3 are -3 and 1 or 3 and -1. Try various combinations until one works.

$2x^2 - 5x - 3 = (2x + 1)(x - 3)$

16. $2a^2 - 17a + 30 = (2a - 5)(a - 6)$

18. $21m^2 + 13mn + 2n^2$

$= (7m + 2n)(3m + n)$

20. $32z^5 - 20z^4a - 12z^3a^2$

$= 4z^3(8z^2 - 5za - 3a^2)$

$= 4z^3(8z + 3a)(z - a)$

22. $9m^2 - 25 = (3m)^2 - (5)^2$

$= (3m + 5)(3m - 5)$

24. $9x^2 + 64$ is the *sum* of two perfect squares. It cannot be factored. It is prime.

26. $m^2 - 6mn + 9n^2$

$= (m)^2 - 2(3mn) + (3n)^2$

$= (m - 3n)^2$

28. $a^3 - 216$

$= (a)^3 - (6)^3$

$= (a - 6)[(a)^2 + (a)(6) + (6)^2]$

$= (a - 6)(a^2 + 6a + 36)$

30. $64m^3 + 125$

$= (4m)^3 + (5)^3$

$= (4m + 5)[(4m)^2 - (4m)(5) + (5)^2]$

$= (4m + 5)(16m^2 - 20m + 25)$

Section R.3

When writing rational expressions in lowest terms in the following exercises, first write numerators and denominators in factored form. Then use the fundamental property of rational expressions.

2. $\dfrac{25p^3}{10p^2} = \dfrac{5 \cdot 5 \cdot p \cdot p \cdot p}{2 \cdot 5 \cdot p \cdot p} = \dfrac{5p}{2}$

4. $\dfrac{3(t + 5)}{(t + 5)(t - 3)} = \dfrac{3}{t - 3}$

6. $\dfrac{36y^2 + 72y}{9y} = \dfrac{36y(y + 2)}{9y}$

$\qquad = \dfrac{9 \cdot 4 \cdot y(y + 2)}{9 \cdot y}$

$\qquad = 4(y + 2)$

8. $\dfrac{r^2 - r - 6}{r^2 + r - 12} = \dfrac{(r - 3)(r + 2)}{(r + 4)(r - 3)}$

$\qquad = \dfrac{r + 2}{r + 4}$

10. $\dfrac{z^2 - 5z + 6}{z^2 - 4} = \dfrac{(z - 3)(z - 2)}{(z + 2)(z - 2)}$

$\qquad = \dfrac{z - 3}{z + 2}$

12. $\dfrac{6y^2 + 11y + 4}{3y^2 + 7y + 4}$

$\qquad = \dfrac{(3y + 4)(2y + 1)}{(3y + 4)(y + 1)}$

$\qquad = \dfrac{2y + 1}{y + 1}$

14. $\dfrac{15p^3}{9p^2} \div \dfrac{6p}{10p^2}$

$\qquad = \dfrac{15p^3}{9p^2} \cdot \dfrac{10p^2}{6p}$

$\qquad = \dfrac{5 \cdot 3 \cdot p \cdot p \cdot p}{3 \cdot 3 \cdot p \cdot p} \cdot \dfrac{2 \cdot 5 \cdot p \cdot p}{2 \cdot 3 \cdot p}$

$\qquad = \dfrac{5 \cdot 5 \cdot p \cdot p}{3 \cdot 3}$

$\qquad = \dfrac{25p^2}{9}$

16. $\dfrac{a - 3}{16} \div \dfrac{a - 3}{32} = \dfrac{(a - 3)}{16} \cdot \dfrac{32}{(a - 3)}$

$\qquad = \dfrac{(a - 3)}{16} \cdot \dfrac{16 \cdot 2}{(a - 3)}$

$\qquad = \dfrac{2}{1}$

$\qquad = 2$

18. $\dfrac{9y - 18}{6y + 12} \cdot \dfrac{3y + 6}{15y - 30}$

$\qquad = \dfrac{9(y - 2)}{6(y + 2)} \cdot \dfrac{3(y + 2)}{15(y - 2)}$

$\qquad = \dfrac{9 \cdot 3}{6 \cdot 15}$

$\qquad = \dfrac{3 \cdot 3 \cdot 3}{2 \cdot 3 \cdot 3 \cdot 5} = \dfrac{3}{10}$

20. $\dfrac{6r - 18}{9r^2 + 6r - 24} \cdot \dfrac{12r - 16}{4r - 12}$

$\qquad = \dfrac{6(r - 3)}{3(3r^2 + 2r - 8)} \cdot \dfrac{4(3r - 4)}{4(r - 3)}$

$\qquad = \dfrac{6(r - 3)}{3(3r - 4)(r + 2)} \cdot \dfrac{4(3r - 4)}{4(r - 3)}$

$\qquad = \dfrac{6}{3(r + 2)}$

$\qquad = \dfrac{2}{r + 2}$

22. $\dfrac{m^2 + 3m + 2}{m^2 + 5m + 4} \div \dfrac{m^2 + 5m + 6}{m^2 + 10m + 24}$

$\qquad = \dfrac{m^2 + 3m + 2}{m^2 + 5m + 4} \cdot \dfrac{m^2 + 10m + 24}{m^2 + 5m + 6}$

$\qquad = \dfrac{(m + 1)(m + 2)}{(m + 4)(m + 1)} \cdot \dfrac{(m + 6)(m + 4)}{(m + 3)(m + 2)}$

$\qquad = \dfrac{m + 6}{m + 3}$

24. $\dfrac{6n^2 - 5n - 6}{6n^2 + 5n - 6} \cdot \dfrac{12n^2 - 17n + 6}{12n^2 - n - 6}$

$\qquad = \dfrac{(2n - 3)(3n + 2)}{(2n + 3)(3n - 2)}$

$\qquad \cdot \dfrac{(3n - 2)(4n - 3)}{(3n + 2)(4n - 3)}$

$\qquad = \dfrac{2n - 3}{2n + 3}$

26. $\dfrac{3}{p} + \dfrac{1}{2}$

Multiply the first term by 2/2 and the second by p/p.

$$\frac{2 \cdot 3}{2 \cdot p} + \frac{p \cdot 1}{p \cdot 2} = \frac{6}{2p} + \frac{p}{2p}$$

$$= \frac{6 + p}{2p}$$

$$= \frac{2y(y + 2) - y(y + 4)}{(y + 4)(y + 3)(y + 2)}$$

$$= \frac{2y^2 + 4y - y^2 - 4y}{(y + 4)(y + 3)(y + 2)}$$

$$= \frac{y^2}{(y + 4)(y + 3)(y + 2)}$$

28. $\dfrac{1}{6m} + \dfrac{2}{5m} + \dfrac{4}{m}$

$$= \frac{5 \cdot 1}{5 \cdot 6m} + \frac{6 \cdot 2}{6 \cdot 5m} + \frac{30 \cdot 4}{30 \cdot m}$$

$$= \frac{5}{30m} + \frac{12}{30m} + \frac{120}{30m}$$

$$= \frac{5 + 12 + 120}{30m}$$

$$= \frac{137}{30m}$$

36. $\dfrac{4m}{3m^2 + 7m - 6} - \dfrac{m}{3m^2 - 14m + 8}$

$$= \frac{4m}{(3m - 2)(m + 3)}$$

$$- \frac{m}{(3m - 2)(m - 4)}$$

$$= \frac{4m(m - 4)}{(3m - 2)(m + 3)(m - 4)}$$

$$- \frac{m(m + 3)}{(3m - 2)(m - 4)(m + 3)}$$

$$= \frac{4m(m - 4) - m(m + 3)}{(3m - 2)(m - 4)(m + 3)}$$

$$= \frac{4m^2 - 16m - m^2 - 3m}{(3m - 2)(m + 3)(m - 4)}$$

$$= \frac{3m^2 - 19m}{(3m - 2)(m + 3)(m - 4)}$$

$$= \frac{m(3m - 19)}{(3m - 2)(m + 3)(m - 4)}$$

30. $\dfrac{6}{r} - \dfrac{5}{r - 2}$

$$= \frac{6(r - 2)}{r(r - 2)} - \frac{5r}{r(r - 2)}$$

$$= \frac{6(r - 2) - 5r}{r(r - 2)}$$

$$= \frac{6r - 12 - 5r}{r(r - 2)}$$

$$= \frac{r - 12}{r(r - 2)}$$

Section R.4

2. $\dfrac{5}{6}k - 2k + \dfrac{1}{3} = \dfrac{2}{3}$

Multiply both sides of the equation by 6.

$$6\left(\frac{5}{6}k\right) - 6(2k) + 6\left(\frac{1}{3}\right) = 6\left(\frac{2}{3}\right)$$

$$5k - 12k + 2 = 4$$

$$-7k + 2 = 4$$

$$-7k + 2 - 2 = 4 - 2$$

$$-7k = 2$$

$$\left(-\frac{1}{7}\right)(-7k) = \left(-\frac{1}{7}\right)(2)$$

$$k = -\frac{2}{7}$$

32. $\dfrac{2}{5(k - 2)} + \dfrac{3}{4(k - 2)}$

$$= \frac{4 \cdot 2}{4 \cdot 5(k - 2)} + \frac{5 \cdot 3}{5 \cdot 4(k - 2)}$$

$$= \frac{8}{20(k - 2)} + \frac{15}{20(k - 2)}$$

$$= \frac{8 + 15}{20(k - 2)}$$

$$= \frac{23}{20(k - 2)}$$

34. $\dfrac{2y}{y^2 + 7y + 12} - \dfrac{y}{y^2 + 5y + 6}$

$$= \frac{2y}{(y + 4)(y + 3)} - \frac{y}{(y + 3)(y + 2)}$$

$$= \frac{2y(y + 2)}{(y + 4)(y + 3)(y + 2)}$$

$$- \frac{y(y + 4)}{(y + 3)(y + 2)(y + 4)}$$

The solution is -2/7.

4. $2[m - (4 + 2m) + 3] = 2m + 2$

$2[m - 4 - 2m + 3] = 2m + 2$

$2[-m - 1] = 2m + 2$

$-2m - 2 = 2m + 2$

$-2m - 2 + 2 = 2m + 2 + 2$

$-2m = 2m + 4$

$-2m - 2m = 2m + 4 - 2m$

$-4m = 4$

$\left(-\frac{1}{4}\right)(-4m) = \left(-\frac{1}{4}\right)(4)$

$m = -1$

The solution is −1.

6. $|4 - 7x| = 15$

$4 - 7x = 15$

$4 - 7x - 4 = 15 - 4$

$-7x = 11$

$-\frac{1}{7}(-7x) = -\frac{1}{7}(11)$

$x = -\frac{11}{7}$

or

$-(4 - 7x) = 15$

$-4 + 7x = 15$

$-4 + 7x + 4 = 15 + 4$

$7x = 19$

$\frac{1}{7}(7x) = \frac{1}{7}(19)$

$x = \frac{19}{7}$

The solutions are −11/7 and 19/7.

8. $|5x + 2| = |8 - 3x|$

Rewrite the equation as follows.

$5x + 2 = 8 - 3x$

$5x + 2 - 2 = 8 - 3x - 2$

$5x = 6 - 3x$

$5x + 3x = 6 - 3x + 3x$

$8x = 6$

$\frac{1}{8}(8x) = \frac{1}{8}(6)$

$x = \frac{6}{8}$

$x = \frac{3}{4}$

or

$-(5x + 2) = 8 - 3x$

$-5x - 2 = 8 - 3x$

$-5x - 2 + 2 = 8 - 3x + 2$

$-5x = 10 - 3x$

$-5x + 3x = 10 - 3x + 3x$

$-2x = 10$

$-\frac{1}{2}(-2x) = -\frac{1}{2}(10)$

$x = -5$

The solutions are 3/4 and −5.

10. $x^2 = 3 + 2x$

$x^2 - 2x - 3 = 0$

$(x - 3)(x + 1) = 0$

$x - 3 = 0 \quad \text{or} \quad x + 1 = 0$

$x = 3 \qquad\qquad x = -1$

The solutions are 3 and −1.

12. $2k^2 - k = 10$

$2k^2 - k - 10 = 0$

$(2k - 5)(k + 2) = 0$

$2k - 5 = 0 \quad \text{or} \quad k + 2 = 0$

$k = \frac{5}{2} \qquad\qquad k = -2$

The solutions are 5/2 and −2.

14. $m(m - 7) = -10$

$m^2 - 7m + 10 = 0$

$(m - 5)(m - 2) = 0$

$m - 5 = 0$ or $m - 2 = 0$

$m = 5$ $m = 2$

The solutions are 5 and 2.

16. $z(2z + 7) = 4$

$2z^2 + 7z - 4 = 0$

$(2z - 1)(z + 4) = 0$

$2z - 1 = 0$ or $z + 4 = 0$

$z = \frac{1}{2}$ $z = -4$

The solutions are 1/2 and −4.

18. $3x^2 - 5x + 1 = 0$

Use the quadratic formula.

$x = \dfrac{-(-5) \pm \sqrt{(-5)^2 - 4(3)(1)}}{2(3)}$

$= \dfrac{5 \pm \sqrt{25 - 12}}{6}$

$x = \dfrac{5 + \sqrt{13}}{6}$ or $x = \dfrac{5 - \sqrt{13}}{6}$

≈ 1.434 $\approx .232$

The solutions are $(5 + \sqrt{13})/6 \approx 1.434$ and $(5 - \sqrt{13})/6 \approx .232$.

20. $p^2 + p - 1 = 0$

$p = \dfrac{-1 \pm \sqrt{1^2 - 4(1)(-1)}}{2(1)}$

$= \dfrac{-1 \pm \sqrt{5}}{2}$

The solutions are $(-1 + \sqrt{5})/2 \approx .618$ and $(-1 - \sqrt{5})/2 \approx -1.618$.

22. $2x^2 + 12x + 5 = 0$

$x = \dfrac{-12 \pm \sqrt{(12)^2 - 4(2)(5)}}{2(2)}$

$= \dfrac{-12 \pm \sqrt{104}}{4} = \dfrac{-12 \pm \sqrt{4 \cdot 26}}{4}$

$= \dfrac{-12 \pm \sqrt{4}\sqrt{26}}{4} = \dfrac{-12 \pm 2\sqrt{26}}{4}$

$= \dfrac{2(-6 \pm \sqrt{26})}{2 \cdot 2} = \dfrac{-6 \pm \sqrt{26}}{2}$

The solutions are $(-6 + \sqrt{26})/2 \approx -.450$ and $(-6 - \sqrt{26})/2 \approx -5.550$.

24. $2x^2 - 7x + 30 = 0$

$x = \dfrac{-(-7) \pm \sqrt{(-7)^2 - 4(2)(30)}}{2(2)}$

$x = \dfrac{7 \pm \sqrt{49 - 240}}{4}$

$x = \dfrac{7 \pm \sqrt{-191}}{4}$

Since there is a negative number under the radical sign, $\sqrt{-191}$ is not a real number. Thus, there are no real-number solutions.

26. $5m^2 + 5m = 0$

$5m(m + 1) = 0$

$5m = 0$ or $m + 1 = 0$

$m = \dfrac{0}{5}$ $m = -1$

$m = 0$ $m = -1$

The solutions are 0 and −1.

28. $\dfrac{x}{3} - 7 = 6 - \dfrac{3x}{4}$

Multiply both sides by 12, a common denominator of 3 and 4.

$12\left(\dfrac{x}{3} - 7\right) = 12\left(6 - \dfrac{3x}{4}\right)$

$12\left(\dfrac{x}{3}\right) - (12)(7) = (12)(6) - (12)\left(\dfrac{3x}{4}\right)$

$4x - 84 = 72 - 9x$

$4x - 84 + 9x = 72 - 9x + 9x$

$13x - 84 = 72$

$13x - 84 + 84 = 72 + 84$

$13x = 156$

$$\frac{1}{13}(13x) = \frac{1}{13}(156)$$

$$x = 12$$

The solution is 12.

30. $\dfrac{5}{2p + 3} - \dfrac{3}{p - 2} = \dfrac{4}{2p + 3}$

Multiply both sides by
$(2p + 3)(p - 2)$. Note that
$p \neq -3/2$ and $p \neq 2$.

$$(2p + 3)(p - 2)\left(\frac{5}{2p + 3} - \frac{3}{p - 2}\right)$$
$$= (2p + 3)(p - 2)\left(\frac{4}{2p + 3}\right)$$

$$(2p + 3)(p - 2)\left(\frac{5}{2p + 3}\right) - (2p + 3)(p - 2)\left(\frac{3}{p - 2}\right)$$
$$= (2p + 3)(p - 2)\left(\frac{4}{2p + 3}\right)$$

$$(p - 2)(5) - (2p + 3)(3)$$
$$= (p - 2)(4)$$

$$5p - 10 - 6p - 9 = 4p - 8$$

$$-p - 19 = 4p - 8$$

$$-5p - 19 = -8$$

$$-5p = 11$$

$$p = -\frac{11}{5}$$

The solution is $-11/5$.

32. $\dfrac{2y}{y - 1} = \dfrac{5}{y} + \dfrac{10 - 8y}{y^2 - y}$

$$\frac{2y}{y - 1} = \frac{5}{y} + \frac{10 - 8y}{y(y - 1)}$$

Multiply both sides by $y(y - 1)$.
Note that $y \neq 0$ and $y \neq 1$.

$$y(y - 1)\left(\frac{2y}{y - 1}\right) = y(y - 1)\left[\frac{5}{y} + \frac{10 - 8y}{y(y - 1)}\right]$$

$$y(y - 1)\left(\frac{2y}{y - 1}\right) = y(y - 1)\left(\frac{5}{y}\right)$$
$$+ y(y - 1)\left[\frac{10 - 8y}{y(y - 1)}\right]$$

$$y(2y) = (y - 1)(5) + (10 - 8y)$$

$$2y^2 = 5y - 5 + 10 - 8y$$

$$2y^2 = 5 - 3y$$

$$2y^2 + 3y - 5 = 0$$

$$(2y + 5)(y - 1) = 0$$

$$2y + 5 = 0 \quad \text{or} \quad y - 1 = 0$$

$$y = -\frac{5}{2} \qquad y = 1$$

Since $y \neq 1$, 1 is not a solution.
The solution is $-5/2$.

34. $\dfrac{5}{a} + \dfrac{-7}{a + 1} = \dfrac{a^2 - 2a + 4}{a^2 + a}$

$$a(a + 1)\left(\frac{5}{a} + \frac{-7}{a + 1}\right) = a(a + 1)\left(\frac{a^2 - 2a + 4}{a^2 + a}\right)$$

Note that $a \neq 0$ and $a \neq -1$.

$$5(a + 1) + (-7)(a) = a^2 - 2a + 4$$

$$5a + 5 - 7a = a^2 - 2a + 4$$

$$5 - 2a = a^2 - 2a + 4$$

$$5 = a^2 + 4$$

$$0 = a^2 - 1$$

$$0 = (a + 1)(a - 1)$$

$$a + 1 = 0 \quad \text{or} \quad a - 1 = 0$$

$$a = -1 \qquad a = 1$$

Since -1 would make two denominators
zero, 1 is the only solution.

Section R.5

2. $\quad 6k - 4 < 3k - 1$

$$6k - 4 + 4 < 3k - 1 + 4$$

$$6k < 3k + 3$$

$$6k + (-3k) < 3k + 3 + (-3k)$$

$$3k < 3$$

$$\frac{1}{3}(3k) < \frac{1}{3}(3)$$

$$k < 1$$

The solution in interval notation is $(-\infty, 1)$.

4.
$$-2(3y - 8) \geq 5(4y - 2)$$
$$-6y + 16 \geq 20y - 10$$
$$-6y + 16 + (-16) \geq 20y - 10 + (-16)$$
$$-6y \geq 20y - 26$$
$$-6y + (-20y) \geq 20y - 26$$
$$-26y \geq -26$$
$$-\frac{1}{26}(-26)y \leq -\frac{1}{26}(-26)$$
$$y \leq 1$$

The solution is $(-\infty, 1]$.

6.
$$x + 5(x + 1) > 4(2 - x) + x$$
$$x + 5x + 5 > 8 - 4x + x$$
$$6x + 5 > 8 - 3x$$
$$6x + 5 + (-5) > 8 - 3x + (-5)$$
$$6x > 3 - 3x$$
$$6x + (3x) > 3 - 3x + (3x)$$
$$9x > 3$$
$$\frac{1}{9}(9x) > \frac{1}{9}(3)$$
$$x > \frac{1}{3}$$

The solution is $(1/3, \infty)$.

8.
$$8 \leq 3r + 1 \leq 13$$
$$8 + (-1) \leq 3r + 1 + (-1) \leq 13 + (-1)$$
$$7 \leq 3r \leq 12$$
$$\frac{1}{3}(7) \leq \frac{1}{3}(3r) \leq \frac{1}{3}(12)$$
$$\frac{7}{3} \leq r \leq 4$$

The solution is $[7/3, 4]$.

10.
$$-1 \leq \frac{5y + 2}{3} \leq 4$$
$$3(-1) \leq 3\left(\frac{5y + 2}{3}\right) \leq 3(4)$$
$$-3 \leq 5y + 2 \leq 12$$
$$-3 + (-2) \leq 5y + 2 + (-2) \leq 12 + (-2)$$
$$-5 \leq 5y \leq 10$$
$$\frac{1}{5}(-5) \leq \frac{1}{5}(5y) \leq \frac{1}{5}(10)$$
$$-1 \leq y \leq 2$$

The solution is $[-1, 2]$.

12.
$$\frac{8}{3}(z - 4) \leq \frac{2}{9}(3z + 2)$$
$$(9)\frac{8}{3}(z - 4) \leq (9)\frac{2}{9}(3z + 2)$$
$$24(z - 4) \leq 2(3z + 2)$$
$$(24)z + (24)(-4) \leq (2)(3z) + (2)(2)$$
$$24z - 96 \leq 6z + 4$$
$$24z - 96 + (96) \leq 6z + 4 + (96)$$
$$24z \leq 6z + 100$$
$$24z + (-6z) \leq 6z + 100 + (-6z)$$
$$18z \leq 100$$
$$\frac{1}{18}(18z) \leq \frac{1}{18}(100)$$

$$z \le \frac{100}{18}$$

$$z \le \frac{2(50)}{2(9)}$$

$$z \le \frac{50}{9}$$

The solution is $(-\infty, 50/9]$.

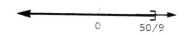

14. $(t + 6)(t - 1) \ge 0$

Solve $(t + 6)(t - 1) = 0$.

$(t + 6)(t - 1) = 0$

$t = -6$ or $t = 1$

Intervals: $(-\infty, -6)$, $(-6, 1)$, $(1, \infty)$

For $(-\infty, -6)$, choose -7 to test for t.

$(-7 + 6)(-7 - 1) = (-1)(-8) = 8 \ge 0$

For $(-6, 1)$, choose 0.

$(0 + 6)(0 - 1) = (6)(-1) = -6 \not\ge 0$

For $(1, \infty)$, choose 2.

$(2 + 6)(2 - 1) = (8)(1) = 8 \ge 0$

Because the symbol $\ge$ is used, the endpoints -6 and 1 are included in the solution, $(-\infty, -6] \cup [1, \infty)$.

16. $2k^2 + 7k - 4 > 0$

Solve $2k^2 + 7k - 4 = 8$.

$2k^2 + 7k - 4 = 0$

$(2k - 1)(k + 4) = 0$

$k = \frac{1}{2}$ or $k = -4$

Intervals: $\left(-\infty, -4\right)$, $\left(-4, \frac{1}{2}\right)$, $\left(\frac{1}{2}, \infty\right)$

For $(-\infty, -4)$, choose -5.

$2(-5)^2 + 7(-5) - 4 = 11 > 0$

For $\left(-4, \frac{1}{2}\right)$, choose 0.

$2(0)^2 + 7(0) - 4 = -4 \not> 0$

For $\left(\frac{1}{2}, \infty\right)$, choose 1.

$2(1)^2 + 7(1) - 4 = 5 > 0$

The solution is $\left(-\infty, -4\right) \cup \left(1/2, \infty\right)$.

18. $2k^2 - 7k - 15 \le 0$

Solve $2k^2 - 7k - 15 = 0$.

$2k^2 - 7k - 15 = 0$

$(2k + 3)(k - 5) = 0$

$k = -\frac{3}{2}$ or $k = 5$

Intervals: $\left(-\infty, -\frac{3}{2}\right)$, $\left(-\frac{3}{2}, 5\right)$, $(5, \infty)$

For $\left(-\infty, -\frac{3}{2}\right)$, choose -2.

$2(-2)^2 - 7(-2) - 15 = 7 \not\le 0$

For $\left(-\frac{3}{2}, 5\right)$, choose 0.

$2(0)^2 - 7(0) - 15 = -15 \le 0$

For $(5, \infty)$, choose 6.

$2(6)^2 - 7(6) - 15 \not< 0$

The solution is $[-3/2, 5]$.

$$-3/2 \quad 0 \qquad\qquad 5$$

20. $10r^2 + r \leq 2$

Solve $10r^2 + r = 2$.

$$10r^2 + r = 2$$
$$10r^2 + r - 2 = 0$$
$$(5r - 2)(2r + 1) = 0$$
$$r = \frac{2}{5} \quad \text{or} \quad r = -\frac{1}{2}$$

Intervals: $\left(-\infty, -\frac{1}{2}\right)$, $\left(-\frac{1}{2}, \frac{2}{5}\right)$, $\left(\frac{2}{5}, \infty\right)$

For $\left(-\infty, -\frac{1}{2}\right)$, choose -1.

$$10(-1)^2 + (-1) = 9 \not\leq 2$$

For $\left(-\frac{1}{2}, \frac{2}{5}\right)$, choose 0.

$$10(0)^2 + 0 = 0 \leq 2$$

For $\left(\frac{2}{5}, \infty\right)$, choose 1.

$$10(1)^2 + 1 = 11 \not\leq 2$$

The solution is $[-1/2, 2/15]$.

$$-1/2 \quad 0 \quad 2/5$$

22. $3a^2 + a > 10$

Solve $3a^2 + a = 10$.

$$3a^2 + a = 10$$
$$3a^2 + a - 10 = 0$$
$$(3a - 5)(a + 2) = 0$$
$$a = \frac{5}{3} \quad \text{or} \quad a = -2$$

Intervals: $\left(-\infty, -2\right)$, $\left(-2, \frac{5}{3}\right)$, $\left(\frac{5}{3}, \infty\right)$

For $(-\infty, -2)$, choose -3.

$$3(-3)^2 + (-3) = 24 > 10$$

For $\left(-2, \frac{5}{3}\right)$, choose 0.

$$3(0)^2 + 0 = 0 \not> 10$$

For $\left(\frac{5}{3}, \infty\right)$, choose 2.

$$3(2)^2 + 2 = 14 > 10$$

The solution is $(-\infty, -2) \cup (5/3, \infty)$.

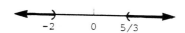

$$-2 \quad 0 \quad 5/3$$

24. $p^2 - 16p > 0$

Solve $\qquad p^2 - 16p = 0$

$$p(p - 16) = 0$$
$$p = 0 \quad \text{or} \quad p = 16$$

Intervals: $(-\infty, 0)$, $(0, 16)$, $(16, \infty)$.

For $(-\infty, 0)$, choose -1.

$$(-1)^2 - 16(-1) = 17 > 0$$

For $(0, 16)$, choose 1.

$$(1)^2 - 16(1) = -15 \not> 0$$

For $(16, \infty)$, choose 17.

$$(17)^2 - 16(17) = 17 > 0$$

The solution is $(-\infty, 0) \cup (16, \infty)$.

$$0 \qquad\qquad 16$$

26. $\dfrac{r + 1}{r - 1} > 0$

Solve the equation $\dfrac{r + 1}{r - 1} = 0$.

$$\dfrac{r + 1}{r - 1} = 0$$

$$(r - 1)\dfrac{r + 1}{r - 1} = (r - 1)(0)$$

$$r + 1 = 0$$

$$r = -1$$

Find the value for which the denominator equals zero.

$$r - 1 = 0$$

$$r = 1$$

Intervals: $(-\infty, -1)$, $(-1, 1)$, $(1, \infty)$

For $(-\infty, -1)$, choose -2.

$$\dfrac{-2 + 1}{-2 - 1} = \dfrac{-1}{-3} = \dfrac{1}{3} > 0$$

For $(-1, 1)$, choose 0.

$$\dfrac{0 + 1}{0 - 1} = \dfrac{1}{-1} = -1 \not> 0$$

For $(1, \infty)$, choose 2.

$$\dfrac{2 + 1}{2 - 1} = \dfrac{3}{1} = 3 > 0$$

The solution is $(-\infty, -1) \cup (1, \infty)$.

28. $\dfrac{a - 5}{a + 2} < -1$

Solve the equation $\dfrac{a - 5}{a + 2} = -1$.

$$\dfrac{a - 5}{a + 2} = -1$$

$$a - 5 = -1(a + 2)$$

$$a - 5 = -a - 2$$

$$2a = 3$$

$$a = \dfrac{3}{2}$$

Set the denominator equal to zero and solve for a.

$$a + 2 = 0$$

$$a = -2$$

Intervals: $\left(-\infty, -2\right)$, $\left(-2, \dfrac{3}{2}\right)$, $\left(\dfrac{3}{2}, \infty\right)$

For $(-\infty, -2)$, choose -3.

$$\dfrac{-3 - 5}{-3 + 2} = \dfrac{-8}{-1} = 8 \not< -1$$

For $\left(-2, \dfrac{3}{2}\right)$, choose 0.

$$\dfrac{0 - 5}{0 + 2} = \dfrac{-5}{2} < -1$$

For $\left(\dfrac{3}{2}, \infty\right)$, choose 2.

$$\dfrac{2 - 5}{2 + 2} = \dfrac{-3}{4} \not< -1$$

The solution is $(-2, 3/2)$.

30. $\dfrac{a + 2}{3 + 2a} \leq 5$

For the equation $\dfrac{a + 2}{3 + 2a} = 5$.

$$\dfrac{a + 2}{3 + 2a} = 5$$

$$a + 2 = 5(3 + 2a)$$

$$a + 2 = 15 + 10a$$

$$-9a = 13$$

$$a = -\dfrac{13}{9}$$

Set the denominator equal to zero and solve for a.

$$3 + 2a = 0$$

$$2a = -3$$

$$a = -\dfrac{3}{2}$$

Intervals: $\left(-\infty, -\frac{3}{2}\right)$, $\left(-\frac{3}{2}, -\frac{13}{9}\right)$

$\left(-\frac{13}{9}, \infty\right)$

For $\left(-\infty, -\frac{3}{2}\right)$, choose -2.

$$\frac{-2 + 2}{3 + 2(-2)} = \frac{0}{-1} = 0 \leq 5$$

For $\left(-\frac{3}{2}, -\frac{13}{9}\right)$, choose -1.46.

$$\frac{-1.46 + 2}{3 + 2(-1.46)} = \frac{.54}{.08} = 6.75 \not\leq 5$$

For $\left(-\frac{13}{9}, \infty\right)$, choose 0.

$$\frac{0 + 2}{3 + 2(0)} = \frac{2}{3} \leq 5$$

The value $-3/2$ cannot be included in the solution since it would make the denominator zero. The solution is $(-\infty, -3/2) \cup [-13/9, \infty)$.

32. $\dfrac{5}{p + 1} > \dfrac{12}{p + 1}$

Solve the equation $\dfrac{5}{p + 1} = \dfrac{12}{p + 1}$.

$$\frac{5}{p + 1} = \frac{12}{p + 1}$$
$$5 = 12$$

The equation has no solution.
Set the denominator equal to zero and solve for p.

$$p + 1 = 0$$
$$p = -1$$

Intervals: $(-\infty, -1)$, $(-1, \infty)$

For $(-\infty, -1)$, choose -2.

$$\frac{5}{-2 + 1} > \frac{12}{-2 + 1}$$
$$-5 > -12$$

For $(-1, \infty)$, choose 0.

$$\frac{5}{0 + 1} \not> \frac{12}{0 + 1}$$
$$5 \not> 12$$

The solution is $(-\infty, -1)$.

34. $\dfrac{8}{p^2 + 2p} > 1$

Solve the equation $\dfrac{8}{p^2 + 2p} = 1$.

$$\frac{8}{p^2 + 2p} = 1$$
$$8 = p^2 + 2p$$
$$0 = p^2 + 2p - 8$$
$$0 = (p + 4)(p - 2)$$
$$p + 4 = 0 \quad \text{or} \quad p - 2 = 0$$
$$p = -4 \qquad\qquad p = 2$$

Set the denominator equal to zero and solve for p.

$$p^2 + 2p = 0$$
$$p(p + 2) = 0$$
$$p = 0 \quad \text{or} \quad p + 2 = 0$$
$$p = -2$$

Intervals: $(-\infty, -4)$, $(-4, -2)$, $(-2, 0)$, $(0, 2)$, $(2, \infty)$

For $(-\infty, -4)$, choose -5.

$$\frac{8}{(-5)^2 + 2(-5)} = \frac{8}{15} \not> 1$$

For $(-4, -2)$, choose -3.

$$\frac{8}{(-3)^2 + 2(-3)} = \frac{8}{9 - 6} = \frac{8}{3} > 1$$

For $(-2, 0)$, choose -1.

$$\frac{8}{(-1)^2 + 2(-1)} = \frac{8}{-1} = -8 \not> 1$$

For $(0, 2)$, choose 1.

$$\frac{8}{(1)^2 + 2(1)} = \frac{8}{3} > 1$$

For $(2, \infty)$, choose 3.

$$\frac{8}{(3)^2 + (2)(3)} = \frac{8}{15} \not> 1$$

The solution is $(-4, -2) \cup (0, 2)$.

36. $\dfrac{a^2 + 2a}{a^2 - 4} \leq 2$

Solve the equation $\dfrac{a^2 + 2a}{a^2 - 4} = 2$.

$$\frac{a^2 + 2a}{a^2 - 4} = 2, \quad a \neq \pm 2$$
$$a^2 + 2a = 2(a^2 - 4)$$
$$a^2 + 2a = 2a^2 - 8$$
$$0 = a^2 - 2a - 8$$
$$0 = (a - 4)(a + 2)$$
$$a - 4 = 0 \quad \text{or} \quad a + 2 = 0$$
$$a = 4 \qquad\qquad a = -2$$

But -2 is not a possible solution. Set the denominator equal to zero and solve for a.

$$a^2 - 4 = 0$$
$$(a + 2)(a - 2) = 0$$
$$a + 2 = 0 \quad \text{or} \quad a - 2 = 0$$
$$a = -2 \qquad\qquad a = 2$$

Intervals: $(-\infty, -2)$, $(-2, 2)$, $(2, 4)$, $(4, \infty)$

For $(-\infty, -2)$, choose -3.

$$\frac{(-3)^2 + 2(-3)}{(-3)^2 - 4} = \frac{9 - 6}{9 - 4} = \frac{3}{5} \leq 2$$

For $(-2, 2)$, choose 0.

$$\frac{(0)^2 + 2(0)}{0 - 4} = \frac{0}{-4} = 0 \leq 2$$

For $(2, 4)$, choose 3.

$$\frac{(3)^2 + 2(3)}{(3)^2 - 4} = \frac{9 + 6}{9 - 5} = \frac{15}{4} \not\leq 2$$

For $(4, \infty)$, choose 5.

$$\frac{(5)^2 + 2(5)}{(5)^2 - 4} = \frac{25 + 10}{25 - 4} = \frac{35}{21} \leq 2$$

The value 4 will satisfy the original inequality, but the values -2 and 2 will not since they make the denominator zero. The solution is $(-\infty, -2) \cup (-2, 2) \cup [4, \infty)$.

Section R.6

2. $3^{-4} = \dfrac{1}{3^4} = \dfrac{1}{3 \cdot 3 \cdot 3 \cdot 3} = \dfrac{1}{81}$

4. $5^0 = 1$, by definition.

6. $2^{-1} + 4^{-1} = \dfrac{1}{2} + \dfrac{1}{4} = \dfrac{2 \cdot 1}{2 \cdot 2} + \dfrac{1}{4}$

$\qquad = \dfrac{2}{4} + \dfrac{1}{4} = \dfrac{2 + 1}{4} = \dfrac{3}{4}$

8. $(-2)^{-4} = \dfrac{1}{(-2)^4} = \dfrac{1}{(-2)(-2)(-2)(-2)}$

$\qquad\qquad = \dfrac{1}{16}$

10. $-(-3^{-2}) = -[(-1)(3)^{-2}] = -\left(-1 \cdot \dfrac{1}{3^2}\right)$

$\qquad = -\left(-1 \cdot \dfrac{1}{9}\right) = -\left(-\dfrac{1}{9}\right) = \dfrac{1}{9}$

12. $\left(\frac{6}{7}\right)^3 = \frac{(6)^3}{(7)^3} = \frac{6 \cdot 6 \cdot 6}{7 \cdot 7 \cdot 7} = \frac{216}{343}$

14. $\left(\frac{1}{5}\right)^{-3} = \frac{1}{\left(\frac{1}{5}\right)^3} = \frac{1}{\frac{(1)^3}{(5)^3}} = \frac{1}{\frac{1 \cdot 1 \cdot 1}{5 \cdot 5 \cdot 5}}$

$= \frac{1}{\frac{1}{125}} = 1 \div \frac{1}{125}$

$= 1 \cdot \frac{125}{1} = 125$

16. $\left(\frac{4}{3}\right)^{-3} = \frac{1}{\left(\frac{4}{3}\right)^3} = \frac{1}{\frac{(4)^3}{(3)^3}} = \frac{1}{\frac{4 \cdot 4 \cdot 4}{3 \cdot 3 \cdot 3}}$

$= \frac{1}{\frac{64}{27}} = 1 \div \frac{64}{27} = 1 \cdot \frac{27}{64}$

$= \frac{27}{64}$

18. $\frac{3^{-4}}{3^2} = 3^{(-4)-2} = 3^{-4-2} = 3^{-6} = \frac{1}{3^6}$

20. $\frac{6^{-1}}{6} = \frac{6^{-1}}{6^1} = 6^{(-1)-(1)} = 6^{-1-1}$

$= 6^{-2} = \frac{1}{6^2}$

22. $\frac{8^9 \cdot 8^{-7}}{8^{-3}} = 8^{9+(-7)-(-3)} = 8^{9-7+3} = 8^5$

24. $\left(\frac{5^{-6} \cdot 5^3}{5^{-2}}\right)^{-1} = \left(5^{-6+3-(-2)}\right)^{-1}$

$= \left(5^{-6+3+2}\right)^{-1} = \left(5^{-1}\right)^{-1}$

$= 5^{(-1)(-1)} = 5^1 = 5$

26. $\frac{y^9 y^7}{y^{13}} = y^{9+7-13} = y^3$

28. $\frac{(3z^2)^{-1}}{z^5} = \frac{3^{-1}(z^2)^{-1}}{z^5} = \frac{3^{-1}z^{2(-1)}}{z^5}$

$= \frac{3^{-1}z^{-2}}{z^5} = 3^{-1}a^{-2-5}$

$= 3^{-1}z^{-7} = \frac{1}{3} \cdot \frac{1}{z^7} = \frac{1}{3z^7}$

30. $\frac{5^{-2}m^2y^{-2}}{5^2m^{-1}y^{-2}} = \frac{5^{-2}}{5^2} \cdot \frac{m^2}{m^{-1}} \cdot \frac{y^{-2}}{y^{-2}}$

$= 5^{-2-2}m^{2-(-1)}y^{-2-(-2)}$

$= 5^{-2-2}m^{2+1}y^{-2+2}$

$= 5^{-4}m^3y^0 = \frac{1}{5^4} \cdot m^3 \cdot 1$

$= \frac{m^3}{5^4}$

32. $\left(\frac{2c^2}{d^3}\right)^{-2} = \frac{(2)^{-2}(c^2)^{-2}}{(d^3)^{-2}}$

$= \frac{(2)^{-2}c^{(2)(-2)}}{d^{(3)(-2)}} = \frac{(2)^{-2}c^{-4}}{d^{-6}}$

$= 2^{-2} \cdot c^{-4} \div d^{-6}$

$= \frac{1}{2^2} \cdot \frac{1}{c^4} \div \frac{1}{d^6}$

$= \frac{1}{2^2} \cdot \frac{1}{c^4} \cdot \frac{d^6}{1} = \frac{d^6}{2^2c^4}$

For Exercises 34–38, $a = 2$ and $b = -3$.

34. $b^{-2} - a = (-3)^{-2} - (2) = \frac{1}{(-3)^2} - 2$

$= \frac{1}{9} - 2 = \frac{1}{9} - \frac{18}{9} = \frac{1 - 18}{9}$

$= -\frac{17}{9}$

36. $\frac{3a^2 - b^2}{b^{-3} + 2a^{-1}} = \frac{3(2)^2 - (-3)^2}{(-3)^{-3} + 2(2)^{-1}}$

$= \frac{3(4) - (9)}{\frac{1}{(-3)^3} + 2 \cdot \frac{1}{(2)^1}}$

$= \frac{12 - 9}{\frac{1}{-27} + \frac{2}{2}} = \frac{3}{-\frac{1}{27} + 1}$

$= \frac{3}{\frac{-1}{27} + \frac{27}{27}} = \frac{3}{\frac{-1 + 27}{27}}$

$= \frac{3}{\frac{26}{27}} = 3 \div \frac{26}{27} = 3 \cdot \frac{27}{26}$

$= \frac{81}{26}$

38. $\left(\dfrac{2b}{5}\right)^2 - 3\left(\dfrac{a^{-1}}{4}\right) = \left(\dfrac{2(-3)}{5}\right)^2 - 3\left(\dfrac{(2)^{-1}}{4}\right)$

$\qquad = \left(\dfrac{-6}{5}\right)^2 - 3\left(\dfrac{\frac{1}{2}}{4}\right)$

$\qquad = \dfrac{(-6)^2}{(5)^2} - 3\left(\dfrac{1}{2} \cdot \dfrac{1}{4}\right)$

$\qquad = \dfrac{36}{25} - 3\left(\dfrac{1}{8}\right)$

$\qquad = \dfrac{36}{25} - \dfrac{3}{8}$

$\qquad = \dfrac{36 \cdot 8}{25 \cdot 8} - \dfrac{3 \cdot 25}{8 \cdot 25}$

$\qquad = \dfrac{288}{200} - \dfrac{75}{200}$

$\qquad = \dfrac{288 - 75}{200} = \dfrac{213}{200}$

40. $27^{1/3} = (3^3)^{1/3} = 3^{(3)(1/3)} = 3^1 = 3$

42. $1000^{2/3} = (10^3)^{2/3} = (10)^{(3)(2/3)}$
$\qquad = 10^2 = 100$

44. $-125^{2/3} = -1 \cdot 125^{2/3} = -1 \cdot (5^3)^{2/3}$
$\qquad = -1 \cdot 5^{(3)(2/3)} = -1 \cdot 5^2$
$\qquad = -1 \cdot 25 = -25$

46. $\left(\dfrac{64}{27}\right)^{1/3} = \left(\dfrac{4^3}{3^3}\right)^{1/3} = \left[\left(\dfrac{4}{3}\right)^3\right]^{1/3}$

$\qquad = \left(\dfrac{4}{3}\right)^{(3)(1/3)} = \left(\dfrac{4}{3}\right)^1 = \dfrac{4}{3}$

48. $625^{-1/4} = (5^4)^{-1/4} = 5^{(4)(-1/4)}$
$\qquad = 5^{-1} = \dfrac{1}{5}$

50. $\left(\dfrac{121}{100}\right)^{-3/2} = \left(\dfrac{11^2}{10^2}\right)^{-3/2} = \left[\left(\dfrac{11}{10}\right)^2\right]^{-3/2}$

$\qquad = \left(\dfrac{11}{10}\right)^{(2)(-3/2)} = \left(\dfrac{11}{10}\right)^{-3}$

$\qquad = \dfrac{1}{\left(\dfrac{11}{10}\right)^3} = \dfrac{1}{\dfrac{(11)^3}{(10)^3}}$

$\qquad = 1 \div \dfrac{(11)^3}{(10)^3} = 1 \cdot \dfrac{(10)^3}{(11)^3}$

$\qquad = 1 \cdot \dfrac{1000}{1331} = \dfrac{1000}{1331}$

52. $27^{2/3} \cdot 27^{-1/3} = 27^{(2/3)+(-1/3)}$
$\qquad = 27^{2/3 - 1/3}$
$\qquad = 27^{1/3}$

54. $\dfrac{3^{-5/2} \cdot 3^{3/2}}{3^{7/2} \cdot 3^{-9/2}}$

$\qquad = 3^{(-5/2)+(3/2)-(7/2)-(-9/2)}$

$\qquad = 3^{-5/2 + 3/2 - 7/2 + 9/2}$

$\qquad = 3^0 = 1$

56. $\dfrac{12^{3/4} \cdot 12^{5/4} \cdot y^{-2}}{12^{-1} \cdot (y^{-3})^{-2}}$

$\qquad = \dfrac{12^{3/4 + 5/4} \cdot y^{-2}}{12^{-1} \cdot y^{(-3)(-2)}} \cdot \dfrac{12^{8/4} \cdot y^{-2}}{12^{-1} \cdot y^6}$

$\qquad = \dfrac{12^2 \cdot y^{-2}}{12^{-1} y^6} = \dfrac{12^2}{12^{-1}} \cdot \dfrac{y^{-2}}{y^6}$

$\qquad = 12^{2-(-1)} \cdot y^{-2-(-6)} = 12^3 y^{-8}$

$\qquad = 12^3 \cdot \dfrac{1}{y^8} = \dfrac{12^3}{y^8}$

58. $\dfrac{8p^{-3}(4p^2)^{-2}}{p^{-5}} = \dfrac{8p^{-3} \cdot 4^{-2} p^{(2)(-2)}}{p^{-5}}$

$\qquad = \dfrac{8p^{-3} 4^{-2} p^{-4}}{p^{-5}}$

$\qquad = 8 \cdot 4^{-2} p^{(-3)+(-4)-(-5)}$

$\qquad = 8 \cdot 4^{-2} p^{-3-4+5}$

$\qquad = 8 \cdot 4^{-2} p^{-2}$

$\qquad = 8 \cdot \dfrac{1}{4^2} \cdot \dfrac{1}{p^2}$

$$= 8 \cdot \frac{1}{16} \cdot \frac{1}{p^2}$$

$$= \frac{8}{16p^2} = \frac{8}{8 \cdot 2p^2}$$

$$= \frac{1}{2p^2}$$

60. $\dfrac{x^{1/3} \cdot y^{2/3} \cdot z^{1/4}}{x^{5/3} \cdot y^{-1/3} \cdot z^{3/4}}$

$$= x^{1/3 - (5/3)} y^{(2/3) - (-1/3)} z^{1/4 - (3/4)}$$

$$= x^{1/3 - 5/3} y^{2/3 + 1/3} z^{1/4 - 3/4}$$

$$= x^{-4/3} y^{3/3} z^{-2/4}$$

$$= \frac{2}{x^{4/3}} y^1 \frac{1}{z^{2/4}} = \frac{y}{x^{4/3} z^{2/4}}$$

$$= \frac{y}{x^{4/3} z^{1/2}}$$

62. $\dfrac{m^{7/3} \cdot n^{-2/5} \cdot p^{3/8}}{m^{-2/3} \cdot n^{3/5} \cdot p^{-5/8}}$

$$= m^{7/3 - (-2/3)} n^{-2/5 - (3/5)} p^{3/8 - (-5/8)}$$

$$= m^{7/3 + 2/3} n^{-2/5 - 3/5} p^{3/8 + 5/8}$$

$$= m^{9/3} n^{-5/5} p^{8/8}$$

$$= m^3 n^{-1} p^1 = m^3 \cdot \frac{1}{n^1} p^1$$

$$= \frac{m^3 p^1}{n^1} = \frac{m^3 p}{n}$$

64. $(3x - 1)(5x + 2)^{1/2}(15) + (5x + 2)^{-1/2}(5)$

$$= (3x - 1)(5x + 2)^{-1/2}(5x + 2)^1(5)(3)$$

$$\quad + (5x + 2)^{-1/2}(5)$$

$$= (5x + 2)^{-1/2}(5)$$

$$\quad \cdot [(3x - 1)(5x + 2)(3) + 1]$$

$$= 5(5x + 2)^{-1/2}$$

$$\quad \cdot [(15x^2 + 6x - 5x - 2)(3) + 1]$$

$$= 5(5x + 2)^{-1/2}$$

$$\quad \cdot [45x^2 + 18x - 15x - 6 + 1]$$

$$= 5(5x + 2)^{-1/2}(45x^2 + 3x - 5)$$

66. $(4x^2 + 1)^2(2x - 1)^{-1/2}$

$$+(2x - 1)^{1/2}(2)(4x^2 + 1)$$

$$= (4x^2 + 1)(4x^2 + 1)(2x - 1)^{-1/2}$$

$$\quad + (2x - 1)^{-1/2}(2x - 1)^1(2)(4x^2 + 1)$$

$$= (4x^2 + 1)(2x - 1)^{-1/2}$$

$$\quad \cdot [(4x^2 + 1) + (2x - 1)(2)]$$

$$= (4x^2 + 1)(2x - 1)^{-1/2}$$

$$\quad \cdot (4x^2 + 1 + 4x - 2)$$

$$= (4x^2 + 1)(2x - 1)^{-1/2}(4x^2 + 4x - 1)$$

Section R.7

2. $\sqrt[4]{1296} = \sqrt[4]{6^4} = (6^4)^{1/4} = 6^{4/4}$

$$= 6^1 = 6$$

4. $\sqrt{50} = \sqrt{25 \cdot 2} = \sqrt{25}\sqrt{2} = 5\sqrt{2}$

6. $\sqrt{32y^5} = \sqrt{(16y^4)(2y)} = \sqrt{16y^4}\sqrt{2y}$

$$= 4y^2\sqrt{2y}$$

8. $4\sqrt{3} - 5\sqrt{12} + 3\sqrt{75}$

$$= 4\sqrt{3} - 5(\sqrt{4}\sqrt{3}) + 3(\sqrt{25}\sqrt{3})$$

$$= 4\sqrt{3} - 5(2\sqrt{3}) + 3(5\sqrt{3})$$

$$= 4\sqrt{3} - 10\sqrt{3} + 15\sqrt{3}$$

$$= (4 - 10 + 15)\sqrt{3} = 9\sqrt{3}$$

10. $3\sqrt{28} - 4\sqrt{63} + \sqrt{112}$

$$= 3(\sqrt{4}\sqrt{7}) - 4(\sqrt{9}\sqrt{7}) + (\sqrt{16}\sqrt{7})$$

$$= 3(2\sqrt{7}) - 4(3\sqrt{7}) + (4\sqrt{7})$$

$$= 6\sqrt{7} - 12\sqrt{7} + 4\sqrt{7}$$

$$= (6 - 12 + 4)\sqrt{7}$$

$$= -2\sqrt{7}$$

12. $2\sqrt[3]{3} + 4\sqrt[3]{24} - \sqrt[3]{81}$

$$= 2\sqrt[3]{3} + 4\sqrt[3]{8 \cdot 3} - \sqrt[3]{27 \cdot 3}$$

$$= 2\sqrt[3]{3} + 4(2)\sqrt[3]{3} - 3\sqrt[3]{3}$$

$$= 2\sqrt[3]{3} + 8\sqrt[3]{3} - 3\sqrt[3]{3}$$

$$= 7\sqrt[3]{3}$$

14. $\sqrt{2x^3y^2z^4} = \sqrt{x^2y^2z^4 \cdot 2x}$
$\qquad = xyz^2\sqrt{2x}$

16. $\sqrt[3]{16z^5x^8y^4} = \sqrt[3]{8z^3x^6y^3 \cdot 2z^2x^2y}$
$\qquad = 2zx^2y\sqrt[3]{2z^2x^2y}$

18. $\sqrt{a^3b^5} - 2\sqrt{a^7b^3} + \sqrt{a^3b^9}$
$\qquad = \sqrt{a^2b^4ab} - 2\sqrt{a^6b^2ab} + \sqrt{a^2b^8ab}$
$\qquad = ab^2\sqrt{ab} - 2a^3b\sqrt{ab} + ab^4\sqrt{ab}$
$\qquad = (ab^2 - 2a^3b + ab^4)\sqrt{ab}$
$\qquad = ab\sqrt{ab}(b - 2a^2 + b^3)$

20. $\dfrac{5}{\sqrt{7}} = \dfrac{5}{\sqrt{7}} \cdot \dfrac{\sqrt{7}}{\sqrt{7}} = \dfrac{5\sqrt{7}}{7}$

22. $\dfrac{-3}{\sqrt{12}} = \dfrac{-3}{\sqrt{4 \cdot 3}} = \dfrac{-3}{2\sqrt{3}} \cdot \dfrac{\sqrt{3}}{\sqrt{3}}$
$\qquad = \dfrac{-3\sqrt{3}}{6}$
$\qquad = -\dfrac{\sqrt{3}}{2}$

24. $\dfrac{3}{1 - \sqrt{5}} = \dfrac{3}{1 - \sqrt{5}} \cdot \dfrac{1 + \sqrt{5}}{1 + \sqrt{5}}$
$\qquad = \dfrac{3(1 + \sqrt{5})}{1 - 5}$
$\qquad = \dfrac{-3(1 + \sqrt{5})}{4}$

26. $\dfrac{-2}{\sqrt{3} - \sqrt{2}}$
$\qquad = \dfrac{-2}{\sqrt{3} - \sqrt{2}} \cdot \dfrac{\sqrt{3} + \sqrt{2}}{\sqrt{3} + \sqrt{2}}$
$\qquad = \dfrac{-2(\sqrt{3} + \sqrt{2})}{3 - 2} = \dfrac{-2(\sqrt{3} + \sqrt{2})}{1}$
$\qquad = -2(\sqrt{3} + \sqrt{2})$

28. $\dfrac{1}{\sqrt{r} - \sqrt{3}}$
$\qquad = \dfrac{1}{\sqrt{r} - \sqrt{3}} \cdot \dfrac{\sqrt{r} + \sqrt{3}}{\sqrt{r} + \sqrt{3}}$
$\qquad = \dfrac{\sqrt{r} + \sqrt{3}}{r - 3}$

30. $\dfrac{y - 5}{\sqrt{y} - \sqrt{5}}$
$\qquad = \dfrac{y - 5}{\sqrt{y} - \sqrt{5}} \cdot \dfrac{\sqrt{y} + \sqrt{5}}{\sqrt{y} + \sqrt{5}}$
$\qquad = \dfrac{(y - 5)(\sqrt{y} + \sqrt{5})}{y - 5}$
$\qquad = \sqrt{y} + \sqrt{5}$

32. $\dfrac{\sqrt{x} + \sqrt{x + 1}}{\sqrt{x} - \sqrt{x + 1}}$
$\qquad = \dfrac{\sqrt{x} + \sqrt{x + 1}}{\sqrt{x} - \sqrt{x + 1}} \cdot \dfrac{\sqrt{x} + \sqrt{x + 1}}{\sqrt{x} + \sqrt{x + 1}}$
$\qquad = \dfrac{x + 2\sqrt{x(x + 1)} + (x + 1)}{x - (x + 1)}$
$\qquad = \dfrac{2x + 2\sqrt{x(x + 1)} + 1}{-1}$
$\qquad = -2x - 2\sqrt{x(x + 1)} - 1$

34. $\dfrac{1 + \sqrt{2}}{2} = \dfrac{(1 + \sqrt{2})(1 - \sqrt{2})}{2(1 - \sqrt{2})}$
$\qquad = \dfrac{1 - 2}{2(1 - \sqrt{2})}$
$\qquad = -\dfrac{1}{2(1 - \sqrt{2})}$

36. $\dfrac{\sqrt{x} + \sqrt{x + 1}}{\sqrt{x} - \sqrt{x + 1}}$
$\qquad = \dfrac{\sqrt{x} + \sqrt{x + 1}}{\sqrt{x} - \sqrt{x + 1}} \cdot \dfrac{\sqrt{x} - \sqrt{x + 1}}{\sqrt{x} - \sqrt{x + 1}}$
$\qquad = \dfrac{x - (x + 1)}{x - 2\sqrt{x} \cdot \sqrt{x + 1} + (x + 1)}$
$\qquad = \dfrac{-1}{2x - 2\sqrt{x(x + 1)} + 1}$

38. $\sqrt{16 - 8x + x^2}$

$= \sqrt{(4 - x)(4 - x)}$

$= \sqrt{(4 - x)^2}$

$= |4 - x|$

Since $\sqrt{}$ denotes the nonnegative root we must have $4 - x \geq 0$.

40. $\sqrt{4 - 25z^2} = \sqrt{(2 + 5z)(2 - 5z)}$

This factorization does not produce a perfect square, so the expression $\sqrt{4 - 25z^2}$ cannot be simplified.

FUNCTIONS AND GRAPHS

Section 1.1

2. The x—value of 27 corresponds to two y—values, 69 and 50. In a function, each x must correspond to exactly one y.
The rule is not a function.

4. 9 corresponds to 3 and −3, 4 corresponds to 2 and −2, and 1 corresponds to −1 and 1.
The rule is a not a function.

6. $y = \sqrt{x}$

Each x—value corresponds to exactly one y—value.
The rule is a function.

8. $x = y^4 - 1$
Solve the rule for y.

$y^4 = 1 + x$ or $y = \pm\sqrt[4]{1 + x}$

Each value of x (except −1) corresponds to two y—values

$y = \sqrt[4]{1 + x}$ and $y = -\sqrt[4]{1 + x}$.
The rule is not a function.

In Exercises 10−24, the domain is $\{-2, -1, 0, 1, 2, 3\}$.

10. $y = 2x + 3$

x	−2	−1	0	1	2	3
y	−1	1	3	5	7	9

Pairs: (−2, −1), (−1, 1), (0, 3), (1, 5), (2, 7), (3, 9)
Range: $\{-1, 1, 3, 5, 7, 9\}$

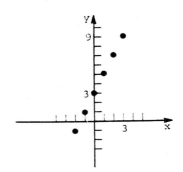

12. $y = -6x + 12$

x	−2	−1	0	1	2	3
y	24	18	12	6	0	−6

Pairs: (−2, 24), (−1, 18), (0, 12), (1, 6), (2, 0), (3, −6)
Range: $\{-6, 0, 6, 12, 18, 24\}$

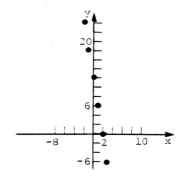

14. $3x + y = 16$
$y = -3x + 16$

x	−2	−1	0	1	2	3
y	22	19	16	13	10	7

Pairs: (−2, 22), (−1, 19), (0, 16), (1, 13), (2, 10), (3, 7)
Range: $\{7, 10, 13, 16, 19, 22\}$

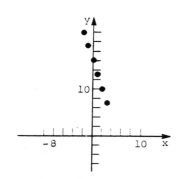

16. 6x − y = −3

  −y = −6x − 3

  y = 6x + 3

x	−2	−1	0	1	2	3
y	−9	−3	3	9	15	21

Pairs: (−2, −9), (−1, −3), (0, 3),
   (1, 9), (2, 15), (3, 21)

Range: {−9, −3, 3, 9, 15, 21}

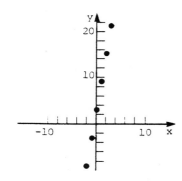

18. y = (x − 2)(x − 3)

  y = x² − 5x + 6

x	−2	−1	0	1	2	3
y	20	12	6	2	0	0

Pairs: (−2, 20), (−1, 12), (0, 6),
   (1, 2), (2, 0), (3, 0)

Range: {0, 2, 6, 12, 20}

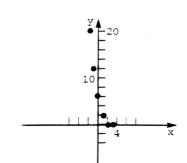

20. y = −2x²

x	−2	−1	0	1	2	3
y	−8	−2	0	−2	−8	−18

Pairs: (−2, −8), (−1, −2), (0, 0),
   (1, −2), (2, −8), (3, −18)

Range: {−18, −8, −2, 0}

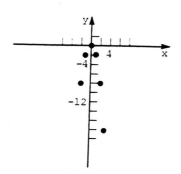

22. $y = \dfrac{-2}{x + 4}$

x	−2	−1	0	1	2	3
y	−1	−2/3	−1/2	−2/5	−1/3	−2/7

Pairs: (-2, -1), (-1, -2/3),

       (0, -1/2), (1, -2/5),

       (2, -1/3), (3, -2/7)

Range:

$\{-1, -2/3, -1/2, -2/5, -1/3, -2/7\}$

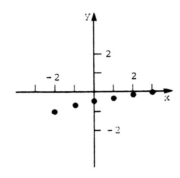

24. $y = \dfrac{2x + 1}{x + 3}$

x	-2	-1	0	1	2	3
y	-3	-1/2	1/3	3/4	1	7/6

Pairs: (-2, -3), (-1, -1/2),

       (0, 1/3), (1, 3/4),

       (2, 1), (3, 7/6)

Range: $\{-3, -1/2, 1/3, 3/4, 1, 7/6\}$

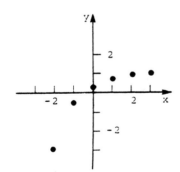

26. $x \geq -3$

This expression represents all numbers greater than or equal to -3, or $[-3, \infty)$. The number -3 is included in the interval.

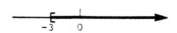

28. $-5 < x \leq -4$

This expression represents all numbers greater than -5 and less than or equal to -4, or $(-5, -4]$. The number -5 is not included in the interval, but the number -4 is included.

30. $6 \leq x$

This expression represents all numbers greater than or equal to 6, or $[6, \infty)$. The number 6 is included in the interval.

32. $[2, 7)$

This interval represents all numbers greater than or equal to 2 but less than 7. 2 is included in the interval, but 7 is not. As an inequality, this is represented as

$$2 \leq x < 7.$$

34. $(3, \infty)$

This interval represents all numbers greater than 3. 3 is not included in the interval. As an inequality, this is represented as

$$x > 3.$$

36.   The interval represents all numbers between 0 and 8. Neither 0 nor 8 is included. As an inequality, this is represented as

$$0 < x < 8.$$

38.   This interval represents all numbers less than 0 or greater than or equal to 3. 0 is not included in the interval but 3 is included. As an inequality, this is represented as

$$x < 0 \quad \text{or} \quad x \geq 3.$$

40. $f(x) = x + 2$

x can take on any value, so the domain is the set of real numbers, which is written $(-\infty, \infty)$.

42. $f(x) = (x - 2)^2$

x can take on any value, so the domain is the set of real numbers, $(-\infty, \infty)$.

44. $f(x) = |x - 1|$

x can take on any value, so the domain is the set of real numbers, $(-\infty, \infty)$.

46. $f(x) = (3x + 5)^{1/2} = \sqrt{3x + 5}$

For $f(x)$ to be a real number,

$$3x + 5 \geq 0$$
$$3x \geq -5$$
$$\frac{1}{3}(3x) \geq \frac{1}{3}(-5)$$
$$x \geq -\frac{5}{3}.$$

In interval notation, the domain is

$$[-\frac{5}{3}, \infty).$$

48. $f(x) = \dfrac{-8}{x^2 - 36}$

In order for $f(x)$ to be a real number, $x^2 - 36$ cannot be equal to 0.

When $x^2 - 36 = 0$,
$$x^2 = 36$$
$$x = 6 \quad \text{or} \quad x = -6$$

Thus, the domain is any real number except 6 or −6. In interval notation, the domain is

$$(-\infty, -6) \cup (-6, 6) \cup (6, \infty).$$

50. $f(x) = -\sqrt{\dfrac{5}{x^2 + 36}}$

x can take on any value. No choice for x will produce a zero in the denominator. Also, no choice for x will produce a negative number under the radical. The domain is $(-\infty, \infty)$.

52. $f(x) = \sqrt{15x^2 + x - 2}$

The expression under the radical must be nonnegative.

$$15x^2 + x - 2 \geq 0$$
$$(5x + 2)(3x - 1) \geq 0$$

Solve $(5x + 2)(3x - 1) = 0$.

$$5x + 2 = 0 \quad \text{or} \quad 3x - 1 = 0$$
$$5x = -2 \qquad\qquad 3x = 1$$
$$x = -\frac{2}{5} \qquad\qquad x = \frac{1}{3}$$

Use these numbers to divide the number line into 3 intervals, $(-\infty, -2/5)$, $(-2/5, 1/3)$, and $(1/3, \infty)$.

Only values in the intervals $(-\infty, -2/5)$ and $(1/3, \infty)$ satisfy the inequality. The domain is $\left(-\infty, -\frac{2}{5}\right] \cup \left[\frac{1}{3}, \infty\right)$.

54. $f(x) = \sqrt{\dfrac{x + 1}{x - 1}}$

For $f(x)$ to be a real number,

$$\frac{x + 1}{x - 1} \geq 0.$$

Solve $\dfrac{x + 1}{x - 1} = 0$.

$$(x - 1)\left(\frac{x + 1}{x - 1}\right) = (x - 0)(0)$$
$$x + 1 = 0$$
$$x = -1$$

Also, $x \neq 1$ since this will cause the denominator to be zero.

Use the numbers -1 and 1 to divide the number line into 3 intervals, $(-\infty, -1)$, $(-1, 1)$, and $(1, \infty)$. Only the values in the intervals $(-\infty, -1]$ and $(1, \infty)$ satisfy the inequality. The value -1 is included, since the numerator may be zero, but the value 1 is not included since it would make the denominator zero. The domain is $(-\infty, -1] \cup (1, \infty)$.

56. By reading the graph, the domain is all numbers greater than or equal to -5. The range is all numbers greater than or equal to 0.
Domain: $[-5, \infty]$ Range: $[0, \infty]$

58. By reading the graph, both x and y can take on any values.
Domain: $(-\infty, \infty)$ Range: $(-\infty, \infty)$

60. $f(x) = 5x - 6$

(a) $f(4) = 5(4) - 6 = 20 - 6 = 14$

(b) $f(-3) = 5(-3) - 6 = -15 - 6 = -21$

(c) $f\left(-\frac{1}{2}\right) = 5\left(-\frac{1}{2}\right) - 6 = -\frac{5}{2} - 6 = \frac{-5}{2} - \frac{12}{2} = -\frac{17}{2}$

(d) $f(a) = 5(a) - 6 = 5a - 6$

(e) $f\left(\frac{2}{m}\right) = 5\left(\frac{2}{m}\right) - 6 = \frac{10}{m} - 6$ or $\frac{10 - 6m}{m}$

62. $f(x) = (x + 3)(x - 4)$

  (a) $f(4) = (4 + 3)(4 - 4)$

     $= (7)(0) = 0$

  (b) $f(-3) = (-3 + 3)(3 - 4)$

     $= (0)(-1) = 0$

  (c) $f\left(-\frac{1}{2}\right) = \left(-\frac{1}{2} + 3\right)\left(-\frac{1}{2} - 4\right)$

     $= \left(\frac{5}{2}\right)\left(\frac{-9}{2}\right) = -\frac{45}{4}$

  (d) $f(a) = [(a) + 3][(a) - 4]$

     $= (a + 3)(a - 4)$

  (e) $f\left(\frac{2}{m}\right) = \left(\frac{2}{m} + 3\right)\left(\frac{2}{m} - 4\right)$

     $= \left(\frac{2 + 3m}{m}\right)\left(\frac{2 - 4m}{m}\right)$

     $= \frac{(2 + 3m)(2 - 4m)}{m^2}$

    or $\frac{(2 + 3m)(2)(1 - 2m)}{m^2}$

     $= \frac{2(2 + 3m)(1 - 2m)}{m^2}$

64. $f(x) = \frac{3x - 5}{2x + 3}$

  (a) $f(4) = \frac{3(4) - 5}{2(4) + 3} = \frac{12 - 5}{8 + 3} = \frac{7}{11}$

  (b) $f(-3) = \frac{3(-3) - 5}{2(-3) + 3} = \frac{-9 - 5}{-6 + 3}$

     $= \frac{-14}{-3} = \frac{14}{3}$

  (c) $f\left(-\frac{1}{2}\right) = \frac{3\left(-\frac{1}{2}\right) - 5}{2\left(-\frac{1}{2}\right) + 3} = \frac{-\frac{3}{2} - 5}{-1 + 3}$

     $= \frac{-\frac{3}{2} - \frac{10}{2}}{2} = \frac{-\frac{13}{2}}{2} = -\frac{13}{4}$

  (d) $f(a) = \frac{3(a) - 5}{2(a) + 3}$

     $= \frac{3a - 5}{2a + 3}$

  (e) $f\left(\frac{2}{m}\right) = \frac{3\left(\frac{2}{m}\right) - 5}{2\left(\frac{2}{m}\right) + 3}$

     $= \frac{\frac{6}{m} - \frac{5m}{m}}{\frac{4}{m} + \frac{3m}{m}} = \frac{\frac{6 - 5m}{m}}{\frac{4 + 3m}{m}}$

     $= \frac{6 - 5m}{m} \cdot \frac{m}{4 + 3m}$

     $= \frac{6 - 5m}{4 + 3m}$

In Exercises 66–68, count squares on the grid. On the horizontal axis, not that two squares correspond to one unit.

66.   (a) $f(-2) = 5$

    (b) $f(0) = 0$

    (c) $f\left(\frac{1}{2}\right) = 1$

    (d) $f(4) = 4$

68.   (a) $f(-2) = 3$

    (b) $f(0) = 3$

    (c) $f\left(\frac{1}{2}\right) = 3$

    (d) $f(4) = 3$

In Exercises 70–74, $f(x) = 6x - 2$ and $g(x) = x^2 - 2x + 5$.

70. $f(2r - 1) = 6(2r - 1) - 2$

     $= 12r - 6 - 2$

     $= 12r - 8$

72. $g(z - p)$

    $= (z - p)^2 - 2(z - p) + 5$

    $= z^2 - 2zp + p^2 - 2z + 2p + 5$

74. $g\left(-\dfrac{5}{z}\right) = \left(-\dfrac{5}{z}\right)^2 - 2\left(-\dfrac{5}{z}\right) + 5$

$= \dfrac{25}{z^2} + \dfrac{10}{z} + 5$

$= \dfrac{25}{z^2} + \dfrac{10z}{z^2} + \dfrac{5z^2}{z^2}$

$= \dfrac{25 + 10z + 5z^2}{z^2}$

76. A vertical line drawn anywhere through the graph will intersect the graph in only one place. The graph represents a function.

78. A vertical line drawn through the graph will intersect the graph in two or more places. The graph does not represent a function.

80. A vertical line is not a function since the one x-value in the domain corresponds to more than one, in fact, infinitely many y-values. The graph does not represent a function.

82. $f(x) = 8 - 3x^2$

(a) $f(x + h) = 8 - 3(x + h)^2$

$ = 8 - 3(x^2 + 2xh + h^2)$

$ = 8 - 3x^2 - 6xh - 3h^2$

(b) $f(x + h) - f(x)$

$= (8 - 3x^2 - 6xh - 3h^2)$

$ - (8 - 3x^2)$

$= 8 - 3x^2 - 6xh - 3h^2 - 8$

$ + 3x^2$

$= -6xh - 3h^2$

(c) $\dfrac{f(x + h) - f(x)}{h}$

$= \dfrac{-6xh - 3h^2}{h}$

$= \dfrac{h(-6x - 3h)}{h}$

$= -6x - 3h$

84. $f(x) = 4x - 11$

(a) $f(x + h) = 4(x + h) - 11$

$ = 4x + 4h - 11$

(b) $f(x + h) - f(x)$

$= (4x + 4h - 11) - (4x - 11)$

$= 4x + 4h - 11 - 4x + 11$

$= 4h$

(c) $\dfrac{f(x + h) - f(x)}{h} = \dfrac{4h}{h} = 4$

86. $f(x) = -\dfrac{1}{x^2}$

(a) $f(x + h) = -\dfrac{1}{(x + h)^2}$

$ = -\dfrac{1}{x^2 + 2xh + h^2}$

(b) $f(x + h) - f(x)$

$= -\dfrac{1}{x^2 + 2xh + h^2} - \left(-\dfrac{1}{x^2}\right)$

$= -\dfrac{1}{x^2 + 2xh + h^2} + \dfrac{1}{x^2}$

$= -\dfrac{x^2}{x^2(x^2 + 2xh + h^2)}$

$ + \dfrac{(x^2 + 2xh + h^2)}{x^2(x^2 + 2xh + h^2)}$

$= \dfrac{-x^2 + x^2 + 2xh + h^2}{x^2(x^2 + 2xh + h^2)}$

$= \dfrac{2xh + h^2}{x^2(x^2 + 2xh + h^2)}$

(c) $\dfrac{f(x + h) - f(x)}{h}$

$= \dfrac{2xh + h^2}{x^2(x^2 + 2xh + h^2)} \div h$

$= \dfrac{2xh + h^2}{hx^2(x^2 + 2xh + h^2)}$

$= \dfrac{h(2x + h)}{hx^2(x^2 + 2xh + h^2)}$

$= \dfrac{2x + h}{x^2(x^2 + 2xh + h^2)}$

88. If x is a whole number of days, the cost of renting a saw in dollars is $S(x) = 7x + 4$. For x in whole days and a fraction of a day, substitute the next whole number for x in $7x + 4$, because a fraction of a day is charged as a whole day.

(a) $S\left(\dfrac{1}{2}\right) = S(1)$

$= 7(1) + 4 = 11$

The cost is $11.00.

(b) $S(1) = 7(1) + 4 = 11$

The cost is $11.00.

(c) $S\left(1\dfrac{1}{4}\right) = S(2) = 7(2) + 4 = 14 + 4$

$= 18$

The cost is $18.00.

(d) $S\left(3\dfrac{1}{2}\right) = S(4)$

$= 7(4) + 4 = 28 + 4$

$= 32$

The cost is $32.00.

(e) $S(4) = 7(4) + 4 = 28 + 4$

$= 32$

The cost is $32.00.

$S\left(4\dfrac{1}{10}\right) = S(5)$

$= 7(5) + 4 = 35 + 4$

$= 39$

The cost is $39.00.

(g) $S\left(4\dfrac{9}{10}\right) = S(5)$

$= 7(5) + 4 = 35 + 4$

$= 39$

The cost is $39.00.

(h) To continue the graph, continue the horizontal bars up and to the right.

(i) The independent variable is x, the number of full and partial days.

(j) The dependent variable is S, the cost of renting a saw.

Section 1.2

2. Find the slope of the line through $(5,-4)$ and $(1, 3)$.

$m = \dfrac{3 - (-4)}{1 - 5}$

$= \dfrac{3 + 4}{-4} = -\dfrac{7}{4}$

4. Find the slope of the line through $(1, 5)$ and $(-2, 5)$.

$m = \dfrac{5 - 5}{-2 - 1} = \dfrac{0}{-3} = 0$

6. $y = 3x - 2$

This is in the slope-intercept form, $y = mx + b$. Thus, the coefficient of the x-term, 3, is the slope.

8. $4x + 7y = 1$

Rewrite the equation in slope-intercept form.

$$7y = 1 - 4x$$
$$\tfrac{1}{7}(7y) = \tfrac{1}{7}(1) - \tfrac{1}{7}(4x)$$
$$y = \tfrac{1}{7} - \tfrac{4}{7}x$$
$$y = -\tfrac{4}{7}x + \tfrac{1}{7}$$

The slope is $-4/7$.

10. The x-axis is the horizontal line $y = 0$. Horizontal lines have a slope of 0.

12. Find the slope of the line perpendicular to $6x = y - 3$.
$6x = y - 3$ is the given line.
Solve for y.

$$6x + 3 = y$$

This line has a slope of 6. The line perpendicular to it has a slope which is the negative reciprocal of 6, or

$$m = -\tfrac{1}{6}.$$

14. Find the slope of the line through $(11.72, 9.811)$ and $(-12.67, -5.009)$. (Note that there are four digits in each number.)

$$m = \frac{-5.009 - 9.811}{-12.67 - 11.72}$$
$$= \frac{-14.82}{-24.39}$$
$$= .6076$$

(We give the answer correct to four significant digits.)

16. As shown on the graph, the line goes through the points $(-2, 0)$ and $(0, -4)$.

$$m = \frac{-4 - 0}{0 - (-2)} = \frac{-4}{2} = -2$$

18. As shown on the graph, the line goes through the points $(1, 0)$ and $(0, -6)$.

$$m = \frac{-6 - 0}{0 - 1} = \frac{-6}{-1} = 6$$

20. The line goes through $(2, 4)$, with slope $m = -1$.
Use point-slope form.

$$y - 4 = -1(x - 2)$$
$$y - 4 = -x + 2$$
$$y = -x + 6$$
$$x + y = 6$$

22. The line goes through $(-8, 1)$, with undefined slope.
Since the slope is undefined, the line is vertical. The equation of a vertical line passing through $(-8, 1)$ is

$$x = -8.$$

24. The line goes through $(8, -1)$ and $(4, 3)$.

Find the slope, then use point-slope form with either of the two given points.

$$m = \frac{3 - (-1)}{4 - 8}$$

$$= \frac{3 + 1}{-4}$$

$$= \frac{4}{-4} = -1$$

$$y - (-1) = -1(x - 8)$$

$$y + 1 = -x + 8$$

$$x + y = 7$$

26. The line goes through $(-2, 3/4)$ and $(2/3, 5/2)$.

$$m = \frac{\frac{5}{2} - \frac{3}{4}}{\frac{2}{3} - (-2)} = \frac{\frac{10}{4} - \frac{3}{4}}{\frac{2}{3} + \frac{6}{3}}$$

$$= \frac{\frac{7}{4}}{\frac{8}{3}} = \frac{21}{32}$$

$$y - \frac{3}{4} = \frac{21}{32}[x - (-2)]$$

$$y - \frac{3}{4} = \frac{21}{32}x + \frac{42}{32}$$

$$32\left(y - \frac{3}{4}\right) = 32\left(\frac{21}{32}x + \frac{42}{32}\right)$$

$$32y - 24 = 21x + 42$$

$$-21x + 32y = 66$$

$$21x - 32y = -66$$

28. The line has x-intercept -2 and y-intercept 4.

Two points on the line are $(-2, 0)$ and $(0, 4)$. Find the slope, then use slope-intercept form.

$$m = \frac{4 - 0}{0 - (-2)} = \frac{4}{2} = 2$$

$$y = mx + b$$

$$y = 2x + 4$$

$$2x - y = -4$$

30. The line is horizontal, through $(8, 7)$.

The line has an equation of the form $y = k$ where k is the y-coordinate of the point, in this case, $k = 7$. So the equation is

$$y = 7.$$

32. The line goes through $(5.469, 11.08)$ with slope 4.723.

Use point-slope form.

$$y - 11.08 = 4.723(x - 5.469)$$

$$y - 11.08 = 4.723x - 25.83$$

$$y = 4.723x - 25.83 + 11.08$$

$$4.723x - y = 14.75$$

34. The line goes through $(-2, 8)$; $m = -1$. The slope is -1, so $m = \frac{\Delta y}{\Delta x} = \frac{-1}{1}$. Thus, $\Delta y = -1$ and $\Delta x = 1$. Another point on the line has coordinates $[(-2 + 1), (8 - 1)]$ $= (-1, 7)$.

Thus, $(-2, 8)$ and $(-1, 7)$ are two points on the line.

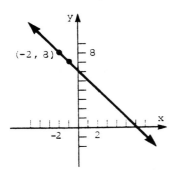

Let y = 0.

$$2x - 3(0) = 12$$
$$2x = 12$$
$$x = 6$$

A second point is (6, 0).
Use the points (0, -4) and (6, 0) to graph the line.

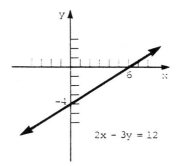

36. The line goes through (-2, -3);
m = -3/4.
One point on the line is (-2, -3).
The slope is -3/4. So

$$m = \frac{\Delta y}{\Delta x} = \frac{-3}{4}.$$

Thus, Δy = -3 and Δx = 4.
Another point on the line is
[(-2 + 4), -3 + (-3)].

So, a second point on the line is
(2, -6).

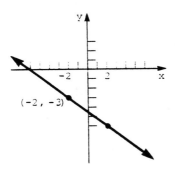

38. Graph the line 2x - 3y = 12.
Let x = 0.

$$2(0) - 3y = 12$$
$$-3y = 12$$
$$y = \frac{12}{-3}$$
$$y = -4$$

One point is (0, -4).

40. Graph line x + 3y = 9.
Let x = 0.

$$0 + 3y = 9$$
$$3y = 9$$
$$y = 3$$

One point on the line is (0, 3).
Let y = 0.

$$x + 3(0) = 9$$
$$x + 0 = 9$$
$$x = 9$$

Another point on the line is (9, 0).
Use the points (0, 3) and (9, 0) to graph the line.

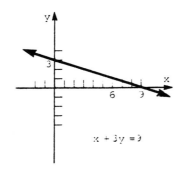

$$x + 3y = 3$$

42. Graph the line $3x - y = 0$.
Let $x = 0$.

$$3(0) - y = 0$$
$$0 - y = 0$$
$$y = 0$$

One point on the line is $(0, 0)$.
Let $x = 1$.

$$3(1) - y = 0$$
$$3 - y = 0$$
$$-y = -3$$
$$y = 3$$

Another point on the line is $(1, 3)$.
Use the points $(0, 0)$ and $(1, 3)$ to
graph the line.

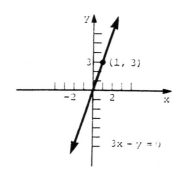

$$3x - y = 0$$

44. $y + 2 = 0$

$$y = -2$$

This is a horizontal line through
the point $(0, -2)$.

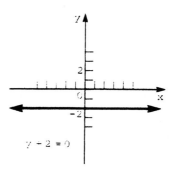

$$y + 2 = 0$$

46. $x = 5$

This is a vertical line through the
point $(5, 0)$.

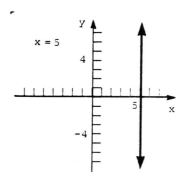

$$x = 5$$

48. Write the equation of the line
through $(2, -5)$, parallel to
$y - 4 = 2x$. Rewrite the equation
in slope-intercept form.

$$y - 4 = 2x$$
$$y = 2x + 4$$

The slope of this line is 2.

Use m = 2 and the point (2, −5) in the point−slope form.

$$y - (-5) = 2(x - 2)$$
$$y + 5 = 2x - 4$$
$$-2x + y = -9$$

50. Write the equation of the line through (−2, 6), perpendicular to 2x + 3y = 5.

Rewrite equation in slope−intercept form.

$$2x - 3y = 5$$
$$-3y = 5 - 2x$$
$$y = \frac{5}{-3} - \frac{2x}{-3}$$
$$y = -\frac{5}{3} + \frac{2}{3}x$$

The slope of this line is 2/3. To find the slope of a perpendicular line, solve

$$\frac{2}{3}m = -1.$$
$$m = -\frac{3}{2}$$

Use $m = -\frac{3}{2}$ and (−2, 6) in the point−slope form.

$$y - 6 = -\frac{3}{2}[x - (-2)]$$
$$y - 6 = -\frac{3}{2}(x + 2)$$
$$2y - 12 = -3(x + 2)$$
$$2y - 12 = -3x - 6$$
$$3x + 2y = 6$$

52. Write the equation of the line with y−intercept 3, parallel to x + y = 4. Rewrite the equation in slope−intercept form.

$$x + y = 4$$
$$y = 4 - x$$

The slope of this line is −1. Since the lines are parallel, −1 is the slope of the needed line. The y−intercept of this line is 3. Using the slope−intercept form of the line with m = −1 and b = 3, we have the equation of the desired line

$$y = (-1)x + 3$$
$$y = -x + 3$$
$$x + y = 3.$$

54. Write the equation of the line with x−intercept −2/3, perpendicular to 2x − y = 4.

Find the slope of the given line.

$$2x - y = 4$$
$$2x - 4 = y$$

The slope of this line is 2. Since the lines are perpendicular, the slope of the needed line is −1/2. The line also has an x−intercept of −2/3. Thus, it passes through the point (−2/3, 0).

Using the point-slope form, we have

$$y - 0 = -\frac{1}{2}\left[x - \left(-\frac{2}{3}\right)\right]$$

$$y = -\frac{1}{2}\left(x + \frac{2}{3}\right)$$

$$y = -\frac{1}{2}x - \frac{1}{3}$$

$$6y = -3x - 2$$

$$3x + 6y = -2.$$

56. (a) Write the given line in slope-intercept form.

$$3y + 2x = 6$$

$$3y = -2x + 6$$

$$y = -\frac{2}{3}x + 2$$

This line has a slope of $-2/3$. The desired line has a slope of $-2/3$ since it is parallel to the given line. Use the definition of slope.

$$m = \frac{y_2 - y_1}{x_2 - x_1}$$

$$-\frac{2}{3} = \frac{2 - (-1)}{k - 4}$$

$$\frac{-2}{3} = \frac{3}{k - 4}$$

$$-2(k - 4) = (3)(3)$$

$$-2k + 8 = 9$$

$$-2k = 1$$

$$k = -\frac{1}{2}$$

(b) Write the given line in slope-intercept form.

$$2y - 5x = 1$$

$$2y = 5x + 1$$

$$y = \frac{5}{2}x + \frac{1}{2}$$

This line has a slope of 5/2. The desired line has a slope of $-2/5$ since it is perpendicular to the given line. Use the definition of slope.

$$m = \frac{y_2 - y_1}{x_2 - x_1}$$

$$= \frac{2 - (-1)}{k - 4}$$

$$-\frac{2}{5} = \frac{2 + 1}{k - 4}$$

$$\frac{-2}{5} = \frac{3}{k - 4}$$

$$-2(k - 4) = (3)(5)$$

$$-2k + 8 = 15$$

$$-2k = 7$$

$$k = -\frac{7}{2}$$

58. The following sketch shows the given points and the diagonals of the square.

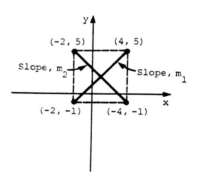

$$m_1 = \frac{5 - (-1)}{4 - (-2)} = \frac{5 + 1}{4 + 2} = \frac{6}{6} = 1$$

$$m_2 = \frac{5 - (-1)}{-2 - 4} = \frac{5 + 1}{-6} = \frac{6}{-6} = -1$$

Since the product of slopes $m_1 m_2 = -1$, the lines are perpendicular

60. First, use the definition of slope with $x_1 = 0$, $y_1 = b$, $x_2 = x_1$, and $y = y_1$.

$$\text{slope} = m = \frac{y_2 - y_1}{x_2 - x_1}$$

$$= \frac{y_1 - b}{x_1 - 0}$$

$$= \frac{y_1 - b}{x_1}$$

Now use the equation $y = mx + b$, let $y = y_1$, $x = x_1$ and solve for m.

$$y_1 = mx_1 + b$$
$$y - b = mx_1$$
$$\frac{y_1 - b}{x_1} = m$$

62. **(a)**

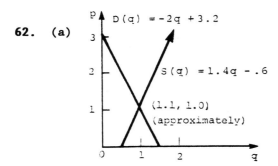

(b) $S(q) = p = 1.4q - .6$
$D(q) = p = -2q + 3.2$

Set supply equal to demand and solve for q.

$$1.4q - .6 = -2q + 3.2$$
$$1.4q + 2q = .6 + 3.2$$
$$3.4q = 3.8$$
$$q = \frac{3.8}{3.4}$$
$$q \approx 1.1$$

The equilibrium quantity is about 1.1 units.

(c) The equilibrium price is found by substituting the value we got for equilibrium quantity in the demand equation $p = -2q + 3.2$.

$$p \approx 1.0$$

The equilibrium price is about $1.

64. **(a)** Let $x_1 = 20$ and $y_1 = 13,900$.
Let $x_2 = 10$ and $y_2 = 7500$.

$$m = \frac{y_2 - y_1}{x_2 - x_1} = \frac{7500 - 13,900}{10 - 20}$$

$$= \frac{-6400}{-10}$$

$$m = 640$$

The equation can be found using the point-slope form of the equation of a line.

$$y - y_1 = m(x - x_1)$$
$$y - 13,900 = 640(x - 20)$$
$$y - 13,900 = 640x - 12,800$$
$$y = 640x + 1100$$

(b) Let $y = 20,000$.

$$20,000 = 640x + 1100$$
$$18,900 = 640x$$
$$29.53 \approx x$$

The company can make 29 trailers for $20,000.

(c) Let $y = 1000$.

$$1000 = 640x + 1100$$
$$-100 = 640x$$
$$-.16 \approx x$$

The company cannot make any trailers for $1000.

66. (a) Let $x_1 = 3$ and $y_1 = 37{,}000$.

Let $x_2 = 12$ and $y_2 = 28{,}000$.

$$m = \frac{y_2 - y_1}{x_2 - x_1} = \frac{28{,}000 - 37{,}000}{12 - 3}$$

$$= \frac{-9000}{9} = -1000$$

The equation of the line is

$$y - y_1 = m(x - x_1)$$
$$y - 37{,}000 = -1000(x - 3)$$
$$y - 37{,}000 = -1000x + 3000$$
$$y = -1000x + 40{,}000.$$

(b) If the fish population is eliminated, $y = 0$.

$$0 = -1000x + 40{,}000$$
$$-40{,}000 = -1000x$$
$$40 = x$$

The fish population is eliminated when 40 tons of pollutant are introduced.

(c) Let $y = 45{,}000$.

$$45{,}000 = -1000x + 40{,}000$$
$$5000 = -1000x$$
$$-5 = x$$

This negative answer indicates that it is not possible to maintain a fish population of 45,000.

68. (a) Let $r_1 = 24$ and $h_1 = 167$.

Let $r_2 = 26$ and $h_2 = 174$.

The slope is $m = \dfrac{h_2 - h_1}{r_2 - r_1}$.

$$m = \frac{174 - 167}{26 - 24} = \frac{7}{2} = 3.5$$

The equation of the line is

$$h - h_1 = m(r - r_1).$$
$$h - 167 = 3.5(r - 24)$$
$$h - 167 = 3.5r - 84$$
$$h = 3.5r + 83$$

(b) Let $r = 23$.

$$h = 3.5(23) + 83$$
$$= 80.5 + 83$$
$$= 163.5$$

Let $r = 27$.

$$h = 3.5(27) + 83$$
$$= 94.5 + 83$$
$$= 177.5$$

The heights would have been about 163.5 cm to 177.5 cm.

(c) Let $h = 17$.

$$170 = 3.5r + 83$$
$$170 - 83 = 3.5r$$
$$87 = 3.5r$$
$$24.85 = r$$

The length of the radius bone is about 25 cm.

70. (a) Find the slope using $(45, 32.5)$ and $(60, 70)$.

$$m = \frac{y_2 - y_1}{x_2 - x_1} = \frac{70 - 32.5}{60 - 45}$$

$$= \frac{37.5}{15} = 2.5$$

Use point-slope form with $(45, 32.5)$.

$$y - 32.5 = 2.5(x - 45)$$

$$y - 32.5 = 2.5x - 112.5$$
$$y = 2.5x - 80$$

(b) Let y = 60.

$$60 = 2.5x - 80$$
$$140 = 2.5x$$
$$56 = x$$

The Republicans would need 56% of the vote.

Section 1.3

2. $45 is the fixed cost and $2 is the cost per mile.

Let x = number of miles and

C(x) = cost of hauling a trailer for x miles.

So,

C(x) = fixed cost + (cost per mile) • (number of miles)

C(x) = 45 + 2x.

4. $44 is the fixed cost and $.28 is the cost per mile.

Let x = the number of miles and

R(x) = the cost of venting for x miles.

So,

R(x) = fixed cost + (cost per mile) • (number of miles)

R(x) = 44 + .28x.

6. Fixed cost, $400; 10 items cost $650 to produce.

C(x) = cost of producing x items.

C(x) = mx + b, where b is the fixed cost.

C(x) = mx + 400

Now,

C(x) = 650 when x = 10.

$$650 = m(10) + 400$$
$$650 - 400 = 10m$$
$$250 = 10m$$
$$25 = m$$

Thus, C(x) = 25x + 400.

8. Fixed cost, $8500; 75 items cost $11,875 to produce.

$$C(x) = mx + 8500$$

Now, C(x) = 11,875 when x = 75.

$$11,875 = m(75) + 8500$$
$$11,875 - 8500 = 75m$$
$$3375 = 75m$$
$$45 = m$$

Thus, C(x) = 45x + 8500.

10. Marginal cost, $120; 100 items cost $15,800 to produce.

Let x = number of items produced and

C(x) = cost of producing x items.

C(x) = mx + b, where m is the marginal cost.

C(x) = 120x + b

Now, C(x) = 15,800 when x = 100.

$$15,800 = 120(100) + b$$
$$15,800 = 12,000 + b$$
$$3800 = b$$

Thus, C(x) = 120x + 3800.

12. Marginal cost, $120; 700 items cost $96,500 to produce.

$$C(x) = 120x + b$$

Now, $C(x) = 96,500$ when $x = 700$.

$$96,500 = 120(700) + b$$
$$96,500 = 84,000 + b$$
$$12,500 = b$$

Thus, $C(x) = 120x + 12,500$.

14. (a) Let $S(x)$ represent sales. Let $x = 0$ represent 1982,

$$y = 850,000.$$

Then $x = 5$ represents 1987,

$$y = 1,262,500.$$

Sales is represented by a linear function, so

$$y = mx + b.$$

$$m = \frac{y_2 - y_1}{x_2 - x_1}$$

$$= \frac{1,262,500 - 850,000}{5 - 0}$$

$$= \frac{412,500}{5} = 82,500$$

The value of y when $x = 0$ is the y-intercept of the line, or b. So

$$b = 850,000.$$

Thus,

$$y = 82,500x + 850,000$$

(b) 1994: $x = 12$

$$y = 82,500(12) + 850,000$$
$$= 990,000 + 850,000$$
$$= \$1,840,000$$

(c) Let sales, y, be $2,170,000.

$$2,170,000 = 82,500x + 850,000$$
$$1,320,000 = 82,500x$$
$$16 = x$$

Since $x = 0$ represents 1982, $x = 16$ represents 1998.

16. (a) $C(x) = 500,000 + 4.75x$

$$C(100,000)$$
$$= 500,000 + 4.75(100,000)$$
$$= 500,000 + 475,000$$
$$= \$975,000$$

(b) Marginal cost is equal to the slope of the line representing the cost function. So,

$$\text{marginal cost} = \$4.75.$$

18. $\overline{C}(x) = \dfrac{C(x)}{x} = \dfrac{500,000 + 4.75x}{x}$

$$= \frac{500,000}{x} + \frac{4.75x}{x}$$

$$\overline{C}(x) = \frac{500,000}{x} + 4.75$$

(a) $\overline{C}(1000) = \dfrac{500,000}{1000} + 4.75$

$$= 500 + 4.75$$
$$\overline{C}(1000) = \$504.75$$

(b) $\overline{C}(5000) = \dfrac{500,000}{5000} + 4.75$

$$= 100 + 4.75$$
$$\overline{C}(5000) = \$104.75$$

(c) $\overline{C}(10,000) = \dfrac{500,000}{10,000} + 4.75$

$$= 100 + 4.75$$
$$\overline{C}(10,000) = \$54.75$$

20. $C(x) = 100x + 6000$

$R(x) = 500x$

Let $C(x) = R(x)$ to find the number of units at the break-even point.

$$100x + 6000 = 500x$$
$$6000 = 400x$$
$$15 = x$$

The break-even point is 15 units.

22. $C(x) = 105x + 6000$

$R(x) = 250x$

Set $C(x) = R(x)$ to find the break-even point.

$$105x + 6000 = 250x$$
$$6000 = 145x$$
$$41.38 = x$$

The break-even point is about 41 units, so you decide to produce.

24. $C(x) = 1000x + 5000$

$R(x) = 900x$

$$900x = 1000x + 5000$$
$$-5000x = 100x$$
$$-50 = x$$

It is impossible to make a profit when the break-point is -50 items. Cost will always be greater than revenue.

26. The value of x where the two curves intersect occurs when $x \approx 95$ units, or about 95 units are produced in about 1977.

28. (a) $y = mx + b$

$$m = \frac{11.2 - 10.3}{3 - 0}$$
$$= \frac{.9}{3}$$
$$= .3$$

Since b is the percent in the year zero, or 10.3%

$$y = .3x + 10.3.$$

(b) The average rate of change

$$= \frac{\text{Total change}}{\text{Number of years}}$$
$$= \frac{.9}{3} = .3\% \text{ per year.}$$

The slope and the average rate of change are the ame.

30. (a) The population is a linear function of years. So the equation has the form

$$y = mx + b.$$

Let $x = 0$ represent 1980;

y (in millions) in 1980 was 31.2.

Let $x = 6$ represent 1986;

y (in millions) in 1986 was 30.3.

So points on the line are (0, 31.2) and (6, 30.3).

Thus,

$$m = \frac{y_2 - y_1}{x_2 - x_1} = \frac{30.3 - 31.2}{6 - 0}$$
$$= \frac{-.9}{6} = -.15.$$

Since $y = 31.2$ when $x = 0$, 31.2 represents the y-intercept or b.

The equation, measured in millions, is

$$y = -.15x + 31.2.$$

(b) The average rate of change of

$$y = \frac{y_2 - y_1}{x_2 - x_1} = \frac{30.3 - 31.2}{6 - 0}$$

$$= \frac{-.9}{6}$$

$$= -.15 \text{ million per year.}$$

32. JND is given by

$$y = .03x.$$

(a) x = 10

$$y = .03(10)$$

$$= .3 \text{ cm}$$

(b) x = 20

$$y = .03(20)$$

$$= .6 \text{ cm}$$

(c) x = 50

$$y = .03(50)$$

$$= 1.5 \text{ cm}$$

(d) x = 100

$$y = .03(100)$$

$$= 3 \text{ cm}$$

(e) The rate of change in JND with respect to the original length of the line of the slope:

$$m = .03.$$

34. m = .85 and b = -5

$$y = mx + b$$

$$y = .85x - 5$$

(a) x = 15

$$y = .85(15) + 1.2$$

$$= 13.95 \text{ min}$$

(b) x = 30

$$y = .85(30) + 1.2$$

$$= 26.7 \text{ min}$$

(c) x = 60

$$y = .85(60) + 1.2$$

$$= 52.2 \text{ min}$$

(d) x = 120

$$y = .85(120) + 1.2$$

$$= 103.2 \text{ min}$$

(e)   y = 60

$$60 = .85x + 1.2$$

$$58.8 = .85x$$

$$x = \frac{58.8}{.85}$$

$$\approx 69 \text{ min}$$

(f)   y = 90

$$90 = .85x + 1.2$$

$$88.8 = .85x$$

$$x = \frac{88.8}{.85}$$

$$\approx 104.5 \text{ min}$$

36. $C = \frac{5}{9}(F - 32)$ and $F = \frac{9}{5}C + 32$

(a) $C = \frac{5}{9}(98.6 - 32)$

$$= \frac{5}{9}(66.6)$$

$$= 37$$

$$98.6° \text{ F} = 37° \text{ C}$$

(b) $F = \frac{9}{5}(20) + 32$

$$= 36 + 32$$

$$= 68$$

$$20° \text{ C} = 68° \text{ F}$$

38. If the temperatures are numerically equal, then F = C.

$$F = \frac{9}{5}C + 32$$

$$C = \frac{9}{5}C + 32$$

$$-\frac{4}{5}C = 32$$

$$C = -40$$

The Celsius and Fahrenheit temperatures are numerically equal at −40°.

40. Let x be the diameter and y be the length of the drill bit.

For Example 6, $y = \frac{38}{3}x + \frac{5}{6}$.

(a)
$$4\frac{1}{4} = \frac{38}{3}x + \frac{5}{6}$$

$$\frac{17}{4} - \frac{5}{6} = \frac{38}{3}x$$

$$\frac{41}{12} = \frac{38}{3}x$$

$$\frac{123}{456} = x$$

$$\frac{41}{152} = x$$

Since the diameter must be a multiple of 1/64, solve $\frac{n}{64} = \frac{41}{152}$ for n.

$$152n = 2624$$

$$n \approx 17.3$$

We must round up to 18.
The drill bit should have a diameter of 18/64 = 9/32 in.

(b)
$$5\frac{1}{2} = \frac{38}{3}x + \frac{5}{6}$$

$$\frac{11}{2} - \frac{5}{6} = \frac{38}{3}x$$

$$\frac{56}{12} = \frac{38}{3}x$$

$$\frac{168}{456} = x$$

$$\frac{7}{19} = x$$

$$\frac{n}{64} = \frac{7}{19}$$

$$19n = 448$$

$$n \approx 23.6$$

We must round up to 24.
The drill bit should have a diameter of 24/64 = 3/8 in.

Section 1.4

2. (a) Vertex is (0, 0).

Plot points:

x	1	−1	2	−2
y	1/2	1/2	2	2

(b) Same graph as part (a) except it is reflected about x-axis.

(c) Plot points:

x	0	1	−1	2	−2
y	0	4	4	16	16

(d) Same graph as part (c) except it is reflected about x-axis.

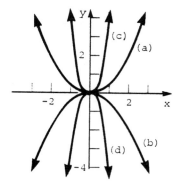

(e) The negative sign causes the graph to be reflected about the x-axis.

4.   (a) Plot the points:

x	0	1	2	3	4
y	4	1	0	1	4

(b) Plot the points:

x	-3	-2	-1	0	1
y	4	1	0	1	4

(c) Plot the points:

x	-5	-4	-3	-2	-1
y	4	1	0	1	4

(d) Plot the points:

x	2	3	4	5	6
y	4	1	0	1	4

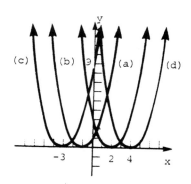

(e) The graphs are shifted to the left or right.

6. $y = x^2 - 10x + 21$
      $= (x - 7)(x - 3)$

Set y = 0 to find the x-intercepts.

$0 = (x - 7)(x - 3)$
$x = 7, \ x = 3$

The x-intercepts are 7 and 3.
Set x = 0 to find the y-intercept.

$y = 0^2 - 10(0) + 21$
$y = 21$

The y-intercept is 21.
The x-coordinate of the vertex is

$x = \dfrac{-b}{2a} = \dfrac{10}{2} = 5.$

Substitute to find the y-coordinate.

$y = 5^2 - 10(5) + 21$
$= 25 - 50 + 21$
$= -4$

The vertex is (5, -4).
The axis is x = 5, the vertical line through the vertex.

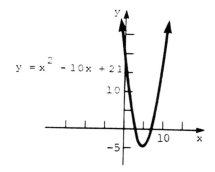

8. y = x² + 8x + 16

   = (x + 4)(x + 4)

Let y = 0.

0 = (x + 4)(x + 4)

x = -4

-4 is the x-intercept.

Let x = 0.

y = 0² + 8(0) + 16

  = 16

16 is the y-intercept.

Vertex: x = $\frac{-b}{2a}$ = $\frac{-8}{2}$ = -4

   y = (-4)² + 8(-4) + 16

     = 16 - 32 + 16

     = 0

The vertex is (-4, 0).

The axis is x = -4, the vertical
line through the vertex.

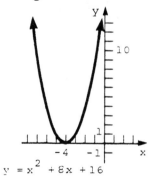

$y = x^2 + 8x + 16$

10. y = -3x² + 12x - 11

   Let y = 0.

   The equation does not factor.
   Use the quadratic formula.

   0 = -3x² + 12x - 11

x = $\frac{-12 \pm \sqrt{12^2 - 4(-3)(-11)}}{2(-3)}$

  = $\frac{-12 \pm \sqrt{144 - 132}}{-6}$

  = $\frac{-12 \pm \sqrt{12}}{-6}$ = $\frac{-12 \pm 2\sqrt{3}}{-6}$

  = 2 ± $\frac{\sqrt{3}}{3}$

The x-intercepts are 2 + √3/3 ≈ 2.58
and 2 - √3/3 ≈ 1.42.

Let x = 0.

y = -3(0)² + 12(0) - 11

y = -11

-11 is the y-intercept.

Vertex: x = $\frac{-b}{2a}$ = $\frac{-12}{2(-3)}$ = $\frac{-12}{-6}$ = 2

y = -3(2)² + 12(2) - 11

  = -12 + 24 - 11

  = 1

The vertex is (2, 1).

The axis is x = 2, the vertical line
through the vertex.

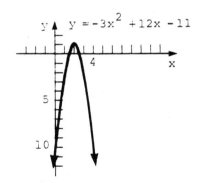

$y = -3x^2 + 12x - 11$

12. y = x² - 2x + 3

   Let y = 0.

   0 = x² - 2x + 3

$$x = \frac{-(-2) \pm \sqrt{(-2)^2 - 4(1)(3)}}{2(1)}$$

$$= \frac{2 \pm \sqrt{4 - 12}}{2} = \frac{2 \pm \sqrt{-8}}{2}$$

Since the radicand is negative, there are no x—intercepts.

Let x = 0.

$$y = 0^2 - 2(0) + 3$$

$$y = 3$$

3 is the y—intercept.

Vertex: $x = \frac{-b}{2a} = \frac{-(-2)}{2(1)} = \frac{2}{2} = 1$

$$y = (1)^2 - 2(1) + 3$$

$$= 1 - 2 + 3$$

$$= 2$$

The vertex is (1, 2).

The axis is x = 1.

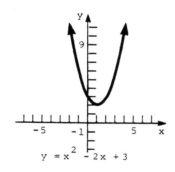

14. $y = -x^2 - 4x + 2$

Let y = 0.

$$0 = -x^2 - 4x + 2$$

$$x = \frac{-(-4) \pm \sqrt{(-4)^2 - 4(-1)(2)}}{2(-1)}$$

$$= \frac{4 \pm \sqrt{16 + 8}}{-2} = \frac{4 \pm \sqrt{24}}{-2}$$

$$= \frac{4 \pm 2\sqrt{6}}{-2} = -2 \pm \sqrt{6}$$

The x—intercepts are $-2 + \sqrt{6} \approx .45$ and $-2 - \sqrt{6} \approx -4.45$.

Let x = 0.

$$y = -0^2 - 4(0) + 2$$

$$y = 2$$

2 is the y—intercept.

Vertex: $x = \frac{-b}{2a} = \frac{-(-4)}{2(-1)} = \frac{4}{-2} = -2$

$$y = -(-2)^2 - 4(-2) + 2$$

$$= -4 + 8 + 2 = 6$$

The vertex is (-2, 6).

The axis is x = -2.

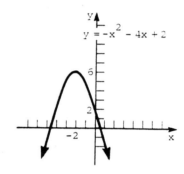

16. $y = 2x^2 - 4x + 5$

Let y = 0.

$$0 = 2x^2 - 4x + 5$$

$$x = \frac{-(-4) \pm \sqrt{(-4)^2 - 4(2)(5)}}{2(2)}$$

$$= \frac{4 \pm \sqrt{16 - 40}}{4} = \frac{4 \pm \sqrt{-24}}{4}$$

Since the radicand is negative, there are no x—intercepts.

Let x = 0.

$y = 2(0)^2 - 4(0) + 5$

$y = 5$

5 is the y-intercept.

Vertex: $x = \dfrac{-b}{2a} = \dfrac{-(-4)}{2(2)} = \dfrac{4}{4} = 1$

$y = 2(1)^2 - 4(1) + 5$

$\quad = 2 - 4 + 5$

$\quad = 3$

The vertex is (1, 3).

The axis is x = 1.

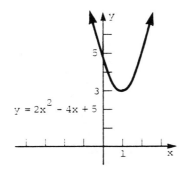

$y = 2x^2 - 4x + 5$

18. $y = -\dfrac{1}{3}x^2 + 2x + 4$

Let y = 0.

$0 = -\dfrac{1}{3}x^2 + 2x + 4$

$x = \dfrac{-2 \pm \sqrt{2^2 - 4\left(-\frac{1}{3}\right)(4)}}{2\left(-\frac{1}{3}\right)}$

$\quad = \dfrac{-2 \pm \sqrt{4 + \frac{16}{3}}}{-\frac{2}{3}} = \dfrac{-2 \pm \sqrt{\frac{28}{3}}}{-\frac{2}{3}}$

$\quad = -2\left(-\dfrac{3}{2}\right) \pm \dfrac{3}{2}\sqrt{\dfrac{28}{3}}$

$\quad = -2\left(-\dfrac{3}{2}\right) \pm \dfrac{3\sqrt{28}}{2\sqrt{3}} \cdot \dfrac{\sqrt{3}}{\sqrt{3}}$

$\quad = 3 \pm \dfrac{\sqrt{84}}{2} = 3 \pm \dfrac{\sqrt{4}\sqrt{21}}{2} = 3 \pm \sqrt{21}$

The x-intercepts are $3 + \sqrt{21} \approx 7.58$ and $3 - \sqrt{21} \approx -1.58$.

Let x = 0.

$y = -\dfrac{1}{3}(0)^2 + 2(0) + 4$

$y = 4$

4 is the y-intercept.

Vertex: $x = \dfrac{-b}{2a} = \dfrac{-2}{2\left(-\frac{1}{3}\right)} = \dfrac{-2}{-\frac{2}{3}} = 3$

$y = -\dfrac{1}{3}(3)^2 + 2(3) + 4$

$\quad = -3 + 6 + 4$

$\quad = 7$

The vertex is (3, 7).

The axis is x = 3.

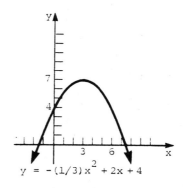

$y = -(1/3)x^2 + 2x + 4$

20. $y = -\dfrac{1}{2}x^2 - x - \dfrac{7}{2}$

Let y = 0.

$0 = -\dfrac{1}{2}x^2 - x - \dfrac{7}{2}$

$x = \dfrac{-(-1) \pm \sqrt{(-1)^2 - 4\left(-\frac{1}{2}\right)\left(-\frac{7}{2}\right)}}{2\left(-\frac{1}{2}\right)}$

$\quad = \dfrac{1 \pm \sqrt{1 - 7}}{-1} = \dfrac{1 \pm \sqrt{-6}}{-1}$

Since the radicand is negative, there are no x-intercepts.

Let x = 0.

$$y = -\frac{1}{2}(0)^2 - 0 - \frac{7}{2} = -\frac{7}{2}$$

-7/2 is the y-intercept.

Vertex: $x = \frac{-b}{2a} = \frac{-(-1)}{2(-\frac{1}{2})} = \frac{1}{-1} = -1$

$$y = -\frac{1}{2}(-1)^2 - (-1) - \frac{7}{2}$$

$$= -\frac{1}{2} + 1 - \frac{7}{2}$$

$$= -3$$

The vertex is (-1, -3).

The axis is x = -1.

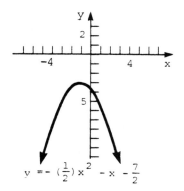

$$y = -\left(\frac{1}{2}\right)x^2 - x - \frac{7}{2}$$

22. $y = \frac{1}{2}x^2 + 2x + \frac{7}{2}$

Let y = 0.

$$0 = \frac{1}{2}x^2 + 2x + \frac{7}{2}$$

$$x = \frac{-2 \pm \sqrt{2^2 - 4\left(\frac{1}{2}\right)\left(\frac{7}{2}\right)}}{2\left(\frac{1}{2}\right)}$$

$$= \frac{-2 \pm \sqrt{4 - 7}}{1}$$

$$= -2 \pm \sqrt{-3}$$

Since the radicand is negative, there are no x-intercepts.

Let x = 0.

$$y = \frac{1}{2}(0)^2 + 2(0) + \frac{7}{2} = \frac{7}{2}$$

7/2 is the y-intercept.

Vertex: $x = \frac{-b}{2a} = \frac{-2}{2(\frac{1}{2})} = \frac{-2}{1} = -2$

$$y = \frac{1}{2}(-2)^2 + 2(-2) + \frac{7}{2}$$

$$= 2 - 4 + \frac{7}{2}$$

$$= \frac{3}{2}$$

The vertex is (-2, 3/2).

The axis is x = -2.

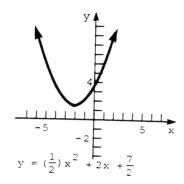

$$y = \left(\frac{1}{2}\right)x^2 + 2x + \frac{7}{2}$$

24. $C(x) = 2x^2 - 20x + 360$

(a) The minimum cost will occur at the vertex.

$$x = \frac{-b}{2a} = \frac{20}{4} = 5$$

$$y = 2(5)^2 - 20(5) + 360$$

$$= 50 - 100 + 360$$

$$= 310$$

The vertex is (5, 310). George will minimize cost if he sells 5 batches of sandwiches.

(b) As shown in Part (a), the vertex is (5, 310). The 5 batches of sandwiches will cost George $310 to produce.

(c) The average daily cost is given by

$$A(x) = \frac{C(x)}{x} = \frac{2x^2 - 20x + 360}{x}$$

$$= 2x - 20 + \frac{360}{x}.$$

(d) $A(4) = 2(4) - 20 + \frac{360}{4}$

$= 8 - 20 + 90$

$= 78$

The average daily cost of producing 4 batches is $78 per batch.

(e) $A(7) = 2(7) - 20 + \frac{360}{7}$

$= 14 - 20 + \frac{360}{7}$

$\approx -6 + 51.4$

≈ 45.43

The average daily cost of producing 7 batches is about $45.43 per batch.

26. (a) The revenue is
    R(x) = (Price per ticket)
          • (Number of people flying).

Number of people flying = 100 - x
Price per ticket = 200 + 4x
R(x) = (200 + 4x)(100 - x)
     = 20,000 + 200x - 4x²

(b) $R(x) = -4x^2 + 200x + 20,000$

x-intercepts:

$0 = (200 + 4x)(100 - x)$

$x = -50$ or $x = 100$

y-intercept:

$y = -4(0)^2 + 200(0) + 20,000$

$= 20,000.$

Vertex:

$x = \frac{-b}{2a} = \frac{-200}{-8} = 25$

$y = -4(25)^2 + 200(25) + 20,000$

$= 22,500$

This is a parabola which opens downward. The vertex is at (25, $22,500).

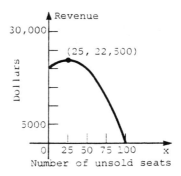

(c) The maximum revenue occurs at the vertex or (25, $22,500). This will happen when x = 25, or there are 25 unsold seats.

(d) The maximum revenue is $22,500, as seen from the graph.

28. Let x = the number of weeks to wait.

(a) Income per pound (in cents):

$$40 - 2x$$

(b) Yield in pounds per tree:

$$100 + 5x$$

(c) Revenue per tree (in cents):
$$R(x) = (100 + 5x)(40 - 2x)$$
$$R(x) = 4000 - 10x^2$$

(d) Find the vertex.

$$x = \frac{-b}{2a} = \frac{0}{-20} = 0$$

$$y = 4000 - 10(0)^2$$
$$= 4000$$

The vertex is (0, 4000).
To produce maximum revenue, wait 0
weeks. Pick the peaches now.

(e) $R(0) = 4000 - 10(0)^2$
$$= 4000$$

or the maximum revenue is 4000 cents
per tree or $40.00 per tree.

30. $M(x) = 10x - x^2$
$$= -x^2 + 10x$$

Find the vertex.

$$x = \frac{-b}{2a} = \frac{-10}{-2} = 5$$

$$y = -5^2 + 10(5)$$
$$= 25$$

The vertex is (5, 25). The rainfall
that produces the maximum number of
mosquitoes is the x-value of this
vertex or 5 in.

32. $C(x) = 10x + 5$ on $[1, 5]$
$C(x) = -20(x - 5)^2 + 100$ on $[5, 7]$

x	1	2	4	5	6	7
y	60	70	90	100	80	20

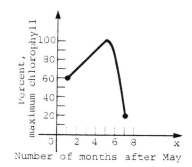

Production is at a maximum when
x = 5, which corresponds to
October.

34. $h = -16t^2 - 64t$

Find the vertex:

$$x = \frac{-b}{2a} = \frac{-64}{-32} = 2$$

$$y = -16(2)^2 + 64(2)$$
$$= -64 + 128$$
$$= 64$$

This is a parabola with vertex
(2, 64) which opens downward. The
maximum height is the value of h
at the vertex, or 64 ft.
The object reaches the ground when
h = 0.

$$0 = -16t^2 + 64t$$
$$0 = 16t(-t + 4)$$
$$16t = 0 \quad \text{or} \quad -t + 4 = 0$$
$$t = 0 \quad \text{or} \quad t = 4$$

When t = 0, the object is about to be thrown. When t = 4, the object hits the ground; that is, after 4 sec.

36. Let x = the length of the lot and
y = the width of the lot.
The perimeter is given by

$$P = 2x + 2y.$$
$$320 = 2x + 2y$$
$$160 = x + y$$
$$160 - x = y$$

Area = xy (quantity to be maximized)

$$A = x(160 - x)$$
$$= 160x - x^2$$
$$= -x^2 + 160x$$

Find the vertex:

$$x = \frac{-b}{2a} = \frac{-160}{-2} = 80$$

$$y = -(80)^2 + 160(80)$$
$$= 6400$$

This is a parabola with vertex (80, 6400) that opens downward. The maximum area is the value of A at the vertex, or 6400 sq ft.

38. Let x = one number.
and 45 - x = second number.
The quantity to be maximized is the product, p, of these two numbers.

$$p = x(45 - x)$$
$$= 45x - x^2$$
$$= -x^2 + 45x$$

Find the vertex.

$$x = \frac{-b}{2a} = \frac{-45}{-2} = 22.5$$

$$y = -(22.5)^2 + 45(22.5)$$
$$= 506.25$$

This is a parabola with vertex (22.5, 506.25) which opens downward. The maximum value occurs at the vertex or when x = 22.5.

Second number = 45 - x
$$= 45 - 22.5$$
$$= 22.5$$

Thus the numbers are both 22.5.

40. Sketch the culvert on the xy-axes as a parabola that opens upward with vertex at (0, 0).

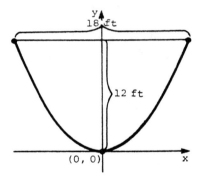

The equation is of the form $y = ax^2$. Since the culvert is 18 ft wide at 12 ft from its vertex, the points (9, 12) and (-9, 12) are on the parabola.
Use (9, 12) as one point on the parabola.

$$12 = a(9)^2$$

$$12 = 81a$$

$$\frac{12}{81} = a$$

$$\frac{4}{27} = a$$

So $y = \frac{4}{27}x^2.$

To find the width from the top, find the points with

$$y\text{-value} = 12 - 8 = 4.$$

Thus,

$$4 = \frac{4}{27}x^2$$

$$108 = 4x^2$$

$$27 = x^2$$

$$x^2 = 27$$

$$x = \pm\sqrt{27}$$

$$x = \pm 3\sqrt{3}.$$

The width of the culvert is
$3\sqrt{3} + |-3\sqrt{3}| = 6\sqrt{3}$ ft ≈ 10.39 ft.

Section 1.5

2. The range is $(-\infty, \infty)$, so the degree is odd. There are 4 turning points, so the degree is 5 or greater. Possible values for the degree are 5, 7, and so on. The shape is similar to the first graph of Figure 33, so the sign of the x^n term is +.

4. Range: of the form $[-k, \infty)$

    The function is of even degree.
    Turning points: 3

The function is of degree 4 or greater. Possible values for the degree: 4, 6, and so on. Shape: similar to the first graph of Figure 34. The sign of the x^n term is +.

6. Range: of the form $[-k, \infty)$

    The function is of even degree.
    Turning points: 5
    The function is of degree 6 or greater. Possible values for degree: 6, 8, and so on. Shape: similar to the first graph of Figure 34. The sign of the x^n term is +.

8. Range: $(-\infty, \infty)$

    The function is of odd degree.
    Turning points: 6
    The function is of degree 7 or higher. Possible values for degree: 7, 9, and so on. Shape: similar to the first graph of Figure 33. The sign of the x^n term is +.

10. $y = \dfrac{-1}{x + 3}$

    Vertical asymptote occurs when $x + 3 = 0$ or when $x = -3$, since this value makes the denominator 0.

x	-6	-5	-4	-2	-1	0
$x + 3$	-3	-2	-1	1	2	3
y	$1/3$	$1/2$	1	-1	$-1/2$	$-1/3$

As $|x|$ gets larger, $\frac{-1}{x+3}$ approaches 0, so $y = 0$ is a horizontal asymptote.

Asymptotes: $y = 0$, $x = -3$

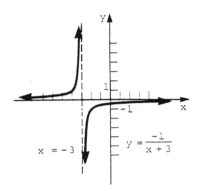

x-intercept:

none, since the x-axis is an asymptote

y-intercept:

$-1/3$, the value when $x = 0$

12. $y = \dfrac{4}{5 + 3x}$

Undefined for

$$5 + 3x = 0$$
$$3x = -5$$
$$x = -\frac{5}{3}$$

Since $x = -5/3$ causes the denominator to equal 0, $x = -5/3$ is a vertical asymptote.

x	-4	-3	-2	-1	0	1
5 + 3x	-7	-4	-1	2	5	8
y	-.571	-1	-4	2	.8	.5

The graph approaches $y = 0$, so the line $y = 0$ is a horizontal asymptote.

Asymptote: $y = 0$, $x = -5/3$

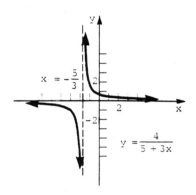

x-intercept:

none, since the x-axis is an asymptote

y-intercept:

$.8 = 4/5$, the value when $x = 0$

14. $y = \dfrac{4x}{3 - 2x}$

Since $x = 3/2$ causes the denominator to equal 0, $x = 3/2$ is a vertical asymptote.

x	-3	-2	-1	0	1	2	3	4
4x	-12	-8	-4	0	4	8	12	16
3 - 2x	9	7	5	3	1	-1	-3	-5
y	-1.33	-1.14	-.8	0	4	-8	-4	-3.2

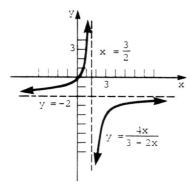

As x gets larger, $\dfrac{4x}{3 - 2x} \approx \dfrac{4x}{-2x} = -2$.

Thus, the line y = -2 is a horizontal asymptote.

Asymptotes: y = -2, x = 3/2

x-intercept:

0, the value when y = 0

y-intercept:

0, the value when x = 0

16. $y = \dfrac{x - 3}{x + 5}$

Since x = -5 causes the denominator to equal 0, x = -5 is a vertical asymptote.

x	-8	-7	-6	-4	-3	-2	-1	0
x - 3	-11	-10	-9	-7	-6	-5	-4	-3
x + 5	-3	-2	-1	1	2	3	4	5
y	3.67	5	9	-7	-3	-1.67	-1	-.6

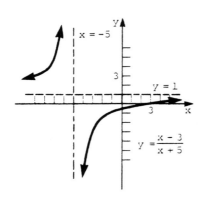

As x gets larger, $\dfrac{x - 3}{x + 5} \approx \dfrac{x}{x} = 1$.

Thus, the line y = 1 is a horizontal asymptote.

Asymptotes: y = 1, x = -5

x-intercept:

3, the value when y = 0

y-intercept:

-.6 = -3/5, the value when x = 0

18. $y = \dfrac{6 - 3x}{4x + 12}$

4x + 12 = 0 when 4x = -12 or x = -3, so x = -3 is a vertical asymptote.

x	-6	-5	-4	-2	-1	0
6 - 3x	24	21	18	12	9	6
4x + 12	-12	-8	-4	4	8	12
y	-2	-2.625	-4.5	3	1.125	.5

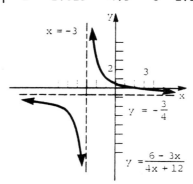

As x gets larger, $\dfrac{6 - 3x}{4x + 12} \approx \dfrac{-3x}{4x} = -\dfrac{3}{4}$.

The line y = -3/4 is a horizontal asymptote.

Asymptotes: y = -3/4, x = -3

x-intercept:

2, the value when y = 0

y-intercept:

.5 = 1/2, the value when x = 0

20. $y = \dfrac{-x + 8}{2x + 5}$

$2x + 5 = 0$ when $2x = -5$ or $x = -5/2$, so $x = -5/2$ is a vertical asymptote.

x	-5	-4	-3	-2	-1	0
-x + 8	13	12	11	10	9	8
2x + 5	-5	-3	-1	1	3	5
y	-2.6	-4	-11	10	3	1.6

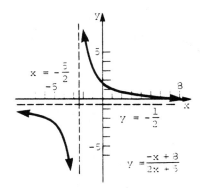

As x gets larger, $\dfrac{-x + 8}{2x + 5} \approx \dfrac{-x}{2x} = -\dfrac{1}{2}$.

The line $y = -1/2$ is a horizontal asymptote.

Asymptotes: $y = -1/2$, $x = -5/2$

x-intercept:

8, the value when $y = 0$

y-intercept:

1.6 = 8/5, the value when $x = 0$

22. $y = \dfrac{110,000}{x + 225}$

(a) If $x = 25$,

$$y = \frac{110,000}{25 + 225} = \frac{110,000}{250} = 440.$$

If $x = 50$,

$$y = \frac{110,000}{50 + 225} = \frac{110,000}{275} = 400.$$

If $x = 100$,

$$y = \frac{110,000}{110 + 225} = \frac{110,000}{325} = 338.$$

If $x = 200$,

$$y = \frac{110,000}{200 + 225} = \frac{110,000}{425} = 259.$$

If $x = 300$,

$$y = \frac{110,000}{300 + 225} = \frac{110,000}{525} = 210.$$

If $x = 400$,

$$y = \frac{110,000}{400 + 225} = \frac{110,000}{25} = 176.$$

(b) Use the following ordered pairs:
(25, 440), (50, 400), (100, 338),
(200, 259), (300, 210), (400, 176).

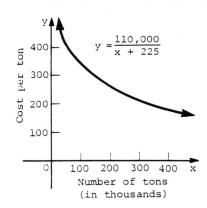

24. Quadratic functions with roots at $x = 0$ and $x = 100$ are of the form $f(x) = ax(100 - x)$.

$f_1(x)$ has a maximum of 100, which occurs at the vertex. The x coordinate of the vertex lies between the two roots.

The vertex is (50, 100).

$$100 = a(50)(100 - 50)$$
$$100 = a(50)(50)$$
$$\frac{100}{2500} = a$$
$$\frac{1}{25} = a$$

$f_1(x) = \frac{1}{25}x(100 - x)$ or $\frac{x(100 - x)}{25}$

$f_2(x)$ has a maximum of 250, occuring at (50, 250).

$$250 = a(50)(100 - 50)$$
$$250 = a(50)(50)$$
$$\frac{250}{2500} = a$$
$$\frac{1}{10} = a$$

$f_2(x) = \frac{1}{10}x(100 - x)$ or $\frac{x(100 - x)}{10}$

$f_1(x)f_2(x)$

$$= \left[\frac{x(100 - x)}{25}\right]\left[\frac{x(100 - x)}{10}\right]$$

$$= \frac{x^2(100 - x)^2}{250}$$

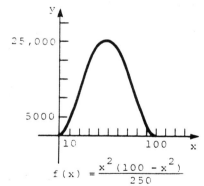

$$f(x) = \frac{x^2(100 - x^2)}{250}$$

26. $y = \frac{80x - 8000}{x - 110}$

(a) $y = \frac{80(55) - 8000}{55 - 110} = \frac{4400 - 8000}{-55}$

$$= \frac{-3600}{-55} = 65.5$$

$65.5(10,000,000) = \$655,000,000$

(b) $y = \frac{80(60) - 8000}{60 - 110} = \frac{4800 - 8000}{-50}$

$$= \frac{-3200}{-50} = 64$$

$64(10,000,000) = \$640,000,000$

(c) $y = \frac{80(70) - 8000}{70 - 110} = \frac{5600 - 8000}{-40}$

$$= \frac{-2400}{-40} = 60$$

$60(10,000,000) = \$600,000,000$

(d) $y = \frac{80(90) - 8000}{90 - 110} = \frac{7200 - 8000}{-20}$

$$= \frac{-800}{-20} = 40$$

$40(10,000,000) = \$400,000,000$

(e) $y = \frac{80(100) - 8000}{100 - 110} = \frac{8000 - 8000}{-10}$

$$= \frac{0}{-10} = \$0$$

(f)

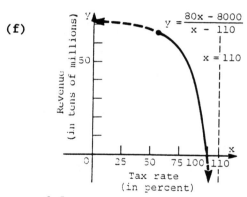

28. $y = \frac{6.5x}{102 - x}$

$y =$ cost in thousands of dollars

$x =$ percent of pollutant

(a) $x = 0$

$$y = \frac{6.5(0)}{102 - 0} = \frac{0}{102} = \$0$$

(b) x = 50

$$y = \frac{6.5(50)}{102 - 50} = \frac{325}{52} = 6.25$$

6.25(1000) = $6250

(c) x = 80

$$y = \frac{6.5(80)}{102 - 80} = \frac{520}{22} = 23.636$$

(23.636)(1000) = $23,636

≈ $24,000

(d) x = 90

$$y = \frac{6.5(90)}{102 - 90} = \frac{585}{12} = 48.75$$

(48.75)(1000) = $48,750

≈ $48,800

(e) x = 95

$$y = \frac{6.5(95)}{102 - 95} = \frac{617.5}{7} = 88.214$$

(88.214)(1000) = 88,214

≈ $88,000

(f) x = 99

$$y = \frac{6.5(99)}{102 - 99} = \frac{643.5}{3} = 214.333$$

(214.333)(1000) = 214,333

≈ $214,500

(g) x = 100

$$y = \frac{6.5(100)}{102 - 100} = \frac{650}{2} = 325$$

(325)(1000) = $325,000

(h)

30. $D(x) = -.125x^5 + 3.125x^4 + 4000$

(a)

x	0	5	10	15
D(x)	4000	5563	22,750	67,281

x	20	25
D(x)	104,000	4000

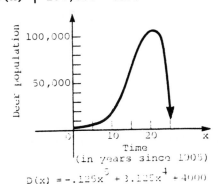

$$D(x) = -.125x^5 + 3.125x^4 + 4000$$

(b) D(x) increases from x = 0 to x = 20. This corresponds to an increasing population from 1905 to 1925. Nevertheless, D(x) does not change much from x = 0 to x = 5. This corresponds to a relatively stable population from 1905 to 1910.

D(x) decreases from x = 20 to x = 25. This corresponds to a decreasing population from 1925 to 1930.

32. $d(x) = \frac{Dx}{x + 12}$

$$d(x) = \frac{70x}{x + 12}$$

(a) A vertical asymptote occurs when x + 12 = 0 or when x = -12.

(b) As x gets larger,

$$\frac{70x}{x + 12} \approx \frac{70x}{x} = 70.$$

(c)

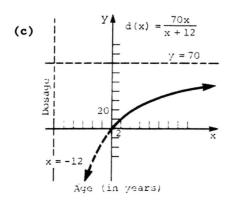

The line y = 70 is a horizontal asymptote.

34. (a) A reasonable domain for the function is $[0, \infty)$. Populations are not measured using negative numbers and they may get extremely large.

(b) $f(x) = \dfrac{Kx}{A + x}$

When K = 5 and A = 2,

$$f(x) = \frac{5x}{2 + x}.$$

Horizontal asymptote at y = 5 since

$$\frac{5x}{2 + x} \approx \frac{5x}{x} = 5$$

as x gets larger.

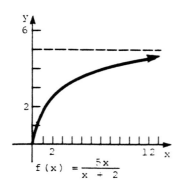

(c) $f(x) = \dfrac{Kx}{A + x}$

As x gets larger,

$$\frac{Kx}{A + x} \approx \frac{Kx}{x} = K.$$

Thus, y = K will always be a horizontal asymptote for this function.

(d) K represents the maximum growth rate. The function approaches this value asymptotically, showing that although the growth rate can get very close to K, it can never reach the maximum, K.

(e) $f(x) = \dfrac{Kx}{A + x}$

Let A = x, the quantity of food present.

$$f(x) = \frac{Kx}{A + x} = \frac{Kx}{2x} = \frac{K}{2}$$

K is the maximum growth rate, so K/2 is half the maximum. Thus, A represents the quantity of food for which the growth rate is half of its maximum.

36. $P(t) = t^3 - 25t^2 + 200t$

(a)

t	0	5	6	7	8	9
P(t)	0	500	516	518	512	504

t	10	11	12
P(t)	500	506	528

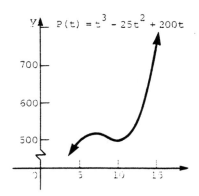

$P(t) = t^3 - 25t^2 + 200t$

(b) As t changes from 0 to about 7 yr, P(t) increases. Also as x increases past 10 yr, P(t) increases.

P(t) decreases for values of t between 7 yr and 10 yr.

38. $f(x) = \frac{x^4}{4} + \frac{a}{2}x^2 + bx$

(a) $a = -5$, $b = 1$

$$f(x) = \frac{x^4}{4} - \frac{5}{2}x^2 + x$$

x	-1	0	1	2	3	4
f(x)	-3.25	0	-1.25	-2	.75	28

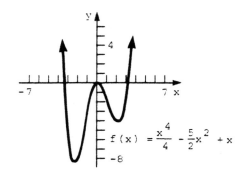

$f(x) = \frac{x^4}{4} - \frac{5}{2}x^2 + x$

(b) $a = 1$, $b = -6$

$$f(x) = \frac{x^4}{4} + \frac{1}{2}x^2 - 6x$$

x	-3	-2	-1	0	1	2	3
f(x)	42.75	20	6.75	0	-5.25	-6	6.75

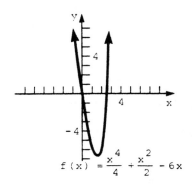

$f(x) = \frac{x^4}{4} + \frac{x^2}{2} - 6x$

40. $f(x) = x^3 - 7x - 9$

x	-4	-3	-2	-1	0	1	2	3	4
f(x)	-45	-15	-3	-3	-9	-15	-15	-3	27

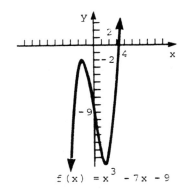

$f(x) = x^3 - 7x - 9$

42. $f(x) = -6x^3 - 11x^2 + x + 6$

x	-3	-2	-1	0	1	2	3
f(x)	66	8	0	6	-10	-84	-252

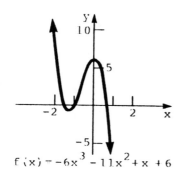

$$f(x) = -6x^3 - 11x^2 + x + 6$$

44. $f(x) = x^4 - 5x^2 + 7$

x	-3	-2	-1	0	1	2	3
f(x)	43	3	3	7	3	3	43

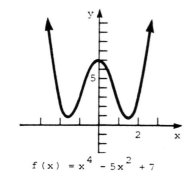

$$f(x) = x^4 - 5x^2 + 7$$

46. $f(x) = -8x^4 + 2x^3 + 47x^2 + 52x + 15$

x	-2	-1	0	1	2	3	4
f(x)	-45	0	15	108	195	0	-945

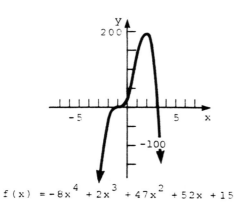

$$f(x) = -8x^4 + 2x^3 + 47x^2 + 52x + 15$$

48. $f(x) = x^5 - 2x^4 - x^3 + 3x^2 + x + 2$

x	-2	-1	0	1	2
f(x)	-44	2	2	4	8

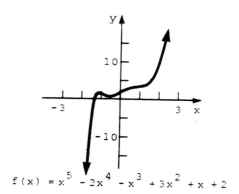

$$f(x) = x^5 - 2x^4 - x^3 + 3x^2 + x + 2$$

52. $f(x) = \dfrac{3x + 2}{x^2 - 4}$

Vertical asymptotes:

$$x^2 - 4 = 0$$
$$(x + 2)(x - 2) = 0$$
$$x = -2, \ x = 2$$

Horizontal asymptotes:

y = 0, since f(x) approaches zero as |x| gets larger.

x	-4	-3	-1	0	1	3	4
f(x)	-.83	-1.4	.3	-.5	-1.7	2.2	1.17

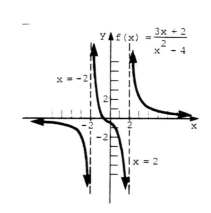

$$f(x) = \dfrac{3x + 2}{x^2 - 4}$$

54. $f(x) = \dfrac{4x^2 - 1}{x^2 + 1}$

Vertical asymptote:

None, since the denominator can never be zero.

Horizontal asymptote:

$y = 4$, since $\dfrac{4x^2 - 1}{x^2 + 1} \approx 4$ as x gets larger.

x	−3	−2	−1	0	1	2	3
f(x)	3.5	3	1.5	−1	1.5	3	3.5

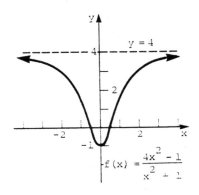

56. $f(x) = \dfrac{5x + 4}{2x^2 - 1}$

Vertical asymptote:

$$2x^2 - 1 = 0$$
$$2x^2 = 1$$
$$x^2 = \frac{1}{2}$$
$$x = \pm\sqrt{\frac{1}{2}} \approx \pm.7$$

Horizontal asymptote:

$y = 0$, since $f(x)$ approaches zero as $|x|$ gets larger.

x	−3	−2	−1	0	1	2	3
f(x)	−.6	−.9	−1	−4	9	2	1.1

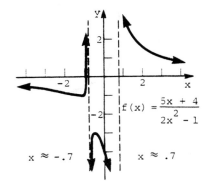

Section 1.6

2. $f(x) = (x - 3)^3$

Translate the graph of $f(x) = x^3$ 3 units right.

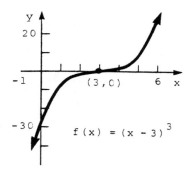

4. $f(x) = (1 - x)^3 - 3$
$= -(x - 1)^3 - 3$

Translate the graph of $f(x) = x^3$ 1 unit right and 3 units down.

Reflect it vertically.

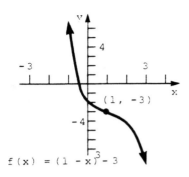

6. $f(x) = -3(x - 2)^3 - 2$

Translate the graph of $f(x) = x^3$ 2 units right and 2 units down. Reflect the graph vertically and stretch it vertically by a factor of 3.

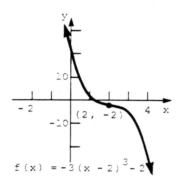

8. $f(x) = (x - 1)^6 - 4$

Translate the graph of $f(x) = x^6$ 1 unit right and 4 units down.

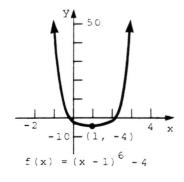

10. $f(x) = \dfrac{3}{x - 2} + 3$

Translate the graph of $f(x) = \dfrac{1}{x}$ 2 units right and 3 units up. Stretch it vertically by a factor of 3.

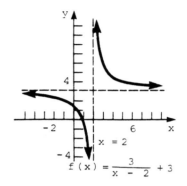

12. $f(x) = \dfrac{-1}{x + 4} - 1$

Translate the graph of $f(x) = \dfrac{1}{x}$ 4 unit left and 1 unit down. Reflect it vertically.

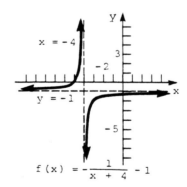

14. $f(x) = \sqrt{x + 1} - 4$

Translate the graph of $f(x) = \sqrt{x}$
1 unit left and 4 units down.

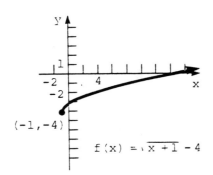

16. $f(x) = -\sqrt{2 - x} + 2$

$\qquad = -\sqrt{-(x - 2)} + 2$

Translate the graph of $f(x) = \sqrt{x}$
2 units right and 2 units up.
Reflect vertically and horizontally.

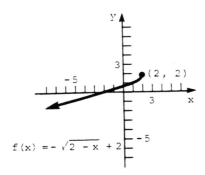

18. $f(x) = x^2 + 4x + 6$

$\qquad = x^2 + 4x + \left(\frac{4}{2}\right)^2 - \left(\frac{4}{2}\right)^2 + 6$

$\qquad = (x^2 + 4x + 4) - 4 + 6$

$\qquad = (x + 2)^2 + 6$

Translate: 2 units left
2 units up

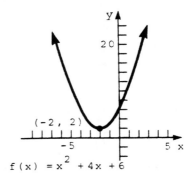

20. $f(x) = x^2 + 6x + 8$

$\qquad = x^2 + 6x + \left(\frac{6}{2}\right)^2 - \left(\frac{6}{2}\right)^2 + 8$

$\qquad = (x^2 + 6x + 9) - 9 + 8$

$\qquad = (x + 3)^2 - 1$

Translate: 3 units left
1 unit down

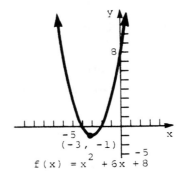

22. $f(x)$

$\qquad = 3x^2 - 12x + 10$

$\qquad = 3(x^2 - 4x) + 10$

$\qquad = 3[x^2 - 4x + \left(-\frac{4}{2}\right)^2 - \left(-\frac{4}{2}\right)^2] + 10$

$\qquad = 3(x^2 - 4x + 4) - 3(4) + 10$

$\qquad = 3(x - 2)^2 - 2$

Translate: 2 units right
          2 units down
Stretch the graph vertically by
a factor of 3.

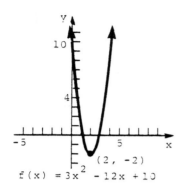

$f(x) = 3x^2 - 12x + 10$

24. $f(x) = -2x^2 - 8x - 13$
$$= -2(x^2 + 4x) - 13$$
$$= -2\left[x^2 + 4x + \left(\frac{4}{2}\right)^2 - \left(\frac{4}{2}\right)^2\right] - 13$$
$$= -2(x^2 + 4x + 4) - 2(-4) - 13$$
$$= -2(x + 2)^2 - 5$$

Translate: 2 units left
          5 units down
Reflect: vertically
Stretch it vertically by a factor
of 2.

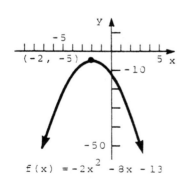

$f(x) = -2x^2 - 8x - 13$

26. If $1 < a$, the graph of $f(ax)$ will be
taller and thinner than the graph of
$f(x)$. Multiplying x by a constant
greater than 1 increases the
corresponding y—values.

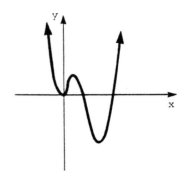

28. If $a < -1$, the graph of $f(ax)$ will
be reflected horizontally, since a
is negative. It will be taller and
thinner because multiplying x by a
constant greater than 1 will increase the corresponding y—values.

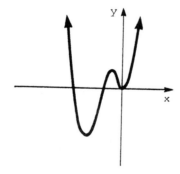

30. If $1 < a$, the graph of $af(x)$ will
be taller than the graph of $f(x)$.
The absolute value of the y—value
will be larger than the original
y—values, while the x—values will
remain the same.

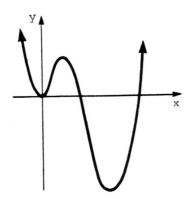

32. If $a < -1$, the graph of $af(x)$ will be reflected vertically. It will also be taller than the graph of $f(x)$ since the absolute value of each y-value will be larger than the original y-values, while the x-values stay the same.

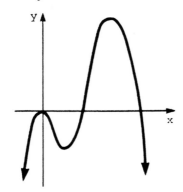

34. $C(x) = 10\sqrt{x} + 50$

   (a) $C(100) = 10\sqrt{100} + 50$

   $= 10 \cdot 10 + 50$

   $= 100 + 50$

   $= \$150$

   (b) The fixed cost is

   $C(0) = 10\sqrt{0} + 50$

   $= 0 + 50$

   $= \$50.$

   (c) Translate the graph of $f(x) = \sqrt{x}$ up 50 units and stretch vertically by a factor of 10.

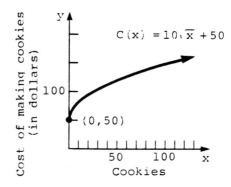

   (d) $A(x) = \bar{C}(x) = \dfrac{C(x)}{x} = \dfrac{10\sqrt{x} + 50}{x}$

   (e) $A(100) = \dfrac{10\sqrt{100} + 50}{100} = \dfrac{150}{100}$

   $= \$1.50$ per cookie

   (f) $A(1600) = \dfrac{10\sqrt{1600} + 50}{1600} = \dfrac{450}{1600}$

   $\approx \$.28$ per cookie

Chapter 1 Review Exercises

For Exercises 6–14, the domain is $\{-3, -2, -1, 0, 1, 2, 3\}$.

6. $3x - 7y = 21$

   $7y = -3x + 21$

   $y = -\dfrac{3}{7}x + 3$

x	−3	−2	−1	0	1	2	3
y	30/7	27/7	24/7	3	18/7	15/7	12/7

   Pairs: $(-3, 30/7)$, $(-2, 27/7)$,

   $(-1, 24/7)$, $(0, 3)$,

   $(1, 18/7)$, $(2, 15/7)$,

   $(3, 12/7)$,

Range: $\{12/7, 15/7, 18/7, 3,$
        $24/7, 27/7, 30/7\}$

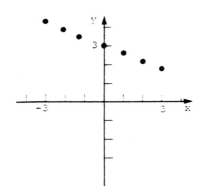

Range: $\{-7, -4, 5, 20\}$

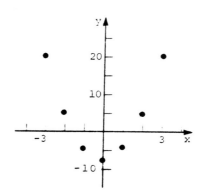

8. $y = (x + 4)(x + 3)$
        $= x^2 + 7x + 12$

x	-3	-2	-1	0	1	2	3
y	0	2	6	12	20	30	42

Pairs: (-3, 0), (-2, 2), (-1, 6),
        (0, 12), (1, 20), (2, 30),
        (3, 42)

Range: $\{0, 2, 6, 12, 20, 30, 42\}$

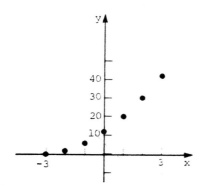

10. $y = 3x^2 - 7$

x	-3	-2	-1	0	1	2	3
y	20	5	-4	-7	-4	5	20

Pairs: (-3, 20), (-2, 5), (-1, -4),
        (0, -7), (1, -4), (2, 5),
        (3, 20)

12. $y = \dfrac{-3 + x}{x + 10}$

x	-3	-2	-1	0	1	2	3
y	-6/7	-5/8	-4/9	-3/10	-2/11	-1/12	0

Pairs: (-3, -6/7), (-2, -5/8),
        (-1, -4/9), (0, -3/10),
        (1, -2/11), (2, -1/12),
        (3, 0)

Range: $\{-6/7, -5/8, -4/9, -3/10,$
        $-2/11, -1/12, 0\}$

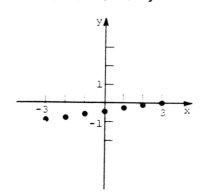

14. $y = 3$

x	-3	-2	-1	0	1	2	3
y	3	3	3	3	3	3	3

Pairs: (-3, 3), (-2, 3), (-1, 3),
       (0, 3), (1, 3), (2, 3),
       (3, 3)

Range: {3}

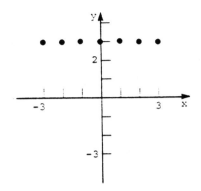

16. f(x) = 3 - 4x

(a) f(6) = 3 - 4(6) = 3 - 24 = -21

(b) f(-2) = 3 - 4(-2)
          = 3 + 8
          = 11

(c) f(-4) = 3 - 4(-4)
          = 3 + 16
          = 19

(d) f(r + 1) = 3 - 4(r + 1)
             = 3 - 4r - 4
             = -1 - 4r

18. f(x) = 8 - x - x²

(a) f(6) = 8 - 6 - (6)²
         = 8 - 6 - 36
         = -34

(b) f(-2) = 8 - (-2) - (-2)²
          = 8 + 2 - 4 = 6

(c) f(-4) = 8 - (-4) - (-4)²
          = 8 + 4 - 16 = -4

(d) f(r + 1)
    = 8 - (r + 1) - (r + 1)²
    = 8 - r - 1 - (r² + 2r + 1)
    = 8 - r - 1 - r² - 2r - 1
    = 6 - 3r - r²

20. y = 6 - 2x

Let x = 0.

        y = 6 - 2(0)
          = 6

Let y = 0.

        0 = 6 - 2x
       2x = 6
        x = 3

Draw the line through (0, 6)
and (3, 0).

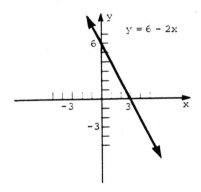

22. 2x + 7y = 14

When x = 0, y = 2.
When y = 0, x = 7.
Draw the line through (0, 2) and
(7, 0).

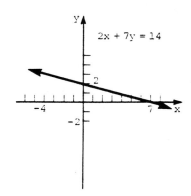

24. $y = 1$

This is the horizontal line passing through $(0, 1)$.

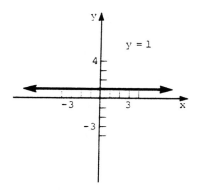

26. $x + 3y = 0$

When $x = 0$, $y = 0$.
When $x = 3$, $y = -1$.
Draw the line through $(0, 0)$ and $(3, -1)$.

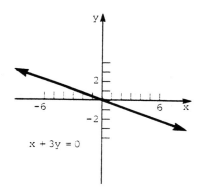

28. **Through $(4, -1)$ and $(3, -3)$**

$$m = \frac{-3 - (-1)}{3 - 4}$$
$$= \frac{-3 + 1}{-1}$$
$$= \frac{-2}{-1} = 2$$

30. **Through the origin and $(0, 7)$**

$$m = \frac{7 - 0}{0 - 0} = \frac{7}{0}$$

The slope of the line is not defined.

32. $4x - y = 7$

$$-y = -4x + 7$$
$$y = 4x - 7$$
$$m = 4$$

34. $3y - 1 = 14$

$$3y = 14 + 1$$
$$3y = 15$$
$$y = 5$$

This is a horizontal line. The slope of a horizontal line is 0.

36. **Through $(8, 0)$, with slope $-\frac{1}{4}$**

Use point-slope form.

$$y - 0 = -\frac{1}{4}(x - 8)$$
$$y = -\frac{1}{4}x + 2$$
$$4y = -x + 8$$
$$x + 4y = 8$$

38. Through $(2, -3)$ and $(-3, 4)$

$$m = \frac{4 - (-3)}{-3 - 2} = -\frac{7}{5}$$

Use point–slope form.

$$y - (-3) = -\frac{7}{5}(x - 2)$$

$$y + 3 = -\frac{7}{5}x + \frac{14}{5}$$

$$5y + 15 = -7x + 14$$

$$7x + 5y = -1$$

40. Slope 0, through $(-2, 5)$

Horizontal lines have 0 slope and an equation of the form $y = k$.
The line passes through $(-2, 5)$ so $k = 5$. An equation of the line is

$$y = 5.$$

42. Through $(2, -1)$, parallel to
$3x - y = 1$

Solve $3x - y = 1$ for y.

$$-y = 1 - 3x$$

$$y = -1 + 3x$$

$$m = 3$$

The desired line has the same slope.
Use point–slope form.

$$y - (-1) = 3(x - 2)$$

$$y + 1 = 3x - 6$$

$$3x - y = 7$$

44. Through $(2, -10)$, perpendicular
to a line with undefined slope
A line with undefined slope is a
vertical line. A line perpendicular to a vertical line is a
horizontal line with equation of
the form $y = k$. The desired line
passes through $(2, -10)$, so $k = -10$.

Thus, an equation of the desired
line is

$$y = -10.$$

46. Through $(-7, 4)$, perpendicular
to $y = 8$
The given line, $y = 8$, is a horizontal line. A line perpendicular
to a horizontal line is a vertical
line with equation of the form
$x = h$.
The desired line passes through
$(-7, 4)$ so $h = -7$. Thus, an
equation of the desired line is

$$x = -7.$$

48. Through $(0, 5)$, $m = -\frac{2}{3}$

One point on the line is $(0, 5)$.

Slope $= \frac{-2}{3} = \frac{\Delta y}{\Delta x}$

So $\Delta y = -2$ and $\Delta x = 3$.

$$x_2 = x_1 + \Delta x = 0 + 3 = 3$$

$$y_2 = y_1 + \Delta y = 5 - 2 = 3$$

A second point on the line is
$(3, 3)$.
Draw the line through these points.

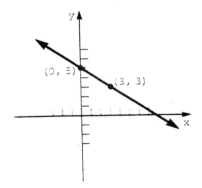

50. Through $(-3, -2)$, $m = -1$

One point on the line is $(-3, -2)$.

Slope $= -1 = \dfrac{-1}{1} = \dfrac{\Delta y}{\Delta x}$

So $\Delta y = -1$ and $\Delta x = 1$.

Thus $x_2 = x_1 + \Delta x = -3 + 1 = -2$
$\qquad y_2 = y_1 + \Delta y = -2 + (-1) = -3$.

A second point on the line is $(-2, -3)$.

Plot the points $(-3, -2)$ and $(-2, -3)$.

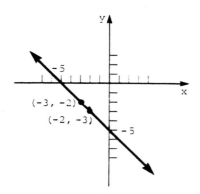

52. $y = 6 - x^2$
$\quad = -x^2 + 6$

The graph is a parabola.
Let $y = 0$.

$$0 = -x^2 + 6$$
$$x^2 = 6$$

$x = \pm\sqrt{6}$ are the x-intercepts.
Let $x = 0$.

$y = 6$ is the y-intercept.

Vertex: $x = \dfrac{-b}{2a} = \dfrac{-0}{2(-1)} = 0$

$y = 6 - (0)^2 = 6$

The vertex is $(0, 6)$.

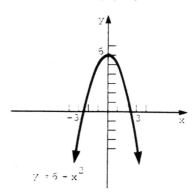

54. $y = -\dfrac{1}{4}x^2 + x + 2$

The graph is a parabola.
Let $y = 0$.

$$0 = -\frac{1}{4}x^2 + x + 2$$

Multiply by 4.

$$0 = -1x^2 + 4x + 8$$

$$x = \frac{-4 \pm \sqrt{4^2 - 4(-1)(8)}}{2(-1)}$$

$$= \frac{-4 \pm \sqrt{48}}{-2}$$

$$= 2 \pm 2\sqrt{3}$$

The x-intercepts are $2 + 2\sqrt{3} \approx 5.46$ and $2 - 2\sqrt{3} \approx -1.46$.
Let $x = 0$.

$$y = -\frac{1}{4}(0)^2 + 0 + 2$$

$y = 2$ is the y-intercept.

Vertex: $x = \dfrac{-b}{2a} = \dfrac{-1}{2\left(-\frac{1}{4}\right)} = 2$

$$y = -\frac{1}{4}(2)^2 + 2 + 2$$

$$= -1 + 4$$

$$= 3$$

The vertex is (2, 3).

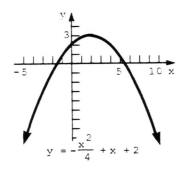

$$y = -\frac{x^2}{4} + x + 2$$

56. $y = -3x^2 - 12x - 1$

x-intercepts: 4.08 and −.08

y-intercept: −1

Vertex: (−2, 11)

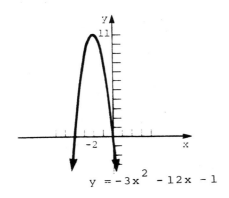

$$y = -3x^2 - 12x - 1$$

58. $f(x) = 1 - x^4$

$\qquad = -x^4 + 1$

Translate the graph of $f(x) = x^4$
1 unit up and reflect vertically.

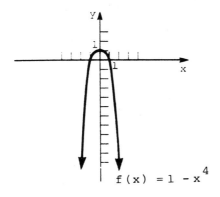

$$f(x) = 1 - x^4$$

60. $y = -(x + 2)^4 - 2$

Translate the graph of $y = x^4$
2 units left and 2 units down.
Reflect vertically.

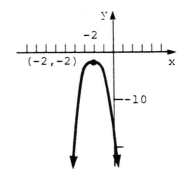

62. $y = -\sqrt{x - 4} + 2$

Translate the graph of $y = \sqrt{x}$
4 units right and 2 units up.
Reflect vertically.

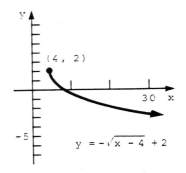

$$y = -\sqrt{x - 4} + 2$$

64. $f(x) = \dfrac{2}{3x - 1}$

Vertical asymptote: $3x - 1 = 0$
or $x = 1/3$

Horizontal asymptote: $y = 0$, since

$\dfrac{2}{3x - 1}$ approaches zero as x gets

larger.

x	0	1	-1	2	-2
y	-2	1	-1/2	2/5	-2/7

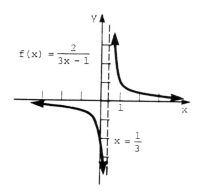

$$f(x) = \frac{2}{3x - 1}$$

$$x = \frac{1}{3}$$

66. $f(x) = \dfrac{6x}{x + 2}$

Vertical asymptote: $x = -2$

Horizontal asymptote: $y = 6$

x	-5	-4	-3	-1	0	1	2
y	10	12	18	-6	0	2	3

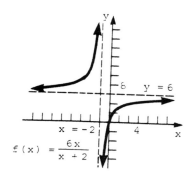

$$y = 6$$

$$x = -2$$

$$f(x) = \frac{6x}{x + 2}$$

68. Exercise 54 is

$$y = -\frac{1}{4}x^2 + x + 2.$$

Completing the square produces

$$y = \frac{-(x - 2)^2}{4} + 3.$$

Translate $y = x^2$ 2 units right and
3 units up. Reflect vertically and
stretch vertically by a factor of
1/4.

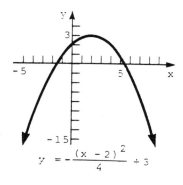

$$y = -\frac{(x - 2)^2}{4} + 3$$

70. Exercise 56 is

$$y = -3x^2 - 12x - 1.$$

Completing the square produces

$$y = -3(x + 2)^2 + 11.$$

Translate $y = x^2$ 2 units left and
11 units up. Reflect vertically and
stretch vertically by a factor of 3.

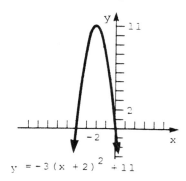

$$y = -3(x + 2)^2 + 11$$

72. $x_1 = 72$ $x_2 = 104$

$p_1 = 6$ $p_2 = 10$

Slope $= \dfrac{p_2 - p_1}{x_2 - x_1} = \dfrac{10 - 6}{104 - 72}$

$= \dfrac{4}{32} = \dfrac{1}{8}$

Use point–slope form.

$$p - 6 = \frac{1}{8}(x - 72)$$

$$p - 6 = \frac{1}{8}x - 9$$

$$8p - 48 = x - 72$$

$$8p = x - 72 + 48$$

$$8p = x - 24$$

$$p = \frac{x}{8} - 3$$

74. Twelve units cost $445, 50 units cost $1585. Points on the line are (12, 445), (50, 1585).

$$m = \frac{1585 - 445}{50 - 12} = 30$$

Use point–slope form.

$$y - 445 = 30(x - 12)$$

$$y - 445 = 30x - 360$$

$$y = 30x + 85$$

$$C(x) = 30x + 85$$

$$A(x) = \frac{C(x)}{x} = \frac{30x + 85}{x} = 30 + \frac{85}{x}$$

76. $C(x) = 20x + 100$

$R(x) = 40x$

(a) Break–even occurs when
$C(x) = R(x)$.

$$20x + 100 = 40x$$

$$100 = 20x$$

$$5 = x$$

Break–even occurs when 5 birdcages are produced.

(b) $R(x) = 40x = 40(5) = \$200$

78. $F(x) = -\frac{2}{3}x^2 + \frac{14}{3}x + 96$

The maximum fever occurs at the vertex of the parabola.

$$x = \frac{-b}{2a} = \frac{-\dfrac{14}{3}}{-\dfrac{4}{3}} = \frac{7}{2}$$

$$y = -\frac{2}{3}\left(\frac{7}{2}\right)^2 + \frac{14}{3}\left(\frac{7}{2}\right) + 96$$

$$= -\frac{2}{3}\left(\frac{49}{4}\right) + \frac{49}{3} + 96$$

$$= -\frac{49}{6} + \frac{49}{3} + 96$$

$$= -\frac{49}{6} + \frac{98}{6} + \frac{576}{6} = \frac{625}{6} \approx 104.2$$

The maximum fever occurs on the third day. It is about 104.2° F.

80. $y = \dfrac{7x}{100 - x}$

(a) $y = \dfrac{7(80)}{100 - 80} = \dfrac{560}{20} = 28$

The cost is $28,000.

(b) $y = \dfrac{7(50)}{100 - 50} = \dfrac{350}{50} = 7$

The cost is $7000.

(c) $\dfrac{7(90)}{100 - 90} = \dfrac{630}{10} = 63$

The cost is $63,000.

(d) Plot the points (80, 28), (50, 7), and (90, 63).

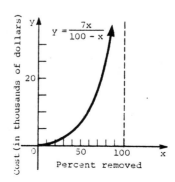

(e) No, because all of the pollutant would be removed when x = 100,
at which point the denominator of
the function would be zero.

82. $C(x) = 30 + 27x$ where x is the
number of ounces over 1 oz.

(a) The weight is between 3 and 4
so x = 3.

$$C(x) = 30 + 27(3)$$
$$C(x) = 30 + 81$$
$$C(x) = 111¢$$

(b) The weight is between 1 and 2
so x = 1.

$$C(x) = 30 + 27(1)$$
$$C(x) = 30 + 27$$
$$C(x) = 57¢$$

(c) The weight is between 5 and 6
so x = 5.

$$C(x) = 30 + 27(5)$$
$$C(x) = 30 + 135$$
$$C(x) = 165¢$$

(d) The weight = 10 oz so x = 9.

$$C(x) = 30 + 27(9)$$
$$C(x) = 30 + 243$$
$$C(x) = 273¢$$

(e)

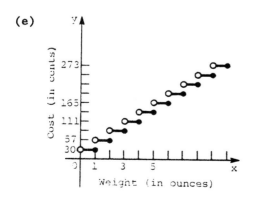

(f) Domain: $(0, \infty)$, since the letter
can weigh as much as you want.
Range:
$\{30, 57, 84, 111, 138, 165, \ldots\}$

84. $C(x) = x^2 + 4x + 7$

(a)

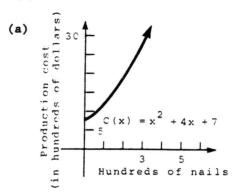

(b) $C(x + 1) - C(x)$

$$= (x + 1)^2 + 4(x + 1) + 7$$
$$\quad - (x^2 + 4x + 7)$$
$$= x^2 + 2x + 1 + 4x + 4 + 7$$
$$\quad - x^2 - 4x - 7$$
$$= 2x + 5$$

(c) $A(x) = \dfrac{C(x)}{x} = \dfrac{x^2 + 4x + 7}{x}$

$$= x + 4 + \frac{7}{x}$$

(d) $A(x + 1) - A(x)$

$$= (x + 1) + 4 + \frac{7}{x + 1}$$
$$\quad - \left(x + 4 + \frac{7}{x}\right)$$
$$= x + 1 + 4 + \frac{7}{x + 1} - x - 4 - \frac{7}{x}$$
$$= 1 + \frac{7}{x + 1} - \frac{7}{x}$$
$$= 1 + \frac{7x - 7(x + 1)}{x(x + 1)}$$
$$= 1 + \frac{7x - 7x - 7}{x(x + 1)}$$
$$= 1 - \frac{7}{x(x + 1)}$$

86. I(x) = CPI + .25(x) where CPI is the percent increase in the Consumer Price Index and x is the percent increase in student enrollment.

(a) I(-3) when CPI = 6.5%.

$$I(-3) = 6.5 + .25(-3)$$
$$= 6.5 - .75$$
$$= 5.75$$

However, the minimum increase is 6% so I(-3) = 6%.

(b) I(-2) = 6.5 + .25(-2)
$$= 6.5 - .5$$
$$= 6\%$$

(c) I(4) = 6.5 + .25(4)
$$= 6.5 + 1$$
$$= 7.5\%$$

(d) I(7) = 6.5 + .25(7)
$$= 6.5 + 1.75$$
$$= 8.25\%$$

However, the maximum increase is 8%, so I(7) = 8%.

(e)

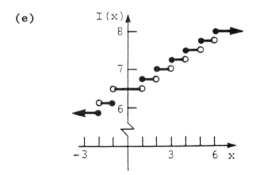

(f) The range starts at 6% and increases 1/4% until it reaches the maximum of 8%.
Range:
$\{6, 6.25, 6.5, \ldots, 7.75, 8\}$

CHAPTER 2   THE DERIVATIVE

Section 2.1

2.   By reading the graph, as x gets closer to 2 from the left or the right, F(x) gets closer to 4.

$$\lim_{x \to 2} F(x) = 4$$

4.   By reading the graph, as x gets closer to 3 from the left or the right, g(x) gets closer to 2.

$$\lim_{x \to 3} g(x) = 2$$

6.   By reading the graph, as x approaches 0 from the left or the right, f(x) approaches 0.

$$\lim_{x \to 0} f(x) = 0$$

10. $f(x) = 2x^2 - 4x + 3$, find $\lim_{x \to 1} f(x)$.
Substitute .9 for x in the expression at the right to get f(.9) = 1.02.
Continue substituting to complete the table.

x	.9	.99	.999
f(x)	1.02	1.0002	1.000002

x	1.001	1.01	1.1
f(x)	1.000002	1.0002	1.02

As x approaches 1 from the left or the right, f(x) approaches 1.

$$\lim_{x \to 1} f(x) = 1$$

12. $f(x) = \dfrac{2x^3 + 3x^2 - 4x - 5}{x + 1}$, find $\lim_{x \to -1} f(x)$.

x	-1.1	-1.01	-1.001
f(x)	-3.68	-3.969	-3.996

x	-.999	-.99	-.9
f(x)	-4.002	-4.02	-4.28

As x approaches -1 from the left or the right, f(x) approaches -4.

$$\lim_{x \to -1} f(x) = -4$$

14. $f(x) = \dfrac{\sqrt{x} - 3}{x - 3}$, find $\lim_{x \to 3} f(x)$.

x	2.9	2.99	2.999
f(x)	12.9706	127.0838	1268.237

x	3.001	3.01	3.1
f(x)	-1267.66	-126.506	-12.6795

$$\lim_{x \to 3^-} f(x) = \infty$$

$$\lim_{x \to 3^+} f(x) = -\infty$$

Thus, $\lim_{x \to 3} f(x)$ does not exist.

16. $\lim_{x \to 4} [g(x) \cdot f(x)]$

$= \left[\lim_{x \to 4} g(x)\right] \cdot \left[\lim_{x \to 4} f(x)\right]$

$= 8 \cdot 16$

$= 128$

18. $\lim_{x \to 4} [3 \cdot f(x)]$

$= 3 \cdot \lim_{x \to 4} f(x)$

$= 3 \cdot 16 = 48$

20. $\lim\limits_{x \to 4} \sqrt[3]{g(x)}$

$= \lim\limits_{x \to 4} [g(x)]^{1/3}$

$= \left[\lim\limits_{x \to 4} g(x) \right]^{1/3}$

$= 8^{1/3} = 2$

22. $\lim\limits_{x \to 4} [1 + f(x)]^2$

$= \left[\lim\limits_{x \to 4} (1 + f(x)) \right]^2$

$= \left[\lim\limits_{x \to 4} 1 + \lim\limits_{x \to 4} f(x) \right]^2$

$= (1 + 16)^2$

$= 17^2$

$= 289$

24. $\lim\limits_{x \to 4} \dfrac{5g(x) + 2}{1 - f(x)}$

$= \dfrac{\lim\limits_{x \to 4} [5g(x) + 2]}{\lim\limits_{x \to 4} [1 - f(x)]}$

$= \dfrac{5 \lim\limits_{x \to 4} g(x) + \lim\limits_{x \to 4} 2}{\lim\limits_{x \to 4} 1 - \lim\limits_{x \to 4} f(x)}$

$= \dfrac{5 \cdot 8 + 2}{1 - 16}$

$= -\dfrac{42}{15}$

26. $\lim\limits_{x \to -2} \dfrac{x^2 - 4}{x + 2} = \lim\limits_{x \to -2} \dfrac{(x + 2)(x - 2)}{(x + 2)}$

$= \lim\limits_{x \to -2} (x - 2)$

$= -2 - 2 = -4$

28. $\lim\limits_{x \to 5} \dfrac{x^2 - 3x - 10}{x - 5}$

$= \lim\limits_{x \to 5} \dfrac{(x - 5)(x + 2)}{(x - 5)}$

$= \lim\limits_{x \to 5} (x + 2)$

$= 5 + 2 = 7$

30. $\lim\limits_{x \to 0} \dfrac{-x^5 - 9x^3 + 8x^2}{5x}$

$= \lim\limits_{x \to 0} \dfrac{x(-x^4 - 9x^2 + 8x)}{5x}$

$= \lim\limits_{x \to 0} \dfrac{-x^4 - 9x^2 + 8x}{5}$

$= \dfrac{-(0)^4 - 9(0)^2 + 8(0)}{5}$

$= \dfrac{0}{5} = 0$

32. $\lim\limits_{x \to 0} \dfrac{\dfrac{-1}{x + 2} - \dfrac{1}{2}}{x}$

$= \lim\limits_{x \to 0} \left(\dfrac{-1}{x + 2} - \dfrac{1}{2} \right)\left(\dfrac{1}{x} \right)$

$= \lim\limits_{x \to 0} \left[\dfrac{-2}{2(x + 2)} + \dfrac{x + 2}{2(x + 2)} \right]\left(\dfrac{1}{x} \right)$

$= \lim\limits_{x \to 0} \dfrac{-2 + x + 2}{2(x + 2)(x)}$

$= \lim\limits_{x \to 0} \dfrac{x}{2x(x + 2)}$

$= \lim\limits_{x \to 0} \dfrac{1}{2(x + 2)}$

$= \dfrac{1}{2(0 + 2)}$

$= \dfrac{1}{4}$

34. $\lim\limits_{x \to 36} \dfrac{\sqrt{x} - 6}{x - 36}$

$= \lim\limits_{x \to 36} \dfrac{\sqrt{x} - 6}{x - 36} \cdot \dfrac{\sqrt{x} + 6}{\sqrt{x} + 6}$

$= \lim\limits_{x \to 36} \dfrac{(x - 36)}{(x - 36)(\sqrt{x} + 6)}$

$= \lim\limits_{x \to 36} \dfrac{1}{\sqrt{x} + 6}$

$= \dfrac{1}{\sqrt{36} + 6}$

$= \dfrac{1}{6 + 6}$

$= \dfrac{1}{12}$

36. $\lim\limits_{h \to 0} \dfrac{(x + h)^3 - x^3}{h}$

$= \lim\limits_{h \to 0} \dfrac{(x^3 + 3x^2h + 3xh^2 + h^3) - x^3}{h}$

$= \lim\limits_{h \to 0} \dfrac{3x^2h + 3xh^2 + h^3}{h}$

$= \lim\limits_{h \to 0} \dfrac{h(3x^2 + 3xh + h^2)}{h}$

$= \lim\limits_{h \to 0} (3x^2 + 3xh + h^2)$

$= 3x^2 + 3x(0) + (0)^2$

$= 3x^2$

38. $G(x) = \dfrac{-6}{(x - 4)^2}$

(a)

x	3	3.9	3.99
G(x)	-6	-600	-60,000

x	4.01	4.1	5
G(x)	-60,000	-600	-6

$\lim\limits_{x \to 4} G(x) = -\infty$

(b) The vertical asymptote occurs when $(x - 4)^2 = 0$, or $x = 4$.

(c) The answers to (a) and (b) are related. Since $x = 4$ is a vertical asymptote, the $\lim\limits_{x \to 4} G(x)$ does not exist.

40. The function has a gap at $x = -1$ so the function is discontinuous at $x = -1$.

$f(-1) = 2$, since the heavy dot above $x = -1$ is at 2.

$\lim\limits_{x \to 1^-} f(x) = 2$

$\lim\limits_{x \to 1^+} f(x) = 4$

Thus, $\lim\limits_{x \to -1} f(x)$ does not exist.

42. By reading the graph, the function is discontinuous at $x = -2$ and $x = 3$.

$f(-2) = 1$ and $f(3) = 1$ because the heavy dots at both $x = -2$ and $x = 3$ are at 1.

$\lim\limits_{x \to -2} f(x) = -1$ because as x approaches -2 from the left or the right, $f(x)$ approaches -1.

$\lim\limits_{x \to 3} f(x) = -1$ because as x approaches 3 from the left or the right, $f(x)$ approaches -1.

44. By reading the graph, the function is discontinuous at $x = 0$ and $x = 2$.

$f(0)$ does not exist since $x = 0$ is a vertical asymptote.

$f(2)$ does not exist since there is no value shown on the graph for $x = 2$.

$\lim\limits_{x \to 0} f(x)$ is $-\infty$.

$\lim\limits_{x \to 2} f(x) = -2$ because as x approaches 2 from the left or the right, $f(x)$ approaches -2.

46. $g(x) = \dfrac{-2x}{(2x + 1)(3x + 6)}$;

x = 0, x = -1/2, x = -2

Since g is a rational function, it will not be continuous when (2x + 1)(3x + 6) = 0. Therefore, g is not continuous for x = -1/2 or x = -2, but is continuous at all other points, including x = 0.

48. $f(x) = \dfrac{4 - x}{x - 9}$;

x = 0, x = 4, x = 9

Since f is a rational function, it will not be continuous when x - 9 = 0. Therefore, f is not continuous for x = 9, but is continuous at all other points, including x = 0 and x = 4.

50. $h(x) = \dfrac{x^2 - 25}{x + 5}$;

x = 0, x = 5, x = -5

Since h is a rational function, it will not be continuous when x + 5 = 0. Therefore, f is not continuous for x = -5, but is continuous at all other points, including x = 0 and x = 5.

52. $g(x) = -3x^3 + 2x^2 - 4x + 1$

Since g(x) is a polynomial function, it is continuous at all real values of x, including x = -2, x = 3, and x = 1.

54. $r(x) = \dfrac{|5 - x|}{x - 5}$; x = -5, x = 0, x = 5

Since r is a rational function, it is not continuous at x = 5, but is continuous at all other points, including x = -5 and x = 0.

56. (a) $\lim\limits_{x \to 6} P(x)$

As x approaches 6 from the left or the right, the value of P(x) for the corresponding point on the graph approaches 500.

Thus, $\lim\limits_{x \to 6} P(x) = \$500$.

(b) $\lim\limits_{x \to -10} P(x) = \$1500$

because as x approaches 10 from the left, P(x) approaches $1500.

(c) $\lim\limits_{x \to 10^+} P(x) = \$1000$ because as x approaches 10 from the right, P(x) approaches $1000.

(d) Since $\lim\limits_{x \to 10^+} P(x) \neq \lim\limits_{x \to 10^-} P(x)$,

$\lim\limits_{x \to 10} P(x)$ does not exist.

(e) From the graph, the function is discontinuous at x = 10. This may be the result of a change of shifts.

(f) From the graph, the second shift will be as profitable as the first shift when 15 units are produced.

58. In dollars,

F(x) = 1.20x if 0 < x ≤ 100

F(x) = 1.0x if x > 100.

(a) F(80) = 1.20(80) = $96

(b) F(150) = 1.0(150) = $150

(c) F(100) = 120(100) = $120

(d) F is discontinuous at x = 100 because the price changes occur at that value.

60. (a) $\lim\limits_{x \to 80} T(x)$ = 6 cents because T(x) is constant at 6 cents as x approaches 80 from the left or the right.

(b) $\lim\limits_{x \to 73^-} T(x)$ = 5 cents because as x approaches 73 from the left, T(x) is constant at 5 cents.

(c) $\lim\limits_{x \to 73^+} T(x)$ = 6 cents because as x approaches 73 from the right T(x) is constant at 6 cents.

(d) $\lim\limits_{x \to 73} T(x)$ does not exist because $\lim\limits_{x \to 73^-} T(x) \neq \lim\limits_{x \to 73^+} T(x)$.

(e) The graph is discontinuous at the years 1935, 1943, 1949, 1967, 1973, and 1991. Any three of these years would be acceptable.

62. This graph has no breaks or gaps. Thus, the graph is discontinuous for no value of Q.

Section 2.2

2. $y = -4x^2 - 6 = f(x)$ between x = 2 and x = 5

Average rate of change

$$= \frac{f(5) - f(2)}{5 - 2}$$

$$= \frac{(-106) - (-22)}{5 - 2}$$

$$= \frac{-106 + 22}{3}$$

$$= \frac{-84}{3}$$

$$= -28$$

4. $y = -3x^3 + 2x^2 - 4x + 1 = f(x)$ between x = 0 and x = 1

Average rate of change

$$= \frac{f(1) - f(0)}{1 - 0}$$

$$= \frac{(-4) - (1)}{1 - 0}$$

$$= \frac{-5}{1}$$

$$= -5$$

6. $y = \sqrt{3x - 2} = f(x)$ between x = 1 and x = 2

Average rate of change

$$= \frac{f(2) - f(1)}{2 - 1}$$

$$= \frac{2 - 1}{2 - 1}$$

$$= \frac{1}{1}$$

$$= 1$$

8. $y = \dfrac{-5}{2x - 3} = f(x)$ between $x = 2$ and

$x = 4$

Average rate of change

$= \dfrac{f(4) - f(2)}{4 - 2}$

$= \dfrac{-1 - (-5)}{4 - 2}$

$= \dfrac{-1 + 5}{2}$

$= \dfrac{4}{2}$

$= 2$

10. $s(t) = t^2 + 5t + 2$

$\displaystyle\lim_{h \to 0} \dfrac{s(1 + h) - s(1)}{h}$

$= \displaystyle\lim_{h \to 0} \dfrac{[(1+h)^2 + 5(1+h) + 2] - [(1)^2 + 5(1) + 2]}{h}$

$= \displaystyle\lim_{h \to 0} \dfrac{[1 + 2h + h^2 + 5 + 5h + 2] - [1 + 5 + 2]}{h}$

$= \displaystyle\lim_{h \to 0} \dfrac{8 + 7h + h^2 - 8}{h}$

$= \displaystyle\lim_{h \to 0} \dfrac{7h + h^2}{h}$

$= \displaystyle\lim_{h \to 0} \dfrac{h(7 + h)}{h}$

$= \displaystyle\lim_{h \to 0} (7 + h)$

$= 7$

12. $s(t) = t^3 + 2t + 9$

$\displaystyle\lim_{h \to 0} \dfrac{s(1 + h) - s(1)}{h}$

$= \displaystyle\lim_{h \to 0} \dfrac{[(1+h)^3 + 2(1+h) + 9] - [(1)^3 + 2(1) + 9]}{h}$

$= \displaystyle\lim_{h \to 0} \dfrac{[1 + 3h + 3h^2 + h^3 + 2 + 2h + 9] - [1 + 2 + 9]}{h}$

$= \displaystyle\lim_{h \to 0} \dfrac{h^3 + 3h^2 + 5h + 12 - 12}{h}$

$= \displaystyle\lim_{h \to 0} \dfrac{h^3 + 3h^2 + 5h}{h}$

$= \displaystyle\lim_{h \to 0} \dfrac{h(h^2 + 3h + 5)}{h}$

$= \displaystyle\lim_{h \to 0} (h^2 + 3h + 5)$

$= 5$

14. $f(x) = x^2 + 2x$ at $x = 0$

$\displaystyle\lim_{h \to 0} \dfrac{f(0 + h) - f(0)}{h}$

$= \displaystyle\lim_{h \to 0} \dfrac{(0 + h)^2 + 2(0 + h) - [0^2 + 2(0)]}{h}$

$= \displaystyle\lim_{h \to 0} \dfrac{h^2 + 2h}{h}$

$= \displaystyle\lim_{h \to 0} \dfrac{h(h + 2)}{h}$

$= \displaystyle\lim_{h \to 0} h + 2$

$= 2$

16. $g(t) = 1 - t^2$ at $t = -1$

$\displaystyle\lim_{h \to 0} \dfrac{g(-1 + h) - g(-1)}{h}$

$= \displaystyle\lim_{h \to 0} \dfrac{1 - (-1 + h)^2 - [1 - (-1)^2]}{h}$

$= \displaystyle\lim_{h \to 0} \dfrac{1 - (1 - 2h + h^2) - 1 + 1}{h}$

$= \displaystyle\lim_{h \to 0} \dfrac{2h - h^2}{h}$

$= \displaystyle\lim_{h \to 0} \dfrac{h(2 - h)}{h}$

$= \displaystyle\lim_{h \to 0} (2 - h)$

$= 2$

20. Let $s(x)$ be the function representing sales in thousands of dollars of
x thousand catalogs.

(a) $s(20) = 40$

$s(10) = 30$

Average rate of change

$$= \frac{s(20) - s(10)}{20 - 10}$$

$$= \frac{40 - 30}{10}$$

$$= 1$$

As catalog distribution changes from 10,000 to 20,000, sales will have an average increase of $1000. Thus, on the average, sales will increase $1000 for each additional 1000 catalogs distributed.

(b) $s(30) = 46$
    $s(20) = 40$

Average rate of change

$$= \frac{s(30) - s(20)}{30 - 20}$$

$$= \frac{46 - 40}{10}$$

$$= \frac{6}{10}$$

$$= \frac{3}{5}$$

As catalog distribution changes from 20,000 to 30,000, on the average, sales will increase $600 for each additional 1000 catalogs distributed.

(c) $s(40) = 50$
    $s(30) = 46$

Average rate of change

$$= \frac{s(40) - s(30)}{40 - 30}$$

$$= \frac{50 - 46}{10}$$

$$= \frac{4}{10}$$

$$= \frac{2}{5}$$

As catalog distribution changes from 30,000 to 40,000, on the average, sales will increase $400 for each additional 1000 catalogs distributed.

(d) As more catalogs are distributed, overall sales increase at a smaller and smaller rate.

22. (a) $s(1985) = 32$
     $s(1986) = 27$

Average rate of change

$$= \frac{s(1986) - s(1985)}{1986 - 1985}$$

$$= \frac{27 - 32}{1}$$

$$= -5$$

(b) $s(1986) = 27$
    $s(1986) = 24$

Average rate of change

$$= \frac{s(1988) - s(1986)}{1988 - 1986}$$

$$= \frac{24 - 27}{2}$$

$$= -\frac{3}{2}$$

(c) $s(1988) = 24$
    $s(1989) = 23.5$

Average rate of change

$$= \frac{s(1989) - s(1988)}{1989 - 1988}$$

$$= \frac{23.5 - 24}{5}$$

$$= -.5$$

(d) s(1989) = 23.5

   s(1990) = 22.5

   Average rate of change = $\dfrac{s(1990) - s(1989)}{1990 - 1989} = \dfrac{22.5 - 23.5}{1} = -1$

(e) The decline in market share seems to be tapering off since the average rate of change is getting less negative, that is, it is increasing overall.

(f) The decline was the greatest when the average rate of change was the most negative, that is the least, from 1985 to 1986.

24. $P(x) = 2x^2 - 5x + 6$

(a) P(4) = 18

   P(2) = 4

   Average rate of change of profit = $\dfrac{P(4) - P(2)}{4 - 2} = \dfrac{18 - 4}{2} = \dfrac{14}{2} = 7$

(b) P(3) = 9

   P(2) = 4

   Average rate of change of profit = $\dfrac{P(3) - P(2)}{3 - 2} = \dfrac{9 - 4}{1} = 5$

(c) For h = .01,

   $\dfrac{P(2 + h) - P(2)}{h} = \dfrac{.0302}{.01} = 3.02$

   For h = .001,

   $\dfrac{P(2 + h) - P(2)}{h} = \dfrac{.003002}{.001} = 3.002$

   For h = .0001,

   $\dfrac{P(2 + h) - P(2)}{h} = \dfrac{.00030002}{.0001} = 3.0002$

(d) As $h \to 0$, $\dfrac{P(2 + h) - P(2)}{h} \to 3$.

(e) $\lim\limits_{h \to 0} \dfrac{P(2 + h) - P(2)}{h}$

$= \lim\limits_{h \to 0} \dfrac{[2(2 + h)^2 - 5(2 + h) + 6] - [2(2)^2 - 5(2) + 6]}{h}$

$= \lim\limits_{h \to 0} \dfrac{[2(4 + 4h + h^2) - 10 - 5h + 6] - [4]}{h}$

$= \lim\limits_{h \to 0} \dfrac{[8 + 8h + 2h^2 - 10 - 5h + 6 - 4]}{h}$

$= \lim\limits_{h \to 0} \dfrac{2h^2 + 3h}{h}$

$= \lim\limits_{h \to 0} \dfrac{h(2h + 3)}{h}$

$= \lim\limits_{h \to 0} (2h + 3)$

$= 3$

(f) The limit in part (e) represents the instantaneous rate of change of profit when x = 2. The value of the instantaneous rate of change when x = 2 is 3.

26. $R = 10x - .002x^2$

(a) Average rate of change $= \dfrac{R(1001) - R(1000)}{1001 - 1000} = \dfrac{8005.998 - 8000}{1} = 5.998$

The average rate of change is $5998.

(b) Marginal revenue

$= \lim\limits_{h \to 0} \dfrac{R(1000 + h) - R(1000)}{h}$

$= \lim\limits_{h \to 0} \dfrac{[10(1000 + h) - .002(1000 + h)^2] - [10(1000) - .002(1000)^2]}{h}$

$= \lim\limits_{h \to 0} \dfrac{[10,000 + 10h - .002(1,000,000 + 2000h + h^2] - 8000}{h}$

$= \lim\limits_{h \to 0} \dfrac{10,000 + 10h - 2000 - 4h - .002h^2 - 8000}{h}$

$= \lim\limits_{h \to 0} \dfrac{6h - .002h^2}{h}$

$= \lim\limits_{h \to 0} \dfrac{h(6 - .002h)}{h}$

$= \lim\limits_{h \to 0} (6 - .002h) = 6$

The marginal revenue is $6000.

(c) Additional revenue

    = R(1001) − R(1000)

    = [10(1001) − .002(1001)²]

      − [10(1000) − .002(1000)²]

    = 8005.998 − 8000

    = 5.998

The additional revenue is $5998.

(d) The answers to parts (a) and (c) are the same.

28. (a) P(2) = 5, P(1) = 3

Average rate of change

$$= \frac{P(2) - P(1)}{2 - 1}$$

$$= \frac{5 - 3}{2 - 1}$$

$$= \frac{2}{1}$$

$$= 2$$

From 1 min to 2 min, the population of bacteria increases, on the average, 2 million per min.

(b) P(3) = 4.2, P(2) = 5

Average rate of change

$$= \frac{P(3) - P(2)}{3 - 2}$$

$$= \frac{4.2 - 5}{3 - 2}$$

$$= \frac{-.8}{1}$$

$$= -.8$$

From 2 min to 3 min, the population of bacteria decreases, on the average, −.8 million or 800,000 per min.

(c) P(3) = 4.2, P(4) = 2

Average rate of change

$$= \frac{P(4) - P(3)}{4 - 3}$$

$$= \frac{2 - 4.2}{4 - 3}$$

$$= \frac{-2.2}{1}$$

$$= -2.2$$

From 3 min to 4 min, the population of bacteria decreases, on the average, −2.2 million per min.

(d) P(4) = 2, P(5) = 1

Average rate of change

$$= \frac{P(5) - P(4)}{5 - 4}$$

$$= \frac{1 - 2}{5 - 4}$$

$$= \frac{-1}{1}$$

$$= -1$$

From 4 min to 5 min, the population decreases, on the avaerage, −1 million per min.

(e) The population increased up to 2 min after the bactericide was introduced, but decreased after 2 min.

(f) The bacteria were decreasing fastest between 3 and 4 min after the bactericide was introduced; the rate began to decrease after about 4 min.

30. $R(t) = -.03t^2 + 15$

    (a)   Instantaneous rate of change where $t = 5$ is

$$\lim_{h\to0} \frac{-.03(5+h)^2 + 15 - [-.03(5)^2 + 15]}{h} = \lim_{h\to0} \frac{-.75 - .3h + .03h^2 + 15 + .75 - 15}{h}$$

$$= \lim_{h\to0} \frac{-.3h + .03h^2}{h}$$

$$= -.3 \text{ word per min.}$$

    (b)   At $t = 15$, the instantaneous rate of change is

$$\lim_{h\to0} \frac{-.03(15+h)^2 + 15 - [-.03(15)^2 + 15]}{h}$$

$$= \lim_{h\to0} \frac{-.03(225 + 30h + h^2) + 15 + .03(225) - 15}{h}$$

$$= \lim_{h\to0} \frac{-.9h + h^2}{h}$$

$$= -.9 \text{ word per minute.}$$

32.   **(a)** $T(1000) = 15,000°$, $T(3000) = 21,000°$

        Average rate of change of temperature $= \dfrac{T(3000) - T(1000)}{3000 - 1000}$

$$= \frac{21,000° - 15,000°}{2000}$$

$$= \frac{6000°}{2000} = 3°$$

On the average, the temperature will rise about $3°$ per thousand ft from 1000 to 3000 ft.

    (b) $T(1000) = 15,000°$, $T(5000) = 20,000°$

        Average rate of change of temperature $= \dfrac{T(5000) - T(1000)}{5000 - 1000}$

$$= \frac{20,000° - 15,000°}{5000 - 1000}$$

$$= \frac{5000°}{4000} = 1.25°$$

On the average, the temperature will rise about $1.25°$ per thousand ft from 1000 to 5000 ft.

    (c) $T(3000) = 21,000°$, $T(9000) = 14,000°$

        Average rate of change of temperature $= \dfrac{T(9000) - T(3000)}{9000 - 3000}$

$$= \frac{14,000° - 21,000°}{9000 - 3000}$$

$$= \frac{-7000°}{6000} = -\frac{7°}{6}$$

On the average, the temperature will drop about $-7/6°$ per thousand ft from 3000 to 9000 ft.

(d) $T(1000) = 15,000°$, $T(9000) = 14,000°$

$$\text{Average rate of change of temperature} = \frac{T(9000) - T(1000)}{9000 - 1000}$$

$$= \frac{14,000° - 15,000°}{9000 - 1000}$$

$$= \frac{-1000°}{8000} = -\frac{1°}{8}$$

On the average, the temperature will drop about $-1/8°$ per thousand ft from 1000 to 9000 ft.

(e)   The temperature is highest at the crest of the curve or 3000 ft; it is lowest at 1000 ft. From the graph, it appears that temperature continues to decrease; the temperature would be lowest at 10,000 ft.

(f)   At 9000 ft the temperature is the same as 1000 ft.

34. $s(t) = t^2 + 5t - 2$

(a)   Average velocity $= \dfrac{s(6) - s(4)}{6 - 4} = \dfrac{64 - 34}{6 - 4} = \dfrac{30}{2} = 15$ ft per sec

(b)   Average velocity $= \dfrac{s(5) - s(4)}{5 - 4} = \dfrac{48 - 34}{5 - 1} = \dfrac{14}{1} = 14$ ft per sec

(c)   For $h = .01$,

$$\frac{s(4 + h) - s(4)}{h} = \frac{.1301}{.01} = 13.01$$

For $h = .0001$,

$$\frac{s(4 + h) - s(4)}{h} = \frac{.013001}{.001} = 13.001$$

For $h = .0001$,

$$\frac{s(4 + h) - s(4)}{h} = \frac{.00130001}{.0001} = 13.0001$$

(d)   As h gets smaller ($h \to 0$),

$$\frac{s(4 + h) - s(4)}{h} \text{ approaches } 13.$$

Thus,

$$\lim_{h \to 0} \frac{s(4 + h) - s(4)}{h} = 13$$

This represents instantaneous velocity when t = 4.

Section 2.3

2. $f(x) = 6x^2 - 4x$; x = -1

Step 1 $f(x + h)$

$= 6(x + h)^2 - 4(x + h)$

$= 6(x^2 + 2xh + h^2) - 4x - 4h$

$= 6x^2 + 12xh + 6h^2 - 4x - 4h$

Step 2 $f(x + h)f(x)$

$= 6x^2 + 12xh + 6h^2 - 4x - 4h$

$- 6x^2 + 4x$

$= 6h^2 + 12xh - 4h$

$= h(6h + 12x - 4)$

Step 3 $\dfrac{f(x + h) - f(x)}{h}$

$= \dfrac{h(6h + 12x - 4)}{h}$

$= 6h + 12x - 4$

Step 4 $f'(x) = \lim_{h \to 0} \dfrac{f(x + h) - f(x)}{h}$

$= \lim_{h \to 0} (6h + 12x - 4)$

$= 12x - 4$

$f'(-1) = 12(-1) - 4 = -16$ is the slope of the tangent line at x = -1.

4. $f(x) = \dfrac{6}{x}$; x = -1

$f(x + h) = \dfrac{6}{x + h}$

$f(x + h) - f(x) = \dfrac{6}{x + h} - \dfrac{6}{x}$

$= \dfrac{6x - 6(x + h)}{x(x + h)}$

$= \dfrac{-6h}{x(x + h)}$

$\dfrac{f(x + h) - f(x)}{h} = \dfrac{-6h}{hx(x + h)}$

$= \dfrac{-6}{x(x + h)}$

$f'(x) = \lim_{h \to 0} \dfrac{f(x + h) - f(x)}{h}$

$= \lim_{h \to 0} \dfrac{-6}{x(x + h)}$

$= \dfrac{-6}{x^2}$

$f'(-1) = \dfrac{-6}{(-1)^2} = -6$ is the slope of the tangent line at x = -1.

6. $f(x) = -3\sqrt{x}$; x = 1

Steps 1–3 are combined.

$\dfrac{f(x + h) - f(x)}{h}$

$= \dfrac{-3\sqrt{x + h} + 3\sqrt{x}}{h}$

Rationalize the numerator.

$= \dfrac{-3\sqrt{x + h} + 3\sqrt{x}}{h} \cdot \dfrac{-3\sqrt{x + h} - 3\sqrt{x}}{-3\sqrt{x + h} - 3\sqrt{x}}$

$= \dfrac{9(x + h) - 9x}{h(-3\sqrt{x + h} - 3\sqrt{x})}$

$= \dfrac{9x + 9h - 9x}{h(-3\sqrt{x + h} - 3\sqrt{x})}$

$= \dfrac{9}{-3\sqrt{x + h} - 3\sqrt{x}}$

$= \dfrac{3}{-\sqrt{x + h} - \sqrt{x}}$

$f'(x) = \lim_{h \to 0} \dfrac{3}{-\sqrt{x + h} - \sqrt{x}}$

$= \dfrac{3}{-\sqrt{x} - \sqrt{x}} = \dfrac{3}{-2\sqrt{x}}$

$f'(1) = \dfrac{3}{-2\sqrt{1}} = -\dfrac{3}{2}$ is the slope of the tangent line at x = 1.

8. $f(x) = 6 - x^2;\ x = -1$

$$\frac{f(x + h) - f(x)}{h}$$

$$= \frac{[6 - (x + h)^2] - [6 - (x)^2]}{h}$$

$$= \frac{[6 - (x^2 + 2xh + h^2)] - [6 - x^2]}{h}$$

$$= \frac{6 - x^2 - 2xh - h^2 - 6 + x^2}{h}$$

$$= \frac{-2xh - h^2}{h} = \frac{h(-2x - h)}{h} = -2x - h$$

$$f'(x) = \lim_{h \to 0} -2x - h = -2x$$

$f'(-1) = -2(-1) = 2$ is the slope of the tangent line at $x = -1$. Use $m = 2$ and $(-1, 5)$ in the point-slope form.

$$y - 5 = 2(x + 1)$$
$$y - 5 = 2x + 2$$
$$2x - y = -7$$

10. $f(x) = \frac{-3}{x + 1};\ x = 1$

$$\frac{f(x + h) - f(x)}{h}$$

$$= \frac{\dfrac{-3}{(x + h) + 1} - \dfrac{-3}{x + 1}}{h}$$

$$= \frac{\dfrac{-3(x + 1) + 3(x + h + 1)}{(x + 1)(x + h + 1)}}{h}$$

$$= \frac{\dfrac{-3x - 3 + 3x + 3h + 3}{(x + 1)(x + h + 1)}}{h}$$

$$= \frac{3h}{h(x + 1)(x + h + 1)}$$

$$f'(x) = \lim_{h \to 0} \frac{3}{(x + 1)(x + h + 1)}$$

$$= \frac{3}{(x + 1)^2}$$

$f'(1) = \dfrac{3}{(1 + 1)^2} = \dfrac{3}{4}$ is the slope of the tangent line at $x = 1$. Use $m = \dfrac{3}{4}$ and $\left(1, -\dfrac{3}{2}\right)$ in the point-slope form.

$$y - \left(-\frac{3}{2}\right) = \frac{3}{4}(x - 1)$$
$$y + \frac{3}{2} = \frac{3}{4}x - \frac{3}{4}$$
$$4y + 6 = 3x - 3$$
$$3x - 4y = 9$$

12. $f(x) = \sqrt{x}$

$$\frac{f(x + h) - f(x)}{h}$$

$$= \frac{\sqrt{x + h} - \sqrt{x}}{h}$$

$$= \frac{\sqrt{x + h} - \sqrt{x}}{h} \cdot \frac{\sqrt{x + h} + \sqrt{x}}{\sqrt{x + h} + \sqrt{x}}$$

$$= \frac{x + h - x}{h(\sqrt{x + h} + \sqrt{x})}$$

$$= \frac{h}{h(\sqrt{x + h} + \sqrt{x})} = \frac{1}{\sqrt{x + h} + \sqrt{x}}$$

$$f'(x) = \lim_{h \to 0} \frac{1}{\sqrt{x + h} + \sqrt{x}} = \frac{1}{2\sqrt{x}}$$

$$f'(25) = \frac{1}{2\sqrt{25}} = \frac{1}{2 \cdot 5} = \frac{1}{10}$$

Use $m = \dfrac{1}{10}$ and $(25, 5)$ in the point-slope form.

$$y - 5 = \frac{1}{10}(x - 25)$$
$$10y - 50 = x - 25$$
$$\text{or}\quad 10y - x = 25$$

For Exercises 14–18, choose any two convenient points on each of the tangent lines.

14. Using the points $(2, 2)$ and $(-2, 6)$, we have

$$m = \frac{6 - 2}{-2 - 2} = \frac{4}{-4} = -1.$$

16. Using the points $(3, -1)$ and $(-3, 4)$, we have

$$m = \frac{4 - (-1)}{-3 - 3} = \frac{5}{-6} = -\frac{5}{6}.$$

18. The line tangent to the curve at $(4, 2)$, is a vertical line. A vertical line has undefined slope.

20. (a) $g(x) = \sqrt[3]{x}$

$$g'(x) = \lim_{h \to 0} \frac{g(x + h) - g(x)}{h}$$

$$= \lim_{h \to 0} \frac{\sqrt[3]{x + h} - \sqrt[3]{x}}{h}$$

$$g'(0) = \lim_{h \to 0} \frac{\sqrt[3]{0 + h} - \sqrt[3]{0}}{h}$$

$$= \lim_{h \to 0} \frac{\sqrt[3]{h}}{h}$$

This limit does not exist, because it is not defined for $h = 0$ and the expression cannot be simplified to eliminate h in the denominator.

(b) The derivative does not exist where the tangent line is vertical because the derivative doesn't exist there.

22. $f(x) = -4x^2 + 11x$

$$\frac{f(x + h) - f(x)}{h}$$

$$= \frac{-4(x + h)^2 + 11x - (-4x^2 + 11x)}{h}$$

$$= \frac{-8xh - 4h^2 + 11h}{h}$$

$$f'(x) = \lim_{h \to 0} (-8x - 4h + 11)$$

$$= -8x + 11$$

$$f'(2) = -8(2) + 11 = -5$$

$$f'(0) = -8(0) + 11 = 11$$

$$f'(-3) = -8(-3) + 11 = 35$$

24. $f(x) = 8x + 6$

$$\frac{f(x + h) - f(x)}{h}$$

$$= \frac{[8(x + h) + 6] - (8x + 6)}{h}$$

$$= \frac{(8x + 8h + 6) - (8x + 6)}{h}$$

$$= \frac{8h}{h}$$

$$= 8$$

$$f'(x) = \lim_{h \to 0} 8 = 8$$

$$f'(2) = 8; \; f'(0) = 8; \; f(-3) = 8$$

26. $f(x) = -\dfrac{2}{x}$

$$\frac{f(x + h) - f(x)}{h} = \frac{\dfrac{-2}{x + h} - \left(\dfrac{-2}{x}\right)}{h}$$

$$= \frac{\dfrac{-2x + 2(x + h)}{(x + h)x}}{h}$$

$$= \frac{2h}{h(x + h)x}$$

$$= \frac{2}{(x + h)x}$$

$$f'(x) = \lim_{h \to 0} \frac{2}{(x + h)x} = \frac{2}{x^2}$$

$$f'(2) = \frac{2}{2^2} = \frac{1}{2}$$

$f'(0) = \dfrac{2}{0^2}$ is undefined, so $f'(0)$

does not exist.

$$f'(3) = \frac{2}{3^2} = \frac{2}{9}$$

28. $f(x) = \sqrt{x}$

$$\frac{f(x + h) - f(x)}{h}$$

$$= \frac{\sqrt{x + h} - \sqrt{x}}{h} \cdot \frac{\sqrt{x + h} + \sqrt{x}}{\sqrt{x + h} + \sqrt{x}}$$

$$= \frac{(x + h) - x}{h(\sqrt{x + h} + \sqrt{x})}$$

$$= \frac{h}{h(\sqrt{x + h} + \sqrt{x})}$$

$$= \frac{1}{\sqrt{x + h} + \sqrt{x}}$$

$$f'(x) = \lim_{h \to 0} \frac{1}{\sqrt{x + h} + \sqrt{x}} = \frac{1}{2\sqrt{x}}$$

$$f'(2) = \frac{1}{2\sqrt{2}}$$

$f'(0) = \dfrac{1}{2\sqrt{0}}$ is undefined so $f'(0)$

does not exist.

$f'(-3) = \dfrac{1}{2\sqrt{-3}}$ is not a real number so

$f'(-3)$ does not exist.

30. At $x = 0$, the graph of $f(x)$ has a sharp point. Therefore, there is no derivative for $x = 0$.

32. For $x = \pm 6$, the graph of $f(x)$ has sharp points. Therefore, there is no derivative for $x = 6$ or $x = -6$.

34. For $x = -3$ and $x = 0$, the tangent to the graph of $f(x)$ is vertical. For $x = -1$, there is a gap in the function $f(x)$. For $x = 2$ the function $f(x)$ does not exist. For $x = 3$ and $x = 5$, the graph $f(x)$ has sharp points. Therefore, no derivative exists for $x = -3$, $x = -1$, $x = 0$, $x = 2$, $x = 3$, and $x = 5$.

36. If the rate of change of $f(x)$ is zero when $x = a$, the tangent line at that point must have a slope of zero. Thus, the tangent line is horizontal at that point.

38. The zeros of graph (b) correspond to the turning points of graph (a), the points where the derivative is zero. Graph (a) gives the distance while graph (b) gives the velocity.

40. $D(p) = -2p^2 + 4p + 6$

    D is demand, p is price.

    (a) Given that $D'(p) = -4p + 4$, the rate of change of demand with respect to price is $-4p + 4$, the derivative of the function $D(p)$.

(b) $D'(10) = -4(10) + 4$
$$= -36$$

The demand is decreasing at the rate of about 36 items for each increase in price of \$1.

42. $P(x) = 1000 + 32x - 2x^2$

Marginal Profit $= P'(x) = 32 - 4x$

(a) \$8000 is 8 thousand so $x = 8$.

$P'(8) = 32 - 4(8) = 32 - 32 = 0$

No, the firm should not increase production, since the marginal profit is 0.

(b) \$6000, $x = 6$

$P'(6) = 32 - 4(6) = 32 - 24 = 8$

Yes, the firm should increase production, since the marginal profit is positive.

(c) \$12,000, $x = 12$

$P'(12) = 32 - 4(12)$
$$= 32 - 48 = -16$$

No, because the marginal profit is negative.

(d) \$20,000, $x = 20$

$P'(20) = 32 - 4(20)$
$$= 32 - 80 = -48$$

No, because the marginal profit is negative.

44. $C(x) = 1000 + .24x^2$
$0 \le x \le 30,000$

(a) The marginal cost is given by
$C'(x) = .48x, \ 0 \le x \le 30,000.$

(b) $C'(100) = .48(100) = 48$

This represents the fact that the cost of producing the next (101st) taco is approximately 48.

(c) The exact cost to produce the 101st taco is

$C(101) - C(100)$
$$= [1000 + .24(101)^2]$$
$$- [1000 + .24(100)^2]$$
$$= 1000 + 2448.24 - 1000 - 2400$$
$$= 48.24.$$

(d) The exact cost of producing the 101st taco is .24 greater than the approximate cost.

46. The derivative is equal to the slope of the tangent line.
At the first point,

$$m = \frac{4000 - 2000}{2 - 0}$$
$$= 1000.$$

The shellfish are increasing at a rate of 1000 shellfish per unit of time.
At the second point,

$$m = \frac{12,000 - 10,000}{13 - 10}$$
$$\approx 700.$$

The population is increasing more slowly, at a rate of about 700 shellfish per unit of time.
At the third point,

$$m = \frac{12,000 - 11,000}{16 - 12}$$
$$= 250.$$

The population growth is increasing much slower, at a rate of 250 shellfish per unit of time.

h	500	1500	3500	5000
f'(h)	−.005	.008	0	−.00125

48. The slope of the tangent line to the graph at the first point is found by finding two points on the tangent line.

$(x_1, y_1) = 1000, 13.5)$

$(x_2, y_2) = (0, 18.5)$

$$m = \frac{18.5 - 13.5}{0 - 1000} = \frac{5}{-1000} = -.005$$

At the second point, we have

$(x_1, y_1) = (1000, 13.5)$

$(x_2, y_2) = (2000, 21.5).$

$$m = \frac{21.5 - 13.5}{2000 - 1000} = \frac{8}{1000} = .008$$

At the third point, we have

$(x_1, y_1) = (5000, 20)$

$(x_2, y_2) = (3000, 22.5).$

$$m = \frac{22.5 - 20}{3000 - 5000} = \frac{2.5}{-2000} = -.00125$$

At 500 ft, the temperature decreases .005° per foot. At about 1500 ft, the temperature increases .008° per foot. At 5000 ft, the temperature decreases .00125° per foot.

50. (a) Use the slopes found in Exercise 48 to complete the chart. Note that 3500 corresponds to the turning point of f(x) where f'(h) = 0.

(b)

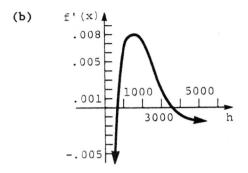

Section 2.4

2. $y = 3x^3 - x^2 - \dfrac{x}{12}$

$y' = 3(3x^{3-1}) - 2x^{2-1} - \dfrac{1}{12}x^{1-1}$

$= 9x^2 - 2x - \dfrac{1}{12}$

4. $y = 3x^4 + 11x^3 + 2x^2 - 4x$

$y' = 3(4x^{4-1}) + 11(3x^{3-1})$
$\quad + 2(2x^{2-1}) - 4x^{1-1}$

$= 12x^3 + 33x^2 + 4x - 4$

6. $f(x) = -2x^{2.5} + 8x^{.5}$

$f'(x) = -2(2.5x^{2.5-1}) + 8(.5x^{.5-1})$

$= -5x^{1.5} + 4x^{-.5}$

or $-5x^{1.5} + \dfrac{4}{x^{.5}}$

8. $y = -24t^{5/2} - 6t^{1/2}$

$y' = -24\left(\dfrac{5}{2}t^{5/2-1}\right) - 6\left(\dfrac{1}{2}t^{1/2-1}\right)$

$= -60t^{3/2} - 3t^{-1/2}$

or $-60t^{3/2} - \dfrac{3}{t^{1/2}}$

10. $y = -100\sqrt{x} - 11x^{2/3}$

$\qquad = -100x^{1/2} - 11x^{2/3}$

$\quad y' = -100\left(\frac{1}{2}x^{1/2\,-\,1}\right) - 11\left(\frac{2}{3}x^{2/3-1}\right)$

$\qquad = -50x^{-1/2} - \dfrac{22x^{-1/3}}{3}$

$\qquad$ or $\quad \dfrac{-50}{x^{1/2}} - \dfrac{22}{3x^{1/3}}$

12. $y = 10x^{-2} + 3x^{-4} - 6x$

$\quad y' = 10(-2x^{-2-1}) + 3(-4x^{-4-1}) - 6x^{1-1}$

$\qquad = -20x^{-3} - 12x^{-5} - 6$

$\qquad$ or $\quad \dfrac{-20}{x^3} - \dfrac{12}{x^5} - 6$

14. $f(t) = \dfrac{6}{t} - \dfrac{8}{t^2}$

$\qquad\quad = 6t^{-1} - 8t^{-2}$

$\quad f'(t) = 6(-1t^{-1-1}) - 8(-2t^{-2-1})$

$\qquad\quad = -6t^{-2} + 16t^{-3}$

$\qquad\qquad$ or $\quad \dfrac{-6}{t^2} + \dfrac{16}{t^3}$

16. $y = \dfrac{9}{x^4} - \dfrac{8}{x^3} + \dfrac{2}{x}$

$\qquad = 9x^{-4} - 8x^{-3} + 2x^{-1}$

$\quad y' = 9(-4x^{-5}) - 8(-3x^{-4}) + 2(-x^{-2})$

$\qquad = -36x^{-5} + 24x^{-4} - 2x^{-2}$

$\qquad$ or $\quad \dfrac{-36}{x^5} + \dfrac{24}{x^4} - \dfrac{2}{x^2}$

18. $p(x) = -10x^{-1/2} + 8x^{-3/2}$

$\quad p'(x) = -10\left(-\frac{1}{2}x^{-3/2}\right) + 8\left(-\frac{3}{2}x^{-5/2}\right)$

$\qquad\quad = 5x^{-3/2} - 12x^{-5/2}$

$\qquad\qquad$ or $\quad \dfrac{5}{x^{3/2}} - \dfrac{12}{x^{5/2}}$

20. $y = \dfrac{6}{4\sqrt{x}} = 6x^{-1/4}$

$\quad y' = 6\left(-\frac{1}{4}\right)x^{-5/4}$

$\qquad = -\dfrac{3}{2}x^{-5/4}$

$\qquad$ or $\quad \dfrac{-3}{2x^{5/4}}$

22.   A quadratic function has degree 2.
When the derivative is taken, the
power will decrease by 1 and the
derivative function will be linear;
choice (b).

24. $y = -3x^{-2} - 4x^{-5}$

$\quad \dfrac{dy}{dx} = -3(-2x^{-2-1}) - 4(-5x^{-5-1})$

$\qquad = 6x^{-3} + 20x^{-6}$

$\qquad$ or $\quad \dfrac{6}{x^3} + \dfrac{20}{x^6}$

26. $D_x\left[\dfrac{8}{\sqrt[4]{x}} - \dfrac{3}{\sqrt{x^3}}\right]$

$\qquad = D_x\left[8x^{-1/4} - 3x^{-3/2}\right]$

$\qquad = 8\left(-\frac{1}{4}x^{-5/4}\right) - 3\left(-\frac{3}{2}x^{-5/2}\right)$

$\qquad = -2x^{-5/4} + \dfrac{9x^{-5/2}}{2}$

$\qquad$ or $\quad \dfrac{-2}{x^{5/4}} + \dfrac{9}{2x^{5/2}}$

28. $f(x) = \dfrac{x^3}{9} - 8x^2$

$\qquad\quad = \dfrac{1}{9}x^3 - 8x^2$

$\quad f'(x) = \dfrac{1}{9}(3x^2) - 8(2x)$

$\qquad\quad = \dfrac{1}{3}x^2 - 16x$

$$f'(3) = \frac{1}{3}(3)^2 - 16(3)$$

$$= 3 - 48 = -45$$

30. $\dfrac{d}{dx}(4x^3 - 6x^{-2})$

$$= 4(3x^2) - 6(-2x^{-3})$$

$$= 12x^2 + 12x^{-3}$$

$$= 12x^2 + \frac{12}{x^3} \qquad choice~(c)$$

$$= \frac{12x^2(x^3) + 12}{x^3}$$

$$= \frac{12x^5 + 12}{x^3} \qquad choice~(b)$$

Neither choice (a) nor choice (d) equals

$$\frac{d}{dx}(4x^3 - 6x^{-2}).$$

32. $y = x^4 - 5x^3 + 2;~ x = 2$

$$y' = 4x^3 - 15x^2$$

$$y'(2) = 4(2)^3 - 15(2)^2$$

$$= -28 \text{ is the slope of tangent line at } x = 2.$$

Use (2, -22) to obtain the equation.

$$y - (-22) = -28(x - 2)$$

$$y = -28x + 34$$

$$28x + y = 34$$

34. $y = -2x^{1/2} + x^{3/2}$

$$y' = -2\left[\frac{1}{2}x^{-1/2}\right] + \frac{3}{2}x^{1/2}$$

$$= -x^{-1/2} + \frac{3}{2}x^{1/2}$$

$$= -\frac{1}{x^{1/2}} + \frac{3x^{1/2}}{2}$$

$$y'(4) = \frac{-1}{(4)^{1/2}} + \frac{3(4)^{1/2}}{2}$$

$$= \frac{-1}{2} + \frac{3(2)}{2}$$

$$= -\frac{1}{2} + 3$$

$$= \frac{5}{2} \text{ is the slope of the tangent line at } x = 4.$$

36. $f(x) = 9x^2 - 8x + 4$

$$f'(x) = 18x - 8$$

Let $f'(x) = 0$ to find the point where the slope of the tangent line is zero.

$$18x - 8 = 0$$

$$18x = 8$$

$$x = \frac{8}{18} = \frac{4}{9}$$

Find the y-coordinate.

$$f(x) = 9x^2 - 8x + 4$$

$$f\left(\frac{4}{9}\right) = 9\left(\frac{4}{9}\right)^2 - 8\left(\frac{4}{9}\right) + 4$$

$$= 9\left(\frac{16}{81}\right) - \frac{32}{9} + 4$$

$$= \frac{16}{9} - \frac{32}{9} + \frac{36}{9}$$

$$= \frac{20}{9}$$

The slope of the tangent line at $\left(\frac{4}{9}, \frac{20}{9}\right)$ is zero.

38.   (a) From the graph, $f(1) = 2$. because the curve goes through (1, 2).

(b) $f'(1)$ gives the slope of the tangent line to f at 1. The line goes through $(-1, 1)$ and $(1, 2)$.

$$m = \frac{2 - 1}{1 - (-1)} = \frac{1}{2}, \text{ so}$$

$$f'(1) = \frac{1}{2}.$$

(c) The domain of f is $[-1, \infty)$ because the x-coordinates of the points on f start at $x = -1$ and continue infinitely through the positive real numbers.

(d) The range of f is $[0, \infty)$ because the y-coordinates of the points on f start at $y = 0$ and continue infinitely through the positive real numbers.

40. Demand is $x = 5000 - 100p$

Solve for p: $p = \frac{5000 - x}{100}$

$$R(x) = x\left(\frac{5000 - x}{100}\right)$$

$$= \frac{5000x - x^2}{100}$$

$$R'(x) = \frac{5000 - 2x}{100}$$

(a) $R'(1000) = \frac{5000 - 2000}{100}$

$$= 30$$

(b) $R'(2500) = \frac{5000 - 2(2500)}{100}$

$$= 0$$

(c) $R'(3000) = \frac{5000 - 2(3000)}{100}$

$$= -10$$

42. $p(x) = \frac{1000}{x} + 1000$

$$= 1000x^{-1} + 1000$$

$$p'(x) = (-1)(1000)x^{-2} = -1000x^{-2}$$

$$p'(10) = -1000(10)^{-2} = -\frac{1000}{100} = -10$$

44. The profit in dollars from the sale of x thousand recorders is

$P(x) = x^3 - 5x^2 + 7x.$

$P'(x) = 3x^2 - 10x + 7$

(a) $x = 1$ for 1000 recorders

$P'(1) = 3 - 10 + 7$

$\qquad = \$0$

(b) $x = 2$ for 2000 recorders

$P'(2) = 3(4) - 10(2) + 7$

$\qquad = -\$1$

(c) $x = 5$ for 5000 recorders

$P'(5) = 3(25) - 10(5) + 7$

$\qquad = \$32$

(d) $x = 10$ for 10,000 recorders

$P'(10) = 3(100) - 10(10) + 7$

$\qquad = \$207$

(e) The profit will not change when sales are increased from 1000 to 1001. The profit will decrease by \$1 when sales are increased from 2000 to 2001. The profit will increase by \$32 when sales are increased from 5000 to 5001. The profit will increase by \$207 when sales are increased from 10,000 to 10,001.

46. $G(x) = -.2x^2 + 450$

(a) $G(0) = -.2(0)^2 + 450 = 450$

(b) $G(25) = -.2(25)^2 + 450$
$$= -125 + 450$$
$$= 325$$

$G'(x) = -2(.2)x = -.4x$

(c) $G'(10) = -.4(10) = -4$

When 10 units of insulin are injected, the blood sugar level is decreasing at a rate of 4 points per unit of insulin.

(d) $G'(25) = -.4(25)$
$$= -10$$

When 10 units of insulin are injected, the blood sugar level is decreasing at a rate of 10 points per unit of insulin.

48. $M(t) = 4t^{3/2} + 2t^{1/2}$

(a) $M(16) = 4 \cdot 16^{3/2} + 2 \cdot 16^{1/2}$
$$= 256 + 8$$
$$= 264$$

(b) $M(25) = 4 \cdot 25^{3/2} + 2 \cdot 25^{1/2}$
$$= 500 + 10$$
$$= 510$$

(c) $M'(t) = \frac{3}{2} \cdot 4t^{1/2} + \frac{1}{2} \cdot 2t^{-1/2}$
$$= 6t^{1/2} + t^{-1/2}$$
$M'(16) = 6 \cdot 16^{1/2} + 16^{-1/2}$
$$= 6 \cdot 4 + \frac{1}{4}$$
$$= 24 + \frac{1}{4}$$
$$= \frac{97}{4} \text{ or } 24.25$$

The rate of change is about 97/4 or 24.25 matings per degree.

50. $s(t) = 11t^2 + 4t + 2$

(a) $v(t) = s'(t) = 22t + 4$

(b) $v(0) = 22(0) + 4 = 4$
$v(5) = 22(5) + 4 = 114$
$v(10) = 22(10) + 4 = 224$

52. $s(t) = 4t^3 + 8t^2$

(a) $v(t) = s'(t) = 12t^2 + 16t$

(b) $v(0) = 12(0)^2 + 16(0) = 0$
$v(5) = 12(5)^2 + 16(5)$
$$= 300 + 80 = 380$$
$v(10) = 12(10)^2 + 16(10)$
$$= 1200 + 160 = 1360$$

54. $s(t) = -16t^2 + 144$

velocity $= s'(t)$
$$= -32t$$

(a) $s'(1) = -32 \cdot 1 = -32$ ft per sec
$s'(2) = -32 \cdot 2$
$$= -64 \text{ ft per sec}$$

(b) The rock will hit the ground when $s(t) = 0$.
$$-16t^2 + 144 = 0$$
$$t = \sqrt{\frac{144}{16}}$$
$$= 3 \text{ sec}$$

(c) The velocity at impact is the velocity at 3 sec.
$$s(3) = -32 \cdot 3$$
$$= -96 \text{ ft per sec}$$

56. $f(x) = -.023x^3 + .3x^2 - .4x + 11.6$

$f'(x) = -.023(3x^2) + .3(2x) - .4$

$\quad = -.069x^2 + .6x - .4$

(a) 1981; $x = 0$

$\quad f'(0) = -.069(0)^2 + .6(0) - .4$

$\qquad = -.4$

(b) 1983; $x = 2$

$\quad f'(2) = -.069(2)^2 + .6(2) - .4$

$\qquad = .524$

(c) 1988; $x = 7$

$\quad f'(7) = -.069(7)^2 + .6(7) - .4$

$\qquad = .419$

(d) 1989; $x = 8$

$\quad f'(8) = -.069(8)^2 + .6(8) - .4$

$\qquad = -.016$

(e) 1990; $x = 9$

$\quad f'(9) = -.069(9)^2 + .6(9) - .4$

$\qquad = -.589$

(f) Living standards were decreasing in 1981 but then began to increase before decreasing again in 1989. The increase slowed in the late 80's and then living standards began to decrease.

Section 2.5

2. $y = (3x + 7)(x - 1)$

$y' = (3x + 7)(1) + (3)(x - 1)$

$\quad = 3x + 7 + 3x - 3$

$\quad = 6x + 4$

4. $y = (5x^2 - 1)(4x + 3)$

$y' = (5x^2 - 1)(4) + (10x)(4x + 3)$

$\quad = 20x^2 - 4 + 40x^2 + 30x$

$\quad = 60x^2 + 30x - 4$

6. $y = (9x^2 + 7x)(x^2 - 1)$

$y' = (9x^2 + 7x)(2x) + (x^2 - 1)(18x + 7)$

$\quad = 18x^3 + 14x^2 + 18x^3 + 7x^2 - 18x - 7$

$\quad = 36x^3 + 21x^2 - 18x - 7$

8. $y = (2x - 5)^2 = (2x - 5)(2x - 5)$

$y' = (2x - 5)(2) + (2x - 5)(2)$

$\quad = 4x - 10 + 4x - 10$

$\quad = 8x - 20$

10. $k(t) = (t^2 - 1)^2$

$\qquad = (t^2 - 1)(t^2 - 1)$

$k'(t) = (t^2 - 1)(2t) + (t^2 - 1)(2t)$

$\qquad = 2t^3 - 2t + 2t^3 - 2t$

$\qquad = 4t^3 - 4t$

12. $y = (x + 1)(\sqrt{x} + 2)$

$\quad = (x + 1)(x^{1/2} + 2)$

$y' = (x + 1)\left(\frac{1}{2}x^{-1/2}\right) + (x^{1/2} + 2)(1)$

$\quad = \frac{1}{2}x^{1/2} + \frac{1}{2}x^{-1/2} + x^{1/2} + 2$

$\quad = \frac{3}{2}x^{1/2} + \frac{1}{2}x^{-1/2} + 2$

or $\dfrac{3x^{1/2}}{2} + \dfrac{1}{2x^{1/2}} + 2$

14. $g(x) = (5\sqrt{x} - 1)(2\sqrt{x} + 1)$

$\qquad = (5x^{1/2} - 1)(2x^{1/2} + 1)$

$g'(x) = (5x^{1/2} - 1)(x^{-1/2})$

$\qquad\quad + (2x^{1/2} + 1)\left(\frac{5}{2}x^{-1/2}\right)$

$\qquad = 5 - x^{-1/2} + 5 + \frac{5}{2}x^{-1/2}$

$\qquad = 10 + \frac{3}{2}x^{-1/2}$ or $10 + \dfrac{3}{2x^{1/2}}$

16. $f(x) = \dfrac{7x + 1}{3x + 8}$

$f'(x) = \dfrac{(3x + 8)(7) - (7x + 1)(3)}{(3x + 8)^2}$

$ = \dfrac{21x + 56 - 21x - 3}{(3x + 8)^2}$

$ = \dfrac{53}{(3x + 8)^2}$

18. $y = \dfrac{2}{3x - 5}$

$y' = \dfrac{(3x - 5)(0) - 2(3)}{(3x - 5)^2}$

$ = \dfrac{-6}{(3x - 5)^2}$

20. $y = \dfrac{5 - 3t}{4 + t}$

$y' = \dfrac{(4 + t)(-3) - (5 - 3t)(1)}{(4 + t)^2}$

$ = \dfrac{-12 - 3t - 5 + 3t}{(4 + t)^2}$

$ = \dfrac{-17}{(4 + t)^2}$

22. $y = \dfrac{x^2 + x}{x - 1}$

$y' = \dfrac{(x - 1)(2x + 1) - (x^2 + x)(1)}{(x - 1)^2}$

$ = \dfrac{2x^2 + x - 2x - 1 - x^2 - x}{(x - 1)^2}$

$ = \dfrac{x^2 - 2x - 1}{(x - 1)^2}$

24. $f(t) = \dfrac{4t + 11}{t^2 - 3}$

$f'(t) = \dfrac{(t^2 - 3)(4) - (4t + 11)(2t)}{(t^2 - 3)^2}$

$ = \dfrac{4t^2 - 12 - 8t^2 - 22t}{(t^2 - 3)^2}$

$ = \dfrac{-4t^2 - 22t - 12}{(t^2 - 3)^2}$

26. $g(x) = \dfrac{x^2 - 4x + 2}{x + 3}$

$g'(x) = \dfrac{(x + 3)(2x - 4) - (x^2 - 4x + 2)(1)}{(x + 3)^2}$

$ = \dfrac{2x^2 - 4x + 6x - 12 - x^2 + 4x - 2}{(x + 3)^2}$

$ = \dfrac{x^2 + 6x - 14}{(x + 3)^2}$

28. $p(t) = \dfrac{\sqrt{t}}{t - 1}$

$ = \dfrac{t^{1/2}}{t - 1}$

$p'(t) = \dfrac{(t - 1)\left(\frac{1}{2}t^{-1/2}\right) - t^{1/2}(1)}{(t - 1)^2}$

$ = \dfrac{\frac{1}{2}t^{1/2} - \frac{1}{2}t^{-1/2} - t^{1/2}}{(t - 1)^2}$

$ = \dfrac{-\frac{1}{2}t^{1/2} - \frac{1}{2}t^{-1/2}}{(t - 1)^2}$

$ = \dfrac{-\frac{\sqrt{t}}{2} - \frac{1}{2\sqrt{t}}}{(t - 1)^2} \quad \text{or} \quad \dfrac{-t - 1}{2\sqrt{t}(t - 1)^2}$

30. $y = \dfrac{5x + 6}{\sqrt{x}} = \dfrac{5x + 6}{x^{1/2}}$

$y' = \dfrac{(x^{1/2})(5) - (5x + 6)\left(\frac{1}{2}x^{-1/2}\right)}{(x^{1/2})^2}$

$ = \dfrac{5x^{1/2} - \frac{5}{2}x^{1/2} - 3x^{-1/2}}{x}$

$ = \dfrac{\frac{5}{2}x^{1/2} - 3x^{-1/2}}{x}$

$ = \dfrac{\frac{5\sqrt{x}}{2} - \frac{3}{\sqrt{x}}}{x} \quad \text{or} \quad \dfrac{5x - 6}{2x\sqrt{x}}$

32. The denominator, $(x^3)^2$, was omiitted. The correct work follows.

$$D_x \left(\frac{x^2 - 4}{x^3}\right) = \frac{x^3(2x) - (x^2 - 4)(3x^2)}{(x^3)^2}$$

$$= \frac{2x^4 - 3x^4 + 12x^2}{x^6}$$

$$= \frac{-x^4 + 12x^2}{x^6}$$

$$= \frac{x^2(-x^2 + 12)}{x^2(x^4)}$$

$$= \frac{-x^2 + 12}{x^4}$$

34. $f(x) = \dfrac{u(x)}{v(x)}$

$f(x + h) = \dfrac{u(x + h)}{v(x + h)}$

$f'(x) = \lim\limits_{h \to 0} \dfrac{f(x + h) - f(x)}{h} = \lim\limits_{h \to 0} \dfrac{\dfrac{u(x + h)}{v(x + h)} - \dfrac{u(x)}{v(x)}}{h}$

$= \lim\limits_{h \to 0} \dfrac{u(x + h)v(x) - u(x)v(x + h)}{h} \cdot \dfrac{1}{v(x)v(x + h)}$

$= \lim\limits_{h \to 0} \left[\dfrac{u(x + h)v(x) - u(x)v(x) + u(x)v(x) - u(x)v(x + h)}{h} \cdot \dfrac{1}{v(x)v(x + h)}\right]$

$= \lim\limits_{h \to 0} \left\{v(x)\left[\dfrac{u(x + h) - u(x)}{h}\right] - u(x)\left[\dfrac{v(x + h) - v(x)}{h}\right]\right\} \cdot \dfrac{1}{v(x)v(x + h)}$

$= \dfrac{v(x) \lim\limits_{h \to 0} \dfrac{u(x + h) - u(x)}{h} - u(x) \lim\limits_{h \to 0} \dfrac{v(x + h) - v(x)}{h}}{\lim\limits_{h \to 0} [v(x)v(x + h)]}$

$= \dfrac{v(x)u'(x) - u(x)v'(x)}{[v(x)]^2}$

36. $P(x) = \dfrac{5x - 6}{2x + 3}$

$\overline{P}(x) = \dfrac{P(x)}{x} = \dfrac{5x - 6}{2x^2 + 3x}$

(a) $\overline{P}(8) = \dfrac{5(8) - 6}{2(8)^2 + 3(8)} = \dfrac{34}{152}$

$\approx .224$ tens of dollars or \$2.24 per book

(b) $\overline{P}(15) = \dfrac{5(15) - 6}{2(15)^2 + 3(15)} = \dfrac{69}{495}$

$\approx .139$ tens of dollars

or $1.39 per book

(c) $\overline{P}(x) = \dfrac{5x - 6}{2x^2 + 3x}$ per book

(d) $\overline{P}'(x)$

$= \dfrac{(2x^2 + 3x)(5) - (5x - 6)(4x + 3)}{(2x^2 + 3x)^2}$

$= \dfrac{10x^2 + 15x - 20x^2 - 15x + 24x + 18}{(2x^2 + 3x)^2}$

$= \dfrac{-10x^2 + 24x + 18}{(2x^2 + 3x)^2}$

38. $M(d) = \dfrac{200d}{3d + 10}$

(a) $M'(d) = \dfrac{(3d + 10)(200) - (200d)(3)}{(3d + 10)^2}$

$= \dfrac{600d + 2000 - 600d}{(3d + 10)^2}$

$= \dfrac{2000}{(3d + 10)^2}$

(b) $M'(2) = \dfrac{2000}{[3(2) + 10]^2}$

$= \dfrac{2000}{(16)^2}$

$= \dfrac{2000}{256}$

$= 7.8125$

$M'(5) = \dfrac{2000}{[3(5) + 10]^2}$

$= \dfrac{2000}{(25)^2}$

$= \dfrac{2000}{625}$

$= 3.2$

The new employee can assemble about 7.8 additional bicycles per day after 2 days of training and 3.2 additional bicycles per day after 5 days of training.

40. $N(t) = (t - 10)^2(2t) + 50$

(a) $N(t) = (t^2 - 20t + 100)(2t) + 50$

$= 2t^3 - 40t^2 + 200t + 50$

$N'(t) = 6t^2 - 80t + 200$

(b) $N'(8) = 6(8)^2 - 80(8) + 200$

$= 6(64) - 640 + 200$

$= -56$

The rate of change is -56 million per hour.

(c) $N'(11) = 6(11)^2 - 80(11) + 200$

$= 6(121) - 880 + 200$

$= 46$

The rate of change is 46 million per hour.

(d) The population first declines and then increases.

Section 2.6

For Exercises 2-6, $f(x) = 4x^2 - 2x$ and $g(x) = 8x + 1$.

2. $g(-5) = 8(-5) + 1$

$= -40 + 1 = -39$

$f[g(-5)] = f[-39]$

$= 4(-39)^2 - 2(-39)$

$= 6084 + 78 = 6162$

4. $f(-5) = 4(-5)^2 - 2(-5)$

$= 100 + 10 = 110$

$g[f(-5)] = g[110]$

$= 8(110) + 1$

$= 880 + 1 = 881$

6. $f(5z) = 4(5z)^2 - 2(5z)$

$\qquad = 4(25z^2) - 10z$

$\qquad = 100z^2 - 10z$

$g[f(5z)] = 8(100z^2 - 10z) + 1$

$\qquad\quad = 800z^2 - 80z + 1$

8. $f(x) = -6x + 9$; $g(x) = \dfrac{x}{5} + 7$

$f[g(x)] = -6\left[\dfrac{x}{5} + 7\right] + 9$

$\qquad = \dfrac{-6x}{5} - 42 + 9$

$\qquad = \dfrac{-6x}{5} - 33$

$\qquad = \dfrac{-6x - 165}{5}$

$g[f(x)] = \dfrac{-6x + 9}{5} + 7$

$\qquad = \dfrac{-6x + 9}{5} + \dfrac{35}{5}$

$\qquad = \dfrac{-6x + 44}{5}$

10. $f(x) = \dfrac{2}{x^4}$; $g(x) = 2 - x$

$f[g(x)] = \dfrac{2}{(2 - x)^4}$

$g[f(x)] = 2 - \left(\dfrac{2}{x^4}\right) = 2 - \dfrac{2}{x^4}$

12. $f(x) = 9x^2 - 11x$; $g(x) = 2\sqrt{x + 2}$

$f[g(x)] = 9(2\sqrt{x + 2})^2 - 11(2\sqrt{x + 2})$

$\qquad = 9[4(x + 2)] - 22\sqrt{x + 2}$

$\qquad = 36(x + 2) - 22\sqrt{x + 2}$

$\qquad = 36x + 72 - 22\sqrt{x + 2}$

$g[f(x)] = 2\sqrt{(9x^2 - 11x) + 2}$

$\qquad = 2\sqrt{9x^2 - 11x + 2}$

14. $f(x) = \dfrac{8}{x}$; $g(x) = \sqrt{3 - x}$

$f[g(x)] = \dfrac{8}{\sqrt{3 - x}}$

$\qquad = \dfrac{8}{\sqrt{3 - x}} \cdot \dfrac{\sqrt{3 - x}}{\sqrt{3 - x}}$

$\qquad = \dfrac{8\sqrt{3 - x}}{3 - x}$

$g[f(x)] = \sqrt{3 - \dfrac{8}{x}} = \sqrt{\dfrac{3x - 8}{x}}$

$\qquad = \dfrac{\sqrt{3x - 8}}{\sqrt{x}} \cdot \dfrac{\sqrt{x}}{\sqrt{x}}$

$\qquad = \dfrac{\sqrt{3x^2 - 8x}}{x}$

16. $y = (3x - 7)^{1/3}$

If $f(x) = x^{1/3}$ and $g(x) = 3x - 7$, then $y = f[g(x)] = (3x - 7)^{1/3}$.

18. $y = \sqrt{9 - 4x}$

If $f(x) = \sqrt{x}$ and $g(x) = 9 - 4x$, then $y = f[g(x)] = \sqrt{9 - 4x}$.

20. $y = (x^{1/2} - 3)^2 + (x^{1/2} - 3) + 5$

If $f(x) = x^2 + x + 5$ and $g(x) = x^{1/2} - 3$, then

$y = f[g(x)]$

$\quad = (x^{1/2} - 3)^2 + (x^{1/2} - 3) + 5$.

24. $y = (8x^4 - 3x^2)^3$

Let $f(x) = x^3$ and $g(x) = 8x^4 - 3x^2$. Then $(8x^4 - 3x^2)^3 = f[g(x)]$.

Use the alternate form of the chain rule.

$D_x (8x^4 - 3x^2)^3 = f'[g(x)] \cdot g'(x)$

$f'(x) = 3x^2$

$f'[g(x)] = 3[g(x)]^2$

$\qquad = 3(8x^4 - 3x^2)^2$

$g'(x) = 32x^3 - 6x$

$D_x (8x^4 - 3x^2)^3$

$\quad = 3(8x^4 - 3x^2)^2(32x^3 - 6x)$

26. $k(x) = -2(12x^2 + 5)^6$

Use the generalized power rule with $u = 12x^2 + 5$, $n = 6$ and $u' = 24x$.

$k'(x) = -2[6(12x^2 + 5)^5 \cdot 24x]$

$\qquad = -2[144x(12x^2 + 5)^5]$

$\qquad = -288x(12x^2 + 5)^5$

28. $s(t) = 45(3t^3 - 8)^{3/2}$

Use the generalized power rule with $u = 3t^3 - 8$, $n = 3/2$ and $u' = 9t^2$.

$s'(t) = 45\left[\frac{3}{2}(3t^3 - 8)^{1/2} \cdot 9t^2\right]$

$\qquad = 45\left[\frac{27}{2}t^2(3t^3 - 8)^{1/2}\right]$

$\qquad = \frac{1215}{2}t^2(3t^3 - 8)^{1/2}$

30. $g(t) = -3\sqrt{7t^3 - 1}$

$\qquad = -3(7t^3 - 1)^{1/2}$

Use the generalized power rule with $u = 7t^3 - 1$, $n = 1/2$ and $u' = 21t^2$.

$g'(t) = -3\left[\frac{1}{2}(7t^3 - 1)^{-1/2} \cdot 21t^2\right]$

$\qquad = -3\left[\frac{21}{2}t^2(7t^3 - 1)^{-1/2}\right]$

$\qquad = \frac{-63}{2}t^2 \cdot \frac{1}{(7t^3 - 1)^{1/2}}$

$\qquad = \frac{-63t^2}{2\sqrt{7t^3 - 1}}$

32. $m(t) = -6t(5t^4 - 1)^2$

Use the product rule and the power rule.

$m'(t) = -6t[2(5t^4 - 1) \cdot 20t^3]$

$\qquad + (5t^4 - 1)^2(-6)$

$\qquad = -6t[40t^3(5t^4 - 1)]$

$\qquad - 6(5t^4 - 1)^2$

$\qquad = -6(5t^4 - 1)[40t^4 + (5t^4 - 1)]$

$\qquad = -6(5t^4 - 1)(45t^4 - 1)$

34. $y = (3x^4 + 1)^2(x^3 + 4)$

$y' = (3x^4 + 1)^2(3x^2) + (x^3 + 4)$

$\qquad \cdot [2(3x^4 + 1) \cdot 12x^3]$

$\quad = 3x^2(3x^4 + 1)^2$

$\qquad + 24x^3(x^3 + 4)(3x^4 + 1)$

$\quad = 3x^2(3x^4 + 1)[(3x^4 + 1) + 8x(x^3 + 4)]$

$\quad = 3x^2(3x^4 + 1)(3x^4 + 1 + 8x^4 + 32x)$

$\quad = 3x^2(3x^4 + 1)(11x^4 + 32x + 1)$

36. $y = 2(3x^4 + 5)^2\sqrt{x}$

$\quad = 2(3x^4 + 5)^2 x^{1/2}$

$y' = 2(3x^4 + 5)^2\left(\frac{1}{2}x^{-1/2}\right)$

$\qquad + x^{1/2}[2 \cdot 2(3x^4 + 5) \cdot 12x^3]$

$\quad = (3x^4 + 5)^2(x^{-1/2})$

$\qquad + x^{1/2}[48x^3(3x^4 + 5)]$

$\quad = (3x^4 + 5)(x^{-1/2})(3x^4 + 5 + x \cdot 48x^3)$

$\quad = \frac{(3x^4 + 5)(51x^4 + 5)}{x^{1/2}}$

$\quad = \frac{(3x^4 + 5)(51x^4 + 5)}{\sqrt{x}}$

38. $y = \frac{-5}{(2x^3 + 1)^2} = -5(2x^3 + 1)^{-2}$

$y' = -5[-2(2x^3 + 1)^{-3} \cdot 6x^2]$

$\quad = -5[-12x^2(2x^3 + 1)^{-3}]$

$\quad = 60x^2(2x^3 + 1)^{-3}$

$\quad = \frac{60x^2}{(2x^3 + 1)^3}$

40. $r(t) = \dfrac{(5t - 6)^4}{3t^2 + 4}$

$r'(t)$

$= \dfrac{(3t^2 + 4)[4(5t - 6)^3 \cdot 5] - (5t - 6)^4(6t)}{(3t^2 + 4)^2}$

$= \dfrac{20(3t^2 + 4)(5t - 6)^3 - 6t(5t - 6)^4}{(3t^2 + 4)^2}$

$= \dfrac{2(5t - 6)^3[10(3t^2 + 4) - 3t(5t - 6)]}{(3t^2 + 4)^2}$

$= \dfrac{2(5t - 6)^3(30t^2 + 40 - 15t^2 + 18t)}{(3t^2 + 4)^2}$

$= \dfrac{2(5t - 6)^3(15t^2 + 18t + 40)}{(3t^2 + 4)^2}$

$= \dfrac{2(5t - 6)^3(15t^2 + 18t + 40)}{(3t^2 + 4)^2}$

42. $y = \dfrac{3x^2 - x}{(2x - 1)^5}$

y'

$= \dfrac{(2x - 1)^5(6x - 1) - (3x^2 - x)[5(2x - 1)^4 \cdot 2]}{[(2x - 1)^5]^2}$

$= \dfrac{(2x - 1)^5(6x - 1) - 10(3x^2 - x)(2x - 1)^4}{(2x - 1)^{10}}$

$= \dfrac{(2x - 1)^4[(2x - 1)(6x - 1) - 10(3x^2 - x)]}{(2x - 1)^{10}}$

$= \dfrac{12x^2 - 2x - 6x + 1 - 30x^2 + 10x}{(2x - 1)^6}$

$= \dfrac{-18x^2 + 2x + 1}{(2x - 1)^6}$

44. (a) $D_x\,(g[f(x)])$ at $x = 1$

$= g'[f(x)] \cdot f'(1)$

$= g'(2) \cdot (-6)$

$= \dfrac{3}{7}(-6)$

$= -\dfrac{18}{7}$

(b) $D_x\,(g[f(x)])$ at $x = 2$

$= g'[f(2)] \cdot f'(2)$

$= g'(4) \cdot (-7)$

$= \dfrac{5}{7}(-7)$

$= -5$

46. $R(x) = 1000\left(1 - \dfrac{x}{500}\right)^2$

$R'(x) = 1000\left[2\left(1 - \dfrac{x}{500}\right)\left(-\dfrac{1}{500}\right)\right]$

$= 1000\left[\dfrac{-2}{500}\left(1 - \dfrac{x}{500}\right)\right]$

$= -4\left(1 - \dfrac{x}{500}\right)$

(a) $R'(400) = -4\left(1 - \dfrac{400}{500}\right)$

$= -4(1 - .8)$

$= -4(.2) = -.8$

(b) $R'(500) = -4\left(1 - \dfrac{500}{500}\right)$

$= -4(1 - 1)$

$= -4(0) = 0$

(c) $R'(600) = -4\left(1 - \dfrac{600}{500}\right)$

$= -4(1 - 1.2)$

$= -4(-.2)$

$= .8$

(d) $\bar{R}(x) = \dfrac{R(x)}{x}$

$= \dfrac{1000}{x}\left(1 - \dfrac{x}{500}\right)^2$

(e) $\bar{R}'(x) = \dfrac{1000}{x}\left[2\left(1 - \dfrac{x}{500}\right)\left(-\dfrac{1}{500}\right)\right]$

$+ \left(1 - \dfrac{x}{500}\right)^2\left(-\dfrac{1000}{x^2}\right)$

$= \dfrac{1000}{x}\left(1 - \dfrac{x}{500}\right)$

$\cdot \left[-\dfrac{1}{250} - \dfrac{1}{x}\left(1 - \dfrac{x}{500}\right)\right]$

$= \dfrac{1000}{x}\left(1 - \dfrac{x}{500}\right)$

$\cdot \left(-\dfrac{1}{250} - \dfrac{1}{x} + \dfrac{1}{500}\right)$

$= \dfrac{1000}{x}\left(1 - \dfrac{x}{500}\right)\left(-\dfrac{1}{500} - \dfrac{1}{x}\right)$

$= \left(1 - \dfrac{x}{500}\right)\left(-\dfrac{2}{x} - \dfrac{1000}{x^2}\right)$

48. $x = 30\left(5 - \dfrac{p}{\sqrt{p^2 + 1}}\right)$

$\qquad = 150 - \dfrac{30p}{\sqrt{p^2 + 1}}$

$\qquad = 150 - \dfrac{30p}{(p^2 + 1)^{1/2}}$

$\dfrac{dx}{dp} = 0 - \left[\dfrac{(p^2 + 1)^{1/2} D_p(30p) - (30p)D_p(p^2 + 1)^{1/2}}{[(p^2 + 1)^{1/2}]^2}\right]$

$\qquad = -\left[\dfrac{(p^2 + 1)^{1/2}(30) - (30p)\left(\frac{1}{2}\right)(p^2 + 1)^{-1/2}(2p)}{(p^2 + 1)}\right]$

$\qquad = -\left[\dfrac{(p^2 + 1)^{1/2}(30) - (30p)(p)(p^2 + 1)^{-1/2}}{(p^2 + 1)}\right]$

$\qquad = -\left[\dfrac{(30)(p^2 + 1)^{-1/2}([p^2 + 1] - p^2)}{(p^2 + 1)}\right]$

$\qquad = \dfrac{-(30)(p^2 + 1)^{-1/2}(1)}{(p^2 + 1)}$

$\qquad = -\dfrac{30}{(p^2 + 1)^{3/2}}$

50. $C = 2000x + 3500$

$x = \sqrt{15,000 - 1.5p}$

Solve for p: $x = \sqrt{15,000 - 1.5p}$

$\qquad\qquad\quad x^2 = 15,000 - 1.5p$

$\dfrac{x^2 - 15,000}{-1.5} = p$

$\dfrac{x^2}{-1.5} + \dfrac{15,000}{1.5} = p$

$\dfrac{-2x^2}{3} + 10,000 = p$

(a) $\quad R = xp = x\left(\dfrac{-2x^2}{3} + 10,000\right)$

$\qquad\qquad = \dfrac{-2x^3}{3} + 10,000x$

$\qquad\qquad = \dfrac{-2x^3 + 30,000x}{3}$

$\qquad\qquad = \dfrac{30,000x - 2x^3}{3}$

(b) $P(x) = R(x) - C(x)$

$$= \frac{30,000x - 2x^3}{3}$$

$$- (2000x + 3500)$$

$$= \left(\frac{-2x^2}{3} + 10,000x\right)$$

$$- (2000x + 3500)$$

$$= \frac{-2x^2}{3} + 8000x - 3500$$

$$= 8000x - \frac{2x^3}{3} - 3500$$

$P(x)$ is the profit function.

(c) $P'(x) = D_x\left(8000x - \frac{2x^3}{3} - 3500\right)$

$$= 8000 - 2x^2$$

$P'(x)$ gives the marginal profit.

(d) If $p = \$25$ and

$$x = \sqrt{15,000 - 1.5p},$$

then $x = \sqrt{15,000 - 1.5(25)}$

$$= \sqrt{15,000 - 37.5}$$

$$= \sqrt{14,962.50}.$$

Thus, $x^2 = 14,962.50$.

$P'(x) = 8000 - 2x^2$

$$= 8000 - 2(14,962.50)$$

$$= 8000 - 29.925$$

$$= -\$21,925$$

52. $p = \frac{200}{x^{1/2}} = 200x^{-1/2}$

$\frac{dp}{dx} = -100x^{-3/2} = \frac{-100}{x^{3/2}}$

If n is the number of employees, $x = 15n$.

$\frac{dx}{dn} = 15$

$\frac{dR}{dn} = \left(p + x\frac{dp}{dx}\right)\frac{dx}{dn}$

$$= \left[\frac{200}{x^{1/2}} + x\left(\frac{-100}{x^{3/2}}\right)\right](15)$$

$$= \left(\frac{200}{x^{1/2}} - \frac{100}{x^{1/2}}\right)(15)$$

$$= \left(\frac{100}{x^{1/2}}\right)(15)$$

$$= \frac{1500}{x^{1/2}}$$

Now $n = 25$,

$\quad x = 15n = 15(25) = 375$.

Thus,

$$\frac{dR}{dn} = \frac{1500}{x^{1/2}} = \frac{1500}{(375)^{1/2}}$$

$$= \$77.46.$$

54. $A(r) = \pi r^2$

$\quad r(t) = t^2$

$A[r(t)] = \pi[t^2]^2$

$$= \pi(t^4)$$

$$= \pi t^4$$

This function represents the area of the oil slick as a function of time t after the beginning of the leak.

56. $N(t) = 2t(5t + 9)^{1/2} + 12$

$N'(t) = (2t)\left[\frac{1}{2}(5t + 9)^{-1/2}(5)\right]$

$$+ 2(5t + 9)^{1/2} + 0$$

$$= 5t(5t + 9)^{-1/2} + 2(5t + 9)^{1/2}$$

$$= (5t + 9)^{-1/2}[5t + 2(5t + 9)]$$

$$= (5t + 9)^{-1/2}(15t + 18)$$

$$= \frac{15t + 18}{(5t + 9)^{1/2}}$$

(a) $N'(0) = \dfrac{15(0) + 18}{[5(0) + 9]^{1/2}}$

$= \dfrac{18}{9^{1/2}} = 6$

(b) $N'\left(\dfrac{7}{5}\right) = \dfrac{15\left(\dfrac{7}{5}\right) + 18}{\left[5\left(\dfrac{7}{5}\right) + 9\right]^{1/2}}$

$= \dfrac{21 + 8}{(7 + 9)^{1/2}}$

$= \dfrac{39}{(16)^{1/2}}$

$= \dfrac{39}{4} = 9.75$

(c) $N'(8) = \dfrac{15(8) + 18}{[5(8) + 9]^{1/2}}$

$= \dfrac{120 + 18}{(49)^{1/2}}$

$= \dfrac{138}{7} \approx 19.71$

58. (a) $R(Q) = Q\left(C - \dfrac{Q}{3}\right)^{1/2}$

$R'(Q) = Q\left[\dfrac{1}{2}\left(C - \dfrac{Q}{3}\right)^{-1/2}\left(-\dfrac{1}{3}\right)\right]$

$\qquad + \left(C - \dfrac{Q}{3}\right)^{1/2}(1)$

$= -\dfrac{1}{6}Q\left(C - \dfrac{Q}{3}\right)^{-1/2} + \left(C - \dfrac{Q}{3}\right)^{1/2}$

$= -\dfrac{Q}{6\left(C - \dfrac{Q}{3}\right)^{1/2}} + \left(C - \dfrac{Q}{3}\right)^{1/2}$

(b) $R'(Q) = -\dfrac{Q}{6\left(C - \dfrac{Q}{3}\right)^{1/2}} + \left(C - \dfrac{Q}{3}\right)^{1/2}$

If $Q = 87$ and $C = 59$, then

$R'(Q) = \left(59 - \dfrac{87}{3}\right)^{1/2} - \dfrac{87}{6\left(59 - \dfrac{87}{3}\right)^{1/2}}$

$= (30)^{1/2} - \dfrac{87}{6(30)^{1/2}}$

$= 5.48 - \dfrac{87}{32.88}$

$= 5.48 - 2.65$

$= 2.83.$

(c) Because $R'(Q)$ is positive, the patient's sensitivity to the drug is increasing.

Chapter 2 Review Exercises

4. $\lim\limits_{x \to -1} g(x)$ does not exist since

$\lim\limits_{x \to -1^+} g(x) = 2$

and $\lim\limits_{x \to -1^-} g(x) = -2.$

6. Let $f(x) = \dfrac{x^2 - 5}{2x}$.

x	-.1	-.01	-.001
f(x)	24.95	250.0	2500

x	.1	.01	.001
f(x)	-24.95	-250.0	-2500

As x approaches 0 from the left, $f(x)$ gets infinitely larger. As x approaches 0 from the right $f(x)$ gets infinitely smaller. Therefore,

$\lim\limits_{x \to 0} \dfrac{x^2 - 5}{2x}$ does not exist

8. $\lim\limits_{x \to 2} (-x^2 + 4x + 1)$

$= -(2)^2 + 4(2) + 1$

$= -4 + 8 + 1 = 5$

10. Let $f(x) = \dfrac{2x + 5}{x - 3}$.

x	2.9	2.99	2.999
f(x)	-108	-1098	-10,998

x	3.1	3.01	3.001
f(x)	112	1102	11,002

As x approaches 3 from the left, f(x) gets infinitely smaller. As x approaches 3 from the right, f(x) gets infinitely larger. Therefore,

$\lim\limits_{x \to 3} \dfrac{2x + 5}{x - 3}$ does not exist.

12. $\lim\limits_{x \to 2} \dfrac{x^2 + 3x - 10}{x - 2}$

$= \lim\limits_{x \to 2} \dfrac{(x + 5)(x - 2)}{x - 2}$

$= \lim\limits_{x \to 2} (x + 5) = 2 + 5 = 7$

14. $\lim\limits_{x \to 3} \dfrac{3x^2 - 2x - 21}{x - 3}$

$= \lim\limits_{x \to 3} \dfrac{(3x + 7)(x - 3)}{(x - 3)}$

$= \lim\limits_{x \to 3} (3x + 7) = 9 + 7 = 16$

16. $\lim\limits_{x \to 16} \dfrac{\sqrt{x} - 4}{x - 16}$

$= \lim\limits_{x \to 16} \dfrac{\sqrt{x} - 4}{x - 16} \cdot \dfrac{\sqrt{x} + 4}{\sqrt{x} + 4}$

$= \lim\limits_{x \to 16} \dfrac{x - 16}{(x - 16)(\sqrt{x} + 4)}$

$= \lim\limits_{x \to 16} \dfrac{1}{\sqrt{x} + 4} = \dfrac{1}{\sqrt{16} + 4}$

$= \dfrac{1}{4 + 4} = \dfrac{1}{8}$

18. As shown on the graph, f(x) is discontinuous at x_1 and x_4.

20. $f(x) = \dfrac{2 - 3x}{(1 + x)(2 - x)}$,

x = 2/3, -1, 2, 0

Since f is a rational function, it is discontinuous when
$(1 + x)(2 - x) = 0$, or for $x = -1$ and $x = 2$.

It is continuous at x = 2/3 and x = 0.

22. $f(x) = \dfrac{x^2 - 9}{x + 3}$; x = 3, -3, 0

Since f is a rational function, it is discontinuous when $x + 3 = 0$, or when $x = -3$. It is continuous at x = 3 and x = 0.

24. $f(x) = 2x^2 - 5x - 3$; x = -1/2, 3, 0

Since f(x) is a polynomial function, it is continuous for all values of x, including x = -1/2, x = 3 and x = 0.

26. $y = 6x^2 + 2 = f(x)$

$f(4) = 6(4)^2 + 2 = 98$

$f(1) = 6(1)^2 + 2 = 8$

Average rate of change

$= \dfrac{98 - 8}{4 - 1} = \dfrac{90}{3} = 30$

$y' = 12x$

Instantaneous rate of change at x = 1:

$12(1) = 12$

28. $y = \dfrac{-6}{3x - 5} = f(x)$

$f(9) = \dfrac{-6}{3(9) - 5} = \dfrac{-6}{22} = -\dfrac{3}{11}$

$f(4) = \dfrac{-6}{3(4) - 5} = -\dfrac{6}{7}$

Average rate of change

$$= \frac{\frac{-3}{11} - \left(-\frac{6}{7}\right)}{9 - 4}$$

$$= \frac{\frac{-21 + 66}{77}}{5}$$

$$= \frac{45}{5(77)} = \frac{9}{77}$$

$$y' = \frac{(3x - 5)(0) - (-6)(3)}{(3x - 5)^2}$$

$$= \frac{18}{(3x - 5)^2}$$

Instantaneous rate of change at
$x = 4$:

$$\frac{18}{(3 \cdot 4 - 5)^2} = \frac{18}{7^2} = \frac{18}{49}$$

30. $y = 4x + 3 = f(x)$

$$y' = \lim_{h \to 0} \frac{f(x + h) - f(x)}{h}$$

$$= \lim_{h \to 0} \frac{[4(x + h) + 3] - [4x + 3]}{h}$$

$$= \lim_{h \to 0} \frac{4x + 4h + 3 - 4x - 3}{h}$$

$$= \lim_{h \to 0} \frac{4h}{h} = \lim_{h \to 0} 4$$

$$= 4$$

32. $y = -x^3 + 7x = f(x)$

$$y' = \lim_{h \to 0} \frac{f(x + h) - f(x)}{h}$$

$$= \lim_{h \to 0} \frac{[-(x + h)^3 + 7(x + h)] - [-x^3 + 7x]}{h}$$

$$= \lim_{h \to 0} \left(\frac{-x^3 - 2x^2h - xh^2 - hx^2 - 2xh^2}{h} \right.$$

$$\left. + \frac{-h^3 + 7x + 7h + x^3 - 7x}{h} \right)$$

$$= \lim_{h \to 0} \frac{-2x^2h - xh^2 - hx^2 - 2xh^2 - h^3 + 7h}{h}$$

$$= \lim_{h \to 0} -2x^2 - xh - x^2 - 2xh - h^2 + 7$$

$$= -3x^2 + 7$$

34. $y = 8 - x^2$; $x = 1$

$$y = 8 - x^2$$

$$y' = -2x$$

$$\text{slope} = y'(1) = -2(1) = -2$$

Use $(1, 7)$ and point-slope form.

$$y - 7 = -2(x - 1)$$

$$y - 7 = -2x + 2$$

$$2x + y = 9$$

36. $y = (3x^2 - 5x)(2x)$, tangent at $x = -1$

$$y' = (3x^2 - 5x)(2) + (2x)(6x - 5)$$

$$= 6x^2 - 10x + 12x^2 - 10x$$

$$= 18x^2 - 20x$$

$$\text{slope} = y'(-1) = 18(-1)^2 - 20(-1)$$

$$= 18 + 20 = 38$$

Use $(-1, -16)$ and point-slope form.

$$y - (-16) = 38[x - (-1)]$$

$$y + 16 = 38x + 38$$

$$y = 38x + 22$$

38. $y = \sqrt{6x - 2}$, tangent at $x = 3$

$$y = \sqrt{6x - 2} = (6x - 2)^{1/2}$$

$$y' = \frac{1}{2}(6x - 2)^{-1/2}(6)$$

$$= 3(6x - 2)^{-1/2}$$

$$\text{slope} = y'(3) = 3(6 \cdot 3 - 2)^{-1/2}$$

$$= 3(16)^{-1/2}$$

$$= \frac{3}{16^{1/2}}$$

$$= \frac{3}{4}$$

Use $(3, 4)$ and point-slope form.

$$y - 4 = \frac{3}{4}(x - 3)$$

$$4y - 16 = 3x - 9$$

$$4y = 3x + 7$$

42. $y = 5x^2 - 7x - 9$

$y' = 5(2x) - 7$

$\quad = 10x - 7$

44. $y = 6x^{7/3}$

$y' = 6\left(\frac{7}{3}\right)x^{4/3}$

$\quad = \frac{42}{3}x^{4/3}$

$\quad = 14x^{4/3}$

46. $f(x) = x^{-3} + \sqrt{x}$

$\quad\quad = x^{-3} + x^{1/2}$

$f'(x) = -3x^{-4} + \left(\frac{1}{2}\right)x^{-1/2}$

$\quad\quad$ or $\dfrac{-3}{x^4} + \dfrac{1}{2x^{1/2}}$

48. $y = (3t^2 + 7)(t^3 - t)$

$y' = (3t^2 + 7)(3t^2 - 1) + (t^3 - t)(6t)$

$\quad = 9t^4 + 18t^2 - 7 + 6t^4 - 6t^2$

$\quad = 15t^4 + 12t^2 - 7$

50. $g(t) = -3t^{-1/3}(5t + 7)$

$g'(t) = (-3t^{-1/3})(5)$

$\quad\quad\quad + (5t + 7)\left[-3\left(-\frac{1}{3}t^{-4/3}\right)\right]$

$\quad\quad = -15t^{-1/3} + (5t + 7)t^{-4/3}$

$\quad\quad = -15t^{-1/3} + 5t^{-1/3} + 7t^{-4/3}$

$\quad\quad = -10t^{-1/3} + 7t^{-4/3}$

$\quad\quad$ or $-\dfrac{10}{t^{1/3}} + \dfrac{7}{t^{4/3}}$

52. $y = 12x^{-3/4}\left(\dfrac{x}{3} + 5\right)$

$y' = 12x^{-3/4}\left(\dfrac{1}{3}\right) + \left(\dfrac{x}{3} + 5\right)$

$\quad\quad \cdot \left[12\left(-\dfrac{3}{4}x^{-7/4}\right)\right]$

$\quad = 4x^{-3/4} - 9x^{-7/4}\left(\dfrac{x}{3} + 5\right)$

$\quad = 4x^{-3/4} - 3x^{-3/4} - 45x^{-7/4}$

$\quad = x^{-3/4} - 45x^{-7/4}$

$\quad$ or $\dfrac{1}{x^{3/4}} - \dfrac{45}{x^{7/4}}$

54. $k(x) = \dfrac{3x}{x + 5}$

$k'(x) = \dfrac{(x + 5)(3) - (3x)(1)}{(x + 5)^2}$

$\quad\quad = \dfrac{3x + 15 - 3x}{(x + 5)^2}$

$\quad\quad = \dfrac{15}{(x + 5)^2}$

56. $y = \dfrac{x^2 - x + 1}{x - 1}$

$y' = \dfrac{(x - 1)(2x - 1) - (x^2 - x + 1)(1)}{(x - 1)^2}$

$\quad = \dfrac{2x^2 - 3x + 1 - x^2 + x - 1}{(x - 1)^2}$

$\quad = \dfrac{x^2 - 2x}{(x - 1)^2}$

58. $f(x) = (3x - 2)^4$

$f'(x) = 4(3x - 2)^3(3)$

$\quad\quad = 12(3x - 2)^3$

60. $y = \sqrt{2t - 5}$

$\quad\quad = (2t - 5)^{1/2}$

$y' = \dfrac{1}{2}(2t - 5)^{-1/2}(2)$

$\quad = (2t - 5)^{-1/2}$ or $\dfrac{1}{(2t - 5)^{1/2}}$

62. $y = 3x(2x + 1)^3$

$y' = 3x(3)(2x + 1)^2(2) + (2x + 1)^3(3)$

$\quad = (18x)(2x + 1)^2 + 3(2x + 1)^3$

$\quad = 3(2x + 1)^2[6x + (2x + 1)]$

$\quad = 3(2x + 1)^2(8x + 1)$

64. $r(t) = \dfrac{5t^2 - 7t}{(3t + 1)^3}$

$r'(t)$

$= \dfrac{(3t + 1)^3(10t - 7) - (5t^2 - 7t)3(3t + 1)^2(3)}{[(3t + 1)^3]^2}$

$= \dfrac{(3t + 1)^3(10t - 7) - 9(5t^2 - 7t)(3t + 1)^2}{(3t + 1)^6}$

$= \dfrac{(3t + 1)(10t - 7) - 9(5t^2 - 7t)}{(3t + 1)^4}$

$= \dfrac{30t^2 - 11t - 7 - 45t^2 + 63t}{(3t + 1)^4}$

$= \dfrac{-15t^2 + 52t - 7}{(3t + 1)^4}$

66. $D_x \left[\dfrac{\sqrt{x} + 1}{\sqrt{x} - 1} \right]$

$= D_x \left[\dfrac{x^{1/2} + 1}{x^{1/2} - 1} \right]$

$= \dfrac{(x^{1/2} - 1)\left(\frac{1}{2}x^{-1/2}\right) - (x^{1/2} + 1)\left(\frac{1}{2}x^{-1/2}\right)}{(x^{1/2} - 1)^2}$

$= \dfrac{\frac{1}{2} - \frac{1}{2}x^{-1/2} - \frac{1}{2} - \frac{1}{2}x^{-1/2}}{(x^{1/2} - 1)^2}$

$= \dfrac{-x^{-1/2}}{(x^{1/2} - 1)^2}$

$= \dfrac{-1}{x^{1/2}(x^{1/2} - 1)^2}$

68. $y = \sqrt{t^{1/2} + t}$

$= (t^{1/2} + t)^{1/2}$

$\dfrac{dy}{dt} = \dfrac{1}{2}(t^{1/2} + t)^{-1/2}\left(\frac{1}{2}t^{-1/2} + 1\right)$

$= \dfrac{\left(\frac{1}{2}t^{-1/2} + 1\right)}{2(t^{1/2} + t)^{1/2}}$

$= \dfrac{2t^{1/2}}{2t^{1/2}} \cdot \left[\dfrac{\left(\frac{1}{2}t^{-1/2} + 1\right)}{2(t^{1/2} + t)^{1/2}} \right]$

$= \dfrac{1 + 2t^{1/2}}{4t^{1/2}(t^{1/2} + t)^{1/2}}$

70. $f(x) = \dfrac{\sqrt{8 + x}}{x + 1}$

$= \dfrac{(8 + x)^{1/2}}{x + 1}$

$f'(x)$

$= \dfrac{(x + 1)\left(\frac{1}{2}\right)(8 + x)^{-1/2}(1) - (8 + x)^{1/2}(1)}{(x + 1)^2}$

$= \dfrac{\left(\frac{1}{2}\right)(x + 1)(8 + x)^{-1/2} - (8 + x)^{1/2}}{(x + 1)^2}$

$f'(1)$

$= \dfrac{\left(\frac{1}{2}\right)(1 + 1)(8 + 1)^{-1/2} - (8 + 1)^{1/2}}{(1 + 1)^2}$

$= \dfrac{\left(\frac{1}{2}\right)(2)(9)^{-1/2} - (9)^{1/2}}{2^2}$

$= \dfrac{\frac{1}{3} - 3}{4} = \dfrac{-\frac{8}{3}}{4} = -\dfrac{2}{3}$

74. $C(x) = \sqrt{x + 1}$

$\overline{C}(x) = \dfrac{C(x)}{x}$

$= \dfrac{\sqrt{x + 1}}{x} = \dfrac{(x + 1)^{1/2}}{x}$

$\overline{C}'(x) = \dfrac{x\left[\frac{1}{2}(x + 1)^{-1/2}\right] - (x + 1)^{1/2}(1)}{x^2}$

$= \dfrac{\frac{1}{2}x(x + 1)^{-1/2} - (x + 1)^{1/2}}{2x}$

$= \dfrac{x(x + 1)^{-1/2} - 2(x + 1)^{1/2}}{2x^2}$

$= \dfrac{(x + 1)^{-1/2}[x - 2(x + 1)]}{2x^2}$

$= \dfrac{(x + 1)^{-1/2}(-x - 2)}{2x^2}$

$= \dfrac{-x - 2}{2x^2(x + 1)^{1/2}}$

76. $C(x) = (x^2 + 3)^3$

$\overline{C}(x) = \dfrac{C(x)}{x} = \dfrac{(x^2 + 3)^3}{x}$

$\overline{C}'(x)$

$= \dfrac{x[3(x^2 + 3)^2(2x)] - (x^2 + 3)^3(1)}{x^2}$

$= \dfrac{6x^2(x^2 + 3)^2 - (x^2 + 3)^3}{x^2}$

$= \dfrac{(x^2 + 3)^2[6x^2 - (x^2 + 3)]}{x^2}$

$= \dfrac{(x^2 + 3)^2(5x^2 - 3)}{x^2}$

78. $S(x) = 1000 + 50\sqrt{x} + 10x$

$= 1000 + 50x^{1/2} + 10x$

$\dfrac{dS}{dx} = 50\left(\dfrac{1}{2}\right)x^{-1/2} + 10$

$= 25x^{-1/2} + 10 = \dfrac{25}{\sqrt{x}} + 10$

(a) $\dfrac{dS}{dx}(9) = \dfrac{25}{\sqrt{9}} + 10$

$= \dfrac{25}{3} + 10$

$= \dfrac{55}{3}$

Sales will increase by 55 million dollars when 3 thousand more dollars are spent on research.

(b) $\dfrac{dS}{dx}(16) = \dfrac{25}{\sqrt{16}} + 10$

$= \dfrac{25}{4} + 10$

$= \dfrac{65}{4}$

Sales will increase by 65 million dollars when 4 thousand more dollars are spent on research.

(c) $\dfrac{dS}{dx}(25) = \dfrac{25}{\sqrt{25}} + 10$

$= 5 + 10$

$= 15$

Sales will increase by 15 million dollars when 1 thousand more dollars are spent on research.

(d) As more money is spent on research, the rate of increase in sales declines. When x = 9, the rate of increase was $\dfrac{55}{3} \approx 18.3$, but when x = 25, the rate of increase had declined to 15.

80. $T(x) = \dfrac{1000 + 50x}{x + 1}$

$T'(x) = \dfrac{(x + 1)(50) - (1000 + 50x)(1)}{(x + 1)^2}$

$= \dfrac{-950}{(x + 1)^2}$

(a) $T'(9) = \dfrac{-950}{(9 + 1)^2}$

$= \dfrac{-950}{100}$

$= -9.5$

Costs will decrease by \$9500 for the next \$100 spent on training.

(b) $T'(19) = \dfrac{-950}{(19 + 1)^2}$

$= \dfrac{-950}{400}$

$= -\dfrac{19}{8} = -2.375$

Costs will decrease by $2375 for the next $100 spent on training.

(c) Costs will always decrease because $T'(x) = \dfrac{-950}{(x + 1)^2}$ will always be negative.

82. $C(x) = \begin{cases} 1.50x & \text{for } 0 < x \le 125 \\ 1.35x & \text{for } x > 125 \end{cases}$

(a) $C(100) = 1.50(100) = \$150$

(b) $C(125) = 1.50(125) = \$187.50$

(c) $C(140) = 1.35(140) = \$189$

(d)

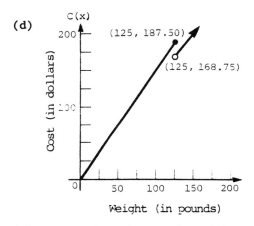

(e) By reading the graph, $C(x)$ is discontinuous at $x = \$125$.

The average cost per pound is given by $\overline{C}(x) = \dfrac{C(x)}{x}$.

$\overline{C}(x) = \begin{cases} 1.50 & \text{for } 0 < x \le 125 \\ 1.35 & \text{for } x > 125 \end{cases}$

(f) $\overline{C}(100) = \$1.50$

(g) $\overline{C}(125) = \$1.50$

(h) $\overline{C}(140) = \$1.35$

The marginal cost is given by

$C(x) = \begin{cases} 1.50 & \text{for } 0 < x \le 125 \\ 1.35 & \text{for } x > 125 \end{cases}$

(i) $C'(100) = 1.50$; the 101st pound will cost $1.50.

(j) $C'(140) = 1.35$; the 141st pound will cost $1.35.

84. $V(t) = -t^2 + 6t - 4$

(a)

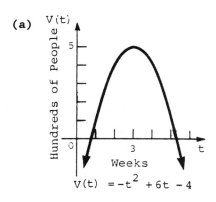

$V(t) = -t^2 + 6t - 4$

(b) The x-intercepts of the parabola are .8 and 5.2, so a reasonable domain would be $[.8, 5.2]$.

(c) The number of cases reaches a maximum at the vertex; $x = \dfrac{-b}{2a} = \dfrac{-6}{-2} = 3$ weeks. The maximum number of cases is $V(3) = -3^2 + 6(3) - 4 = 5$ hundred cases.

(d) $V'(t) = -2t + 6$

(e) $V'(3) = -2(3) + 6 = 0$

(f) The sign of the rate of change up to the maximum is +, because the function is increasing. The sign of the rate of change after the maximum is − because the function is decreasing.

For Exercises 86 and 88, use a computer
or a graphing calculator. Solutions will
vary depending on the program that is
used. Answers are given.

86.   (a) The graph shows that the derivative is positive where x is in
the intervals $(-.3, .4)$ and
$(1, \infty)$.

(b) $k'(x) = 0$ when $x = -.3$, $x = .4$,
and $x = 1$

(c) The graph shows that the derivative is negative where x is in
the intervals $(-\infty, -.3)$ and
$(.4, 1)$.

(d) The derivative is zero at the low
points and high point of the
graph of k(x). The derivative is
positive where k(x) is increasing
and negative where k(x) is
decreasing.

88.   (a) The graph shows that the derivative is positive for values of x
in the interval $(.5, \infty)$.

(b) The derivative is never zero.

(c) The graph shows that the derivative is negative for values of x
in the interval $(-\infty, .5)$.

(d) The derivative does not exist at
$x = .5$, which corresponds to a
sharp point on the graph of K(x).
The derivative is positive where
K(x) is increasing and negative
where K(x) is decreasing.

CHAPTER 3 CURVE SKETCHING

Section 3.1

2. By reading the graph, $f(x)$ is

    (a) increasing on $(-\infty, 4)$ and

    (b) decreasing on $(4, \infty)$.

4. By reading the graph, $g(x)$ is

    (a) increasing on $(3, \infty)$ and

    (b) decreasing on $(-\infty, 3)$.

6. By reading the graph, $h(x)$ is

    (a) increasing on $(1, 5)$ and

    (b) decreasing on $(-\infty, 1)$ and $(5, \infty)$.

8. By reading the graph, $f(x)$ is

    (a) increasing on $(-3, 0)$ and $(3, \infty)$ and

    (b) decreasing on $(-\infty, -3)$ and $(0, 3)$.

10. $f(x) = x^2 - 9x + 4$

    $f'(x) = 2x - 9$

    $f'(x)$ is zero when

    $2x - 9 = 0$

    $x = \dfrac{9}{2}.$

Since $f(x)$ is polynomial function, there are no values where f fails to exist. 9/2 is the only critical number.

9/2 determines two intervals on a number line.

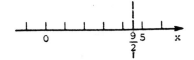

Testing a point (any point will do other than the one where x = 9/2) in each interval, we find the following.

(a) $f'(5) = 1 > 0$, so $f(x)$ is increasing on $(9/2, \infty)$.

(b) $f'(0) = -9 < 0$, so $f(x)$ is decreasing on $(-\infty, 9/2)$.

12. $y = .3 + .4x - .2x^2$

    $y' = .4 - .4x$

    y' is zero when

    $.4 - .4x = 0$

    $x = 1.$

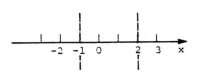

Test a point in each interval.

(a) When $x = 0$, $y' = .4 > 0$, so y is increasing on $(-\infty, 1)$.

(b) When $x = 2$, $y' = -.4 < 0$, so y is decreasing on $(1, \infty)$.

14. $f(x) = \dfrac{2}{3}x^3 - x^2 - 4x + 2$

    $f'(x) = 2x^2 - 2x - 4$

    $ = 2(x^2 - x - 2)$

    $ = 2(x + 1)(x - 2)$

    $f'(x)$ is zero when $x = -1$ or $x = 2$.

Test a point in each interval.

$f'(-2) = 8 > 0$

$f'(0) = -4 < 0$

$f'(3) = 8 > 0$

(a) $f(x)$ is increasing on $(-\infty, -1)$ and $(2, \infty)$.

(b) $f(x)$ is decreasing on $(-1, 2)$.

16. $f(x) = 4x^3 - 9x^2 - 30x + 6$

$f'(x) = 12x^2 - 18x - 30$

$= 6(2x^2 - 3x - 5)$

$= 6(2x - 5)(x + 1)$

$f'(x)$ is zero when $x = \frac{5}{2}$ or $x = -1$.

$f(-2) = 54 > 0$

$f(0) = -30 < 0$

$f(3) = 24 > 0$

(a) $f(x)$ is increasing on $(-\infty, -1)$ and $(5/2, \infty)$.

(b) $f(x)$ is decreasing on $(-1, 5/2)$.

18. $y = 6x - 9$

$y' = 6 > 0$

(a) Since y' is always positive, the function is increasing everywhere, or on the interval $(-\infty, \infty)$.

(b) y' is never negative so the function is decreasing on no interval.

20. $f(x) = \dfrac{x + 3}{x - 4}$

$f'(x) = \dfrac{(1)(x - 4) - (1)(x + 3)}{(x - 4)^2}$

$= \dfrac{x - 4 - x - 3}{(x - 4)^2}$

$= \dfrac{-7}{(x - 4)^2}$

$f(x)$ is never 0, but it fails to exist at $x = 4$. Since $f(x)$ also does not exist at $x = 4$, 4 is not a critical number. However, the line $x = 4$ is an asymptote of the graph, so the function might change direction from one side of the asymptote to the other.

$f'(0) = -\dfrac{7}{16} < 0$

$f'(5) = -7 < 0$

(a) $f'(x)$ is always negative, so $f(x)$ is increasing on no interval.

(b) $f'(x)$ is always negative so $f(x)$ is decreasing everywhere that is defined. Since $f(x)$ is not defined at $x = 4$, these intervals are $(-\infty, 4)$ and $(4, \infty)$.

22. $y = -|x - 3| = \begin{cases} -(x - 3) & \text{if } x \geq 3 \\ (x - 3) & \text{if } x < 3 \end{cases}$

Therefore, $y = \begin{cases} -x + 3 & \text{if } x \geq 3 \\ x - 3 & \text{if } x < 3 \end{cases}.$

$y' = \begin{cases} -1 & \text{if } x \geq 3 \\ 1 & \text{if } x < 3 \end{cases}$

(a) y is increasing on $(-\infty, 3)$.

(b) y is decreasing on $(3, \infty)$.

24. $f(x) = \sqrt{5 - x} = (5 - x)^{1/2}$

Note that $f(x)$ is defined only for $x \le 5$ and exists for all such values.

$f'(x) = \frac{1}{2}(5 - x)^{-1/2}(-1)$

$= -\frac{1}{(5 - x)^{1/2}}$

$= \frac{-1}{\sqrt{5 - x}}$

(a) $f'(x)$ is never positive so $f(x)$ is increasing on no intervals.

(b) $f'(x)$ is negative for all values of x for which $f(x)$ is defined, or on $(-\infty, 5)$. Thus, $f(x)$ is decreasing on $(-\infty, 5)$.

26. $y = x\sqrt{9 - x^2} = x(9 - x^2)^{1/2}$

Use the product rule.

$y' = (1)(9 - x^2)^{1/2}$

$+ \frac{1}{2}(9 - x^2)^{-1/2}(-2x)(x)$

$= (9 - x^2)^{1/2} - x^2(9 - x^2)^{-1/2}$

$= (9 - x^2)^{-1/2}(9 - x^2 - x^2)$

$= (9 - x^2)^{-1/2}(9 - 2x^2)$

$= \frac{9 - 2x^2}{\sqrt{9 - x^2}}$

Critical values occur when $y' = 0$ or when y' fails to exist.
$y' = 0$ when

$9 - 2x^2 = 0$

$x = \frac{\pm 3}{\sqrt{2}} = \frac{\pm 3\sqrt{2}}{2}.$

y' fails to exist when

$9 - x^2 = 0$

$x = \pm 3.$

These four values determine three intervals since $f(x)$ is defined only on $[-3, 3]$. Note that $\pm\frac{3\sqrt{2}}{2} \approx \pm 2.12$.

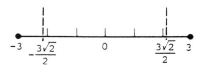

$f(-2.5) = -2.11 < 0$
$f(0) = 3 > 0$
$f(2.5) = -2.11 < 0$

(a) $f(x)$ is increasing on

$\left(-\frac{3\sqrt{2}}{2}, \frac{3\sqrt{2}}{2}\right).$

(b) $f(x)$ is decreasing on

$\left(-3, -\frac{3\sqrt{2}}{2}\right)$ and $\left(\frac{3\sqrt{2}}{2}, 3\right).$

28. $f(x) = (x + 1)^{4/5}$

$f'(x) = \frac{4}{5}(x + 1)^{-1/5}$

$= \frac{4}{5(x + 1)^{1/5}}$

$f'(x)$ is never zero, but fails to exist when $x = -1$.

$f'(-2) = -\frac{4}{5} < 0$

$f'(0) = \frac{4}{5} > 0$

(a) $f(x)$ is increasing on $(-1, \infty)$.

(b) $f(x)$ is decreasing on $(-\infty, -1)$.

30. $f(x) = ax^2 + bx + c$, $a < 0$

$f'(x) = 2ax + b$

Let $f'(x) = 0$ to find the critical number.

$$2ax + b = 0$$
$$2ax = -b$$
$$x = \frac{-b}{2a}$$

Choose a value in the interval $(-\infty, -b/2a)$. Since $a < 0$,

$$\frac{-b}{2a} - \frac{-1}{2a} = \frac{-b + 1}{2a} < \frac{-b}{2a}.$$

$$f'\left(\frac{-b + 1}{2a}\right) = 2a\left(\frac{-b + 1}{2a}\right) + b$$
$$= -1 > 0$$

Choose a value in the interval $(-b/2a, \infty)$, since $a < 0$,

$$\frac{-b}{2a} - \frac{-1}{2a} = \frac{-b - 1}{2a} > \frac{-b}{2a}.$$

$$f'\left(\frac{-b - 1}{2a}\right) = 2a\left(\frac{-b - 1}{2a}\right) + b$$
$$= -1 < 0$$

$f'(x)$ is increasing on $(-\infty, -b/(2a))$ and decreasing on $(-b/(2a), \infty)$. This tells us that the curve opens downward and $x = -b/2a$ is the x-coordinate of the vertex.

$$f\left(\frac{-b}{2a}\right) = a\left(\frac{-b}{2a}\right)^2 + b\left(\frac{-b}{2a}\right) + c$$
$$= \frac{ab^2}{4a^2} - \frac{b^2}{2a} + c$$
$$= \frac{b^2}{4a} - \frac{2b^2}{4a} + \frac{4ac}{4a}$$
$$= \frac{4ac - b^2}{4a}$$

The vertex is $\left(-\dfrac{b}{2a}, \dfrac{4ac - b^2}{4a}\right)$.

32. $H(r) = \dfrac{300}{1 + .03r^2} = 300(1 + .03r^2)^{-1}$

$H'(r) = 300[-1(1 + .03r^2)^{-2}(.06r)]$

$$= \frac{-18r}{(1 + .03r^2)^2}$$

Since r is a mortgage rate (in percent), it is always positive. Thus, $H'(r)$ is always negative.

(a) $H(r)$ is increasing on no interval.

(b) $H(r)$ is decreasing on $(0, \infty)$.

34. $P(x) = \dfrac{1}{3}x^3 - \dfrac{7}{2}x^2 + 10x - 2$

$P'(x) = x^2 - 7x + 10$
$$= (x - 5)(x - 2)$$

Profit is increasing when $P'(x) > 0$ and decreasing when $P'(x) < 0$.

$P'(x) = 0$ when

$$x = 5 \quad \text{or} \quad x = 2.$$

$P'(0) = 10 > 0$

$P'(3) = -2 < 0$

$P'(6) = 4 > 0$

(a) $P(x)$ is increasing on $(-\infty, 2)$ and $(5, \infty)$.

Since x is positive and represents quantity in hundreds per month, profit is increasing on the intervals $(0, 200)$ and $(500, 800)$.

(b) Similarly, $P(x)$ is decreasing on $(2, 5)$, or the profit is decreasing on the interval $(200, 500)$.

36. $A(x) = -.015x^3 + 1.058x$

$A'(x) = -.045x^2 + 1.058$

$A'(x) = 0$ when

$$-.045x^2 + 1.058 = 0$$

$$-.045x^2 = -1.058$$

$$x^2 \approx 23.5$$

$$x \approx \pm 4.8.$$

The function only applies for the interval [0, 8], so we disregard the solution −4.8.

Then, 4.8 divides [0, 8] into two intervals.

$A'(4) = .338 > 0$

$A'(5) = -.067 < 0$

(a) $A(x)$ is increasing on the interval (0, 4.8).

(b) $A(x)$ is decreasing on the interval (4.8, 8).

38. $K(t) = \dfrac{5t}{t^2 + 1}$

$K'(t) = \dfrac{5(t^2 + 1) - 2t(5t)}{(t^2 + 1)^2}$

$= \dfrac{5t^2 + 5 - 10t^2}{(t^2 + 1)^2}$

$= \dfrac{5 - 5t^2}{(t^2 + 1)^2}$

$K'(t) = 0$ when

$$\dfrac{5 - 5t^2}{(t^2 + 1)^2} = 0$$

$$5 - 5t^2 = 0$$

$$5t^2 = 5$$

$$t = \pm 1.$$

Since t is the time after a drug is administered, the function applies

only for [0, ∞), so we discard t = −1. Then 1 divides the interval into two intervals.

$K'(.5) = 2.4 > 0$

$K'(2) = -.6 < 0$

(a) $K(t)$ is increasing on (0, 1).

(b) $K(t)$ is decreasing on (1, ∞).

Section 3.2

2. As shown on the graph, the relative maximum of 1 occurs when x = 4.

4. As shown on the graph, the relative minimum of −4 occurs when x = 3.

6. As shown on the graph, the relative minimum of −6 occurs when x = 1 and the relative maximum of 2 occurs when x = 5.

8. As shown on the graph, the relative maximum of 4 occurs when x = 0; the relative minimum of 0 occurs when x = −3 and x = 3.

10. $f(x) = x^2 - 4x + 6$

$f'(x) = 2x - 4$

$= 2(x - 2)$

$f'(x)$ is zero when x = 2.

f'(0) = 2(0) - 4 = -4 < 0

f'(3) = 2(3) - 4 = 2 > 0

Thus, f(x) is decreasing on (-∞, 2) and increasing on (2, ∞), so f(2) is a relative minimum.

$$f(2) = (2)^2 - 4(2) + 6$$
$$= 4 - 8 + 6 = 2$$

Relative minimum of 2 at 2

12. $f(x) = 3 - .4x - .2x^2$

$f'(x) = -.4 - .4x$

$\quad\quad = -.4(1 + x)$

f'(x) is zero when x = -1.

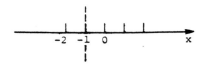

f'(-2) = .4 > 0

f'(0) = -.4 < 0

f(x) is increasing on (-∞, -1) and decreasing on (-1, ∞). f(-1) is a relative maximum.

$$f(-1) = 3 - .4(-1) - .2(-1)^2$$
$$= 3 + .4 - .2$$
$$= 3.2$$

Relative maximum of 3.2 at -1

14. $f(x) = x^3 + 3x^2 - 24x + 2$

$f'(x) = 3x^2 + 6x - 24$

$\quad\quad = 3(x^2 + 2x - 8)$

$\quad\quad = 3(x + 4)(x - 2)$

f'(x) is zero when x = -4 and x = 2.

f'(-5) = 21 > 0

f'(0) = -24 < 0

f'(3) = 21 > 0

f(x) is increasing on (-∞, -4) and decreasing on (-4, 2). Thus, a relative maximum occurs at x = -4. f(x) is decreasing on (-4, 2) and increasing on (2, ∞). Thus, a relative minimum occurs at x = 2.

$$f(-4) = (-4)^3 + 3(-4)^2 - 24(-4) + 2$$
$$= 82$$
$$f(2) = (2)^3 + 3(2)^2 - 24(2) + 2$$
$$= -26$$

Relative maximum of 82 at -4; relative minimum of -26 at 2

16. $f(x) = -\frac{2}{3}x^3 - \frac{1}{2}x^2 + 3x - 4$

$f'(x) = -2x^2 - x + 3$

$\quad\quad = -(2x^2 + x - 3)$

$\quad\quad = -(2x + 3)(x - 1)$

f'(x) is zero when $x = -\frac{3}{2}$ or x = 1.

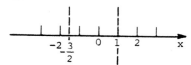

f'(-2) = -3

f'(0) = 3

f'(2) = -7

f(x) is decreasing on (-∞, -3/2), increasing on (-3/2, 1). Thus, a relative minimum occurs at x = -3/2. f(x) is increasing on (-3/2, 1) and decreasing on (1, ∞). Thus, a relative maximum occurs at x = 1.

$$f\left(-\frac{3}{2}\right) = -\frac{59}{8}$$

$$f(1) = -\frac{13}{6}$$

Relative maximum of -13/6 at 1;
relative minimum of -59/8 at -3/2

18. $f(x) = 2x^3 + 15x^2 + 36x - 4$

$f'(x) = 6x^2 + 30x + 36$

$\qquad = 6(x^2 + 5x + 6)$

$\qquad = 6(x + 3)(x + 2)$

$f'(x)$ is zero when $x = -3$ or $x = -2$.

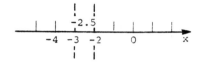

$f'(-4) = 12$

$f'(-2.5) = -1.5$

$f'(0) = 36$

$f(x)$ is increasing on $(-\infty, -3)$ and
decreasing on $(-3, -2)$. Thus, a
relative maximum occurs at $x = -3$.
$f(x)$ is decreasing on $(-3, -2)$ and
increasing on $(-2, \infty)$. Thus, a
relative minimum occurs at $x = -2$.
$f(-3) = -31$
$f(-2) = -32$

Relative maximum of -31 at -3;
relative minimum of -32 at -2

20. $f(x) = x^4 - 8x^2 + 9$

$f'(x) = 4x^3 - 16x$

$\qquad = 4x(x^2 - 4)$

$\qquad = 4x(x + 2)(x - 2)$

$f'(x)$ is zero when $x = 0$ or $x = -2$
or $x = 2$.

$f'(-3) = -60 < 0$

$f'(-1) = 12 > 0$

$f'(1) = -12 < 0$

$f(3) = 60 > 0$

$f(x)$ is increasing on $(-2, 0)$ and
$(2, \infty)$; $f(x)$ is decreasing on
$(-\infty, -2)$ and $(0, 2)$.

$f(-2) = -7$

$f(0) = 9$

$f(2) = -7$

Relative maximum of 9 at 0;
relative minimum of -7 at -2
and 2

22. $f(x) = (2 - 9x)^{2/3}$

$f'(x) = \frac{2}{3}(2 - 9x)^{-1/3}(-9)$

$\qquad = \frac{-6}{(2 - 9x)^{1/3}}$

Critical number:

$$2 - 9x = 0$$

$$x = \frac{2}{9}$$

$f'(0) = -4.76 < 0$

$f'(1) = 3.14 > 0$

$f(x)$ is decreasing on $(-\infty, 2/9)$ and
increasing on $(2/9, \infty)$.

$$f\left(\frac{2}{9}\right) = 0$$

Relative minimum of 0 at 2/9

24. $f(x) = 3x^{5/3} - 15x^{2/3}$

$f'(x) = 5x^{2/3} - 10x^{-1/3}$

$= 5x^{-1/3}(x - 2)$

$= \dfrac{5(x - 2)}{x^{1/3}}$

Critical numbers:

$5(x - 2) = 0$ $\qquad$ $x^{1/3} = 0$

$\qquad x = 2$ $\qquad\qquad$ $x = 0$

$f'(-1) = 15 > 0$

$f'(1) = -15 < 0$

$f'(3) = 3.47 > 0$

f(x) is increasing on $(-\infty, 0)$ and $(2, \infty)$.

f(x) is decreasing on $(0, 2)$.

$f(x) = 3x^{2/3}(x - 5)$

$f(0) = 3 \cdot 0(0 - 5) = 0$

$f(2) = 3 \cdot 2^{2/3}(2 - 5)$

$= -9 \cdot 2^{2/3} \approx -14.287$

Relative maximum of 0 at 0; relative minimum of $-9 \cdot 2^{2/3} \approx -14.287$ at 2

26. $f(x) = x^2 + \dfrac{1}{x} = x^2 + x^{-1}$

$f'(x) = 2x - x^{-2}$

$= 2x - \dfrac{1}{x^2}$

$= \dfrac{2x^3 - 1}{x^2}$

Critical number:

$2x^3 - 1 = 0$

$x = \dfrac{1}{\sqrt[3]{2}} = \dfrac{\sqrt[3]{4}}{2}$

Note that both f(x) and f'(x) do not exist at x = 0, so 0 is not a critical number.

$f'(-1) = -3 < 0$

$f'(1) = 1 > 0$

f(x) is decreasing on $(-\infty, \sqrt[3]{4}/2)$ and increasing on $(\sqrt[3]{4}/2, \infty)$.

$f\left(\dfrac{\sqrt[3]{4}}{2}\right) = \left(\dfrac{\sqrt[3]{4}}{2}\right)^2 + \left(\dfrac{\sqrt[3]{4}}{2}\right)^{-1}$

$= \left(\dfrac{\sqrt[3]{4}}{2}\right)^{-1}\left[\left(\dfrac{\sqrt[3]{4}}{2}\right)^3 + 1\right]$

$= \dfrac{2}{\sqrt[3]{4}}\left(\dfrac{4}{8} + 1\right) = \dfrac{2}{\sqrt[3]{4}}\left(\dfrac{3}{2}\right) \cdot \dfrac{\sqrt[3]{2}}{\sqrt[3]{2}}$

$= \dfrac{3\sqrt[3]{2}}{2} \approx 1.890$

Relative minimum of $3\sqrt[3]{2}/2 \approx 1.890$ at $\sqrt[3]{4}/2$

28. $f(x) = \dfrac{x^2}{x - 3}$

$f'(x) = \dfrac{2x(x - 3) - (1)(x^2)}{(x - 3)^2}$

$= \dfrac{2x^2 - 6x - x^2}{(x - 3)^2}$

$= \dfrac{x^2 - 6x}{(x - 3)^2}$

$= \dfrac{x(x - 6)}{(x - 3)^2}$

Find critical numbers:

$x(x - 6) = 0$ $x - 3 = 0$

$x = 0$ or $x = 6$ $x = 3$

Note that $f(x)$ and $f'(x)$ do not exist at $x = 3$, so 3 is not a critical number.

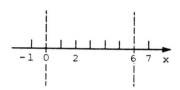

$f'(-1) = .4375 > 0$

$f'(2) = -8 < 0$

$f'(7) = .4375 > 0$

$f(x)$ is increasing on $(-\infty, 0)$ and $(6, \infty)$. $f(x)$ is decreasing on $(0, 6)$.

$$f(0) = 0$$

$$f(6) = 12$$

Relative maximum of 0 at 0; relative minimum of 12 at 6

30. $f(x) = \dfrac{x^2 - 6x + 9}{x + 2}$

$f'(x) = \dfrac{(2x - 6)(x + 2) - (1)(x^2 - 6x + 9)}{(x + 2)^2}$

$= \dfrac{x^2 + 4x - 21}{(x + 2)^2}$

$= \dfrac{(x + 7)(x - 3)}{(x + 2)^2}$

Find critical numbers:

$(x + 7)(x - 3) = 0$ $x + 2 = 0$

$x = -7$ or $x = 3$ $x = -2$

$f'(-8) = \dfrac{11}{36} > 0$

$f'(-3) = -24 < 0$

$f'(0) = -\dfrac{21}{4} < 0$

$f(4) = \dfrac{11}{36} > 0$

$f(x)$ is increasing on $(-\infty, -7)$ and $(3, \infty)$.

$f(x)$ is decreasing on $(-7, 3)$

$$f(-7) = -20$$

$$f(3) = 0$$

Relative maximum of -20 at -7; relative minimum of 0 at 3

32. $y = 3x^2 - 12x + 2$

$y' = 6x - 12$

$= 6(x - 2)$

The vertex occurs when $y' = 0$ or when

$$6(x - 2) = 0$$

$$x = 2.$$

$3(2)^2 - 12(2) + 2 = -10$

The vertex is at $(2, -10)$.

34. $y = ax^2 + bx + c$

$y' = 2ax + b$

The vertex occurs when $y' = 0$ or when $2ax + b = 0$

$$x = \dfrac{-b}{2a}.$$

$$a\left(\frac{-b}{2a}\right)^2 + b\left(\frac{-b}{2a}\right) + c$$

$$= \frac{ab^2}{4a^2} - \frac{b^2}{2a} + c$$

$$= \frac{b^2}{4a} - \frac{2b^2}{4a} + \frac{4ac}{4a}$$

$$= \frac{4ac - b^2}{4a}$$

The vertex is at $\left(\frac{-b}{2a}, \frac{4ac - b^2}{4a}\right)$.

36. $C(x) = 25x + 5000;\ p = 80 - .01x$

$$P(x) = R(x) - C(x)$$
$$= px - C(x)$$
$$= (80 - .01x)x - (25x + 5000)$$
$$= 55x - .01x^2 - 5000$$

$P'(x) = 55 - .02x$

$P'(x) = 0$ when $x = 2750$.

(a) $p = 80 - .01x$

     $= 80 - .01(2750) = 52.50$,

     the price per unit that

     produces maximum profit.

(b) As shown above, the maximum

     profit occurs when 2750 units

     are sold.

(c) $P(x) = 55x - .01x^2 - 5000$

$P(2750) = 55(2750) - .01(2750)^2$

           $- 5000$

           $= 70,625$

The maximum profit is 70,625.

38. $P(x) = -x^3 + 3x^2 + 72x$

(a) $P'(x) = -3x^2 + 6x + 72$

         $= -3(x^2 - 2x - 24)$

$P'(x) = 0$ when $x^2 - 2x - 24 = 0$

                 $(x - 6)(x + 4) = 0$

$x = 6$ or $x = -4$.

Disregard the negative value.
6 units should be sold to maximize profit.

(b) **Maximize profit:**

$P(6) = -(6)^3 + 3(6)^2 + 72(6)$

     $= \$324$

40. $C(x) = .002x^3 - 9x + 4000$

$\overline{C}(x) = \frac{C(x)}{x} = .002x^2 - 9 + \frac{4000}{x}$

$\overline{C}'(x) = .004x - \frac{4000}{x^2}$

$$\frac{.004x^3 - 4000}{x^2} = 0$$

        $.004x^3 = 4000$

           $x = 100$, the
value of x that produces minimum cost.

42. $D(x) = -x^4 + 8x^3 + 80x^2$

$D'(x) = -4x^3 + 24x^2 + 160x$

        $= -4x(x^2 - 6x - 40)$

        $= -4x(x + 4)(x - 10)$

$D'(x) = 0$ when $x = 0$, $x = -4$, or $x = 10$.

Disregard the nonpositive value.
Verify that $x = 10$ gives a maximum:

    $D'(9) = 468 > 0$

    $D'(11) = -660 < 0$

The speaker should aim for a degree of discrepancy of 10.

44. $s(t) = -16t^2 + 64t + 3$

    $s'(t) = -32t + 64$

When $s'(t) = 0$,

        $0 = -32t + 64$

      $32t = 64$

        $t = 2$.

Verify that t = 2 gives a maximum:

$$s'(1) = 32 > 0$$
$$s'(3) = -32 < 0$$
$$s(2) = -16(2)^2 + 64(2) + 3$$
$$= 67$$

Therefore, the maximum height is 67 ft.

Exercises 46 and 48 should be solved by computer or graphing calculator methods. The solutions will vary according to the method or computer program that is used.

46. $f(x) = -x^5 - x^4 + 2x^3 - 25x^2 + 9x + 12$

The answer is that there is a relative maximum of 13 at .18 and a relative minimum of -140 at -2.7.

48. $f(x) = -.001x^6 - .005x^5 - .5x^4 + 7x^3$
$- 8x^2 + 15x + 43$

The answer is that there is a relative maximum of 53,000 at 20.

Section 3.3

2. As shown on the graph, the absolute minimum occurs at x_1; there is no absolute maximum. (There is no functional value that is greater than all others.)

4. As shown on the graph, there are no absolute extrema.

6. As shown on the graph, the absolute maximum occurs at x_1; there is no absolute minimum.

8. As shown on the graph, the absolute maximum occurs at x_2; the absolute minimum occurs at x_1.

10. $f(x) = x^2 - 4x + 1$; $[-6, 5]$

Find critical number(s):

$$f'(x) = 2x - 4 = 0$$
$$x = 2$$

Evaluate the function at 2 and at the endpoints.

x	f(x)	
-6	61	Absolute maximum
2	-3	Absolute minimum
5	6	

12. $f(x) = 9 - 6x - 3x^2$; $[-4, 3]$

Find critical number(s).

$$f'(x) = -6 - 6x = 0$$
$$x = -1$$

x	f(x)	
-4	-15	
-1	12	Absolute maximum
3	-36	Absolute minimum

14. $f(x) = x^3 - 6x^2 + 9x - 8$; $[0, 5]$

Find critical numbers:

$$f'(x) = 3x^2 - 12x + 9 = 0$$
$$x^2 - 4x + 3 = 0$$
$$(x - 3)(x - 1) = 0$$
$$x = 1 \text{ or } 3$$

x	f(x)	
0	-8	Absolute minimum
1	-4	
3	-8	Absolute minimum
5	12	Absolute maximum

16. $f(x) = \frac{1}{3}x^3 - \frac{3}{2}x^2 - 4x + 1$; $[-5, 2]$

Find critical numbers:

$f'(x) = x^2 + 3x - 4 = 0$

$(x + 4)(x - 1) = 0$

$x = -4$ or 1

x	f(x)	
-4	$\frac{59}{3} = 19.67$	Absolute maximum
1	$-\frac{7}{6} = -1.17$	Absolute minimum
-5	$\frac{21}{6} \approx 3.5$	
2	$\frac{5}{3} = 1.67$	

18. $f(x) = x^4 - 18x^2 + 1$; $[-4, 4]$

$f'(x) = 4x^3 - 36x = 0$

$4x(x^2 - 9) = 0$

$4x(x + 3)(x - 3) = 0$

$x = 0, -3$ or 3

x	f(x)	
-4	-31	
-3	-80	Absolute minimum
0	1	Absolute maximum
3	-80	Absolute minimum
4	-31	

20. $f(x) = \frac{-2}{x + 3}$; $[1, 4]$

$f'(x) = \frac{2}{(x + 3)^2}$

No critical numbers; $f'(x)$ is never zero or undefined when $f(x)$ is undefined.

x	f(x)	
1	$-\frac{1}{2}$	Absolute minimum
4	$-\frac{2}{7}$	Absolute maximum

22. $f(x) = \frac{1 - x}{3 + x}$; $[0, 3]$

$f'(x) = \frac{-4}{(3 + x)^2}$

No critical numbers

x	f(x)	
0	$\frac{1}{3}$	Absolute maximum
3	$-\frac{1}{3}$	Absolute minimum

24. $f(x) = \frac{x - 1}{x^2 + 2}$; $[1, 5]$

$f'(x) = \frac{-x^2 + 2x + 1}{(x^2 + 1)^2}$

$-x^2 + 2x + 1 = 0$

Critical numbers are $x = 1 + \sqrt{2}$, $1 - \sqrt{2}$. $1 - \sqrt{2}$ is not in $[1, 5]$.

x	f(x)	
1	0	Absolute minimum
5	$\frac{4}{26} \approx .15$	Absolute maximum
$1 + \sqrt{2}$	.14	

26. $f(x) = (x^2 - 4)^{1/3}$; $[-2, 2]$

$f'(x) = \frac{2x}{3(x^2 - 4)^{2/3}} = 0$

$x = 0$

x	f(x)	
-2	0	Absolute maximum
0	-1.59	Absolute minimum
2	0	Absolute maximum

28. $f(x) = (x - 3)(x - 1)^3$; $[-2, 3]$

$f'(x) = (1)(x-1)^3 + 3(x-1)^2(x-3)$

$= (x - 1)^2(4x - 10) = 0$

$= 2(x - 1)^2(2x - 5) = 0$

$$x = 1 \text{ or } \frac{5}{2}$$

x	f(x)	
-2	135	Absolute maximum
1	0	
$\frac{5}{2}$	-1.687	Absolute minimum
3	0	

30. $f(x) = \dfrac{3}{\sqrt{x^2 + 4}}$; $[-2, 2]$

$$f'(x) = \frac{-3x}{(x^2 + 4)^{3/2}} = 0$$

$$x = 0$$

x	f(x)	
-2	$\frac{3}{\sqrt{8}} \approx 1.06$	Absolute minimum
0	$\frac{3}{2} = 1.5$	Absolute maximum
2	$\frac{3}{\sqrt{8}} \approx 1.06$	Absolute minimum

32. $P(x) = -x^3 + 9x^2 + 120x - 400$,

$x \geq 5$

$$\begin{aligned}P'(x) &= -3x^2 + 18x + 120 \\ &= -3(x^2 - 6x - 40) \\ &= -3(x - 10)(x + 4) = 0 \\ & \qquad\qquad x = 10 \text{ or } -4\end{aligned}$$

-4 is not relevant since $x \geq 5$.

Critical number is $x = 10$.

The graph of $P'(x)$ is a parabola that opens downward so $P'(x) > 0$ in the interval $[5, 10)$ and $P'(x) < 0$ in the interval $(10, \infty)$. Thus, $P(x)$ is a maximum at $x = 10$.

Since x is measured in hundred thouands, 10 hundred thousand or 1,000,000 tires must be sold to maximize profit.

Also,

$$P(10) = -(10)^3 + 9(10)^2 + 120(10) - 400$$

$$P(10) = 700.$$

So the maximum profit is $700,000.

34. $C(x) = x^3 + 37x + 250$

(a) $1 \leq x \leq 10$

$$\begin{aligned}\overline{C}(x) = \frac{C(x)}{x} &= \frac{x^3 + 37x + 250}{x} \\ &= x^2 + 37 + \frac{250}{x}\end{aligned}$$

$$\begin{aligned}\overline{C}'(x) &= 2x - \frac{250}{x^2} \\ &= \frac{2x^3 - 250}{x^2} = 0 \text{ when}\end{aligned}$$

$$2x^3 = 250$$
$$x^3 = 125$$
$$x = 5.$$

Test for relative minimum.

$\overline{C}'(4) = -7.625 < 0$

$\overline{C}'(6) \approx 5.0556 > 0$

$\overline{C}(5) = 112$

$\overline{C}(1) = 1 + 37 + 250 = 288$

$\overline{C}(10) = 100 + 37 + 25 = 162$

The minimum for $1 \leq x \leq 10$ is 112.

(b) $10 \leq x \leq 20$

There are no critical values in this interval. Check the endpoints.

$\overline{C}(10) = 162$

$\overline{C}(20) = 400 + 37 + 12.5 = 449.5$

The minimum for $10 \leq x \leq 20$ is 162.

36. $S(x) = -x^3 + 3x^2 + 360x + 5000;$

$6 \leq x \leq 20$

$S'(x) = -3x^2 + 6x + 360$

$= -3(x^2 - 2x - 120)$

$S'(x) = -3(x - 12)(x + 10) = 0$

$x = 12$ or $x = -10$ (not in the interval)

x	f(x)
6	7052
12	8024
10	7900

$x = 12°$ is the temperature that produces the maximum number of salmon.

38. $M(x) = -.018x^2 + 1.24x + 6.2,$

$30 \leq x \leq 60$

$M'(x) = -.036x + 1.24 = 0$

$x = 34.4$

x	M(x)
30	27.2
34.4	27.6
60	15.8

The absolute minimum of 15.8 mpg occurs at 60 mph.
The absolute maximum of 27.6 mpg occurs at 34.4 mph.

40. Total area = A(x)

$$= \pi\left(\frac{x}{2\pi}\right)^2 + \left(\frac{12 - x}{4}\right)^2$$

$$= \frac{x^2}{4\pi} + \frac{(12 - x)^2}{16}$$

$$A'(x) = \frac{x}{2\pi} - \frac{12 - x}{8} = 0$$

$$\frac{4x - \pi(12 - x)}{8\pi} = 0$$

$$x = \frac{12\pi}{4 + \pi} \approx 5.28$$

x	Area
0	9
5.28	5.04
12	11.46

The total area is maximized when all 12 feet of wire are used to form the circle.

Exercises 42 and 44 should be solved by computer or graphing calculator methods. The solutions will vary according to the method or computer program that is used.

42. $f(x) = \dfrac{-5x^4 + 2x^3 + 3x^2 + 9}{x^4 - x^3 + x^2 + 7};$ $[-1, 1]$

The answer is that the absolute maximum is at .61 and the absolute minimum is at −1.

44. $f(x) = x^{10/3} - x^{4/3} - 4x^2 - 8x;$
$[0, 4]$

The answer is that the absolute maximum is at 0 and the absolute minimum is at 2.64.

Section 3.4

2. $f(x) = x^3 + 4x^2 + 2$

$f'(x) = 3x^2 + 8x$

$f''(x) = 6x + 8$

$f''(0) = 6(0) + 8 = 8$

$f''(2) = 6(2) + 8 = 20$

$f''(-3) = 6(-3) + 8 = -10$

4. $f(x) = -x^4 + 2x^3 - x^2$

$f'(x) = -4x^3 + 6x^2 - 2x$

$f''(x) = -12x^2 + 12x - 2$

$f''(0) = -12(0)^2 + 12(0) - 2 = -2$

$f''(2) = -12(2)^2 + 12(2) - 2 = -26$

$f''(-3) = -12(-3)^2 + 12(-3) - 2$
$= -146$

6. $f(x) = 8x^2 + 6x + 5$

$f'(x) = 16x + 6$

$f''(x) = 16$

$f''(0) = 16$

$f''(2) = 16$

$f''(-3) = 16$

8. $f(x) = (x - 2)^3$

$f'(x) = 3(x - 2)^2$

$f''(x) = 6(x - 2)$

$f''(0) = 6(0 - 2) = -12$

$f''(2) = 6(2 - 2) = 0$

$f''(-3) = 6(-3 - 2) = -30$

10. $f(x) = \dfrac{x + 1}{x - 1}$

$f'(x) = \dfrac{(x - 1)(1) - (x + 1)(1)}{(x - 1)^2}$

$= \dfrac{-2}{(x - 1)^2} = -2(x - 1)^{-2}$

$f''(x) = 4(x - 1)^{-3} = \dfrac{4}{(x - 1)^3}$

$f''(0) = \dfrac{4}{(0 - 1)^3} = -4$

$f''(2) = \dfrac{4}{(2 - 1)^3} = 4$

$f''(-3) = \dfrac{4}{(-3 - 1)^3} = -\dfrac{1}{16}$

12. $f(x) = \dfrac{-x}{1 - x^2}$

$f'(x) = \dfrac{(1 - x^2)(-1) - (-x)(-2x)}{(1 - x^2)^2}$

$= \dfrac{-1 + x^2 - 2x^2}{(1 - x^2)^2}$

$= \dfrac{-1 - x^2}{(1 - x^2)^2}$

$f''(x)$

$= \dfrac{(1-x^2)^2(-2x)-(-1-x^2)2(1-x^2)(-2x)}{(1 - x^2)^4}$

$= \dfrac{(1 - x^2)[-2x(1 - x^2) + 4x(-1 - x^2)]}{(1 - x^2)^4}$

$= \dfrac{-2x^3 - 6x}{(1 - x^2)^3} = \dfrac{-2x(x^2 + 3)}{(1 - x^2)^3}$

$f''(0) = \dfrac{-2(0)(0^2 + 3)}{[1 - (0)^2]^3} = 0$

$f''(2) = \dfrac{-2(2)(4 + 3)}{[1 - (2)^2]^3} = \dfrac{-28}{-27} = \dfrac{28}{27}$

$f''(-3) = \dfrac{-2(-3)(9 + 3)}{(1 - 9)^3} = -\dfrac{9}{64}$

14. $f(x) = \sqrt{2x + 9} = (2x + 9)^{1/2}$

$f'(x) = \dfrac{1}{2}(2x + 9)^{-1/2} \cdot 2$

$= (2x + 9)^{-1/2}$

$f''(x) = -\dfrac{1}{2}(2x + 9)^{-3/2} \cdot 2$

$= -1(2x + 9)^{-3/2}$

$= \dfrac{-1}{(2x + 9)^{3/2}}$

$f''(0) = \dfrac{-1}{9^{3/2}} = -\dfrac{1}{27}$

$f''(2) = -\dfrac{1}{13^{3/2}} \approx -.0213$

$f''(-3) = -\dfrac{1}{3^{3/2}} \approx -.1925$

16. $f(x) = -2x^{2/3}$

$f'(x) = -\frac{4}{3}x^{-1/3}$

$f''(x) = \frac{4}{9}x^{-4/3} = \frac{4}{9x^{4/3}}$

$f''(0)$ does not exist.

$f''(2) = \frac{4}{9(2)^{4/3}} = \frac{4}{9 \cdot 2 \cdot 2^{1/3}}$

$= \frac{2}{9 \cdot 2^{1/3}} \approx -.1764$

$f''(-3) = \frac{4}{9(-3)^{4/3}}$

$= \frac{4}{9 \cdot (-3)(-3)^{1/3}}$

$= -\frac{4}{27(-3)^{1/3}}$

$\approx .1027$

18. $f(x) = 2x^4 - 3x^3 + x^2$

$f'(x) = 8x^3 - 9x^2 + 2x$

$f''(x) = 24x^2 - 18x + 2$

$f'''(x) = 48x - 18$

$f^{(4)}(x) = 48$

20. $f(x) = 3x^5 - x^4 + 2x^3 - 7x$

$f'(x) = 15x^4 - 4x^3 + 6x^2 - 7$

$f''(x) = 60x^3 - 12x^2 + 12x$

$f'''(x) = 180x^2 - 24x + 12$

$f^{(4)}(x) = 360x - 24$

22. $f(x) = \frac{x + 1}{x}$

$f'(x) = \frac{(1)(x) - 1(x + 1)}{x^2}$

$= -\frac{1}{x^2} = -x^{-2}$

$f''(x) = 2x^{-3}$

$f'''(x) = -6x^{-4} = -\frac{6}{x^4}$

$f^{(4)}(x) = 24x^{-5} = \frac{24}{x^5}$

24. $f(x) = \frac{x}{2x + 1}$

$f'(x) = \frac{(1)(2x + 1) - (2)(x)}{(2x + 1)^2}$

$= \frac{1}{(2x + 1)^2} = (2x + 1)^{-2}$

$f''(x) = -2(2x + 1)^{-3}(2)$

$= -4(2x + 1)^{-3}$

$f'''(x) = 12(2x + 1)^{-4}(2)$

$= 24(2x + 1)^{-4}$

$= \frac{24}{(2x + 1)^4}$

$f^{(4)}(x) = -96(2x + 1)^{-5}(2)$

$= -192(2x + 1)^{-5}$

$= \frac{-192}{(2x + 1)^5}$

26.   Concave upward on $(-\infty, 3)$

Concave downward on $(3, \infty)$

Point of inflection at $(3, 7)$

28.   Concave upward on $(-2, 6)$

Concave downward on $(-\infty, -2)$ and $(6, \infty)$

Points of inflection at $(-2, -4)$ and $(6, -1)$

30.   Concave upward on $(-\infty, 0)$

Concave downward on $(0, \infty)$

No points of inflection

32. $f(x) = 8 - 6x - x^2$

$f'(x) = -6 - 2x$

$f''(x) = -2 < 0$ for all x.

Always concave downward

No points of inflection

34. $f(x) = 2x^3 - 3x^2 - 12x + 1$

$f'(x) = 6x^2 - 6x - 12$

$f''(x) = 12x - 6$

$f''(x) = 12x - 6 > 0$ when

$\qquad 6(2x - 1) > 0$

$\qquad\qquad x > \frac{1}{2}.$

Concave upward on $(\frac{1}{2}, \infty)$

$f''(x) = 12x - 6 < 0$ when

$\qquad 6(2x - 1) < 0$

$\qquad\qquad x < \frac{1}{2}.$

Concave downward on $(-\infty, \frac{1}{2})$

$f''(x) = 12x - 6 = 0$

$\qquad 6(2x - 1) = 0$

$\qquad\qquad x = \frac{1}{2}$

$f(\frac{1}{2}) = -\frac{11}{2}$

Point of inflection at $(\frac{1}{2}, -\frac{11}{2})$

36. $f(x) = -x^3 - 12x^2 - 45x + 2$

$f'(x) = -3x^2 - 24x - 45$

$f''(x) = -6x - 24$

$f''(x) = -6x - 24 > 0$ when

$\qquad -6(x + 4) > 0$

$\qquad\qquad x + 4 < 0$

$\qquad\qquad\qquad x < -4.$

Concave upward on $(-\infty, -4)$

$f''(x) = -6x - 24 < 0$ when

$\qquad -6(x + 4) < 0$

$\qquad\qquad x + 4 > 0.$

$\qquad\qquad\qquad x > -4.$

Concave downward on $(-4, \infty)$

$f''(x) = -6x - 24 = 0$ when

$\qquad -6(x + 4) = 0$

$\qquad\qquad x = -4.$

$f(-4) = 54$

Point of inflection at $(-4, 54)$

38. $f(x) = \frac{-2}{x + 1} = -2(x + 1)^{-1}$

$f'(x) = 2(x + 1)^{-2}$

$f''(x) = -4(x + 1)^{-3} = \frac{-4}{(x + 1)^3}$

$f''(x) = \frac{-4}{(x + 1)^3} > 0$ when

$\qquad x + 1 < 0$

$\qquad\qquad x < -1.$

Concave upward on $(-\infty, -1)$

$f''(x) = \frac{-4}{(x + 1)^3} < 0$ when

$\qquad x + 1 > 0$

$\qquad\qquad x > -1.$

Concave downward on $(-1, \infty)$

$f''(x) \neq 0$ for any value of x; it does not exist when $x = -1$. There is a change of concavity there, but no point of inflection since $f(-1)$ does not exist.

40. $f(x) = -x(x - 3)^2$

$f'(x) = -1(x - 3)^2 + 2(x - 3)(-x)$

$\qquad = -(x - 3)^2 - 2x^2 + 6x$

$f''(x) = -2(x - 3) - 4x + 6$

$\qquad = -2x + 6 - 4x + 6$

$\qquad = -6x + 12$

$f''(x) = -6x + 12 > 0$ when

$$-6(x - 2) > 0$$
$$x - 2 < 0$$
$$x < 2.$$

Concave upward on $(-\infty, 2)$

$f''(x) = -6x + 12 < 0$ when

$$-6(x - 2) < 0$$
$$x - 2 > 0$$
$$x > 2.$$

Concave downward on $(2, \infty)$

$f''(x) = -6x + 12 = 0$ when $x = 2$.

$f(2) = -2$

Point of inflection at $(2, -2)$

42. $f(x) = x^2 - 12x + 36$

$f'(x) = 2x - 12$

$$2x - 12 = 0$$

Critical number:

$$x = 6$$

$f''(x) = 2 > 0$ for all x.

The curve is concave upward, which means a relative minimum occurs at $x = 6$.

44. $f(x) = 2x^3 - 4x^2 + 2$

$f'(x) = 6x^2 - 8x$

$$6x^2 - 8x = 0$$
$$2x(3x - 4) = 0$$

Critical numbers: $x = 0$ or $x = \dfrac{4}{3}$

$f''(x) = 12x - 8$

$f''(0) = -8 < 0$, which means that a relative maximum occurs at $x = 0$.

$f''\left(\dfrac{4}{3}\right) = 8 > 0$, which means that a relative minimum occurs at $x = 4/3$.

46. $f(x) = x^3$

$f'(x) = 3x^2$

$$3x^2 = 0$$

Critical number: $x = 0$

$f''(x) = 6x$

$f''(0) = 0$

The second derivative test fails. Use the first derivative test.

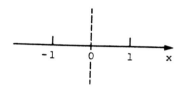

$f'(-1) = 3(-1)^2 = 3 > 0$

This indicates that f is increasing on $(-\infty, 0)$.

$f'(1) = 3(1)^2 = 3 > 0$

This indicates that f is increasing on $(0, \infty)$.

Neither a relative maximum nor relative minimum occur at $x = 0$.

48. $R(x) = 10,000 - x^3 + 42x^2 + 800x$;

$0 \le x \le 20$

$R'(x) = -3x^2 + 84x + 800$

$R''(x) = -6x + 84$

A point of diminishing returns occurs at a point of inflection, or where $R''(x) = 0$.

$$-6x + 84 = 0$$
$$x = 14$$

Test $R''(x)$ to determine whether concavity changes at $x = 14$.

$R''(12) = 12 > 0$

$R''(16) = -12 < 0$

$R(x)$ is concave up on $(0, 14)$ and concave down on $(14, 20)$.

$$R(14) = 10,000 - (14)^3 + 42(14)^2$$
$$- 800(14)$$
$$= 4288$$

The point of diminishing returns is $(14, 4288)$.

50. $I(M) = \dfrac{-U''(M)}{U'(M)}$

$U(M) = \sqrt{M} = M^{1/2}$

$U'(M) = \dfrac{1}{2}M^{-1/2}$

$U''(M) = -\dfrac{1}{4}M^{-3/2}$

$I(M) = \dfrac{-\left(-\dfrac{1}{4}M^{-3/2}\right)}{\dfrac{1}{2}M^{-1/2}}$

$= \dfrac{1}{2}M^{-1}$

$= \dfrac{1}{2M}$

$U(M) = M^{2/3}$

$U'(M) = \dfrac{2}{3}M^{-1/3}$

$U''(M) = -\dfrac{2}{9}M^{-4/3}$

$I(M) = \dfrac{-\left(-\dfrac{2}{9}M^{-4/3}\right)}{\dfrac{2}{3}M^{-1/3}}$

$= \dfrac{1}{3}M^{-1}$

$= \dfrac{1}{3M}$

$U(M) = \sqrt{M}$ indicates a greater risk aversion because $\dfrac{1}{2M} > \dfrac{1}{3M}$ for $0 < M < 1$.

52. (a) f_0 represents initial population $(t = 0)$.

(b) $(a, f(a))$ is the point where the graph changes concavity or the point of inflection.

(c) f_M is the maximum carrying capacity.

54. $K(x) = \dfrac{3x}{x^2 + 4};\ x > 0$

(a) $K'(x) = \dfrac{3(x^2 + 4) - (2x)(3x)}{(x^2 + 4)^2}$

$= \dfrac{-3x^2 + 12}{(x^2 + 4)^2} = 0$

$-3x^2 + 12 = 0$

$x^2 = 4$

$x = 2$ or $x = -2$

-2 is not in the domain of $K(x)$.

$K''(x)$

$= \dfrac{(x^2 + 4)^2(-6x) - (-3x^2 + 12)2(x^2 + 4)(2x)}{(x^2 + 4)^4}$

$= \dfrac{-6x(x^2 + 4) - 4x(-3x^2 + 12)}{(x^2 + 4)^3}$

$= \dfrac{6x^3 - 72x}{(x^2 + 4)^3}$

$K''(2) = \dfrac{-96}{512} = -\dfrac{3}{16} < 0$ implies that $K(x)$ is maximized at $x = 2$ hours.

(b) $K(2) = \dfrac{3(2)}{(2)^2 + 4} = \dfrac{3}{4}$

The maximum concentration is $\dfrac{3}{4}$%.

56. $V(x) = 12x(100 - x)$

$\qquad = 1200x - 12x^2$

$V'(x) = 1200 - 24x$

Set $V'(x) = 0$.

$1200 - 24x = 0$

$\qquad\qquad x = 50$

$V''(x) = -24$

$V''(50) = -24$

Thus, a value of 50 will produce a maximum rate of reaction.

58. $s(t) = -3t^2 - 6t + 2$

$v(t) = s'(t) = -6t - 6$

$a(t) = v'(t) = s''(t) = -6$

$v(0) = -6$ cm/sec

$v(4) = -30$ cm/sec

$a(0) = -6$ cm/sec^2

$a(4) = -6$ cm/sec^2

60. $s(t) = 3t^3 - 4t^2 + 8t - 9$

$v(t) = s'(t) = 9t^2 - 8t + 8$

$a(t) = v'(t) = s''(t) = 18t - 8$

$v(0) = 8$ cm/sec

$v(4) = 120$ cm/sec

$a(0) = -8$ cm/sec^2

$a(4) = 64$ cm/sec^2

62. $s(t) = \dfrac{1}{t + 3} = (t + 3)^{-1}$

$v(t) = -1(t + 3)^{-2} = \dfrac{-1}{(t + 3)^2}$

$a(t) = 2(t + 3)^{-3} = \dfrac{2}{(t + 3)^3}$

$v(0) = \dfrac{-1}{(0 + 3)^2} = -\dfrac{1}{9}$ cm/sec

$v(4) = \dfrac{-1}{(4 + 3)^2} = -\dfrac{1}{49}$ cm/sec

$a(0) = \dfrac{2}{(0 + 3)^3} = \dfrac{2}{27}$ cm/sec^2

$a(4) = \dfrac{2}{(4 + 3)^3} = \dfrac{2}{343}$ cm/sec^2

64. $s(t) = 256t - 16t^2$

$v(t) = s'(t) = 256 - 32t$

$a(t) = v'(t) = s''(t) = -32$

To find when the maximum height occurs, set $s'(t) = 0$.

$256 - 32t = 0$

$\qquad\qquad t = 8$

Find the maximum height:

$s(8) = 256(8) - 16(8^2)$

$\qquad = 1024$ ft.

The object hits the ground when $s = 0$.

$256t - 16t^2 = 0$

$16t(16 - t) = 0$

$t = 0$ (initial moment)

$t = 16$ (final monent)

The object hits the ground 16 seconds after being thrown.

Exercises 66 and 68 should be solved by computer or graphing calculator methods. The solutions will vary according to the method or computer program that is used.

66. $f(x) = 10x^3(x - 1)^2$; $(-2, 2)$ in steps of .3

The answers are

(a) increasing on $(-2, .4)$ and $(1.3, 2)$; decreasing on $(.7, 1)$

(b) maximum between .4 and .7; minimum at 0

(c) concave downward on $(-2, -.2)$ and $(.4, .7)$; concave upward on $(1, 2)$

(d) inflection points between $-.2$ and .1, .1 and .4, and .7 and 1.

68. $f(x) = \dfrac{x}{x^2 + 1};\ (-3, 3)$ in steps of .4

The answers are

(a) decreasing on $(-3, -1)$ and $(1, 3)$; increasing on $(-1, .6)$

(b) minimum between -1.4 and -1; maximum between .6 and 1

(c) concave downward on $(-3, -1.8)$ and $(.2, 3)$; concave upward on $(-1.4, -.2)$

(d) inflection points between -1.8 and -1.4 and between $-.2$ and .2.

Section 3.5

2. As x decreases without bound, $g(x)$ continues to increase. Since $g(x)$ does not approach any fixed number, $g(x)$ has no limit as x approaches $-\infty$. Therefore,

$$\lim_{x \to -\infty} g(x)$$

does not exist.

4. $\lim\limits_{x \to \infty} \dfrac{5x}{3x - 1}$

$$= \lim_{x \to \infty} \frac{\dfrac{5x}{x}}{\dfrac{3x - 1}{x}}$$

$$= \lim_{x \to \infty} \frac{5}{3 - \dfrac{1}{x}}$$

$$= \frac{\lim\limits_{x \to \infty} 5}{\lim\limits_{x \to \infty} 3 - \lim\limits_{x \to \infty} \dfrac{1}{x}}$$

$$= \frac{5}{3 - 0} = \frac{5}{3}$$

6. $\lim\limits_{x \to -\infty} \dfrac{8x + 2}{2x - 5}$

$$= \lim_{x \to -\infty} \frac{8 + \dfrac{2}{x}}{2 - \dfrac{5}{x}}$$

$$= \frac{\lim\limits_{x \to -\infty} 8 + \lim\limits_{x \to -\infty} \dfrac{2}{x}}{\lim\limits_{x \to -\infty} 2 - \lim\limits_{x \to -\infty} \dfrac{5}{x}}$$

$$= \frac{8 + 0}{2 - 0}$$

$$= \frac{8}{2} = 4$$

8. $\lim\limits_{x \to \infty} \dfrac{x^2 + 2x - 5}{3x^2 + 2}$

$$= \lim_{x \to \infty} \frac{1 - \dfrac{2}{x} - \dfrac{5}{x^2}}{3 + \dfrac{2}{x^2}}$$

$$= \frac{\lim\limits_{x \to \infty} 1 - \lim\limits_{x \to \infty} \dfrac{2}{x} - \lim\limits_{x \to \infty} \dfrac{5}{x^2}}{\lim\limits_{x \to \infty} 3 + \lim\limits_{x \to \infty} \dfrac{2}{x^2}}$$

$$= \frac{1 - 0 - 0}{3 + 0}$$

$$= \frac{1}{3}$$

10. $\lim\limits_{x\to\infty}\dfrac{2x^2-1}{3x^4+2}$

$= \lim\limits_{x\to\infty}\dfrac{\dfrac{2}{x^2}-\dfrac{1}{x^4}}{3+\dfrac{2}{x^4}}$

$= \dfrac{\lim\limits_{x\to\infty}\dfrac{2}{x^2}-\lim\limits_{x\to\infty}\dfrac{1}{x^4}}{\lim\limits_{x\to\infty}3+\lim\limits_{x\to\infty}\dfrac{2}{x^4}} = \dfrac{0-0}{3+0}$

$= \dfrac{0}{3} = 0$

12. $\lim\limits_{x\to\infty}(x-\sqrt{x^2-9})$

$= \lim\limits_{x\to\infty}(x-\sqrt{x^2-9})\cdot\dfrac{(x+\sqrt{x^2-9})}{(x+\sqrt{x^2-9})}$

$= \lim\limits_{x\to\infty}\dfrac{x^2-(x^2-9)}{(x+\sqrt{x^2-9})}$

$= \lim\limits_{x\to\infty}\dfrac{9}{x+\sqrt{x^2-9}}$

$= \dfrac{\lim\limits_{x\to\infty}9}{\lim\limits_{x\to\infty}(x+\sqrt{x^2-9})}$

$= \dfrac{\lim\limits_{x\to\infty}\dfrac{9}{x}}{\lim\limits_{x\to\infty}\left(1+\sqrt{1-\dfrac{9}{x^2}}\right)}$

$= \dfrac{0}{\lim\limits_{x\to\infty}1+\lim\limits_{x\to\infty}\sqrt{\left(1-\dfrac{9}{x^2}\right)}}$

$= \dfrac{0}{1+1} = \dfrac{0}{2}$

$= 0$

14. $f(x) = -2x^3 - 9x^2 + 60x - 8$

$f'(x) = -6x^2 - 18x + 60$

$= -6(x^2 + 3x - 10)$

$= -6(x + 5)(x - 2) = 0$

Critical numbers: $x = -5$ and $x = 2$

Critical points: $(-5, -283)$ and $(2, 60)$

$f''(x) = -12x - 18$

$f''(-5) = 42 > 0$

$f''(2) = -42 < 0$

Relative maximum at 2, relative minimum at -5

Increasing on $(-5, 2)$

Decreasing on $(-\infty, -5)$ and $(2, \infty)$

$f''(x) = -12x - 18 = 0$

$-6(2x + 3) = 0$

$x = -\dfrac{3}{2}$

Point of inflection at $(-1.5, -111.5)$

Concave up on $(-\infty, -1.5)$

Concave down on $(-1.5, \infty)$

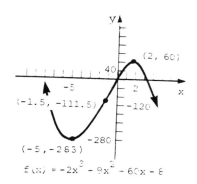

16. $f(x) = x^3 - \dfrac{15}{2}x^2 - 18x - 1$

$f'(x) = 3x^2 - 15x - 18$

$= 3(x^2 - 5x - 6)$

$= 3(x - 6)(x + 1) = 0$

Critical numbers: $x = 6$ and $x = -1$

Critical points: (6, -163) and

(-1, 8.5)

$$f''(x) = 6x - 15$$

$$f''(6) = 21 > 0$$

$$f''(-1) = -21 < 0$$

Relative maximum at x = -1, relative

minimum at x = 6

Increasing on (-∞, -1) and (6, ∞)

Decreasing on (-1, 6)

$$f''(x) = 6x - 15 = 0$$

$$x = \frac{5}{2}$$

Point of inflection at

(5/2, -77.25)

Concave up on (5/2, ∞)

Concave down on (-∞, 5/2)

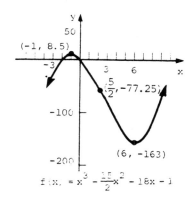

18. $f(x) = x^4 - 8x^2$

$$f'(x) = 4x^3 - 16x$$

$$= 4x(x^2 - 4)$$

$$= 4x(x + 2)(x - 2)$$

Critical numbers x = 0, x = -2, and

x = 2

Critical points: (0, 0), (-2, -16)

and (2, -16)

$$f''(x) = 12x^2 - 16$$

$$f''(0) = -16 < 0$$

$$f''(-2) = 32 > 0$$

$$f''(2) = 32 > 0$$

Relative maximum at 0,

relative minimum at -2 and 2

Increasing on (-2, 0) and (2, ∞)

Decreasing on (-∞, -2) and (0, 2)

$$f''(x) = 12x^2 - 16 = 0$$

$$4(3x^2 - 4) = 0$$

$$x = \pm\sqrt{\frac{4}{3}}$$

Points of inflection at

$(\sqrt{4/3}, -80/9)$ and $(-\sqrt{4/3}, -80/9)$

Concave up on $(-∞, -\sqrt{4/3})$ and

$(\sqrt{4/3}, ∞)$

Concave down on $(-\sqrt{4/3}, \sqrt{4/3})$

x-intercepts: $0 = x^4 - 8x^2$

$$0 = x^2(x^2 - 8)$$

$$x = 0 \quad or \quad x = \pm 2\sqrt{2}$$

y-intercept: $y = 0^4 - 8(0)^2 = 0$

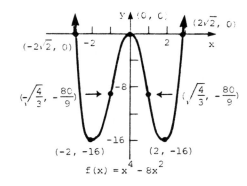

20. $f(x) = x^5 - 15x^3$

$$f'(x) = 5x^4 - 45x^2 = 0$$

$$5x^2(x^2 - 9) = 0$$

$$5x^2(x + 3)(x - 3) = 0$$

Critical numbers: $x = 0$ and $x = -3$
and $x = 3$

Critical points: $(0, 0)$ and
$(-3, 162)$ and $(3, -162)$

$f''(x) = 20x^3 - 90x$

$f''(0) = 0$

$f''(-3) = -270 < 0$

$f''(3) = 270 > 0$

Relative maximum at -3

Relative minimum at 3

No relative extrema at 0

Increasing on $(-\infty, -3)$ and $(3, \infty)$

Decreasing on $(-3, 3)$

$f''(x) = 20x^3 - 90x = 0$

$10x(2x^2 - 9) = 0$

$x = 0$ or $x = \pm\dfrac{3}{\sqrt{2}}$

Points of inflection at $(0, 0)$ and
$(-3/\sqrt{2}, 100.23)$ and $(3/\sqrt{2}, -100.23)$

Concave up on $(-3/\sqrt{2}, 0)$ and
$(3/\sqrt{2}, \infty)$

Concave down on $(-\infty, -3/\sqrt{2})$ and

$(0, 3/\sqrt{2})$

x-intercepts: $0 = x^5 - 15x^3$

$0 = x^3(x^2 - 15)$

$x = 0,\ x = \pm\sqrt{15}$

y-intercept: $y = 0^5 - 15(0)^3 = 0$

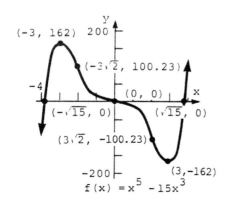

22. $f(x) = 2x + \dfrac{8}{x}$

Vertical asymptote at $x = 0$

$f'(x) = 2 - \dfrac{8}{x^2} = 0$

$\dfrac{2x^2 - 8}{x^2} = 0$

$2x^2 - 8 = 0$

$2(x^2 - 4) = 0$

Critical numbers: $x = -2$ and $x = 2$

Critical points: $(-2, -8)$ and
$(2, 8)$

$f''(x) = \dfrac{16}{x^3}$

$f''(-2) = -2 < 0$

$f''(2) = 2 > 0$

Relative maximum at -2

Relative minimum at 2

Increasing on $(-\infty, -2)$ and $(2, \infty)$

Decreasing on $(-2, 0)$ and $(0, 2)$

(Recall that $f(x)$ does not exist at
$x = 0$.)

$f''(x) = \dfrac{16}{x^3}$ is never zero.

There are no points of inflection.

Concave up on $(0, \infty)$

Concave down on $(-\infty, 0)$

$f(x)$ is never zero, so there are no
x-intercepts.

$f(x)$ does not exist at $x = 0$, so
there is no y-intercept.

$y = x$ is an oblique asymptote.

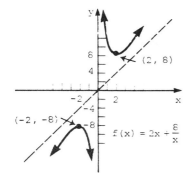

f(x) does not exist at x = 0, so there is no y-intercept.

y = x is an oblique asymptote.

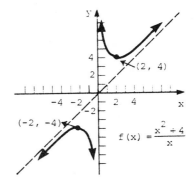

24. $f(x) = \dfrac{x^2 + 4}{x} = x + \dfrac{4}{x}$

Vertical asymptote at x = 0

$f'(x) = 1 - \dfrac{4}{x^2} = 0$

$\dfrac{x^2 - 4}{x^2} = 0$

$x^2 - 4 = 0$

$(x + 2)(x - 2) = 0$

Critical numbers: x = −2 and x = 2
Critical points: (−2, −4) and (2, 4)

$f''(x) = \dfrac{8}{x^3}$

$f''(2) = 1 > 0$

$f''(-2) = -1 < 0$

Relative maximum at −2,
relative minimum at 2

Increasing on (−∞, −2) and (2, ∞)

Decreasing on (−2, 0) and (0, 2)

(Recall that f(x) does not exist at x = 0.)

$f''(x) = \dfrac{8}{x^3}$ is never zero.

There are no points of inflection.

Concave up on (0, ∞)

Concave down on (−∞, 0)

f(x) is never zero, so there are no x-intercepts.

26. $f(x) = \dfrac{x}{x + 1}$

Vertical asymptote at x = −1
Horizontal asymptote at y = 1

$f'(x) = \dfrac{(1)(1 + x) - (1)(x)}{(1 + x)^2}$

$= \dfrac{1}{(1 + x)^2}$

f'(x) is never zero.
f'(x) fails to exist for x = −1.

$f''(x) = \dfrac{(1 + x)^2(0) - 1(2)(1 + x)}{(1 + x)^4}$

$= \dfrac{-2(1 + x)}{(1 + x)^4}$

$= \dfrac{-2}{(x + 1)^3}$

f''(x) fails to exist for x = −1.

No critical values, no maximum nor minimum

Increasing on (−∞, −1) and (−1, ∞)

(Recall that f(x) does not exist at x = −1.)

No points of inflection

$f''(-2) = 2 > 0$

$f''(0) = -2 < 0$

Concave up on $(-\infty, -1)$

Concave down on $(-1, \infty)$

x-intercept: $0 = \dfrac{x}{1 + x}$

$0 = x$

y-intercept: $y = \dfrac{0}{1 + 0} = 0$

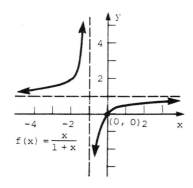

$f(x) = \dfrac{x}{1 + x}$

28. $f(x) = \dfrac{1}{x^2 + 1}$

Horizontal asymptote at $y = 0$

$f'(x) = \dfrac{(x^2 + 1)(0) - 1(2x)}{(x^2 + 1)^2}$

$= \dfrac{-2x}{(x^2 + 1)^2} = 0$

Critical number: $x = 0$

Critical point: $(0, 1)$

$f''(x)$

$= \dfrac{(x^2 + 1)^2(-2) - (-2x)(2)(x^2 + 1)(2x)}{(x^2 + 1)^4}$

$= \dfrac{6x^2 - 2}{(x^2 + 1)^3}$

$f''(0) = -2 < 0$

Relative maximum at 0

Increasing on $(-\infty, 0)$

Decreasing on $(0, \infty)$

$f''(x) = \dfrac{6x^2 - 2}{(x^2 + 1)^3} = 0$

$6x^2 - 2 = 0$

$2(3x^2 - 1) = 0$

$x = \pm\dfrac{1}{\sqrt{3}}$

Points of inflection at $\left(1/\sqrt{3},\ 3/4\right)$

$\left(-1/\sqrt{3},\ 3/4\right)$

Concave up on $\left(-\infty, -\dfrac{1}{\sqrt{3}}\right)$ and $\left(\dfrac{1}{\sqrt{3}}, \infty\right)$

Concave down on $\left(-\dfrac{1}{\sqrt{3}}, \dfrac{1}{\sqrt{3}}\right)$

$f(x)$ is never zero, so there is no x-intercept.

y-intercept: $y = \dfrac{0}{0^2 + 1} = 1$

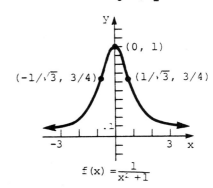

$f(x) = \dfrac{1}{x^2 + 1}$

30. $f(x) = \dfrac{x}{x^2 - 1}$

Vertical asymptotes at $x = 1$ and $x = -1$

Horizontal asymptote at $y = 0$

$f'(x) = \dfrac{(x^2 - 1)(1) - x(2x)}{(x^2 - 1)^2}$

$= \dfrac{-x^2 - 1}{(x^2 - 1)^2}$

$f'(x)$ is never zero.

No critical values, no maximum nor minimum

Decreasing on $(-\infty, -1)$, $(-1, 1)$, $(1, \infty)$

(Recall that f(x) does not exist at x = -1 and x = 1.)

f''(x)

$= \dfrac{(x^2 - 1)^2(-2x) - (-x^2 - 1)(2)(x^2 - 1)(2x)}{(x^2 - 1)^4}$

$= \dfrac{2x^3 + 6x}{(x^2 - 1)^3} = 0$

$2x^3 + 6x = 0$

$2x(x^2 + 3) = 0$

$x = 0$

Point of inflection at (0, 0).

$f''(-3) = -\dfrac{9}{64} < 0$

$f''\left(-\dfrac{1}{2}\right) = \dfrac{208}{125} > 0$

$f''\left(\dfrac{1}{2}\right) = -\dfrac{208}{125} < 0$

$f''(3) = \dfrac{9}{24} > 0$

Concave up on $(-1, 0)$ and $(1, \infty)$

Concave down on $(-\infty, -1)$ and $(0, 1)$

y-intercept: $0 = \dfrac{x}{x^2 - 1}$

$0 = x$

y-intercept: $y = \dfrac{0}{0 - 1} = 0$

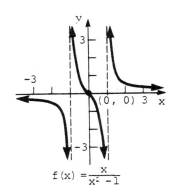

$f(x) = \dfrac{x}{x^2 - 1}$

Graphs for Exercises 32 and 34 may vary. Examples are given.

32. (a) indicates that the curve may not contain breaks.

(b) and (c) indicate relative maxima at -2 and 3 and a relative minimum at 0.

(d) shows that concavity does not change at 0.

(d) and (e) are consistent with (i).

(f) shows critical values.

(g) and (h) indicate that the function is not differentiable at 0, and is differentiable everywhere else. Thus, a sharp corner must exist at 0.

(i) indicates that concavity changes just once, at (5, 1).

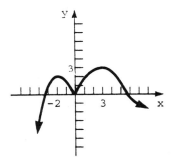

34. (a) indicates a smooth, continuous curve except where there is a vertical asymptote.

(b) indicates the function decreases on both sides of the asymptote so there are no relative extrema.

(c) gives the horizontal asymptote $y = 2$.

(d) and (e) indicate that concavity does not change left of the asymptote, but that the right portion of the graph changes concavity at $x = 2$ and $x = 4$. There are points of inflection at 2 and 4.

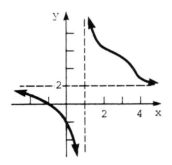

36. $P(s) = \dfrac{75s}{s + 8}$

$$\lim_{s \to \infty} P(s) = \lim_{s \to \infty} \frac{s(75)}{s\left(1 + \frac{8}{s}\right)}$$

$$= \lim_{s \to \infty} \frac{75}{1 + \frac{8}{s}}$$

$$= \frac{\lim_{s \to \infty} 75}{\lim_{s \to \infty} 1 + \lim_{s \to \infty} \frac{8}{s}}$$

$$= \lim_{s \to \infty} \frac{75}{1}$$

$$= 75$$

The number of pieces of work a new employee can do gets closer and closer to 75 as the number of training days increases.

38. $p_n = \frac{1}{2} + \left(p_0 - \frac{1}{2}\right)(1 - 2p)^n$ with $p_0 = .7$ and $p = .2$

(a) $p_2 = \frac{1}{2} + \left(.7 - \frac{1}{2}\right)[1 - 2(.2)]^2$

$\quad = .5 + (.2)(1 - .4)^2$

$\quad = .5 + (.2)(.6)^2$

$\quad = .5 + (.2)(.36)$

$\quad = .5 + .072$

$\quad = .572$

This indicates that the probability that the congressman will vote "yes" on the second roll call is .572.

(b) $p_4 = \frac{1}{2} + \left(.7 - \frac{1}{2}\right)[1 - 2(.2)]^4$

$\quad = .5 + (.2)(1 - .4)^4$

$\quad = .5 + (.2)(.6)^4$

$\quad = .5 + .02592$

$\quad \approx .526$

The probability that he will vote "yes" on the fourth vote is .526.

(c) $p_8 = \frac{1}{2} + \left(.7 - \frac{1}{2}\right)[1 - .2(.2)]^8$

$\quad p_8 = .5 + (.2)(1 - .4)^8$

$\quad p_8 = .5 + (.2)(.6)^8$

$\quad p_8 = .5 + .0034$

$\quad p_8 \approx .503$

The probability that he will vote "yes" on the eighth vote is .503.

(d) As the number of roll calls increases ($n \to \infty$), p_n approaches .5. So $\lim_{n \to \infty} p_n = .5$.

This means that, as the number of roll calls increases, the probability that the congressman will vote "yes" gets close to .5 but is never less than .5.

Exercises 40–46 should be solved by computer or graphing calculator methods. The solutions will vary according to the method or computer program that is used.

40. $\lim\limits_{x \to -\infty} \dfrac{\sqrt{9x^2 + 5}}{2x}$

(a) The answer is −1.5.

42. $\lim\limits_{x \to \infty} \dfrac{\sqrt{36x^2 + 2x + 7}}{3x}$

(a) The answer is 2.

44. $\lim\limits_{x \to -\infty} \dfrac{(1 + 5x^{1/3} + 2x^{5/3})^3}{x^5}$

(a) The answer is 8.

Chapter 3 Review Exercises

6. $f(x) = -2x^2 - 3x + 4$

$f'(x) = -4x - 3 = 0$

Critical number: $x = -\dfrac{3}{4}$

$f''(x) = -4 < 0$ for all x.

f(x) is a maximum at x = −3/4.

f(x) is increasing on (−∞, −3/4) and decreasing on (−3/4, ∞).

8. $f(x) = 4x^3 + 3x^2 - 18x + 1$

$f'(x) = 12x^2 + 6x - 18$

$f'(x) = 6(2x^2 + x - 3)$

$f'(x) = 6(2x + 3)(x - 1) = 0$

2x + 3 = 0 or x − 1 = 0

Critical numbers: $x = -\dfrac{3}{2}$ or x = 1

$f''(x) = 24x + 6$

$f''\left(-\dfrac{3}{2}\right) = -30 < 0$

$f''(1) = 30 > 0$

f(x) is a maximum at x = −3/2 and minimum at 1.

f(x) is increasing on (−∞, −3/2) and (1, ∞) and is decreasing on (−3/2, 1).

10. $f(x) = \dfrac{5}{2x + 1}$

$f'(x) = \dfrac{-10}{(2x + 1)^2} < 0$ for all x,

but not defined for x = −1/2. f(x) is never increasing, it is decreasing on (−∞, −1/2) and (−1/2, ∞).

12. $f(x) = x^2 - 6x + 4$

$f'(x) = 2x - 6 = 0$

Critical number: x = 3

$f''(x) = 2 > 0$ for all x, so f(3) is a relative minimum.

$f(3) = -5$

Relative minimum of −5 at 3.

14. $f(x) = -3x^2 + 2x - 5$

$f'(x) = -6x + 2 = 0$

Critical number: $x = \dfrac{1}{3}$

$f''(x) = -6 < 0$ for all x, $f(\frac{1}{3})$ is

a relative maximum.

$$f(\tfrac{1}{3}) = -\dfrac{14}{3}$$

Relative maximum of $-14/3$ at $1/3$

16. $f(x) = 2x^3 + 3x^2 - 12x + 5$

$f'(x) = 6x^2 + 6x - 12 = 0$

$x^2 + x - 2 = 0$

$(x + 2)(x - 1) = 0$

Critical numbers: $x = -2$, $x = 1$

$f''(x) = 12x + 6$

$f''(-2) = -18 < 0$, so a maximum

occurs at $x = -2$.

$f''(1) = 18 > 0$, so a minimum occurs

at $x = 1$.

$f(-2) = 25$

$f(1) = -2$

Relative maximum of 25 at -2

Relative minimum of -2 at 1

18. $f(x) = 9x^3 + \dfrac{1}{x} = 9x^3 + x^{-1}$

$f'(x) = 27x^2 - x^{-2}$

$f''(x) = 54x + 2x^{-3} = 54x + \dfrac{2}{x^3}$

$f''(1) = 54(1) + \dfrac{2}{(1)^3} = 56$

$f''(-3) = 54(-3) + \dfrac{2}{(-3)^3}$

$= -162 - \dfrac{2}{27} = -\dfrac{4376}{27}$

20. $f(x) = \dfrac{4 - 3x}{x + 1}$

$f'(x) = \dfrac{-3(x + 1) - (1)(4 - 3x)}{(x + 1)^2}$

$= \dfrac{-7}{(x + 1)^2} = -7(x + 1)^{-2}$

$f''(x) = 14(x + 1)^{-3} = \dfrac{14}{(x + 1)^3}$

$f''(1) = \dfrac{14}{(1 + 1)^3} = \dfrac{7}{4}$

$f''(-3) = \dfrac{14}{(-3 + 1)^3} = -\dfrac{7}{4}$

22. $f(t) = -\sqrt{5 - t^2} = -(5 - t^2)^{1/2}$

$f'(t) = -\dfrac{1}{2}(5 - t^2)^{-1/2}(-2t)$

$= t(5 - t^2)^{-1/2}$

$f''(t) = (1)(5 - t^2)^{-1/2}$

$+ t\left[-\dfrac{1}{2}(5 - t^2)^{-3/2}(-2t)\right]$

$= (5 - t^2)^{-1/2} + t[t(5 - t^2)^{-3/2}]$

$= (5 - t^2)^{-3/2}[5 - t^2 + t^2]$

$= \dfrac{5}{(5 - t^2)^{3/2}}$

$f''(1) = \dfrac{5}{(5 - 1)^{3/2}} = \dfrac{5}{8}$

$f''(-3) = \dfrac{5}{(5 - 9)^{3/2}}$

This value does not exist since

$(-4)^{3/2}$ does not exist.

24. $f(x) = 4x^2 - 8x - 3$; $[-1, 2]$

$f'(x) = 8x - 8 = 0$ when $x = 1$.

$f(-1) = 9$

$f(1) = -7$

$f(2) = -3$

Absolute maximum of 9 at -1;

absolute minimum of -7 at 1

26. $f(x) = -2x^3 - 2x^2 + 2x - 1;\ [-3, 1]$

$f'(x) = -6x^2 - 4x + 2 = 0$

$\qquad 3x^2 + 2x - 1 = 0$

$\qquad (3x - 1)(x + 1) = 0 \text{ when}$

$\qquad x = \dfrac{1}{3} \text{ or } x = -1.$

$f(-3) = 29$

$f(-1) = -3$

$f\left(\dfrac{1}{3}\right) = -\dfrac{17}{27}$

$f(1) = -3$

Absolute maximum of 29 at -3;

absolute minimum of -3 at -1 and 1

28. $\displaystyle\lim_{x \to \infty} f(x) = -3$ because $f(x)$

approaches the horizontal asymptote

$y = -3$ as x gets larger and larger.

30. $\displaystyle\lim_{x \to \infty} \dfrac{x^2 + 6x + 8}{x^3 + 2x + 1}$

$\qquad = \displaystyle\lim_{x \to \infty} \dfrac{\dfrac{1}{x} + \dfrac{6}{x^2} + \dfrac{8}{x^3}}{1 + \dfrac{2}{x^2} + \dfrac{1}{x^3}}$

$\qquad = \dfrac{0 + 0 + 0}{1 + 0 + 0} = \dfrac{0}{1} = 0$

32. $\displaystyle\lim_{x \to -\infty} \left(\dfrac{9}{x^4} + \dfrac{1}{x^2} - 3\right) = (0 + 0 - 3)$

$\qquad\qquad\qquad\qquad = -3$

34. $f(x) = -\dfrac{4}{3}x^3 + x^2 + 30x - 7$

$f'(x) = -4x^2 + 2x + 30$

$\qquad = -2(2x^2 - x - 15)$

$\qquad = -2(2x + 5)(x - 3) = 0$

Critical numbers: $x = -5/2$ and

$x = 3$

Critical points: $(-5/2, -54.91)$

and $(3, 56)$

$f''(x) = -8x + 2$

$f''\left(-\dfrac{5}{2}\right) = 22 > 0$

$f''(3) = -22 < 0$

Relative maximum at 3

Relative minimum at $-5/2$

Increasing on $(-5/2, 3)$

Decreasing on $(-\infty, -5/2)$ and $(3, \infty)$

$f''(x) = -8x + 2 = 0$

$\qquad x = \dfrac{1}{4}$

Point of inflection at $(\dfrac{1}{4}, .54)$

Concave up on $(-\infty, \dfrac{1}{4})$

Concave down on $(\dfrac{1}{4}, \infty)$

y-intercept:

$\qquad y = -\dfrac{4}{3}(0)^3 + (0)^3 + 30(0)^2 - 7$

$\qquad = -7$

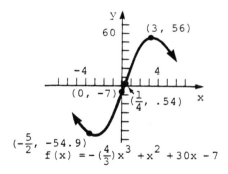

36. $f(x) = -\dfrac{2}{3}x^3 + \dfrac{9}{2}x^2 + 5x + 1$

$f'(x) = -2x^2 + 9x + 5 = 0$

$\qquad (-2x - 1)(x - 5) = 0$

Critical numbers: $x = -\dfrac{1}{2}$ and $x = 5$

Critical points: $(-\frac{1}{2}, -.29)$ and

$(5, 55.17)$

$f''(x) = -4x + 9$

$f''(-\frac{1}{2}) = 11 > 0$

$f''(5) = -11 < 0$

Relative maximum at 5

Relative minimum at $-\frac{1}{2}$

Increasing on $(-\frac{1}{2}, 5)$

Decreasing on $(-\infty, -\frac{1}{2})$ and $(5, \infty)$

$f''(x) = -4x + 9 = 0$

$$x = \frac{9}{4}$$

Point of inflection at $\left(\frac{9}{4}, 27.44\right)$

Concave up on $\left(-\infty, \frac{9}{4}\right)$

Concave down on $\left(\frac{9}{4}, \infty\right)$

y-intercept:

$y = -\frac{2}{3}(0)^3 + \frac{9}{2}(0)^2 + 5(0) + 1 = 1$

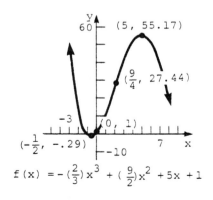

$f(x) = -\left(\frac{2}{3}\right)x^3 + \left(\frac{9}{2}\right)x^2 + 5x + 1$

38. $f(x) = \dfrac{2x - 5}{x + 3}$

Vertical asymptote at $x = -3$

Horizontal asymptote at $y = 2$

$f'(x) = \dfrac{2(x + 3) - (2x - 5)}{(x + 3)^2}$

$ = \dfrac{11}{(x + 3)^2}$

f' is never zero.

$f(x)$ has no extrema.

$f''(x) = \dfrac{-22}{(x + 3)^3}$

$f''(-4) = 22 > 0$

$f''(-2) = -22 < 0$

Concave up on $(-\infty, -3)$

Concave down on $(-3, \infty)$

x-intercept: $\dfrac{2x - 5}{x + 3} = 0$

$ x = \dfrac{5}{2}$

y-intercept: $\dfrac{2(0) - 5}{0 + 3} = -\dfrac{5}{3}$

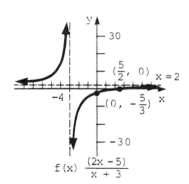

$f(x) = \dfrac{(2x - 5)}{x + 3}$

40. $f(x) = x^3 + \dfrac{5}{2}x^2 - 2x - 3$

$f'(x) = 3x^2 + 5x - 2$

$ = (3x - 1)(x + 2) = 0$

Critical numbers: $x = \dfrac{1}{3}$ and $x = -2$

Critical points: $(\frac{1}{3}, -3.35)$ and

$(-2, 3)$

$f''(x) = 6x + 5$

$f''(\frac{1}{3}) = 7 > 0$

$f''(-2) = -7 < 0$

Relative maximum at -2

Relative minimum at $\frac{1}{3}$

Increasing on $(-\infty, -2)$ and $(\frac{1}{3}, \infty)$

Decreasing on $(-2, \frac{1}{3})$

$f''(x) = 6x + 5 = 0$

$x = -\frac{5}{6}$

Point of inflection at $(-\frac{5}{6}, -.18)$

Concave up on $(-\frac{5}{6}, \infty)$

Concave down on $(-\infty, -\frac{5}{6})$

x-intercept: $(0, -3)$

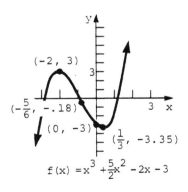

$$f(x) = x^3 + \frac{5}{2}x^2 - 2x - 3$$

42. $f(x) = 6x^3 - x^4$

$f'(x) = 18x^2 - 4x^3$

$= 2x^2(9 - 2x) = 0$

Critical numbers: $x = 0$ and $x = \frac{9}{2}$

Critical points: $(0, 0)$ and

$(\frac{9}{2}, 136.7)$

$f''(x) = 36x - 12x^2$

$= 12x(3 - x)$

$f''(0) = 0$

$f''(\frac{9}{2}) = -81 < 0$

Relative maximum at $\frac{9}{2}$

No relative extrema at 0

Increasing on $(-\infty, \frac{9}{2})$

Decreasing on $(\frac{9}{2}, \infty)$

$f''(x) = 12x(3 - x) = 0$

$x = 0, x = 3$

Points of inflection at $(0, 0)$ and

$(3, 81)$

Concave up on $(0, 3)$

Concave down on $(-\infty, 0)$ and $(3, \infty)$

x-intercepts: $6x^3 - x^4 = 0$

$x^3(6 - x) = 0$

$x = 0, x = 6$

y-intercept: $y = 0$

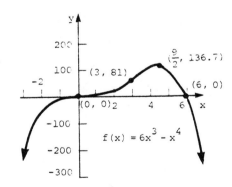

$$f(x) = 6x^3 - x^4$$

44. $f(x) = x + \dfrac{8}{x}$

Vertical asymptote at $x = 0$

Oblique asymptote at $y = x$

$f'(x) = 1 - \dfrac{8}{x^2}$

$\qquad = \dfrac{x^2 - 8}{x^2} = 0$

Critical numbers: $x = \pm 2\sqrt{2}$

Critical points: $(2\sqrt{2}, 4\sqrt{2})$,

$(-2\sqrt{2}, -4\sqrt{2})$

$\qquad f''(x) = \dfrac{16}{x^3}$

$f''(-2\sqrt{2}) = -\dfrac{\sqrt{2}}{2} < 0$

$f''(2\sqrt{2}) = \dfrac{\sqrt{2}}{2} > 0$

Relative maximum at $-2\sqrt{2}$

Relative minimum at $2\sqrt{2}$

Increasing on $(-\infty, -2\sqrt{2})$ and

$(2\sqrt{2}, \infty)$

Decreasing on $(-2\sqrt{2}, 0)$ and $(0, 2\sqrt{2})$

$f''(x) = \dfrac{16}{x^3} > 0$ for all x.

No inflection points

Concave up on $(0, \infty)$

Concave down on $(-\infty, 0)$

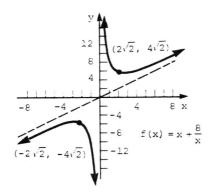

46. $f(x) = \dfrac{-4x}{1 + 2x}$

Vertical asymptote at $x = -\dfrac{1}{2}$

Horizontal asymptote at $y = -2$

$f'(x) = \dfrac{-4(1 + 2x) - 2(-4x)}{(1 + 2x)^2}$

$\qquad = \dfrac{-4 - 8x + 8x}{(1 + 2x)^2}$

$\qquad = \dfrac{-4}{(1 + 2x)^2}$

$f'(x)$ is never zero.

No critical values; no relative extrema

$f'(0) = -4 < 0$

$f'(-1) = -4 < 0$

Decreasing on $\left(-\infty, -\dfrac{1}{2}\right)$ and $\left(-\dfrac{1}{2}, \infty\right)$

$f''(x) = \dfrac{16}{(1 + 2x)^3}$

$f''(x)$ is never zero; no points of inflection.

$f''(0) = 16 > 0$

$f''(-1) = -16 < 0$

Concave up on $\left(-\dfrac{1}{2}, \infty\right)$

Concave down on $\left(-\infty, -\dfrac{1}{2}\right)$

x-intercept and y-intercept at $(0, 0)$

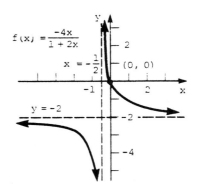

CHAPTER 4 APPLICATIONS OF THE DERIVATIVE

Section 4.1

2. $x + y = 250$

    $P = xy$

    (a) $y = 250 - x$

    (b) $P = xy = x(250 - x)$

    $\qquad = 250x - x^2$

    (c) Since $y = 250 - x$ and x and y are nonnegative numbers, $x \geq 0$ and $250 - x \geq 0$ or $x \leq 250$. The domain of P is $[0, 250]$.

    (d) $P' = 250 - 2x$

    $\qquad 250 - 2x = 0$

    $\qquad 2(125 - x) = 0$

    $\qquad\qquad\qquad x = 125$

    (e)

x	P
0	0
125	15,625
250	0

    (f) From the chart, the maximum value of P is 15,625; this occurs when $x = 125$ and $y = 125$.

4. $x + y = 30$

    $P = x^2 + y^2$

    (a) $y = 30 - x$

    (b) $P = x^2 + (30 - x)^2$

    $\qquad = x^2 + 900 - 60x + x^2$

    $\qquad = 2x^2 - 60x + 900$

    (c) Since $y = 30 - x$ and x and y are nonnegative numbers, the domain of P is $[0, 30]$.

    (d) $P' = 4x - 60$

    $\qquad 4x - 60 = 0$

    $\qquad 4(x - 15) = 0$

    $\qquad\qquad\qquad x = 15$

    (e)

x	P
0	900
15	450
30	900

    (f) The minimum value of P is 450; this occurs when $x = 15$ and $y = 15$.

6. $x + y = 45$

    Maximize xy^2.

    (a) $y = 45 - x$

    (b) Let $P = xy^2 = x(45 - x)^2$

    $\qquad\qquad\qquad = x(2025 - 90x + x^2)$

    $\qquad\qquad\qquad = 2025x - 90x^2 + x^3$

    (c) Since $y = 45 - x$ and x and y are nonnegative numbers, the domain of P is $[0, 45]$.

    (d) $P' = 2025 - 180x + 3x^2$

    $\qquad 3x^2 - 180x + 2025 = 0$

    $\qquad 3(x^2 - 60x + 675) = 0$

    $\qquad 3(x - 15)(x - 45) = 0$

    $\qquad\qquad x = 15 \quad \text{or} \quad x = 45$

    (e)

x	P
0	0
15	13,500
45	0

    (f) The maximum value of xy^2 occurs when $x = 15$ and $y = 30$. The maximum value is 13,500.

8. $x - y = 3$

Minimize xy.

(a) $y = x - 3$

(b) Let $P = xy = x(x - 3)$
$$= x^2 - 3x$$

(c) Since $y = x - 3$ and x and y are nonnegative numbers, the domain of P is $[3, \infty)$.

(d) $P' = 2x - 3$
$$2x - 3 = 0$$
$$x = \frac{3}{2}$$

Note that $3/2$ is not in the domain.

(e)

x	P
3	0

(f) $P'(3) = 3 > 0$ implies that $P(3)$ is a minimum. The minimum value of xy occurs when $x = 3$ and $y = 0$. The minimum value is 0.

10. Let x = length
y = width.

Perimeter = $P = 2x + 2y = 200$.
$$x + y = 100$$
$$y = 100 - x$$

Area = $xy = x(100 - x)$
$$= 100x - x^2$$
$A' = 100 - 2x = 0$
$$x = 50$$

$A'' = -2$, which implies that $x = 50$ is the location of a maximum. If $x = 50$,

$y = 100 - x = 100 - 50 = 50$.

A maximum area occurs when the length is 50 m and the width is 50 m.

12. Let $8 - x$ = the distance the hunter will travel on the river.

Then $\sqrt{9 + x^2}$ = the distance he will travel on land.

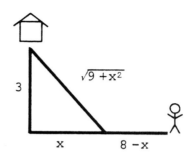

Since the rate on the river is 5 mph, the rate on land is 2 mph, and $t = d/r$, $\frac{8 - x}{5}$ = the time on the river, $\frac{\sqrt{9 + x^2}}{2}$ = the time on land. The total time is

$$T(x) = \frac{8 - x}{5} + \frac{\sqrt{9 + x^2}}{2}$$
$$= \frac{8}{5} - \frac{1}{5}x + \frac{1}{2}(9 + x^2)^{1/2}.$$
$$T' = -\frac{1}{5} + \frac{1}{4} \cdot 2x(9 + x^2)^{-1/2}$$
$$-\frac{1}{5} + \frac{x}{2(9 + x^2)^{1/2}} = 0$$
$$\frac{1}{5} = \frac{x}{2(9 + x^2)^{1/2}}$$
$$2(9 + x^2)^{1/2} = 5x$$
$$4(9 + x^2) = 25x^2$$
$$36 + 4x^2 = 25x^2$$
$$36 = 21x^2$$
$$\frac{6}{\sqrt{21}} = x$$
$$\frac{6\sqrt{21}}{21} = \frac{2\sqrt{21}}{7} = x$$
$$1.31 \approx x$$

x	T(x)
0	3.1
1.31	2.98
8	4.27

Since the minimum time is 2.98 hr, the hunter should travel 8 - 1.31 or about 6.7 miles along the river.

14. Let   x = the length and
           y = the width = the height.
   Then, 4y = the girth.

   $$x + 4y = 108$$

   Maximize volume, xy^2.

   $$x = 108 - 4y$$

   Let $V = xy^2 = (108 - 4y)y^2$
   $$= 108y^2 - 4y^3.$$

   $$V' = 216y - 12y^2$$

   $$216y - 12y^2 = 0$$
   $$12y(18 - y) = 0$$
   $$y = 0 \quad \text{or} \quad y = 18$$

y	V
0	0
18	11,664

   Since $x + 4y = 108$,

   $$\begin{aligned} x &= 108 - 4y \\ &= 108 - 4(18) \\ &= 108 - 72 \\ &= 36. \end{aligned}$$

The volume will be maximized if the box is 36 in by 18 in by 18 in.

16. $p(x) = 6 - \dfrac{x}{8}$

   (a) Revenue from x thousand tapes:

   $$\begin{aligned} R(x) &= 1000xp \\ &= 1000x\left(6 - \frac{x}{8}\right) \\ &= 6000x - 125x^2 \end{aligned}$$

   (b) $R'(x) = 6000 - 250x$
   $$6000 - 250x = 0$$
   $$6000 = 250x$$
   $$24 = x$$

   The maximum revenue occurs when 24 thousand tapes are sold.

   (c) $R(24) = 6000(24) - 125(24)^2$
   $$= 72,000$$

   The maximum revenue is $72,000.

18. $G(x) = \dfrac{1}{50}\left(\dfrac{200}{x} + \dfrac{x}{15}\right)$

   The total cost is
   $$\begin{aligned} C &= G(x) \times (\text{Cost per gallon}) \\ &\quad \times (\text{miles traveled}) \\ &= \frac{1}{50}\left(\frac{200}{x} + \frac{x}{15}\right) \times (\$2) \times (250) \\ &= \frac{2000}{x} + \frac{10x}{15}. \end{aligned}$$

   (a) $C' = \dfrac{-2000}{x^2} + \dfrac{2}{3} = 0$

   $$\frac{-2000}{x^2} = -\frac{2}{3}$$
   $$x^2 = 3000$$
   $$x \approx 54.8$$

   $C''(x) = \dfrac{4000}{x^3} > 0$ for $x > 0$ which implies $C(x)$ is minimized when $x \approx 54.8$ mph.

(b) $C(54.8) = \dfrac{2000}{54.8} + \dfrac{10(54.8)}{15}$

$\qquad \approx 36.50 + 36.53$

$\qquad = 73.03$

The minimum total cost is $73.03.

20. Let x = the length at $4 per meter

y = the width of $2 per meter.

$xy = 15,625$

$y = \dfrac{15,625}{x}$

Perimeter $= x + 2y = x + \dfrac{31,250}{x}$

Cost $= x(4) + \dfrac{31,250}{x}(2)$

$\qquad = 4x + \dfrac{62,500}{x}$

Minimize cost.

$C' = 4 - \dfrac{62,500}{x^2}$

$4 - \dfrac{62,500}{x^2} = 0$

$\qquad\qquad 4x^2 = 62,500$

$\qquad\qquad x^2 = 15,625$

$\qquad\qquad x = 125$

$\qquad\qquad y = \dfrac{15,625}{125} = 125$

125 m at $4 per meter will cost
$500. 250 m at $2 per m will cost
$500. The total cost will be $1000.

22. Let x = number of days to wait.

$\dfrac{12,000}{100} = 120 =$ the number of 100-lb
groups collected al-
ready.

Then $4 - .10x =$ the price per 100 lb

$\qquad\qquad 4x =$ the number of 100-lb
groups collected per
day

120 + 4x = total number of 100-lb
groups collected.

Revenue $= R(x)$

$\qquad = (4 - .10x)(120 + 4x)$

$\qquad = 480 + 4x - .4x^2$

$R'(x) = 4 - .8x = 0$

$\qquad\qquad x = 5$

$R''(x) = -.8 < 0$ so $R(x)$ is maximized
at $x = 5$.

So the scouts should wait 5 days
at which time their income will be
maximized at

$R(x) = 480 + 4(5) - .4(5)^2 = \$490.$

24. (a) Let x = the number of refunds.

Then 425 - 5x = the cost per passenger

$\qquad 75 + x =$ the number of passengers.

Revenue $= R(x) = (425 - 5x)(75 + x)$

$\qquad\qquad = 31,875 + 50x - 5x^2$

$\qquad R'(x) = 50 - 10x = 0$

$\qquad\qquad\qquad x = 5$

$R''(x) = -10 < 0$ so $R(x)$ is maximized
when $x = 5$.

Thus, the number of passengers that
will maximize revenue is $75 + 5 = 80$.

(b) $R(5) = 31,875 + 50(5) - 5(5)^2$

$\qquad = \$32,000$

26. Let   x = the length of a side of
the top and bottom.

Then $x^2 =$ the area of the top and
bottom and

$(\$3)(2x^2) =$ the cost for the top
and bottom.

Let y = depth of box.

Then xy = the area of one side and

4xy = the total area of the sides.

($1.50)(4xy) = the cost of the sides.

The total cost is

C(x) = (3)(2x²) + (1.50)(4xy)

= 6x² + 6xy.

The volume is

V = 16,000 = x²y.

$$y = \frac{16,000}{x^2}$$

$$C(x) = 6x^2 + 6x\left(\frac{16,000}{x^2}\right)$$

$$= 6x^2 + \frac{96,000}{x}$$

$$C'(x) = 12x - \frac{96,000}{x^2} = 0$$

$$x^3 = 8000$$

$$x = 20$$

$$C''(x) = 12 + \frac{192,000}{x^2} > 0 \text{ at } x = 20,$$

which implies that C(x) is minimixed when x = 20.

$$y = \frac{16,000}{(20)^2} = 40$$

So the dimensions of the box are x by x by y, or 20 cm by 20 cm by 40 cm.

$$C(20) = 6(20)^2 + \frac{96,000}{20} = \$7200 \text{ is}$$

the minimum total cost.

30. Let   x = the length of the side of the cutout square.

Then 3 - 2x = the width of the box

8 - 2x = the length of the box.

$$V(x) = x(3 - 2x)(8 - 2x)$$

$$= 4x^3 - 22x^2 + 24x$$

The domain of V is (0, 3/2).

Maximize the volume.

$$V'(x) = 12x^2 - 44x + 24$$

$$12x^2 - 44x + 24 = 0$$

$$4(3x^2 - 11x + 6) = 0$$

$$4(3x - 2)(x - 3) = 0$$

$$x = \frac{2}{3} \text{ or } x = 3$$

3 is not in the domain of V.

$$V''(x) = 24x - 44$$

$$V''\left(\frac{2}{3}\right) = -28 < 0$$

which implies that V is maximized when x = 2/3.

The box will have maximum volume when x = 2/3 ft or 8 in.

32. Distance on shore: 9 - x miles

Cost on shore: $400 per mile

Distance underwater: $\sqrt{x^2 + 36}$

Cost underwater: $500 per mile

Find the distance from A, that is, (9 - x), to minimize cost, C(x).

$$C(x) = (9 - x)(400) + (\sqrt{x^2 + 36})(500)$$

$$= 3600 - 400x + 500(x^2 + 36)^{1/2}$$

$$C'(x) = -400 + 500\left(\frac{1}{2}\right)(x^2 + 36)^{-1/2}(2x)$$

$$= -400 + \frac{500x}{\sqrt{x^2 + 36}}$$

If C'(x) = 0,

$$\frac{500x}{\sqrt{x^2 + 36}} = 400$$

$$\frac{5x}{4} = \sqrt{x^2 + 36}$$

$$\frac{25}{16}x^2 = x^2 + 36$$

$$\frac{9}{16}x^2 = 36$$

$$x^2 = \frac{36 \cdot 16}{9}$$

$$x = \frac{6 \cdot 4}{3} = 8.$$

(Discard the negative solution.)
Then the distance should be

$$9 - x = 9 - 8$$
$$= 1 \text{ mile from point A.}$$

34. Let x = the number of additional
      tables.

Then 90 - .25x

      = the cost per table and

300 + x = the number of tables
      ordered.

$$R = (90 - .25x)(300 + x)$$
$$= 27{,}000 + 15x - .25x^2$$
$$R' = 15 - .5x = 0$$
$$x = 30$$

$R'' = -.5 < 0$ so when 300 + 30 = 330
tables are ordered, revenue is maximum.

Thus, the maximum revenue is

$$= 27{,}000 + 15(30) - .25(30)^2$$
$$= \$27{,}225.$$

Minimum revenue is found by letting
R = 0.

$$(90 = .25x)(300 + x) = 0$$

90 - .25x = 0 or   300 + x = 0

       x = 360   x = -300
                        (impossible)

So when 300 + 360 = 660 tables are
ordered, revenue is 0, that is, each
table is free.

I would fire the assistant.

36. $H(S) = f(S) - S$

$f(S) = -S^2 + 2.2S$

$H(S) = -S^2 + 2.2S - S$

$\quad\quad = -S^2 + 1.2S$

$H'(S) = -2S + 1.2 = 0$

$$S = .6$$

The number of creatures needed to
sustain the population is $S_0 = .6$
thousand.

$H''(S) = -2 < 0$ so $H(S)$ is maximized
when $S_0 = .6$ thousand.

$H(.6) = -(.6)^2 + 1.2(.6) = .36$

The maximum sustainable harvest is
.36 thousand.

38. $H(S) = f(S) - S$

$f(S) = 12S^{.25}$

$H(S) = 12S^{.25} - S$

$H'(S) = 3S^{-.75} - 1 = 0$

$$S^{-.75} = \frac{1}{3}$$

$$\frac{1}{S^{.75}} = \frac{1}{3}$$

$$S^{.75} = 3$$

$$S^{3/4} = 3$$

$$S = 3^{4/3}$$

$$S = 4.327$$

The number of creatures needed to
sustain the population is $S_0 = 4.327$
thousand.

$H''(S) = \dfrac{-2.25}{S^{1.75}} < 0$ when $S = 4.327$

so $H(S)$ is maximized.

$H(4.327) = 12(4.327)^{.25} - 4.327$

$$\approx 12.98$$

The maximum sustainable harvest is
12.98 thousand.

40. $H(S) = f(S) - S$

$f(S) = .999S$

$H(S) = .999S - S$

$\quad = -.001S$

$H'(S) = -.001$

No harvest is possible since the population is always declining.

42. Let x = distance from P to A.

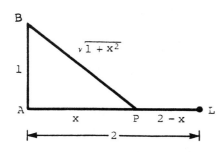

Energy used over land: 1 unit per mile

Energy used over watewr: 10/9 units per mile

Distance over land: $(2 - x)$ mi

Distance over water: $\sqrt{1 + x^2}$ mi

Find the location of P to minimize energy used.

$E(x) = 1(2 - x) + \dfrac{10}{9}\sqrt{1 + x^2}$

$E'(x) = -1 + \dfrac{10}{9}\left(\dfrac{1}{2}\right)(1 + x^2)^{-1/2}(2x)$

If $E'(x) = 0$,

$\dfrac{10}{9}x(1 + x^2)^{-1/2} = 1$

$\dfrac{10x}{9(1 + x^2)^{1/2}} = 1$

$\dfrac{10}{9}x = (1 + x^2)^{1/2}$

$\dfrac{100}{81}x^2 = 1 + x^2$

$\dfrac{19}{81}x^2 = 1$

$x^2 = \dfrac{81}{19}$

$x = \dfrac{9}{\sqrt{19}}$

$\quad = \dfrac{9\sqrt{19}}{19}$

$\quad \approx 2.06.$

This is impossible, since the total distance from A to L is just 2 miles. Thus,

Point P must be at Point L.

44. (a) Write F as a function of r only, where

$F = \pi\dfrac{(P - P_0)}{2k}r^4;$

$P - P_0 = \dfrac{r - r_0}{a}.$

$F = \dfrac{\pi(r - r_0)}{2ak}r^4$

Find value of r that maximizes F.

$F = \dfrac{\pi(r - r_0)r^4}{2ak} = \dfrac{\pi r^5 - \pi r_0 r^4}{2ak}$

$F' = \dfrac{\pi}{2ak}(5r^4 - 4r_0 r^3)$

If $F' = 0$,

$5r^4 - 4r_0 r^3 = 0$

$\quad\quad 5r^4 = 4r_0 r^3$

$\quad\quad\quad r = \dfrac{4r_0}{5}.$

Test for maximum or minimum.

$F'' = \dfrac{\pi}{2ak}(20r^3 - 12r_0 r^2)$

$\quad = \dfrac{4\pi r^2}{2ak}(5r - 3r_0)$

Since $r > r_0$ and $a < 0$, $F'' < 0$.

Therefore $r = \dfrac{4r_0}{5}$ maximizes the flow.

(b) Write $\bar{v}$ as a function of r only.

$$\bar{v} = \frac{P - P_0}{2k}r^2$$

$$= \frac{\frac{(r - r_0)}{a}r^2}{2k}$$

$$= \frac{(r - r_0)r^2}{2ak}$$

Write $v(0)$ as a function of r, where

$$v = \frac{P - P_0}{k}(r^2 - x^2);$$

$$P - P_0 = \frac{(r - r_0)}{a}.$$

$$v = \frac{(r - r_0)(r^2 - x^2)}{ak}.$$

When $x = 0$,

$$v(0) = \frac{(r - r_0)r^2}{ak}.$$

Find the value of r that maximizes $\bar{v}$.

$$\bar{v} = \frac{(r - r_0)r^2}{2ak} = \frac{r^3 - r_0r^2}{2ak}$$

$$\bar{v}' = \frac{3r^2 - 2rr_0}{2ak}$$

$$= \frac{r(3r - 2r_0)}{2ak}$$

If $\bar{v}' = 0$,

$$\frac{r(3r - 2r_0)}{2ak} = 0$$

$$3r^2 - 2rr_0 = 0$$

$$3r^2 = 2rr_0$$

$$r = \frac{2r_0}{3}.$$

Check $r = 2r_0/3$ for maximum or minimum.

$$\bar{v}'' = \frac{6r - 2r_0}{2ak} = \frac{3r - r_0}{ak}$$

Since $r > r_0$ and $a < 0$, $\bar{v}'' < 0$. Therefore, $r = 2r_0/3$ maximizes the average velocity.

Find the value of r that maximizes $v(0)$.

$$v(0) = \frac{(r - r_0)r^2}{ak} = \frac{r^3 - r^2r_0}{ak}$$

$$v'(0) = \frac{3r^2 - 2rr_0}{ak}$$

If $v'(0) = 0$,

$$\frac{3r^2 - 2rr_0}{ak} = 0$$

$$3r^2 - 2rr_0 = 0$$

$$3r^2 = 2rr_0$$

$$r = \frac{2r_0}{3}.$$

Check $r = 2r_0/3$ for maximum or minimum.

$$v''(0) = \frac{6r - 2r_0}{ak}$$

Since $r > r_0$ and $a < 0$, $v''(0) < 0$. Therefore, $r = 2r_0/3$ maximizes $v(0)$, the velocity in the center of the airway.

Exercises 46–50 should be solved by computer methods. The solutions will vary according to the computer programs that are needed.

46. The answer is the radius is 5.454 cm, the height is 10.70 cm.

48. $C(x) = \frac{1}{2}x^3 + 2x^2 - 3x + 35$

The answer is $A(x) = x^2/2 + 2x - 3 + 35/x$, $x = 2.722$.

50. $C(x) = 10 + 20x^{1/2} + 16x^{3/2}$

The answer is $A(x) = 10/x + 20x^{-1/2} + 16x^{1/2}$, $x = 2.110$.

Section 4.2

2. The annual number of batches will depend only on fixed setup costs and storage costs.

4. Use equation (3) with

M = 16,800 cases of sugar

k = $3, the cost to store one unit for one year

f = $7, the cost to produce each batch

x = the number of batches per year.

$$x = \sqrt{\frac{kM}{2f}} = \sqrt{\frac{(3)(16,800)}{(2)(7)}}$$
$$= \sqrt{3600} = 60$$

6. From Exercise 4, the number of batches is 60 and the number of cases is 16,800. The number of cases per batch is $\frac{16,800}{60} = 280$.

8. Use equation (3) with

f = fixed cost for one order

= $5

M = total number of units in one year

= 900

k = cost of storing one unit for one year

= $1

x = number of units annually.

$$x = \sqrt{\frac{kM}{2f}} = \sqrt{\frac{(1)(900)}{2(5)}}$$
$$\approx 9 \text{ or } 10 \text{ (The number of units must be an integer.)}$$

The optimum number of bottles per order is

$$\frac{M}{x} = \frac{900}{9} = 100 \text{ or } \frac{900}{10} = 90.$$

10. Since k = $6 times the maximum number of books stored, use

$$x = \sqrt{\frac{kM}{f}}$$

from Exercise 9.

M = 5000 copies per year

f = $1000 fixed cost

$$x = \sqrt{\frac{kM}{f}}$$
$$= \sqrt{\frac{6(5000)}{1000}}$$
$$= \sqrt{30}$$
$$\approx 5$$

Five print runs should be scheduled.

$$\frac{5000 \text{ total books}}{5 \text{ print runs}} = 1000 \text{ books per print run.}$$

12. Because there is a cost for storing each unit, plus an annual cost per case, use

$$x = \sqrt{\frac{(k_1 + 2k_2)M}{2f}}$$

from Exercise 11.

$k_1 = \$1$

$k_2 = \$2$

$M = 30,000$

$f = \$750$

$g = \$8$

$x = \sqrt{\dfrac{(1 + 2 \cdot 2)(30,000)}{2(750)}}$

$= \sqrt{\dfrac{15,000}{1500}}$

$= \sqrt{100} = 10$

She should have 10 production runs each year.

14. $q = 50 - \dfrac{p}{4}$

(a) $\dfrac{dq}{dp} = -\dfrac{1}{4}$

$E = -\dfrac{p}{q} \cdot \dfrac{dq}{dp}$

$= -\dfrac{p}{50 - \dfrac{p}{4}}\left(-\dfrac{1}{4}\right)$

$= -\dfrac{p}{\dfrac{200 - p}{4}}\left(-\dfrac{1}{4}\right)$

$= \dfrac{p}{200 - p}$

(b) $R = pq$

$\dfrac{dR}{dp} = q(1 - E)$

When R is maximum, $q(1 - E) = 0$.
Since $q = 0$ means no revenue,
set $1 - E = 0$.

$E = 1$

From (a),

$\dfrac{p}{200 - p} = 1$

$p = 200 - p$

$p = 100.$

$q = 50 - \dfrac{p}{4}$

$= 50 - \dfrac{100}{4}$

$= 25$

Total revenue is maximized if $q = 25$.

16. $q = \sqrt[3]{\dfrac{2000}{p}}$

$= \left(\dfrac{2000}{p}\right)^{1/3}$

$= (2000p^{-1})^{1/3}$

$= 2000^{1/3}\, p^{-1/3}$

$\dfrac{dq}{dp} = 2000^{1/3}\left(-\dfrac{1}{3}\right)p^{-4/3}$

$= -\dfrac{2000^{1/3}}{3p^{4/3}}$

(a) $E = -\dfrac{p}{q} \cdot \dfrac{dq}{dp}$

$= -\dfrac{p}{2000^{1/3}\, p^{-1/3}} \cdot \dfrac{-(2000)^{1/3}}{3p^{4/3}}$

$= \dfrac{p}{3p} = \dfrac{1}{3}$

(b) $R = pq$

$\dfrac{dR}{dp} = q(1 - E)$

$= q\left(1 - \dfrac{1}{3}\right)$

$= \dfrac{2}{3}q$

The only way for $\dfrac{dR}{dp}$ to be zero is if $q = 0$, yielding no revenue. Thus, there are no values of q that maximize total revenue.

18. $q = 400 - .2p^2$

$$\frac{dq}{dp} = -.4p$$

$$E = -\frac{p}{q} \cdot \frac{dq}{dp}$$

$$E = -\frac{p}{400 - .2p^2}(-.4p)$$

$$= \frac{.4p^2}{400 - .2p^2}$$

(a) If $p = \$20$,

$$E = \frac{(.4)(20)^2}{400 - .2(20)^2}$$

$$= .5 < 1$$

$E = .5$; inelastic; total revenue increases as price increases.

(b) If $p = \$40$,

$$E = \frac{(.4)(40)^2}{400 - .2(40)^2}$$

$$= 8 > 1$$

$E = 8$; elastic; total revenue decreases as price increases.

20. $q = m - np$ for $0 \le p \le \frac{m}{n}$

$$\frac{dq}{dp} = -n$$

$$E = -\frac{p}{q} \cdot \frac{dq}{dp}$$

$$E = -\frac{p}{m - np}(-n)$$

$$E = \frac{pn}{m - np} = 1$$

$$pn = m - np$$

$$2np = m$$

$$p = \frac{m}{2n}$$

Thus, $E = 1$ when $p = m/2n$, or at the midpoint of the demand curve on the interval $0 \le p \le m/n$.

22. When increase in price results in an increase of demand, $dq/dp > 0$. Since $p > 0$ and $q > 0$, $E = -\frac{p}{q} \cdot \frac{dq}{dp}$ is negative.

Section 4.3

2. $2x^2 - 5y^2 = 4$

$$\frac{d}{dx}(2x^2 - 5y^2) = \frac{d}{dx}(4)$$

$$\frac{d}{dx}(2x^2) - \frac{d}{dx}(5y^2) = \frac{d}{dx}(4)$$

$$4x - 10y\frac{dy}{dx} = 0$$

$$10y\frac{dy}{dx} = 4x$$

$$\frac{dy}{dx} = \frac{2x}{5y}$$

4. $-3xy - 4y^2 = 2$

$$\frac{d}{dx}(-3xy - 4y^2) = \frac{d}{dx}(2)$$

$$\frac{d}{dx}(-3xy) - \frac{d}{dx}(4y^2) = \frac{d}{dx}(2)$$

$$-3x\frac{dy}{dx} - 3y - 8y\frac{dy}{dx} = 0$$

$$\frac{dy}{dx}(-3x - 8y) = 3y$$

$$\frac{dy}{dx} = \frac{3y}{-3x - 8y}$$

$$= \frac{-3y}{3x + 8y}$$

6. $-4y^2x^2 - 3x + 2 = 0$

$$\frac{d}{dx}(-4y^2x^2 - 3x + 2) = \frac{d}{dx}(0)$$

$$-4y^2\frac{d}{dx}(x^2) + x^2\frac{d}{dx}(-4y^2) - \frac{d}{dx}(3x) + \frac{d}{dx}(2)$$

$$= \frac{d}{dx}(0)$$

$$-8xy^2 + x^2(-8y)\frac{dy}{dx} - 3 + 0 = 0$$

$$-8xy^2 - 8x^2y\frac{dy}{dx} - 3 = 0$$

$$-8x^2y\frac{dy}{dx} = 3 + 8xy^2$$

$$\frac{dy}{dx} = \frac{3 + 8xy^2}{-8x^2y}$$

$$= \frac{-8xy^2 - 3}{8x^2y}$$

$$-\frac{3}{2x^2} = \frac{1}{y^2} \cdot \frac{dy}{dx} + \frac{dy}{dx}$$

$$-\frac{3}{2x^2} = \left(\frac{1}{y^2} + 1\right)\frac{dy}{dx}$$

$$-\frac{3}{2x^2} = \left(\frac{1 + y^2}{y^2}\right)\frac{dy}{dx}$$

$$\frac{-3y^2}{2x^2(1 + y^2)} = \frac{dy}{dx}$$

8. $8x^2 = 6y^2 + 2xy$

$$\frac{d}{dx}(8x^2) = \frac{d}{dx}(6y^2 + 2xy)$$

$$16x = \frac{d}{dx}(6y^2) + \frac{d}{dx}(2xy)$$

$$16x = 12y\frac{dy}{dx} + 2x\frac{d}{dx}(y) + y\frac{d}{dx}(2x)$$

$$16x = 12y\frac{dy}{dx} + 2x\frac{dy}{dx} \cdot 1 + 2y$$

$$16x - 2y = \frac{dy}{dx}(12y + 2x)$$

$$\frac{16x - 2y}{12y + 2x} = \frac{dy}{dx}$$

$$\frac{8x - y}{6y + x} = \frac{dy}{dx}$$

10. $x^3 - 6y^2 = 10$

$$\frac{d}{dx}(x^3 - 6y^2) = \frac{d}{dx}(10)$$

$$\frac{d}{dx}(x^3) - \frac{d}{dx}(6y^2) = 0$$

$$3x^2 - 12y\frac{dy}{dx} = 0$$

$$-12y\frac{dy}{dx} = -3x^2$$

$$\frac{dy}{dx} = \frac{x^2}{4y}$$

12. $\frac{3}{2x} + \frac{1}{y} = y$

$$\frac{d}{dx}\left(\frac{3}{2x} + \frac{1}{y}\right) = \frac{d}{dx}(y)$$

$$\frac{d}{dx}\left(\frac{3}{2x}\right) + \frac{d}{dx}\left(\frac{1}{y}\right) = \frac{d}{dx}(y)$$

$$-\frac{3}{2x^2} - \frac{1}{y^2} \cdot \frac{dy}{dx} = \frac{dy}{dx}$$

14. $2y^2 = \frac{5 + x}{5 - x}$

$$\frac{d}{dx}(2y^2) = \frac{d}{dx}\left(\frac{5 + x}{5 - x}\right)$$

$$4y\frac{dy}{dx} = \frac{(1)(5 - x) - (-1)(5 + x)}{(5 - x)^2}$$

$$4y\frac{dy}{dx} = \frac{5 - x + 5 + x}{(5 - x)^2} = \frac{10}{(5 - x)^2}$$

$$\frac{dy}{dx} = \frac{10}{4y(5 - x)^2} = \frac{5}{2y(5 - x)^2}$$

16. $2xy^2 + 2y^3 + 5x = 0$

$$\frac{d}{dx}(2xy^2 + 2y^3 + 5x) = \frac{d}{dx}(0)$$

$$2y^2 + (2x)\left(2y\frac{dy}{dx}\right) + 6y^2\frac{dy}{dx} + 5 = 0$$

$$2y^2 + 4xy\frac{dy}{dx} + 6y^2\frac{dy}{dx} + 5 = 0$$

$$(4xy + 6y^2)\frac{dy}{dx} = -2y^2 - 5$$

$$\frac{dy}{dx} = \frac{-2y^2 - 5}{4xy + 6y^2}$$

18. $2\sqrt{x} - \sqrt{y} = 1$

$$\frac{d}{dx}(2x^{1/2} - y^{1/2}) = \frac{d}{dx}(1)$$

$$x^{-1/2} - \frac{1}{2}y^{-1/2}\frac{dy}{dx} = 0$$

$$-\frac{1}{2}y^{-1/2}\frac{dy}{dx} = -x^{-1/2}$$

$$\frac{dy}{dx} = -2y^{1/2}(-x^{-1/2})$$

$$= \frac{2y^{1/2}}{x^{1/2}}$$

20. $\sqrt{2xy} - 1 = 3y^2$

$$\frac{d}{dx}(\sqrt{2xy} - 1) = \frac{d}{dx}(3y^2)$$

$$\frac{d}{dx}(2xy)^{1/2} - \frac{d}{dx}(1) = \frac{d}{dx}(3y^2)$$

$$\frac{1}{2}(2xy)^{-1/2}\left(2y + 2x\frac{dy}{dx}\right) - 0 = 6y\frac{dy}{dx}$$

$$\frac{y + x\frac{dy}{dx}}{(2xy)^{1/2}} = 6y\frac{dy}{dx}$$

$$y + x\frac{dy}{dx} = 6y(2xy)^{1/2}\frac{dy}{dx}$$

$$x\frac{dy}{dx} - 6y(2xy)^{1/2}\frac{dy}{dx} = -y$$

$$\frac{dy}{dx}\left[x - 6y(2xy)^{1/2}\right] = -y$$

$$\frac{dy}{dx} = \frac{-y}{x - 6y(2xy)^{1/2}}$$

22. $(xy)^{4/3} + x^{1/3} = y^6 + 1$

$$\frac{d}{dx}\left[(xy)^{4/3} + x^{1/3}\right] = \frac{d}{dx}(y^6 + 1)$$

$$\frac{d}{dx}(x^{4/3}y^{4/3}) + \frac{d}{dx}(x^{1/3}) = \frac{d}{dx}(y^6) + \frac{d}{dx}(1)$$

$$x^{4/3} \cdot \frac{4}{3}y^{1/3}\frac{dy}{dx} + \frac{4}{3}x^{1/3}y^{4/3} + \frac{1}{3}x^{-2/3}$$

$$= 6y^5\frac{dy}{dx} + 0$$

$$\frac{4}{3}x^{1/3}y^{4/3} + \frac{1}{3}x^{-2/3} = 6y^5\frac{dy}{dx}$$
$$- \frac{4}{3}x^{4/3}y^{1/3}\frac{dy}{dx}$$

$$4x^{1/3}y^{4/3} + x^{-2/3} = 18y^5\frac{dy}{dx}$$
$$- 4x^{4/3}y^{1/3}\frac{dy}{dx}$$

$$4x^{1/3}y^{4/3} + x^{-2/3} = (18y^5 - 4x^{4/3}y^{1/3})$$
$$\cdot \frac{dy}{dx}$$

$$\frac{4x^{1/3}y^{4/3} + x^{-2/3}}{18y^5 - 4x^{4/3}y^{1/3}} = \frac{dy}{dx}$$

$$\frac{x^{2/3}}{x^{2/3}} \cdot \frac{4x^{1/3}y^{4/3} + x^{-2/3}}{18y^5 - 4x^{4/3}y^{1/3}} = \frac{dy}{dx}$$

$$\frac{4xy^{4/3} + 1}{18x^{2/3}y^5 - 4x^2y^{1/3}} = \frac{dy}{dx}$$

24. $\sqrt{x^2 + y^2} = x^{3/2} - y - 2$

$$\frac{d}{dx}\sqrt{x^2 + y^2} = \frac{d}{dx}(x^{3/2} - y - 2)$$

$$\frac{d}{dx}(x^2 + y^2)^{1/2} = \frac{d}{dx}(x^{3/2}) - \frac{d}{dx}(y)$$
$$- \frac{d}{dx}(2)$$

$$\frac{1}{2}(x^2 + y^2)^{-1/2}\frac{d}{dx}(x^2 + y^2) = \frac{3}{2}x^{1/2} - \frac{dy}{dx} - 0$$

$$\frac{1}{2}(x^2 + y^2)^{-1/2}\left(2x + 2y\frac{dy}{dx}\right) = \frac{3}{2}x^{1/2} - \frac{dy}{dx}$$

$$x(x^2 + y^2)^{-1/2} + y(x^2 + y^2)^{-1/2}\frac{dy}{dx}$$
$$= \frac{3}{2}x^{1/2} - \frac{dy}{dx}$$

$$y(x^2 + y^2)^{-1/2}\frac{dy}{dx} + \frac{dy}{dx} = \frac{3}{2}x^{1/2}$$
$$- x(x^2 + y^2)^{-1/2}$$

$$\frac{dy}{dx}[y(x^2 + y^2)^{-1/2} + 1] = \frac{3}{2}x^{1/2}$$
$$- x(x^2 + y^2)^{-1/2}$$

$$\frac{dy}{dx} = \frac{\frac{3}{2}x^{1/2} - x(x^2 + y^2)^{-1/2}}{y(x^2 + y^2)^{-1/2} + 1}$$

$$= \frac{2(x^2 + y^2)^{1/2}}{2(x^2 + y^2)^{1/2}} \cdot \frac{\frac{3}{2}x^{1/2} - x(x^2 + y^2)^{-1/2}}{y(x^2 + y^2)^{-1/2} + 1}$$

$$= \frac{3x^{1/2}(x^2 + y^2)^{1/2} - 2x}{2y + 2(x^2 + y^2)^{1/2}}$$

$$= \frac{3x^{1/2}\sqrt{x^2 + y^2} - 2x}{2(y + \sqrt{x^2 + y^2})}$$

26. $x^2 + y^2 = 100$; tangent at $(8, -6)$

$$\frac{d}{dx}(x^2 + y^2) = \frac{d}{dx}(100)$$

$$2x + 2y\frac{dy}{dx} = 0$$

$$\frac{dy}{dx} = -\frac{x}{y}$$

$$m = -\frac{x}{y} = -\frac{8}{-6} = \frac{4}{3}$$

$$y - y_1 = m(x - x_1)$$

$$y + 6 = \frac{4}{3}(x - 8)$$

$$3y + 18 = 4x - 32$$

$$3y = 4x - 50$$

28. $x^2y^3 = 8$; tangent at $(-1, 2)$

$$\frac{d}{dx}(x^2y^3) = \frac{d}{dx}(8)$$

$$2xy^3 + 3x^2y^2\frac{dy}{dx} = 0$$

$$\frac{dy}{dx} = \frac{-2xy^3}{3x^2y^2}$$

$$m = -\frac{2xy^3}{3x^2y^2} = -\frac{2(-1)(2)^3}{3(-1)^2(2)^2}$$

$$= \frac{16}{12} = \frac{4}{3}$$

$$y - 2 = \frac{4}{3}(x + 1)$$

$$3y - 6 = 4x + 4$$

$$3y = 4x + 10$$

30. $2y^2 - \sqrt{x} = 4$; tangent at $(16, 2)$

$$\frac{d}{dx}(2y^2 - \sqrt{x}) = \frac{d}{dx}(4)$$

$$4y\frac{dy}{dx} - \frac{1}{2}x^{-1/2} = 0$$

$$4y\frac{dy}{dx} = \frac{1}{2x^{1/2}}$$

$$\frac{dy}{dx} = \frac{1}{8yx^{1/2}}$$

$$m = \frac{1}{8yx^{1/2}} = \frac{1}{8(2)(16)^{1/2}}$$

$$= \frac{1}{8(2)(4)} = \frac{1}{64}$$

$$y - 2 = \frac{1}{64}(x - 16)$$

$$64y - 128 = x - 16$$

$$64y = x + 112$$

32. $x + \frac{\sqrt{y}}{3x} = 2$; tangent at $(1, 9)$

$$\frac{d}{dx}\left(x + \frac{\sqrt{y}}{3x}\right) = \frac{d}{dx}(2)$$

$$\frac{d}{dx}\left(x + \frac{1}{3}x^{-1}y^{1/2}\right) = \frac{d}{dx}(2)$$

$$1 + \left(-\frac{1}{3}x^{-2}\right)(y^{1/2}) + \left(\frac{1}{2}y^{-1/2}\right)\frac{dy}{dx}\left(\frac{1}{3}x^{-1}\right) = 0$$

$$1 + \frac{-y^{1/2}}{3x^2} + \frac{1}{6xy^{1/2}}\frac{dy}{dx} = 0$$

$$\frac{1}{6xy^{1/2}}\frac{dy}{dx} = \frac{y^{1/2} - 3x^2}{3x^2}$$

$$\frac{dy}{dx} = \frac{(y^{1/2} - 3x^2)6xy^{1/2}}{3x^2}$$

$$= \frac{(y^{1/2} - 3x^2)(2y^{1/2})}{x}$$

$$m = \frac{[9^{1/2} - 3(1)^2] \cdot 2(9)^{1/2}}{1}$$

$$= \frac{(3 - 3) \cdot 6}{1} = 0$$

$$y - 9 = 0(x - 1)$$
$$y = 9$$

34. $xy = 1$

$$\frac{d}{dx}(xy) = \frac{d}{dx}(1)$$

$$y + x\frac{dy}{dx} = 0$$

$$\frac{dy}{dx} = -\frac{y}{x}$$

(a) At $x = -1$, $y = \frac{1}{x} = -1$.

$$m = -\frac{-1}{-1} = -1$$

tangent at $(-1, -1)$:

$$y - (-1) = -1[x - (-1)]$$
$$y + 1 = -x - 1$$
$$x + y = -2$$

At $x = 1$, $y = \frac{1}{x} = 1$.

$$m = -\frac{1}{1} = -1$$

tangent at $(1, 1)$:

$$y - 1 = -1(x - 1)$$
$$y - 1 = -x + 1$$
$$x + y = 2$$

(b)

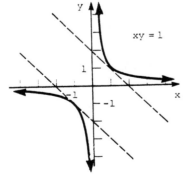

36. $3(x^2 + y^2)^2 = 25(x^2 - y^2)$; tangent at $(2, 1)$

$$\frac{d}{dx}[3(x^2 + y^2)^2] = \frac{d}{dx}[25(x^2 - y^2)]$$

$$6(x^2 + y^2)\frac{d}{dx}(x^2 + y^2) = 25\frac{d}{dx}(x^2 - y^2)$$

$$6(x^2 + y^2)\left(2x + 2y\frac{dy}{dx}\right) = 25\left(2x - 2y\frac{dy}{dx}\right)$$

$$12x(x^2 + y^2) + 12y(x^2 + y^2)\frac{dy}{dx} = 50x - 50y\frac{dy}{dx}$$

$$12y(x^2 + y^2)\frac{dy}{dx} + 50y\frac{dy}{dx} = 50x$$
$$\qquad\qquad - 12x(x^2 + y^2)$$

$$\frac{dy}{dx} = \frac{50x - 12x(x^2 + y^2)}{12y(x^2 + y^2) + 50y}$$

$$m = \frac{50x - 12x(x^2 + y^2)}{12y(x^2 + y^2) + 50y}$$

$$= \frac{100 - 24(5)}{12(5) + 50}$$

$$= \frac{-20}{110} = -\frac{2}{11}$$

$$y - 1 = -\frac{2}{11}(x - 2)$$
$$11y - 11 = -2x + 4$$
$$11y = -2x + 15$$

38. $\sqrt{u} + \sqrt{2v + 1} = 5$

$$\frac{du}{dv}(\sqrt{u} + \sqrt{2v + 1}) = \frac{du}{dv}(5)$$

$$\frac{1}{2}u^{-1/2}\frac{du}{dv} + \frac{1}{2}(2v + 1)^{-1/2}(2) = 0$$

$$\frac{1}{2}u^{-1/2}\frac{du}{dv} = -\frac{1}{(2v + 1)^{1/2}}$$

$$\frac{du}{dv} = -\frac{2u^{1/2}}{(2v + 1)^{1/2}}$$

40. $2p^2 + q^2 = 1600$

(a) $4p + 2q\frac{dq}{dp} = 0$

$$4p = -2q\frac{dq}{dp}$$

$$\frac{-2p}{q} = \frac{dq}{dp}$$

This is the rate of change of demand with respect to price.

(b) $4p\frac{dp}{dq} + 2q = 0$

$$\frac{dp}{dq} = \frac{-q}{2p}$$

This is the rate of change of price with respect to demand.

42. $s^3 - 4st + 2t^3 - 5t = 0$

$$3s^2\frac{ds}{dt} - \left(4t\frac{ds}{dt} + 4s\right) + 6t^2 - 5 = 0$$

$$3s^2\frac{ds}{dt} - 4t\frac{ds}{dt} - 4s + 6t^2 - 5 = 0$$

$$\frac{ds}{dt}(3s^2 - 4t) = 4s - 6t^2 + 5$$

$$\frac{ds}{dt} = \frac{4s - 6t^2 + 5}{3s^2 - 4t}$$

Section 4.4

2. $y = \frac{3x + 2}{1 - x}; \quad \frac{dx}{dt} = -1, \quad x = 3$

$$\frac{dy}{dt} = \frac{3(1 - x) - (3x + 2)(-1)}{(1 - x)^2}\frac{dx}{dt}$$

$$= \frac{3 - 3x + 3x + 2}{(1 - x)^2}\frac{dx}{dt}$$

$$= \frac{5}{(1 - x)^2}\frac{dx}{dt}$$

$$= \frac{5}{(1 - 3)^2}(-1) = -\frac{5}{4}$$

4. $8y^3 + x^2 = 1; \quad \frac{dx}{dt} = 2, \quad x = 3, \quad y = -1$

$$24y^2\frac{dy}{dt} + 2x\frac{dx}{dt} = 0$$

$$\frac{dy}{dt} = \frac{-2x\frac{dx}{dt}}{24y^2} = -\frac{x\frac{dx}{dt}}{12y^2}$$

$$= -\frac{(3)(2)}{12(-1)^2}$$

$$= -\frac{1}{2}$$

6. $4x^3 - 9xy^2 + y = -80; \quad \frac{dx}{dt} = 4, \quad x = -3,$

$y = 1$

$$12x^2\frac{dx}{dt} - \left(9y^2\frac{dx}{dt} + 18xy\frac{dy}{dt}\right) + \frac{dy}{dt} = 0$$

$$12x^2\frac{dx}{dt} - 9y^2\frac{dx}{dt} - 18xy\frac{dy}{dt} + \frac{dy}{dt} = 0$$

$$(1 - 18xy)\frac{dy}{dt} = (9y^2 - 12x^2)\frac{d}{d}$$

$$\frac{dy}{dt} = \frac{3(3y^2 - 4x^2)\frac{dx}{dt}}{1 - 18xy}$$

$$= \frac{3(3 \cdot 1 - 4 \cdot 9)(4)}{1 - 18(-3)(1)}$$

$$= \frac{-396}{55} = -\frac{36}{5}$$

8. $\frac{y^3 - x^2}{x + 2y} = \frac{17}{7}; \quad \frac{dx}{dt} = 1, \quad x = -3, \quad y = -2$

$$7(y^3 - x^2) = 17(x + 2y)$$

$$7y^3 - 7x^2 = 17x + 34y$$

$$21y^2\frac{dy}{dt} - 14x\frac{dx}{dt} = 17\frac{dx}{dt} + 34\frac{dy}{dt}$$

$$(21y^2 - 34)\frac{dy}{dt} = (17 + 14x)\frac{dx}{dt}$$

$$\frac{dy}{dt} = \frac{(17 + 14x)\frac{dx}{dt}}{21y^2 - 34}$$

$$= \frac{[17 + 14(-3)] \cdot 1}{21 \cdot 4 - 34}$$

$$= \frac{-25}{50} = -\frac{1}{2}$$

10. $C = \dfrac{R^2}{400,000} + 10,000;$ $\dfrac{dC}{dx} = 10,$

  $R = 20,000$

  $\dfrac{dC}{dx} = \dfrac{R}{200,000}\dfrac{dR}{dx}$

  $10 = \dfrac{20,000}{200,000}\dfrac{dR}{dx}$

  $10 = .1\dfrac{dR}{dx}$

  $100 = \dfrac{dR}{dx}$

  Revenue is changing at a rate of $100 per unit.

12. $R = 50x - .4x^2,$ $C = 5x + 15;$ $x = 200,$

  $\dfrac{dx}{dt} = 50$

  (a) $\dfrac{dR}{dt} = 50\dfrac{dx}{dt} - .8x\dfrac{dx}{dt}$

  $= 50(50) - .8(200)(50)$

  $= 2500 - 8000$

  $= -5500$

  Revenue is decreasing at a rate of $5500 per day.

  (b) $\dfrac{dC}{dt} = (5)\dfrac{dx}{dt}$

  $= (5)(50)$

  $= 250$

  Cost is increasing at a rate of $250 per day.

  (c) $P = R - C$

  $\dfrac{dP}{dt} = \dfrac{dR}{dt} - \dfrac{dC}{dt}$

  $= -5500 - 250$

  $= -5750$

  Profit is decreasing at a rate of $5750 per day.

14. $p = 70 - \dfrac{q^2}{120};$ $\dfrac{dq}{dt} = 25,$ $q = 20$

  $R = qp = q\left(70 - \dfrac{q^2}{120}\right)$

  $= 70q - \dfrac{q^3}{120}$

  $\dfrac{dR}{dt} = \left(70 - \dfrac{q^2}{40}\right)\dfrac{dq}{dt}$

  $= \left(70 - \dfrac{(20)^2}{40}\right)(25)$

  $= (70 - 10)(25)$

  $= 1500$

  Demand is increasing at a rate of $1500 per day.

16. $V = k(R^2 - r^2);$ $k = 4,$ $r = 1$ mm,

  $\dfrac{dr}{dt} = .004$ mm/min, R is constant.

  $V = k(R^2 - r^2)$

  $V = 4(R^2 - r^2)$

  $\dfrac{dV}{dt} = 4\left(0 - 2r\dfrac{dr}{dt}\right)$

  $= 4(-2)(1)(.004)$

  $= -.032$ mm/min

18. $C = \dfrac{1}{10}(T - 60)^2 + 100$

  $\dfrac{dC}{dt} = \dfrac{1}{5}(T - 60)\dfrac{dT}{dt}$

  If $T = 76°$ and $\dfrac{dT}{dt} = 8,$

  $\dfrac{dC}{dt} = \dfrac{1}{5}(76 - 60)(8) = \dfrac{1}{5}(16)(8)$

  $= 25.6$ crimes per month.

20. $W(t) = \dfrac{-.02t^2 + t}{t + 1}$

$\dfrac{dW}{dt} = \dfrac{(.-04t + 1)(t + 1) - (1)(-.02t^2 + t)}{(t + 1)^2}$

If $t = 5$,

$\dfrac{dW}{dt} = \dfrac{(-.2 + 1)(6) - (-.5 + 5)}{(6)^2}$

$\phantom{\dfrac{dW}{dt}} = \dfrac{4.8 - 4.5}{36}$

$\phantom{\dfrac{dW}{dt}} = .008$

22.   Let x = the distance one car travels west

y = the distance the other car travels north

s = the distance between the two cars.

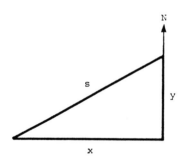

$s^2 = x^2 + y^2$

$2s\dfrac{ds}{dt} = 2x\dfrac{dx}{dt} + 2y\dfrac{dy}{dt}$

$s\dfrac{ds}{dt} = x\dfrac{dx}{dt} + y\dfrac{dy}{dt}$

Use $d = rt$ to find x and y.

$x = (40)(2) = 80$ mi

$y = (30)(2) = 60$ mi

$s = \sqrt{x^2 + y^2}$

$ = \sqrt{(80)^2 + (60)^2}$

$ = 100$ mi

$\dfrac{dx}{dt} = 40$ mph and $\dfrac{dy}{dt} = 30$ mph

So

$(100)\dfrac{ds}{dt} = (80)(40) + (60)(30)$

$\dfrac{ds}{dt} = \dfrac{5000}{100} = 50$ mph.

24. $V = \dfrac{4}{3}\pi r^3$, $r = 4$ in, and $\dfrac{dr}{dt} = -\dfrac{1}{4}$ in/hr

$\dfrac{dV}{dt} = 4\pi r^2 \dfrac{dr}{dt}$

$\phantom{\dfrac{dV}{dt}} = 4\pi (4)^2 \left(-\dfrac{1}{4}\right)$

$\phantom{\dfrac{dV}{dt}} = -16\pi$ in^3/hr

26.   Let y = the length of the man's shadow

x = the distance of the man from the lamp post

h = the height of the lamp post.

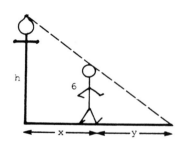

$\dfrac{dx}{dt} = 50$ ft/min

Find $\dfrac{dy}{dt}$ when $x = 25$ ft.

Now $\dfrac{h}{x + y} = \dfrac{6}{y}$, by similar triangles.

When $x = 8$, $y = 10$,

$\dfrac{h}{18} = \dfrac{6}{10}$

$h = 10.8$.

So $\dfrac{10.8}{x + y} = \dfrac{6}{y}$.

$$10.8y = 6x + 6y$$
$$4.8y = 6x$$
$$y = 1.25x$$

$$\frac{dy}{dt} = 1.25\frac{dx}{dt}$$
$$= 1.25(50)$$
$$\frac{dy}{dt} = 62.5 \text{ ft/min}$$

28. Let x = the distance from the docks
s = the length of the rope.

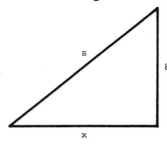

$$\frac{ds}{dt} = 1 \text{ ft/sec}$$
$$s^2 = x^2 + (8)^2$$
$$2s\frac{ds}{dt} = 2x\frac{dx}{dt} + 0$$
$$s\frac{ds}{dt} = x\frac{dx}{dt}$$

If x = 8,

$$s = \sqrt{(8)^2 + (8)^2} = \sqrt{128} = 8\sqrt{2}.$$

So

$$8\sqrt{2}(1) = 8\frac{dx}{dt}$$
$$\frac{dx}{dt} = \sqrt{2} \text{ ft/sec}.$$

Section 4.5

2. $y = -8x^4$
$$dy = 4(-8x^3)dx$$
$$= -32x^3dx$$

4. $y = -3x^3 + 2x^2$
$$dy = [-3(3x^2) + 2(2x)]dx$$
$$= (-9x^2 + 4x)dx$$

6. $y = 8\sqrt{2x - 1}$
$$= 8(2x - 1)^{1/2}$$
$$dy = 8 \cdot \frac{1}{2}(2x - 1)^{-1/2} \cdot 2dx$$
$$= 8(2x - 1)^{-1/2} dx$$

8. $y = \dfrac{-4x + 7}{3x - 1}$
$$dy = \frac{-4(3x - 1) - (3)(-4x + 7)}{(3x - 1)^2} dx$$
$$= \frac{-12x + 4 + 12x - 21}{(3x - 1)^2} dx$$
$$= \frac{-17}{(3x - 1)^2} dx$$

10. $y = -x^3\left(2 + \dfrac{3}{x^2} - \dfrac{5}{x}\right)$
$$= -2x^3 - 3x + 5x^2$$
$$dy = (-6x^2 - 3 + 10x)dx$$

12. $y = \left(9 - \dfrac{2}{x^2}\right)\left(3 + \dfrac{1}{x}\right)$
$$= (9 - 2x^{-2})(3 + x^{-1})$$
$$dy = [(4x^{-3})(3 + x^{-1}) + (-x^{-2})(9 - 2x^{-2})]dx$$
$$= (12x^{-3} + 4x^{-4} - 9x^{-2} + 2x^{-4})dx$$
$$= (12x^{-3} + 6x^{-4} - 9x^{-2})dx$$

14. $y = x^2 - 3x$; $x = 3$, $\Delta x = .1$

$dy = (2x - 3)dx$

$\approx (2x - 3)\Delta x$

$= [2(3) - 3](.1)$

$= (3)(.1)$

$= .3$

16. $y = 2x^3 + x^2 - 4x$; $x = 2$, $\Delta x = -.2$

$dy = (6x^2 + 2x - 4)dx$

$\approx (6x^2 + 2x - 4)\Delta x$

$= [6(2)^2 + 2(2) - 4](-.2)$

$= (24 + 4 - 4)(-.2)$

$= -4.8$

18. $y = \sqrt{4x - 1}$; $x = 5$, $\Delta x = .08$

$dy = \frac{1}{2}(4x - 1)^{-1/2}(4)dx$

$= 2(4x - 1)^{-1/2}dx$

$\approx 2(4x - 1)^{-1/2}\Delta x$

$= 2[4(5) - 1]^{-1/2}(.08)$

$= 2(19)^{-1/2}(.08)$

$= \frac{2}{(19)^{1/2}}(.08)$

$= .037$

20. $y = \frac{6x - 3}{2x + 1}$; $x = 3$, $\Delta x = -.04$

$dy = \frac{6(2x + 1) - 2(6x - 3)}{(2x + 1)^2}dx$

$= \frac{12}{(2x + 1)^2}dx$

$\approx \frac{12}{(2x + 1)^2}\Delta x$

$= \frac{12}{[2(3) + 1]^2}(-.04)$

$= \frac{-.48}{49}$

$= -.010$

22. $y = 9\left(3 + \frac{1}{x^4}\right)$; $x = -2$, $\Delta x = -.015$

$= 27 + 9x^{-4}$

$dy = (-36x^{-5})dx$

$= \frac{-36dx}{x^5}$

$\approx \frac{-36\Delta x}{x^5}$

$= \frac{(-36)(-.015)}{(-2)^5}$

$= -.017$

24. $y = \frac{2 - 5x}{\sqrt{x + 1}}$; $x = 3$, $\Delta x = .02$

$dy = \frac{-5\sqrt{x + 1} - \frac{1}{2}(x + 1)^{-1/2}(2 - 5x)}{(\sqrt{x + 1})^2}dx$

$\approx \frac{-5\sqrt{x + 1} - \frac{1}{2}(x + 1)^{-1/2}(2 - 5x)}{x + 1}\Delta x$

$= \frac{-5\sqrt{4} - \frac{1}{2}(4)^{-1/2}(2 - 15)}{4}(.02)$

$= \frac{-10 - \frac{1}{4}(-13)}{4}(.02)$

$= -.034$

26. $A(x) = .04x^3 + .1x^2 + .5x + 6$

(a) $x = 3$, $\Delta x = 1$

$dA = (.12x^2 + .2x + .5)dx$

$\approx (.12x^2 + .2x + .5)\Delta x$

$= [(.12)(3)^2 + (.2)(3) + (.5)](1)$

$= 2.18$

(b) $x = 5$, $\Delta x = 1$

$dA \approx [(.12)(5)^2 + (.2)(5) + (.5)](1)$

$= 4.5$

28. $R(x) = 625 + .03x + .0001x^2$
$x = 1000, \Delta x = 1$

$dR = (.03 + .0002x)dx$

$\approx (.03 + .0002x)\Delta x$

$= [.03 + .0002(1000)](1)$

$= \$.23$

30. If a cube is given a coating .1 in thick, each edge increases in length by twice that amount, or .2 in, because there is a face at both ends of the edge.

$V = x^3, x = 4, \Delta x = .2$

$dV = 3x^2dx$

$\Delta V \approx 3x^2\Delta x$

$= 3(4^2)(.2)$

$= 9.6$

For 1000 cubes 9.6(1000) = 9600 in³ o coating should be ordered.

32. $C = \dfrac{5x}{9 + x^2}$

$dC = \dfrac{5(9 + x^2) - 2x(5x)}{(9 + x)^2} dx$

$= \dfrac{45 + 5x^2 - 10x^2}{(9 + x^2)^2} dx$

$= \dfrac{45 - 5x^2}{(9 + x^2)^2} dx$

$\approx \dfrac{45 - 5x^2}{(9 + x^2)^2} \Delta x$

(a) $x = 1, \Delta x = .5$

$dC \approx \dfrac{45 - 5(1)^2}{(9 + 1)^2}(.5)$

$= \dfrac{40}{100}(.5)$

$= .2$

(b) $x = 2, \Delta x = .25$

$dC \approx \dfrac{45 - 5(2)^2}{(9 + 4)^2}(.25)$

$= .037$

34. $A = \pi r^2, r = 17$ mm, $\Delta r = -1$ mm

$dA = 2\pi r dr$

$\Delta A \approx 2\pi r \Delta r$

$= 2\pi(17)(-1)$

$= -34\pi$ mm²

36. $A = \pi r^2, r = 1.2$ mi, $\Delta r = .2$ mi

$dA = 2\pi r dr$

$\Delta A \approx 2\pi r \Delta r$

$= 2\pi(1.2)(.2)$

$= .48\pi$ mi²

38. $V = \dfrac{4}{3}\pi r^3, r = 4$ cm, $\Delta r = .2$ cm

$dV = 4\pi r^2 dr$

$\Delta V \approx 4\pi r^2 \Delta r$

$= 4\pi(4)^2(.2)$

$= 12.8\pi$ cm³

40. $A = x^2; x = 3.45, \Delta x = \pm.002$

$dA = 2x dx$

$\Delta A \approx 2x \Delta x$

$= 2(3.45)(\pm.002)$

$= \pm.0138$ sq in

42. $V = \dfrac{4}{3}\pi r^3; r = 5.81, \Delta r = \pm.003$

$dV = \dfrac{4}{3}\pi(3r^2)dr$

$\Delta V \approx \dfrac{4}{3}\pi(3r^2)\Delta r$

$= 4\pi(5.81)^2(\pm.003)$

$= \pm.405\pi \approx \pm1.273$ in³

Chapter 4 Review Exercises

6. $\dfrac{x}{y} - 4y = 3x$

$$\frac{d}{dx}\left(\frac{x}{y} - 4y\right) = \frac{d}{dx}(3x)$$

$$\frac{(1)y - \left(\frac{dy}{dx}\right)x}{y^2} - 4\frac{dy}{dx} = 3$$

$$y - x\frac{dy}{dx} - 4y^2\,\frac{dy}{dx} = 3y^2$$

$$y - 3y^2 = x\frac{dy}{dx} + 4y^2\,\frac{dy}{dx}$$

$$y - 3y^2 = (x + 4y^2)\frac{dy}{dx}$$

$$\frac{y - 3y^2}{4y^2 + x} = \frac{dy}{dx}$$

8. $2\sqrt{y - 1} = 8x^{2/3}$

$$\frac{d}{dx}\left[2(y - 1)^{1/2}\right] = \frac{d}{dx}(8x^{2/3})$$

$$2 \cdot \frac{1}{2} \cdot (y - 1)^{-1/2}\frac{dy}{dx} = \frac{16}{3}x^{-1/3}$$

$$(y - 1)^{-1/2}\frac{dy}{dx} = \frac{16}{3x^{1/3}}$$

$$\frac{dy}{dx} = \frac{16(y - 1)^{1/2}}{3x^{1/3}}$$

10. $\dfrac{6 + 5x}{2 - 3y} = \dfrac{1}{5x}$

$$5x(6 + 5x) = 2 - 3y$$

$$30x + 25x^2 = 2 - 3y$$

$$\frac{d}{dx}(30x + 25x^2) = \frac{d}{dx}(2 - 3y)$$

$$30 + 50x = -3\frac{dy}{dx}$$

$$\frac{-(30 + 50x)}{3} = \frac{dy}{dx}$$

12. $(8x + y^{1/2})^3 = 9y^2$

$$\frac{d}{dx}(8x + y^{1/2})^3 = \frac{d}{dx}(9y^2)$$

$$3(8x + y^{1/2})^2\left(8 + \frac{1}{2}y^{-1/2}\frac{dy}{dx}\right) = 18y\frac{dy}{dx}$$

$$24(8x + y^{1/2})^2 + \frac{3}{2}y^{-1/2}(8x + y^{1/2})^2\frac{dy}{dx} = 18y\frac{dy}{dx}$$

$$24(8x + y^{1/2})^2 = 18y\frac{dy}{dx} - \frac{3}{2y^{1/2}}(8x + y^{1/2})^2\frac{dy}{dx}$$

$$\frac{24(8x + y^{1/2})^2}{18y - \frac{3}{2y^{1/2}}(8x + y^{1/2})^2} = \frac{dy}{dx}$$

$$\frac{48y^{1/2}(8x + y^{1/2})^2}{36y^{3/2} - 3(8x + y^{1/2})^2} = \frac{dy}{dx}$$

$$\frac{16y^{1/2}(8x + y^{1/2})^2}{12y^{3/2} - (8x + y^{1/2})^2} = \frac{dy}{dx}$$

14. $x^2 + y^2 = 25$

$2x + 2y\dfrac{dy}{dx} = 0$

$\dfrac{dy}{dx} = -\dfrac{x}{y}$

When $x = -3$, $y = \pm\sqrt{25 - (-3)^2} = \pm 4$.

If $y = 4$, $\dfrac{dy}{dx} = \dfrac{-(-3)}{4} = \dfrac{3}{4}$.

If $y = -4$, $\dfrac{dy}{dx} = \dfrac{-(-3)}{4} = -\dfrac{3}{4}$.

Tangent 1:

$$y - 4 = \frac{3}{4}(x + 3)$$

$$4y - 16 = 3x + 9$$

$$4y = 3x + 25$$

Tangent 2:

$$y + 4 = -\frac{3}{4}(x + 3)$$

$$4y + 16 = -3x - 9$$

$$4y + 3x = -25$$

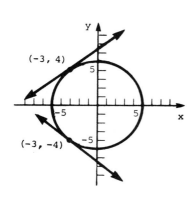

(-3, 4)

(-3, -4)

16. $y = \dfrac{9 - 4x}{3 + 2x}$; $\dfrac{dy}{dx} = -1$, $x = -3$

$$\dfrac{dy}{dx} = \dfrac{(-4)(3 + 2x) - (2)(9 - 4x)}{(3 + 2x)^2}\dfrac{dx}{dt}$$

$$= \dfrac{-30}{(3 + 2x)^2}\dfrac{dx}{dt}$$

$$= \dfrac{-30}{[3 + 2(-3)]^2}(-1) = \dfrac{30}{9} = \dfrac{10}{3}$$

18. $\dfrac{x^2 + 5y}{x - 2y} = 2$; $\dfrac{dx}{dt} = 1$, $x = 2$, $y = 0$

$x^2 + 5y = 2(x - 2y)$

$x^2 + 5y = 2x - 4y$

$9y = -x^2 + 2x$

$y = \dfrac{1}{9}(-x^2 + 2x)$

$\quad = -\dfrac{1}{9}x^2 + \dfrac{2}{9}x$

$\dfrac{dy}{dt} = \left(-\dfrac{2}{9}x + \dfrac{2}{9}\right)\dfrac{dx}{dt}$

$\quad = \left[\left(-\dfrac{2}{9}\right)(2) + \dfrac{2}{9}\right](1)$

$\quad = -\dfrac{4}{9} + \dfrac{2}{9} = -\dfrac{2}{9}$

20. $y = 8x^3 - 2x^2$

$dy = (24x^2 - 4x)dx$

22. $y = \dfrac{6 - 5x}{2 + x}$

$dy = \dfrac{(2 + x)(-5) - (6 - 5x)(1)}{(2 + x)^2}dx$

$\quad = \dfrac{-16}{(2 + x)^2}dx$

24. $y = 8 - x^2 + x^3$, $x = -1$,

$\Delta x = .02$

$dy = (-2x + 3x^2)dx$

$\quad \approx (-2x + 3x^2)\Delta x$

$\quad = [-2(-1) + 3(-1)^2](.02)$

$\quad = .1$

28.   Let x and y be the numbers.

$x + y = 25$

$\quad y = 25 - x$

$f(x) = xy$

$f(x) = x(25 - x)$

$\quad = 25x - x^2$

$f'(x) = 25 - 2x$

At a maximum, $f' = 0$ and $f'' < 0$.

$25 - 2x = 0$

$\quad 2x = 25$

$\quad x = \dfrac{25}{2}$

$f'' = -2 < 0$

So $f(x)$ is maximum at $x = 25/2$.

$y = 25 - \dfrac{25}{2}$

$\quad = \dfrac{25}{2}$

The numbers are 25/2 and 25/2.

30. $P(x) = 40x - x^2$;

x = the price in hundreds of dollars

(a) $P'(x) = 40 - 2x$

If $P'(x) = 0$,

$$2x = 40$$

$$x = 20.$$

$$P''(x) = -2 < 0$$

So the maximum profit occurs at 20(100) or $2000.

(b) Maximum profit is found by

$$P(20) = 40(20) - (20)^2$$

$$= 400.$$

The maximum profit is $40,000.

32. Let x = the length and width of a side of base and

h = the height.

Volume = 32 cu m; square base; no top. Find height, length, and width for minimum surface area.

Volume = $x^2 h$

$$x^2 h = 32$$

$$h = \frac{32}{x^2}$$

Surface area = $x^2 + 4xh$

$$A = x^2 + 4x\left(\frac{32}{x^2}\right)$$

$$= x^2 + 128x^{-1}$$

$$A' = 2x - 128x^{-2}$$

If $A' = 0$,

$$\frac{2x^3 - 128}{x^2} = 0$$

$$x^3 = 64$$

$$x = 4.$$

$$A''(x) = 2 + 2(128)x^{-3}$$

$$A''(4) = 6 > 0$$

So the minimum is at x = 4 where

$$h = \frac{32}{4^2}$$

$$= 2.$$

The dimensions are 2 m by 4 m by 4 m.

34. Volume of cylinder = $\pi r^2 h$

Surface area of cylinder open at one end = $2\pi rh + \pi r^2$.

$$V = \pi r^2 h = 27\pi$$

$$h = \frac{27\pi}{\pi r^2} = \frac{27}{r^2}$$

$$A = 2\pi r\left(\frac{27}{r^2}\right) + \pi r^2$$

$$= 54\pi r^{-1} + \pi r^2$$

$$A' = -54\pi r^{-2} + 2\pi r$$

If $A' = 0$,

$$2\pi r = \frac{54\pi}{r^2}$$

$$r^3 = 27$$

$$r = 3.$$

$$A'' = 108\pi r^{-3} + 2\pi > 0$$

So for the minimum cost,

$$r = 3 \text{ in.}$$

36. $x = \sqrt{\dfrac{kM}{2f}}$

M = 320,000 rolls sold per year

k = .10, cost to store 1 roll for 1 yr

f = 10, fixed cost for order

x = number of orders per year

$$x = \sqrt{\frac{(.10)(32,000)}{2(10)}}$$

$$= \sqrt{1600} = 40 \text{ orders per year}$$

$$\text{Lot size} = \frac{\text{Total number of rolls}}{\text{Number of orders}}$$

$$= \frac{320,000}{40}$$

$$= 8000$$

38. M = 128,000 cases sold per year

k = 1, cost to store 1 case for 1 yr

f = 10, fixed cost for order

x = number of lots per year

$$x = \sqrt{\frac{kM}{2f}}$$

$$= \sqrt{\frac{(1)(128,000)}{2(10)}}$$

$$= \sqrt{6400}$$

$$= 80$$

40. $A = \pi r^2$; $\frac{dr}{dt} = 4$ ft/min, r = 7 ft

$$\frac{dA}{dt} = 2\pi r \frac{dr}{dt}$$

$$\frac{dA}{dt} = 2\pi(7)(4)$$

$$\frac{dA}{dt} = 56\pi \text{ ft}^2/\text{min}$$

42. $\frac{dV}{dt} = 1.2$ ft³/min

Find $\frac{dr}{dt}$ when r = 1.2 ft.

$$V = \frac{4}{3}\pi r^3$$

$$\frac{dV}{dt} = \frac{4}{3}\pi(3)r^2 \frac{dr}{dt}$$

$$= 4\pi r^2 \frac{dr}{dt}$$

$$1.2 = 4\pi(1.2)^2 \frac{dr}{dt}$$

$$\frac{1.2}{4\pi(1.2)^2} = \frac{dr}{dt}$$

$$\frac{dr}{dt} = \frac{1}{4.8\pi} \approx .0663 \text{ ft/min}$$

44. $V = \frac{4}{3}\pi r^3$, r = 4 in, Δr = .02 in

$$dV = 4\pi r^2 dr$$

$$\Delta V \approx 4\pi r^2 \Delta r$$

$$= 4\pi(4)^2(.02)$$

$$= 1.28\pi \text{ in}^3 \text{ or about } 4.021 \text{ in}^3$$

46. Let x = width of play area

y = length of play area.

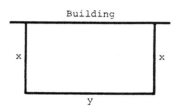

An equation describing the amount of fencing is

$$900 = 2x + y$$

$$y = 900 - 2x.$$

$$A = xy$$

$$A(x) = x(900 - 2x)$$

$$= 900x - 2x^2$$

If A′(x) = 900 − 4x = 0,

$$x = 225.$$

Then y = 900 − 2(225) = 450.

A″(x) = −4 < 0 so the area is maximized if the dimensions are 225 m by 450 m.

CHAPTER 5 EXPONENTIAL AND LOGARITHMIC FUNCTIONS

Section 5.1

2. $y = 4^x$

x	-2	-1	0	1	2
y	1/16	1/4	1	4	16

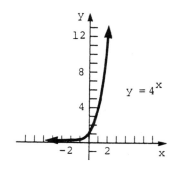

4. $y = 4^{-x/3}$

x	-6	-3	0	3	6
y	16	4	1	1/4	1/16

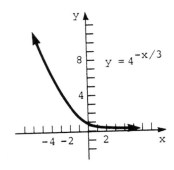

6. $y = \left(\frac{1}{3}\right)^x - 2$

x	-2	-1	0	1	2
y	7	1	-1	-5/3	-17/9

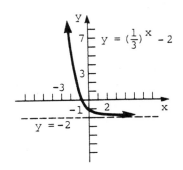

8. $y = -3x^{2-1}$

x	-2	-1	0	1	2
$x^2 - 1$	3	0	-1	0	3
y	-27	-1	-1/3	-1	-27

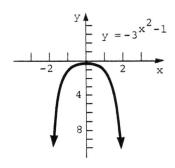

10. $y = e^{x+1}$

x	-2	-1	0	1	2
y	.37	1	2.72	7.39	20.09

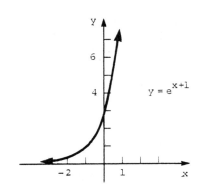

12. $y = 100 - 80e^{-x}$

x	-1	0	1	2	3
y	-117.46	20	70.57	89.17	96.02

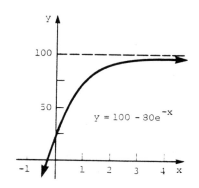

$$y = 100 - 30e^{-x}$$

14. $y = x^2 \cdot 2^x$

x	-3	-2	-1	0	1	2
y	1.125	1	.5	0	2	16

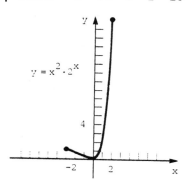

$$y = x^2 \cdot 2^x$$

16. $y = \dfrac{e^x + e^{-x}}{2}$

x	-3	-2	-1	0	1	2
y	10.07	3.76	1.54	1	1.54	3.76

$$y = \frac{e^x + e^{-x}}{2}$$

18. $2^x = \dfrac{1}{8}$

$\quad\quad 2^x = \dfrac{1}{2^3}$

$\quad\quad 2^x = 2^{-3}$

$\quad\quad\; x = -3$

20. $e^x = e^2$

$\quad\quad x = 2$

22. $\quad\quad 4^x = 8^{x+1}$

$\quad (2^2)^x = (2^3)^{x+1}$

$\quad\quad 2^{2x} = 2^{3x+3}$

$\quad\quad\; 2x = 3x + 3$

$\quad\quad -x = 3$

$\quad\quad\;\; x = -3$

24. $\quad\quad 16^{-x+1} = 8^x$

$\quad (2^4)^{-x+1} = (2^3)^x$

$\quad\quad 2^{-4x+4} = 2^{3x}$

$\quad\quad -4x + 4 = 3x$

$\quad\quad\quad\quad 4 = 7x$

$\quad\quad\quad \dfrac{4}{7} = x$

26. $(e^4)^{-2x} = e^{-x+1}$

$\quad\quad e^{-8x} = e^{-x+1}$

$\quad\quad -8x = -x + 1$

$\quad\quad -7x = 1$

$\quad\quad\quad x = -\dfrac{1}{7}$

28. $2^{|x|} = 16$

$\quad\; 2^{|x|} = 2^4$

$\quad\;\; |x| = 4$

$\quad x = 4 \quad \text{or} \quad x = -4$

30.

$$2^{x^2-4x} = \left(\frac{1}{16}\right)^{x-4}$$

$$2^{x^2-4x} = (2^{-4})^{x-4}$$

$$2^{x^2-4x} = 2^{-4x+16}$$

$$x^2 - 4x = -4x + 16$$

$$x^2 - 16 = 0$$

$$(x + 4)(x - 4) = 0$$

$$x = -4 \quad \text{or} \quad x = 4$$

32.

$$8^{x^2} = 2^{5x+2}$$

$$(2^3)^{x^2} = 2^{5x+2}$$

$$2^{3x^2} = 2^{5x+2}$$

$$3x^2 = 5x + 2$$

$$3x^2 - 5x - 2 = 0$$

$$(3x + 1)(x - 2) = 0$$

$$x = -\frac{1}{3} \quad \text{or} \quad x = 2$$

34. $f(x) = 2^x$

(a) $\dfrac{f(1) - f(0)}{1 - 0} = \dfrac{2^1 - 2^0}{1}$

$$= \frac{2 - 1}{1} = 1$$

(b) $\dfrac{f(.1) - f(0)}{.1 - 0} = \dfrac{2^{.1} - 2^0}{.1} = .718$

(c) $\dfrac{f(.01) - f(0)}{.01 - 0} = \dfrac{2^{.01} - 2^0}{.01}$

$$= .696$$

(d) $\dfrac{f(.001) - f(0)}{.001 - 0} = \dfrac{2^{.001} - 2^0}{.001}$

$$= .693$$

(e) The slope of the graph of $f(x)$ at $x = 0$ is about .693.

36. The graph is a sequence of points, one for each rational number.

38. $A = P\left(1 + \dfrac{r}{m}\right)^{tm}$, $P = 10,000$, $r = .06$, $t = 5$

(a) annually, $m = 1$

$$A = 10,000\left(1 + \frac{.06}{1}\right)^{5 \cdot 1}$$

$$= 10,000(1.06)^5$$

$$= \$13,382.26$$

Interest $= \$13,382.26 - \$10,000$
$$= \$3382.26$$

(b) semiannually, $m = 2$

$$A = 10,000\left(1 + \frac{.06}{2}\right)^{5 \cdot 2}$$

$$= 10,000(1.03)^{10}$$

$$= \$13,439.16$$

Interest $= \$13,439.16 - \$10,000$
$$= \$3439.16$$

(c) quarterly, $m = 4$

$$A = 10,000\left(1 + \frac{.06}{4}\right)^{5 \cdot 4}$$

$$= 10,000(1.015)^{20}$$

$$= \$13,468.55$$

Interest $= \$13,468.55 - \$10,000$
$$= \$3468.55$$

(d) monthly, $m = 12$

$$A = 10,000\left(1 + \frac{.06}{12}\right)^{5 \cdot 12}$$

$$= 10,000(1.005)^{60}$$

$$= \$13,488.50$$

Interest $= \$13,488.50 - \$10,000$
$$= \$3488.50$$

40. $A = P\left(1 + \dfrac{r}{m}\right)^{tm}$, $P = 9430$, $r = .06$,

$m = 4$, $t = 4$

$A = 9430\left(1 + \dfrac{.06}{4}\right)^{4 \cdot 4}$

$\quad = \$11,966.53$

42. $P = 18,000$, $t = 1.5$

For $r = .08$, $m = 2$,

$A = 18,000\left(1 + \dfrac{.08}{2}\right)^{1.5(2)}$

$\quad = 18,000(1.04)^3$

$\quad = \$20,247.55.$

For $r = .075$, $m = 12$,

$A = 18,000\left(1 + \dfrac{.075}{12}\right)^{1.5(12)}$

$\quad = 18,000(1.00625)^{18}$

$\quad = \$20,136.25.$

The difference in interest is

$20,247.55 - 20,136.25$

$\quad = \$111.30.$

If David chooses the 8% investment, he would earn \$111.30 additional interest.

44. $y = (.92)^t$

(a)

t	y
1	$(.92)^1 = .92$
2	$(.92)^2 = .85$
3	$(.92)^3 = .78$
4	$(.92)^4 = .72$
6	$(.92)^6 = .61$
7	$(.92)^7 = .56$
8	$(.92)^8 = .51$
9	$(.92)^9 = .47$

(b)

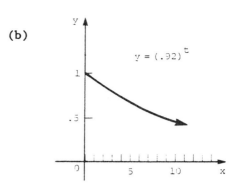

(c) Let x = the cost of the house in 10 yr.

Then, $.43x = 165,000$

$\quad\quad\quad x = 383,721$

$\quad\quad\quad\quad$ or   about \$384,000.

(d) Let x = the cost of the book in 8 yr.

Then, $.51x = 20$

$\quad\quad\quad x = 39.2$

$\quad\quad\quad\quad$ or about \$39.

46. $A = P\left(1 + \dfrac{r}{m}\right)^{tm}$

$A = 1000\left(1 + \dfrac{j}{2}\right)^{5 \cdot 2}$

$\quad = 1000\left(1 + \dfrac{j}{2}\right)^{10}$

This represents the amount in Bank X on January 1, 1985.

$A = P\left(1 + \dfrac{r}{m}\right)^{tm}$

$\quad = \left[1000\left(1 + \dfrac{j}{2}\right)^{10}\right]\left(1 + \dfrac{k}{4}\right)^{3 \cdot 4}$

$\quad = = 1000\left(1 + \dfrac{j}{2}\right)^{10}\left(1 + \dfrac{k}{4}\right)^{12}$

This represents the amount in Bank Y on January 1, 1988, \$1990.76.

$$A = P\left(1 + \frac{r}{m}\right)^{tm}$$

$$= 1000\left(1 + \frac{k}{4}\right)^{8 \cdot 4}$$

$$= 1000\left(1 + \frac{k}{4}\right)^{32}$$

This represents the amount he could have had from January 1, 1980, to January 1, 1988, at a rate of k per annum compounded quarterly, $2203.76.
So,

$$1000\left(1 + \frac{j}{2}\right)^{10}\left(1 + \frac{k}{2}\right)^{12} = 1990.76$$

and

$$1000\left(1 + \frac{k}{4}\right)^{32} = 2203.76.$$

$$\left(1 + \frac{k}{4}\right)^{32} = 2.20376$$

$$1 + \frac{k}{4} = (2.20376)^{1/32}$$

$$1 + \frac{k}{4} = 1.025$$

$$\frac{k}{4} = .025$$

$$k = .1 \quad \text{or} \quad 10\%$$

Substituting, we have

$$1000\left(1 + \frac{j}{2}\right)^{10}\left(1 + \frac{.1}{4}\right)^{12} = 1990.76$$

$$1000\left(1 + \frac{j}{2}\right)^{10}(1.025)^{12} = 1990.76$$

$$\left(1 + \frac{j}{2}\right)^{10} = 1.480$$

$$1 + \frac{j}{2} = (1.480)^{1/10}$$

$$1 + \frac{j}{2} = 1.04$$

$$\frac{j}{2} = .04$$

$$j = .08$$

$$\text{or} \quad 8\%.$$

The ratio $\frac{k}{j} = \frac{.1}{.08} = 1.25$, choice (a).

48. $E(t) = 1,000,000 \cdot 2^{t/30}$

(a) Initially, $t = 0$.

$$E(0) = 1,000,000 \cdot 2^{0/30}$$

$$= 1,000,000 \cdot 2^0$$

$$= 1,000,000$$

(b) $E(30) = 1,000,000 \cdot 2^{30/30}$

$$= 1,000,000 \cdot 2$$

$$= 2,000,000$$

(c) From parts (a) and (b), the bacteria double every 30 min.

(d) Find t such that

$$32,000,000 = 1,000,000 \cdot 2^{t/30}$$

$$32 = 2^{t/30}$$

$$2^5 = 2^{t/30}$$

$$5 = \frac{t}{30}$$

$$150 = t$$

The bacteria will increase to 32,000,000 in 150 min.

50. $P(t) = 1,000,000(2^{.2t})$

$$= 10^6(2^{.2t})$$

(a) $P(5) = 10^6(2^{.2(5)})$

$$= 10^6(2)$$

$$= 2,000,000$$

(b) $8,000,000 = 1,000,000(2^{.2t})$

$$8 = 2^{.2t}$$

$$2^3 = 2^{.2t}$$

$$3 = .2t$$

$$15 = t$$

It will take 15 yr.

52. $f(x) = .88(1.03)^x$

(a) 1975: $t = 3$

     $f(3) = .88(1.03)^3$

           $= .96$ million

(b) 1980: $t = 8$

     $f(8) = .88(1.03)^8$

           $= 1.11$ million

(c) 1985: $t = 13$

     $f(13) = .88(1.03)^{13}$

           $= 1.29$ million

(d) 1990: $t = 18$

     $f(18) = .88(1.03)^{18}$

           $= 1.50$ million

54. This exercise should be solved by a graphing calculator or computer methods. The solution will vary according to the method that is used.

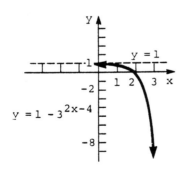

56. This exercise should be solved by a graphing calculator or computer methods. The solution will vary according to the method that is used.

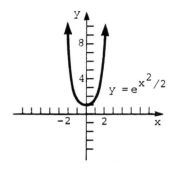

Section 5.2

2. $5^2 = 25$

Since $a^y = x$ means $y = \log_a x$, the equation in logarithmic form is

$$\log_5 25 = 2.$$

4. $6^3 = 216$

$$\log_6 216 = 3$$

6. $\left(\dfrac{3}{4}\right)^{-2} = \dfrac{16}{9}$

$$\log_{3/4} \dfrac{16}{9} = -2$$

8. $\log_3 81 = 4$

Since $y = \log_a x$ means $a^y = x$, the equation in exponential form is

$$3^4 = 81.$$

10. $\log_2 \frac{1}{8} = -3$

$2^{-3} = \frac{1}{8}$

12. $\log .00001 = -5$

$\log_{10} .00001 = -5$

$10^{-5} = .00001$

When no base is written, $\log_{10}$ is understood.

14. Let $\log_9 81 = x$.

Then, $9^x = 81$

$9^x = 9^2$

$x = 2$.

Thus, $\log_9 81 = 2$.

16. $\log_6 216 = x$

$6^x = 216$

$6^x = 6^3$

$x = 3$

18. $\log_3 \frac{1}{27} = x$

$3^x = \frac{1}{27}$

$3^x = 3^{-3}$

$x = -3$

20. $\log_8 \sqrt[4]{\frac{1}{2}} = x$

$8^x = \sqrt[4]{\frac{1}{2}} = \left(\frac{1}{2}\right)^{1/4}$

$(2^3)^x = 2^{-1/4}$

$3x = -\frac{1}{4}$

$x = -\frac{1}{12}$

22. $\ln e^2 = x$

Recall that $\ln$ is $\log_e$.

$e^x = e^2$

$x = 2$

24. $\ln 1 = x$

$e^x = 1$

$e^x = e^0$

$x = 0$

28. $y = 1 - \log x$

Use a calculator to find plotting points.

x	1	2	5	10	20	30
y	1	.7	.3	0	−.3	−.5

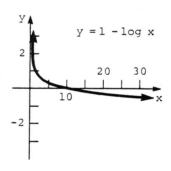

30. $y = \log_{1/2} (1 + x)$

$\left(\frac{1}{2}\right)^y = 1 + x$

$\left(\frac{1}{2}\right)^y - 1 = x$

To find plotting points, use values of y to find x.

x	3	1	0	-1/2	-3/4
y	-2	-1	0	1	2

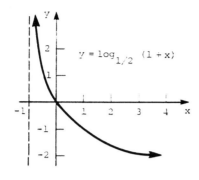

$y = \log_{1/2}(1 + x)$

32. $y = \ln |x|$

x	-4	-3	-2	-1	0
y	1.39	1.1	.69	0	does not exist

x	1	2	3	4
y	0	.69	1.1	1.39

x cannot be zero because there is no value of y such that $e^y = 0$.

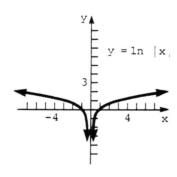

$y = \ln |x|$

34. $\log_5 (8p) = \log_5 8 + \log_5 p$

36. $\log_7 \dfrac{11p}{13y}$

$= \log_7 11p - \log_7 13y$

$= (\log_7 11 + \log_7 p)$

$\quad - (\log_7 13 + \log_7 y)$

$= \log_7 11 + \log_7 p - \log_7 13$

$\quad - \log_7 y$

38. $\log_2 \dfrac{9\sqrt[3]{5}}{\sqrt[4]{3}}$

$= \log_2 9\sqrt[3]{5} - \log_2 \sqrt[4]{3}$

$= \log_2 9 \cdot 5^{1/3} - \log_2 3^{1/4}$

$= \log_2 9 + \log_2 5^{1/3} - \log_2 3^{1/4}$

$= \log_2 9 + \dfrac{1}{3} \log_2 5 - \dfrac{1}{4} \log_2 3$

40. $\log_b 24$

$= \log_b (8 \cdot 3) = \log_b (2^3 \cdot 3)$

$= \log_b 2^3 + \log_b 3$

$= 3 \log_b 2 + \log_b 3$

$= 3a + c$

42. $\log_b (4b^2) = \log_b 4 + \log_b b^2$

$= \log_b 2^2 + \log_b b^2$

$= 2 \log_b 2 + 2 \log_b b$

$= 2a + 2(1)$

$= 2a + 2$

44. $\log_{12} 170 = \dfrac{\ln 170}{\ln 12}$

≈ 2.07

46. $\log_{2.8} .12 = \dfrac{\ln .12}{\ln 2.8}$

≈ -2.06

48. $\log_2 4.5^{-.8} = -.8 \log_2 4.5$

$= -.8\left(\dfrac{\ln 4.5}{\ln 2}\right)$

≈ -1.74

50. $\log_9 27 = m$

$$9^m = 27$$
$$(3^2)^m = 3^3$$
$$3^{2m} = 3^3$$
$$2m = 3$$
$$m = \frac{3}{2}$$

52. $\log_y 8 = \frac{3}{4}$

$$y^{3/4} = 8$$
$$(y^{3/4})^{4/3} = 8^{4/3}$$
$$y = (8^{1/3})^4$$
$$= 2^4 = 16$$

54. $\log_3 (5x + 1) = 2$

$$3^2 = 5x + 1$$
$$9 = 5x + 1$$
$$5x = 8$$
$$x = \frac{8}{5}$$

56. $\log_4 x - \log_4 (x + 3) = -1$

$$\log_4 \frac{x}{x + 3} = -1$$
$$4^{-1} = \frac{x}{x + 3}$$
$$\frac{1}{4} = \frac{x}{x + 3}$$
$$4x = x + 3$$
$$3x = 3$$
$$x = 1$$

58. $3^x = 5$

$$\ln 3^x = \ln 5$$
$$x \ln 3 = \ln 5$$
$$x = \frac{\ln 5}{\ln 3} \approx 1.47$$

60. $e^{k-1} = 4$

$$\ln e^{k-1} = \ln 4$$
$$(k - 1) \ln e = \ln 4$$
$$k - 1 = \frac{\ln 4}{\ln e}$$
$$k - 1 = \frac{\ln 4}{1}$$
$$k = 1 + \ln 4$$
$$\approx 2.39$$

62. $2e^{5a+2} = 8$

$$e^{5a+2} = 4$$
$$\ln e^{5a+2} = \ln 4$$
$$(5a + 2) \ln e = \ln 4$$
$$5a + 2 = \ln 4$$
$$a = \frac{\ln 4 - 2}{5}$$
$$a \approx -.12$$

64. Prove: $\log_a \frac{x}{y} = \log_a x - \log_a y$.

Let $x = a^m$ and $y = a^n$.

Then $m = \log_a x$ and $n = \log_a y$.

$$\frac{x}{y} = \frac{a^m}{a^n}$$
$$\frac{x}{y} = a^{m-n}$$

This equation in logarithmic form is

$$\log_a \frac{x}{y} = m - n.$$

Since $m = \log_a x$ and $n = \log_a y$,

$$\log_a \frac{x}{y} = \log_a x - \log_a y.$$

66. From Example 8, the doubling time t in years when $m = 1$ is given by

$$t = \frac{\ln 2}{\ln (1 + r)}$$

(a) Let r = .03.

$$t = \frac{\ln 2}{\ln 1.03}$$

$$= 23.4 \text{ yr}$$

(b) Let r = .06.

$$t = \frac{\ln 2}{\ln 1.06}$$

$$= 11.9 \text{ yr}$$

(c) Let r = .08.

$$t = \frac{\ln 2}{\ln 1.06}$$

$$= 9.0 \text{ yr}$$

(d) Since .001 ≤ .03 ≤ .05, for r = .03, we use the rule of 70.

$$\frac{70}{100r} = \frac{70}{100(.03)} = 23.3 \text{ yr}$$

Since .05 ≤ .06 ≤ .12, for r = .06, we use the rule of 72.

$$\frac{72}{100r} = \frac{72}{100(.06)} = 12 \text{ yr}$$

For r = .08, we use the rule of 72.

$$\frac{72}{100(.08)} = 9 \text{ yr}$$

68. The total number of individuals in the community is 50 + 50, or 100.

Let $P_1 = \frac{50}{100} = .5$, $P_2 = .5$.

$$H = \frac{-1}{\ln 2}[P_1 \ln P_1 + P_2 \ln P_2]$$

$$= \frac{-1}{\ln 2}[.5 \ln .5 + .5 \ln .5]$$

$$= 1$$

70. F(t) = 50 ln (2t + 3)

(a) F(0) = 50 ln (2 · 0 + 3)

$$= 50 \ln 3$$

$$\approx 55$$

(b) F(3) = 50 ln (2 · 3 + 3)

$$= 50 \ln 9$$

$$\approx 110$$

(c) F(15) = 50 ln (2 · 15 + 3)

$$= 50 \ln 33$$

$$\approx 175$$

(d)

(e) From Part (a), F(0) = 50 ln 3. Find t such that

$$2(50 \ln 3) = 50 \ln (2t + 3).$$

$$100 \ln 3 = 50 \ln (2t + 3)$$

$$2 \ln 3 = \ln (2t + 3)$$

$$\ln 3^2 = \ln (2t + 3)$$

$$\ln 9 = \ln (2t + 3)$$

$$9 = 2t + 3$$

$$6 = 2t$$

$$3 = t$$

The population will double in 3 yr.

72. N(r) = −5000 ln r

(a) N(.9) = −5000 ln (.9)

$$\approx 530$$

(b) N(.5) = −5000 ln (.5)

$$\approx 3500$$

(c) $N(.3) = -5000 \ln (.3)$

≈ 6000

(d) $N(.7) = -5000 \ln (.7)$

≈ 1800

(e) $1000 = -5000 \ln r$

$-.2 = \ln r$

$e^{-.2} = r$

$r \approx .8$

74. Richter scale rating is $\log \dfrac{I}{I_0}$.

(a) $I = 1,000,000 I_0$

Richter scale rating is

$\log \dfrac{10^6 \cdot I_0}{I_0} = \log 10^6$

$= 6.$

(b) $I = 100,000,000 I_0$

Richter scale rating is

$\log \dfrac{10^8 \cdot I_0}{I_0} = \log 10^8$

$= 8.$

(c) Let $x = \dfrac{I}{I_0}$. Then $I = x I_0$.

$8.3 = \log x$

$10^{8.3} = x$

$199,526,231.5 \approx x$

The intensity was about $200,000,000 I_0$.

(d) $7.1 = \log x$

$10^{7.1} = x$

$12,589,254.12 \approx x$

The intensity was about $12,600,000 I_0$.

(e) $\dfrac{200,000,000 I_0}{12,600,000 I_0} \approx 15.9$

The 1906 earthquake was almost 16 times as powerful as the 1989 earthquake.

Exercises 76 and 78 should be solved by graphing calculator or computer methods. The solutions will vary according to the method that is used.

76.

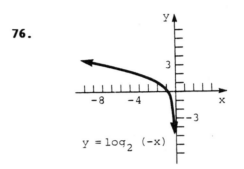

$y = \log_2 (-x)$

78.

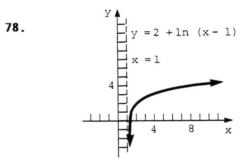

$y = 2 + \ln (x - 1)$

$x = 1$

Section 5.3

2. $r = 15\%$ compounded quarterly, $m = 4$

$r_E = \left(1 + \dfrac{r}{m}\right)^m - 1$

$= \left(1 + \dfrac{.15}{4}\right)^4 - 1$

$\approx .1587$

$= 15.87\%$

4. $r = 18\%$ compounded monthly, $m = 12$

$$r_E = \left(1 + \frac{.18}{12}\right)^{12} - 1$$

$$\approx .1956$$

$$= 19.56\%$$

6. $r = 7\%$ compounded continuously

$$r_E = e^r - 1$$

$$= e^{.07} - 1$$

$$\approx .0725$$

$$= 7.25\%$$

8. $A = \$10,000$, $r = 12\%$, $m = 2$, $t = 5$

$$P = A\left(1 + \frac{r}{m}\right)^{-tm}$$

$$= 10,000\left(1 + \frac{.12}{2}\right)^{-5(2)}$$

$$\approx \$5583.95$$

10. $A = \$45,678.93$, $r = 12.6\%$, $m = 12$, $t = 11$ months

$$P = A\left(1 + \frac{r}{m}\right)^{-tm}$$

$$= 45,678.93\left(1 + \frac{.126}{12}\right)^{-(11/12)(12)}$$

$$\approx \$40,720.81$$

12. $A = \$25,000$, $r = 9\%$ compounded continuously, $t = 8$

$$A = Pe^{rt}$$

$$P = \frac{A}{e^{rt}}$$

$$= \frac{25,000}{e^{.09(8)}}$$

$$\approx \$12,168.81$$

14. In the exponential growth function, $y = y_0 e^{kt}$, y_0 represents the amount present at time 0 and k represents the rate of growth or decay.

16. The half-life of a quantity is the time period it takes for the quantity to decay to one-half the initial amount.

18. $y = y_0 e^{kT}$, $t = T$, $y(T) = \frac{1}{2} y_0$

$$\frac{1}{2} y_0 = y_0 e^{kT}$$

$$\frac{1}{2} = e^{kT}$$

$$\ln \frac{1}{2} = \ln e^{kT}$$

$$\ln \frac{1}{2} = kT$$

$$\frac{\ln \frac{1}{2}}{T} = k.$$

So,

$$y = y_0 e^{[(\ln 1/2)/T]t}$$
$$= y_0 e^{(\ln 1/2)(t/T)}.$$

Since $e^{\ln a} = a$,

$$y = y_0 \left(\frac{1}{2}\right)^{t/T}.$$

20. $P = \$25,000$, $r = 9\%$

$$A = Pe^{rt}$$

(a) $t = 1$

$$A = 25,000e^{.09(1)}$$

$$= \$27,354.36$$

(b) $t = 5$

$$A = 25,000e^{.09(5)}$$

$$= \$39,207.80$$

(c) $t = 10$,

$A = 25,000e^{.09(10)}$

$= \$61,490.08$

22. $r = 9\%$ compounded semiannually

$r_E = \left(1 + \dfrac{.09}{2}\right)^2 - 1$

$\approx .0920$

$\approx 9.20\%$

24. $r = 6\%$ compounded monthly

$r_E = \left(1 + \dfrac{.06}{12}\right)^{12} - 1$

$\approx .0617$

$\approx 6.17\%$

26. (a) $A = \$307,000$, $t = 3$, $r = 6\%$, $m = 2$

$A = P\left(1 + \dfrac{r}{m}\right)^{mt}$

$307,000 = P\left(1 + \dfrac{.06}{1}\right)^{3(2)}$

$307,000 = P(1.03)^6$

$\dfrac{307,000}{(1.03)^6} = P$

$\$257,107.67 = P$

(b) Interest $= 307,000 - 257,107.67$
$= \$49,892.33$

(c) $P = \$200,000$

$A = 200,000(1.03)^6$

$= 238,810.46$

The additional needed is

$307,000 - 238,810.46$

$= \$68,189.54.$

28. $S(t) = S_0 e^{-at}$

(a) $S(t) = \$45,000$, $S_0 = \$50,000$

$45,000 = 50,000e^{-a(1)}$

$.9 = e^{-a(1)}$

$\ln .9 = -a$

$-.105 = -a$

$.105 = a$

So $S(t) = 50,000e^{-.105t}$

(b) $S(2) = 50,000e^{-.105(2)}$

$= 40,529$

$\approx 40,500$

(c) $S(t) = \$40,000$

$40,000 = 50,000e^{-.105t}$

$.8 = e^{-.105t}$

$\ln (.8) = -.105t$

$2.1 \approx t$

It would take about 2.1 yr.

(d) $\lim\limits_{t \to \infty} S_0 e^{-at} = 0$

As t grows larger, e^{-at} grows smaller and smaller. Thus, the limit is zero.

30. $S(x) = 5000 - 4000e^{-x}$

(a) $S(0) = 5000 - 4000e^0$

$= 1000$

Since $S(x)$ represents sales in thousands, in year 0 the sales are \$1,000,000.

(b) Let $S(x) = 4500$.

$4500 = 5000 - 4000e^{-x}$

$-500 = -4000e^{-x}$

$.125 = e^{-x}$

$-\ln .125 = x$

$x \approx 2$ yr

(c) $\lim\limits_{x \to \infty} (5000 - 4000e^{-x})$

$\quad = \lim\limits_{x \to \infty} 5000 - \lim\limits_{x \to \infty} 4000e^{-x}$

$\quad = 5000 - 0$

$\quad = 5000$

32. $y = y_0 e^{kt}$

$y = 40{,}000$, $y_0 = 25{,}000$, $t = 10$

(a) $40{,}000 = 25{,}000e^{k(10)}$

$\quad 1.6 = e^{10k}$

$\quad \ln 1.6 = 10k$

$\quad .047 = k$

The equation is

$\quad y = 25{,}000e^{.047t}.$

(b) $y = 60{,}000$

$\quad 60{,}000 = 25{,}000e^{.047t}$

$\quad 2.4 = e^{.047t}$

$\quad \ln 2.4 = .047t$

$\quad 18.6 = t$

There will be 60,000 bacteria in about 18.6 hr.

34. $f(t) = 500e^{.1t}$

(a) $f(t) = 3000$

$\quad 3000 = 500e^{.1t}$

$\quad 6 = e^{.1t}$

$\quad \ln 6 = .1t$

$\quad 17.9 = t$

It will take 17.9 days.

(b) If $t = 0$ corresponds to January 1, the date January 17 should be placed on the product. January 18 would be more than 17.9 days.

36. $y = 300 - 290e^{-.693t}$

(a) $t = 0$

$\quad y = 300 - 290e^{-.693(0)}$

$\quad = 300 - 290e^0$

$\quad = 10$

(b) $\lim\limits_{x \to \infty} (300 - 290e^{-.693t})$

$\quad = \lim\limits_{x \to \infty} 300 - \lim\limits_{x \to \infty} 290 e^{-.693t}$

$\quad = 300 - 0$

$\quad = 300$

(c) $y = 150$

$\quad 150 = 300 - 290e^{-.693t}$

$\quad -150 = -290e^{-.693t}$

$\quad \dfrac{15}{29} = e^{-.693t}$

$\quad \ln \dfrac{15}{29} = -.693t$

$\quad \dfrac{\ln 15 - \ln 29}{-.693} = t$

$\quad .95 \approx t$

The population will reach 150 in about 1 day.

38. $W(t) = 60 - 30e^{-.5t}$

(a) $W_0 = W(0) = 60 - 30e^{-.5(0)}$

$\qquad\qquad\quad = 60 - 30 = 30$

(b) $W(1) = 60 - 30e^{-.5(1)} \approx 42$

(c) $W(4) = 60 - 30e^{-.5(4)} \approx 56$

(d) $\quad 45 = 60 - 30e^{-.5t}$

$\quad -15 = -30 e^{-.5t}$

$\quad .5 = e^{-.5t}$

$\quad \ln(.5) = -.5t$

$\quad 1.386 = t$

$\quad 1.4 \approx t$

A new typist will type 45 words per min at about 1.4 mo.

(e) $\lim\limits_{t \to \infty} (60 - 30e^{-.5t})$

$= \lim\limits_{t \to \infty} 60 - \lim\limits_{t \to \infty} 30e^{-.5t}$

$= 60 - 0 = 60$

(f)

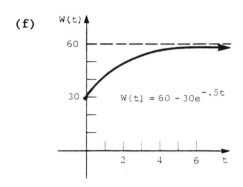

$W(t) = 60 - 30e^{-.5t}$

40. $y(t) = \dfrac{y_0 e^{kt}}{1 - y_0(1 - e^{kt})}$

(a) $y(10) = \dfrac{.05e^{.1(10)}}{1 - .05(1 - e^{.1(10)})}$

$y(10) = .125$

(b) $y(5) = \dfrac{.10e^{.2(5)}}{1 - .1(1 - e^{.2(5)})}$

$= \dfrac{.1e}{1 - .1 + .1e}$

$= \dfrac{.1e}{.9 + .1e}$

$\approx .23$

(c)

$.5 = \dfrac{.02e^{.1t}}{1 - .02(1 - e^{.1t})} = \dfrac{.02e^{.1t}}{1 - .02 + .02e^{.1t}}$

$.5(1 - .02 + .02e^{.1t}) = .02e^{.1t}$

$.5 - .01 + .01e^{.1t} = .02e^{.1t}$

$.49 = .01e^{.1t}$

$49 = e^{.1t}$

$\ln 49 = .1t$

$38.9 = t$

$39 \approx t$

Half the people hear the rumor in 39 days.

(d) $\lim\limits_{t \to \infty} \dfrac{y_0 e^{kt}}{1 - y_0(1 - e^{kt})}$

$= \dfrac{\lim\limits_{t \to \infty} y_0 e^{kt}}{\lim\limits_{t \to \infty} 1 - \lim\limits_{t \to \infty} y_0 + \lim\limits_{t \to \infty} y_0 e^{kt}}$

As $t \to \infty$, $y_0 e^{kt}$ gets larger and larger. The terms 1 and y_0 remain constant. Thus, the fraction approaches 1, or 100%.

42. $\dfrac{1}{2}A_0 = A_0 e^{-.053t}$

$\dfrac{1}{2} = e^{-.053t}$

$\ln \dfrac{1}{2} = -.053t$

$\ln 1 - \ln 2 = -.053t$

$\dfrac{0 - \ln 2}{-.053} = t$

$13 \approx t$

The half-life of plutonium 241 is about 13 yr.

44. $\dfrac{1}{2}A_0 = A_0 e^{-.087t}$

$\dfrac{1}{2} = e^{-.087t}$

$\ln \dfrac{1}{2} = -.087t$

$\ln 1 - \ln 2 = -.087t$

$\dfrac{0 - \ln 2}{-.087} = t$

$8 \approx t$

The half-life of iodine 131 is about 8 yr.

46. $P(t) = 100e^{-.1t}$

(a) $P(4) = 100e^{-.1(4)} \approx 67\%$

(b) $P(10) = 100e^{-.1(10)} \approx 37\%$

(c) $10 = 100e^{-.1t}$

$.1 = e^{-.1t}$

$\ln (.1) = -.1t$

$\dfrac{-\ln (.1)}{.1} = t$

$23 \approx t$

It would take about 23 days.

(d) $1 = 100e^{-.1t}$

$.01 = e^{-.1t}$

$\ln (.01) = -.1t$

$\dfrac{-\ln (.01)}{.1} = t$

$46 \approx t$

It would take about 46 days.

48. $t = 9$, $T_0 = 18$, $C = 5$, $k = .6$

$f(t) = T_0 = Ce^{-kt}$

$f(t) = 18 + 5e^{-.6(9)}$

$= 18 + 5e^{-5.4}$

$\approx 18.02°$

50. $C = -14.6$, $k = .6$, $T_0 = 18°$,

$f(t) = 10°$

$f(t) = T_0 + Ce^{-kt}$

$f(t) = 18 + (-14.6)e^{-.6t}$

$-8 = -14.6e^{-.6t}$

$.5479 = e^{-.6t}$

$\ln .5479 = -.6t$

$\dfrac{-\ln .5479}{.6} = t$

$1 \approx t$

It would take about 1 hr.

Section 5.4

2. $y = \ln (-4x)$

$y' = \dfrac{d}{dx}[\ln (-4x)]$

$= \dfrac{d}{dx}[\ln (-4) + \ln x]$

$= \dfrac{d}{dx}[\ln (-4)] + \dfrac{d}{dx}(\ln x)$

$= 0 + \dfrac{1}{x}$

$= \dfrac{1}{x}$

4. $y = \ln (1 + x^2)$

$g(x) = 1 + x^2$

$g'(x) = 2x$

$y' = \dfrac{g'(x)}{g(x)}$

$= \dfrac{2x}{1 + x^2}$

6. $y = \ln |-8x^2 + 6x|$

$g(x) = -8x^2 + 6x$

$g'(x) = -16x + 6$

$y' = \dfrac{-16x + 6}{-8x^2 + 6x}$

$= \dfrac{2(-8x + 3)}{2(-4x^2 + 3x)}$

$= \dfrac{-8x + 3}{-4x^2 + 3x}$

8. $y = \ln \sqrt{2x + 1} = \ln (2x + 1)^{1/2}$

$g(x) = (2x + 1)^{1/2}$

$g'(x) = \dfrac{1}{2}(2x + 1)^{-1/2} (2)$

$= (2x + 1)^{-1/2}$

$y' = \dfrac{(2x + 1)^{-1/2}}{(2x + 1)^{1/2}}$

$= \dfrac{1}{2x + 1}$

10. $y = \ln |(5x^3 - 2x)^{3/2}|$

$= \frac{3}{2} \ln |5x^3 - 2x|$

$y' = \frac{3}{2} D_x |\ln 5x^3 - 2x|$

$g(x) = 5x^3 - 2x$

$g'(x) = 15x^2 - 2$

$y' = \frac{3}{2}\left(\frac{15x^2 - 2}{5x^3 - 2x}\right)$

$= \frac{3(15x^2 - 2)}{2(5x^3 - 2x)}$

12. $y = (3x + 1) \ln (x - 1)$

Use the product rule.

$y' = (3x + 1)\frac{1}{x - 1} + 3 \ln (x - 1)$

$= \frac{3x + 1}{x - 1} + 3 \ln (x - 1)$

14. $y = x \ln |2 - x^2|$

Use the product rule.

$y' = x\left(\frac{1}{2 - x^2}\right)(-2x) + \ln |2 - x^2|$

$= \frac{-2x^2}{2 - x^2} + \ln |2 - x^2|$

16. $y = \frac{\ln x}{x^3}$

Use the quotient rule.

$y' = \frac{x^3\left(\frac{1}{x}\right) - (\ln x)(3x^2)}{(x^3)^2}$

$= \frac{x^2 - 3x^2 \ln x}{x^6}$

$= \frac{x^2(1 - 3 \ln x)}{x^6}$

$= \frac{1 - 3 \ln x}{x^4}$

18. $y = \frac{-2 \ln x}{3x - 1}$

Use the quotient rule.

$y' = \frac{(3x - 1)(-2)\left(\frac{1}{x}\right) - (-2 \ln x)(3)}{(3x - 1)^2}$

$= \frac{\frac{-2(3x - 1)}{x} + 6 \ln x}{(3x - 1)^2}$

$= \frac{-2(3x - 1) + 6x \ln x}{x(3x - 1)^2}$

$= \frac{-2(3x - 1 - 3x \ln x)}{x(3x - 1)^2}$

20. $y = \frac{x^3 - 1}{2 \ln x}$

$y' = \frac{(2 \ln x)(3x^2) - (x^3 - 1)(2)\left(\frac{1}{x}\right)}{(2 \ln x)^2}$

$= \frac{6x^2 \ln x - \frac{2}{x}(x^3 - 1)}{(2 \ln x)^2} \cdot \frac{x}{x}$

$= \frac{6x^3 \ln x - 2(x^3 - 1)}{4x (\ln x)^2}$

$= \frac{3x^3 \ln x - (x^3 - 1)}{2x (\ln x)^2}$

22. $y = \sqrt{\ln |x - 3|} = (\ln |x - 3|)^{1/2}$

$y' = \frac{1}{2}(\ln |x + 3|)^{-1/2}\frac{d}{dx}(\ln |x - 3|)$

$= \frac{1}{2(\ln |x - 3|)^{1/2}}\left(\frac{1}{x - 3}\right)$

$= \frac{1}{2(x - 3)(\ln |x - 3|)^{1/2}}$

$= \frac{1}{2(x - 3)\sqrt{\ln |x - 3|}}$

24. $y = (\ln 4)(\ln |3x|)$

$y' = (\ln 4)\left(\dfrac{1}{3x}\right)(3)$

$\quad = \dfrac{3 \ln 4}{3x}$

$\quad = \dfrac{\ln 4}{x}$

Recall, $\ln 4$ is a constant.

26. $y = \log_2 x = \dfrac{\ln x}{\ln 2} = \dfrac{1}{\ln 2}(\ln x)$

$y' = \dfrac{1}{\ln 2}\left(\dfrac{1}{x}\right) = \dfrac{1}{(\ln 2)x}$

Choice (b) is the derivative of $y = \log_2 x$.

28. $y = \log (2x - 3) = \dfrac{\ln (2x - 3)}{\ln 10}$

$y' = \dfrac{1}{\ln 10} \cdot \dfrac{d}{dx}[\ln (2x - 3)]$

$\quad = \dfrac{1}{\ln 10} \cdot \dfrac{2}{2x - 3}$

$\quad = \dfrac{2}{(\ln 10)(2x - 3)}$

30. $y = \log |-3x| = \dfrac{\ln |-3x|}{\ln 10}$

$y' = \dfrac{1}{\ln 10} \cdot \dfrac{-3}{-3x}$

$\quad = \dfrac{1}{x \ln 10}$

32. $y = \log_7 \sqrt{2x - 3} = \dfrac{\ln \sqrt{2x - 3}}{\ln 7}$

$\quad = \dfrac{1}{\ln 7} \cdot \ln (2x - 3)^{1/2}$

$\quad = \dfrac{1}{\ln 7} \cdot \dfrac{1}{2} \ln (2x - 3)$

$y' = \dfrac{1}{2 \ln 7} \cdot \dfrac{2}{2x - 3}$

$\quad = \dfrac{1}{(\ln 7)(2x - 3)}$

34. $y = \log_2 |(2x^2 - x)^{5/2}|$

$\quad = \dfrac{\ln |(2x^2 - x)^{5/2}|}{\ln 2}$

$\quad = \dfrac{1}{\ln 2} \cdot \dfrac{5}{2} \ln |(2x^2 - x)|$

$y' = \dfrac{5}{2 \ln 2} \cdot \dfrac{4x - 1}{2x^2 - x}$

$\quad = \dfrac{5(4x - 1)}{2(\ln 2)(2x^2 - x)}$

36. $y = x - \ln x, \; x > 0$

To find any maxima or minima, find the first derivative.

$$y = x - \ln x$$

$$y' = 1 - \dfrac{1}{x}$$

Set the derivative equal to 0.

$$\dfrac{x - 1}{x} = 0.$$

$$x - 1 = 0$$

$$x = 1$$

$y = 1 - \ln 1$

$\quad = 1$

Find the second derivative to determine whether y is a maximum or minimum at $x = 1$.

$$y'' = \dfrac{1}{x^2} > 0 \text{ since } x > 0.$$

$x = 1$ gives a minimum value of $y = 1$.

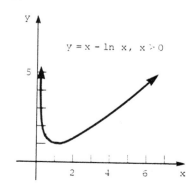

38. $y = x - \ln |x|$

$$y' = 1 - \frac{1}{x}$$

$$1 - \frac{1}{x} = 0$$

$$x = 1$$

$$y(1) = 1 - \ln |1| = 1$$

$$y'' = \frac{1}{x^2}$$

$$y''(1) = 1 > 0$$

A relative minimum of 1 occurs at x = 1.

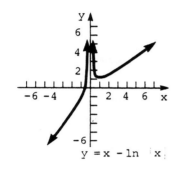

$y = x - \ln |x|$

40. $y = \frac{\ln x^2}{x^2}$

$$y' = \frac{\left(\frac{2x}{x^2}\right)(x^2) - (2x)(\ln x^2)}{(x^2)^2}$$

$$= \frac{2x - 2x \ln x^2}{x^4}$$

$$= \frac{2x(1 - \ln x^2)}{x^4}$$

$$= \frac{2(1 - \ln x^2)}{x^3}$$

Set y' = 0.

$$1 - \ln x^2 = 0$$

$$1 = \ln x^2$$

$$e = x^2$$

$$\pm\sqrt{e} = x$$

$$y'' = \frac{x^3\left(-\frac{2x}{x^2}\right) - 3x^2(1 - \ln x^2)}{x^6}$$

$$= \frac{-2 - 3(1 - \ln x^2)}{x^4}$$

$$= \frac{-5 + 3 \ln x^2}{x^4}$$

Use a calculator to show that y'' is negative for $x = \pm\sqrt{e}$.

So, relative maxima occur at $x = \pm\sqrt{e}$.

Now $y = \frac{\ln (\pm\sqrt{e})^2}{e} = \frac{\ln e}{e} = \frac{1}{e}$.

So a relative maximum of 1/e occurs at $x = \sqrt{e}$ and $x = -\sqrt{e}$.

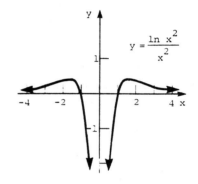

$$y = \frac{\ln x^2}{x^2}$$

42. $f(x) = \ln x$

(a) $f'(x) = \frac{1}{x} = x^{-1}$

$f''(x) = -1x^{-2}$

$f'''(x) = (-2)(-1)x^{-3} = 2x^{-3}$

$f^{(4)}(x) = (-3)(-2)(-1)x^{-4} = -6x^{-4}$

$f^{(5)}(x) = (-4)(-3)(-2)(-1)x^{-5}$

$\qquad = 25x^{-5}$

(b) $f^n(x)$

$= [-(n-1)][-(n-2)] \cdot$

$\quad \cdots \cdot (-1)x^{-n}$

$= \frac{(-1)^{n-1}[1 \cdot 2 \cdot 3 \cdots \cdot (n-1)]}{x^n}$

$= \frac{(-1)^{n-1}(n-1)!}{x^n}$

44. $R(x) = 30 \ln (2x + 1)$

$C(x) = \dfrac{x}{2}$

$P = R - C = 30 \ln (2x + 1) - \dfrac{x}{2}$

$P' = 30\left(\dfrac{1}{2x + 1}\right)(2) - \dfrac{1}{2}$

$\quad = \dfrac{60}{2x + 1} - \dfrac{1}{2}$

Now, $\dfrac{60}{2x + 1} - \dfrac{1}{2} = 0$ when

$\qquad \dfrac{60}{2x + 1} = \dfrac{1}{2}$

$\qquad 120 = 2x + 1$

$\qquad \dfrac{119}{2} = x.$

$P''(x) = \dfrac{-120}{(2x + 1)^2} < 0$ for all x.

Thus, a maximum profit occurs when x = 119/2 or, in a practical sense, when 59 or 60 items are manufactured. Both 59 and 60 give the same profit.

46. $C(x) = 100x + 100$

(a) The marginal cost is given by $C'(x)$.

$\quad C'(x) = 100$

(b) $P(x) = R(x) - C(x)$

$\qquad = x\left(100 + \dfrac{50}{\ln x}\right)$

$\qquad \quad - (100x + 100)$

$\qquad = 100x + \dfrac{50x}{\ln x} - 100x - 100$

$\qquad = \dfrac{50x}{\ln x} - 100$

(c) The profit from one more unit is is $\dfrac{dP}{dx}$ for x = 8.

$\dfrac{dP}{dx} = \dfrac{(\ln x)(50) - 50x\left(\frac{1}{x}\right)}{(\ln x)^2}$

$\qquad = \dfrac{50 \ln x - 50}{(\ln x)^2} = \dfrac{50(\ln x - 10)}{(\ln x)^2}$

When x = 8, the profit from one more unit is

$\dfrac{50(\ln 8 - 1)}{(\ln 8)^2} = \$12.48.$

(d) The manager can use the information from part (c) to decide whether it is profitable to make and sell additional items.

48. $M(t) = (.1t + 1) \ln \sqrt{t}$

(a) $M(15) = [.1(15) + 1] \ln \sqrt{15}$

$\qquad = 3.385$

So, M(15) is about 3.

(b) $M(25) = [.1(25) + 1] \ln \sqrt{25}$

$\qquad = 5.663$

So, M(25) is about 6.

(c) $M(t) = (.1t + 1) \ln \sqrt{t}$

$\qquad = (.1t + 1) \ln t^{1/2}$

$M'(t) = (.1t + 1)\left(\dfrac{1}{2} \cdot \dfrac{1}{t}\right)$

$\qquad \quad + (\ln t^{1/2})(.1)$

$\qquad = .1 \ln \sqrt{t} + \dfrac{1}{2t}(.1t + 1)$

$M'(15) = .1 \ln \sqrt{15}$

$\qquad \quad + \dfrac{1}{2 \cdot 15}[(.1)(15) + 1]$

$\qquad \approx .22$

50. $I(p) = -p \ln p - (1 - p) \ln (1 - p)$

(a) $I'(p) = \left[(-1) \ln p + (-p)\left(\frac{1}{p}\right) \right]$

$\qquad - \left[(-1) \ln (1 - p) \right.$

$\qquad + \left. \left(\frac{-1}{1 - p}\right)(1 - p) \right]$

$\qquad = (-\ln p - 1)$

$\qquad - [-\ln (1 - p) - 1]$

$\qquad = -\ln p - 1 + \ln (1 - p) + 1$

$\qquad = -\ln p + \ln (1 - p)$

(b) $\qquad\qquad I'(p) = 0$

$-\ln p + \ln (1 - p) = 0$

$\qquad\qquad \ln p = \ln (1 - p)$

$\qquad\qquad p = 1 - p$

$\qquad\qquad 2p = 1$

$\qquad\qquad p = \frac{1}{2}$

$I''(p) = -\frac{1}{p} + \frac{-1}{1 - p}$

$\qquad = \frac{-(1 - p) - p}{p(1 - p)}$

$\qquad = \frac{-1}{p - p^2}$

$I''\left(\frac{1}{2}\right) = -4 < 0$

So, $I(p)$ is a maximum at $p = 1/2$.

(c) Since the same basic message may be given in more than one way, the information in (b) can be used to phrase a message to get maximum information content.

52. This exercise should be solved by a graphing calculator or computer methods. The solution will vary according to the method used. A minimum of 1 occurs at $x = 1$.

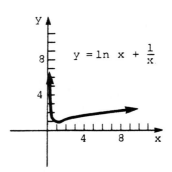

$y = \ln x + \frac{1}{x}$

Section 5.5

2. $\qquad\qquad y = e^{-2x}$

Let $\quad g(x) = -2x,$

with $g'(x) = -2.$

$\qquad\qquad y' = -2e^{-2x}$

4. $\quad y = .2e^{5x}$

$\quad y' = .2(5e^{5x})$

$\qquad = e^{5x}$

6. $\quad y = -4e^{-.1x}$

$\quad y' = -4(-.1e^{-.1x})$

$\qquad = .4e^{-.1x}$

8. $\quad y = e^{-x^2}$

$\quad g(x) = -x^2$

$\quad g'(x) = -2x$

$\qquad y' = -2xe^{-x^2}$

10. $\qquad y = -5e^{4x^3}$

$\quad g(x) = 4x^3$

$\quad g'(x) = 12x^2$

$\qquad y' = (-5)(12x^2)e^{4x^3}$

$\qquad = -60x^2e^{4x^3}$

12. $y = -3e^{3x^2+5}$

$g(x) = 3x^2 + 5$

$g'(x) = 6x$

$y' = (-3)(6x)e^{3x^2+5}$

$\quad = -18xe^{3x^2+5}$

14. $y = x^2e^{-2x}$

Use the product rule.

$y' = x^2(-2e^{-2x}) + 2xe^{-2x}$

$\quad = -2x^2e^{-2x} + 2xe^{-2x}$

$\quad = 2x(1 - x)e^{-2x}$

16. $y = (3x^2 - 4x)e^{-3x}$

Use the product rule.

$y' = (3x^2 - 4x)(-3)(e^{-3x})$

$\qquad + (6x - 4)e^{-3x}$

$\quad = (-9x^2 + 12x)(e^{-3x})$

$\qquad + (6x - 4)e^{-3x}$

$\quad = (6x - 4 - 9x^2 + 12x)e^{-3x}$

$\quad = (-9x^2 + 18x - 4)e^{-3x}$

18. $y = e^{2x-1} \ln (2x - 1), \ x > \dfrac{1}{2}$

$y' = (2)e^{2x-1} \ln (2x - 1)$

$\qquad + (e^{2x-1})\left(\dfrac{1}{2x - 1}\right)(2)$

$\quad = 2e^{2x-1} \ln (2x - 1) + \dfrac{2e^{2x-1}}{2x - 1}$

20. $y = \dfrac{\ln x}{e^x}, \ x > 0$

Use the quotient rule.

$y' = \dfrac{\left(\dfrac{1}{x}\right)e^x - (e^x) \ln x}{(e^x)^2}$

$\quad = \dfrac{\dfrac{e^x}{x} - e^x \ln x}{e^{2x}} \cdot \dfrac{x}{x}$

$\quad = \dfrac{e^x - xe^x \ln x}{xe^{2x}}$

$\quad = \dfrac{e^x(1 - x \ln x)}{xe^{2x}}$

$\quad = \dfrac{1 - x \ln x}{xe^x}$

22. $y = \dfrac{e^x}{2x + 1}$

$y' = \dfrac{e^x(2x + 1) - (2)(e^x)}{(2x + 1)^2}$

$\quad = \dfrac{e^x(2x + 1 - 2)}{(2x + 1)^2}$

$\quad = \dfrac{e^x(2x - 1)}{(2x + 1)^2}$

24. $y = \dfrac{e^x - e^{-x}}{x}$

$y' = \dfrac{x(e^x - (-1)e^{-x}) - (e^x - e^{-x})(1)}{x^2}$

$\quad = \dfrac{xe^x + xe^{-x} - e^x + e^{-x}}{x^2}$

$\quad = \dfrac{e^x(x - 1) + e^{-x}(x + 1)}{x^2}$

26. $y = \dfrac{600}{1 - 50e^{.2x}}$

$y' = \dfrac{(1 - 50e^{.2x}) \cdot 0 - 600[0 - 50(.2)e^{.2x}]}{(1 - 50e^{.2x})^2}$

$\quad = \dfrac{6000e^{.2x}}{(1 - 50e^{.2x})^2}$

28. $y = \dfrac{500}{12 + 5e^{-.5x}}$

$y' = \dfrac{(12 + 5e^{-.5x}) \cdot 0 - 500[0 + 5(-.5)e^{-.5x}]}{(12 + 5e^{-.5x})^2}$

$\quad = \dfrac{1250e^{-.5x}}{(12 + 5e^{-.5x})^2}$

30. $y = (e^{2x} + \ln x)^3, \quad x > 0$

Use the chain rule.

$$y' = 3(e^{2x} + \ln x)^2\left[(2)e^{2x} + \frac{1}{x}\right] = 3(e^{2x} + \ln x)^2\left(\frac{2xe^{2x} + 1}{x}\right)$$

$$= \frac{3(e^{2x} + \ln x)^2(2xe^{2x} + 1)}{x}$$

32. $y = 2^{-x} = e^{\ln 2^{-x}} = e^{-x \ln 2}$

$\quad y' = -(\ln 2)e^{-x \ln 2} = -(\ln 2)2^{-x}$

34. $y = -10^{3x^2-4} = -e^{\ln(10^{3x^2-4})} = -e^{(3x^2-4)\ln 10}$

$\quad y' = -\ln 10(6x)e^{(3x^2-4)\ln 10} = -6x(\ln 10)(10^{3x^2-4}) = -6x(10^{3x^2-4})\ln 10$

36. $y = 5 \cdot 7^{\sqrt{x-2}} = 5 \cdot e^{\ln 7\sqrt{x-2}} = 5 e^{\sqrt{x-1}(\ln 7)}$

$\quad y' = 5(\ln 7)\frac{1}{2}(x-2)^{-1/2}e^{\sqrt{x-2}\ln 7} = \frac{5(\ln 7)e^{\sqrt{x-2}\ln 7}}{2(x-2)^{1/2}} = \frac{(5\ln 7)(7^{\sqrt{x-2}})}{2\sqrt{x-2}}$

38. $G(t) = \dfrac{2{,}000{,}000}{200 + 9800e^{-.1t}} = \dfrac{10{,}000}{1 + 49e^{-.1t}} = 10{,}000(1 + 49e^{-.1t})^{-1}$

$G'(t) = -10{,}000(1 + 49e^{-.1t})^{-2}(-4.9e^{-.1t}) = 49{,}000 \, e^{-.1t}(1 + 49e^{-.1t})^{-2}$

$G''(t) = 49{,}000e^{-.1t}[-2(1 + 49e^{-.1t})^{-3}(-4.9e^{-.1t})] + (1 + 49e^{-.1t})^{-2}(-4900e^{-.1t})$

$\qquad = 480{,}200e^{-.2t}(1 + 49e^{-.1t})^{-3} - 4900e^{-.1t}(1 + 49e^{-.1t})^{-2}$

$\qquad = 4900e^{-.1t}(1 + 49e^{-.1t})^{-3}[98e^{-.1t} - (1 + 49e^{-.1t})]$

$\qquad = 4900e^{-.1t}(1 + 49e^{-.1t})^{-3}(49e^{-.1t} - 1)$

$G''(t) = 0$ when $49e^{-.1t} - 1 = 0$.

$$49e^{-.1t} = 1$$

$$e^{-.1t} = \frac{1}{49}$$

$$-.1t = \ln 1 - \ln 49$$

$$t = \frac{0 - \ln 49}{-.1} \approx 39$$

$G(39) = \dfrac{10{,}000}{1 + 49e^{-.1(39)}} \approx 5020$

The inflection point is approximately (39, 5000).

40. $y = xe^{-x}$

$y' = (1)e^{-x} + x(-e^{-x})$

$\quad = e^{-x} - xe^{-x}$

Set $y' = 0$ for critical points.

$\quad e^{-x}(1 - x) = 0$

$\qquad\qquad e^{-x} = 0$ has no solution.

$\qquad\qquad x = 1$

Check second derivative for concavity.

$y'' = -e^{-x} + (1 - x)(-e^{-x})$

$\quad = -e^{-x} - e^{-x} + xe^{-x}$

$\quad = -2e^{-x} + xe^{-x}$

At $x = 1$, $y'' = -2e^{-1} + e^{-1} = -e^{-1} < 0$.

Now, $y(1) = 1e^{-1} = e^{-1}$.

So there is a relative maximum of e^{-1} at $x = 1$.

Set $y'' = 0$ to find inflection points.

$-2e^{-x} + xe^{-x} = 0$

$-e^{-x}(2 - x) = 0$

$\qquad\qquad x = 2$

$\qquad\qquad y = 2e^{-2}$

Inflection point at $(2, 2e^{-2})$

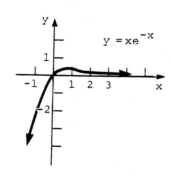

42. $y = (x - 1)e^{-x}$

$y' = e^{-x} + (x - 1)(-e^{-x})$

$\quad = e^{-x}(2 - x)$

Critical points:

$e^{-x}(2 - x) = 0$

$\qquad 2 - x = 0$

$\qquad\qquad 2 = x$

Check second derivative for concavity.

$y''(x) = -e^{-x}(2 - x) + (-1)(e^{-x})$

$\qquad\quad = -e^{-x}(2 - x) - e^{-x}$

$\qquad\quad = -e^{-x}(3 - x)$

If $x = 2$, $y'' = -e^{-2} < 0$, y is concave down, maximum and $y = e^{-2}$.

Maximum of e^{-2} occurs at $x = 2$.

Set $y'' = 0$ to find inflection points.

$-e^{-x}(3 - x) = 0$

$\qquad\qquad x = 3$

$y = (3 - 1)e^{-3}$

$\quad \approx .1$

Inflection point at $(3, .1)$

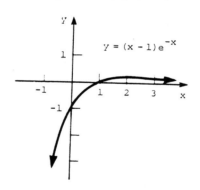

44. $y = -x^2e^x$

$y' = (-2x)e^x + (-x^2)e^x$

$\quad = -2xe^x - x^2e^x$

$\quad = xe^x(-2 - x)$

$\qquad xe^x(-2 - x) = 0$ when

x = 0   or   -2 - x = 0

$$-2 = x.$$

Critical numbers are x = 0 and x = -2.

$$y'' = -2e^x - 2xe^x - 2xe^x - x^2e^x$$

$$= -e^x(x^2 + 4x + 2)$$

$$y''(0) = -2 < 0$$

$$y''(-2) = 2e^{-2} > 0$$

$$y(0) = 0$$

$$y(-2) = -4e^{-2}$$

There is a relative maximum of 0 at x = 0 and a relative minimum of $-4e^{-2}$ at x = -2.

Set y'' = 0 for inflection points.

$$-e^x(x^2 + 4x + 2) = 0$$

$$x = \frac{-4 \pm \sqrt{16 - 8}}{2} = -2 \pm \sqrt{2}$$

$$x \approx -.6 \quad \text{or} \quad x = -3.4$$

$$y = -(-.6)^2e^{-.6}$$

$$\approx -.2$$

$$y = -(-3.4)^2e^{-3.4}$$

$$\approx -.4$$

Inflection points at (-.6, -.2) and (-3.4, -.4)

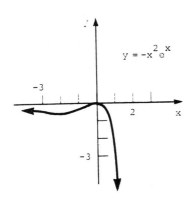

46. $f(x) = e^x$

The slope of the tangent line is $f'(x) = e^x$.

(a) $\lim\limits_{x \to -\infty} e^x = 0$

As x → -∞, the slope approaches 0.

(b) $\lim\limits_{x \to 0} e^x = 1$

As x → 0, the slope approaches 1, the slope of a 45° line, or the line y = x.

48. $S(t) = 100 - 90e^{-.3t}$

$$S'(t) = -90(-.3)e^{-.3t}$$

$$= 27e^{-.3t}$$

(a) $S'(1) = 27e^{-.3(1)}$

$$= 27e^{-.3}$$

$$\approx 20$$

(b) $S'(5) = 27e^{-.3(5)}$

$$= 27e^{-1.5}$$

$$\approx 6$$

(c) As time goes on, the rate of change of sales is decreasing.

(d) $S'(t) = 27e^{-.3t} \neq$ but,

$$\lim\limits_{t \to 0} S'(t) = \lim\limits_{t \to 0} 27e^{-.3t} = 0.$$

Although the rate of change of sales never equals zero, it gets closer and closer to zero.

50. $y = 100e^{-.03045t}$

(a) For t = 0,

$$y = 100e^{-.03045(0)}$$

$$= 100e^0$$

$$= 100\%.$$

(b) For $t = 2$,

$$y = 100e^{-.03045(2)}$$
$$= 100e^{-.0609}$$
$$\approx 94\%.$$

(c) For $t = 4$,

$$y = 100e^{-.03045(4)}$$
$$\approx 89\%.$$

(d) For $t = 6$,

$$y = 100e^{-.03045(6)}$$
$$\approx 83\%.$$

(e) $y' = 100(-.03045)e^{-.03045t}$

$$= -3.045e^{-.03045t}$$

For $t = 0$,

$$y' = -3.045e^{-.03045(0)}$$
$$= -3.045.$$

(f) For $t = 2$,

$$y' = -3.045e^{-.03045(2)}$$
$$\approx -2.865.$$

(g) The percent of these cars on the road is decreasing, but at a slower rate as they age.

52. $P(x) = .04e^{-4x}$

(a) $P(.5) = .04e^{-4(.5)}$

$$= .04e^{-2}$$
$$\approx .005$$

(b) $P(1) = .04e^{-4(1)}$

$$= .04e^{-4}$$
$$\approx .0007$$

(c) $P(2) = .04e^{-4(2)}$

$$= .04e^{-8}$$
$$\approx .000013$$

$P'(x) = .04(-4)e^{-4x} = -.16e^{-4x}$

(d) $P'(.5) = -.16e^{-4(.5)}$

$$= -.16e^{-2}$$
$$\approx -.022$$

(e) $P'(1) = -.16e^{-4(1)}$

$$= -.16e^{-4}$$
$$\approx -.0029$$

(f) $P'(2) = -.16e^{-4(2)}$

$$= -.16e^{-8}$$
$$\approx -.000054$$

54. $H(N) = 1000(1 - e^{-kN})$, $k = .1$

$$H' = -1000e^{-.1N}(-.1)$$
$$= 100e^{-.1N}$$

(a) $H'(10) = 100e^{-.1(10)}$

$$\approx 36.8.$$

(b) $H'(100) = 100e^{-.1(100)}$

$$\approx .00454.$$

(c) $H'(1000) = 100e^{-.1(1000)}$

$$\approx 0$$

(d) $1000e^{-.1N}$ is always positive since powers of e are never negative. This means that repetition always makes a habit stronger.

56. This exercise should be solved by a graphing calculator or computer methods. The solution will vary according to the method that is used. A minimum occurs at approximately $(.96, 7)$ and an inflection point occurs at approximately $(2.7, 4.3)$.

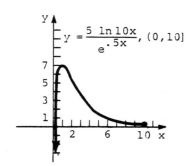

$$y = \frac{5 \ln 10x}{e^{.5x}}, (0,10]$$

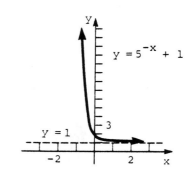

$$y = 5^{-x} + 1$$

Chapter 5 Review Exercises

4. $\left(\frac{9}{16}\right)^x = \frac{3}{4}$

$\left(\frac{3}{4}\right)^{2x} = \left(\frac{3}{4}\right)^1$

$2x = 1$

$x = \frac{1}{2}$

6. $\left(\frac{1}{2}\right) = \left(\frac{b}{4}\right)^{1/4}$

$\left(\frac{1}{2}\right)^4 = \frac{b}{4}$

$4\left(\frac{1}{2}\right)^4 = b$

$4\left(\frac{1}{16}\right) = b$

$\frac{1}{4} = b$

8. $y = 5^{-x} + 1$

x	−2	−1	0	1	2
y	26	6	2	6/5	26/5

10. $y = \left(\frac{1}{2}\right)^{x-1}$

x	−2	−1	0	1	2
y	8	4	2	1	1/2

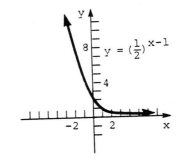

$$y = \left(\frac{1}{2}\right)^{x-1}$$

12. $y = 1 + \log_3 x$

$y - 1 = \log_3 x$

$3^{y-1} = x$

x	1/9	1/3	1	3	9
y	−1	0	1	2	3

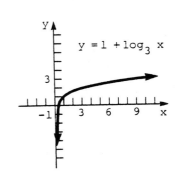

$$y = 1 + \log_3 x$$

14. $y = 2 - \ln x^2$

x	-4	-3	-2	-1	1	2	3	4
y	-.8	-.2	.6	2	2	.6	-.2	-.8

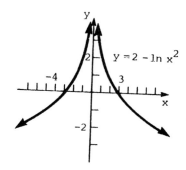

16. $3^{1/2} = \sqrt{3}$

$\log_3 \sqrt{3} = \frac{1}{2}$

18. $10^{1.07918} = 12$

$\log_{10} 12 = 1.07918$

20. $\log_{10} 100 = 2$

$10^2 = 100$

22. $\log 15.46 = 1.18921$

$10^{1.18921} = 15.46$

Recall: $\log_{10}$ is understood.

24. $\log_{1/3} 81 = x$

$\left(\frac{1}{3}\right)^x = 81$

$3^{-x} = 81$

$3^{-x} = 3^4$

$-x = 4$

$x = -4$

26. $\log_{25} 5 = x$

$25^x = 5$

$5^{2x} = 5^1$

$2x = 1$

$x = \frac{1}{2}$

28. $\log_{1/2} 4 = x$

$\left(\frac{1}{2}\right)^x = 4$

$2^{-x} = 2^2$

$-x = 2$

$x = -2$

30. $\log_3 2y^3 - \log_3 8y^2$

$= \log_3 \left(\frac{2y^3}{8y^2}\right)$

$= \log_3 \left(\frac{y}{4}\right)$

32. $5 \log_4 r - 3 \log_4 r^2$

$= \log_4 r^5 - \log_4 (r^2)^3$

$= \log_4 \left(\frac{r^5}{r^6}\right)$

$= \log_4 \left(\frac{1}{r}\right)$

$= \log_4 r^{-1}$

$= -\log_4 r$

34. $3^{z-2} = 11$

$\ln 3^{z-2} = \ln 11$

$(z - 2) \ln 3 = \ln 11$

$z - 2 = \frac{\ln 11}{\ln 3}$

$z = \frac{\ln 11}{\ln 3} + 2$

≈ 4.183

36. $15^{-k} = 9$

$\ln 15^{-k} = \ln 9$

$-k \ln 15 = \ln 9$

$k = -\dfrac{\ln 9}{\ln 15}$

$\approx -.811$

38. $e^{3x-1} = 12$

$\ln (e^{3x-1}) = \ln 12$

$3x - 1 = \ln 12$

$3x = 1 + \ln 12$

$x = \dfrac{1 + \ln 12}{3}$

≈ 1.162

40. $\left(1 + \dfrac{2p}{5}\right)^2 = 3$

$1 + \dfrac{2p}{5} = \pm\sqrt{3}$

$5 + 2p = \pm 5\sqrt{3}$

$2p = -5 \pm 5\sqrt{3}$

$p = \dfrac{-5 \pm 5\sqrt{3}}{2}$

$p = \dfrac{-5 + 5\sqrt{3}}{2} \approx 1.830$

or $p = \dfrac{-5 - 5\sqrt{3}}{2} \approx -6.830$

42. $y = 8e^{.5x}$

$y' = 8(.5e^{.5x}) = 4e^{.5x}$

44. $y = -4e^{x^2}$

$g(x) = x^2$

$g'(x) = 2x$

$y' = (2x)(-4e^{x^2})$

$= -8xe^{x^2}$

46. $y = -7x^2e^{-3x}$

Use the product rule.

$y' = (-7x^2)(-3e^{-3x}) + e^{-3x}(-14x)$

$= 21x^2e^{-3x} - 14xe^{-3x}$

$= 7xe^{-3x}(3x - 2)$

48. $y = \ln(5x + 3)$

$g(x) = 5x + 3$

$g'(x) = 5$

$y' = \dfrac{5}{5x + 3}$

50. $y = \dfrac{\ln |2x - 1|}{x + 3}$

$y' = \dfrac{(x + 3)\left(\dfrac{2}{2x - 1}\right) - (\ln |2x - 1|)(1)}{(x + 3)^2} \cdot \dfrac{2x - 1}{2x - 1}$

$= \dfrac{2(x + 3) - (2x - 1) \ln |2x - 1|}{(2x - 1)(x + 3)^2}$

52. $y = \dfrac{(x^2 + 1)e^{2x}}{\ln x}$

$y' = \dfrac{\ln x[(x^2 + 1)(2e^{2x}) + (e^{2x})(2x)] - (x^2 + 1)e^{2x}\left(\dfrac{1}{x}\right)}{(\ln x)^2} \cdot \dfrac{x}{x}$

$= \dfrac{x \ln x[2e^{2x}(x^2 + 1) + 2xe^{2x}] - (x^2 + 1)e^{2x}}{x(\ln x)^2}$

$= \dfrac{e^{2x}[2x \ln x(x^2 + 1 + x) - (x^2 + 1)]}{x(\ln x)^2}$

54. $y = (e^{2x+1} - 2)^4$

Use the chain rule.

$y' = 4(e^{2x+1} - 2)^3[2e^{2x+1}] = 8e^{2x+1}(e^{2x+1} - 2)^3$

56. $y = 3xe^{-x}$

Find the first derivative and set it equal to zero.

$y' = 3x(-e^{-x}) + e^{-x}(3)$

$= -3xe^{-x} + 3e^{-x}$

$= 3e^{-x}(1 - x)$

$3e^{-x}(1 - x) = 0$

$1 - x = 0$

$x = 1$

To determine minimum or maximum, check second derivative.

$$y'' = 3e^{-x}(-1) + (1 - x)(-3e^{-x})$$
$$= -3e^{-x} - 3e^{-x} + 3xe^{-x}$$
$$= -6e^{-x} + 3xe^{-x}$$
$$= 3e^{-x}(-2 + x)$$

At x = 1,

$$y'' = 3e^{-1}(-1)$$
$$= -3e^{-1} < 0$$

y is concave down, maximum at x = 1.

$$y = 3e^{-1} \approx 1.1$$

Set y'' = 0 to find inflection points.

$$3e^{-x}(-2 + x) = 0$$
$$-2 + x = 0$$
$$x = 2$$
$$y = 3(2)e^{-2}$$
$$= 6e^{-2}$$
$$\approx .81$$

Inflection point at (2, .81)

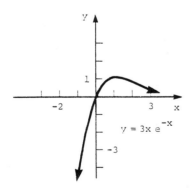

$y = 3x\,e^{-x}$

58. $y = \dfrac{\ln |5x|}{2x}$

$$y' = \frac{2x\left(\frac{5}{5x}\right) - 2\ln |5x|}{(2x)^2}$$

$$\frac{1 - \ln |5x|}{2x^2} = 0$$

$$1 - \ln |5x| = 0$$

$$\ln |5x| = 1$$

$$|5x| = e$$

$$5x = \pm e$$

$$x = \pm \frac{e}{5}$$

$$y\left(\frac{e}{5}\right) = \frac{\ln \left|5\left(\frac{e}{5}\right)\right|}{2\left(\frac{e}{5}\right)}$$

$$= \frac{1}{\frac{2e}{5}} = \frac{5}{2e} \approx .9$$

$$y\left(-\frac{e}{5}\right) = \frac{\ln \left|5\left(-\frac{e}{5}\right)\right|}{2\left(-\frac{e}{5}\right)}$$

$$= \frac{1}{-\frac{2e}{5}} = -\frac{5}{2e} \approx -.9$$

To determine maximum or minimum, check the second derivative.

$$y'' = \frac{4x^2\left(-2 \cdot \frac{5}{5x}\right) - (2 - 2\ln |5x|)(8x)}{(4x^2)^2}$$

$$= \frac{-8x - 16x + 16x \ln |5x|}{16x^4}$$

$$= \frac{-3 + 2\ln |5x|}{2x^3}$$

When x = e/5, y'' < 0 so a maximum occurs at .9.

When x = -e/5, y'' > 0, so a minimum occurs at -.9.

Set $y'' = 0$ to find inflection points.

$$\frac{-3 + 2 \ln |5x|}{2x^3} = 0$$

$$2 \ln |5x| = 3$$

$$\ln |5x| = \frac{3}{2}$$

$$|5x| = e^{3/2}$$

$$5x = \pm e^{3/2}$$

$$x = \pm \frac{e^{3/2}}{5}$$

$$\approx \pm .9$$

$$y = \frac{\ln \left|5\left(\pm\frac{e^{3/2}}{5}\right)\right|}{2\left(\pm\frac{e^{3/2}}{5}\right)}$$

$$= \frac{\ln |e^{3/2}|}{\pm\frac{2e^{3/2}}{5}}$$

$$\approx \pm .84$$

Inflection points at $(.9, .84)$ and $(-.9, -.84)$

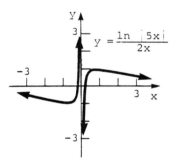

60. $P = \$2781.36$, $r = 8\%$, $t = 6$, $m = 4$

$$A = P\left(1 + \frac{r}{m}\right)^{tm}$$

$$A = 2781.36\left(1 + \frac{.08}{4}\right)^{(6)(4)}$$

$$= 2781.36(1.02)^{24}$$

$$= \$4473.64$$

Interest $= \$4473.64 - \$2781.36$

$$= \$1692.28$$

For Exercises 62 and 64, use $A = Pe^{rt}$.

62. $P = \$12,104$, $r = 8\%$, $t = 4$

$$A = Pe^{rt}$$

$$A = 12,104e^{.08(4)}$$

$$= 12,104e^{.32}$$

$$= \$16,668.75$$

64. $A = \$1500$, $r = .10$, $t = 9$

$$A = 1500e^{.10(9)}$$

$$= 1500e^{.9}$$

$$= \$3689.40$$

66. $r = 7\%$, $m = 4$

$$r_E = \left(1 + \frac{r}{m}\right)^m = 1$$

$$= \left(1 + \frac{.07}{4}\right)^4 - 1$$

$$= .0719 \text{ or } 7.19\%$$

68. $r = 11\%$, $m = 2$

$$r_E = \left(1 + \frac{r}{m}\right)^m - 1$$

$$= \left(1 + \frac{.11}{2}\right)^2 - 1$$

$$= .1130 \text{ or } 11.30\%$$

70. $r = 11\%$ compounded continuously

$$r_E = e^r - 1$$

$$= e^{.11} - 1$$

$$= .1163 \text{ or } 11.63\%$$

72. $A = \$10,000$, $r = 8\%$, $m = 2$, $t = 6$

$$P = A\left(1 + \frac{r}{m}\right)^{-tm}$$

$$= 10,000\left(1 + \frac{.08}{2}\right)^{-2(6)}$$

$$= 10,000(1.04)^{-12}$$

$$= \$6245.97$$

74. $A = \$9760$, $r = 12\%$, $m = 12$, $t = 3$

$$P = A\left(1 + \frac{r}{m}\right)^{-tm}$$

$$P = 9760\left(1 + \frac{.12}{12}\right)^{-12(3)}$$

$$= 9760(1.01)^{-36}$$

$$= \$6821.51$$

76. $r = 10\%$, $t = 8$, $m = 2$, $P = 10,000$

$$A = P\left(1 + \frac{r}{m}\right)^{tm}$$

$$= 10,000\left(1 + \frac{.10}{2}\right)^{8(2)}$$

$$= 10,000(1.05)^{16}$$

$$= \$21,828.75$$

78. $P = \$6000$, $A = \$8000$, $t = 3$

$$A = Pe^{rt}$$

$$8000 = 6000e^{3r}$$

$$\frac{4}{3} = e^{3r}$$

$$\ln 4 - \ln 3 = 3r$$

$$r = \frac{\ln 4 - \ln 3}{3}$$

$$r \approx .0959 \quad \text{or} \quad \text{about } 9.59\%$$

80. $y = 17,000$, $y_0 = 15,000$, $t = 4$

(a)
$$y = y_0 e^{kt}$$

$$17,000 = 15,000e^{4k}$$

$$\frac{17}{15} = e^{4k}$$

$$\ln\left(\frac{17}{15}\right) = 4k$$

$$\frac{.125^2}{4} = k$$

$$.0313 = k$$

So, $y = 15,000e^{.0313t}$.

(b)
$$45,000 = 15,000e^{.0313t}$$

$$3 = e^{.0313t}$$

$$\ln 3 = .0313t$$

$$\frac{\ln 3}{.0313} = t$$

$$35 = t$$

It would take about 35 yr.

82.
$$c(t) = e^{-t} - e^{-2t}$$

$$c'(t) = -e^{-t} + 2e^{-2t}$$

$$= e^{-t}(-1 + 2e^{-t})$$

$$e^{-t}(-1 + 2e^{-t}) = 0$$

$$-1 + 2e^{-t} = 0$$

$$-1 = -2e^{-t}$$

$$\frac{1}{2} = e^{-t}$$

$$\ln\left(\frac{1}{2}\right) = -t$$

$$t = \ln 2$$

$$t \approx .7$$

$$c(\ln 2) = e^{-\ln 2} - e^{-2\ln 2}$$

$$= e^{\ln 2^{-1}} - e^{\ln 2^{-2}}$$

$$= \frac{1}{2} - \frac{1}{4}$$

$$= \frac{1}{4} = .25$$

The maximum concentration of .25 occurs at

$$t = \ln 2 \approx .7 \text{ min.}$$

84. $y = y_0 e^{-kt}$

(a) $128{,}000 = 100{,}000 e^{-k(-5)}$

$128{,}000 = 100{,}000^{5k}$

$$\frac{128}{100} = e^{5k}$$

$$\ln\left(\frac{128}{100}\right) = 5k$$

$$.05 \approx k$$

$y = 100{,}000 e^{-.05t}$

(b) $70{,}000 = 100{,}000 e^{-.05t}$

$$\frac{7}{10} = e^{-.05t}$$

$$\ln\left(\frac{7}{10}\right) = -.05t$$

$$7.1 \approx t$$

It will take about 7.1 yr.

86. (a) $A(t) = A e^{kt}$

$113 = 34 e^{k(30)}$

$3.324 \approx e^{30k}$

$\ln 3.324 = 30k$

$.04 = k$

So, $A(t) = 34 e^{.04t}$

(b) 50% higher than the base year with CPI 100 is 150.

$150 = 34 e^{.04t}$

$4.412 \approx e^{.04t}$

$\ln 4.412 \approx .04t$

$37 \approx t$

Since $t = 0$ corresponds to 1960, the year when costs will be 50% higher than 1983 is 1997.

(c) $100 = 34 e^{.04t}$

$2.94 \approx e^{.04t}$

$\ln 2.94 \approx .04t$

$27 \approx t$

The year was 1987. We don't get 1983 because the exponential function only gives an approximation.

88. $A(t) = 830 e^{.15t}$

where $t = 0$ corresponds to 1965.

(a) $A(10) = 830 e^{.15(10)}$

≈ 3700

(b) $A(15) = 830 e^{.15(15)}$

≈ 7900

(c) $A(20) = 830 e^{.15(20)}$

$\approx 17{,}000$

Using the given function, we expected about 17,000 warheads in 1985, but only 10,012 actually existed. The changing world situation may have caused the growth rate to decrease.

(d) $A'(t) = 830(.15) e^{.15t}$

$= 124.5 e^{.15t}$

According to $A(t)$, growth rate is exponential, that is, increasing faster and faster.

90. $f(x) = \log_a x; \ a > 0, \ a \neq 1$

(a) The domain is $(0, \infty)$.

(b) The range is $(-\infty, \infty)$.

(c) The x-intercept is 1.

(d) There are no discontinuities

(e) x = 0 is an asymptote.

(f) f(x) is increasing when a is greater than 1.

(g) f(x) is decreasing when a is between 0 and 1.

CHAPTER 6   INTEGRATION

Section 6.1

2. $\displaystyle\int 8x\ dx = 8\int x\ dx$

$\displaystyle = 8 \cdot \frac{1}{1+1}x^{1+1} + C$

$\displaystyle = \frac{8x^2}{2} + C$

$\displaystyle = 4x^2 + C$

4. $\displaystyle\int 6x^3\ dx = 6\int x^3\ dx$

$\displaystyle = 6 \cdot \frac{1}{3+1}x^{3+1} + C$

$\displaystyle = 6\frac{x^4}{4} + C = \frac{3x^4}{2} + C$

6. $\displaystyle\int 2\ dy = 2\int 1\ dy = 2\int y^0\ dy$

$\displaystyle = \frac{2}{1}y^{0+1} + C$

$\displaystyle = 2y + C$

8. $\displaystyle\int (3x - 5)\ dx$

$\displaystyle = 3\int x\ dx - 5\int x^0\ dx$

$\displaystyle = 3 \cdot \frac{1}{2}x^2 - 5 \cdot \frac{1}{1}x + C$

$\displaystyle = \frac{3x^2}{2} - 5x + C$

10. $\displaystyle\int (t^2 - 2t)dt = \int t^2\ dt - 2\int t\ dt$

$\displaystyle = \frac{t^3}{3} - 2\frac{t^2}{2} + C$

$\displaystyle = \frac{t^3}{3} - t^2 + C$

12. $\displaystyle\int (5x^2 - 6x + 3)dx$

$\displaystyle = 5\int x^2\ dx - 6\int x\ dx + 3\int x^0\ dx$

$\displaystyle = \frac{5x^3}{3} - \frac{6x^2}{2} + 3x + C$

$\displaystyle = \frac{5x^3}{3} - 3x^2 + 3x + C$

14. $\displaystyle\int (12y^3 + 6y^2 - 8y + 5)dy$

$\displaystyle = 12\int y^3\ dy + 6\int y^2\ dy - 8\int y\ dy$

$\displaystyle \quad + 5\int dy$

$\displaystyle = \frac{12y^4}{4} + \frac{6y^3}{3} - \frac{8y^2}{2} + 5y + C$

$\displaystyle = 3y^4 + 2y^3 - 4y^2 + 5y + C$

16. $\displaystyle\int t^{1/4}\ dt = \frac{t^{1/4+1}}{1/4+1} + C$

$\displaystyle = \frac{t^{5/4}}{5/4} + C$

$\displaystyle = \frac{4t^{5/4}}{5} + C$

18. $\displaystyle\int (4\sqrt{v} - 3v^{3/2})dv$

$\displaystyle = 4\int v^{1/2}\ dv - 3\int v^{3/2}\ dv$

$\displaystyle = \frac{4v^{3/2}}{3/2} - \frac{3v^{5/2}}{5/2} + C$

$\displaystyle = \frac{8v^{3/2}}{3} - \frac{6v^{5/2}}{5} + C$

20. $\displaystyle\int (x^{1/2} - x^{-1/2})dx$

$\displaystyle = \int x^{1/2}\ dx - \int x^{1/2}\ dx$

$\displaystyle = \frac{x^{1/2+1}}{1/2+1} - \frac{x^{-1/2+1}}{-1/2+1} + C$

$\displaystyle = \frac{x^{3/2}}{3/2} - \frac{x^{1/2}}{1/2} + C$

$\displaystyle = \frac{2x^{3/2}}{3} - 2x^{1/2} + C$

22. $\int (56t^{5/2} + 18t^{7/2})dt$

$= 56 \int t^{5/2} dt + 18 \int t^{7/2} dt$

$= \dfrac{56t^{7/2}}{7/2} + \dfrac{18t^{9/2}}{9/2} + C$

$= 16t^{7/2} + 4t^{9/2} + C$

24. $\int \left(\dfrac{4}{x^3}\right)dx = \int 4x^{-3} dx$

$= 4 \int x^{-3} dx$

$= \dfrac{4x^{-2}}{-2} + C$

$= -2x^{-2} + C$

$= \dfrac{-2}{x^2} + C$

26. $\int \left(\sqrt{u} + \dfrac{1}{u^2}\right)du$

$= \int u^{1/2} du + \int u^{-2} du$

$= \dfrac{u^{3/2}}{3/2} + \dfrac{u^{-1}}{-1} + C$

$= \dfrac{2u^{3/2}}{3} - \dfrac{1}{u} + C$

28. $\int (8x^{-3} + 4x^{-1})dx$

$= 8 \int x^{-3} dx + 4 \int x^{-1} dx$

$= \dfrac{8x^{-2}}{-2} + 4 \ln |x| + C$

$= -4x^{-2} + 4 \ln |x| + C$

$= \dfrac{-4}{x^2} + 4 \ln |x| + C$

30. $\int e^{-3y} dy = \dfrac{1}{-3}e^{-3y} + C$

$= \dfrac{-e^{-3y}}{3} + C$

32. $\int -4e^{\cdot 2v} dv = -4 \int e^{\cdot 2v} dv$

$= (-4)\dfrac{1}{.2}e^{\cdot 2v} + C$

$= -20e^{\cdot 2v} + C$

34. $\int \left(\dfrac{9}{x} - 3e^{-\cdot 4x}\right)dx$

$= \int \dfrac{9}{x}dx - 3 \int e^{-\cdot 4x} dx$

$= 9 \ln |x| - 3\left(-\dfrac{1}{.4}\right)e^{-\cdot 4x} + C$

$= 9 \ln |x| + \dfrac{15e^{-\cdot 4x}}{2} + C$

36. $\int \dfrac{2y^{1/2} - 3y^2}{y} dy$

$= \int \dfrac{2y^{1/2}}{y} dy - \int \dfrac{3y^2 dy}{y}$

$= 2 \int y^{-1/2} dy - 3 \int y dy$

$= 2\dfrac{y^{1/2}}{1/2} - \dfrac{3y^2}{2} + C$

$= 4y^{1/2} - \dfrac{3y^2}{2} + C$

38. $\int (v^2 - e^{3v})dv = \int v^2 dv - \int e^{3v} dv$

$= \dfrac{v^3}{3} - \dfrac{e^{3v}}{3} + C$

$= \dfrac{v^3 - e^{3v}}{3} + C$

40. $\int (2y - 1)^2 dy$

$= \int (4y^2 - 4y + 1)dy$

$= \dfrac{4y^3}{3} - \dfrac{4y^2}{2} + y + C$

$= \dfrac{4y^3}{3} - 2y^2 + y + C$

42. $\displaystyle\int \frac{1 - 2\sqrt[3]{z}}{\sqrt[3]{z}}\,dz = \int \left(\frac{1}{\sqrt[3]{z}} + \frac{2\sqrt[3]{z}}{\sqrt[3]{z}}\right) dz$

$\displaystyle = \int (z^{-1/3} - 2)\,dz$

$\displaystyle = \frac{z^{2/3}}{2/3} - 2z + C$

$\displaystyle = \frac{3z^{2/3}}{2} - 2z + C$

44. Find $f(x)$ such that $f'(x) = 6x^2 - 4x + 3$, and $(0, 1)$ is on the curve.

$\displaystyle f(x) = \int (6x^2 - 4x + 3)\,dx$

$\displaystyle = \frac{6x^3}{3} - \frac{4x^2}{2} + 3x + C$

$\displaystyle = 2x^3 - 2x^2 + 3x + C$

Since $(0, 1)$ is on the curve, then $f(0) = 1$.

$f(0) = 2(0)^3 - 2(0)^2 + 3(0) + C = 1$

$\qquad\qquad\qquad\qquad\qquad C = 1$

So, $f(x) = 2x^3 - 2x^2 + 3x + 1$.

46. $C'(x) = 2x + 3x^2$, fixed cost is \$15.

$\displaystyle C(x) = \int (2x + 3x^2)\,dx$

$\displaystyle = \frac{2x^2}{2} + \frac{3x^3}{3} + k$

$\displaystyle = x^2 + x^3 + k$

$C(0) = (0)^2 + (0)^3 + k = k$

Since $C(0) = 15$, $k = 15$.

So, $C(x) = x^2 + x^3 + 15$

48. $C'(x) = .8x^2 - x$, fixed cost is \$5.

$\displaystyle C(x) = \int (.8x^2 - x)\,dx$

$\displaystyle = \frac{.8x^3}{3} - \frac{x^2}{2} + k$

$\displaystyle = \frac{4x^3}{15} - \frac{x^2}{2} + k$

$\displaystyle C(0) = \frac{4(0)^3}{15} + \frac{(0)^2}{2} + k$

Since $C(0) = 5$, $k = 5$.

So, $\displaystyle C(x) = \frac{4x^3}{15} - \frac{x^2}{2} + 5$

50. $C'(x) = x^{1/2}$, 16 units cost is \$45.

$\displaystyle C(x) = \int x^{1/2}\,dx$

$\displaystyle = \frac{x^{3/2}}{3/2} + k$

$\displaystyle = \frac{2}{3}x^{3/2} + k$

$\displaystyle C(16) = \frac{2}{3}(16)^{3/2} + k$

$\displaystyle = \frac{2}{3}(64) + k$

$\displaystyle = \frac{128}{3} + k$

Since $C(16) = 45$,

$\displaystyle \frac{128}{3} + k = 45$

$\displaystyle k = \frac{7}{3}.$

So, $\displaystyle C(x) = \frac{2}{3}x^{3/2} + \frac{7}{3}.$

52. $C'(x) = x^2 - 2x + 3$, 3 units costs \$15, so

$C(3) = 15.$

$\displaystyle C(x) = \int (x^2 - 2x + 3)\,dx$

$\displaystyle = \frac{x^3}{3} - \frac{2x^2}{2} + 3x + k$

$\displaystyle = \frac{x^3}{3} - x^2 + 3x + k$

$\displaystyle C(3) = \frac{3^3}{3} - 3^2 + 3(3) + k$

Since $C(3) = 15$,

$15 = 9 - 9 + 9 + k$

$k = 6$.

So, $C(x) = \dfrac{x^3}{3} - x^2 + 3x + 6$.

54. $C'(x) = \dfrac{1}{x} + 2x$, 7 units cost $58.40,

so

$C(7) = 58.40$.

$C(x) = \displaystyle\int \left(\dfrac{1}{x} + 2x\right) dx$

$= \ln |x| + \dfrac{2x^2}{2} + k$

$= \ln |x| + x^2 + k$

$C(7) = \ln |7| + 7^2 + k$

Since $C(7) = 58.40$,

$58.40 = \ln 7 + 49 + k$

$k = 7.45$.

$C(x) = \ln |x| + x^2 + 7.45$

56. $C'(x) = 1.2^x(\ln 1.2)$, 2 units

cost $9.44 (Hint: recall that

$a^x = e^{x \ln a}$.)

$C(x) = \displaystyle\int 1.2^x(\ln 1.2) dx$

$= \ln 1.2 \displaystyle\int 1.2^x \, dx$

$= \ln 1.2 \displaystyle\int e^{x \ln 1.2} dx$

$= \ln 1.2 \left(\dfrac{1}{\ln 1.2} e^{x \ln 1.2}\right) + k$

$= e^{x \ln 1.2} + k$

$C(2) = e^{2 \ln 1.2} + k = 1.44 + k$

Since $C(2) = 9.44$,

$144 + k = 9.44$

$k = 8$.

So $C(x) = e^{x \ln 1.2} + 8$

$= 1.2^x + 8$.

58. $P'(x) = 4 - 6x + 3x^2$, profit is -40

when 0 hamburgers are sold.

$P(x) = \displaystyle\int (4x - 6x + 3x^2) dx$

$= 4x - 3x^2 + x^3 + k$

$P(0) = 4(0) - 3(0)^2 + (0)^3 + k$

Since $P(0) = -40$,

$-40 = k$.

So, $P(x) = 4x - 3x^2 + x^3 - 40$.

60. **(a)** $c(t) = (c_0 - C)e^{-kAt/V} + M$

$c'(t) = (c_0 - C)\left(\dfrac{-kA}{V}\right)e^{-kAt/V}$

$= \dfrac{-kA}{V}(c_0 - C)e^{-kAt/V}$

(b) Since equation (1) states

$c'(t) = \dfrac{kA}{V}[C - c(t)]$,

then from (a) and by substituting

from equation (2),

$(c_0 - C)\left(\dfrac{-kA}{V}\right)e^{-kAt/V}$

$= \dfrac{kA}{V}C - \dfrac{kA}{V}[(c_0 - C)e^{-kAt/V} + M]$

$\dfrac{-kA}{V}(c_0 - C)e^{-kAt/V} + M$

$= \dfrac{-kA}{V}(c_0 - C)e^{-kAt/V} + \dfrac{kA}{V}C - \dfrac{kA}{V}M$

If $t = 0$, $c(t) = c_0$.

So

$c_0 = (c_0 - C)e^0 + M$ *Equation (2)*

$c_0 = c_0 - C + M$

or $C = M$.

Thus,

$$\frac{-kA}{V}(c_0 - C)e^{-kAt/V}$$

$$= \frac{-kA}{V}(c_0 - C)e^{-kAt/V} + \frac{kA}{V}M - \frac{kA}{V}M$$

or

$$\frac{-kA}{V}(c_0 - C)e^{-kAt/V}$$

$$= \frac{-kA}{V}(c_0 - C)e^{-kAt/V}.$$

62. $v(t) = 6t^2 - \dfrac{2}{t^2}$

$s = \displaystyle\int v(t)dt$

$= \displaystyle\int (6t^2 - 2t^{-2})dt$

$= 2t^3 + 2t^{-1} + C$

$s = 2t^3 + \dfrac{2}{t} + C$

Since $s(1) = 8$,

$8 = 2(1)^3 + \dfrac{2}{1} + C$

$8 = 4 + C$

$4 = C$.

Thus, $s = 2t^3 + \dfrac{2}{t} + 4$.

64. $a(t) = 18t + 8$

$v(t) = \displaystyle\int (18t + 8)\, dt$

$= 9t^2 + 8t + C_1$

$v(1) = 9(1)^2 + 8(1) + C_1 = 17 + C_1$

Since $v(1) = 15$, $C_1 = -2$.

$v(t) = 9t^2 + 8t - 2$

$s(t) = \displaystyle\int (9t^2 + 8t - 2)dt$

$= 3t^3 + 4t^2 - 2t + C_2$

$s(1) = 3(1)^3 + 4(1)^2 - 2(1) + C_2$

$= 5 + C_2$

Since $s(1) = 19$, $C_2 = 14$.

$s(t) = 3t^3 + 4t^2 - 2t + 14$

Section 6.2

2. $\displaystyle\int (-4t + 1)^3\, dt$

$= -\dfrac{1}{4}\displaystyle\int -4(-4t + 1)^3\, dt$

Let $u = (-4t + 1)$, so that

$du = -4\, dt$.

$= -\dfrac{1}{4}\displaystyle\int u^3\, du$

$= -\dfrac{1}{4}\cdot\dfrac{u^4}{4} + C$

$= \dfrac{-u^4}{16} + C$

$= \dfrac{-(-4t + 1)^4}{16} + C$

4. $\displaystyle\int \frac{3\, du}{\sqrt{3u - 5}} = \int 3(3u - 5)^{-1/2}\, du$

Let $w = 3u - 5$, so that

$dw = 3\, du$.

$= \displaystyle\int w^{-1/2}\, dw$

$= \dfrac{w^{1/2}}{1/2} + C$

$= 2w^{1/2} + C$

$= 2(3u - 5)^{1/2} + C$

6. $\displaystyle\int \frac{6x^2 \ dx}{(2x^3 + 7)^{3/2}}$

$\displaystyle= \int 6x^2(2x^3 + 7)^{-3/2} \ dx$

Let $2x^3 + 7 = u$, so that

$\quad 6x^2 \ dx = du$.

$\displaystyle= \int u^{-3/2} \ du$

$\displaystyle= \frac{u^{-1/2}}{-1/2} + C$

$\displaystyle= -2u^{-1/2} + C$

$\displaystyle= \frac{-2}{u^{1/2}} + C$

$\displaystyle= \frac{-2}{(2x^3 + 7)^{1/2}} + C$

8. $\displaystyle\int r\sqrt{r^2 + 2} \ dr = \int r(r^2 + 2)^{1/2} \ dr$

Let $u = r^2 + 2$, so that

$du = 2r \ dr$.

$\displaystyle= \frac{1}{2} \int 2r(r^2 + 2)^{1/2} \ dr$

$\displaystyle= \frac{1}{2} \int u^{1/2} \ du$

$\displaystyle= \frac{1}{2} \cdot \frac{u^{3/2}}{3/2} + C$

$\displaystyle= \frac{u^{3/2}}{3} + C$

$\displaystyle= \frac{(r^2 + 2)^{3/2}}{3} + C$

10. $\displaystyle\int 5e^{-.3g} \ dg = 5 \int e^{-.3g} \ dg$

Let $u = -.3g$, so that

$\quad du = -.3 \ dg$.

$\displaystyle= \frac{5}{-.3} \int (-.3)e^{-.3g} \ dg$

$\displaystyle= \frac{-50}{3} \int e^u \ du$

$\displaystyle= \frac{-50e^u}{3} + C$

$\displaystyle= \frac{-50e^{-.3g}}{3} + C$

12. $\displaystyle\int re^{-r^2} \ dr$

Let $u = -r^2$, so that

$\quad du = -2r \ dr$.

$\displaystyle\int re^{-r^2} \ dr$

$\displaystyle= -\frac{1}{2} \int -2re^{-r^2} \ dr$

$\displaystyle= -\frac{1}{2} \int e^u \ du$

$\displaystyle= \frac{-e^u}{2} + C$

$\displaystyle= \frac{-e^{-r^2}}{2} + C$

14. $\displaystyle\int (x^2 - 1)e^{x^3 - 3x} \ dx$

Let $u = x^3 - 3x$, so that

$du = (3x^2 - 3)dx = 3(x^2 - 1)dx$

$\displaystyle\int (x^2 - 1)e^{x^3 - 3x} \ dx$

$\displaystyle= \frac{1}{3} \int 3(x^2 - 1)e^{x^3 - 3x} \ dx$

$\displaystyle= \frac{1}{3} \int e^u \ du = \frac{e^u}{3} + C$

$\displaystyle= \frac{e^{x^3 - 3x}}{3} + C$

16. $\displaystyle\int \frac{e^{\sqrt{y}}}{2\sqrt{y}} \ dy = \int \frac{e^{y^{1/2}}}{2y^{1/2}} \ dy$

$\displaystyle= \int \frac{1}{2}y^{-1/2}e^{y^{1/2}} \ dy$

Let $u = y^{1/2}$, so that

$\quad du = \frac{1}{2}y^{-1/2} \ dy$.

$\displaystyle= \int e^u \ du = e^u + C$

$\displaystyle= e^{y^{1/2}} + C = e^{\sqrt{y}} + C$

18. $\displaystyle\int \frac{9}{2 + 5t}\, dt = 9 \int \frac{dt}{2 + 5t}$

Let $u = 2 + 5t$, so that
$du = 5\, dt$.

$$= \frac{9}{5} \int \frac{5\, dt}{2 + 5t} = \frac{9}{5} \int \frac{du}{u}$$

$$= \frac{9 \ln |u|}{5} + C$$

$$= \frac{9 \ln |2 + 5t|}{5} + C$$

20. $\displaystyle\int \frac{dw}{5w - 2}$

Let $u = 5w - 2$, so that
$du = 5\, dw$.

$$\int \frac{dw}{5w - 2} = \frac{1}{5} \int \frac{5\, dw}{5w - 2} = \frac{1}{5} \int \frac{du}{u}$$

$$= \frac{\ln |u|}{5} + C$$

$$= \frac{\ln |5w - 2|}{5} + C$$

22. $\displaystyle\int \frac{x\, dx}{(2x^2 - 5)^3} = \int x(2x^2 - 5)^{-3}\, dx$

Let $u = 2x^2 - 5$, so that
$du = 4x\, dx$.

$$= \frac{1}{4} \int 4x(2x^2 - 5)^{-3}\, dx$$

$$= \frac{1}{4} \int u^{-3}\, du$$

$$= \frac{1}{4} \cdot \frac{u^{-2}}{-2} + C$$

$$= -\frac{1}{8} \cdot \frac{1}{u^2} + C$$

$$= \frac{-1}{8u^2} + C$$

$$= \frac{-1}{8(2x^2 - 5)^2} + C$$

24. $\displaystyle\int \frac{2x + 1}{(x^2 + x)^3}\, dx$

$$= \int (2x + 1)(x^2 + x)^{-3}\, dx$$

Let $u = x^2 + x$, so that
$du = (2x + 1)dx$

$$= \int u^{-3}\, du = \frac{u^{-2}}{-2} + C$$

$$= \frac{-1}{2u^2} + C$$

$$= \frac{-1}{2(x^2 + x)^2} + C$$

26. $\displaystyle\int \left(\frac{2}{A} - A\right)\left(\frac{-2}{A^2} - 1\right)dA$

$$= \int (2A^{-1} - A)(-2A^{-2} - 1)dA$$

Let $u = 2A^{-1} - A$, so that
$du = (-2A^{-2} - 1)dA$.

$$= \int u\, du = \frac{u^2}{2} + C$$

$$= \frac{(2A^{-1} - A)^2}{2} + C$$

$$= \frac{\left(\frac{2}{A} - A\right)^2}{2} + C$$

28. $\displaystyle\int \frac{B^3 - 1}{(2B^4 - 8B)^{3/2}}\, dB$

$$= \int (B^3 - 1)(2B^4 - 8B)^{-3/2}\, dB$$

Let $u = 2B^4 - 8B$, so that
$du = (8B^3 - 8)dB = 8(B^3 - 1)dB$.

$$= \frac{1}{8} \int 8(B^3 - 1)(2B^4 - 8B)^{-3/2}\, dB$$

$$= \frac{1}{8} \int u^{-3/2}\, du = \frac{1}{8} \cdot \frac{u^{-1/2}}{-1/2} + C$$

$$= -\frac{1}{4} u^{-1/2} + C = \frac{-1}{4u^{1/2}} + C$$

$$= \frac{-1}{4(2B^4 - 8B)^{1/2}} + C$$

30. $\int x^3 (1 + x^2)^{1/4} \, dx$

Let $u = 1 + x^2$, so that
$du = 2x$; also, $u - 1 = x^2$.

$\int x^3 (1 + x^2)^{1/4} \, dx$

$= \frac{1}{2} \int 2x(x^2)(1 + x^2)^{1/4}$

$= \frac{1}{2} \int (u - 1)u^{1/4} \, du$

$= \frac{1}{2} \int (u^{5/4} - u^{1/4}) du$

$= \frac{1}{2} \left(\frac{u^{9/4}}{9/4} \right) - \frac{1}{2} \left(\frac{u^{5/4}}{5/4} \right) + C$

$= \frac{2u^{9/4}}{9} - \frac{2u^{5/4}}{5} + C$

$= \frac{2(1 + x^2)^{9/4}}{9} - \frac{2(1 + x^2)^{5/4}}{5} + C$

32. $\int 4r\sqrt{8 - r} \, dr$

$= \int 4r(8 - r)^{1/2} \, dr$

Let $u = 8 - r$, so that
$du = -dr$; also, $r = 8 - u$.

$= -4 \int -r(8 - r)^{1/2} \, dr$

$= -4 \int (8 - u)u^{1/2} \, du$

$= -4 \int (8u^{1/2} - u^{3/2}) du$

$= -4 \left(\frac{8u^{3/2}}{3/2} - \frac{u^{5/2}}{5/2} \right) + C$

$= \frac{8(8 - r)^{5/2}}{5} - \frac{64(8 - r)^{3/2}}{3} + C$

34. $\int \frac{2x}{(x + 5)^6} \, dx$

$= \int 2x(x + 5)^{-6} \, dx$

$= 2 \int x(x + 5)^{-6} \, dx$

Let $u = x + 5$, so that
$du = dx$; also, $u - 5 = x$.

$= 2 \int (u - 5)u^{-6} \, du$

$= 2 \int (u^{-5} - 5u^{-6}) du$

$= 2 \left(\frac{u^{-4}}{-4} \right) - 10 \left(\frac{u^{-5}}{-5} \right) + C$

$= -\frac{u^{-4}}{2} + 2u^{-5} + C$

$= \frac{-1}{2(x + 5)^4} + \frac{2}{(x + 5)^5} + C$

36. $\int (\sqrt{x^2 - 6x})(x - 3) dx$

$= \int (x^2 - 6x)^{1/2} (x - 3) dx$

Let $u = x^2 - 6x$, so that
$du = (2x - 6) dx = 2(x - 3) dx$.

$= \frac{1}{2} \int (x^2 - 6x)^{1/2} \, 2(x - 3) dx$

$= \frac{1}{2} \int u^{1/2} \, du = \frac{1}{2} \left(\frac{u^{3/2}}{3/2} \right) + C$

$= \frac{u^{3/2}}{3} + C$

$= \frac{(x^2 - 6x)^{3/2}}{3} + C$

38. $\int \frac{-4x}{x^2 + 3} \, dx$

Let $u = x^2 + 3$, so that
$du = 2x \, dx$.

$\int \frac{-4x}{x^2 + 3} \, dx$

$= -2 \int \frac{2x \, dx}{x^2 + 3}$

$= -2 \int \frac{du}{u}$

$= -2 \ln |u| + C$

$= -2 \ln (x^2 + 3) + C$

40. $\int x^2 e^{-x^3} \, dx$

Let $u = -x^3$, so that
$du = -3x^2 \, dx$.

$\int x^2 e^{-x^3} \, dx$

$= -\dfrac{1}{3} \int -3x^2 e^{-x^3} \, dx$

$= -\dfrac{1}{3} \int e^u \, du = \dfrac{-e^u}{3} + C$

$= \dfrac{-e^{-x^3}}{3} + C$

42. $\int \dfrac{\sqrt{2 + \ln x}}{x} \, dx$

Let $u = 2 + \ln x$, so that
$du = \dfrac{1}{x} \, dx$.

$\int \dfrac{\sqrt{2 + \ln x}}{x} dx = \int \sqrt{u} \, du$

$= \int u^{1/2} \, du$

$= \dfrac{u^{3/2}}{3/2} + C$

$= \dfrac{2}{3} u^{3/2} + C$

$= \dfrac{2}{3}(2 + \ln x)^{3/2} + C$

44. $\int \dfrac{1}{x(\ln x)} \, dx$

Let $u = \ln x$, so that
$du = \dfrac{1}{x} \, dx$.

$\int \dfrac{1}{x(\ln x)} \, dx = \int \dfrac{1}{u} \, du$

$= \ln |u| + C$

$= \ln |\ln x| + C$

46. (a)

$M'(x) = \sqrt{x^2 + 12x}(2x + 12)$

$\qquad = (x^2 + 12x)^{1/2}(2x + 12)$

$M(x) = \int M'(x) \, dx$

$\qquad = \int (x^2 + 12x)^{1/2}(2x + 12) \, dx$

Let $u = x^2 + 12x$, so that
$du = (2x + 12) \, dx$.

$M(x) = \int u^{1/2} \, du = \dfrac{u^{3/2}}{3/2} + C$

$\qquad = \dfrac{2u^{3/2}}{3} + C$

$M(x) = \dfrac{2(x^2 + 12x)^{3/2}}{3} + C$

Now, when $x = 4$, $M = 612$.

$612 = \dfrac{2[(4)^2 + 12(4)]^{3/2}}{3} + C$

$612 = \dfrac{2(16 + 48)^{3/2}}{3} + C$

$612 = \dfrac{2(64)^{3/2}}{3} + C$

$270.67 = C$

So

$M(x) = \dfrac{2}{3}(x^2 + 12x)^{3/2} + 270.67.$

(b)

$M(x) = \dfrac{2}{3}(x^2 + 12x)^{3/2} + 270.67 = 2000$

$\dfrac{2}{3}(x^2 + 12x)^{3/2} = 1729.33$

$(x^2 + 12x)^{3/2} = 2593.995$

$x^2 + 12x = 188.79$

$x^2 + 12x - 188.79 = 0$

$x = \dfrac{-12 \pm \sqrt{12^2 - 4(1)(-188.79)}}{2(1)}$

$x = \dfrac{-12 \pm 29.99}{2}$

$x = 8.99 \quad \text{or} \quad x = -20.99$

9 yr must pass.

48. (a) $C'(x) = -100(x + 10)^{-2}$

$$C(x) = \int [-100(x + 10)^{-2}]dx$$

$$= -100 \int (x + 10)^{-2}dx$$

$$= -100\left[\frac{1}{-1}(x + 10)^{-1}\right] + k$$

$$= \frac{100}{x + 10} + k$$

$$C(0) = 10 + k$$

Since $C(0) = 10$, $k = 0$.

So, $C(x) = \dfrac{100}{x + 10}$.

(b) $C(5) = \dfrac{100}{15}$

$$C(5) = 6.\overline{6}$$

So, the total cost in 5 yr is $6666.67. No, they should not add the new line.

50. (a) $S'(t) = 4.4e^{.16t}$

$$S(t) = \int 4.4e^{.16t} \, dt$$

$$= \frac{4.4}{.16}e^{.16t} + k$$

$$= 27.5e^{.16t} + k$$

$$S(0) = 27.5e^{.16(0)} + k$$

$$= 27.5 + k$$

Since $S(0) = 27.3$, $k = -.2$.

So $S(t) = 27.5e^{.16t} - .2$.

(b)

$$S(t) = 27.5e^{.16t} - .2. = 2(27.3)$$

$$27.5e^{.16t} = 54.8$$

$$e^{.16t} = 1.99\overline{27}$$

$$\ln e^{.16t} = \ln 1.99\overline{27}$$

$$.16t \, (\ln e) = \ln 1.99\overline{27}$$

$$t = \frac{\ln 1.99\overline{27}}{.16}$$

$$t \approx 4.3$$

The Canadian cross-border shoppers will double in 4.3 yr.

Section 6.3

2. $\displaystyle\sum_{i=1}^{6} (-5i)$

$$= (-5) \sum_{i=1}^{6} i$$

$$= (-5)(1 + 2 + 3 + 4 + 5 + 6)$$

$$= (-5)(21) = -105$$

4. $\displaystyle\sum_{i=1}^{10} (5i - 8)$

$$= 5\sum_{i=1}^{10} i - \sum_{i=1}^{10} 8$$

$$= 5(1 + 2 + 3 + 4 + 5 + 6 + 7$$
$$+ 8 + 9 + 10) - 8(10)$$

$$= 5(55) - 80$$

$$= 275 - 80$$

$$= 195$$

6. $x_1 = 10$, $x_2 = 15$, $x_3 = -8$, $x_4 = -12$,
$\qquad x_5 = 0$

$$\sum_{i=1}^{5} x_i = x_1 + x_2 + x_3 + x_4 + x_5$$

$$= 10 + 15 + (-8) + (-12) + 0$$

$$= 5$$

8. $f(x) = x^2 + 1$ and $x_1 = -2$, $x_2 = 0$,
$\qquad x_3 = 2$, $x_4 = 4$

$$\sum_{i=1}^{4} f(x_i)$$

$$= f(x_1) + f(x_2) + f(x_3) + f(x_4)$$

$f(x_1) = f(-2) = (-2)^2 + 1 = 5$

$f(x_2) = f(0) = (0)^2 + 1 = 1$

$f(x_3) = f(2) = (2)^2 + 1 = 5$

$f(x_4) = f(4) = (4)^2 + 1 = 17$

So

$$\sum_{i=1}^{4} f(x_i) = 5 + 1 + 5 + 17 = 28.$$

10. $f(x) = \dfrac{1}{x}$ and $x_1 = \dfrac{1}{2}$, $x_2 = 1$, $x_3 = \dfrac{3}{2}$,

   $x_4 = 2$ and $\Delta x = \dfrac{1}{2}$

   (a) $\displaystyle\sum_{i=1}^{4} f(x_i)\Delta x$

   $= f(x_1)\Delta x + f(x_2)\Delta x + f(x_3)\Delta x$
   $\quad + f(x_4)\Delta x$

   $f(x_1) = f\left(\dfrac{1}{2}\right) = \dfrac{1}{\frac{1}{2}} = 2$

   $f(x_2) = f(1) = \dfrac{1}{1} = 1$

   $f(x_3) = f\left(\dfrac{3}{2}\right) = \dfrac{1}{\frac{3}{2}} = \dfrac{2}{3}$

   $f(x_4)\ f(2) = \dfrac{1}{2}$

   So

   $\displaystyle\sum_{i=1}^{4} f(x_i)\Delta x$

   $= (2)\left(\dfrac{1}{2}\right) + (1)\left(\dfrac{1}{2}\right) + \left(\dfrac{2}{3}\right)\left(\dfrac{1}{2}\right)$
   $\quad + \left(\dfrac{1}{2}\right)\left(\dfrac{1}{2}\right)$

   $= 1 + \dfrac{1}{2} + \dfrac{1}{3} + \dfrac{1}{4}$

   $= \dfrac{12 + 6 + 4 + 3}{12}$

   $= \dfrac{25}{12}.$

(b)

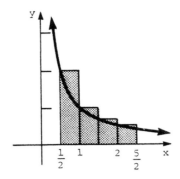

$$\int_{1/2}^{5/2} \frac{1}{x}\, dx$$

12. $f(x) = -2x + 1$ from $x = -4$ to $x = 0$
   For $n = 2$ rectangles:

   $$\Delta x = \frac{0 - (-4)}{2} = \frac{4}{2} = 2$$

i	x_i	$f(x_i)$
1	$x_1 = -4$	$f(-4) = 9$
2	$x_2 = -2$	$f(-2) = 5$

   $A = \displaystyle\sum_{i=1}^{2} f(x_i)\Delta x$

   $= f(x_1)\Delta x + f(x_2)\Delta x$

   $= (9)(2) + (5)(2)$

   $= 28$

   For $n = 4$ rectangles:

   $$\Delta x = \frac{0 - (-4)}{4} = \frac{4}{4} = 1$$

i	x_1	$f(x_i)$
1	$x_1 = -4$	9
2	$x_2 = -3$	7
3	$x_3 = -2$	5
4	$x_4 = -1$	3

$A = \sum_{i=1}^{4} f(x_i)\Delta x$

$= f(x_1)\Delta x + f(x_2)\Delta x + f(x_3)\Delta x$

$\quad + f(x_4)\Delta x$

$= (9)(1) + (7)(1) + (5)(1) + (3)(1)$

$= 24$

14. $f(x) = 3 + x$ from $x = 1$ to $x = 3$

For $n = 2$ rectangles:

$$\Delta x = \frac{3 - 1}{2} = 1$$

i	x_i	$f(x_i)$
1	$x_1 = 1$	$f(1) = 4$
2	$x_2 = 2$	$f(2) = 5$

$A = \sum_{i=1}^{2} f(x_i)\Delta x$

$= f(1)\Delta x + f(2)\Delta x$

$= (4)(1) + (5)(1)$

$= 9$

For $n = 4$ rectangles:

$$\Delta x = \frac{3 - 1}{4} = \frac{1}{2}$$

i	x_i	$f(x_i)$
1	$x_1 = 1$	$f(1) = 4$
2	$x_2 = \frac{3}{2}$	$f\left(\frac{3}{2}\right) = \frac{9}{2}$
3	$x_3 = 2$	$f(2) = 5$
4	$x_4 = \frac{5}{2}$	$f\left(\frac{5}{2}\right) = \frac{11}{2}$

$A = \sum_{i=1}^{4} f(x_i)\Delta x$

$= (4)\left(\frac{1}{2}\right) + \left(\frac{9}{2}\right)\left(\frac{1}{2}\right) + (5)\left(\frac{1}{2}\right) + \left(\frac{11}{2}\right)\left(\frac{1}{2}\right)$

$= 2 + \frac{9}{4} + \frac{5}{2} + \frac{11}{4}$

$= \frac{8 + 9 + 10 + 11}{4}$

$= \frac{19}{2}$

16. $f(x) = x^2$ from $x = 0$ to $x = 4$

For $n = 2$ rectangles:

$$\Delta x = \frac{4 - 0}{2} = 2$$

i	x_i	$f(x_i)$
1	0	$(0)^2 = 0$
2	2	$(2)^2 = 4$

$A = \sum_{i=1}^{2} f(x_i)\Delta x$

$= f(0)\Delta x + f(2)\Delta x$

$= (0)(2) + 4(2)$

$= 8$

For $n = 4$ rectangles:

$$\Delta x = \frac{4 - 0}{4} = 1$$

i	x_i	$f(x_i)$
1	0	$(0)^2 = 0$
2	1	$(1)^2 = 1$
3	2	$(2)^2 = 4$
4	3	$(3)^2 = 9$

$A = \sum_{i=1}^{4} f(x_i)\Delta x$

$= (0)(1) + (1)(1) + (4)(1) + (9)(1)$

$= 14$

18. $f(x) = -x^2 + 4$ from $x = -2$ to $x = 2$

For $n = 2$ rectangles:

$$\Delta x = \frac{2 - (-2)}{2} = 2$$

i	x_i	$f(x_i)$
1	-2	$-(-2)^2 + 4 = 0$
2	0	$-(0)^2 + 4 = 4$

$$A = \sum_{i=1}^{2} f(x_i)\Delta x$$

$$= f(-2)\Delta x + f(0)\Delta x$$

$$= (0)(2) + (4)(2)$$

$$= 8$$

For n = 4 rectangles:

$$\Delta x = \frac{2 - (-2)}{4} = 1$$

i	x_i	$f(x_i)$
1	-2	$-(-2)^2 + 4 = 0$
2	-1	$-(-1)^2 + 4 = 3$
3	0	$-(0)^2 + 4 = 4$
4	1	$-(1)^2 + 4 = 3$

$$A = \sum_{i=1}^{4} f(x_i)\Delta x$$

$$= (0)(1) + (3)(1) + (4)(1) + (3)(1)$$

$$= 10$$

20. $f(x) = e^x + 1$ from x = -2 to x = 2

For n = 2 rectangles:

$$\Delta x = \frac{2 - (-2)}{2} = 2$$

i	x_i	$f(x_i)$
1	-2	$e^{-2} + 1$
2	0	$e^0 + 1 = 2$

$$A = \sum_{i=1}^{2} f(x_i)\Delta x$$

$$= (e^{-2} + 1)(2) + (2)(2)$$

$$\approx 6.27$$

For n = 4 rectangles:

$$\Delta x = \frac{2 - (-2)}{4} = 1$$

i	x_i	$f(x_i)$
1	-2	$e^{-2} + 1$
2	-1	$e^{-1} + 1$
3	0	$e^0 + 1 = 2$
4	1	$e^1 + 1$

$$A = \sum_{i=1}^{4} f(x_i)\Delta x$$

$$= \sum_{i=1}^{4} f(x_i)(1)$$

$$= \sum_{i=1}^{4} f(x_i)$$

$$= (e^{-2} + 1) + (e^{-1} + 1) + 2 + e^1 + 1$$

$$\approx 8.22$$

22. $f(x) = \frac{2}{x}$ from x = 1 to x = 9

For n = 2 rectangles:

$$\Delta x = \frac{9 - 1}{2} = 4$$

i	x_i	$f(x_i)$
1	1	$\frac{2}{1} = 2$
2	5	$\frac{2}{5} = .4$

$$A = \sum_{i=1}^{2} f(x_i)\Delta x$$

$$= (2)(4) + (.4)(4)$$

$$= 9.6$$

For n = 4 rectangles:

$$\Delta x = \frac{9 - 1}{4} = 2$$

i	x_i	$f(x_i)$
1	1	$\frac{2}{1} = 2$
2	3	$\frac{2}{3}$
3	5	$\frac{2}{5} = .4$
4	7	$\frac{2}{7}$

$A = \sum_{i=1}^{4} f(x_i) \Delta x$

$= (2)(2) + \left(\frac{2}{3}\right)(2) + (.4)(2) + \left(\frac{2}{7}\right)(2)$

$= 6.7$

24. $\int_{0}^{5} (5 - x)\,dx$

Graph $y = 5 - x$.

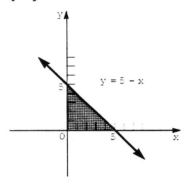

$\int_{0}^{5} (5 - x)\,dx$ is the area of a tri-

angle with base = 5 − 0 = 5 and
altitude = 5.

Area $= \frac{1}{2}$(altitude)(base)

$= \frac{1}{2}(5)(5) = 12.5$

26. $\int_{1}^{5} \frac{7}{2}\,dx$

Graph $y = \frac{7}{2}$.

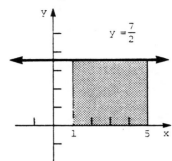

$\int_{1}^{5} \frac{7}{2}\,dx$ is the area of a rectangle

with width 7/2 and length 4.

Area = (length)(width)

$= (4)\left(\frac{7}{2}\right)$

$= 14$

28. $\int_{-4}^{0} \sqrt{16 - x^2}\,dx$

Graph $y = \sqrt{16 - x^2}$.

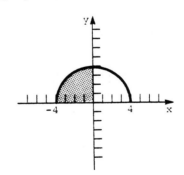

$$\int_{-4}^{0} \sqrt{16 - x^2} \, dx \text{ is the area of the}$$

portion of the circle in the second quadrant; that is, it is one—fourth of a circle. The circle has radius 4.

$$\text{Area} = \frac{1}{4}\pi r^2$$

$$= \frac{1}{4}\pi(4)^2$$

$$= 4\pi$$

30. $\displaystyle\int_{2}^{5} (1 + 2x) \, dx$

Graph $y = 1 + 2x$.

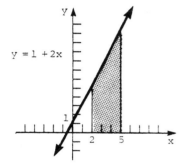

$\displaystyle\int_{2}^{5} (1 + 2x) \, dx$ is the area of the

trapezoid with B = 11, b = 5, and h = 3. The formula for the area is

$$A = \frac{1}{2}(B + b)h.$$

$$A = \frac{1}{2}(11 + 5)(3)$$

$$= 24$$

For Exercises 32—38, readings on the graphs and answers may vary.

32. Read values of the function on the graph for every 2 hr from midnight to 10 P.M. These are the left sides of rectangles with width $\Delta x = 2$.

$$\sum_{i=1}^{12} f(x_i)\Delta x$$

$$A = 3(2) + 3.5(2) + 3.8(2) + 4.2(2)$$
$$+ 5(2) + 6.2(2) + 8(2) + 11(2)$$
$$+ 11.5(2) + 9.5(2) + 6(2) + 4(2)$$
$$\approx 150$$

The total usage on the day is about 150 million kwh.

34. Read values of the function on the graph at every hour from 0 to 7. These are left sides of rectangles with $\Delta x = 1$ as width.

$$\sum_{i=1}^{8} f(x_i)\Delta x$$

$$\approx 0(1) + 1(1) + 2(1) + 3(1) + 3.4(1)$$
$$+ 3.6(1) + 3.2(1) + 2.4(1)$$
$$\approx 18.6$$

The total concentration is about 19 units.

36. Read the value of the function for every 3 sec from x = 3 to x = 18. These are the right sides of rectangles with width $\Delta x = 3$. Then read the function for x = 19, which is the right side of a rectangle with width $\Delta x = 1$.

$$\sum_{i=1}^{7} f(x_i)\Delta x$$

$$\approx 34(3) + 54(3) + 66(3) + 80(3)$$
$$+ 90(3) + 98(3) + 100(1)$$
$$\approx 1366$$

$$\frac{1366}{3600}(5280) \approx 2004$$

The Porsche 928 traveled about 2004 ft.

38. **(a)** Read values of the function on the plain glass graph every 2 hr from 6 to 6. These are at midpoints of the widths $\Delta x = 2$ and represent the heights of the rectangles.

$$f(x_i)\Delta x$$
$$= 132(2) + 215(2) + 150(2) + 44(2)$$
$$+ 34(2) + 26(2) + 12(2)$$
$$\approx 1230 \text{ BTUs}$$

(b) Read values on the ShadeScreen graph every 2 hr from 6 to 6.

$$\sum f(x_i)\Delta x$$
$$= 38(2) + 25(2) + 16(2) + 12(2)$$
$$+ 10(2) + 10(2) + 5(2)$$
$$\approx 230 \text{ BTUs}$$

Exercises 40 and 42 should be solved using computer methods. The solutions will vary depending on the computer program that is used.

40. $f(x) = x \ln x;\ [1, 5]$

The answer is 13.9572.

42. $f(x) = \dfrac{\ln x}{x};\ [1, 5]$

The answer is 1.28857.

Section 6.4

2. $\displaystyle\int_{-4}^{1} 6x\ dx = 6\int_{-4}^{1} x\ dx$

$$= 3 \cdot x^2 \Big|_{-4}^{1}$$

$$= 3[1^2 - (-4)^2]$$
$$= 3(1 - 16)$$
$$= -45$$

4. $\displaystyle\int_{-2}^{2} (4z + 3)\,dz$

$$= 4\int_{-2}^{2} z\ dz + 3\int_{-2}^{2} dz$$

$$= 2z^2 \Big|_{-2}^{2} + 3z \Big|_{-2}^{2}$$

$$= 2[2^2 - (-2)^2] + 3[2 - (-2)]$$

$$= 2(4 - 4) + 3(4)$$
$$= 12$$

6. $\displaystyle\int_{-2}^{3} (-x^2 - 3x + 5)\,dx$

$$= -\int_{-2}^{3} x^2\ dx - 3\int_{-2}^{3} x\ dx + 5\int_{-2}^{3} dx$$

$$= -\frac{1}{3}x^3 \Big|_{-2}^{3} - \frac{3}{2}x^2 \Big|_{-2}^{3} + 5x \Big|_{-2}^{3}$$

$$= -\frac{1}{3}[3^3 - (-2)^3] - \frac{3}{2}[3^2 - (-2)^2]$$
$$+ 5[3 - (-2)]$$

$$= -\frac{1}{3}(27 + 8) - \frac{3}{2}(9 - 4) + 5(5)$$

$$= -\frac{35}{3} - \frac{15}{2} + 25$$

$$= \frac{35}{6}$$

8. $\displaystyle\int_3^9 \sqrt{2r-2}\ dr$

$\displaystyle= \int_3^9 (2r-2)^{1/2}\ dr$

Let $u = 2r - 2$, so that
$\quad du = 2\ dr$.
If $r = 9$, $u = 2 \cdot 9 - 2 = 16$.
If $r = 3$, $u = 2 \cdot 3 - 2 = 4$.

$\displaystyle\int_3^9 (2r-2)^{1/2}\ dr$

$\displaystyle= \frac{1}{2}\int_3^9 (2r-2)^{1/2}\ 2\ dr$

$\displaystyle= \frac{1}{2}\int_4^{16} u^{1/2}\ du$

$\displaystyle= \frac{1}{2} \cdot \frac{u^{3/2}}{3/2}\ \Big|_4^{16}$

$\displaystyle= \frac{1}{3} \cdot u^{3/2}\ \Big|_4^{16}$

$\displaystyle= \frac{1}{3}(16^{3/2} - 4^{3/2})$

$\displaystyle= \frac{1}{3}(64 - 8)$

$\displaystyle= \frac{56}{3}$

10. $\displaystyle\int_0^4 -(3x^{3/2} + x^{1/2})dx$

$\displaystyle= -3\int_0^4 x^{3/2}\ dx - \int_0^4 x^{1/2}\ dx$

$\displaystyle= -3\frac{x^{5/2}}{5/2}\ \Big|_0^4 - \frac{x^{3/2}}{3/2}\ \Big|_0^4$

$\displaystyle= -\frac{6}{5}(32) - \frac{2}{3}(8)$

$\displaystyle= -\frac{192}{5} - \frac{16}{3} = -\frac{656}{15}$

12. $\displaystyle\int_4^9 (4\sqrt{r} - 3r\sqrt{r})dr$

$\displaystyle= 4\int_4^9 r^{1/2}\ dr - 3\int_4^9 r^{3/2}\ dr$

$\displaystyle= 4\frac{r^{3/2}}{3/2}\ \Big|_4^9 - 3\frac{r^{5/2}}{5/2})\ \Big|_4^9$

$\displaystyle= \frac{8}{3}r^{3/2}\ \Big|_4^9 - \frac{6}{5}r^{5/2}\ \Big|_4^9$

$\displaystyle= \frac{8}{3}(27 - 8) - \frac{6}{5}(243 - 32)$

$\displaystyle= \frac{8}{3} \cdot 19 - \frac{6}{5}(211)$

$\displaystyle= \frac{760}{15} - \frac{3798}{15}$

$\displaystyle= -\frac{3038}{15}$

14. $\displaystyle\int_1^4 \frac{-3}{(2p+1)^2}\ dp$

$\displaystyle= -3\int_1^4 (2p+1)^{-2}\ dp$

Let $u = 2p + 1$, so that
$\quad du = 2\ dp$.
If $p = 4$, $u = 2 \cdot 4 + 1 = 9$.
If $p = 1$, $u = 2 \cdot 1 + 1 = 3$.

$\displaystyle-3\int_1^4 (2p+1)^{-2}\ dp$

$\displaystyle= -\frac{3}{2}\int_3^9 u^{-2}\ du$

$\displaystyle= -\frac{3}{2} \cdot \frac{u^{-1}}{-1}\ \Big|_3^9$

$\displaystyle= \frac{3}{2u}\ \Big|_3^9$

$\displaystyle= \frac{3}{18} - \frac{3}{6} = -\frac{1}{3}$

16. $\displaystyle\int_{2}^{3} (3x^{-3} - x^{-4})dx$

$\displaystyle = 3\int_{2}^{3} x^{-3}\, dx - \int_{2}^{3} x^{-4}\, dx$

$\displaystyle = 3\frac{x^{-2}}{-2}\bigg|_{2}^{3} - \frac{x^{-3}}{-3}\bigg|_{2}^{3}$

$\displaystyle = -\frac{3}{2x^2}\bigg|_{2}^{3} + \frac{1}{3x^3}\bigg|_{2}^{3}$

$\displaystyle = -\frac{3}{2}\left(\frac{1}{9} - \frac{1}{4}\right) + \frac{1}{81} - \frac{1}{24}$

$\displaystyle = -\frac{1}{6} + \frac{3}{8} + \frac{1}{81} - \frac{1}{24}$

$\approx .179$

18. $\displaystyle\int_{1}^{2} \left(\frac{-1}{B} + 3e^{.2B}\right)dB$

$\displaystyle = \int_{1}^{2} -\frac{1}{B}\, dB + \frac{3}{.2}\int_{1}^{2} .2e^{.2B}\, dB$

$\displaystyle = -\ln B\bigg|_{1}^{2} + \frac{3}{.2}e^{.2B}\bigg|_{1}^{2}$

$\displaystyle = -\ln 2 + 15e^{.4} - 15e^{.2}$

≈ 3.363

20. $\displaystyle\int_{.5}^{1} \left(p^3 - e^{4p}\right)dp$

$\displaystyle = \int_{.5}^{1} p^3\, dp - \int_{.5}^{1} e^{4p}\, dp$

$\displaystyle = \frac{p^4}{4}\bigg|_{.5}^{1} - \frac{e^{4p}}{4}\bigg|_{.5}^{1}$

$\displaystyle = \frac{1}{4} - \frac{1}{64} - \left(\frac{e^4}{4} - \frac{e^2}{4}\right)$

$\displaystyle = \frac{15}{64} - \frac{e^4}{4} + \frac{e^2}{4}$

≈ -11.568

22. $\displaystyle\int_{0}^{3} m^2(4m^3 + 2)^3\, dm$

Let $u = 4m^3 + 2$ so that,

$\quad du = 12m^2\, dm$ and $\dfrac{1}{12}\, du = m^2\, dm.$

Also,

$\quad$ when $m = 3$, $u = 4(3^3) + 2 = 110$

and

$\quad$ when $m = 0$, $u = 4(0^3) + 2 = 2.$

$\displaystyle \frac{1}{12}\int_{2}^{110} u^3\, du = \frac{1}{12}\cdot\frac{u^4}{4}\bigg|_{2}^{110}$

$\displaystyle = \frac{1}{48}u^4\bigg|_{2}^{110}$

$\displaystyle = \frac{146,410,000}{48} - \frac{16}{48}$

$\displaystyle = \frac{146,409,984}{48}$

$\displaystyle = \frac{9,150,624}{3}$

$\displaystyle = 3,050,208$

24. $\displaystyle\int_{1}^{8} \frac{3 - y^{1/3}}{y^{2/3}}\, dy$

$\displaystyle = \int_{1}^{8} (3y^{-2/3} - y^{-1/3})\, dy$

$\displaystyle = \int_{1}^{8} 3y^{-2/3}\, dy - \int_{1}^{8} y^{-1/3}\, dy$

$\displaystyle = \frac{3y^{1/3}}{1/3}\bigg|_{1}^{8} - \frac{y^{2/3}}{2/3}\bigg|_{1}^{8}$

$\displaystyle = 9y^{1/3}\bigg|_{1}^{8} - \frac{3y^{2/3}}{2}\bigg|_{1}^{8}$

$$= 9(2 - 1) - \frac{3}{2}(4 - 1)$$

$$= 9 - \frac{9}{2}$$

$$= \frac{9}{2}$$

26. $\displaystyle\int_{1}^{3} \frac{\sqrt{\ln x}}{x} \, dx$

Let $u = \ln x$, so that

$$du = \frac{1}{x} \, dx.$$

When $x = 3$, $u = \ln 3$, and
when $x = 1$, $u = \ln 1 = 0$.

$$\int_{0}^{\ln 3} \sqrt{u} \, du = \int_{0}^{\ln 3} u^{1/2} \, du$$

$$= \frac{u^{3/2}}{3/2} \Big|_{0}^{\ln 3}$$

$$= \frac{2}{3} u^{3/2} \Big|_{0}^{\ln 3}$$

$$= \frac{2}{3}(\ln 3)^{3/2} - \frac{2}{3}(0)^{3/2}$$

$$\approx .76767$$

28. $\displaystyle\int_{1}^{2} \frac{3}{x(1 + \ln x)} \, dx$

Let $u = 1 + \ln x$, so that

$$du = \frac{1}{x} \, dx.$$

When $x = 2$, $u = 1 + \ln 2$, and
when $x = 1$, $u = 1 + \ln 1 = 1$.

$$\int_{1}^{1+\ln 2} \frac{3}{u} \, du$$

$$= 3 \ln |u| \Big|_{1}^{1+\ln 2}$$

$$= 3 \ln (1 + \ln 2) - 3 \ln 1$$

$$\approx 1.5798$$

30. $\displaystyle\int_{0}^{1} \frac{e^{2x}}{\sqrt{1 + e^{2x}}} \, dx$

Let $u = 1 + e^{2x}$, so that

$$du = 2e^{2x} \, dx \text{ and } \frac{1}{2} \, du = e^{2x} \, dx.$$

When $x = 1$, $u = 1 + e^2$, and
when $x = 0$, $u = 1 + e^0 = 2$.

$$\frac{1}{2} \int_{2}^{1+e^2} \frac{1}{\sqrt{u}} \, du = \frac{1}{2} \int_{2}^{1+e^2} u^{-1/2} \, du$$

$$= \frac{1}{2} \cdot \frac{u^{1/2}}{1/2} \Big|_{2}^{1+e^2}$$

$$= u^{1/2} \Big|_{2}^{1+e^2}$$

$$= \sqrt{1 + e^2} - \sqrt{2}$$

$$\approx 1.4822$$

32. $\displaystyle\int_{1}^{8} \frac{(1 + x^{1/3})^6}{x^{2/3}} \, dx$

Let $u = 1 + x^{1/3}$, so that

$$du = \frac{1}{3} x^{-2/3} \, dx \text{ and } 3 \, du = \frac{1}{x^{2/3}} \, dx.$$

When $x = 8$, $u = 1 + 8^{1/3} = 3$,
when $x = 1$, $u = 1 + 1^{1/3} = 2$.

$$3 \int_{2}^{3} u^6 \, du = 3 \cdot \frac{u^7}{7} \Big|_{2}^{3}$$

$$= \frac{3}{7} u^7 \Big|_{2}^{3}$$

$$= \frac{3}{7}(3)^7 - \frac{3}{7}(2)^7$$

$$= \frac{3}{7}(2187 - 128) = \frac{6177}{7}$$

$$\approx 882.43$$

34. f(x) = 4x – 7; [5, 10]

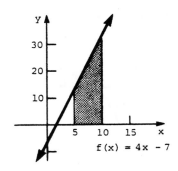

The area of the region is

$$\int_{5}^{10} (4x - 7)dx$$

$$= \left(2x^2 - 7x\right)\Big|_{5}^{10}$$

$$= (200 - 70) - (50 - 35)$$

$$= 115.$$

36. f(x) = 9 – x²; [0, 6]

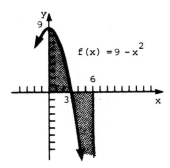

The graph crosses the x-axis at

$$0 = 9 - x^2$$

$$x^2 = 9$$

$$x = \pm 3$$

In the interval, the graph crosses at x = 3.

The area of the region is

$$\int_{0}^{3} (9 - x^2)dx + \left|\int_{3}^{6} (9 - x^2)dx\right|$$

$$= \left(9x - \frac{x^3}{3}\right)\Big|_{0}^{3} + \left|\left(9x - \frac{x^3}{3}\right)\Big|_{3}^{6}\right|$$

$$= (27 - 9) + \left|(54 - 72) - (27 - 9)\right|$$

$$= 18 + \left|-36\right|$$

$$= 18 + 36 = 54.$$

38. f(x) = x² – 6x + 5; [–1, 4]

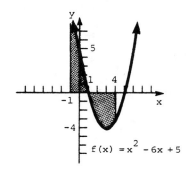

The graph crosses the x-axis at

$$0 = x^2 - 6x + 5$$

$$x = \frac{6 \pm \sqrt{36 - 20}}{2} = \frac{6 \pm 4}{2}$$

$$x = 5 \quad \text{or} \quad x = 1.$$

The area of the region is

$$\int_{-1}^{1} (x^2 - 6x + 5)dx + \left|\int_{1}^{4} (x^2 - 6x + 5)dx\right|$$

$$= \left(\frac{x^3}{3} - 3x^2 + 5x\right)\Big|_{-1}^{1} + \left|\left(\frac{x^3}{3} - 3x^2 + 5x\Big|_{1}^{4}\right)\right|$$

$$= \left(\frac{1}{3} - 3 + 5\right) - \left(-\frac{1}{3} - 3 - 5\right)$$

$$+ \left|\left(\frac{64}{3} - 48 + 20\right) - \left(\frac{1}{3} - 3 + 5\right)\right|$$

$$= \frac{32}{3} + |-9|$$

$$= \frac{32}{3} + 9$$

$$= \frac{59}{3}.$$

40. $f(x) = x^3 - 2x$; $[-2, 4]$

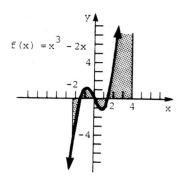

The graph crosses the x-axis at

$$0 = x^3 - 2x$$
$$= x(x^2 - 2)$$

$x = 0$, $x = \sqrt{2}$, and $x = -\sqrt{2}$.
These locations are all in the interval.

The area of the region is

$$\left| \int_{-2}^{-\sqrt{2}} (x^3 - 2x)\,dx \right| + \left| \int_{-\sqrt{2}}^{0} (x^3 - 2x)\,dx \right|$$

$$+ \left| \int_{0}^{-\sqrt{2}} (x^3 - 2x)\,dx \right| + \left| \int_{\sqrt{2}}^{4} (x^3 - 2x)\,dx \right|$$

$$= \left| \left(\frac{x^4}{4} - x^2 \right) \Big|_{-2}^{-\sqrt{2}} \right| + \left| \left(\frac{x^4}{4} - x^2 \right) \Big|_{-\sqrt{2}}^{0} \right|$$

$$+ \left| \left(\frac{x^4}{4} - x^2 \right) \Big|_{0}^{\sqrt{2}} \right| + \left| \left(\frac{x^4}{4} - x^2 \right) \Big|_{\sqrt{2}}^{4} \right|$$

$$= |(1-2)-(4-4)| + |0-(1-2)|$$
$$+ |(1-2)-0 + |(64-16)-1-2)|$$
$$= |-1| + |1| + |-1| + |49|$$
$$= 1 + 1 + 1 + 49$$
$$= 52.$$

42. $f(x) = 1 - e^{-x}$; $[-1, 2]$

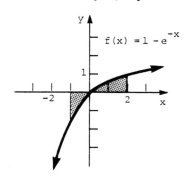

The graph crosses the x-axis at

$$0 = 1 - e^{-x}$$
$$e^{-x} = 1$$
$$-x \ln e = \ln 1$$
$$-x = 0$$
$$x = 0.$$

The area of the region is

$$\left| \int_{-1}^{0} (1 - e^{-x})\,dx \right| + \int_{0}^{2} (1 - e^{-x})\,dx$$

$$= \left| (x + e^{-x}) \Big|_{-1}^{0} \right| + (x + e^{-x}) \Big|_{0}^{2}$$

$$= |(1) - (-1 + e^1)| + (2 + e^{-2}) - (e^0)$$
$$= |2 - e| + 2 + e^{-2} - 1$$
$$= |-.718| + 1 + e^{-2}$$
$$= .718 + 1.135$$
$$= 1.854.$$

44. $f(x) = \frac{1}{x}$; $[e, e^2]$

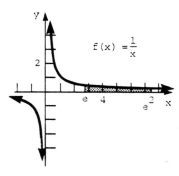

The graph does not cross the x-axis.

$$\int_{e}^{e^2} \frac{1}{x} \, dx = \ln x \Big|_{e}^{e^2}$$

$$= \ln e^2 - \ln e$$

$$= 2 - 1 = 1$$

46. $f(x) = x^2 - 2x$; $[-1, 2]$

From the graph, we see that the total area is

$$\int_{-1}^{0} (x^2 - 2x) \, dx + \left| \int_{0}^{2} (x^2 - 2x) \, dx \right|$$

$$= \left(\frac{x^3}{3} - x^2 \right) \Big|_{-1}^{0} + \left| \left(\frac{x^3}{3} - x^2 \right) \Big|_{0}^{2} \right|$$

$$= -\left(-\frac{1}{3} - 1 \right) + \left| \frac{8}{3} - 4 \right|$$

$$= \frac{4}{3} + \left| -\frac{4}{3} \right|$$

$$= \frac{4}{3} + \frac{4}{3}$$

$$= \frac{8}{3}$$

48. $y = e^x - e$; $[0, 2]$

From the graph, we see that the total area is

$$\left| \int_{0}^{1} (e^x - e) \, dx \right| + \int_{1}^{2} (e^x - e) \, dx$$

$$= \left| (e^x - xe) \Big|_{0}^{1} \right| + (e^x - xe) \Big|_{1}^{2}$$

$$= \left| (e^1 - e) - (e^0 + 0) \right|$$
$$\quad + (e^2 - 2e) - (e^1 - e)$$

$$= |-1| + e^2 - 2e$$

$$= 1 + e^2 - 2e$$

$$\approx 2.9525.$$

50. Let $F'(x) = f(x)$, and hence $F(x)$ is an antiderivative of $f(x)$. Since $kF'(x) = kf(x)$, $kF(x)$ is an antiderivative of $kf(x)$.

$$\int_{a}^{b} kf(x) \, dx = kF(x) \Big|_{a}^{b}$$

$$= kF(b) - kF(a)$$

$$= k[F(b) - F(a)]$$

$$= k \left(F(x) \Big|_{a}^{b} \right)$$

$$= k \int_{a}^{b} f(x) \, dx$$

52. $\int_{-1}^{4} f(x) \, dx$

$$= \int_{-1}^{0} (2x + 3) \, dx + \int_{0}^{4} \left(-\frac{x}{4} - 3 \right) dx$$

$$= (x^2 + 3x) \Big|_{-1}^{0} + \left(-\frac{x^2}{8} - 3x \right) \Big|_{0}^{4}$$

$$= -(1 - 3) + (-2 - 12)$$

$$= 2 - 14$$

$$= -12$$

54. $I'(x) = 100 - x$ is the rate of income per day in hundreds of dollars.

(a) The total income for the first 10 days is

$$\int_{0}^{10} (100 - x) \, dx$$

$$= \left(100x - \frac{x^2}{2} \right) \Big|_{0}^{10}$$

$$= (1000 - 50)$$

$$= 950$$

Since $950(100) = 95,000$, the total income is $95,000.

(b) The total income from the tenth to the twentieth day is:

$$\int_{10}^{20} (100 - x)\,dx$$

$$= \left(100x - \frac{x^2}{2}\right)\Big|_{10}^{20}$$

$$= (2000 - 200) - (1000 - 50)$$

$$= 850$$

that is, $85,000 is earned.

(c) The total income in a days is

$$I(a) = \int_{0}^{a} (100 - x)\,dx$$

$$= \left(100x - \frac{x^2}{2}\right)\Big|_{0}^{a}$$

$$= 100a - \frac{a^2}{2}.$$

If at least $5000, or $50(100)$, is earned,

$$50 \le 100a - \frac{a^2}{2}$$

$$100 \le 200a - a^2.$$

Solve $a^2 - 200a + 100 = 0$.

$$a = \frac{200 \pm \sqrt{200^2 - 4(100)}}{2}$$

$$= \frac{200 \pm \sqrt{39,600}}{2}$$

$$a \approx 199.5 \quad \text{or} \quad a \approx .5$$

To earn at least $5000, the job must last about 1/2 day.

56. $H'(x) = 20 - 2x$ is the rate of change of the number of hours it takes a worker to produce the xth item.

(a) The total number of hours required to produce the first 5 items is

$$\int_{0}^{5} (20 - 2x)\,dx$$

$$= (20x - x^2)\Big|_{0}^{5}$$

$$= 100 - 25$$

$$= 75.$$

It would take 75 hr to produce 5 items.

(b) The total number of hours required to produce the first 10 items is

$$\int_{0}^{10} (20 - 2x)\,dx$$

$$= (20x - x^2)\Big|_{0}^{10}$$

$$= (200 - 100) - (0)$$

$$= 100.$$

It would take 100 hr to produce the first 10 items.

58. The tanker is leaking oil at a rate in barrels per hour of

$$L'(t) = \frac{80 \ln (t + 1)}{t + 1}.$$

(a) $\displaystyle\int_{0}^{24} \frac{80 \ln (t + 1)}{t + 1}\, dt$

Let $u = \ln (t + 1)$ so that

$$du = \frac{1}{t + 1}\, dt.$$

When $t = 24$, $u = \ln 25$. When $t = 0$, $u = \ln 1 = 0$.

$$80 \int_{0}^{\ln 25} u\, du = 80\frac{u^2}{2}\Big|_{0}^{\ln 25}$$

$$= 40u^2 \Big|_{0}^{\ln 25}$$

$$= 40(\ln 25)^2 - 40(0)^2$$

$$\approx 414 \text{ barrels of oil}$$

(b) $\displaystyle\int_{24}^{48} \frac{80 \ln (t + 1)}{t + 1}\, dt$

Let $u = \ln (t + 1)$ so that the limits of integration with respect to u are $\ln 25$ and $\ln 49$.

$$80 \int_{\ln 25}^{\ln 49} u\, du$$

$$= 40u^2 \Big|_{\ln 25}^{\ln 49}$$

$$= 40(\ln 49)^2 - 40(\ln 25)^2$$

$$\approx 191 \text{ barrels of oil}$$

(c) $\displaystyle\lim_{t \to \infty} L'(t)$

$$= \lim_{t \to \infty} \frac{80 \ln (t + 1)}{t + 1} = 0$$

The number of barrels of oil leaking per day is decreasing to 0.

60. Total growth after 2.5 days is

$$\int_{0}^{2.5} R'(x)\, dx$$

$$= \int_{0}^{2.5} 200e^{.2x}\, dx$$

$$= 200\frac{e^{.2x}}{.2}\Big|_{0}^{2.5}$$

$$= 1000e^{.2x}\Big|_{0}^{2.5}$$

$$= 1000e^{.5} - 1000e^{0}$$

$$\approx 648.72$$

62. $s = k(R^2 - r^2)$

(a) $Q(R) = \displaystyle\int_{0}^{R} 2\pi sr\, dr$

$$= \int_{0}^{R} 2\pi k(R^2 - r^2)r\, dr$$

$$= 2\pi k \int_{0}^{R} (R^2 r - r^3)\, dr$$

$$= 2\pi k \left(\frac{R^2 r^2}{2} - \frac{r^4}{4}\right)\Big|_{0}^{R}$$

$$= 2\pi k \left(\frac{R^4}{2} - \frac{R^4}{4}\right)$$

$$= 2\pi k \left(\frac{R^4}{4}\right)$$

$$= \frac{\pi k R^4}{2}$$

(b) $Q(.4) = \dfrac{\pi k(.4)^4}{2}$

$$= .04k \text{ mm/min}$$

64. $P(T) = \int_1^T \left(10t - \dfrac{15}{\sqrt{t}}\right) dt$

$\qquad = \int_1^T (10t - 15t^{-1/2}) dt$

$\qquad = \left. \left(5t^2 - \dfrac{15t^{1/2}}{1/2}\right) \right|_1^T$

$\qquad = (5T^2 - 30T^{1/2}) - (5 - 30)$

$\qquad = 5T^2 - 30\sqrt{T} + 25$ tons

66. $c'(t) = 1.2e^{.04t}$

$\qquad c(T) = \int_0^T 1.2e^{.04t}$

$\qquad\quad = \left. \dfrac{1.2}{.04} e^{.04t} \right|_0^T$

$\qquad\quad = 30(e^{.04T} - e^0)$

$\qquad\quad = 30(e^{.04T} - 1)$

In 5 yr,

$\qquad c(5) = 30(e^{.04(5)} - 1)$

$\qquad\quad = 30(e^{.2} - 1)$

$\qquad\quad \approx 6.64$ billion barrels

Section 6.5

2. $x = 1$, $x = 2$, $y = x^3$, $y = 0$

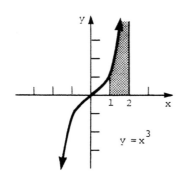

$\int_1^2 (x^3 - 0) dx$

$\qquad = \left. \dfrac{x^4}{4} \right|_1^2$

$\qquad = 4 - \dfrac{1}{4}$

$\qquad = \dfrac{15}{4}$

4. $x = -2$, $x = 0$, $y = 1 - x^2$, $y = 0$

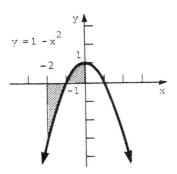

The region is composed of two separate regions in $[-2, 0]$ because $y = 1 - x^2$ intersects $y = 0$ at $x = -1$.

Let $f(x) = 1 - x^2$, $g(x) = 0$.

In interval $[-2, -1]$, $g(x) \geq f(x)$.

In interval $[-1, 0]$, $f(x) \geq g(x)$.

$\int_{-2}^{-1} [0 - (1 - x^2)] dx + \int_{-1}^0 [(1 - x^2) - 0] dx$

$\qquad = \left. \left(-x + \dfrac{x^3}{3}\right) \right|_{-2}^{-1} + \left. \left(x - \dfrac{x^3}{3}\right) \right|_{-1}^0$

$\qquad = \left(1 - \dfrac{1}{3}\right) - \left(2 - \dfrac{8}{3}\right) + 0 - \left(-1 + \dfrac{1}{3}\right)$

$\qquad = 1 - \dfrac{1}{3} - 2 + \dfrac{8}{3} + 1 - \dfrac{1}{3}$

$\qquad = 2$

6. x = 0, x = 6, y = 5x, y = 3x + 10

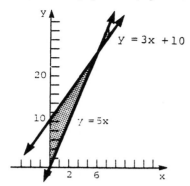

To find the intersection of y = 5x
and y = 3x + 10, substitute for y.

$$5x = 3x + 10$$
$$2x = 10$$
$$x = 5$$

If x = 5, y = 5(5) = 25.

The region is composed of two
separate regions because y = 5x
and y = 3x + 10 intersect at
x = 5 (that is, (5, 25)).

Let f(x) = 3x + 10, g(x) = 5x.

In interval [0, 5], f(x) ≥ g(x).

In interval [5, 6], g(x) ≥ f(x).

$$\int_0^5 (3x + 10 - 5x)\,dx + \int_5^6 [5x - (3x + 10)]\,dx$$

$$= \int_0^5 (-2x + 10)\,dx + \int_5^6 (2x - 10)\,dx$$

$$= \left(\frac{-2x^2}{2} + 10x\right)\Big|_0^5 + \left(\frac{2x^2}{2} - 10x\right)\Big|_5^6$$

$$= (-x^2 + 10x)\Big|_0^5 + (x^2 - 10x)\Big|_5^6$$

$$= -25 + 50 + (36 - 60) - (25 - 50)$$

$$= 26$$

8. y = x² - 18, y = x - 6

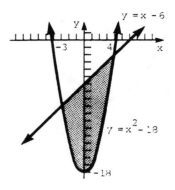

Find the intersection points.

$$x^2 - 18 = x - 6$$
$$x^2 - x - 12 = 0$$
$$(x - 4)(x + 3) = 0$$

The curves intersect at x = -3 and
x = 4.

$$\int_{-3}^4 [(x - 6) - (x^2 - 18)]\,dx$$

$$= \int_{-3}^4 (x - 6 - x^2 + 18)\,dx$$

$$= \int_{-3}^4 (-x^2 + x + 12)\,dx$$

$$= \left(\frac{-x^3}{3} + \frac{x^2}{2} + 12x\right)\Big|_{-3}^4$$

$$= \left(\frac{-64}{3} + 8 + 48\right) - \left(9 + \frac{9}{2} - 36\right)$$

$$= \left(\frac{-64}{3} + 56\right) - \left(-27 + \frac{9}{2}\right)$$

$$= \frac{-64}{3} + 83 - \frac{9}{2}$$

$$= \frac{343}{6}$$

$$\approx 57.167$$

10. $y = x^2$, $y = x^3$

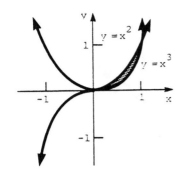

Find the intersection points.

$$x^2 = x^3$$
$$x^2 - x^3 = 0$$
$$x^2(1 - x) = 0$$

The curves intersect at $x = 0$ and $x = 1$.

In the interval $[0, 1]$ $x^2 > x^3$.

$$\int_0^1 (x^2 - x^3)dx = \left(\frac{x^3}{3} - \frac{x^4}{4}\right)\Big|_0^1$$
$$= \frac{1}{3} - \frac{1}{4}$$
$$= \frac{1}{12}$$

12. $x = 0$, $x = 4$, $y = \dfrac{1}{x + 1}$, $y = \dfrac{x - 1}{2}$

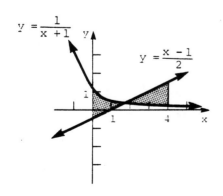

Find the intersection points.

$$\frac{1}{x + 1} = \frac{x - 1}{2}$$
$$x^2 - 1 = 2$$
$$x^2 - 3 = 0$$

In the interval $[0, 4]$, the only intersection point is at $x = \sqrt{3}$.

$$\int_0^{\sqrt{3}}\left(\frac{1}{x + 1} - \frac{x - 1}{2}\right)dx$$
$$+ \int_{\sqrt{3}}^4 \left(\frac{x - 1}{2} - \frac{1}{x + 1}\right)dx$$
$$= \left(\ln|x + 1| - \frac{x^2}{4} + \frac{x}{2}\right)\Big|_0^{\sqrt{3}}$$
$$+ \left(\frac{x^2}{4} - \frac{x}{2} - \ln|x + 1|\right)\Big|_{\sqrt{3}}^4$$
$$= \ln(\sqrt{3} + 1) - \frac{3}{4} + \frac{\sqrt{3}}{2}$$
$$+ \left\{(4 - 2 - \ln 5)\right.$$
$$\left. - \left[\frac{3}{4} - \frac{\sqrt{3}}{2} - \ln(\sqrt{3} + 1)\right]\right\}$$
$$= \ln(\sqrt{3} + 1) - \frac{3}{4} + \frac{\sqrt{3}}{2} + 2$$
$$- \ln 5 - \frac{3}{4} + \frac{\sqrt{3}}{2} + \ln(\sqrt{3} + 1)$$
$$= \ln(\sqrt{3} + 1) + \ln(\sqrt{3} + 1)$$
$$- \ln 5 + \frac{1}{2} + \sqrt{3}$$
$$= \ln\frac{(\sqrt{3} + 1)^2}{5} + \frac{1}{2} + \sqrt{3}$$
$$\approx 2.633$$

14. $x = -1$, $x = 2$, $y = e^{-x}$, $y = e^x$.

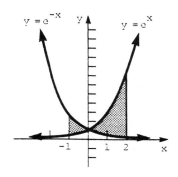

The total area between the curves from $x = -1$ to $x = 2$ is

$$\int_{-1}^{0} (e^{-x} - e^x)dx + \int_{0}^{2} (e^x - e^{-x})dx$$

$$= (-e^{-x} - e^x)\Big|_{-1}^{0} + (e^x + e^{-x})\Big|_{0}^{2}$$

$$= \left[(-1 - 1) - (-e - e^{-1})\right] + \left[(e^2 + e^{-2}) - (1 + 1)\right]$$

$$= -4 + e + \frac{1}{e} + e^2 + \frac{1}{e^2}$$

$$\approx 6.6106.$$

16. $x = 2$, $x = 4$, $y = \frac{x}{2} + 3$, $y = \frac{1}{x - 1}$

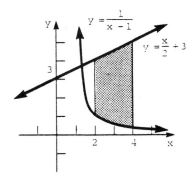

Find the intersection points in $[2, 4]$.

$$\frac{x}{2} + 3 = \frac{1}{x - 1}$$

$$\frac{x + 6}{2} = \frac{1}{x - 1}$$

$$x^2 + 5x - 6 = 2$$

$$x^2 + 5x - 4 = 0$$

$$x = \frac{-5 \pm \sqrt{25 + 4(4)}}{2}$$

$$= \frac{-5 \pm \sqrt{41}}{2}$$

$$x = .7 \quad \text{or} \quad x = -5.7$$

There are no intersection points in the interval.

$$\frac{x}{2} + 3 \geq \frac{1}{x - 1} \text{ in } [2, 4].$$

$$\int_{2}^{4} \left[\left(\frac{x}{2} + 3\right) - \left(\frac{1}{x - 1}\right)\right] dx$$

$$= \left(\frac{x^2}{4} + 3x - \ln|x - 1|\right)\Big|_{2}^{4}$$

$$= (4 + 12 - \ln 3) - (1 + 6 - 0)$$

$$= 16 - \ln 3 - 7$$

$$= 9 - \ln 3$$

$$\approx 7.901$$

18. $y = 2x^3 + x^2 + x + 5$,

$y = x^3 + x^2 + 2x + 5$

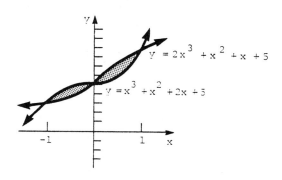

To find the points of intersection, substitute for y.

$$2x^3 + x^2 + x + 5 = x^3 + x^2 + 2x + 5$$
$$x^3 - x = 0$$
$$x(x^2 - 1) = 0$$

The points of intersection are at $x = 0$, $x = -1$, and $x = 1$.

The area of the region between the curves is

$$\int_{-1}^{0} [(2x^3 + x^2 + x + 5) - (x^3 + x^2 + 2x + 5)]\,dx$$

$$+ \int_{0}^{1} [(x^3 + x^2 + 2x + 5) - (2x^3 + x^2 + x + 5)]\,dx$$

$$= \int_{-1}^{0} (x^3 - x)\,dx + \int_{0}^{1} (-x^3 + x)\,dx$$

$$= \left(\frac{x^4}{4} - \frac{x^2}{2}\right)\Big|_{-1}^{0} + \left(-\frac{x^4}{4} + \frac{x^2}{2}\right)\Big|_{0}^{1}$$

$$= \left[0 - \left(\frac{1}{4} - \frac{1}{2}\right)\right] + \left[\left(-\frac{1}{4} + \frac{1}{2}\right) - 0\right]$$

$$= \frac{1}{4} + \frac{1}{4}$$

$$= \frac{1}{2}.$$

20. $y = x^5 - 2\ln(x + 5)$,
$y = x^3 - 2\ln(x + 5)$

To find the points of intersection, substitute for y.

$$x^5 - 2\ln(x + 5) = x^3 - 2\ln(x + 5)$$
$$x^5 - x^3 = 0$$
$$x^3(x^2 - 1) = 0$$

The points of intersection are at $x = 0$ and $x = 1$ and $x = -1$.

In the interval $[-1, 0]$,

$$x^5 - 2\ln(x + 5) > x^3 - 2\ln(x + 5).$$

In the interval $[0, 1]$,

$$x^5 - 2\ln(x + 5) < x^3 - 2\ln(x + 5).$$

The area between the curves is

$$\int_{-1}^{0} [(x^5 - 2\ln(x + 5)) - (x^3 - 2\ln(x + 5))]\,dx$$

$$+ \int_{0}^{1} [(x^3 - 2\ln(x + 5)) - (x^5 - 2\ln(x + 5))]\,dx$$

$$= \int_{-1}^{0} (x^5 - x^3)\,dx + \int_{0}^{1} (x^3 - x^5)\,dx$$

$$= \left(\frac{x^6}{6} - \frac{x^4}{4}\right)\Big|_{-1}^{0} + \left(\frac{x^4}{4} - \frac{x^6}{6}\right)\Big|_{0}^{1}$$

$$= \left[0 - \left(\frac{1}{6} - \frac{1}{4}\right)\right] + \left[\left(\frac{1}{4} - \frac{1}{6}\right) - 0\right]$$

$$= \frac{1}{12} + \frac{1}{12}$$

$$= \frac{1}{6}.$$

22. $y = \sqrt{x}$, $y = x\sqrt{x}$

To find the points of intersection, substitute for y.

$$\sqrt{x} = x\sqrt{x}$$
$$x\sqrt{x} - \sqrt{x} = 0$$
$$\sqrt{x}(x - 1) = 0$$

The points of intersection are at $x = 0$ and $x = 1$.

In $[0, 1]$, $\sqrt{x} > x\sqrt{x}$.

The area between the curves is

$$\int_0^1 (\sqrt{x} - x\sqrt{x})\,dx$$

$$= \int_0^1 (x^{1/2} - x^{3/2})\,dx$$

$$= \left(\frac{x^{3/2}}{3/2} - \frac{x^{5/2}}{5/2}\right)\Bigg|_0^1$$

$$= \left(\frac{2}{3}x^{3/2} - \frac{2}{5}x^{5/2}\right)\Bigg|_0^1$$

$$= \left[\frac{2}{3}(1) - \frac{2}{5}(1)\right] - 0$$

$$= \frac{4}{15}.$$

24. **(a)** $S(x) = C(x)$

$$-x^2 + 4x + 8 = \frac{3}{25}x^2$$

$$-25x^2 + 100x + 200 = 3x^2$$

$$0 = 28x^2 - 100x - 200$$

$$0 = 7x^2 - 25x - 50$$

$$0 = (7x + 10)(x - 5)$$

$$x = -\frac{10}{7} \quad \text{or} \quad x = 5$$

Since time would not be negative, 5 is the only solution.
It will pay to use the device for 5 yr.

(b) The total savings over 5 yr will be

$$\int_0^5 (-x^2 + 4x + 8)\,dx$$

$$= \left(\frac{-x^3}{3} + 2x^2 + 8x\right)\Bigg|_0^5$$

$$= \frac{-125}{3} + 90$$

$$= 48.33.$$

The total cost over 5 yr will be

$$\int_0^5 \frac{3}{25}x^2\,dx = \frac{x^3}{25}\Bigg|_0^5 = 5.$$

Net savings = \$48.33 - \$5

= \$43.33 millions

26. **(a)** It will no longer be profitable when $C(t) > R(t)$.
Find t when $C(t) > R(t)$.

$$.3e^{t/2} > 104 - .4e^{t/2}$$

$$.7e^{t/2} > 104$$

$$e^{t/2} > \frac{104}{.7}$$

$$\ln e^{t/2} > \ln\left(\frac{104}{.7}\right)$$

$$t > 2\ln\left(\frac{104}{.7}\right)$$

$$t > 10 \text{ yr}$$

(b) The total net savings is

$$\int_0^{10} [(104 - .4e^{t/2}) - .3e^{t/2}]\,dt$$

$$= \int_0^{10} (104 - .7e^{t/2})\,dt$$

$$= \left(104t - \frac{.7e^{t/2}}{1/2}\right)\Bigg|_0^{10}$$

$$= (104t - 1.4e^{t/2})\Bigg|_0^{10}$$

$$= [(1040 - 1.4e^5) - (0 - 1.4)]$$

$$= 1041.4 - 1.4e^5$$

$$\approx 834 \text{ thousand dollars.}$$

28. $S(q) = 100 + 3q^{3/2} + q^{5/2}$, equilibrium quantity is $q = 9$.

Producers' surplus is $\int_0^{q_0} [p_0 - S(q)]dq$.

$p_0 = S(9) = 424$

$\int_0^9 [424 - (100 + 3q^{3/2} + q^{5/2})]dq$

$= \int_0^9 (324 - 3q^{3/2} - q^{5/2})dq$

$= \left(324q - \frac{6}{5}q^{5/2} - \frac{2}{7}q^{7/2}\right)\Big|_0^9$

$= \left[\left(324(9) - \frac{6}{5}(9)^{5/2} - \frac{2}{7}(9)^{7/2}\right) - 0\right]$

$= 2916 - \frac{1458}{5} - \frac{4374}{7}$

$= 1999.54$

30. $D(q) = \dfrac{16,000}{(2q + 8)^3}$, equilibrium quantity is $q = 6$.

Consumers' surplus $= \int_0^{q_0} [D(q) - p_0]dq$.

$p_0 = D(6) = \dfrac{16,000}{20^3} = 2$

$\int_0^6 \left[\dfrac{16,000}{(2q + 8)^3} - 2\right]dq$

$= \int_0^6 \dfrac{16,000}{(2q + 8)^3}\,dq - \int_0^6 2\,dq$

Let $u = 2q + 8$ so that

$du = 2\,dq$ and $\frac{1}{2}\,du = dq$.

$= \frac{1}{2}\int_8^{20} \dfrac{16,000}{u^3}\,du - \int_0^6 2\,dq$

$= 8000\int_8^{20} u^{-3}\,du - \int_0^6 2\,dq$

$= 8000 \cdot \dfrac{u^{-2}}{-2}\Big|_8^{20} - 2q\Big|_0^6$

$= \dfrac{-4000}{u^2}\Big|_8^{20} - 2q\Big|_0^6$

$= \left(\dfrac{-4000}{400} + \dfrac{4000}{64}\right) - 12$

$= -10 + 62.5 - 12$

$= 40.5$

32. **(a)** $S(q) = q^2 + \dfrac{11}{4}q$

$D(q) = 150 - q^2$

The graphs of the supply and demand functions are parabolas with vertices at $\left(-\dfrac{11}{8}, -\dfrac{121}{64}\right)$ and $(0, 150)$, respectively.

To find where the graphs interest, substitute for y.

$q^2 + \dfrac{11}{4}q = 150 - q^2$

$2q^2 + \dfrac{11}{4} - 150 = 0$

$8q^2 + 11q - 600 = 0$

$q = \dfrac{-11 \pm \sqrt{121 - 4(8)(-600)}}{2(8)}$

$q = 8 \quad \text{or} \quad q = \dfrac{-150}{16}$

Disregard the negative solution.

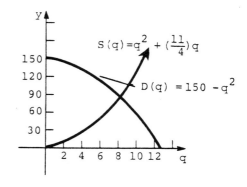

(b) The supply and demand are in equilibrium at q = 8.

$S(8) = 8^2 + \frac{11}{4}(8) = 86.$ (Also,

$D(8) = 150 - 8^2 = 86.$)

The point at which supply and demand are in equilibrium is (8, 86).

(c) Consumers' surplus

$$= \int_0^{q_0} [D(q) - p_0]dq$$

$$p_0 = D(8) = 86$$

$$\int_0^8 [(150 - q^2) - 86]dq$$

$$= \int_0^8 (64 - q^2)dq$$

$$= \left(64q - \frac{1}{3}q^3\right)\Big|_0^8$$

$$= 512 - \frac{512}{3} = \frac{1024}{3}$$

(d) Producers' surplus

$$= \int_0^{q_0} [p_0 - S(q)]dq$$

$$p_0 = S(8) = 86$$

$$\int_0^8 \left[86 - \left(q^2 + \frac{11}{4}q\right)\right]dq$$

$$= \int_0^8 \left(86 - q^2 - \frac{11}{4}q\right)dq$$

$$= 86q - \frac{1}{3}q^3 - \frac{11}{8}q^2\Big|_0^8$$

$$= 688 - \frac{512}{3} - 88$$

$$= \frac{1288}{3}$$

34. $y = \sqrt{x}, \ y = \frac{x}{2}$

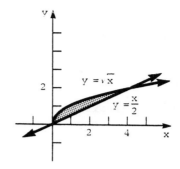

To find the points of intersection, substitute for y.

$$\sqrt{x} = \frac{x}{2}$$

$$\frac{x}{2} - \sqrt{x} = 0$$

$$x - 2\sqrt{x} = 0$$

$$\sqrt{x}(\sqrt{x} - 2) = 0$$

$$x = 0 \quad \text{or} \quad x = 4$$

$$\text{Area} = \int_0^4 \left(\sqrt{x} - \frac{x}{2}\right)dx$$

$$= \int_0^4 \left(x^{1/2} - \frac{x}{2}\right)dx$$

$$= \left(\frac{2}{3}x^{3/2} - \frac{1}{4}x^2\right)\Big|_0^4$$

$$= \frac{16}{3} - 4$$

$$= \frac{4}{3}$$

For Exercises 36 and 38, use computer methods. The solutions will vary depending on the computer program used.

36. y = ln x and y = 4 − x²; [2, 4]

The answer is 12.83.

38. $y = \sqrt{4 - 4x^2}$ and $y = \sqrt{\dfrac{9 - x^2}{3}}$;

[-1, 1]

The answer is .2585.

Chapter 6   Review Exercises

6. $\displaystyle\int (-4)\,dx = -4x + C$

8. $\displaystyle\int (5x - 1)\,dx = \dfrac{5x^2}{2} - x + C$

10. $\displaystyle\int (6 - x^2)\,dx = 6x - \dfrac{x^3}{3} + C$

12. $\displaystyle\int \dfrac{\sqrt{x}}{2}\,dx = \int \dfrac{1}{2}x^{1/2}\,dx$

$\qquad = \dfrac{\frac{1}{2}x^{3/2}}{3/2} + C$

$\qquad = \dfrac{x^{3/2}}{3} + C$

14. $\displaystyle\int (2x^{4/3} + x^{-1/2})\,dx$

$\qquad = \dfrac{2x^{7/3}}{7/3} + \dfrac{x^{1/2}}{1/2} + C$

$\qquad = \dfrac{6x^{7/3}}{7} + 2x^{1/2} + C$

16. $\displaystyle\int \dfrac{5}{x^4}\,dx = \int 5x^{-4}\,dx$

$\qquad = \dfrac{5x^{-3}}{-3} + C$

$\qquad = -\dfrac{5}{3x^3} + C$

18. $\displaystyle\int 5e^{-x}\,dx = -5e^{-x} + C$

20. $\displaystyle\int \dfrac{-4}{x + 2}\,dx = -4\ln|x + 2| + C$

22. $\displaystyle\int 2xe^{x^2}\,dx = e^{x^2} + C$

24. $\displaystyle\int \dfrac{-x}{2 - x^2}\,dx = -\dfrac{1}{2}\int \dfrac{-2x\,dx}{2 - x^2}$

Let $u = 2 - x^2$ so that

$du = -2x\,dx.$

$\qquad = -\dfrac{1}{2}\int \dfrac{du}{u}$

$\qquad = -\dfrac{1}{2}\ln|u| + C$

$\qquad = -\dfrac{1}{2}\ln|2 - x^2| + C$

26. $\displaystyle\int (x^2 - 5x)^4(2x - 5)\,dx$

Let $u = x^2 - 5x$ so that

$du = (2x - 5)\,dx$

$\displaystyle\int (x^2 - 5x)^4(2x - 5)\,dx$

$\qquad = \int u^4\,du$

$\qquad = \dfrac{u^5}{5} + C$

$\qquad = \dfrac{(x^2 - 5x)^5}{5} + C$

28. $\displaystyle\int \dfrac{12(2x + 9)}{x^2 + 9x + 1}\,dx$

Let $u = x^2 + 9x + 1$ so that

$du = (2x + 9)\,dx.$

$\qquad = \int \dfrac{12(2x + 9)}{x^2 + 9x + 1}\,dx$

$\qquad = 12\int \dfrac{du}{u} = 12\ln|u| + C$

$\qquad = 12\ln|x^2 + 9x + 1| + C$

30. $\displaystyle\int e^{3x^2+4}x\ dx$

Let $u = 3x^2 + 4$ so that

$du = 6x\ dx.$

$\displaystyle\int e^{3x^2+4}x\ dx = \frac{1}{6}\int (6x)(e^{3x^2})dx$

$\displaystyle = \frac{1}{6}\int e^u\ du$

$\displaystyle = \frac{1}{6}e^u + C$

$\displaystyle = \frac{e^{3x^2+4}}{6} + C$

32. $\displaystyle\int e^{-4x}\ dx$

Let $u = -4x$ so that

$du = -4\ dx.$

$\displaystyle\int e^{-4x}\ dx = -\frac{1}{4}\int -4e^{-4x}\ dx$

$\displaystyle = -\frac{1}{4}\int e^u\ du$

$\displaystyle = \frac{-e^u}{4} + C$

$\displaystyle = \frac{-e^{-4x}}{4} + C$

34. $f(x) = 3x + 1$, $x_1 = -1$, $x_2 = 0$,
$x_3 = 1$, $x_4 = 2$, $x_5 = 3$

$f(x_1) = -2$, $f(x_2) = 1$, $f(x_3) = 4$,
$f(x_4) = 7$, $f(x_5) = 10$

So

$\displaystyle\sum_{i=1}^{5} f(x_i)$

$= f(1) + f(2) + f(3) + f(4) + f(5)$

$= -2 + 1 + 4 + 7 + 10$

$= 20$

36. $\displaystyle\int_0^4 (2x + 3)dx$

Graph $y = 2x + 3$.

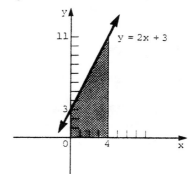

$\displaystyle\int_0^4 (2x + 3)dx$ is the area of a

trapezoid with $B = 11$, $b = 3$, $h = 4$.
The formula for the area is

$A = \frac{1}{2}(B + b)h.$

$A = \frac{1}{2}(11 + 3)(4)$

$A = 28$

so

$\displaystyle\int_0^4 (2x + 3)dx = 28.$

38. $\displaystyle\int_1^2 (3x^2 + 5)dx = \left(\frac{3x^3}{3} + 5x\right)\Big|_1^2$

$= (2^3 + 10) - (1 + 5)$

$= 18 - 6$

$= 12$

40. $\displaystyle\int_1^5 (3x^{-2} + x^{-3})\,dx$

$\displaystyle= \left(\frac{3x^{-1}}{-1} + \frac{x^{-2}}{-2}\right)\Big|_1^5$

$\displaystyle= \left(-\frac{3}{5} - \frac{1}{50}\right) - \left(-3 - \frac{1}{2}\right)$

$\displaystyle= \frac{-31}{50} + \frac{7}{2}$

$\displaystyle= \frac{-31 + 175}{50}$

$\displaystyle= \frac{144}{50}$

$\displaystyle= \frac{72}{25} \approx 2.88$

42. $\displaystyle\int_1^3 2x^{-1}\,dx = 2\int_1^3 \frac{dx}{x}$

$\displaystyle= 2\ln|x|\Big|_1^3$

$= 2\ln 3 - 2\ln 1$

$= 2\ln 3 \quad\text{or}\quad \ln 9$

≈ 2.1972

44. $\displaystyle\int_0^4 2e^x\,dx = 2e^x\Big|_0^4$

$= 2e^4 - 2e^0$

$= 2e^4 - 2$

≈ 107.1963

46. $\displaystyle\int_{\sqrt{5}}^5 2x\sqrt{x^2 - 3}\,dx$

Let $u = x^2 - 3$ so that

$\quad du = 2x\,dx.$

When $x = 5$, $u = 22$. When $x = \sqrt{5}$, $u = 2$.

$\displaystyle= \int_2^{22} \sqrt{u}\,du = \int_2^{22} u^{1/2}\,du$

$\displaystyle= \frac{u^{3/2}}{3/2}\Big|_2^{22} = \frac{2}{3}u^{3/2}\Big|_2^{22}$

$\displaystyle= \frac{2}{3}(22^{3/2}) - \frac{2}{3}(2^{3/2})$

≈ 66.907

48. $f(x) = x\sqrt{x - 1}$; $[1, 10]$

$\displaystyle\text{Area} = \int_1^{10} x\sqrt{x - 1}\,dx$

$\displaystyle= \int_1^{10} x(x - 1)^{1/2}\,dx$

Let $u = x - 1$ so that

$\quad du = dx$ and $x = u + 1$.

When $x = 10$, $u = 9$. When $x = 1$, $u = 0$.

$\displaystyle= \int_0^9 (u + 1)u^{1/2}\,du$

$\displaystyle= \int_0^9 (u^{3/2} + u^{1/2})\,du$

$\displaystyle= \left(\frac{2}{5}u^{5/2} + \frac{2}{3}u^{3/2}\right)\Big|_0^9$

$\displaystyle= \left[\frac{2}{5}(9^{5/2}) + \frac{2}{3}(9^{3/2})\right] - 0$

$\displaystyle= \frac{486}{5} + 18 = \frac{576}{5}$

50. $\displaystyle\int_0^2 e^x\,dx = e^x\Big|_0^2$

$= e^2 - e^0$

$= e^2 - 1$

≈ 6.3891

52. $f(x) = 5 - x^2$, $g(x) = x^2 - 3$

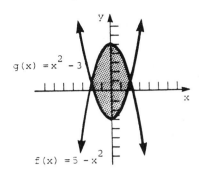

Points of intersection:

$$5 - x^2 = x^2 - 3$$
$$2x^2 - 8 = 0$$
$$2(x^2 - 4) = 0$$
$$x = \pm 2$$

Since $f(x) \geq g(x)$ in $[-2, 2]$, the area between the graphs is

$$\int_{-2}^{2} [f(x) - g(x)]\,dx$$

$$= \int_{-2}^{2} [(5 - x^2) - (x^2 - 3)]\,dx$$

$$= \int_{-2}^{2} (-2x^2 + 8)\,dx$$

$$= \left(\frac{-2x^3}{3} + 8x\right)\Bigg|_{-2}^{2}$$

$$= -\frac{2}{3}(8) + 16 + \frac{2}{3}(-8) - 8(-2)$$

$$= \frac{-32}{3} + 32$$

$$= \frac{64}{3}.$$

54. $f(x) = x^2 - 4x$, $g(x) = x + 1$, $x = 2$, $x = 4$

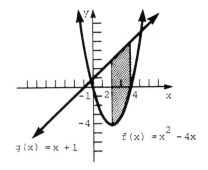

$g(x) > f(x)$ in the interval $[2, 4]$.

$$\int_{2}^{4} [(x + 1) - (x^2 - 4x)]\,dx$$

$$= \int_{2}^{4} (x + 1 - x^2 + 4x)\,dx$$

$$= \int_{2}^{4} (5x + 1 - x^2)\,dx$$

$$= \left(\frac{5x^2}{2} + x - \frac{x^3}{3}\right)\Bigg|_{2}^{4}$$

$$= \left(\frac{5}{2}(4)^2 + 4 - \frac{(4)^3}{3}\right)$$
$$\quad - \left(\frac{5}{2}(2)^2 + 2 - \frac{(2)^3}{3}\right)$$

$$= \left(40 + 4 - \frac{64}{3}\right) - \left(10 + 2 - \frac{8}{3}\right)$$

$$= \frac{40}{3}$$

58. $C'(x) = 2x + 3x^2$; 2 units cost \$12.

$$C(x) = \int (2x + 3x^2)\,dx$$

$$C(x) = x^2 + x^3 + k$$

If $x = 2$, $C(2) = 12$.

So $12 = (2)^2 + (2)^3 + k$

$\quad k = 0$.

Thus, $C(x) = x^2 + x^3$.

60. $C(x) = \dfrac{1}{x + 1}$; fixed cost is \$18.

$$C(x) = \int \frac{dx}{x + 1}$$

$$C(x) = \ln |x + 1| + k$$

If $x = 0$, $C(x) = 18$.

So $18 = \ln |1| + k$

$$k = 18.$$

Thus, $C(x) = \ln |x + 1| + 18$.

62. Total amount

$$= \int_0^t 100,000 e^{.03t}\, dt$$

$$= \frac{100,000 e^{.03t}}{.03}\Bigg|_0^t$$

$$= \frac{10,000,000}{3}(e^{.03t} - 1)$$

Set this expression equal to
4,000,000.

$$\frac{10,000,000}{3}(e^{.03t} - 1) = 4,000,000$$

$$e^{.03t} - 1 = 1.2$$

$$.03t = \ln 2.2$$

$$t \approx 26.3 \text{ yr}$$

64. $S(q) = q^2 + 5q + 100$

$D(q) = 350 - q^2$

$S(q) = D(q)$ at the equilibrium
point.

$$q^2 + 5q + 100 = 350 - q^2$$
$$2q^2 + 5q - 250 = 0$$
$$(-2q + 25)(q - 10) = 0$$
$$q = \frac{-25}{2} \quad \text{or} \quad q = 10$$

Since the number of units produced
would not be negative, the equilibrium point occurs when $q = 10$.

Equilibrium supply

$$= (10)^2 + 5(10) + 100 = 250$$

Equilibrium demand

$$= 350 - (10)^2 = 250$$

(a) Producers' surplus

$$= \int_0^{10} [250 - (q^2 + 5q + 100)]\,dx$$

$$= \int_0^{10} (-q^2 - 5q + 150)\,dx$$

$$= \left(\frac{-q^3}{3} - \frac{5q^2}{2} + 150q\right)\Bigg|_0^{10}$$

$$= \frac{-1000}{3} - \frac{500}{2} + 1500$$

$$= \frac{\$2750}{3}$$

$$\approx \$916.67$$

(b) Consumers' surplus

$$= \int_0^{10} [(350 - q^2) - 250]\,dx$$

$$= \int_0^{10} (100 - q^2)\,dx$$

$$= \left(100q - \frac{q^3}{3}\right)\Bigg|_0^{10}$$

$$= 1000 - \frac{1000}{3}$$

$$= \frac{\$2000}{3}$$

$$\approx \$666.67$$

66. $y' = 100 - \sqrt{2.4t + 1}$

The total number of spiders in the first ten months is

$$\int_0^{10} (100 - \sqrt{2.4t + 1})\,dt,$$

where t is the time in months.

$$= \int_0^{10} 100\,dt - \int_0^{10} (2.4t + 1)^{1/2}\,dt$$

Let $u = 2.4t + 1$ so that $du = 2.4\,dt$ and $\frac{1}{2.4}\,du = dt$

When $t = 10$, $u = 25$. When $t = 0$, $u = 1$.

$$= \int_0^{10} 100\,dt - \frac{1}{2.4}\int_1^{25} u^{1/2}\,du$$

$$= 100t\Big|_0^{10} - \frac{5}{12} \cdot \frac{u^{3/2}}{3/2}\Big|_1^{25}$$

$$= 1000 - \frac{5}{18}u^{3/2}\Big|_1^{25}$$

$$= 1000 - \frac{5}{18}(125) + \frac{5}{18}$$

$$= 1000 - \frac{310}{9}$$

$$\approx 965.56$$

68. $v(t) = t^2 - 2t$

$$s(t) = \int_0^t (t^2 - 2t)\,dt$$

$$s(t) = \frac{t^3}{3} - t^2 + s_0$$

If $t = 3$, $s = 8$.

$$8 = 9 - 9 + s_0$$

$$8 = s_0$$

Thus, $s(t) = \frac{t^3}{3} - t^2 + 8$.

**CHAPTER 7 FURTHER TECHNIQUES AND
APPLICATIONS OF INTEGRATION**

Section 7.1

2. $\int (x + 1)e^x \, dx$

Let $dv = e^x \, dx$ and $u = x + 1$.

Then $v = \int e^x \, dx$ and $du = dx$.

$\qquad v = e^x + C$

Use the formula

$$\int u \, dv = uv - \int v \, du.$$

$\int (x + 1)e^x \, dx = (x + 1)e^x - \int e^x \, dx$

$\qquad\qquad = xe^x + e^x - e^x + C$

$\qquad\qquad = xe^x + C$

4. $\int (6x + 3)e^{-2x} \, dx$

Let $dv = e^{-2x} \, dx$ and $u = 6x + 3$.

Then $v = \int e^{-2x} \, dx$ and $du = 6 \, dx$.

$\qquad v = \dfrac{e^{-2x}}{-2} + C$

$\int (6x + 3)e^{-2x} \, dx$

$\quad = \dfrac{(6x + 3)e^{-2x}}{-2} - \int \dfrac{6e^{-2x}}{-2} \, dx$

$\quad = -\dfrac{1}{2}(6x + 3)e^{-2x} + \dfrac{3e^{-2x}}{-2} + C$

$\quad = -\dfrac{1}{2}(6x + 3)e^{-2x} - \dfrac{3}{2}e^{-2x} + C$

6. $\displaystyle\int_0^1 \dfrac{1 - x}{3e^x} \, dx = \dfrac{1}{3} \int_0^1 (1 - x)e^{-x} \, dx$

Let $dv = e^{-x} \, dx$ and $u = 1 - x$.

Then $v = -e^{-x}$ and $du = -dx$.

$\dfrac{1}{3} \int (1 - x)e^{-x} \, dx$

$\quad = \dfrac{1}{3}\Big[-(1 - x)e^{-x} - \int e^{-x} \, dx\Big]$

$\quad = \dfrac{1}{3}\Big[-(1 - x)e^{-x} + e^{-x}\Big]$

$\quad = \dfrac{1}{3}xe^{-x}$

$\displaystyle\int_0^1 (1 - x)e^{-x} \, dx = \dfrac{1}{3}xe^{-x}\Big|_0^1$

$\qquad\qquad\qquad = \dfrac{1}{3e} \approx .123$

8. $\displaystyle\int_1^2 \ln 5x \, dx$

Let $dv = dx$ and $u = \ln 5x$.

Then $v = x$ and $du = \dfrac{1}{x} \, dx$.

$\int \ln 5x \, dx = x \ln 5x - \int x\Big(\dfrac{1}{x} \, dx\Big)$

$\qquad\qquad = x \ln 5x - x$

$\displaystyle\int_1^2 \ln 5x \, dx$

$\quad = (x \ln 5x - x)\Big|_1^2$

$\quad = 2 \ln 10 - 2 - \ln 5 + 1$

$\quad = \ln \dfrac{10^2}{5} - 1$

$\quad = \ln 20 - 1 \approx 1.996$

10. $\int x^2 \ln x \, dx, \ x > 0$

Let $dv = x^2 \, dx$ and $u = \ln x$.

Then $v = \dfrac{x^3}{3}$ and $du = \dfrac{1}{x} \, dx$.

$$\int x^2 \ln x \, dx = \frac{x^3 \ln x}{3} - \int \frac{x^3}{3}\left(\frac{1}{x}\right) dx$$

$$= \frac{x^3 \ln x}{3} - \frac{1}{3} \int x^2 \, dx$$

$$= \frac{x^3 \ln x}{3} - \frac{x^3}{9} + C$$

12. $A = \displaystyle\int_0^1 xe^x \, dx$

Let $dv = e^x \, dx$ and $u = x$.

Then $v = e^x$ and $du = dx$.

$$\int xe^x \, dx = xe^x - \int e^x \, dx$$

$$= xe^x - e^x = e^x(x - 1)$$

$$A = e^x(x - 1) \Big|_0^1$$

$$= e(0) - 1(-1)$$

$$= 1$$

14. $\displaystyle\int_1^2 (1 - x^2)e^{2x} \, dx$

Let $u = 1 - x^2$ and $dv = e^{2x} \, dx$.

Use column integration.

D	I
$1 - x^2$	e^{2x}
$-2x$	$e^{2x}/2$
-2	$e^{2x}/4$
0	$e^{2x}/8$

$$\int (1 - x^2)e^{2x} \, dx$$

$$= (1 - x^2)e^{2x}/2 - (-2x)e^{2x}/4$$
$$+ (-2)e^{2x}/8$$

$$= \frac{(1 - x^2)e^{2x}}{2} + \frac{xe^{2x}}{2} - \frac{e^{2x}}{4}$$

$$= \frac{e^{2x}}{2}\left(1 - x^2 + x - \frac{1}{2}\right)$$

$$= \frac{e^{2x}}{2}\left(\frac{1}{2} - x^2 + x\right)$$

$$\int_1^2 (1 - x^2)e^{2x} \, dx$$

$$= \frac{e^{2x}}{2}\left(\frac{1}{2} - x^2 + x\right) \Big|_1^2$$

$$= \frac{e^4}{2}\left(-\frac{3}{2}\right) - \frac{e^2}{2}\left(\frac{1}{2}\right)$$

$$= -\frac{e^2}{4}(3e^2 + 1)$$

$$\approx -42.80$$

16. $\displaystyle\int (2x - 1) \ln (3x) \, dx$

Let $dv = (2x - 1) \, dx$ and $u = \ln 3x$.

Then $v = x^2 - x$ and $du = \frac{1}{x} \, dx$.

$$\int (2x - 1) \ln (3x) \, dx$$

$$= (x^2 - x) \ln 3x - \int (x^2 - x)\left(\frac{1}{x} \, dx\right)$$

$$= (x^2 - x) \ln 3x - \int (x - 1) \, dx$$

$$= (x^2 - x) \ln 3x - \frac{x^2}{2} + x + C$$

18. $\displaystyle\int xe^{x^2} \, dx = \frac{1}{2} \int 2xe^{x^2} \, dx$

Let $u = x^2$ and $du = 2x \, dx$.

$$= \frac{1}{2}e^{x^2} + C$$

$$= \frac{e^{x^2}}{2} + C$$

20. $\displaystyle\int_0^1 \frac{x^2\ dx}{2x^3 + 1}$

Let $u = 2x^3 + 1$.

Then $du = 6x^2\ dx$.

$$\int_0^1 \frac{x^2\ dx}{2x^3 + 1} = \frac{1}{6} \int_0^1 \frac{6x^2\ dx}{2x^3 + 1}$$

$$= \frac{1}{6}\left(\ln\ |2x^3 + 1|\ \Big|_0^1\right)$$

$$= \frac{1}{6}(\ln 3)$$

$$\approx .183$$

22. $\displaystyle\int \frac{x^2\ dx}{2x^3 + 1} = \frac{1}{6} \int \frac{6x^2\ dx}{2x^3 + 1}$

Let $u = 2x^3 + 1$.

Then $du = 6x^2\ dx$.

$$= \frac{1}{6}\ \ln\ |2x^3 + 1| + C$$

24. $\displaystyle\int \frac{9}{\sqrt{x^2 + 9}}\ dx = 9 \int \frac{dx}{\sqrt{x^2 + 9}}$

If $a = 3$, this integral matches entry 5 in the table.

$$= 9\ \ln\ |x + \sqrt{x^2 + 9}| + C$$

26. $\displaystyle\int \frac{-12}{x^2 - 16}\ dx$

$$= -12 \int \frac{dx}{x^2 - 16}$$

$$= -12 \int \frac{dx}{x^2 - 4^2}$$

If $a = 4$, this integral matches entry 8 in the table.

$$= -12\left[\frac{1}{2(4)}\ \ln\ \left|\frac{x - 4}{x + 4}\right|\right] + C$$

$$= -\frac{3}{2}\ \ln\ \left|\frac{x - 4}{x + 4}\right| + C$$

28. $\displaystyle\int \frac{3}{x\sqrt{121 - x^2}}\ dx$

$$= 3 \int \frac{dx}{x\sqrt{11^2 - x^2}}$$

If $a = 11$, this integral matches entry 9 in the table.

$$= 3\left(-\frac{1}{11}\ \ln\ \left|\frac{11 + \sqrt{121 - x^2}}{x}\right|\right) + C$$

$$= -\frac{3}{11}\ \ln\ \left|\frac{11 + \sqrt{121 - x^2}}{x}\right| + C$$

30. $\displaystyle\int \frac{6x}{4x - 5}\ dx$

$$= 6 \int \frac{x\ dx}{4x - 5}$$

If $a = 4$ and $b = -5$, this matches entry 11 in the table.

$$= 6\left(\frac{x}{4} - \frac{-5}{4^2}\ \ln\ |4x - 5|\right) + C$$

$$= \frac{3x}{2} + \frac{15}{8}\ \ln\ |4x - 5| + C$$

32. $\displaystyle\int \frac{-4}{3x(2x + 7)}\ dx$

$$= -\frac{4}{3} \int \frac{dx}{x(2x + 7)}$$

With $a = 2$ and $b = 7$, this matches entry 13 in the table.

$$= -\frac{4}{3}\left(\frac{1}{7}\ \ln\ \left|\frac{x}{2x + 7}\right|\right) + C$$

$$= -\frac{4}{21}\ \ln\ \left|\frac{x}{2x + 7}\right| + C$$

34. $\displaystyle\int \frac{-6}{9x^2 - 1}\, dx$

$\displaystyle = -6\int \frac{dx}{9x^2 - 1} = -\frac{6}{9}\cdot\frac{dx}{x^2 - \frac{1}{9}}$

$\displaystyle = -\frac{2}{3}\int \frac{dx}{x^2 - \left(\frac{1}{3}\right)^2}$

With a = 1/3, this matches entry 8 in the table.

$\displaystyle = -\frac{2}{3}\left[\frac{1}{2\left(\frac{1}{3}\right)}\, \ln\left|\frac{x - \frac{1}{3}}{x + \frac{1}{3}}\right|\right] + C$

$\displaystyle = -\ln\left|\frac{x - \frac{1}{3}}{x + \frac{1}{3}}\right| + C$

or $\displaystyle -\ln\left|\frac{3x - 1}{3x + 1}\right| + C$

36. $\displaystyle\int \frac{-2}{x\sqrt{1 - 16x^2}}\, dx$

$\displaystyle = -2\int \frac{dx}{4\sqrt{\frac{1}{16} - x^2}}$

$\displaystyle = \frac{-2}{4}\int \frac{dx}{x\sqrt{\left(\frac{1}{4}\right)^2 - x^2}}$

This matches entry 9 in the table with a = $\frac{1}{4}$.

$\displaystyle = -\frac{1}{2}\left(-\frac{1}{\frac{1}{4}}\, \ln\left|\frac{\frac{1}{4} + \sqrt{\frac{1}{16} - x^2}}{x}\right|\right) + C$

$\displaystyle = 2\, \ln\left|\frac{\frac{1}{4} + \sqrt{\frac{1}{16} - x^2}}{x}\right| + C$

or $\displaystyle 2\, \ln\left|\frac{1 + \sqrt{1 - 16x^2}}{4x}\right| + C$

38. $\displaystyle\int \frac{4x}{6 - x}\, dx$

$\displaystyle = 4\int \frac{x\, dx}{6 - x} = 4\int \frac{x\, dx}{-x + 6}$

This matches entry 11 in the table with a = -1 and b = 6.

$\displaystyle = 4\left[\frac{x}{-1} - \frac{6}{(-1)^2}\, \ln\left|-x + 6\right|\right] + C$

$\displaystyle = -4x - 24\, \ln\left|6 - x\right| + C$

40. $\displaystyle\int \frac{-3}{x(4x + 3)^2}\, dx$

$\displaystyle = -3\int \frac{dx}{x(4x + 3)^2}$

This matches entry 14 in the table with a = 4 and b = 3.

$\displaystyle = -3\left[\frac{1}{3(4x + 3)} + \frac{1}{3^2}\, \ln\left|\frac{x}{4x + 3}\right|\right] + C$

$\displaystyle = \frac{-1}{4x + 3} - \frac{1}{3}\, \ln\left|\frac{x}{4x + 3}\right| + C$

42. $\displaystyle\int x^n e^{ax}\, dx$

Let $dv = e^{ax}dx$ and $u = x^n$; then $v = \frac{1}{a}e^{ax}$ and $du = nx^{n-1}\, dx$.

$\displaystyle \int x^n e^{ax}\, dx$

$\displaystyle = \frac{x^n e^{ax}}{a} - \int \left(\frac{1}{a}e^{ax}\cdot nx^{n-1}\right)dx$

$\displaystyle = \frac{x^n e^{ax}}{a} - \frac{n}{a}\int x^{n-1}e^{ax}\, dx + C$

44. $\displaystyle R(x) = \int_0^{12} \frac{1000}{\sqrt{x^2 + 25}}\, dx$

$\displaystyle = 1000\int_0^{12} \frac{1}{\sqrt{x^2 + 25}}\, dx$

If a = 5, this integral matches entry 5 in the table.

$$1000 \int_0^{12} \frac{1}{\sqrt{x^2 + 25}} \, dx$$

$$= 1000 \left(\ln |x + \sqrt{x^2 + 25}| \, \Big|_0^{12} \right)$$

$$= 1000(\ln 25 - \ln 5)$$

$$= 1000 \ln 5$$

$$\approx \$1609.44$$

46. $\displaystyle\int_0^3 30xe^{2x} \, dx$

Let $dv = e^{2x} \, dx$ and $u = 30x$.

Then $v = \dfrac{e^{2x}}{2}$ and $du = 30 \, dx$.

$$\int 30xe^{2x} \, dx$$

$$= 15xe^{2x} - \int 15e^{2x} \, dx$$

$$= 15xe^{2x} - \frac{15}{2}e^{2x}$$

$$\int_0^3 30xe^{2x} \, dx$$

$$= \left(15xe^{2x} - \frac{15}{2}e^{2x} \right) \Big|_0^3$$

$$= 45e^6 - \frac{15}{2}e^6 - 0 + \frac{15}{2}$$

$$= \frac{75}{2}e^6 + \frac{15}{2}$$

$$= \frac{15}{2}(5e^6 + 1)$$

$$\approx 15,136$$

Section 7.2

2. $\displaystyle\int_0^2 (2x + 1) \, dx$

$n = 4$, $b = 2$, $a = 0$, $f(x) = 2x + 1$

i	x_i	$f(x_i)$
0	0	1
1	1/2	2
2	1	3
3	3/2	4
4	2	5

(a) Trapezoidal rule

$$\int_0^2 (2x + 1) \, dx$$

$$\approx \frac{2 - 0}{4} \left[\frac{1}{2}(1) + 2 + 3 + 4 + \frac{1}{2}(5) \right]$$

$$= \frac{1}{2} \left(\frac{1}{2} + 2 + 3 + 4 + \frac{5}{2} \right)$$

$$= 6$$

(b) Simpson's rule

$$\int_0^2 (2x + 1) \, dx$$

$$\approx \frac{2 - 0}{3(4)} [1 + 4(2) + 2(3) + 4(4) + 5]$$

$$= \frac{1}{6}(36) = 6$$

(c) Exact value

$$\int_0^2 (2x + 1) \, dx = (x^2 + x) \Big|_0^2$$

$$= 4 + 2$$

$$= 6$$

4. $\int_1^5 \dfrac{1}{x+1} \, dx$

$n = 4, \; b = 5, \; a = 1, \; f(x) = \dfrac{1}{x+1}$

i	x_i	$f(x_i)$
0	1	1/2
1	2	1/3
2	3	1/4
3	4	1/5
4	5	1/6

(a) Trapezoidal rule

$\int_1^5 \dfrac{dx}{x+1}$

$\approx \dfrac{5-1}{4}\left[\dfrac{1}{2}\left(\dfrac{1}{2}\right) + \dfrac{1}{3} + \dfrac{1}{4} + \dfrac{1}{5} + \dfrac{1}{2}\left(\dfrac{1}{6}\right)\right]$

$= \dfrac{1}{4} + \dfrac{1}{3} + \dfrac{1}{4} + \dfrac{1}{5} + \dfrac{1}{12}$

≈ 1.1167

(b) Simpson's rule

$\int_1^5 \dfrac{dx}{x+1}$

$\approx \dfrac{5-1}{3(4)}\left[\dfrac{1}{2} + 4\left(\dfrac{1}{3}\right) + 2\left(\dfrac{1}{4}\right) + 4\left(\dfrac{1}{5}\right) + \dfrac{1}{6}\right]$

$= \dfrac{1}{3}\left(\dfrac{1}{2} + \dfrac{4}{3} + \dfrac{1}{2} + \dfrac{4}{5} + \dfrac{1}{6}\right)$

$= 1.1000$

(c) Exact value

$\int_1^5 \dfrac{dx}{x+1} = \ln|x+1|\Big|_1^5$

$= \ln 6 - \ln 2 = \ln \dfrac{6}{2}$

$= \ln 3 \approx 1.0986$

6. $\int_0^3 (2x^2 + 1) \, dx$

$n = 4, \; b = 3, \; a = 0, \; f(x) = 2x^2 + 1$

i	x	f(x)
0	0	1
1	.75	2.125
2	1.5	5.5
3	2.25	11.125
4	3	19

(a) Trapezoidal rule

$\int_0^3 (2x^2 + 1) \, dx$

$= \dfrac{3-0}{4}\left[\dfrac{1}{2}(1) + 2.125 + 5.5 + 11.125 + \dfrac{1}{2}(19)\right]$

$= \dfrac{3}{4}(28.75)$

$= 21.5625$

(b) Simpson's rule

$\int_0^3 (2x^2 + 1) \, dx$

$= \dfrac{3-0}{3(4)}[1 + 4(2.125) + 2(5.5)$

$\quad + 4(11.125) + 19]$

$= \dfrac{1}{4}(1 + 8.5 + 11 + 44.5 + 19)$

$= 21.0000$

(c) Exact value

$\int_0^3 (2x^2 + 1) \, dx = \left(\dfrac{2x^3}{3} + x\right)\Big|_0^3$

$= 18 + 3 = 21$

8. $\displaystyle\int_2^4 \frac{1}{x^3}\,dx$

$n = 4,\ b = 4,\ a = 2,\ f(x) = \frac{1}{x^3}$

i	x_i	$f(x_i)$
0	2	.125
1	2.5	.064
2	3	.03703
3	3.5	.02332
4	4	.015625

(a) Trapezoidal rule

$$\int_2^4 \frac{dx}{x^3} \approx \frac{4-2}{4}\Big[\frac{1}{2}(.125)+.064+.03703$$
$$+\ .02332+\frac{1}{2}(.015625)\Big]$$
$$\approx \frac{1}{2}\,(.19466)$$
$$\approx .0973$$

(b) Simpson's rule

$$\int_2^4 \frac{dx}{x^3} \approx \frac{4-2}{3(4)}[.125+4(.064)+2(.03703)$$
$$+\ 4(.02332)+.015625]$$
$$\approx \frac{1}{6}(.56397)$$
$$\approx .0940$$

(c) Exact value

$$\int_2^4 \frac{dx}{x^3} = \int_2^4 x^{-3}\,dx = \frac{x^{-2}}{-2}\Big|_2^4 = \frac{-1}{2x^2}\Big|_2^4$$
$$= \frac{-1}{32}+\frac{1}{8}=\frac{3}{32}=.09375$$

10. $\displaystyle\int_1^4 x\sqrt{2x-1}\,dx$

$n = 4,\ b = 4,\ a = 1,\ f(x) = x\sqrt{2x-1}$

i	x_i	$f(x_i)$
0	1	1
1	1.75	2.7670
2	2.5	5
3	3.25	7.6219
4	4	10.5830

(a) Trapezoidal rule

$$\int_1^4 x\sqrt{2x-1}\,dx$$
$$= \frac{4-1}{4}\Big[\frac{1}{2}(1)+2.7670+5+7.6219$$
$$+\frac{1}{2}(10.5830)\Big]$$
$$= 15.8853$$

(b) Simpson's rule

$$\int_1^4 x\sqrt{2x-1}\,dx$$
$$= \frac{4-1}{3(4)}[1+4(2.7670+2(5)$$
$$+\ 4(7.6219)+10.5830]$$
$$= 15.7847$$

(c) Let $2x-1=u$,

then $x=\frac{1}{2}(u+1)$

$dx=\frac{1}{2}\,du.$

When $x=1$, $u=1$; when $x=4$, $u=7$.

$$\int_{1}^{4} x\sqrt{2x-1}\ dx$$

$$= \frac{1}{4}\int_{1}^{7} (u+1)u^{1/2}\ du$$

$$= \frac{1}{4}\int_{1}^{7} (u^{3/2} + u^{1/2})\ du$$

$$= \frac{1}{4}\left[\left(\frac{2}{5}u^{5/2} + \frac{2}{3}u^{3/2}\right)\Big|_{1}^{7}\right]$$

$$= \frac{\left(\frac{2}{5}\right)7^{5/2} + \left(\frac{2}{3}\right)7^{3/2} - \frac{2}{5} - \frac{2}{3}}{4}$$

$$\approx 15.7842$$

12. $4x^2 + 9y^2 = 36$

$$y^2 = \frac{36 - 4x^2}{9}$$

$$y = \pm\frac{1}{3}\sqrt{36 - 4x^2}$$

Semiellipse is $y = \frac{1}{3}\sqrt{36 - 4x^2}$.

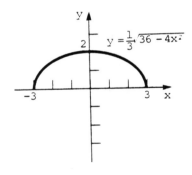

$n = 12$, $b = -3$, $a = 3$

i	x_i	y
0	−3	0
1	−2.5	1.1055
2	−2	1.4907
3	−1.5	1.7321
4	−1	1.8856
5	−.5	1.9720
6	0	2
7	.5	1.9720
8	1	1.8856
9	1.5	1.7321
10	2	1.4907
11	2.5	1.1055
12	3	0

(a) Trapezoidal rule

$$\frac{A}{2} = \frac{6}{12}\Big[\frac{1}{2}(0) + 1.1055 + 1.4907 + 1.7321$$
$$+ 1.8856 + 1.972 + 2 + 1.972$$
$$+ 1.8856 + 1.7321 + 1.4907$$
$$+ 1.1055 + 2(0)\Big]$$
$$= 9.1859$$

(b) Simpson's rule

$$\frac{A}{2} = \frac{6}{3(12)}[0 + 4(1.1055) + 2(1.4907)$$
$$+ 4(1.7321) + 2(1.8856) + 4(1.972)$$
$$+ 2(2) + 4(1.972) + 2(1.8856) + 4(1.7321)$$
$$+ 2(1.4907) + 4(1.155) + 0]$$
$$= \frac{1}{6}(55.982)$$
$$= 9.3304$$

(c) Trapezoidal rule gives the area of the ellipse

$$2(9.1859) = 18.3718.$$

Simpson's rule gives the area of the ellipse

$$2(9.3304) = 18.6608.$$

Exact area is 18.8496.

Simpson's rule is a better approximation.

14. (a)

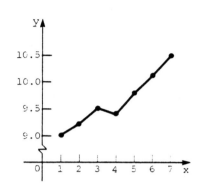

(b) $A = \dfrac{7-1}{6}\left[\frac{1}{2}(9) + 9.2 + 9.5 + 9.4\right.$

$$\left. + 9.8 + 10.1 + \frac{1}{2}(10.5)\right]$$

$$= 57.75$$

(c) $A = \dfrac{7-1}{3(6)}[9.0 + 4(9.2) + 2(9.5)$

$$+ 4(9.4) + 2(9.8) + 4(10.1)$$

$$+ 10.5]$$

$$= \frac{1}{3}(172.9)$$

$$= 57.63$$

16. $y = \displaystyle\int_{1}^{7} \left(\frac{2}{t} + e^{-t^{2}/2}\right) dt$

$$n = 12, \ b = 7, \ a = 1$$

i	x_i	$f(x_i)$
0	1	2.607
1	1.5	1.658
2	2	1.135
3	2.5	.8439
4	3	.6778
5	3.5	.5736
6	4	.5003
7	4.5	.4445
8	5	.4000
9	5.5	.3636
10	6	.3333
11	6.5	.3077
12	7	.2857

(a) Total growth

$$= \dfrac{7-1}{12}\left[\frac{1}{2}(2.607) + 1.658\right.$$

$$+ 1.135 + .8439 + .6778$$

$$+ .5736 + .5003 + .4445$$

$$+ .4000 + .3636 + .3333$$

$$\left. + .3077 + \frac{1}{2}(.2857)\right]$$

$$\approx 4.3421 \text{ ft}$$

(b) Total growth

$$= \dfrac{7-1}{3(12)}[2.607 + 4(1.658)$$

$$+ 2(1.135) + 4(.8439)$$

$$+ 2(.6778) + 4(.5736)$$

$$+ 2(.5003) + 4(.4445)$$

$$+ 4(.3077) + .2857]$$

$$\approx 4.2919 \text{ ft}$$

18. $n = 10$, $b = 20$, $a = 0$

i	x_i	y
0	0	0
1	2	2.0
2	4	3.0
3	6	2.9
4	8	2.5
5	10	2.0
6	12	1.75
7	14	1.0
8	16	.75
9	18	.50
10	20	.25

$A = \dfrac{20 - 0}{10}[\frac{1}{2}(0) + 2 + 3 + 2.9 + 2.5$

$+ 2 + 1.75 + 1.0 + .75 + .5$

$+ \frac{1}{2}(.25)]$

= 33.05 (This answer may vary depending upon readings from the graph.)

The area under the curve, about 33 mcg/ml, represents the total amount of drug available to the patient.

20. The area both under the curve for Formulation B and above the minimum effective concentration line is on the interval (2, 10).
$n = 8$, $b = 10$, $a = 2$

i	x_i	y
0	2	2.0
1	3	2.4
2	4	3.0
3	5	2.8
4	6	2.9
5	7	2.6
6	8	2.5
7	9	2.2
8	10	2.0

Let A_B = area under Formulation B curve between $t = 2$ and $t = 10$.

$A_B = \dfrac{10 - 2}{8}[\frac{1}{2}(2) + 2.4 + 3 + 2.8$

$+ 2.9 + 2.6 + 2.5 + 2.2 + \frac{1}{2}(2)]$

$A_B = 20.4$

Let A_{ME} = area under minimum effective concentration curve between $t = 2$ and $t = 10$.

$$A_{ME} = (10 - 2)(2) = 16$$

So area between A_B and A_{ME} between $t = 2$ and $t = 10$

$$= 20.4 - 16$$
$$= 4.4.$$

This area, about 4.4 mcg/ml, represents the total effective amount of the drug available to the patient. Notice that between $t = 0$ and $t = 2$ and between $t = 10$ and $t = 12$, the graph for Formulation B is below the minimum effective concentration line.

Thus, no area exists under the curve for Formulation B and above the minimum effective concentration line in the intervals $(0, 2)$ and $(10, 12)$.

22. (a)

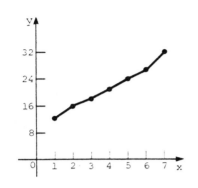

(b) $A = \dfrac{7 - 1}{6}[\dfrac{1}{2}(12) + 16 + 18 + 21$

$\qquad + 24 + 27 + \dfrac{1}{2}(32)]$

$\qquad A = 1(128)$

$\qquad A = 128$

(c) $A = \dfrac{7 - 1}{3(6)}[12 + 4(16) + 2(18)$

$\qquad + 4(21) + 2(24) + 4(27) + 32]$

$\qquad A = 128$

Exercises 24–30 should be solved by computer methods. The solutions will vary according to the computer program that is used. The answer are given.

24. $\displaystyle\int_{-2}^{2} e^{-x^2}\, dx$

Trapezoidal rule: 1.76414
Simpson's rule: 1.76416

26. $\displaystyle\int_{-1}^{1} \sqrt{16 + 5x^2}\, dx$

Trapezoidal rule: 8.39910
Simpson's rule: 8.39903

28. $\displaystyle\int_{1}^{4} (x^3 + 4)^{5/4}\, dx$

Trapezoidal rule: 183.026
Simpson's rule: 183.014

30. Either rule gives 99.9929.

Because of space considerations in Parts (b) of Exercises 32 and 34, tables of data are not shown. Substitutions of these data in the appropriate rules are given, however.

32. (a) $\displaystyle\int_{0}^{1} x^4\, dx$

$\qquad = \left.(\dfrac{1}{5})x^5\right|_{0}^{1}$

$\qquad = \dfrac{1}{5}$

$\qquad = .2$

(b) $n = 4$, $b = 1$, $a = 0$, $f(x) = x^4$

$\displaystyle\int_{0}^{1} x^4\, dx = \dfrac{1 - 0}{4}[\dfrac{1}{2}(0) + \dfrac{1}{256} + \dfrac{1}{16}$

$\qquad + \dfrac{81}{256} + \dfrac{1}{2}(1)]$

$\qquad \approx \dfrac{1}{4}\left(\dfrac{226}{256}\right)$

$\qquad \approx .220703$

$n = 8$, $b = 1$, $a = 0$, $f(x) = x^4$

$$\int_0^1 x^4 \, dx = \frac{1-0}{8}\left[\frac{1}{2}(0) + \frac{1}{4096} + \frac{1}{256}\right.$$

$$+ \frac{81}{4096} + \frac{1}{16} + \frac{625}{4096} + \frac{81}{256}$$

$$\left. + \frac{2401}{4096} + \frac{1}{2}(1)\right]$$

$$\approx \frac{1}{8}\left(\frac{6724}{4096}\right)$$

$$\approx .205200$$

$n = 16$, $b = 1$, $a = 0$, $f(x) = x^4$

$$\int_0^1 x^4 \, dx \approx \frac{1-0}{16}\left[\frac{1}{2}(0) + \frac{1}{65536} + \frac{1}{4096}\right.$$

$$+ \frac{81}{65536} + \frac{1}{256} + \frac{625}{65536}$$

$$+ \frac{81}{4096} + \frac{2401}{65536} + \frac{1}{16}$$

$$+ \frac{6561}{65536} + \frac{625}{4096} + \frac{14641}{65536}$$

$$+ \frac{81}{256} + \frac{28561}{65536} + \frac{2401}{4096}$$

$$\left. + \frac{50625}{65536} + \frac{1}{2}(1)\right]$$

$$\approx \frac{1}{16}\left(\frac{211080}{65536}\right)$$

$$\approx .201302$$

$n = 32$, $b = 1$, $a = 0$, $f(x) = x^4$

$$\int_0^1 x^4 \, dx$$

$$\approx \frac{1-0}{32}\left[\frac{1}{2}(0) + \frac{1}{1048576} + \frac{1}{65536}\right.$$

$$+ \frac{81}{1048576} + \frac{1}{4096} + \frac{625}{1048576} + \frac{81}{65536}$$

$$+ \frac{2401}{1048576} + \frac{1}{256} + \frac{6561}{1048576} + \frac{625}{65536}$$

$$+ \frac{14641}{1048576} + \frac{81}{4096} + \frac{28561}{1048576} + \frac{2401}{65536}$$

$$+ \frac{50625}{1048576} + \frac{1}{16} + \frac{83521}{1048576} + \frac{6561}{65536}$$

$$+ \frac{130321}{1048576} + \frac{625}{4096} + \frac{194481}{1048576} + \frac{14641}{65536}$$

$$+ \frac{279841}{1048576} + \frac{81}{256} + \frac{390625}{1048576} + \frac{28561}{65536}$$

$$+ \frac{531441}{1048576} + \frac{2401}{4096} + \frac{707281}{1048576} + \frac{50625}{65536}$$

$$\left. + \frac{923521}{1048576} + \frac{1}{2}(1)\right]$$

$$\approx \frac{1}{32}\left(\frac{6721808}{1048576}\right) \approx .200325$$

To find error for each value of n, subtract as indicated.

$n = 4$: $(.220703 - .2) = .020703$

$n = 8$: $(.205200 - .2) = .005200$

$n = 16$: $(.201302 - .2) = .001302$

$n = 32$: $(.200325 - .2) = .000325$

(c) $p = 1$:

$$4^1(.020703) = 4(.020703)$$
$$= .082812$$
$$8^1(.005200) = 8(.005200)$$
$$= .0416$$

Since these are not the same, try $p = 2$.

$p = 2$:

$$4^2(.020703) = 16(.020703) = .331248$$
$$8^2(.005200) = 64(.005200) = .3328$$
$$16^2(.001302) = 256(.001302)$$
$$= .333312$$
$$32^2(.000325) = 1024(.000325)$$
$$= .3328$$

Since these values are all approximately the same, the correct choice is $p = 2$.

34. **(a)** $\int_0^1 x^4 \, dx$

$$= \frac{1}{5}x^5 \Big|_0^1$$

$$= \frac{1}{5}$$

$$= .2$$

(b) $n = 4$, $b = 1$, $a = 0$, $f(x) = x^4$

$$\int_0^1 x^4 \, dx \approx \frac{1-0}{3(4)}\left[0 + 4\left(\frac{1}{256}\right) + 2\left(\frac{1}{16}\right)\right.$$

$$\left. + 4\left(\frac{81}{256}\right) + 1\right]$$

$$\approx \frac{1}{12}\left(\frac{154}{16}\right)$$

$$\approx .2005208$$

$n = 8$, $b = 1$, $a = 0$, $f(x) = x^4$

$$\int_0^1 x^4 \, dx \approx \frac{1-0}{3(8)}\left[0 + 4\left(\frac{1}{4096}\right) + 2\left(\frac{1}{256}\right)\right.$$

$$+ 4\left(\frac{81}{4096}\right) + 2\left(\frac{1}{16}\right) + 4\left(\frac{625}{4096}\right)$$

$$\left. + 2\left(\frac{81}{256}\right) + 4\left(\frac{2401}{4096}\right) + 1\right]$$

$$\approx \frac{1}{24}\left(\frac{4916}{1024}\right)$$

$$\approx .2000326$$

$n = 16$, $b = 1$, $a = 0$, $f(x) = x^4$

$$\int_0^1 x^4 \, dx$$

$$\approx \frac{1-0}{3(16)}\left[0 + 4\left(\frac{1}{65536}\right) + 2\left(\frac{1}{4096}\right)\right.$$

$$+ 4\left(\frac{81}{65536}\right] + 2\left(\frac{1}{256}\right) + 4\left(\frac{625}{65536}\right)$$

$$+ 2\left(\frac{81}{4096}\right) + 4\left(\frac{2401}{65536}\right) + 2\left(\frac{1}{16}\right)$$

$$+ 4\left(\frac{6561}{65536}\right) + 2\left(\frac{625}{4096}\right) + 4\left(\frac{14641}{65536}\right)$$

$$+ 2\left(\frac{81}{256}\right) + 4\left(\frac{28561}{65536}\right) + 2\left(\frac{2401}{4096}\right)$$

$$+ 4\left(\frac{50625}{65536}\right) + 1]$$

$$\approx \frac{1}{48}\left(\frac{157288}{16384}\right) \approx .2000020$$

$n = 32$, $b = 1$, $a = 0$, $f(x) = x^4$

$$\int_0^1 x^4 \, dx$$

$$\approx \frac{1-0}{3(32)}\left[0 + 4\left(\frac{1}{1048576}\right) + 2\left(\frac{1}{65536}\right)\right.$$

$$+ 4\left(\frac{81}{1048576}\right) + 2\left(\frac{1}{4096}\right) + 4\left(\frac{625}{1048576}\right)$$

$$+ 2\left(\frac{625}{65536}\right) + 4\left(\frac{14641}{1048576}\right) + 2\left(\frac{81}{4096}\right)$$

$$+ 4\left(\frac{28561}{1048576}\right) + 2\left(\frac{2401}{65536}\right) + 4\left(\frac{50625}{1048576}\right)$$

$$+ 2\left(\frac{1}{16}\right) + 4\left(\frac{83521}{1048576}\right) + 2\left(\frac{6561}{65536}\right)$$

$$+ 4\left(\frac{130321}{1048576}\right) + 2\left(\frac{625}{4096}\right) + 4\left(\frac{194481}{1048576}\right)$$

$$+ 2\left(\frac{14641}{65536}\right) + 4\left(\frac{279841}{1048576}\right) + 2\left(\frac{81}{256}\right)$$

$$+ 4\left(\frac{390625}{1048576}\right) + 2\left(\frac{28561}{65536}\right) + 4\left(\frac{531441}{1048576}\right)$$

$$+ 2\left(\frac{2401}{4096}\right) + 4\left(\frac{707281}{1048576}\right) + 2\left(\frac{50625}{65536}\right)$$

$$+ 4\left(\frac{923521}{1048576}\right) + 1]$$

$$\approx \frac{1}{96}\left(\frac{50033168}{262144}\right) \approx .2000001$$

To find error for each value of n, subtract as indicated.

$n = 4$: $(.2005208 - .2) = .0005208$

$n = 8$: $(.2000326 - .2) = .0000326$

$n = 16$: $(.2000020 - .2) = .0000020$

$n = 32$: $(.2000001 - .2) = .0000001$

p = 1:

$4^1(.0005208) = 4(.0005208)$

$\qquad\qquad\quad = .0020832$

$8^1(.0000326) = 8(.0000326)$

$\qquad\qquad\quad = .0002608$

Try p = 2:

$4^2(.0005208) = 16(.0005208)$

$\qquad\qquad\quad = .0083328$

$8^2(.0000326) = 64(.0000326)$

$\qquad\qquad\quad = .0020864$

Try p = 3:

$4^3(.0005208) = 64(.0005208)$

$\qquad\qquad\quad = .0333312$

$8^3 = (.0000326) = 512(.0000326)$

$\qquad\qquad\qquad = .0166912$

Try p = 4:

$4^4(.0005208) = 256(.0005208)$

$\qquad\qquad\quad = .1333248$

$8^4(.0000326) = 4096(.0000326)$

$\qquad\qquad\quad = .1335296$

$16^4(.0000020) = 65536(.0000020)$

$\qquad\qquad\qquad = .131072$

$32^4(.0000001) = 1048576(.0000001)$

$\qquad\qquad\qquad = .1048576$

These are the closest values we can get; thus, p = 4.

Section 7.3

2. f(x) = 2x, y = 0, x = 0, x = 3
    Graph f(x) = 2x. Then show the
    solid of revolution formed by rota-
    ting about the x-axis the region
    bounded by f(x), x = 0, and x = 3.

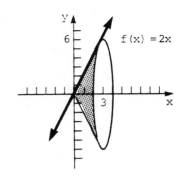

$$V = \pi \int_0^3 (2x)^2 \ dx$$

$$= \pi \int_0^3 4x^2 \ dx$$

$$= \frac{4\pi x^3}{3} \Big|_0^3$$

$$= 36\pi$$

4. f(x) = x − 4, y = 0, x = 4, x = 10

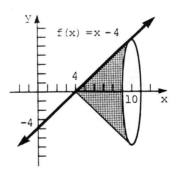

$$V = \pi \int_4^{10} (x - 4)^2 \ dx$$

$$= \frac{\pi(x - 4)^3}{3} \Big|_4^{10}$$

$$= \frac{\pi}{3}[(6)^3 - 0]$$

$$= 72\pi$$

6. $f(x) = \frac{1}{2}x + 4$, $y = 0$, $x = 0$, $x = 5$

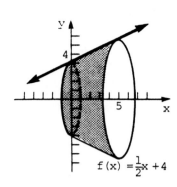

$f(x) = \frac{1}{2}x + 4$

$$V = \pi \int_0^5 \left(\frac{1}{2}x + 4\right)^2 dx$$

$$= 2\pi \int_0^5 \frac{1}{2}\left(\frac{1}{2}x + 4\right)^2 dx$$

$$= 2\pi \frac{\left(\frac{1}{2}x + 4\right)^3}{3} \Bigg|_0^5$$

$$= \frac{2\pi}{3}\left[\left(\frac{5}{2} + 4\right)^3 - (4)^3\right]$$

$$= \frac{2\pi}{3}\left[\left(\frac{13}{2}\right)^3 - 64\right]$$

$$= \frac{2\pi}{3}\left(\frac{2197}{8} - \frac{512}{8}\right)$$

$$= \frac{1685\pi}{12}$$

8. $f(x) = \sqrt{x + 1}$, $y = 0$, $x = 0$, $x = 3$

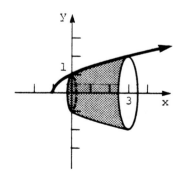

$$V = \pi \int_0^3 (\sqrt{x + 1})^2 dx$$

$$= \pi \int_0^3 (x + 1) dx$$

$$= \pi\left(\frac{x^2}{2} + x\right)\Bigg|_0^3 = \pi\left(\frac{9}{2} + 3\right)$$

$$= \frac{15\pi}{2}$$

10. $f(x) = \sqrt{3x + 2}$, $y = 0$, $x = 1$, $x = 2$

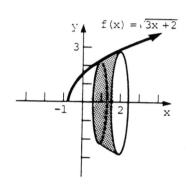

$f(x) = \sqrt{3x + 2}$

$$V = \pi \int_1^2 (\sqrt{3x + 2})^2 dx$$

$$= \pi \int_1^2 (3x + 2) dx$$

$$= \pi\left(\frac{3x^2}{2} + 2x\right)\Bigg|_1^2$$

$$= \pi\left[\left(\frac{3}{2}(2)^2 + 2(2)\right) - \left(\frac{3}{2}(1) + 2(1)\right)\right]$$

$$= \pi\left(10 - \frac{7}{2}\right)$$

$$= \frac{13\pi}{2}$$

12. $f(x) = 2e^x$; $y = 0$, $x = -2$, $x = 1$

$$V = \pi \int_{-2}^{1} (2e^x)^2 \, dx$$

$$= \pi \int_{-2}^{1} 4x^{2x} \, dx$$

$$= \frac{4\pi}{2}(e^{2x}) \Big|_{-2}^{1}$$

$$= 2\pi(e^2 - e^{-4}) \approx 46.3$$

14. $f(x) = \dfrac{1}{\sqrt{x+1}}$, $y = 0$, $x = 0$, $x = 2$

$$V = \pi \int_{0}^{2} \left(\frac{1}{\sqrt{x+1}}\right)^2 \, dx$$

$$= \pi \int_{0}^{2} \frac{dx}{x+1}$$

$$= \pi(\ln |x+1|) \Big|_{0}^{2}$$

$$= \pi \ln 3$$

$$= \pi \ln 3 \approx 3.45$$

16. $f(x) = \dfrac{x^2}{2}$, $y = 0$, $x = 0$, $x = 4$

$$V = \pi \int_{0}^{4} \left(\frac{x^2}{2}\right)^2 \, dx = \pi \int_{0}^{4} \frac{x^4}{4} \, dx$$

$$= \frac{\pi}{4}\left(\frac{x^5}{5}\right) \Big|_{0}^{4} = \frac{\pi}{20}(4^5) = \frac{256\pi}{5}$$

18. $f(x) = 2 - x^2$, $y = 0$

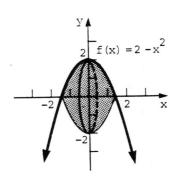

Since $f(x) = 2 - x^2$ intersects $y = 0$ where

$$2 - x^2 = 0$$
$$x = \pm\sqrt{2},$$
$$a = -\sqrt{2} \quad \text{and} \quad b = \sqrt{2}.$$

$$V = \pi \int_{-\sqrt{2}}^{\sqrt{2}} (2 - x^2)^2 \, dx$$

$$= \pi \int_{-\sqrt{2}}^{\sqrt{2}} (4 - 4x^2 + x^4) \, dx$$

$$= \pi\left(4x - \frac{4x^3}{3} + \frac{x^5}{5}\right) \Big|_{-\sqrt{2}}^{\sqrt{2}}$$

$$= \pi\left[\left(4\sqrt{2} - \frac{8}{3}\sqrt{2} + \frac{4}{5}\sqrt{2}\right)\right.$$
$$\left. - \left(-4\sqrt{2} + \frac{8}{3}\sqrt{2} - \frac{4}{5}\sqrt{2}\right)\right]$$

$$= \pi\left(\frac{32}{15}\sqrt{2} + \frac{32}{15}\sqrt{2}\right)$$

$$= \frac{64\pi\sqrt{2}}{15}$$

20. $f(x) = \sqrt{16 - x^2}$, $r = \sqrt{16} = 4$

$$V = \pi \int_{-4}^{4} (\sqrt{16 - x^2})^2 \, dx$$

$$= \pi \int_{-4}^{4} (16 - x^2) \, dx$$

$$= \pi \left(16x - \frac{x^3}{3}\right)\Bigg|_{-4}^{4}$$

$$= \pi \left[\left(64 - \frac{64}{3}\right) - \left(-64 + \frac{64}{3}\right)\right]$$

$$= \pi\left(128 - \frac{128}{3}\right)$$

$$= \frac{256\pi}{3}$$

22. $V = \pi \int_{-a}^{a} \left[\frac{b}{a}\sqrt{a^2 - x^2}\right]^2 \, dx$

$$= \pi \int_{-a}^{a} \frac{b^2}{a^2}(a^2 - x^2) \, dx$$

$$= \frac{\pi b^2}{a^2}\left(a^2 x - \frac{x^3}{3}\right)\Bigg|_{-a}^{a}$$

$$= \frac{\pi b^2}{a^2}\left[\left(a^3 - \frac{a^3}{3}\right) - \left(-a^3 + \frac{a^3}{3}\right)\right]$$

$$= \frac{\pi b^2}{a^2}\left(2a^3 - \frac{2a^3}{3}\right)$$

$$= \frac{\pi b^2}{a^2}\left(\frac{4a^3}{3}\right)$$

$$= \frac{4\pi b^2 a}{3}$$

24. $f(x) = 3 - 2x^2$; $[1, 9]$

Average value

$$= \frac{1}{9 - 1} \int_{1}^{9} (3 - 2x^2) \, dx$$

$$= \frac{1}{8}\left(3x - \frac{2x^3}{3}\right)\Bigg|_{1}^{9}$$

$$= \frac{1}{8}(27 - 486) - \frac{1}{8}\left(3 - \frac{2}{3}\right)$$

$$\approx -57.67$$

26. $f(x) = (2x - 1)^{1/2}$; $[1, 13]$

Average value

$$= \frac{1}{13 - 1} \int_{1}^{13} (2x - 1)^{1/2} \, dx$$

$$= \frac{1}{12}\left(\frac{1}{2}\right) \int_{1}^{13} 2(2x - 1)^{1/2} \, dx$$

$$= \frac{1}{24} \cdot \frac{2}{3}(2x - 1)^{3/2}\Bigg|_{1}^{13}$$

$$= \frac{1}{36}(25^{3/2} - 1)$$

$$= \frac{1}{36}(125) - \frac{1}{36}$$

$$= \frac{124}{36} = \frac{31}{9} \approx 3.44$$

28. $f(x) = e^{.1x}$; $[0, 10]$

Average value

$$= \frac{1}{10 - 0} \int_{0}^{10} e^{.1x} \, dx$$

$$= \frac{10}{10}(e^{.1x})\Bigg|_{0}^{10}$$

$$= e^1 - 1$$

$$= e - 1 \approx 1.718$$

30. $f(x) = x \ln x$; $[1, e]$

Average value

$$= \frac{1}{e - 1} \int_{1}^{e} x \ln x \, dx$$

Let $u = \ln x$ and $dv = x \, dx$.
Use column integration.

D	I
$\ln x$ $\searrow$ $+$	x
$\frac{1}{x}$ $\underline{\qquad -\qquad }$	$\frac{1}{2}x^2$

$\int x \ln x \, dx$

$= \frac{1}{2}x^2 \ln x - \int \left(\frac{1}{x} \cdot \frac{1}{2}x^2\right) dx$

$= \frac{1}{2}x^2 \ln x - \frac{1}{2} \int x \, dx$

$= \frac{1}{2}x^2 \ln x - \frac{1}{4}x^2$

$\frac{1}{e-1} \int_1^e x \ln x \, dx$

$= \frac{1}{e-1}\left(\frac{1}{2}x^2 \ln x - \frac{1}{4}x^2\right)\Big|_1^e$

$= \frac{1}{e-1}\left(\frac{e^2}{2} - \frac{e^2}{4} + \frac{1}{4}\right)$

$= \frac{1}{e-1}\left(\frac{e^2+1}{4}\right)$

$= \frac{e^2+1}{4(e-1)} \approx 1.221$

32. **(a)** $\int_0^R 2\pi rk(R^2 - r^2) \, dr$

$= 2\pi k \int_0^R r(R^2 - r^2) \, dr$

(b) $= 2\pi k \int_0^R (rR^2 - r^3) \, dr$

$= 2\pi k\left[\frac{r^2R^2}{2} - \frac{r^4}{4}\right]\Big|_0^R$

$= 2\pi k\left[\frac{R^4}{2} - \frac{R^4}{4} - 0\right]$

$= 2\pi k\left(\frac{R^4}{4}\right)$

$= \frac{\pi kR^4}{2}$

34. For (a), (b), and (c), use substitution and column integration to
find $\int \ln(t+1) \, dt$.

Let $y = t + 1$; then $dy = dt$.

So $\int \ln(t+1) \, dt = \int \ln y \, dy$.

Let $u = \ln y$ and $dv = dy$.

D	I
$\ln y$	1
$\frac{1}{y}$	y

$\int \ln(t+1) \, dt$

$= \int \ln y \, dy$

$= y \ln y - \int \left(\frac{1}{y} \cdot y\right) dy$

$= y \ln y - \int dy$

$= y \ln y - y + C$

$= (t+1) \ln(t+1) - (t+1) + C$

(a) The average number of items produced daily after 5 days is given by

$\frac{1}{5-0} \int_0^5 35 \ln(t+1) \, dt.$

$\frac{1}{5} \int_0^5 35 \ln(t+1) \, dt$

$= \frac{35}{5} \int_0^5 \ln(t+1) \, dt$

$= 7\left([(t+1) \ln(t+1) - (t+1)]\Big|_0^5\right)$

$= 7(6 \ln 6 - 6 + 1)$

$= 7(6 \ln 6 - 5) \approx 40.254$

(b) After 10 days, the average number of items produced daily is:

$$\frac{1}{10-0} \int_0^{10} 35 \ln(t+1) \, dt$$

$$= \frac{35}{10}\left([(t+1)\ln(t+1) - (t+1)]\Big|_0^{10}\right)$$

$$= \frac{7}{2}(11 \ln 11 - 11 + 1)$$

$$= \frac{7(11 \ln 11 - 10)}{2} \approx 57.319$$

(c) After 15 days, the average number of items produced daily is:

$$\frac{1}{15-0} \int_0^{15} 35 \ln(t+1) \, dt$$

$$= \frac{35}{15}\left([(t+1)\ln(t+1) - (t+1)]\Big|_0^{15}\right)$$

$$= \frac{7}{3}(16 \ln 16 - 16 + 1)$$

$$= \frac{7(16 \ln 16 - 15)}{3} \approx 68.510$$

Section 7.4

2. $f(x) = 300$

(a) $P = \int_0^{10} (300)e^{-.12x} \, dx$

$$= \frac{300}{-.12} e^{-.12x} \Big|_0^{10}$$

$$= -2500(e^{-1.2} - e^0)$$

$$= \$1747.01$$

Store the value for P without rounding in your calculator.

(b) $A = e^{.12(10)} \int_0^{10} 300e^{-.12x} \, dx$

$$= e^{1.2} P$$

$$= \$5800.29$$

4. $f(x) = 2000$

(a) $P = \int_0^{10} 2000e^{-.12x} \, dx$

$$= \frac{2000}{.12} e^{-.12x} \Big|_0^{10}$$

$$= \$16,666.67(e^{-1.2} - e^0)$$

$$= \$11,646.76$$

(b) $A = e^{.12(10)} \int_0^{10} 2000e^{-.12x} \, dx$

$$= e^{1.2} P$$

$$= \$38,668.62$$

6. $f(x) = 800e^{.05x}$

(a) $P = \int_0^{10} 800e^{.05x}e^{-.12x} \, dx$

$$= 800 \int_0^{10} e^{-.07x} \, dx$$

$$= \frac{800}{-.07} e^{-.07x} \Big|_0^{10}$$

$$= -11,428.57(e^{-.7} - 1)$$

$$= \$5753.31$$

(b) $A = e^{.12(10)} \int_0^{10} 800e^{.05x}e^{-.12x} \, dx$

$$= e^{1.2} \int_0^{10} 800e^{-.07x} \, dx$$

$$= e^{1.2} P$$

$$= \$19,101.67$$

8. $f(x) = 1000e^{-.02x}$

(a) $P = 1000 \int_0^{10} e^{-.02x}e^{-.12x} \, dx$

$= 1000 \int_0^{10} e^{-.14x} \, dx$

$= \frac{1000}{-.14} e^{-.14x} \Big|_0^{10}$

$= -7142.86(e^{-1.4} - 1)$

$= \$5381.45$

(b) $A = e^{.12(10)} \int_0^{10} e^{-.02x}e^{-.12x} \, dx$

$= e^{1.2} \int_0^{10} e^{-.14x} \, dx$

$= e^{1.2} P$

$= \$17,867.04$

10. $f(x) = .5x$

(a) $P = \int_0^{10} .5xe^{-.12x} \, dx$

$= .5 \int_0^{10} xe^{-.12x} \, dx$

$.5 \int xe^{-.12x} \, dx$

$= .5 \left(\frac{xe^{-.12x}}{-.12} \right) - \frac{.5}{-.12} \int e^{-.12x} \, dx$

$P = \left[.5 \left(\frac{xe^{-.12x}}{-.12} \right) + \frac{.5}{.12} \left(\frac{e^{-.12x}}{-.12} \right) \right] \Big|_0^{10}$

$= -4.167(10e^{-1.2})$

$+ (-34.72)(e^{-1.2} - 1)$

$= \$11.71$

(b) $A = e^{.12(10)} \int_0^{10} .5xe^{-.12x} \, dx$

$= e^{1.2} P$

$= \$38.89$

12. $f(x) = .05x + 500$

(a) $P = \int_0^{10} (.05x + 500)e^{-.12x} \, dx$

$= .05 \int_0^{10} xe^{-.12x} \, dx$

$+ 500 \int_0^{10} e^{-.12x} \, dx$

$.05 \int xe^{-.12x} \, dx$

$= .05 \left(\frac{xe^{-.12x}}{-.12} - \frac{1}{-.12} \int e^{-.12x} \, dx \right)$

$= .05 \left(\frac{xe^{-.12x}}{-.12} + \frac{1}{.12} \cdot \frac{e^{-.12x}}{-.12} \right)$

$P = \left[.05 \left(\frac{xe^{-.12x}}{-.12} - \frac{e^{-.12x}}{(.12)^2} \right) \right.$

$\left. + \frac{500}{-.12}(e^{-.12x}) \right] \Big|_0^{10}$

$= -.4167(10e^{-1.2}) - 3.472(e^{-1.2} - 1)$

$- 4166.67(e^{-1.2} - 1)$

$= \$2912.86$

(b)

$A = e^{.12(10)} \int_0^{10} (.05x + 500)e^{-.12x} \, dx$

$= e^{1.2} P$

$= \$9671.04$

14. $f(x) = 2000x - 150x^2$

(a) $P = \displaystyle\int_0^{10} (2000x - 150x^2)e^{-.12x}\, dx$

$ = \displaystyle\int_0^{10} 2000xe^{-.12x}\, dx$

$ - \displaystyle\int_0^{10} 150x^2 e^{-.12x}\, dx$

For $\displaystyle\int_0^{10} 2000xe^{-.12x}\, dx$,

let $u = 2000x$ and $dv = e^{-.12x}\, dx$;
then $du = 2000\, dx$ and

$$v = \left(-\frac{1}{.12}\right)e^{-.12x}.$$

$\displaystyle\int 2000xe^{-.12x}\, dx$

$ = \left(\dfrac{-2000x}{.12}\right)e^{-.12x} - \displaystyle\int \dfrac{2000}{-.12}\, e^{-.12x}\, dx$

$ = \dfrac{2000xe^{-.12x}}{-.12} - \dfrac{2000}{(-.12)^2}\, e^{-.12x} + C$

For $\displaystyle\int 150x^2 e^{-.12x}\, dx$, let $u = 150x^2$
and $dv = e^{-.12x}\, dx$.

Use column integration

D	I
$150x^2$	$e^{-.12x}$
$300x$	$\left(\dfrac{1}{-.12}\right)e^{-.12x}$
300	$\dfrac{1}{(-.12)^2}\, e^{-.12x}$
0	$\dfrac{1}{(-.12)^3}\, e^{-.12x}$

$\displaystyle\int 150x^2 e^{-.12x}\, dx$

$ = \dfrac{150x^2 e^{-.12x}}{-.12} - \dfrac{300xe^{-.12x}}{(-.12)^2}$

$ + \dfrac{300e^{-.12x}}{(-.12)^3} + C$

$\displaystyle\int_0^{10} 2000xe^{-.12x}\, dx - \int_0^{10} 150x^2 e^{-.12x}\, dx$

$ = \left[\dfrac{2000xe^{-.12x}}{-.12} - \dfrac{2000e^{-.12x}}{(-.12)^2}\right.$

$ - \dfrac{150x^2 e^{-.12x}}{-.12} + \dfrac{300xe^{-.12x}}{(-.12)^2}$

$ \left. - \dfrac{300e^{-.12x}}{(-.12)^3}\right]$

$ = \dfrac{20000e^{-1.2}}{-.12} - \dfrac{2000e^{-1.2}}{(-.12)^2}$

$ - \dfrac{15000e^{-1.2}}{-.12} + \dfrac{3000e^{-1.2}}{(-.12)^2}$

$ - \dfrac{300e^{-1.2}}{(-.12)^3} + \dfrac{2000}{(-.12)^2} + \dfrac{300}{(-.12)^3}$

$ = \$25,934.95$

(b)

$e^{.12(10)} \displaystyle\int_0^{10} (2000x - 150x^2)e^{-.12x}\, dx$

$ = e^{1.2}P$

$ = \$86,107.05$

16.   (a) Present value

$ = \displaystyle\int_0^6 8000e^{-.12x}\, dx$

$ = \dfrac{8000}{-.12}(e^{-.12x})\Big|_0^6$

$ = -66,666.67(e^{-.72} - 1)$

$ = \$34,216.52$

(b) Present value

$$= \int_0^6 8000e^{-.10x}\, dx$$

$$= \frac{8000}{-.10}(e^{-.10x})\Big|_0^6$$

$$= -80,000(e^{-.6} - 1)$$

$$= \$36,095.07$$

(c) Present value

$$= \int_0^6 8000e^{-.15x}\, dx$$

$$= \frac{8000}{-.15}(e^{-.15x})\Big|_0^6$$

$$= -53,333.33(e^{-.9} - 1)$$

$$= \$31,649.62$$

18. **(a)** Present value

$$= \int_0^4 1000e^{.05x}e^{-.11x}\, dx$$

$$= 1000 \int_0^4 e^{-.06x}\, dx$$

$$= \frac{1000}{-.06}(e^{-.06x})\Big|_0^4$$

$$= -16,666.67(e^{-.2x} - 1)$$

$$= \$3556.20$$

(b) Final amount

$$= e^{.11(4)} \int_0^4 1000e^{.05x}e^{-.11x}\, dx$$

$$= e^{.44}(3556.20)$$

$$= \$5521.74$$

20. $$A = e^{.10(3)} \int_0^3 (1000 - x^2)e^{-.10x}\, dx$$

$$= e^{.3} \int_0^3 1000e^{-.1x}\, dx$$

$$\quad - e^{.3} \int_0^3 x^2 e^{-.1x}\, dx$$

$$= \frac{1000e^{.3}e^{-.1x}}{-.1}\Big|_0^3 - e^{.3}(7.2)$$

$$= -13,498.59(e^{-.3} - 1) - 9.72$$

$$= 3498.59 - 9.72$$

$$= \$3488.84$$

Section 7.5

2. $$\int_5^\infty \frac{1}{x^2}\, dx$$

$$= \lim_{b\to\infty} \int_5^b \frac{dx}{x^2} = \lim_{b\to\infty} \int_5^b x^{-2}\, dx$$

$$= \lim_{b\to\infty} \left(\frac{x^{-1}}{-1}\right)\Big|_5^b = \lim_{b\to\infty} \left(-\frac{1}{x}\right)\Big|_5^b$$

$$= \lim_{b\to\infty} \left(-\frac{1}{b} + \frac{1}{5}\right)$$

As $b \to \infty$, $-\frac{1}{b} \to 0$. The integral is convergent.

$$\int_5^\infty \frac{1}{x^2}\, dx = 0 + \frac{1}{5} = \frac{1}{5}$$

4. $\displaystyle\int_{16}^{\infty} \frac{-3}{\sqrt{x}}\,dx = \lim_{b\to\infty} \int_{16}^{b} -3x^{-1/2}\,dx$

$\displaystyle = \lim_{b\to\infty} \left(\frac{-3x^{1/2}}{1/2}\right)\Big|_{16}^{b}$

$\displaystyle = \lim_{b\to\infty} (-6\sqrt{b} - 6\sqrt{16})$

$\displaystyle = \lim_{b\to\infty} (-6\sqrt{b} - 24)$

As $b\to\infty$, $(-6\sqrt{b} - 24)\to-\infty$, so the integral is divergent.

6. $\displaystyle\int_{-\infty}^{-4} \frac{3}{x^4}\,dx = \lim_{a\to-\infty} \int_{a}^{-4} 3x^{-4}\,dx$

$\displaystyle = \lim_{a\to-\infty} \left(\frac{3x^{-3}}{-3}\right)\Big|_{a}^{-4}$

$\displaystyle = \lim_{a\to-\infty} \left(-\frac{1}{x^3}\right)\Big|_{a}^{-4}$

$\displaystyle = \lim_{a\to-\infty} \left(\frac{1}{64} + \frac{1}{a^3}\right)$

As $a\to-\infty$, $\frac{1}{a^3}\to 0$. The integral is convergent.

$\displaystyle\int_{-\infty}^{-4} \frac{3}{x^4}\,dx = \frac{1}{64} + 0 = \frac{1}{64}$

8. $\displaystyle\int_{1}^{\infty} \frac{1}{x^{.999}}\,dx = \lim_{b\to\infty} \int_{1}^{b} x^{-.999}\,dx$

$\displaystyle = \lim_{b\to\infty} \left(\frac{x^{.001}}{.001}\right)\Big|_{1}^{b}$

$\displaystyle = \lim_{b\to\infty} (1000x^{.001})\Big|_{1}^{b}$

$\displaystyle = \lim_{b\to\infty} (1000b^{.001} - 1000)$

As $b\to\infty$, $(1000b^{.001} - 1000)\to\infty$.
The integral is divergent.

10. $\displaystyle\int_{-\infty}^{-4} x^{-2}\,dx = \lim_{a\to-\infty} \int_{a}^{-4} x^{-2}\,dx$

$\displaystyle = \lim_{a\to-\infty} \left(\frac{x^{-1}}{-1}\right)\Big|_{a}^{-4}$

$\displaystyle = \lim_{a\to-\infty} \left(\frac{-1}{x}\right)\Big|_{a}^{-4}$

$\displaystyle = \lim_{a\to-\infty} \left(\frac{-1}{-4} + \frac{1}{a}\right)$

As $a\to-\infty$, $\frac{1}{a}\to 0$. The integral is convergent.

$\displaystyle\int_{-\infty}^{-4} x^{-2}\,dx = \frac{1}{4} + 0 = \frac{1}{4}$

12. $\displaystyle\int_{-\infty}^{27} x^{-5/3}\,dx$

$\displaystyle = \lim_{a\to-\infty} \int_{a}^{27} x^{-5/3}\,dx$

$\displaystyle = \lim_{a\to-\infty} \left(\frac{x^{-2/3}}{-2/3}\right)\Big|_{a}^{27}$

$\displaystyle = \lim_{a\to-\infty} \left(-\frac{3}{2}x^{-2/3}\right)\Big|_{a}^{27}$

$\displaystyle = \lim_{a\to-\infty} \left[-\frac{3}{2}(27)^{-2/3} + \frac{3}{2}(a)^{-2/3}\right]$

$\displaystyle = \lim_{a\to-\infty} \left(-\frac{1}{6} + \frac{3}{a^{2/3}}\right)$

As $a\to-\infty$, $\frac{3}{a^{2/3}}\to 0$. The integral is convergent.

$\displaystyle\int_{-\infty}^{27} x^{-5/3}\,dx = -\frac{1}{6} + 0 = -\frac{1}{6}$

14. $\displaystyle\int_0^\infty 10e^{-10x}\,dx = \lim_{b\to\infty}\int_0^b 10e^{-10x}\,dx$

$$= \lim_{b\to\infty}\,(-e^{-10x})\Big|_0^b$$

$$= \lim_{b\to\infty}\,(-e^{-10b} + e^0)$$

$$= \lim_{b\to\infty}\,(-e^{-10b} + 1)$$

As $b\to\infty$, $\dfrac{-1}{e^{10b}}\to 0$. The integral is convergent.

$$\int_0^\infty 10e^{-10x}\,dx = 0 + 1 = 1$$

16. $\displaystyle\int_{-\infty}^0 3e^{4x}\,dx = \lim_{a\to-\infty}\int_a^0 3e^{4x}\,dx$

$$= \lim_{a\to-\infty}\left(\frac{3e^{4x}}{4}\right)\Big|_a^0$$

$$= \lim_{a\to-\infty}\left(\frac{3}{4} - \frac{3}{4}e^{4a}\right)$$

As $a\to-\infty$, e^{4a} is in the denominator of the fraction. So, $-\dfrac{3}{4}e^{4a}\to 0$. The integral is convergent.

$$\int_{-\infty}^0 3e^{4x}\,dx = \frac{3}{4} + 0 = \frac{3}{4}$$

18. $\displaystyle\int_1^\infty \ln|x|\,dx = \lim_{b\to\infty}\int_1^b \ln|x|\,dx$

Let $\;u = \ln|x|\;$ and $\;dv = dx$.

Then $du = \dfrac{1}{x}\,dx\;$ and $\;v = x$.

$$\int \ln|x|\,dx = x\ln|x| - \int \frac{x}{x}\,dx$$

$$= x\ln|x| - x + C$$

$\displaystyle\int_1^\infty \ln|x|\,dx$

$$= \lim_{b\to\infty}\,(x\ln|x| - x)\Big|_1^b$$

$$= \lim_{b\to\infty}\,[(b\ln b - b) - (-1)]$$

$$= \lim_{b\to\infty}\,[b\ln b - b + 1]$$

As $b\to\infty$, $(b\ln b - b + 1)\to\infty$. The integral is divergent.

20. $\displaystyle\int_0^\infty \frac{dx}{(2x+1)^3}$

$$= \lim_{b\to\infty}\int_0^b \frac{dx}{(2x+1)^3}$$

$$= \lim_{b\to\infty}\left(\frac{1}{2}\int_0^b 2(2x+1)^{-3}\,dx\right)$$

$$= \lim_{b\to\infty}\left[\frac{1}{2}\cdot\frac{(2x+1)^{-2}}{-2}\right]\Big|_0^b$$

$$= \lim_{b\to\infty}\left[-\frac{1}{4}(2x+1)^{-2}\right]\Big|_0^b$$

$$= \lim_{b\to\infty}\left[-\frac{1}{4}(2b+1)^{-2} + \frac{1}{4}(1)^{-2}\right]$$

As $b\to\infty$, $-\dfrac{1}{4}(2b+1)^{-2}\to 0$. The integral is convergent.

$$\int_0^\infty \frac{dx}{(2x+1)^3} = 0 + \frac{1}{4} = \frac{1}{4}$$

22. $\displaystyle\int_0^\infty \frac{2x + 3}{x^2 + 3x} \, dx$

$\displaystyle = \lim_{b \to \infty} \int_0^b \frac{2x + 3}{x^2 + 3x} \, dx$

$\displaystyle = \lim_{b \to \infty} \left[\ln |x^2 + 3x| \Big|_0^b \right]$

$\displaystyle = \lim_{b \to \infty} [\ln (b^2 + 3b) - \ln 0]$

As $b \to \infty$, $[\ln (b^2 + 3b) - \ln 0] \to \infty$.
The integral is divergent.

24. $\displaystyle\int_2^\infty \frac{1}{x(\ln x)^2} \, dx$

$\displaystyle = \lim_{b \to \infty} \int_2^b \frac{1}{x(\ln x)^2} \, dx$

Use substitution.

$\displaystyle = \lim_{b \to \infty} \left(-\frac{1}{\ln x} \Big|_2^b \right)$

$\displaystyle = \lim_{b \to \infty} \left(\frac{-1}{\ln b} + \frac{1}{\ln 2} \right)$

As $b \to \infty$, $-\dfrac{1}{\ln b} \to 0$. The integral is

convergent.

$\displaystyle\int_2^\infty \frac{1}{x(\ln x)^2} \, dx = 0 + \frac{1}{\ln 2}$

$\displaystyle \qquad\qquad\qquad = \frac{1}{\ln 2}$

26. $\displaystyle\int_{-\infty}^0 xe^{3x} \, dx = \lim_{a \to -\infty} \int_a^0 xe^{3x} \, dx$

Let $dv = e^{3x} \, dx$ and $u = x$.

Then $v = \frac{1}{3}e^{3x}$ and $du = dx$.

$\displaystyle\int xe^{3x} \, dx = \frac{x}{3} e^{3x} - \int \frac{1}{3} e^{3x} \, dx$

$\displaystyle \qquad\qquad = \frac{xe^{3x}}{3} - \frac{1}{9} e^{3x} + C$

$\displaystyle\int_{-\infty}^0 xe^{3x} \, dx$

$\displaystyle = \lim_{a \to -\infty} \left(\frac{xe^{3x}}{3} - \frac{1}{9} e^{3x} \right) \Big|_a^0$

$\displaystyle = \lim_{a \to -\infty} \left(-\frac{1}{9} - \frac{ae^{3a}}{3} + \frac{1}{3a} e^{3a} \right)$

As $a \to -\infty$, e^{3a} is in the denominator
of a fraction. The integral is convergent.

$\displaystyle\int_{-\infty}^0 xe^{3x} \, dx = -\frac{1}{9} - 0 + 0 = -\frac{1}{9}$

28. $\displaystyle\int_1^\infty \frac{7}{2x(5x + 1)} \, dx$

$\displaystyle = \lim_{b \to \infty} \int_1^b \frac{7 \, dx}{2x(5x + 1)}$

$\displaystyle = \lim_{b \to \infty} \frac{7}{2} \int_1^b \frac{dx}{x(5x + 1)}$

$\displaystyle = \lim_{b \to \infty} \frac{7}{2} \ln \left| \frac{x}{5x + 1} \right| \Big|_1^b$

$\displaystyle = \lim_{b \to \infty} \frac{7}{2} \left(\ln \frac{b}{5b + 1} - \ln \frac{1}{6} \right)$

$\displaystyle = \frac{7}{2} \lim_{b \to \infty} \left(\ln \frac{b}{5b + 1} + \ln 6 \right)$

As $b \to \infty$, $\dfrac{b}{5b + 1} \to \dfrac{1}{5}$. The integral is

convergent.

$$\int_1^\infty \frac{7}{2x(5x + 1)}\, dx = \frac{7}{2}\left(\ln \frac{1}{5} + \ln 6\right)$$

$$= \frac{7}{2} \ln \frac{6}{5} \approx .638$$

30. $\displaystyle\int_{-\infty}^{-5} \frac{5\, dx}{4x(x + 2)^2}$

$$= \lim_{a \to -\infty} \int_a^{-5} \frac{5\, dx}{4x(x + 2)^2}$$

$$= \lim_{a \to -\infty} \left(\frac{5}{4} \int_a^{-5} \frac{dx}{x(x + 2)^2}\right)$$

Use entry 14 from the table.

$$= \frac{5}{4} \lim_{a \to -\infty} \left(\frac{1}{2(x + 2)} + \frac{1}{4} \ln \left|\frac{x}{x + 2}\right|\right)\Big|_a^{-5}$$

$$= \frac{5}{4} \lim_{a \to -\infty} \left(\frac{1}{2(-5 + 2)} + \frac{1}{4} \ln \left|\frac{5}{-5 + 2}\right|\right.$$

$$\left. - \frac{1}{2(a + 2)} - \frac{1}{4} \ln \left|\frac{a}{a + 2}\right|\right)$$

As $a \to -\infty$, $-\dfrac{1}{2(a + 2)} \to 0$ and

$\ln \left|\dfrac{a}{a + 2}\right| \to \ln 1 = 0$.

The integral is convergent.

$$\int_{-\infty}^{-5} \frac{5\, dx}{4x(x + 2)^2}$$

$$= \frac{5}{4}\left(-\frac{1}{6}\right) + \frac{5}{4} \cdot \frac{1}{4} \ln \left|-\frac{5}{3}\right|$$

$$= -\frac{5}{24} + \frac{5}{16} \ln \frac{5}{3} \approx -.0487$$

32. $\displaystyle\int_9^\infty \frac{1}{\sqrt{x^2 - 4}}\, dx$

$$= \lim_{b \to \infty} \int_9^b \frac{1}{\sqrt{x^2 - 4}}\, dx$$

Use entry 6 in the table.

$$= \lim_{b \to \infty} \left(\ln \left|x + \sqrt{x^2 - 4}\right|\Big|_9^b\right)$$

$$= \lim_{b \to \infty} [\ln |b + \sqrt{b^2 - 4}|$$

$$- \ln (9 + \sqrt{77})]$$

As $b \to \infty$, $\ln (b + \sqrt{b^2 - 4}) \to \infty$.
The integral is divergent.

34. $f(x) = e^{-x}$ for $(-\infty, e]$

$$\int_{-\infty}^e e^{-x} = \lim_{a \to -\infty} \int_a^e e^{-x}\, dx$$

$$= \lim_{a \to -\infty} (-e^{-x})\Big|_a^e$$

$$= \lim_{a \to -\infty} (-e^{-e} + e^{-a})$$

As $a \to -\infty$, $e^{-a} \to \infty$, and $(-e^{-e} + e^{-a})$
$\to \infty$. The integral is divergent, so
the area cannot be found.

36. $f(x) = \dfrac{1}{(x - 1)^3}$ for $(-\infty, 0]$

$$\int_{-\infty}^0 \frac{1}{(x - 1)^3}\, dx$$

$$= \lim_{a \to -\infty} \int_a^0 \frac{dx}{(x - 1)^3}$$

$$= \lim_{a \to -\infty} \left(\frac{(x - 1)^{-2}}{-2}\right)\Big|_a^0$$

$$= \lim_{a \to -\infty} \left[-\frac{1}{2(x - 1)^2}\right]\Big|_a^0$$

$$= \lim_{a \to -\infty} \left[-\frac{1}{2} + \frac{1}{2(a - 1)^2}\right]$$

$$= -\frac{1}{2}$$

Since area is positive, the area is $|-1/2| = 1/2$.

38. $\displaystyle\int_{-\infty}^{\infty} \frac{x}{(1 + x^2)^2}\, dx$

$\displaystyle = \int_{-\infty}^{c} \frac{x}{(1 + x^2)^2}\, dx$

$\displaystyle \quad + \int_{c}^{\infty} \frac{x}{(1 + x^2)^2}\, dx$

$\displaystyle = \lim_{a \to -\infty} \int_{a}^{c} \frac{x\, dx}{(1 + x^2)^2}$

$\displaystyle \quad + \lim_{b \to \infty} \int_{c}^{b} \frac{x\, dx}{(1 + x^2)^2}$

$\displaystyle = \lim_{a \to -\infty} \left(\frac{-1}{2(1 + x^2)} \right) \Bigg|_{a}^{c}$

$\displaystyle \quad + \lim_{b \to \infty} \left(\frac{-1}{2(1 + x^2)} \right) \Bigg|_{c}^{b}$

$\displaystyle = \lim_{a \to -\infty} \left[\frac{-1}{2(1 + c^2)} + \frac{1}{2(1 + a^2)} \right]$

$\displaystyle \quad + \lim_{b \to \infty} \left[\frac{-1}{2(1 + b^2)} + \frac{1}{2(1 + c^2)} \right]$

$\displaystyle = \frac{-1}{2(1 + c^2)} + 0 + 0 + \frac{1}{2(1 + c^2)}$

$= 0$

42. Capital value

$\displaystyle = \int_{0}^{\infty} 500{,}000 e^{-.06t}\, dt$

$\displaystyle = \lim_{b \to \infty} \int_{0}^{b} 500{,}000 e^{-.06t}\, dt$

$\displaystyle = \lim_{b \to \infty} \frac{500{,}000}{-.06}\, e^{-.06t} \Bigg|_{0}^{b}$

$\displaystyle = -\frac{500{,}000}{.06} \lim_{b \to \infty} (e^{-.06b} - e^0)$

As $b \to \infty$, $\dfrac{1}{e^{.06b}} \to 0$.

$\displaystyle = -\frac{500{,}000}{.06}(-1)$

$= \$8{,}333{,}333.33$

44. Capital value

$\displaystyle = \int_{0}^{\infty} 1000 e^{.02t} e^{-.07t}\, dt$

$\displaystyle = 1000 \lim_{b \to \infty} \int_{0}^{b} e^{-.05t}\, dt$

$\displaystyle = 1000 \lim_{b \to \infty} \frac{e^{-.05t}}{-.05} \Bigg|_{0}^{b}$

$\displaystyle = \frac{1000}{-.05} \lim_{b \to \infty} (e^{-.05b} - e^0)$

$\displaystyle = \frac{1000}{.05} = \$20{,}000$

46. $r'(x) = 2x^2 e^{-x}$

$\displaystyle r(x) = \int_{0}^{\infty} 2x^2 e^{-x}\, dx$

$\displaystyle \quad = \lim_{b \to \infty} \int_{0}^{b} 2x^2 e^{-x}\, dx$

Let $u = 2x^2$ and $dv = e^{-x}\, dx$.

Use column integration to obtain

$\displaystyle \lim_{b \to \infty} \int_{0}^{b} 2x^2 e^{-x}\, dx$

$\displaystyle = \lim_{b \to \infty} \left[(-2x^2 e^{-x} - 4x e^{-x} - 4 e^{-x}) \Bigg|_{0}^{b} \right]$

$\displaystyle = \lim_{b \to \infty} \left[(2x^2 e^{-x} + 4x e^{-x} + 4 e^{-x}) \Bigg|_{0}^{b} \right]$

$\displaystyle = \lim_{b \to \infty} (2b^2 e^{-b} + 4b e^{-b} + 4 e^{-b} - 4)$

$= -(-4)$ (Use hint to evaluate limits.)

$= 4$

48. $\displaystyle\int_0^\infty 50e^{-.04t}\ dt$

$\displaystyle = 50\ \lim_{b\to\infty}\int_0^b e^{-.04t}\ dt$

$\displaystyle = 50\ \lim_{b\to\infty}\ \frac{e^{-.04t}}{-.04}\Big|_0^b$

$\displaystyle = \frac{50}{-.04}\ \lim_{b\to\infty}\left(\frac{1}{e^{.04b}} - 1\right)$

As $b\to\infty$, $\dfrac{1}{e^{.04b}}\to 0$.

$= -1250(-1)$

$= 1250$

Chapter 7 Review Exercises

6. $\displaystyle\int \frac{3x}{\sqrt{x-2}} = \int 3x(x-2)^{-1/2}\ dx$

Let $u = 3x$ and $dv = (x-2)^{-1/2}\,dx$.
Then $du = 3\ dx$ and $v = 2(x-2)^{1/2}$.

$\displaystyle\int \frac{3x\ dx}{\sqrt{x-2}}$

$\displaystyle = 6x(x-2)^{1/2} - 6\int (x-2)^{1/2}\ dx$

$\displaystyle = 6x(x-2)^{1/2} - \frac{6(x-2)^{3/2}}{3/2} + C$

$\displaystyle = 6x(x-2)^{1/2} - 4(x-2)^{3/2} + C$

8. $\displaystyle\int (x+2)e^{-3x}\ dx$

Let $u = x+2$ and $dv = e^{-3x}$.
Then $du = dx$ and $v = -\frac{1}{3}e^{-3x}$.

$\displaystyle\int (x+2)e^{-3x}\ dx$

$\displaystyle = (x+2)\left(-\frac{1}{3}e^{-3x}\right) + \frac{1}{3}\int e^{-3x}\ dx$

$\displaystyle = \frac{-(x+2)e^{-3x}}{3} - \frac{e^{-3x}}{9} + C$

10. $\displaystyle\int (x-1)\ln|x|\ dx$

Let $u = \ln|x|$ and $dv = (x-1)\ dx$.
Then $du = \frac{1}{x}\ dx$ and $v = \left(\frac{x^2}{2} - x\right)$.

$\displaystyle\int (x-1)\ln|x|\ dx$

$\displaystyle = \left(\frac{x^2}{2} - x\right)\ln|x| - \int \left(\frac{x}{2} - 1\right)\ dx$

$\displaystyle = \left(\frac{x^2}{2} - x\right)\ln|x| - \frac{x^2}{4} + x + C$

12. $\displaystyle\int \frac{x}{\sqrt{25 + 9x^2}}\ dx$

Use substitution.
Let $u = 25 + 9x^2$; then $du = 18x\ dx$
and $\frac{1}{18}\ du = x\ dx$.

$\displaystyle\int \frac{x}{\sqrt{25 + 9x^2}}\ dx$

$\displaystyle = \frac{1}{18}\int \frac{1}{u^{1/2}}\ du$

$\displaystyle = \frac{1}{18}\left(\frac{2}{1}\right)(u^{1/2}) + C$

$\displaystyle = \frac{1}{9}u^{1/2} + C$

$\displaystyle = \frac{1}{9}\sqrt{25 + 9x^2} + C$

14. $\displaystyle\int \frac{1}{\sqrt{25 + 9x^2}}\ dx$

Let $u = 3x$, then $du = 3\ dx$.

$$\int \frac{1}{\sqrt{25 + 9x^2}}\ dx$$

$$= \frac{1}{3} \int \frac{3\ dx}{\sqrt{25 + 9x^2}}$$

$$= \frac{1}{3} \int \frac{du}{\sqrt{u^2 + 25}}$$

Use entry 5 in the table.

$$= \frac{1}{3} \ln \left| u + \sqrt{u^2 + 25} \right| + C$$

$$= \frac{1}{3} \ln \left| 3x + \sqrt{9x^2 + 25} \right| + C$$

16. $\displaystyle\int_0^3 \sqrt{16 + x^2}\ dx$

$$= \int_0^3 \sqrt{4^2 + x^2}$$

Use entry 15 in the table.

$$= \left(\frac{x}{2}\sqrt{16 + x^2} + 8\ \ln \left| x + \sqrt{x^2 + 16} \right| \right) \Bigg|_0^3$$

$$= \frac{3}{2}(5) + 8\ \ln\ (3 + 5) - 8\ \ln\ (0 + 4)$$

$$= \frac{15}{2} + 8\ \ln 8 - 8\ \ln 4$$

$$= \frac{15}{2} + 8\ \ln 2$$

$$\approx 13.045$$

18. $\displaystyle\int_0^1 x^2 e^{x/2}\ dx$

Let $u = x^2$ and $dv = e^{x/2}\ dx$.

Use column integration.

D	I
x^2	$e^{x/2}$
$2x$	$2e^{x/2}$
2	$4e^{x/2}$
0	$8e^{x/2}$

$$\int_0^1 x^2 e^{x/2}\ dx$$

$$= \left(2x^2 e^{x/2} - 8xe^{x/2} + 16e^{x/2} \right) \Bigg|_0^1$$

$$= 2e^{1/2} - 8e^{1/2} + 16e^{1/2} - 16$$

$$= 10e^{1/2} - 16$$

$$\approx .48721$$

20. $\displaystyle A = \int_1^3 x^3 (x^2 - 1)^{1/3}\ dx$

Let $u = x^2$ and $dv = x(x^2 - 1)^{1/3}\ dx$.

Then $du = 2x$ and $v = \frac{3}{8}(x^2 - 1)^{4/3}$.

$$\int x^3 (x^2 - 1)^{1/3}\ dx$$

$$= \frac{3x^2}{8}(x^2 - 1)^{4/3} - \frac{3}{4} \int x(x^2 - 1)^{4/3}\ dx$$

$$= \frac{3x^2}{8}(x^2 - 1)^{4/3} - \frac{3}{4}\left[\frac{1}{2} \cdot \frac{3}{7}(x^2 - 1)^{7/3} \right]$$

$$= \frac{3x^2}{8}(x^2 - 1)^{4/3} - \frac{9}{56}(x^2 - 1)^{7/3} + C$$

$$A = \left[\frac{3x^2}{8}(x^2 - 1)^{4/3} - \frac{9}{56}(x^2 - 1)^{7/3} \right] \Bigg|_1^3$$

$$= \frac{3}{8}(144) - \frac{9}{56}(128)$$

$$= 54 - \frac{144}{7} = \frac{234}{7} \approx 33.43$$

22. $\int_{2}^{10} \frac{x \, dx}{x - 1}$

n = 4, b = 10, a = 2, $f(x) = \frac{x}{x - 1}$

i	x_i	$f(x_i)$
0	2	2
1	4	$\frac{4}{3}$
2	6	$\frac{6}{5}$
3	8	$\frac{8}{7}$
4	10	$\frac{10}{9}$

$\int_{2}^{10} \frac{x \, dx}{x - 1}$

$\approx \frac{10 - 2}{4}\left[\frac{1}{2}(2) + \frac{4}{3} + \frac{6}{5} + \frac{8}{7} + \frac{1}{2}\left(\frac{10}{9}\right)\right]$

$\approx 2(5.232)$

≈ 10.46

Exact value:

$\int_{2}^{10} \frac{x}{x - 1} \, dx$

Use entry 11 in the table.

$\int_{2}^{10} \frac{x}{x - 1} \, dx = (x + \ln|x - 1|)\Big|_{2}^{10}$

$= 10 + \ln 9 - 2 - \ln 1$

$= 8 + \ln 9$

≈ 10.20

24. $\int_{2}^{6} \frac{dx}{x^2 - 1}$

n = 4, b = 6, a = 2, $f(x) = \frac{1}{x^2 - 1}$

i	x_i	$f(x_i)$
0	2	$\frac{1}{3}$
1	3	$\frac{1}{8}$
2	4	$\frac{1}{15}$
3	5	$\frac{1}{24}$
4	6	$\frac{1}{35}$

$\int_{2}^{6} \frac{dx}{x^2 - 1}$

$\approx \frac{6 - 2}{3(4)}\left[\frac{1}{3} + 4\left(\frac{1}{8}\right) + 2\left(\frac{1}{15}\right) + 4\left(\frac{1}{24}\right) + \frac{1}{35}\right]$

$\approx \frac{1}{3}(1.162)$

$\approx .3873$

26. $\int_{1}^{5} \ln x \, dx$

n = 4, b = 5, a = 1, $f(x) = \ln x$

i	x_i	$f(x_i)$
0	1	$\ln 1 = 0$
1	2	$\ln 2 = .6931$
2	3	$\ln 3 = 1.0986$
3	4	$\ln 4 = 1.3863$
4	5	$\ln 5 = 1.6094$

$A = \frac{5 - 1}{3(4)}[0 + 4(.6931 + 2(1.0986)$

$\qquad + 4(1.3863) + 1.6094]$

$\approx \frac{1}{3}(12.1242)$

≈ 4.041

28. $A = \int_{-1}^{1} \sqrt{1 - x^2} \; dx$

$n = 6, \; b = 1, \; a = -1, \; f(x) = \sqrt{1 - x^2}$

i	x_i	$f(x_i)$
0	-1	0
1	$-\frac{2}{3}$	.7453
2	$-\frac{1}{3}$	.9428
3	0	1
4	$\frac{1}{3}$	.9428
5	$\frac{2}{3}$	.7453
6	1	0

$A \approx \frac{1 - (-1)}{3(6)}[0 + 4(.7453) + 2(.9428)$

$\qquad + 4(1) + 2(.9428) + 4(.7453) + 0]$

$\approx \frac{1}{9}(13.7336)$

≈ 1.526

30. $f(x) = \sqrt{x - 2}, \; y = 0, \; x = 11$

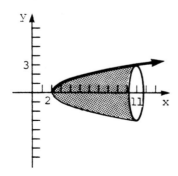

Since $f(x) = \sqrt{x - 2}$ intersects $y = 0$ at $x = 2$, the integral has a lower bound, $a = 2$.

$V = \pi \int_{2}^{11} (\sqrt{x - 2})^2 \; dx$

$\quad = \pi \int_{2}^{11} (x - 2) \; dx$

$\quad = \pi\left(\frac{x^2}{2} - 2x\right)\Big|_{2}^{11}$

$\quad = \pi\left(\frac{121}{2} - 22\right) - \pi(2 - 4)$

$\quad = \pi\left(\frac{121}{2} - 22 + 2\right)$

$\quad = \frac{81\pi}{2} \approx 127.23$

32. $f(x) = \frac{1}{\sqrt{x - 1}}, \; y = 0, \; x = 2, \; x = 4$

$V = \pi \int_{2}^{4} \left(\frac{1}{\sqrt{x - 1}}\right)^2 \; dx$

$\quad = \pi \int_{2}^{4} \frac{dx}{x - 1}$

$\quad = \pi \; (\ln |x - 1|)\Big|_{2}^{4}$

$\quad = \pi \ln 3 \approx 3.451$

34. $f(x) = \frac{x^2}{4}, \; y = 0, \; x = 4$

Since $f(x) = \frac{x^2}{4}$ intersects $y = 0$ at $x = 0$, the integral has a lower bound, $a = 0$.

$$V = \pi \int_0^4 \left(\frac{x^2}{4}\right)^2 dx = \pi \int_0^4 \frac{x^4}{16}$$

$$= \frac{\pi}{16}\left(\frac{x^5}{5}\right)\Big|_0^4$$

$$= \frac{\pi}{16}\left(\frac{1024}{5}\right)$$

$$= \frac{64\pi}{5} \approx 40.21$$

38. Average value

$$= \frac{1}{1-0}\int_0^1 x^2(x^3+1)^5 dx$$

$$= 1\int_0^1 x^2(x^3+1)^5 dx$$

$$= \frac{1}{18}(x^3+1)^6\Big|_0^1$$

$$= \frac{1}{18}(2^6 - 1^6)$$

$$= \frac{1}{18}(64 - 1)$$

$$= \frac{63}{18} = \frac{7}{2}$$

40. $\displaystyle\int_{-\infty}^{-2} x^{-2} dx = \lim_{a\to-\infty}\int_a^{-2} x^{-2} dx$

$$= \lim_{a\to-\infty}(-x^{-1})\Big|_a^{-2}$$

$$= \lim_{a\to-\infty}\left[\left(\frac{1}{2}\right) + \frac{1}{a}\right]$$

As $a \to -\infty$, $\frac{1}{a} \to 0$. The integral

converges.

$$\int_{-\infty}^{-2} x^{-2} dx = \frac{1}{2} + 0 = \frac{1}{2}$$

42. $\displaystyle\int_1^\infty 6e^{-x} dx = \lim_{b\to\infty}\int_1^b 6e^{-x} dx$

$$= \lim_{b\to\infty} -6e^{-x}\Big|_1^b$$

$$= \lim_{b\to\infty}(-6e^{-b} + 6e^{-1})$$

$$= \lim_{b\to\infty}\left(\frac{-6}{e^b} + \frac{6}{e}\right)$$

As $b \to \infty$, $e^b \to \infty$, so $\frac{-6}{e^b} \to 0$. The

integral converges.

$$\int_1^\infty 6e^{-x} dx = 0 + \frac{6}{e} = \frac{6}{e} \approx 2.207$$

44. $\displaystyle\int_{10}^\infty \ln(2x) dx$

$$= \lim_{b\to\infty}\int_{10}^b \ln(2x) dx$$

Let $u = \ln(2x)$ and $dv = dx$,

then $du = \frac{2\,dx}{2x} = \frac{dx}{x}$ and $v = x$.

$$\int \ln(2x) dx = x\ln(2x) - \int \frac{x\,dx}{x}$$

$$= x\ln(2x) - x$$

$$\int_{10}^\infty \ln(2x) dx$$

$$= \lim_{b\to\infty}[x\ln(2x) - x]\Big|_{10}^b$$

$$= \lim_{b\to\infty}(b\ln 2b - b - 10\ln 20 + 10)$$

As $b \to \infty$, $(b\ln 2b - b) \to \infty$.
The integral is divergent.

46. $f(x) = 3e^{-x}$ for $[0, \infty)$

$$A = \int_0^\infty 3e^{-x} \; dx$$

$$= \lim_{b \to \infty} \int_0^b 3e^{-x} \; dx$$

$$= \lim_{b \to \infty} (-3e^{-x}) \Big|_0^b$$

$$= \lim_{b \to \infty} \left(\frac{-3}{e^b} + 3\right)$$

As $b \to \infty$, $\frac{-3}{e^b} \to 0$.

$A = 0 + 3 = 3$

48. $R' = x(x - 50)^{1/2}$

$$R = \int_{50}^{75} x(x - 50)^{1/2} \; dx$$

Let $u = x$ and $dv = (x - 50)^{1/2}$.

Then $du = dx$ and $v = \frac{2}{3}(x - 50)^{3/2}$.

$$\int x(x - 50)^{1/2} \; dx$$

$$= \frac{2}{3}x(x-50)^{3/2} - \frac{2}{3}\int (x - 50)^{3/2} \; dx$$

$$= \frac{2}{3}x(x - 50)^{3/2} - \frac{2}{3} \cdot \frac{2}{5}(x - 50)^{5/2}$$

$$R = \left[\frac{2}{3}x(x - 50)^{3/2} - \frac{4}{15}(x - 50)^{5/2}\right]\Big|_{50}^{75}$$

$$= \frac{2}{3}(75)(25^{3/2}) - \frac{4}{15}(25^{5/2})$$

$$= 6250 - \frac{2500}{3}$$

$$= \frac{16,250}{3} \approx 5416.67$$

50. Sales

$$= \frac{7 - 1}{3(6)}[.7 + 4(1.2) + 2(1.5)$$

$$+ 4(1.9) + 2(2.2) + 4(2.4) + 2]$$

$$= \frac{1}{3}(32.10)$$

$$= 10.7$$

Total sales are \$10.7 million.

52. $f(x) = 25,000$; 12 yr; 10%

$$P = \int_0^{12} 25,000e^{-.10x} \; dx$$

$$= 25,000\left(\frac{e^{-.10x}}{-.10}\right)\Big|_0^{12}$$

$$= 250,000(-.3012 + 1)$$

$$= \$174,701.45$$

54. $f(x) = 30x$; 18 mo; 5%

$$P = \int_0^{1.5} 30xe^{-.05x} \; dx$$

Let $u = 30x$ and $dv = e^{-.05x} \; dx$.

Use column integration.

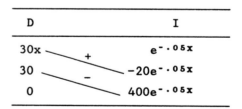

D	I
30x	$e^{-.05x}$
30	$-20e^{-.05x}$
0	$400e^{-.05x}$

$$\int_0^{1.5} 30xe^{-.05x} \; dx$$

$$= (-600xe^{-.05x} - 12,000e^{-.05x})\Big|_0^{1.5}$$

$$= -600(1.5)e^{-.075} - 12,000e^{-.075}$$

$$+ 0 + 12,000e^0$$

$$= -12,900e^{-.075} + 12,000$$

$$\approx \$32.11$$

56. $f(x) = 500e^{-.03x}$; 8 yr; 10% per year

$$e^{.10(8)} \int_0^8 500e^{-.03x}e^{-.10x} \, dx$$

$$= e^{.8} \int_0^8 500e^{-.13x} \, dx$$

$$= \frac{500e^{.8}e^{-.13x}}{-.13} \bigg|_0^8$$

$$= -8559.77(e^{-1.04} - 1)$$

$$= \$5534.28$$

58. $f(x) = 1000 + 200x$; 10 yr; 9% per year

$$e^{(.09)(10)} \int_0^{10} (1000 + 200x)e^{-.09x} \, dx$$

$$= e^{.9} \left[\frac{1000}{-.09} e^{-.09x} \right.$$

$$\left. + \frac{200}{(.09)^2}(-.09x - 1)e^{-.09x} \right] \bigg|_0^{10}$$

$$= e^{.9} \left[\frac{1000}{-.09}(e^{-.9} - 1) \right.$$

$$\left. + \frac{200}{(.09)^2}(-1.9e^{-.9} + 1) \right]$$

$$= \$30,035.17$$

60. $e^{.105(10)} \int_0^{10} 10,000e^{-.105x} \, dx$

$$= e^{1.05} \left(\frac{10,000e^{-.105x}}{-.105} \right) \bigg|_0^{10}$$

$$= \frac{10,000e^{1.05}}{-.105}(e^{-1.05} - 1)$$

$$= -272,157.25(-.65006)$$

$$= \$176,919.15$$

62. $\int_0^5 .5xe^{-x} \, dx$

$$= .5 \int_0^5 xe^{-x} \, dx$$

Let $u = x$ and $dv = e^{-x} \, dx$.

Then $du = dx$ and $v = \frac{e^{-x}}{-1}$.

$$\int xe^{-x} \, dx = \frac{xe^{-x}}{-1} + \int e^{-x} \, dx$$

$$= -xe^{-x} + \frac{e^{-x}}{-1}$$

$$.5 \int_0^5 xe^{-x} \, dx = .5(-xe^{-x} - e^{-x}) \bigg|_0^5$$

$$= .5(-5e^{-5} - e^{-5} + e^0)$$

$$= .480$$

The total reaction over the first 5 hr is .480.

64. **(a)** $\overline{T} = \frac{1}{10 - 0} \int_0^{10} (400 - .25x^2) \, dx$

$$= \frac{1}{10}(400x - \frac{.25x^3}{3}) \bigg|_0^{10}$$

$$= \frac{1}{10}[400(10) - \frac{.25}{3}(10)^3]$$

$$= \frac{1}{10}(3916.7)$$

$$= 391.7$$

(b) $\overline{T} = \frac{1}{40 - 10} \int_{10}^{40} (400 - .25x^2) \, dx$

$$= \frac{1}{30}(400x - \frac{.25x^3}{3}) \bigg|_{10}^{40}$$

$$= \frac{1}{30}\left[\left(400(40) - \frac{.25(40)^3}{3}\right)\right.$$

$$\left. - \left(400(10) - \frac{.25(10)^3}{3}\right)\right]$$

$$= \frac{1}{30}(10{,}666.7 - 3916.67)$$

$$= 225$$

(c) $\overline{T} = \displaystyle\int_{0}^{40} (400 - .25x^2)\ dx$

$$= \frac{1}{40}\left(400x - \frac{.25x^3}{3}\right)\Big|_{0}^{40}$$

$$= \frac{1}{40}\left[(400)(40) - \frac{(.25)(40)^3}{3}\right]$$

$$= \frac{1}{40}[10{,}666.7]$$

$$= 266.7$$

CHAPTER 8   MULTIVARIABLE CALCULUS

Section 8.1

2. $g(x, y) = -x^2 - 4xy + y^3$

(a) $g(-2, 4) = -(-2)^2 - 4(-2)(4)$
$\qquad\qquad + (4)^3$
$\qquad\quad = 92$

(b) $g(-1, -2) = -(-1)^2 - 4(-1)(-2)$
$\qquad\qquad\quad + (-2)^3$
$\qquad\qquad = -17$

(c) $g(-2, 3) = -(-2)^2 - 4(-2)(3)$
$\qquad\qquad\quad + (3)^3$
$\qquad\qquad = 47$

(d) $g(5, 1) = -(5)^2 - 4(5)(1) + (1)^3$
$\qquad\qquad = -44$

4. $f(x, y) = \dfrac{\sqrt{9x + 5y}}{\log x}$

(a) $f(10, 2) = \dfrac{\sqrt{9(10) + 5(2)}}{\log 10}$
$\qquad\qquad = \dfrac{\sqrt{100}}{1} = 10$

(b) $f(100, 1) = \dfrac{\sqrt{9(100) + 5(1)}}{\log 100}$
$\qquad\qquad = \dfrac{\sqrt{905}}{2}$

(c) $f(1000, 0) = \dfrac{\sqrt{9(1000) + 5(0)}}{\log 1000}$
$\qquad\qquad = \dfrac{\sqrt{9000}}{3} = 10\sqrt{10}$

(d) $f\left(\dfrac{1}{10}, 5\right) = \dfrac{\sqrt{9\left(\dfrac{1}{10}\right) + 5(5)}}{\log \dfrac{1}{10}}$
$\qquad\qquad = \dfrac{\sqrt{25.9}}{-1} = -\sqrt{25.9}$

6. $x + y + z = 12$

To find x−intercept, let $y = 0$, $z = 0$.

$\qquad x + 0 + 0 = 12$
$\qquad\qquad x = 12$

To find y−intercept, let $x = 0$, $z = 0$.

$\qquad\qquad y = 12$

To find z−intercept, let $x = 0$, $y = 0$.

$\qquad\qquad z = 12$

Sketch the portion of the plane in the first octant that contains these intercepts.

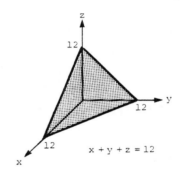

8. $4x + 2y + 3z = 24$

x−intercept: $y = 0$, $z = 0$

$\qquad 4x = 24$
$\qquad x = 6$

y−intercept: $x = 0$, $z = 0$

$\qquad 2y = 24$
$\qquad y = 12$

z−intercept: $x = 0$, $y = 0$

$\qquad 3z = 24$
$\qquad z = 8$

Sketch the portion of the plane in the first octant that contains these intercepts.

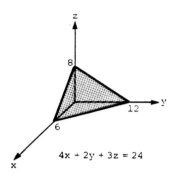

$4x + 2y + 3z = 24$

10. $y + z = 5$

x-intercept: $y = 0$, $z = 0$

$0 = 5$

Impossible, so no x-intercept

y-intercept: $x = 0$, $z = 0$

$y = 5$

z-intercept: $x = 0$, $y = 0$

$z = 5$

Sketch the portion of the plane in the first octant that contains these intercepts and is parallel to the x-axis.

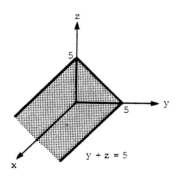

$y + z = 5$

12. $z = 3$

No x-intercept, no y-intercept. Sketch the portion of the plane in the first octant that passes through (0, 0, 3) parallel to the xy-plane.

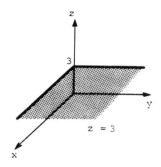

$z = 3$

14. $x + 3y + 2z = 8$

If $z = 0$, we have $x + 3y = 8$. The level curve is a line in the xy-plane with an x-intercept of 8 and a y-intercept of $\frac{8}{3}$.

If $z = 2$, we have $x + 3y = 4$. The level curve is a line in the plane $z = 2$ passing through the points (4, 0, 2) and $(0, \frac{4}{3}, 2)$.

If $z = 4$, we have $x + 3y = 0$. The level curve is a line in the plane $z = 4$ passing through the point (0, 0, 4) on the z-axis.

Sketch segments of these lines in the first octant.

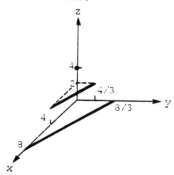

16. $2y - \dfrac{x^2}{3} = z$

    If $z = 0$, we have $y = \dfrac{1}{6}x^2$. The level curve is a parabola in the xy-plane with vertex at the origin.

    If $z = 2$, we have $y = \dfrac{1}{6}x^2 + 1$. The level curve is a parabola in the plane $z = 2$ with vertex at the point $(0, 1, 2)$.

    If $z = 4$, we have $y = \dfrac{1}{6}x^2 + 2$. The level curve is a parabola in the plane $z = 4$ with vertex at the point $(0, 2, 4)$.

    Sketch portions of these curves in the first octant.

    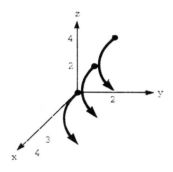

18. $M = f(25, .05, .28)$

    $= \dfrac{(1 + .05)^{25}(1 - .28) + .28}{[1 + (1 - .28)(.05)]^{25}}$

    ≈ 1.12

    Since $M > 1$, the IRA account grows faster.

20. $z = x^{.7}y^{.3}$ and $z = 500$

    so $500 = x^{.7}y^{.3}$.

    $y^{.3} = \dfrac{500}{x^{.7}}$ or $y^{3/10} = \dfrac{500}{x^{7/10}}$

    $y = \left(\dfrac{500}{x^{7/10}}\right)^{10/3} \approx \dfrac{9.9 \times 10^8}{x^{7/3}} \approx \dfrac{10^9}{x^{7/3}}$

    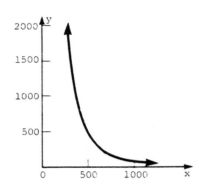

22. $z = x^{.7}y^{.3}$

    If x is doubled, z is multiplied by $2^{.7}$, or approximately 1.6.

    If y is doubled, z is multiplied by $2^{.3}$, or approximately 1.2.

    If both are doubled, z is multiplied by $2^{.7} \cdot 2^{.3} = 2^{1.0} = 2$. Thus, z is doubled.

24. $m = \dfrac{2.5(T - F)}{w^{.67}}$

    (a) $m = \dfrac{2.5(38 - 6)}{(32)^{.67}} \approx 7.85$

    (b) $m = \dfrac{2.5(40 - 20)}{(43)^{.67}} \approx 4.02$

26. The girth is $2H + 2W$. Thus, $f(L, W, H) = L + 2H + 2W$.

28. $f(H, D) = \sqrt{H^2 + D^2}$ with $D = 3.75$ in

(a) $\dfrac{H}{D} = \dfrac{3}{4}$

$H = \dfrac{3}{4}D$

$H = \dfrac{3}{4}(3.75)$

$H = 2.8125$

$f(2.8125, 3.75)$

$= \sqrt{(2.8125)^2 + (3.75)^2}$

≈ 4.69

The length of the ellipse is approximately 4.69 in, and its width is 3.75 in.

(b) $\dfrac{H}{D} = \dfrac{2}{5}$

$H = \dfrac{2}{5}D$

$H = \dfrac{2}{5}(3.75)$

$H = 1.5$

$f(1.5, 3.75)$

$= \sqrt{(1.5)^2 + (3.75)^2}$

≈ 4.04

The length of the ellipse is approximately 4.04 in, and its width is 3.75 in.

30. $z^2 - y^2 - x^2 = 1$

If $z = 0$,

$-(y^2 + x^2) = 1.$

This is impossible so there is no xy-trace.

If $x = 0$.

$z^2 - y^2 = 1.$

yz-trace: hyperbola

If $y = 0$,

$z^2 - x^2 = 1.$

xz-trace: hyperbola

Hyperboloid of two sheets: (f)

32. $z = y^2 - x^2$

If $z = 0$,

$x^2 = y^2$

$x = \pm y.$

xy-trace: two intersecting lines

If $x = 0$,

$z = y^2.$

yz-trace: parabola, opening upward

If $y = 0$,

$z = -x^2.$

xz-trace: parabola, opening downward

Hyperbolic paraboloid

Both (a) and (e) are hyperbolic paraboloids, but only (a) has traces described by this function.

34. $z = 5(x^2 + y^2)^{-1/2}$

$= \dfrac{5}{\sqrt{x^2 + y^2}}$

Note that $z > 0$ for all values of x and y.

xz-trace: $y = 0$

$z = \dfrac{5}{\sqrt{x^2}} = \dfrac{5}{|x|}$

Gives one branch of hyperbola $xz = 5$, where $z > 0$ and $x > 0$, and one branch of hyperbola $xz = -5$, where $z > 0$ and $x < 0$.

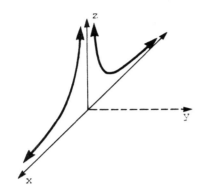

yz–trace: $x = 0$

$$z = \frac{5}{\sqrt{y^2}} = \frac{5}{|y|}$$

Gives one branch of hyperbola $yz = 5$, where $z > 0$ and $y > 0$ and one branch of hyperbola $yz = -5$, where $z > 0$ and $y < 0$.

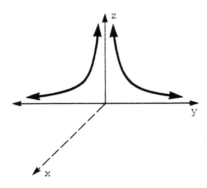

Level curves on planes $z = k$, where $k > 0$, are

$$k = \frac{5}{\sqrt{x^2 + y^2}}$$
$$x^2 + y^2 = \frac{25}{k^2}$$

These are circles with centers $(0, 0, k)$ and radii $5/k$. The graph of $z = 5(x^2 + y^2)^{-1/2}$ is (d).

36. $f(x, y) = 7x^3 + 8y^2$

(a) $\dfrac{f(x + h, y) - f(x, y)}{h}$

$= \dfrac{[7(x + h)^3 + 8y^2] - (7x^3 + 8y^2)}{h}$

$= \dfrac{7x^3 + 21x^2h + 21xh^2 + 7h^3 - 7x^3}{h}$

$= 21x^2 + 21xh + 7h^2$

(b) $\dfrac{f(x, y + h) - f(x, y)}{h}$

$= \dfrac{[7x^3 + 8(y + h)^2] - (7x^3 + 8y^2)}{h}$

$= \dfrac{8y^2 + 16yh + 8h^2 - 8y^2}{h}$

$= 16y + 8h$

Section 8.2

2. $z = g(x, y) = 5x + 9x^2y + y^2$

(a) $\dfrac{\partial g}{\partial x} = 5 + 18xy$

(b) $\dfrac{\partial g}{\partial y} = 9x^2 + 2y$

(c) $\dfrac{\partial z}{\partial y}(-3, 0) = \dfrac{\partial g}{\partial y}(-3, 0)$

$= 9(-3)^2 + 2(0)$

$= 81$

(d) $g_x(2, 1) = \dfrac{\partial g}{\partial x}(2, 1)$

$= 5 + 18(2)(1)$

$= 41$

4. $f(x, y) = 4x^2y - 9y^2$

$f_x = 8xy$

$f_y = 4x^2 - 18y$

$f_x(2, -1) = 8(2)(-1) = -16$

$f_y(-4, 3) = 4(-4)^2 - 18(3) = 10$

6. $f(x, y) = -2x^2y^4$

$f_x = -4xy^4$

$f_y = -8x^2y^3$

$f_x(2, -1) = -4(2)(-1)^4 = -8$

$f_y(-4, 3) = -8(-4)^2(3)^3 = -3456$

8. $f(x, y) = 3e^{2x+y}$

$f_x = 6e^{2x+y}$

$f_y = 3e^{2x+y}$

$f_x(2 - 1) = 6e^{2(2)-1} = 6e^3$

$f_y(-4, 3) = 3e^{2(-4)+3} = 3e^{-5}$

10. $f(x, y) = 8e^{7x-y}$

$f_x = 56e^{7x-y}$

$f_y = -8e^{7x-y}$

$f_x(2, -1) = 56e^{7(2)-(-1)} = 56e^{15}$

$f_y(-4, 3) = -8e^{7(-4)-3} = -8e^{-31}$

12. $f(x, y) = \dfrac{3x^2y^3}{x^2 + y^2}$

$f_x = \dfrac{(x^2 + y^2) \cdot 6xy^3 - 3x^2y^3 \cdot 2x}{(x^2 + y^2)^2}$

$\quad = \dfrac{6xy^5}{(x^2 + y^2)^2}$

$f_y = \dfrac{(x^2 + y^2) \cdot 9x^2y^2 - 3x^2y^3 \cdot 2y}{(x^2 + y^2)^2}$

$\quad = \dfrac{9x^4y^2 + 3x^2y^4}{(x^2 + y^2)^2}$

$f_x(2, -1) = \dfrac{6(2)(-1)^5}{((2)^2 + (-1)^2)^2}$

$\quad = -\dfrac{12}{25}$

$f_y(-4, 3) = \dfrac{9(-4)^4(3)^2 + 3(-4)^2(3)^4}{((-4)^2 + (3)^2)^2}$

$\quad = \dfrac{24,624}{625}$

14. $f(x, y) = \ln\left|2x^5 - xy^4\right|$

$f_x = \dfrac{1}{2x^5 - xy^4} \cdot (10x^4 - y^4)$

$\quad = \dfrac{10x^4 - y^4}{2x^5 - xy^4}$

$f_y = \dfrac{1}{2x^5 - xy^4} \cdot (-4xy^3)$

$\quad = \dfrac{-4xy^3}{2x^5 - xy^4}$

$f_x(2, -1) = \dfrac{10(2)^4 - (-1)^4}{2(2^5) - 2(-1)^4}$

$\quad = \dfrac{159}{62}$

$f_y(-4, 3) = \dfrac{-4(-4)(3)^3}{2(-4)^5 - (-4)(3)^4}$

$\quad = \dfrac{432}{-1724}$

$\quad = -\dfrac{108}{431}$

16. $f(x, y) = y^2e^{x+3y}$

$f_x = y^2e^{x+3y}$

$f_y = y^2 \cdot 3e^{x+3y} + e^{x+3y} \cdot 2y$

$\quad = ye^{x+3y}(3y + 2)$

$f_x(2, -1) = (-1)^2e^{2+3(-1)} = e^{-1}$

$f_y(-4, 3) = 3e^{-4+3(3)}(3(3) + 2)$

$\quad = 33e^5$

18. $g(x, y) = 5xy^4 + 8x^3 - 3y$

$g_x = 5y^4 + 24x^2 \qquad g_y = 20xy^3 - 3$

$g_{xx} = 48x \qquad\qquad g_{yy} = 60xy^2$

$g_{xy} = 20y^3 \qquad\qquad g_{yx} = 20y^3$

20. $h(x, y) = 30y + 5x^2y + 12xy^2$

$h_x = 10xy + 12y^2 \qquad h_y = 30 + 5x^2 + 24xy$

$h_{xx} = 10y \qquad\qquad h_{yy} = 24x$

$h_{xy} = 10x + 24y \qquad h_{yx} = 10x + 24y$

22. $k(x, y) = \dfrac{-5y}{x + 2y} = -5y(x + 2y)^{-1}$

$k_x = 5y(x + 2y)^{-2} = \dfrac{5y}{(x + 2y)^2}$

$k_y = \dfrac{(x + 2y)(-5) - (-5y) \cdot 2}{(x + 2y)^2}$

$\quad = \dfrac{-5x}{(x + 2y)^2} = -5x(x + 2y)^{-2}$

$k_{xx} = -10y(x + 2y)^{-3} = \dfrac{-10y}{(x + 2y)^3}$

$k_{yy} = 10x(x + 2y)^{-3} \cdot 2$

$\quad = \dfrac{20x}{(x + 2y)^3}$

$k_{xy} = \dfrac{(x + 2y)^2 \cdot 5 - 5y \cdot 2(x + 2y) \cdot 2}{(x + 2y)^4}$

$\quad = \dfrac{5x - 10y}{(x + 2y)^3}$

$k_{yx} = \dfrac{(x + 2y)^2 \cdot (-5) - (-5x) \cdot 2(x + 2y)}{(x + 2y)^4}$

$\quad = \dfrac{5x - 10y}{(x + 2y)^3}$

24. $z = -3ye^x$

$z_x = -3ye^x \qquad\qquad z_y = -3e^x$

$z_{xx} = -3ye^x \qquad\qquad z_{yy} = 0$

$z_{xy} = -3e^x \qquad\qquad z_{yx} = -3e^x$

26. $k = \ln|5x - 7y|$

$k_x = \dfrac{5}{5x - 7y} = 5(5x - 7y)^{-1}$

$k_y = \dfrac{-7}{5x - 7y} = -7(5x - 7y)^{-1}$

$k_{xx} = -5(5x - 7y)^{-2} \cdot 5$

$\quad = -25(5x - 7y)^{-2} \quad \text{or} \quad \dfrac{-25}{(5x - 7y)^2}$

$k_{yy} = 7(5x - 7y)^{-2} \cdot (-7)$

$\quad = -49(5x - 7y)^{-2} \quad \text{or} \quad \dfrac{-49}{(5x - 7y)^2}$

$k_{xy} = -5(5x - 7y)^{-2} \cdot (-7)$

$\quad = 35(5x - 7y)^{-2} \quad \text{or} \quad \dfrac{35}{(5x - 7y)^2}$

$k_{yx} = 7(5x - 7y)^{-2} \cdot (5)$

$\quad = 35(5x - 7y)^{-2} \quad \text{or} \quad \dfrac{35}{(5x - 7y)^2}$

28. $z = (y + 1) \ln|x^3y|$

$\quad = (y + 1)(3 \ln|x| + \ln|y|)$

$z_x = (y + 1) \cdot \left(3 \cdot \dfrac{1}{x}\right)$

$\quad = \dfrac{3(y + 1)}{x}$

$\quad = 3x^{-1}(y + 1)$

$z_y = (y + 1) \cdot \left(\dfrac{1}{y}\right)$

$\qquad + (3 \ln|x| + \ln|y|) \cdot 1$

$\quad = \dfrac{y + 1}{y} + 3 \ln|x| + \ln|y|$

$z_{xx} = -3x^{-2}(y + 1) = \dfrac{-3(y + 1)}{x^2}$

$z_{yy} = \dfrac{y \cdot 1 - (y + 1) \cdot 1}{y^2} + \dfrac{1}{y}$

$\quad = -\dfrac{1}{y^2} + \dfrac{1}{y}$

$z_{xy} = 3x^{-1} = \dfrac{3}{x}$

$z_{yx} = 3 \cdot \dfrac{1}{x} = \dfrac{3}{x}$

30. $f(x, y) = 50 + 4x - 5y + x^2 + y^2 + xy$

$f_x = 4 + 2x + y, \quad f_y = -5 + 2y + x$

Solve the system

$\qquad 4 + 2x + y = 0$

$\qquad -5 + x + 2y = 0.$

Multiply the second equation by -2 and add.

$$\begin{aligned} 4 + 2x + y &= 0 \\ \underline{10 - 2x - 4y} &= 0 \\ 14 \qquad\quad - 3y &= 0 \\ y &= \frac{14}{3} \end{aligned}$$

Substitute into the second equation to get $x = -13/3$.

32. $f(x, y) = 2200 + 27x^3 + 72xy + 8y^2$

$f_x = 81x^2 + 72y$, $f_y = 72x + 16y$

Solve the system

$$81x^2 + 72y = 0$$
$$\underline{72x\ \ \ + 16y = 0}$$
$$9x^2 + 8y = 0$$
$$9x\ + 2y = 0$$

From the second equation, $y = -9x/2$.
Substitute into the first equation.

$$9x^2 - 36x = 0$$
$$9x(x - 4) = 0$$
$$x = 0 \ \ \text{or} \ \ x = 4$$

Since $y = -\dfrac{9}{2}x$,

if $x = 0$, $y = 0$;

if $x = 4$, $y = -\dfrac{9}{2}(4) = -18$.

34. $f(x, y, z) = 3x^5 - x^2 + y^5$

$f_x = 15x^4 - 2x$; $f_y = 5y^4$; $f_z = 0$;

$f_{yz} = 0$

36. $f(x, y, z) = \dfrac{2x^2 + xy}{yz - 2}$

$$= \dfrac{1}{yz - 2}(2x^2 + xy)$$

$$= (2x^2 + xy)(yz - 2)^{-1}$$

$f_x = \dfrac{1}{yz - 2}(4x + y) = \dfrac{4x + y}{yz - 2}$

$f_y = \dfrac{(yz - 2) \cdot x - (2x^2 + xy) \cdot z}{(yz - 2)^2}$

$$= \dfrac{-2x - 2x^2z}{(yz - 2)^2}$$

$f_z = -(2x^2 + xy)(yz - 2)^{-2} \cdot y$

$$= -\dfrac{(2x^2y + xy^2)}{(yz - 2)^2}$$

f_{yz}

$$= \dfrac{(yz - 2)^2(-2x^2) - (-2x - 2x^2z) \cdot 2(yz - 2) \cdot y}{(yz - 2)^4}$$

$$= \dfrac{4x^2 + 4xy + 2x^2yz}{(yz - 2)^3}$$

38. $f(x, y, z) = \ln|8xy + 5yz - x^3|$

$f_x = \dfrac{1}{8xy + 5yz - x^3} \cdot (8y - 3x^2)$

$$= \dfrac{8y - 3x^2}{8xy + 5yz - x^3}$$

$f_y = \dfrac{1}{8xy + 5yz - x^3} \cdot (8x + 5z)$

$$= \dfrac{8x + 5z}{8xy + 5yz - x^3}$$

$f_z = \dfrac{1}{8xy + 5yz - x^3} \cdot 5y$

$$= \dfrac{5y}{8xy + 5yz - x^3}$$

$f_{yz} = \dfrac{(8xy + 5yz - x^3) \cdot 5 - (8x + 5z) \cdot 5y}{(8xy + 5yz - x^3)^2}$

$$= \dfrac{-5x^3}{(8xy + 5yz - x^3)^2}$$

40. $R(x, y) = 5x^2 + 9y^2 - 4xy$

(a) $R(9, 5) = 5(9)^2 + 9(5)^2 - 4(9)(5)$

$$= 450$$

$R_x = 10x - 4y$

$R_x(9, 5) = 10(9) - 4(5) = 70$

So R would increase by $70.

(b) $R_y = 18y - 4x$

$R_y(9, 5) = 18(5) - 4(9) = 54$

So R would increase by $54.

42. $P(x, y) = 100\sqrt{x^2 + y^2}$

$$= 100(x^2 + y^2)^{1/2},$$

where x is labor, y is capital.

(a) $\dfrac{\partial P}{\partial x} = 50(x^2 + y^2)^{-1/2} \cdot 2x$

$$= \dfrac{100x}{\sqrt{x^2 + y^2}}$$

$$\frac{\partial P}{\partial x}(4, \ 3) = \frac{100(4)}{\sqrt{(4)^2 + (3)^2}}$$

$$= 80 \text{ units}$$

(b) $\dfrac{\partial P}{\partial y} = 50(x^2 + y^2)^{-1/2} \cdot 2y$

$$= \frac{100x}{\sqrt{x^2 + y^2}}$$

$$\frac{\partial P}{\partial x}(4, \ 3) = \frac{100(3)}{\sqrt{(4)^2 + (3)^2}}$$

$$= 60 \text{ units}$$

44. $z = x^{\cdot 7} y^{\cdot 3}$, where x is labor, y is capital.

Marginal productivity of labor is

$$\frac{\partial z}{\partial x} = .7x^{-\cdot 3} y^{\cdot 3}.$$

Marginal productivity of capital is

$$\frac{\partial z}{\partial y} = .3x^{\cdot 7} y^{-\cdot 7}.$$

46. $f(x, \ y) = 3x^{1/3} y^{2/3}$, where x is labor, y is capital.

(a) $f_x = x^{-2/3} y^{2/3}$

$$= \frac{y^{2/3}}{x^{2/3}} = \left(\frac{y}{x}\right)^{2/3}$$

$$f_x(64, \ 125) = \left(\frac{125}{64}\right)^{2/3}$$

$$= \frac{25}{16}$$

$$= 1.5625,$$

which is the approximate change in production (in thousands of units) for a 1 unit change in labor.

$$f_y = 2x^{1/3} y^{-1/3}$$

$$= 2 \frac{x^{1/3}}{y^{1/3}} = 2\left(\frac{x}{y}\right)^{1/3}$$

$$f_y(64, \ 125) = 2\left(\frac{64}{125}\right)^{1/3}$$

$$= \frac{8}{5} = 1.6,$$

which is the approximate change in production (in thousands of units) for a 1 unit change in capital.

(b) Increasing to 65 units of labor would result in an increase of approximately

$$\frac{25}{16}(1000) \approx 1563 \text{ batteries.}$$

(c) An increase of approximately

$$\frac{16}{5}(1000) = 3200 \text{ batteries}$$

would be the effect of increasing capital to 126 while holding labor at 64. Increasing capital is the better option.

48. $m(T, \ F, \ w) = 2.5(T - F)w^{-\cdot 67}$

$$= 2.5Tw^{-\cdot 67}$$

$$- 2.5Fw^{-\cdot 67}$$

(a) Increasing T from 38°C to 39°C while F remains at 12°C and w remains at 30 kg results in a change in oxygen consumption of

$$m_T(38, \ 12, \ 30) = 2.5w^{-\cdot 67}$$

$$= 2.5(30)^{-\cdot 67}$$

$$\approx .256.$$

(b) Increasing F from 14°C to 15°C while T remains at 36°C and w remains at 25 kg results in a change of oxygen consumption of

$$m_F(36, \ 14, \ 25) = -2.5w^{-\cdot 67}$$

$$= -2.5(25^{-\cdot 67})$$

$$\approx -.289.$$

50. $C(a, b, v) = \dfrac{b}{a - v} = b(a - v)^{-1}$

(a) $C(160, 200, 125) = \dfrac{200}{160 - 125}$

$= \dfrac{200}{35}$

≈ 5.71

(b) $C_a = -b(a - v)^{-2} \cdot 1$

$C_a = -\dfrac{b}{(a - v)^2}$

$C_a(160, 200, 125)$

$= -\dfrac{200}{(160 - 125)^2}$

$= -\dfrac{200}{35^2}$

$\approx -.163$

(c) $C_b = (a - v)^{-1}$

$C_b(160, 200, 125)$

$= (160 - 125)^{-1}$

$= \dfrac{1}{35}$

$\approx .0286$

(d) $C_v = -b(a - v)^{-2} \cdot (-1)$

$= \dfrac{b}{(a - v)^2}$

$C_v(160, 200, 125)$

$= \dfrac{200}{(160 - 125)^2}$

$= \dfrac{200}{35^2}$

$\approx .163$

(e) Changing a 1 unit produces the greatest decrease in the liters of blood pumped, while changing v 1 unit produces the same amount of increase in the liters of blood pumped.

52. $R(x, t) = x^2(a - x)t^2e^{-t}$

$= (ax^2 - x^3)t^2e^{-t}$

(a) $\dfrac{\partial R}{\partial x} = (2ax - 3x^2)t^2e^{-t}$

(b) $\dfrac{\partial R}{\partial t} = x^2(a - x)$

$\cdot [t^2 \cdot (-e^{-t}) + e^{-t} \cdot 2t]$

$= x^2(a - x)(-t^2 + 2t)e^{-t}$

(c) $\dfrac{\partial^2 R}{\partial x^2} = (2a - 6x)t^2e^{-t}$

(d) $\dfrac{\partial^2 R}{\partial x \partial t} = (2ax - 3x^2)(-t^2 + 2t)e^{-t}$

(e) $\dfrac{\partial R}{\partial x}$ gives the rate of change of the reaction per unit of change in the amount of drug administered.

$\dfrac{\partial R}{\partial t}$ gives the rate of change of the reaction for a 1-hr change in the time after the drug is administered.

54. $F = \dfrac{mgR^2}{r^2} = mgR^2r^{-2}$

(a) $F_m = gR^2r^{-2}$ is the approximate rate of change in force when mass is increased by 1 unit while distance is held constant.

$F_r = -2mgR^2r^{-3}$ is the approximate rate of change in force when distance is increased by 1 unit while mass is held constant.

(b) $F_m = \dfrac{gR^2}{r^2}$, where all quantities are positive.

Therefore, $F_m > 0$.

$F_r = \dfrac{-2mgR^2}{r^3}$ where m, g, R^2, and r^3 are positive.

Therefore, $F_r < 0$.

These are reasonable since force increases when mass increases (m is in the numerator) and force decreases when distance increases (r is in the denominator).

Section 8.3

2. $f(x, y) = 4xy + 8x - 9y$

$f_x = 4y + 8$, $f_y = 4x - 9$

$f_x = 0$ and $f_y = 0$ when

$$4y + 8 = 0$$
$$y = -2$$

and $4x - 9 = 0$

$$x = \frac{9}{4}.$$

$f_{xx} = 0$, $f_{yy} = 0$, $f_{xy} = 4$

Since $D = f_{xx}(9/4, -2) \cdot f_{yy}(9/4, -2)$

$$- f_{xy}(9/4, -2)$$
$$= 0 \cdot 0 - 4^2 = -16 < 0,$$

$(9/4, -2)$ is a saddle point.

4. $f(x, y) = x^2 + xy + y^2 - 6x - 3$

$f_x = 2x + y - 6$, $f_y = x + 2y$

$$2x + y - 6 = 0$$
$$\underline{x + 2y \qquad = 0}$$

$$2x + y - 6 = 0$$
$$\underline{-2x - 4y \qquad = 0}$$
$$-3y - 6 = 0$$
$$y = -2$$

$$x + 2(-2) = 0$$
$$x = 4$$

$f_{xx} = 2$, $f_{yy} = 2$, $f_{xy} = 1$

$D = 2 \cdot 2 - 1^2 = 3 > 0$ and $f_{xx} > 0$

Relative minimum at $(4, -2)$

6. $f(x, y) = x^2 + xy + y^2 + 3x - 3y$

$f_x = 2x + y + 3$, $f_y = x + 2y - 3$

$$2x + y + 3 = 0$$
$$\underline{x + 2y - 3 = 0}$$

$$2x + y + 3 = 0$$
$$\underline{-2x - 4y + 6 = 0}$$
$$-3y + 9 = 0$$
$$y = 3$$

$$x + 2(3) - 3 = 0$$
$$x = -3$$

$f_{xx} = 2$, $f_{yy} = 2$, $f_{xy} = 1$

$D = 2 \cdot 2 - 1^2 = 3 > 0$ and $f_{xx} > 0$

Relative minimum at $(-3, 3)$

8. $f(x, y) = 5xy - 7x^2 - y^2 + 3x - 6y - 4$

$f_x = 5y - 14x + 3$, $f_y = 5x - 2y - 6$

$$5y - 14x + 3 = 0$$
$$\underline{-2y + 5x - 6 = 0}$$

$$10y - 28x + 6 = 0$$
$$\underline{-10y + 25x - 30 = 0}$$
$$-3x - 24 = 0$$
$$x = -8$$

$$-2y + 5(-8) - 6 = 0$$
$$-2y = 46$$
$$y = -23$$

$f_{xx} = -14$, $f_{yy} = -2$, $f_{xy} = 5$

$D = (-14)(-2) - 5^2 = 3 > 0$ and $f_{xx} < 0$

Relative maximum at $(-8, -23)$

10. $f(x, y) = x^2 + xy + 3x + 2y - 6$

$f_x = 2x + y + 3$, $f_y = x + 2$

$$2x + y + 3 = 0$$
$$x + 2 = 0$$
$$x = -2$$

$$2(-2) + y + 3 = 0$$
$$y = 1$$

$f_{xx} = 2$, $f_{yy} = 0$, $f_{xy} = 1$

$D = 2 \cdot 0 - 1^2 = -1 < 0$

Saddle point at $(-2, 1)$

12. $f(x, y) = x^2 + xy + y^2 - 3x - 5$

$f_x = 2x + y - 3$, $f_y = x + 2y$

$$2x + y - 3 = 0$$
$$\underline{x + 2y \qquad = 0}$$

$$2x + y - 3 = 0$$
$$\underline{-2x - 4y \qquad = 0}$$
$$-3y - 3 = 0$$
$$y = -1$$

$$x + 2(-1) = 0$$
$$x = 2$$

$f_{xx} = 2$, $f_{yy} = 2$, $f_{xy} = 1$

$D = 2 \cdot 2 - 1^2 = 3 > 0$ and $f_{xx} > 0$

Relative minimum at $(2, -1)$

14. $f(x, y) = 5x^3 + 2y^2 - 60xy - 3$

$f_x = 15x^2 - 60y$, $f_y = 4y - 60x$

$$15x^2 - 60y = 0$$
$$\underline{4y \quad - 60x = 0}$$

$$x^2 - 4y = 0$$
$$y - 15x = 0$$
$$y = 15x$$

Substituting, we have

$$x^2 - 4(15x) = 0$$
$$x^2 - 60x = 0$$
$$x = 0 \quad \text{or} \quad x = 60$$
$$y = 0 \qquad y = 900.$$

$f_{xx} = 30x$, $f_{yy} = 4$, $f_{xy} = -60$

At $(0, 0)$,

$D = 0 \cdot 4 - (-60)^2 = -3600 < 0.$

Saddle point at $(0, 0)$

At $(60, 900)$,

$D = 1800 \cdot 4 - (-60)^2$
$\quad = 3600 > 0$ and $f_{xx} > 0.$

Relative minimum at $(60, 900)$

16. $f(x, y) = 3x^2 + 7y^3 - 42xy + 5$

$f_x = 6x - 42y$, $f_y = 21y^2 - 42x$

$$6x \quad - 42x = 0$$
$$\underline{21y^2 - 42x = 0}$$

$$x - 7y = 0$$
$$y^2 - 2x = 0$$
$$x = 7y$$

Substituting, we have

$$y^2 - 2(7y) = 0$$
$$y^2 - 14y = 0$$
$$y = 0 \quad \text{or} \quad y = 14$$
$$x = 0 \qquad x = 98.$$

$f_{xx} = 6$, $f_{yy} = 42y$, $f_{xy} = -42$

At $(0, 0)$,

$D = 6 \cdot 0 - (-42)^2 = -1764 < 0.$

Saddle point at $(0, 0)$

At (98, 14),

$D = 6 \cdot 588 - (-42)^2$

$\qquad = 1764 > 0$ and $f_{xx} > 0$.

Relative minimum at (98, 14)

18. $f(x, y) = x^2 + e^y$

$f_x = 2x, \quad f_y = e^y$

$2x = 0$

$e^y = 0$

The latter equation has no solutions. No extrema, no saddle points

22. $z = \frac{3}{2}y - \frac{1}{2}y^3 - x^2y + \frac{1}{16}$

$\frac{\partial z}{\partial x} = -2xy, \quad \frac{\partial z}{\partial y} = \frac{3}{2} - \frac{3}{2}y^2 - x^2$

$\qquad\qquad -2xy = 0$

$\qquad\qquad x = 0 \quad \text{or} \quad y = 0$

$\frac{3}{2} - \frac{3}{2}y^2 - x^2 = 0$

If $x = 0$,

$\qquad\qquad \frac{3}{2} - \frac{3}{2}y^2 = 0$

$\qquad\qquad\qquad y = \pm 1.$

If $y = 0$,

$\qquad\qquad \frac{3}{2} - x^2 = 0$

$\qquad\qquad x = \pm\sqrt{\frac{3}{2}} = \pm\frac{\sqrt{6}}{2}.$

$\frac{\partial^2 z}{\partial x^2} = -2y, \quad \frac{\partial^2 z}{\partial y^2} = -3y, \quad \frac{\partial^2 z}{\partial y \partial x} = -2x$

$D = (-2y)(-3y) - (-2x)^2 = 6y^2 - 4x^2$

At (0, 1),

$D = 6 > 0$ and $\frac{\partial^2 z}{\partial x^2} = -2 < 0.$

$z = \frac{3}{2} - \frac{1}{2} + \frac{1}{10} = 1\frac{1}{16}$

Relative maximum of 1 1/16 at (0, 1)

At (0, -1),

$D = 6 > 0$ and $\frac{\partial^2 z}{\partial x^2} = 2 < 0.$

$z = -\frac{3}{2} + \frac{1}{2} + \frac{1}{16} = -\frac{15}{16}$

Relative minimum of -15/16 at (0, -1)

At $\left(\pm\frac{\sqrt{6}}{2}, 0\right)$, $D = -6 < 0.$

Saddle points at $\left(\frac{\sqrt{6}}{2}, 0\right)$ and $\left(-\frac{\sqrt{6}}{2}, 0\right)$

Graph is (d).

24. $z = -2x^3 - 3y^4 + 6xy^2 + \frac{1}{16}$

$\frac{\partial z}{\partial x} = -6x^2 + 6y^2, \quad \frac{\partial z}{\partial y} = -12y^3 + 12xy$

$\qquad\qquad -6x^2 + 6y^2 = 0$

$\qquad\qquad \underline{-12y^3 + 12xy = 0}$

$\qquad\qquad\qquad -x^2 + y^2 = 0$

$\qquad\qquad\qquad\qquad y = \pm x$

$\qquad\qquad\qquad -y^3 + xy = 0$

If $y = x$,

$\qquad\qquad\qquad -x^3 + x^2 = 0$

$\qquad\qquad\qquad -x^2(-x + 1) = 0$

$\qquad\qquad\qquad x = 0 \quad \text{or} \quad x = 1.$

If x = 0, y = 0.

If x = 1, y = 1.

If y = -x,

$$x^3 - x^2 = 0$$
$$x^2(x - 1) = 0$$
$$x = 0 \quad \text{or} \quad x = 1.$$

If x = 0, y = 0.

If x = 1, y = -1.

$\dfrac{\partial^2 z}{\partial x^2} = -12x, \dfrac{\partial^2 z}{\partial y^2} = -36y^2 + 12x.$

$\dfrac{\partial^2 z}{\partial y \partial x} = 12y$

$D = (-12x)(-36y^2 + 12x) - (12y)^2$

At (0, 0), D = 0, which gives no information.

At (1, 1),

$D = -12(-36 + 12) - 144$

$= 144 > 0$ and $\dfrac{\partial^2 z}{\partial x^2} = -12 < 0,$

$z = -2 - 3 + 6 + \dfrac{1}{16} = 1\dfrac{1}{16}$

so relative maximum of 1 1/16 at (1, 1).

At (1, -1),

$D = -12(-36 + 12) - 144$

$= 144 > 0$ and $\dfrac{\partial^2 z}{\partial x^2} = -12 < 0,$

so relative maximum of 1 1/16 at (1, -1).

Graph is (c).

26. $z = -y^4 + 4xy - 2x^2 + \dfrac{1}{16}$

$\dfrac{\partial z}{\partial x} = 4y - 4x, \dfrac{\partial z}{\partial y} = -4y^3 + 4x$

$$4y - 4x = 0$$
$$-4y^3 + 4x = 0$$
$$y - x = 0$$
$$y = x$$
$$-y^3 + x = 0$$

Substituting, we have

$$-x^3 + x = 0$$
$$x(-x^2 + 1) = 0$$
$$x = 0 \quad \text{or} \quad x = 1 \quad \text{or} \quad x = -1.$$

If x = 0, y = 0.

If x = 1, y = 1.

If x = -1, y = -1.

$\dfrac{\partial^2 z}{\partial x^2} = -4, \dfrac{\partial^2 z}{\partial y^2} = = -12y^2, \dfrac{\partial^2 z}{\partial y \partial x} = 4$

$D = -4(-12y^2) - 4^2 = 48y^2 - 16$

At (0, 0), D = -16 < 0.

Saddle point at (0, 0)

At (1, 1) and (-1, -1),

$D = 48 - 16 = 32 > 0$ and

$\dfrac{\partial^2 z}{\partial x^2} = -4 < 0.$

Relative maximum of 1 1/16 at (1, 1) and at (-1, -1)

Graph is (f).

28. $f(x, y) = x^3 + (x - y)^2$

$f_x = 3x^2 + 2(x - y), f_y = -2(x - y)$

$$3x^2 + 2x - 2y = 0$$
$$\underline{\quad\quad -2x + 2y = 0}$$
$$3x^2 = 0$$
$$x = 0$$
$$0 + 2y = 0$$
$$y = 0$$

$f_{xx} = 6x + 2$, $f_{yy} = 2$, $f_{xy} = -2$

$D = (6x + 2)(2) - (-2)^2 = 12x$

At $(0, 0)$, $D = 0$, which gives no information. Examine the graph of $z = x^3 + (x - y)^2$: in the yz-plane, the trace is $z = y^2$, which has a minimum at $(0, 0, 0)$; in the xz-plane, the trace is $z = x^3 + x^2$, which has a minimum at $(0, 0, 0)$. But in the plane $y = x$, the trace is $z = x^3$, which has neither a maximum nor a minimum at $(0, 0, 0)$. So the function has no relative extrema. Notice the orientation of axes in the following figure: This is a back view.

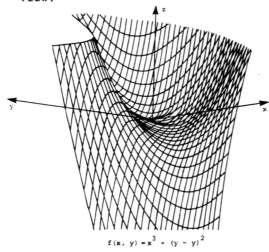

$f(x, y) = x^3 + (y - y)^2$

30. $L(x, y) = \frac{3}{2}x^2 + y^2 - 2x - 2y - 2xy + 68$, where x is skilled hours and y is semiskilled hours.

$L_x = 3x - 2 - 2y$, $L_y = 2y - 2 - 2x$

$$3x - 2 - 2y = 0$$
$$\underline{-2x - 2 + 2y = 0}$$
$$x - 4 \qquad = 0$$
$$x = 4$$

$$-2(4) - 2 + 2y = 0$$
$$2y = 10$$
$$y = 5$$

$L_{xx} = 3$, $L_{yy} = 2$, $L_{xy} = -2$

$D = 3(2) - (-2)^2 = 2 > 0$ and $L_{xx} > 0$.

Relative minimum at $(4, 5)$ is

$L(4, 5) = \frac{3}{2}(4)^2 + (5)^2 - 2(4) - 2(5) - 2(4)(5) + 68 = 59$. So \$59 is a minimum cost, when $x = 4$ and $y = 5$.

32. $R(x, y) = 12 + 74x + 85y - 3x^2 - 5y^2 - 5xy$, where x is number of spas and y is number of solar heaters.

$R_x = 74 - 6x - 5y$, $R_y = 85 - 10y - 5x$

$$74 - 6x - 5y = 0$$
$$\underline{85 - 5x - 10y = 0}$$

$$370 - 30x - 25y = 0$$
$$\underline{-510 + 30x + 60y = 0}$$
$$-140 \qquad + 35y = 0$$
$$y = 4$$

$$85 - 5x - 10(4) = 0$$
$$-5x = -45$$
$$x = 9$$

$R_{xx} = -6$, $R_{yy} = -10$, $R_{xy} = -5$

$D = -6(-10) - (-5)^2$
$= 35 > 0$ and $R_{xx} < 0$

Relative maximum at $(9, 4)$ is

$R(9, 4)$
$= 12 + 74(9) + 85(4) - 3(9)^2 - 5(4)^2 - 5(9)(4)$
$= 515$ in hundreds of dollars.

That is, $R(9, 4) = \$51,500$.

Sell 9 spas and 4 solar heaters for maximum revenue of \$51,500.

Section 8.4

2. Maximize $f(x, y) = 4xy + 2$,
subject to $x + y = 24$.

1. $g(x, y) = x + y - 24$

2. $F(x, y, \lambda)$
$= 4xy + 2 + \lambda(x + y - 24)$

3. $F_x = 4y + \lambda$
$F_y = 4x + \lambda$
$F_\lambda = x + y - 24$

4. $4y + \lambda = 0$
$4x + \lambda = 0$
$x + y - 24 = 0$

5. $\lambda = -4y$ and $\lambda = -4x$
$-4y = -4x$
$y = x$

Since $x + y - 24 = 0$ and $y = x$,
we have $2x - 24 = 0$ so $x = 12$
and $y = 12$.
Maximum is $f(12, 12) = 4(12)(12) + 2$
$= 578$.

4. Maximize $f(x, y) = 4xy^2$,
subject to $3x - 2y = 5$.

1. $g(x, y) = 3x - 2y - 5$

2. $F(x, y, \lambda)$
$= 4xy^2 + \lambda(3x - 2y - 5)$

3. $F_x = 4y^2 + 3\lambda$
$F_y = 8xy - 2\lambda$
$F_\lambda = 3x - 2y - 5$

4. $4y^2 + 3\lambda = 0$
$8xy - 2\lambda = 0$
$3x - 2y - 5 = 0$

5. $\lambda = -\dfrac{4y^2}{3}$ and $\lambda = 4xy$

$-\dfrac{4y^2}{3} = 4xy$

$0 = \dfrac{4}{3}y^2 + 4xy = 4y\left(\dfrac{1}{3}y + x\right)$

$y = 0$ or $y = -3x$

Substituting into $3x - 2y - 5 = 0$,
we have
for $y = 0$, $3x - 5 = 0$ so $x = 5/3$ and
for $y = -3x$, $3x - 2(-3x) - 5 = 0$, so
$x = 5/9$ and $y = -5/3$.

$f\left(\dfrac{5}{3}, 0\right) = 4\left(\dfrac{5}{3}\right)(0)^2 = 0$

$f\left(\dfrac{5}{9}, -\dfrac{5}{3}\right) = 4\left(\dfrac{5}{9}\right)\left(-\dfrac{5}{3}\right)^2 = \dfrac{500}{81}$

The maximum is $f\left(\dfrac{5}{9}, -\dfrac{5}{3}\right) = \dfrac{500}{81} \approx 6.2$.

6. Minimize $f(x, y) = 3x^2 + 4y^2 - xy - 2$,
subject to $2x + y = 21$.

1. $g(x, y) = 2x + y - 21$

2. $F(x, y, \lambda)$
$= 3x^2 + 4y^2 - xy - 2 + \lambda(2x + y - 21)$

3. $F_x = 6x - y + 2\lambda$
$F_y = 8y - x + \lambda$
$F_\lambda = 2x + y - 21$

4. $6x - y + 2\lambda = 0$
$8y - x + \lambda = 0$
$2x + y - 21 = 0$

5. $\lambda = \dfrac{-6x + y}{2}$ and $\lambda = x - 8y$

$\dfrac{-6x + y}{2} = x - 8y$

$y = \dfrac{8}{17}x$

Substituting into $2x + y - 21 = 0$, we have

$2x + \frac{8}{17}x - 21 = 0$ so $x = 17/2$ and $y = 4$.

Minimum is $f\left(\frac{17}{2}, 4\right)$

$= 3\left(\frac{17}{2}\right)^2 + 4(4)^2 - \frac{17}{2}(4) - 2$

$= \frac{979}{4}$

$= 244.75.$

8. Maximize $f(x, y) = 12xy - x^2 - 3y^2$, subject to $x + y = 16$.

1. $g(x, y) = x + y - 16$

2. $F(x, y, \lambda)$
$= 12xy - x^2 - 3y^2 + \lambda(x + y - 16)$

3. $F_x = 12y - 2x + \lambda$
$F_y = 12x - 6y + \lambda$
$F_\lambda = x + y - 16$

4. $12y - 2x + \lambda = 0$
$12x - 6y + \lambda = 0$
$x + y - 16 = 0$

5. $\lambda = 2x - 12y$ and $\lambda = -12x + 6y$

$2x - 12y = -12x + 6y$

$y = \frac{7}{9}x$

Substituting into $x + y - 16 = 0$, we have

$x + \frac{7}{9}x - 16 = 0$ so $x = 9$ and $y = 7$.

Maximum is

$f(9, 7) = 12(9)(7) - (9)^2 - 3(7)^2$
$= 528.$

10. Maximize $f(x, y, z) = xy + 2xz + 2yz$, subject to $xyz = 32$

1. $g(x, y, z) = xyz - 32$

2. $F(x, y, z, \lambda)$
$= xy + 2xz + 2yz + \lambda(xyz - 32)$

3. $F_x = y + 2z + \lambda yz$
$F_y = x + 2x + \lambda xz$
$F_z = 2x + 2y + \lambda xy$
$F_\lambda = xyz - 32$

4. $y + 2z + \lambda yz = 0$
$x + 2z + \lambda xz = 0$
$2x + 2y + \lambda xy = 0$
$xyz - 32 = 0$

5. $\lambda = \frac{-y - 2z}{yz}$, $\lambda = \frac{-x - 2z}{xz}$, and

$\lambda = \frac{-2x - 2y}{xy}$

$\frac{-y - 2z}{yz} = \frac{-x - 2z}{xz}$

$-xyz - 2xz^2 = -xyz - 2yz^2$
$2yz^2 - 2xz^2 = 0$
$2z^2(y - x) = 0$
$z = 0$ or $y = x$

and

$\frac{-y - 2z}{yz} = \frac{-2x - 2y}{xy}$

$-xy^2 - 2xyz = -2xyz - 2y^2z$
$2y^2z - xy^2 = 0$
$y^2(2z - x) = 0$

$y = 0$ or $z = \frac{x}{2}$

Since $xyz = 32$, $z = 0$ and $y = 0$ are impossible.

Substituting $y = x$ and $z = x/2$ into $xyz - 32 = 0$, we have

$x(x)\left(\frac{x}{2}\right) = 32$ so $x = 4$, $y = 4$, and $z = 2$.

Maximum is

$f(4, 4, 2)$

$\quad = 4(4) + 2(4)(2) + 2(4)(2) = 48.$

12. Let x and y be two numbers such that $x + y = 36$.
     Maximize $f(x, y) = x^2y$, subject to $x + y = 36$.

 1. $g(x, y) = x + y - 36$

 2. $F(x, y, \lambda) = x^2y + \lambda(x + y - 36)$

 3. $F_x = 2xy + \lambda$
    $F_y = x^2 + \lambda$
    $F_\lambda = x + y - 36$

 4. $2xy + \lambda = 0$
       $x^2 + \lambda = 0$
    $x + y - 36 = 0$

 5. $\lambda = -2xy$ and $\lambda = -x^2$
       $-2xy = -x^2$
    $x(-2y + x) = 0$

    Since $x = 0$ gives a smaller value of $f(x, y) = x^2y$ than any positive values of x and y, we can assume $x \neq 0$ so $y = x/2$.
    Substituting into $x + y - 36 = 0$, we have

    $x + \dfrac{x}{2} - 36 = 0$ so $x = 24$ and $y = 12$.

14. Let x, y, and z be three positive numbers such that $x + y + z = 240$.
     Maximize $f(x, y, z) = xyz$, subject to $x + y + z = 240$.

 1. $g(x, y) = x + y + z - 240$

 2. $F(x, y, z, \lambda) = xyz + \lambda(x + y + z - 240)$

 3. $F_x = yz + \lambda$
    $F_y = xz + \lambda$
    $F_z = xy + \lambda$
    $F_\lambda = x + y + z - 240$

 4. $yz + \lambda = 0$
    $xz + \lambda = 0$
    $xy + \lambda = 0$
    $x + y + z - 240 - 0$

 5. $\lambda = -yz, \ \lambda = -xz, \ \lambda = -xy$
    $-yz = -xz$
    $z = 0$ (impossible) or $x = y$
    $-xz = -xy$
    $x = 0$ (impossible) or $z = y$
    Thus, $x = y = z$

    $x + x + x - 240 = 0$
    $\qquad\qquad\quad x = 80$

    Thus,

    $\qquad x = y = z = 80.$

    The three numbers are 80, 80, and 80.

18. Let x be the length of the fence opposite the building and y be the length of each end.
     Maximize $f(x, y) = xy$, subject to the total cost

     $\qquad 6x + 8(2y) = 1200.$

 1. $g(x, y) = 6x + 16y - 1200$

 2. $F(x, y, \lambda)$
    $\quad = xy + \lambda(6x + 16y - 1200)$

3. $F_x = y + 6\lambda$

$F_y = x + 16\lambda$

$F_\lambda = 6x + 16y - 1200$

4. $y + 6\lambda = 0$

$x + 16\lambda = 0$

$6x + 16y - 1200 = 0$

5. $\lambda = -\frac{y}{6}$ and $\lambda = -\frac{x}{16}$

$-\frac{y}{6} = -\frac{x}{16}$

$y = \frac{3}{8}x$

Substituting into $6x + 16y - 1200 = 0$ we have

$6x + 16\left(\frac{3}{8}x\right) - 1200 = 0$ so $x = 100$

and $y = \frac{75}{2} = 37.5$.

Thus, the dimensions are 100 ft by 37.5 ft.

20. Maximize $P(x, y) = -x^2 - y^2 + 4x + 8y$, subject to $x + y = 6$.

1. $g(x, y) = x + y - 6$

2. $F(x, y, \lambda)$

$= -x^2 - y^2 + 4x + 8y + \lambda(x + y - 6)$

3. $F_x = -2x + 4 + \lambda$

$F_y = -2y + 8 + \lambda$

$F_\lambda = x + y - 6$

4. $-2x + 4 + \lambda = 0$

$-2y + 8 + \lambda = 0$

$x + y - 6 = 0$

5. $\lambda = 2x - 4$ and $\lambda = 2y - 8$

$2x - 4 = 2y - 8$

$y = x + 2$

Substituting into $x + y - 6 = 0$, we have

$x + (x + 2) - 6 = 0$ so $x = 2$ and $y = 4$.

22. $f(x, y) = 12x^{3/4}y^{2/4}$, where x is labor and y is capital. Maximize $f(x, y)$ subject to $100x + 180y = 25{,}200$.

1. $g(x, y) = 100x + 180y - 25{,}200$

2. $F(x, y, \lambda)$

$= 12x^{3/4}y^{1/4}$

$+ \lambda(100x + 180y - 25{,}200)$

3. $F_x = \frac{3}{4}(12x^{-1/4}y^{1/4}) + 100\lambda$

$= \frac{9y^{1/4}}{x^{1/4}} + 100\lambda$

$F_y = \frac{1}{4}(12x^{3/4}y^{-3/4}) + 180\lambda$

$= \frac{3x^{3/4}}{y^{3/4}} + 180\lambda$

$F_\lambda = 100x + 180y - 25{,}200$

4. $\frac{9y^{1/4}}{x^{1/4}} + 100\lambda = 0$

$\frac{3x^{3/4}}{y^{3/4}} + 180\lambda = 0$

$100x + 180y - 25{,}200 = 0$

5. $\lambda = \frac{-9y^{1/4}}{100x^{1/4}}$ and $\lambda = \frac{-3x^{3/4}}{180y^{3/4}}$

$= \frac{-x^{3/4}}{60y^{3/4}}$

$\frac{-9y^{1/4}}{100x^{1/4}} = \frac{-x^{3/4}}{60y^{3/4}}$

$100x = 540y$

$x = \frac{27y}{5}$

Substitute into

$$100x + 180y - 25,200 = 0.$$

$$100\left(\frac{27y}{5}\right) + 180y = 25,200$$

$$540 + 180y = 25,200$$

$$720y = 25,200$$

$$y = 35$$

$$x = \frac{27(35)}{5} = 189$$

Production will be maximized with 189 units of labor and 35 units of capital.

24.   If x and y are the dimensions of the field, we must maximize $f(x, y) = xy$ subject to $x + 2y = 600$ m.

1. $g(x, y) = x + 2y - 600$

2. $F(x, y, \lambda)$
    $= xy + \lambda(x + 2y - 600)$

3. $F_x = y + \lambda$
    $F_y = x + 2\lambda$
    $F_\lambda = x + 2y - 600$

4. $y + \lambda = 0$
    $x + 2\lambda = 0$
    $x + 2y - 600 = 0$

5. $\lambda = -y$ and $\lambda = -\frac{x}{2}$

$$-y = -\frac{x}{2}$$

$$y = \frac{x}{2}$$

Substituting into $x + 2y - 600 = 0$, we have

$x + 2\left(\frac{x}{2}\right) - 600 = 0$, so $x = 300$ and $y = 150$.

The largest area is $(300)(150)$
   $= 45,000$ m².

26.   Let x be the radius of the can and y be the height.
   Minimize surface area $f(x, y)$
      $= 2\pi xy + 2\pi x^2$, subject to the constraint that $\pi x^2 y = 25$ in³.

1. $g(x, y) = \pi x^2 y - 25$

2. $F(x, y, \lambda)$
    $= 2\pi xy + 2\pi x^2 + \lambda(\pi x^2 y - 25)$

3. $F_x = 2\pi y + 4\pi x + 2\lambda\pi xy$
    $F_y = 2\pi x + \lambda\pi x^2$
    $F_\lambda = \pi x^2 y - 25$

4. $2\pi y + 4\pi x + 2\lambda\pi xy = 0$
    $2\pi x + \lambda\pi x^2 = 0$
    $\pi x^2 y - 25 = 0$

5. $\lambda = -\dfrac{2x + y}{xy}$ and $\lambda = -\dfrac{2}{x}$

$$-\frac{2x + y}{xy} = -\frac{2}{x}$$

$$2x^2 + xy = 2xy$$

$$2x^2 - xy = 0$$

$$x = 0 \text{ or } y = 2x$$

$x = 0$ is impossible.

Substituting $y = 2x$ into $\pi x^2 y - 25 = 0$, we have

$\pi x^2(2x) - 25 = 0$ so $x = \sqrt[3]{\dfrac{25}{2\pi}}$

≈ 1.58 in and $y = 2\sqrt[3]{\dfrac{25}{2\pi}} \approx 3.17$ in.

The can with minimum surface area will have a radius of approximately 1.58 in and a height of approximately 3.17 in.

28. If the box is x by x by y, we must minimize surface area $f(x, y) - 2x^2 + 4xy$, subject to $x^2y = 185$ in^3.

1. $g(x, y) = x^2y - 185$

2. $F(x, y, \lambda)$
$$= 2x^2 + 4xy + \lambda(x^2y - 185)$$

3. $F_x = 4x + 4y + 2\lambda xy$
$F_y = 4x + \lambda x^2$
$F_\lambda = x^2y - 185$

4. $4x + 4y + 2\lambda xy = 0$
$4x + \lambda x^2 = 0$
$x^2y - 185 = 0$

5. $\lambda = -\dfrac{2x + 2y}{xy}$ and $\lambda = -\dfrac{4}{x}$

$$-\frac{2x + 2y}{xy} = -\frac{4}{x}$$
$$2x^2 + 2xy = 4xy$$
$$2x^2 - 2xy = 0$$
$$2x(x - y) = 0$$
$$x = 0 \text{ or } y = x$$

x = 0 is impossible.
Substituting y = x into $x^2y - 185 = 0$, we have

$$y = x = \sqrt[3]{185} \approx 5.70.$$

The dimensions are 5.70 in by 5.70 in by 5.70 in.

30. Let the dimensions of the bottom be x by y, and let the height be z. We must minimize $f(x, y, z) = xy + 2xz + 2yz$ subject to $xyz = 32$.

1. $g(x, y, z) = xyz - 32$

2. $F(x, y, z, \lambda)$
$$= xy + 2xz + 2yz + \lambda(xyz - 32)$$

3. $F_x = y + 2z + \lambda yz$
$F_y = x + 2z + \lambda xz$
$F_z = 2x + 2y + \lambda xy$
$F_\lambda = xyz - 32$

4. $y + 2z + \lambda yz = 0$
$x + 2z + \lambda xz = 0$
$2x + 2y + \lambda xy = 0$
$xyz - 32 = 0$

5. $\lambda = -\dfrac{y + 2z}{yz}$

$\lambda = -\dfrac{x + 2z}{xz}$

$\lambda = -\dfrac{2x + 2y}{xy}$

$xyz = 32$

$$-\frac{y + 2z}{yz} = -\frac{x + 2z}{xz}$$
$$xyz + 2xz^2 = xyz + 2yz^2$$
$$2z^2(x - y) = 0$$
$$z^2 = 0 \text{ or } x - y = 0$$
$$z = 0 \text{ (inpossible)} \text{ or } x = y$$

$$-\frac{x + 2z}{xz} = -\frac{2x + 2y}{xy}$$
$$x^2y + 2xyz = 2x^2z + 2xyz$$
$$x^2(y - 2z) = 0$$
$$x^2 = 0 \text{ or } y - 2z = 0$$
$$x = \text{(impossible)} \text{ or } y = 2z$$

Since x = y and y = 2z and since xyz = 32, we have

$$(2z)(2z)z = 32$$
$$z^3 = 8$$
$$z = 2$$

If z = 2, y = 4 and x = 4.
The dimensions are 4 ft by 4 ft for the base and 2 ft for the height.

Section 8.5

4.

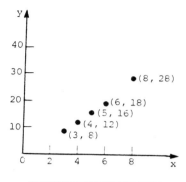

x	y	x²	xy
3	8	9	24
4	12	16	48
5	16	25	80
6	18	36	108
8	28	64	224
Totals 26	82	150	484

$$m = \frac{26(82) - 5(484)}{(26)^2 - 5(150)}$$

$$= \frac{-288}{-74} \approx 3.89$$

Keep value in calculator's memory to find b.

$$b = \frac{82 - m(26)}{5} \approx -3.84$$

Least squares equation is

$$y' = 3.89x - 3.84.$$

If y = 17, then x = 5.4; if y = 26, then x = 7.7.

6. (a)

(b)	x	y	x²	xy
	1	1.0	1	1.0
	2	1.3	4	2.6
	3	1.7	9	5.1
	4	1.9	16	7.6
	5	2.1	25	10.5
Total	15	8.0	55	26.8

n = 5

$$m = \frac{15(8.0) - 5(26.8)}{(15)^2 - 5(55)} = \frac{-14}{-50} = .28$$

$$b = \frac{8.0 - .28(15)}{5} = .76$$

y′ = .28x + .76

(c) y′ = .28(6) + .76 = 2.44

The company's sales will be 2.44 million.

8. (a)

x	y	x²	xy
0	48	0	0
1	59	1	59
2	66	4	132
3	75	9	225
4	80	16	320
5	90	25	450
Totals 15	418	55	1186

n = 6

$$m = \frac{15(418) - 6(1186)}{(15)^2 - 6(55)} = \frac{-846}{-105}$$

$$\approx 8.06$$

$$b = \frac{418 - 8.06(15)}{6} \approx 49.5$$

$$y' = 8.06x + 49.5$$

(b) In year 7, x = 7 and

$$y' = 8.06(7) + 49.5$$
$$y' = 105.9$$

In year 7 the sales will be approximately \$106,000.

10.

x	y	x^2	xy
88.6	20.0	7849.96	1772.00
71.6	16.0	5126.56	1145.60
93.3	19.8	8704.89	1847.34
84.3	18.4	7106.49	1551.12
80.6	17.1	6496.36	1378.26
75.2	15.5	5655.04	1165.60
69.7	14.7	4858.09	1024.59
82.0	17.1	6724.00	1402.20
69.4	15.4	4816.36	1068.76
83.3	16.2	6938.89	1349.46
79.6	15.0	6336.16	1194.00
82.6	17.2	6822.76	1420.72
80.6	16.0	6496.36	1289.60
83.5	17.0	6972.25	1419.50
76.3	14.4	5821.69	1098.72
Totals 1200.6	249.8	96,725.86	20,127.47

n = 15

(a)

$$m = \frac{(1200.6)(249.8) - 15(20,127.47)}{(1200.6)^2 - 15(96,725.86)}$$

$$= \frac{-2002.17}{-9447.54}$$

$$\approx .212$$

$$b = \frac{249.8 - m(1200.6)}{15}$$

$$\approx \frac{-4.637}{15}$$

$$\approx -.309$$

$$y' = .212x - .309$$

(b) If x = 73,

$$y' = .212(73) - .309$$

$$\approx 15.2.$$

If the temperature is 73°F, we would expect approximately 15.2 chirps per sec.

(c) If y' = 18,

$$18 = .212x - .309$$

$$.212x = 18.309$$

$$x = \frac{18.309}{.212}$$

$$x \approx 86.4$$

If the crickets are chirping at a rate of 18 chirps per sec, the temperature is approximately 86.4°F.

12.

x	y	x^2	xy
62	120	3844	7440
62	140	3844	8680
63	130	3969	8190
65	150	4225	9750
66	142	4356	9372
67	130	4489	8710
68	135	4624	9180
68	175	4624	11,900
70	149	4900	10,430
72	168	5184	12,096
Totals 663	1439	44,059	95,748

n = 10

(a) $m = \frac{(663)(1439) - 10(95,748)}{(663)^2 - 10(44,059)}$

$$= \frac{-3423}{-1021} \approx 3.35$$

$$b = \frac{1439 - m(663)}{10}$$

$$= \frac{783.8}{10} \approx 78.4$$

$$y' = 3.35x - 78.4$$

(b) $y' = 3.35(60) - 78.4$

$$= 123 \text{ lb}$$

(c) $y' = 3.35(70) - 78.4$

$$= 156 \text{ lb}$$

14.

x	y	x^2	xy
10	14.7	100	147.0
20	13.0	400	260.0
30	11.3	900	339.0
40	10.8	1600	432.0
50	9.6	2500	480.0
60	9.5	3600	570.0
70	9.5	4900	665.0
80	8.8	6400	704.0
88	8.8	7744	774.4
Totals 448	96.0	28,144	4371.4

$n = 9$

(a) $m = \dfrac{(448)(96.0) - 9(4371.4)}{(448)^2 - 9(28,144)}$

$= \dfrac{3665.4}{-52,592}$

$\approx -.070$

$b = \dfrac{96.0 - m(448)}{9}$

≈ 14.1

$y' = -.070x + 14.1$

(b) For 1920, x = 20. If x = 20,

$y' = -.070(20) + 14.1$

$y' = 12.7.$

For 1950, x = 50. If x = 50,

$y' = -.070(50) + 14.1$

$y' = 10.6.$

For 1980, x = 80. If x = 80,

$y' = -.070(80) + 14.1$

$y' = 8.5.$

(c)

Year	Predicated Rate	Actual Rate
1920	12.7	13.0
1950	10.6	9.6
1980	8.5	8.8

The equation is a reasonable fit because the predicted rates are close to the actual rates.

(d) For 1994, x = 94. If x = 94,

$y' = -.070(94) + 14.1$

$y' \approx 7.5.$

The predicted death rate in 1994 is 7.5.

16. $n = 5,\ \Sigma x = 376,\ \Sigma y = 120,$
$\Sigma xy = 28,050,\ \Sigma x^2 = 62,522$

(a) $m = \dfrac{376(120) - 5(28,050)}{(376)^2 - 5(62,522)}$

$= \dfrac{5}{9} \approx .556$

$b = \dfrac{120 - m(376)}{5} \approx -17.8$

Least squares equation is

$y' = .556x - 17.8.$

(b) If x = 120, then $y' \approx 48.9$.
By this formula, 120°F corresponds to 48.9°C.

Section 8.6

2. $z = x^2 + 7y^4$

$dz = 2x \, dx + 28y^3 \, dy$

4. $z = \dfrac{x + y^2}{y - 2}$

$dz = \dfrac{1}{y - 2} \, dx$

$\quad + \dfrac{(y - 2) \cdot 2y - (x + y^2) \cdot 1}{(y - 2)^2} \, dy$

$= \dfrac{dx}{y - 2} + \dfrac{y^2 - 4y - x}{(y - 2)^2} \, dy$

6. $z = (x^2 + y^2)^{1/2} + x^{1/2} y^{1/2}$

$dz = [x(x^2 + y^2)^{-1/2} + \frac{1}{2}x^{-1/2} y^{1/2}] \, dx$

$\quad + [y(x^2 + y^2)^{-1/2} + \frac{1}{2}x^{1/2} y^{-1/2}] \, dy$

$= \left(\dfrac{x}{\sqrt{x^2 + y^2}} + \dfrac{\sqrt{y}}{2\sqrt{x}}\right) dx$

$\quad + \left(\dfrac{y}{\sqrt{x^2 + y^2}} + \dfrac{\sqrt{x}}{2\sqrt{y}}\right) dy$

8. $z = (5x^2 + 6)(4 + 3y)^{1/2}$

$dz = 10x(4 + 3y)^{1/2} \, dx$

$\quad + (5x^2 + 6) \cdot \frac{3}{2}(4 + 3y)^{-1/2} \, dy$

$= 10x\sqrt{4 + 3y} \, dx + \dfrac{3(5x^2 + 6)}{2\sqrt{4 + 3y}} \, dy$

10. $z = \ln\left(\dfrac{8 + x}{8 - y}\right)$

$= \ln(8 + x) - \ln(8 - y)$

$dz = \dfrac{1}{8 + x} \, dx - \dfrac{-1}{8 - y} \, dy$

$= \dfrac{dx}{8 + x} + \dfrac{dy}{8 - y}$

12. $z = (x + y)e^{-x^2}$

$dz = [(x + y) \cdot (-2xe^{-x^2})$

$\quad + e^{-x^2} \cdot 1] dx + e^{-x^2} dy$

$= (-2x^2 - 2xy + 1)e^{-x^2} \, dx$

$\quad + e^{-x^2} dy$

14. $z = x^2 + 3y - x \ln y$

$dz = (2x - \ln y) dx + \left(3 - \dfrac{x}{y}\right) dy$

16. $w = 6x^3 y^2 z^5$

$dw = 18x^2 y^2 z^5 \, dx + 12x^3 yz^5 \, dy$

$\quad + 30x^3 y^2 z^4 \, dz$

18. $z = 8x^3 + 2x^2 y - y$, $x = 1$, $y = 3$,

$dz = .01$, $dy = .02$

$dz = (24x^2 + 4xy) dx + (2x^2 - 1) dy$

$= (24(1)^2 + 4(1)(3))(.01)$

$\quad + (2(1)^2 - 1)(.02)$

$= .38$

20. $z = \dfrac{y^2 + 3x}{y^2 - x}$, $x = 4$, $y = -4$,

$dx = .01$, $dy = .03$

$dz = \dfrac{(y^2 - x) \cdot 3 - (y^2 + 3x) \cdot (-1)}{(y^2 - x)^2} \, dx$

$\quad + \dfrac{(y^2 - x) \cdot 2y - (y^2 + 3x) \cdot 2y}{(y^2 - x)^2} \, dx$

$= \dfrac{4y^2}{(y^2 - x)^2} \, dx - \dfrac{8xy}{(y^2 - x)^2} \, dy$

$= \dfrac{4(-4)^2}{((-4)^2 - 4)^2}(.01)$

$\quad - \dfrac{8(4)(-4)}{((-4)^2 - 4)^2}(.03)$

$\approx .0311$

22. $z = \ln\left(\dfrac{x + y}{x - y}\right)$

    $= \ln(x + y) - \ln(x - y)$

    $x = 4$, $y = -2$, $dx = .03$, $dy = .02$

    $dz = \left(\dfrac{1}{x + y} - \dfrac{1}{x - y}\right)dx$

    $\qquad + \left(\dfrac{1}{x + y} + \dfrac{1}{x - y}\right)dy$

    $= \left[\dfrac{1}{4 + (-2)} - \dfrac{1}{4 - (-2)}\right](.03)$

    $\qquad + \left[\dfrac{1}{4 + (-2)} - \dfrac{1}{4 - (-2)}\right](.02)$

    $\approx .0233$

24. $w = x \ln(yz) - y \ln\left(\dfrac{x}{z}\right)$

    $= x(\ln y + \ln z) - y(\ln x - \ln z)$,

    $x = 2$, $y = 1$, $z = 4$, $dx = .03$,

    $dy = .02$, $dz = -.01$

    $dw = \left(\ln y + \ln z - \dfrac{y}{x}\right)dx$

    $\qquad + \left(\dfrac{x}{y} - \ln x + \ln z\right)dy + \left(\dfrac{x}{z} + \dfrac{y}{z}\right)dz$

    $= \left(\ln 1 + \ln 4 - \dfrac{1}{2}\right)(.03)$

    $\qquad + \left(\dfrac{2}{1} - \ln 2 + \ln 4\right)(.02)$

    $\qquad + \left(\dfrac{2}{4} + \dfrac{1}{4}\right)(-.01)$

    $\approx .0730$

26. Let r be the radius inside the tumbler and h be the height inside.

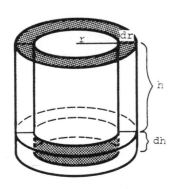

$V = \pi r^2 h$, $r = 1.5$, $h = 9$, $dr = dh$

$= .2$

$dV = 2\pi rh\, dr + \pi r^2\, dh$

$\quad = 2\pi(1.5)(9)(.2) + \pi(1.5)^2(.2)$

$\quad \approx 18.4 \text{ cm}^3 \text{ of material}$

28. $M(x, y) = 40x^2 + 30y^2 - 10xy + 30$

    $x = 4$, $y = 7$, $dx = 5 - 4 = 1$,

    $dy = 6.50 - 7 = -.50$

    $dM = (80x - 10y)dx + (60y - 10x)dy$

    $\quad = [80(4) - 10(7)](1)$

    $\qquad + [60(7) - 10(4)](-.50)$

    $\quad = 60$

Expect costs to increase by approximately \$60.

30. $z = x^{.8}y^{.2}$, $x = 20$, $y = 18$,

    $dx = 21 - 20 = 1$, $dy = 16 - 18 = -2$

    $dz = .8x^{-.2}y^{.2}\, dx + .2x^{.8}y^{-.8}\, dy$

    $\quad = .8\left(\dfrac{y^{.2}}{x^{.2}}\right)dx + .2\left(\dfrac{x^{.8}}{y^{.8}}\right)dy$

    $\quad = .8\left(\dfrac{y}{x}\right)^{.2}dx + .2\left(\dfrac{x}{y}\right)^{.8}dy$

    $\quad = .8\left(\dfrac{18}{20}\right)^{.2}(1) + .2\left(\dfrac{20}{18}\right)^{.8}(-2)$

    $\quad \approx .348$

The change in production is .348 units.

32. Assume blood vessel is cylindrical.

    $V = \pi r^2 h$, $r = .8$, $h = 7.9$, $dr = dh$

    $= \pm.15$

    $dV = 2\pi rh\, dr + \pi r^2\, dh$

    $\quad = 2\pi(.8)(7.9)(\pm.15) + \pi(.8)^2(\pm.15)$

    $\quad \approx \pm 6.26 \text{ cm}^3$

The maximum possible error is 6.26 cm^3.

34. $m = \dfrac{2.5(T - F)}{w^{.67}}$

$T = 38°$, $F = 12°$, $w = 30$ kg,

$dT = (36 - 38) = -2°$,

$dF = (13 - 12) = 1°$,

$dw = (31 - 30) = 1$ kg

$f_T = \dfrac{w^{.67}(2.5)(1) - 2.5(T - F)(0)}{(w^{.67})^2}$

$\quad = \dfrac{2.5}{w^{.67}}$

$f_F = \dfrac{w^{.67}(2.5)(-1) - 2.5(T - F)(0)}{(w^{.67})^2}$

$\quad = \dfrac{-2.5}{w^{.67}}$

$f_w = \dfrac{w^{.67}(0) - 2.5(T - F)(.67)e^{-.33}}{(w^{.67})^2}$

$\quad = \dfrac{-1.675(T - F)}{w^{1.67}}$

$dm = \dfrac{2.5}{w^{.67}}\, dT + \dfrac{-2.5}{w^{.67}}\, DF$

$\qquad + \dfrac{-1.675(T - F)}{w^{1.67}}\, dw$

$dm(38, 12, 30)$

$\quad = \dfrac{2.5}{30^{.67}}(-2) + \dfrac{-2.5}{30^{.67}}(1)$

$\qquad + \dfrac{-1.675(38 - 12)}{30^{1.67}}(1)$

$\quad = -.5120 - .2560 - .1490$

$\quad = -.917$ units

36. $V = \dfrac{1}{3}\pi r^2 h$, $r = 2.9$, $h = 8.4$,

$dr = dh = \pm.1$

$dV = \dfrac{2}{3}\pi rh\pi\, dr + \dfrac{1}{3}r^2\, dh$

$\quad = \dfrac{2}{3}\pi(2.9)(8.4)(\pm.1)$

$\qquad + \dfrac{1}{3}\pi(2.9)^2(\pm.1)$

$\quad \approx \pm 5.98$

The maximum possible error is 5.98 cm^3.

Section 8.7

2. $\displaystyle\int_1^4 (xy^2 - x)\,dy = \left(\dfrac{xy^3}{3} - xy\right)\Big|_1^4$

$\qquad\qquad = \left(\dfrac{64x}{3} - 4x\right) - \left(\dfrac{x}{3} - x\right)$

$\qquad\qquad = 18x$

4. $\displaystyle\int_3^7 (x + 5y)^{1/2}\, dy$

$\quad = \dfrac{2}{15}(x + 5y)^{3/2}\Big|_3^7$

$\quad = \dfrac{2}{15}[(x + 35)^{3/2} - (x + 15)^{3/2}]$

6. $\displaystyle\int_3^6 x\sqrt{x^2 + 3y}\, dx$

Let $u = x^2 + 3y$.

$\quad du = 2x\, dx$

When $x = 6$, $u = 36 + 3y$.

When $x = 3$, $u = 9 + 3y$

$\quad = \dfrac{1}{2}\displaystyle\int_{9+3y}^{36+y} u^{1/2}\, du$

$\quad = \dfrac{1}{2}\cdot\dfrac{2}{3}(u^{3/2})\Big|_{9+3y}^{36+3y}$

$\quad = \dfrac{1}{3}[(36 + 3y)^{3/2} - (9 + 3y)^{3/2}]$

8. $\int_{2}^{7} \dfrac{3 + 5y}{\sqrt{x}}\ dy$

$= \left(\dfrac{3y}{\sqrt{x}} + \dfrac{5y^2}{2\sqrt{x}}\right)\Big|_{2}^{7}$

$= \dfrac{1}{\sqrt{x}}\left[\left(21 + \dfrac{245}{2}\right) - \left(6 + \dfrac{20}{2}\right)\right]$

$= \dfrac{255}{2\sqrt{x}}$

10. $\int_{2}^{6} e^{x+4y}\ dx = e^{x+4y}\Big|_{2}^{6}$

$= e^{6+4y} - e^{2+4y}$

12. $\int_{1}^{6} xe^{x^2+9y}\ dy = \dfrac{x}{y}e^{x^2+9y}\Big|_{1}^{6}$

$= \dfrac{x}{9}(e^{x^2+54} - e^{x^2+9})$

14. (See Exercise 2.)

$\int_{0}^{3}\left[\int_{1}^{4} (xy^2 - x)\,dy\right]dx$

$= \int_{0}^{3} (18x)\,dx = 9x^2\Big|_{0}^{3}$

$= 81$

16. (See Exercise 5.)

$\int_{0}^{3}\left[\int_{4}^{5} x\sqrt{x^2 + 3y}\ dy\right]dx$

$= \int_{0}^{3} \dfrac{2x}{9}\left[(x^2 + 15)^{3/2} - (x^2 + 12)^{3/2}\right]dx$

$= \dfrac{2}{45}\left[(x^2 + 15)^{5/2} - (x^2 + 12)^{5/2}\right]\Big|_{0}^{3}$

$= \dfrac{2}{45}(24^{5/2} - 21^{5/2} - 15^{5/2} + 12^{5/2})$

18. (See Exercise 8.)

$\int_{16}^{25}\left[\int_{2}^{7} \dfrac{3 + 5y}{\sqrt{x}}\ dy\right]dx$

$= \int_{16}^{25} \dfrac{255}{2\sqrt{x}}\ dx$

$= \int_{16}^{25} \dfrac{255}{2}x^{-1/2}\ dx$

$= 255x^{1/2}\Big|_{16}^{25} = 255(5 - 4)$

$= 255$

20. $\int_{1}^{4}\int_{2}^{5} \dfrac{dy\ dx}{x} = \int_{1}^{4} \dfrac{y}{x}\Big|_{2}^{5}\ dx = \int_{1}^{4}\left(\dfrac{5}{x} - \dfrac{2}{x}\right)dx$

$= \int_{1}^{4} \dfrac{3}{x}\ dx = 3\ \ln\ |x|\Big|_{1}^{4}$

$= 3\ \ln\ 4$

22. $\int_{3}^{4}\int_{1}^{2}\left(\dfrac{6x}{5} + \dfrac{y}{x}\right)dx\ dy$

$= \int_{3}^{4}\left(\dfrac{3x^2}{5} + y\ \ln\ x\right)\Big|_{1}^{2}\ dy$

$= \int_{3}^{4}\left(\dfrac{12}{5} + y\ \ln\ 2 - \dfrac{3}{5}\right)dy$

$= \int_{3}^{4}\left(\dfrac{9}{5} + y\ \ln\ 2\right)dy$

$= \left(\dfrac{9y}{5} + \dfrac{y^2}{2}\ \ln\ 2\right)\Big|_{3}^{4}$

$= \dfrac{36}{5} + 8\ \ln\ 2 - \dfrac{27}{5} - \dfrac{9}{2}\ \ln\ 2$

$= \dfrac{9}{5} + \dfrac{7}{2}\ \ln\ 2$

24. $\int_0^2 \int_1^4 (4x^3 + y^2)dx\,dy$

$= \int_0^2 (x^4 + xy^2)\Big|_1^4 \, dy$

$= \int_0^2 (256 + 4y^2 - 1 - y^2)dy$

$= \int_0^2 (255 + 3y^2)dy$

$= (255y + y^3)\Big|_0^2$

$= 510 + 8 = 518$

26. $\int_0^3 \int_0^2 x^2(x^3 + 2y)^{1/2} \, dx\,dy$

$= \int_0^3 \frac{2}{9}(x^3 + 2y)^{3/2}\Big|_0^2 \, dy$

$= \int_0^3 \frac{2}{9}[(8 + 2y)^{3/2} - (2y)^{3/2}]dy$

$= \frac{2}{45}[(8 + 2y)^{5/2} - (2y)^{5/2}]\Big|_0^3$

$= \frac{2}{45}(14^{5/2} - 6^{5/2} - 8^{5/2})$

28. $\int_1^2 \int_0^3 \frac{y}{\sqrt{6x + 5y^2}} \, dx\,dy$

$= \int_1^2 \int_0^3 y(6x + 5y^2)^{-1/2} \, dx\,dy$

$= \int_1^2 \frac{y}{3}(6x + 5y^2)^{1/2}\Big|_0^3 \, dy$

$= \int_1^2 \frac{y}{3}[(18 + 5y^2)^{1/2} - (5y^2)^{1/2}]dy$

$= \int_1^2 \frac{1}{3}[y(18 + 5y^2)^{1/2} - y(5y^2)^{1/2}]dy$

$= \frac{1}{3}\left[\frac{1}{15}(18 + 5y^2)^{3/2} - \frac{(5y^2)^{3/2}}{15}\right]\Big|_1^2$

$= \frac{1}{45}(38^{3/2} - 20^{3/2} - 23^{3/2} + 5^{3/2})$

or $\frac{1}{45}(38^{3/2} - 23^{3/2} - 35\sqrt{5})$

30. $\int_1^3 \int_1^2 x^2 e^{x^3+2y}dx\,dy$

$= \int_1^3 \frac{1}{3}e^{x^3+2y}\Big|_1^2 \, dy$

$= \int_1^3 \frac{1}{3}(e^{8+2y} - e^{1+2y})dy$

$= \frac{1}{6}(e^{8+2y} - e^{1+2y})\Big|_1^3$

$= \frac{1}{6}(e^{14} - e^7 - e^{10} + e^3)$

32. $V = \int_{-2}^1 \int_0^3 (9x + 5y + 12)dx\,dy$

$= \int_{-2}^1 \left(\frac{9x^2}{2} + 5xy + 12x\right)\Big|_0^3 \, dy$

$= \int_{-2}^1 \left(\frac{81}{2} + 15y + 36\right)dy$

$= \int_{-2}^1 \left(\frac{153}{2} + 15y\right)dy$

$$= \left(\frac{153y}{2} + \frac{15y^2}{2}\right)\Bigg|_{-2}^{1}$$

$$= \frac{1}{2}(153 + 15 + 306 - 60)$$

$$= 207$$

34. $\displaystyle\int_0^4 \int_0^9 y^{1/2}\, dy\, dx$

$$= \int_0^4 \frac{2}{3}y^{3/2}\Bigg|_0^9 dx = \int_0^4 \frac{2}{3}(27)\, dx$$

$$= \int_0^4 18\, dx = 18x\Bigg|_0^4$$

$$= 72$$

36. $\displaystyle\int_0^1 \int_0^4 yx(x^2 + y^2)^{1/2}\, dx\, dy$

$$= \int_0^1 \frac{y}{3}(x^2 + y^2)^{3/2}\Bigg|_0^4 dy$$

$$= \int_0^1 \frac{y}{3}[(16 + y^2)^{3/2} - (y^2)^{3/2}]\, dy$$

$$= \int_0^1 \frac{1}{3}[y(16 + y^2)^{3/2} - y^4]\, dy$$

$$= \frac{1}{3}\left[\frac{1}{5}(16 + y^2)^{5/2} - \frac{y^5}{5}\right]\Bigg|_0^1$$

$$= \frac{1}{15}(17^{5/2} - 1 - 16^{5/2})$$

$$= \frac{1}{15}(17^{5/2} - 1 - 1024)$$

$$= \frac{1}{15}(17^{5/2} - 1025)$$

38. $\displaystyle\int_0^1 \int_0^1 e^{x+y}\, dx\, dy = \int_0^1 e^{x+y}\Bigg|_0^1 dy$

$$= \int_0^1 (e^{1+y} - e^y)\, dy$$

$$= (e^{1+y} - e^y)\Bigg|_0^1$$

$$= e^2 - e - e + 1$$
$$= e^2 - 2e + 1$$

40. $\displaystyle\int_0^1 \int_0^1 x^2 e^{2x^3+6y}\, dx\, dy$

$$= \int_0^1 \frac{1}{6}e^{2x^3+6y}\Bigg|_0^1 dy$$

$$= \int_0^1 \frac{1}{6}[e^{2+6y} - e^{6y}]\, dy$$

$$= \frac{1}{36}[e^{2+6y} - e^{6y}]\Bigg|_0^1$$

$$= \frac{1}{36}(e^8 - e^6 - e^2 + 1)$$

42. $\displaystyle\int_0^5 \int_0^{2y} (x^2 + y)\, dx\, dy$

$$= \int_0^5 \left(\frac{x^3}{3} + xy\right)\Bigg|_0^{2y} dy$$

$$= \int_0^5 \left(\frac{8y^3}{3} + 2y^2\right)\Bigg|_0^5 dy$$

$$= \left(\frac{2y^4}{3} + \frac{2y^3}{3}\right)\Bigg|_0^5$$

$$= \frac{2}{3}[625 + 125]$$

$$= 500$$

44. $\displaystyle\int_1^4\int_0^x (x + y)^{1/2}\, dy\, dx$

$\displaystyle = \int_1^4 \frac{2}{3}(x + y)^{3/2}\Big|_0^x dx$

$\displaystyle = \int_1^4 \frac{2}{3}[(2x)^{3/2} - x^{3/2}]dx$

$\displaystyle = \frac{2}{3}\left[\frac{1}{5}(2x)^{5/2} - \frac{2}{5}x^{5/2}\right]\Big|_1^4$

$\displaystyle = \frac{2}{15}(8^{5/2} - 2(4)^{5/2} - 2^{5/2} + 2)$

$\displaystyle = \frac{2}{15}(8^{5/2} - 64 - 2^{5/2} - 2)$

$\displaystyle = = \frac{2}{15}(8^{5/2} - 62 - 2^{5/2})$

46. $\displaystyle\int_1^4\int_x^{x^2} \frac{1}{y}\, dy\, dx = \int_1^4 \ln y\Big|_x^{x^2} dx$

$\displaystyle = \int_1^4 (\ln x^2 - \ln x)dx$

$\displaystyle = \int_1^4 (2\ln x - \ln x)dx$

$\displaystyle = \int_1^4 \ln x\, dx$

$\displaystyle = \left(x\ln x - \int dx\right)\Big|_1^4$

Integration by parts
u = ln x, dv = dx
du = 1/x dx, v = x

$\displaystyle = (x\ln x - x)\Big|_1^4$

$= 4\ln 4 - 4 + 1$

$= 4\ln 4 - 3$

Note: We can say ln y instead ln |y| since x is in [1, 4] and y is in [x, x²], so y > 0.)

48. $\displaystyle\int_0^1\int_{2x}^{4x} e^{x+y}\, dy\, dx$

$\displaystyle = \int_0^1 e^{x+y}\Big|_{2x}^{4x} dx$

$\displaystyle = \int_0^1 (e^{5x} - e^{3x})dx$

$\displaystyle = \left(\frac{1}{5}e^{5x} - \frac{1}{3}e^{3x}\right)\Big|_0^1$

$\displaystyle = \frac{1}{5}e^5 - \frac{1}{3}e^3 - \frac{1}{5} + \frac{1}{3}$

$\displaystyle = \frac{e^5}{5} - \frac{e^3}{3} + \frac{2}{15}$

50. $\displaystyle\int_2^4\int_2^{3x} (3x + 9y)dy\, dx$

$\displaystyle = \int_2^4 \left[3xy + \frac{9y^2}{2}\right]\Big|_2^{3x} dx$

$\displaystyle = \int_2^4 \left[9x^2 + \frac{81x^2}{2} - 6x - 18\right]dx$

$\displaystyle = \int_2^4 \left[\frac{99x^2}{2} - 6x - 18\right]dx$

$\displaystyle = \frac{33x^3}{2} - 3x^2 - 18x\Big|_2^4$

$= 1056 - 48 - 72 - 132 + 12 + 36$

$= 852$

52. $\displaystyle\int_1^2\int_0^{x-1} \frac{dy\, dx}{x} = \int_1^2 \frac{y}{x}\Big|_0^{x-1} dx$

$\displaystyle = \int_1^2 \frac{x-1}{x} dx$

$\displaystyle = \int_1^2 \left[1 - \frac{1}{x}\right]dx$

$$= (x - \ln x) \Big|_1^2$$

$$= 2 - \ln 2 - 1$$

$$= 1 - \ln 2$$

54. $$\int_{-1}^{1} \int_{-x^2}^{x^2} (x^2 - y) \, dy \, dx$$

$$= \int_{-1}^{1} \left[x^2 y - \frac{y^2}{2} \right] \Big|_{-x^2}^{x^2} dx$$

$$= \int_{-1}^{1} \left[x^4 - \frac{x^4}{2} + x^4 + \frac{x^4}{2} \right] dx$$

$$= \int_{-1}^{1} 2x^4 dx = \frac{2x^5}{5} \Big|_{-1}^{1}$$

$$= \frac{2}{5} + \frac{2}{5} = \frac{4}{5}$$

56. R is bounded by $y = x$, $y = 2x$, and $x = 1$.

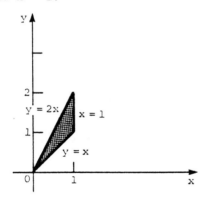

$$\int_{0}^{1} \int_{x}^{2x} x^2 y^2 \, dy \, dx \quad \textit{Notice order of integration}$$

$$= \int_{0}^{1} \frac{x^2 y^3}{3} \Big|_{x}^{2x} dx$$

$$= \int_{0}^{1} \left(\frac{8x^5}{3} - \frac{x^5}{3} \right) dx$$

$$= \int_{0}^{1} \frac{7x^5}{3} \, dx$$

$$= \frac{7x^6}{18} \Big|_{0}^{1}$$

$$= \frac{7}{18}$$

58. R defined by $1 \le x \le 4$, $1 \le y \le 2$
$A = 3 \cdot 1 = 3$
Average value is

$$\frac{1}{3} \int_{1}^{4} \int_{1}^{2} (5xy + 2y) \, dy \, dx$$

$$= \frac{1}{3} \int_{1}^{4} \left[\frac{5xy^2}{2} + y^2 \right] \Big|_{1}^{2} dx$$

$$= \frac{1}{3} \int_{1}^{4} \left[10x + 4 - \frac{5x}{2} - 1 \right] dx$$

$$= \frac{1}{3} \int_{1}^{4} \left[\frac{15x}{2} + 3 \right] dx$$

$$= \frac{1}{3} \left[\frac{15x^2}{4} + 3x \right] \Big|_{1}^{4}$$

$$= \frac{1}{3} \left[60 + 12 - \frac{15}{4} - 3 \right]$$

$$= \frac{87}{4}.$$

60. R defined by $0 \le x \le 2$, $0 \le y \le 2$
$A = 2 \cdot 2 = 4$
Average value is

$\frac{1}{4}\int_0^2\int_0^2 e^{-5y+3x}\ dy\ dx$

$\qquad = \frac{1}{4}\int_0^2 -\frac{1}{5}e^{-5y+3x}\Big|_0^2\ dx$

$\qquad = \frac{1}{4}\int_0^2 -\frac{1}{5}[e^{3x-10}-e^{3x}]dx$

$\qquad = -\frac{1}{20}[\frac{1}{3}e^{3x-10}-\frac{1}{3}e^{3x}]\Big|_0^2$

$\qquad = -\frac{1}{60}[e^{-4}-e^6-e^{-10}+1]$

$\qquad = \dfrac{e^6+e^{-10}-e^{-4}-1}{60}.$

62. The plane that intersects the axes has the equation

$$z = 6 - 2x - 2y.$$

$V = \displaystyle\iint\limits_R f(x,\ y)dA$

$\qquad = \displaystyle\int_0^3\int_0^{-x+3}(6-2x-2y)dy\ dx$

$\qquad = \displaystyle\int_0^3 (6y-2xy-y^2)\Big|_0^{-x+3}\ dx$

$\qquad = \displaystyle\int_0^3 [-6x+18-2x(-x+3)$

$\qquad\qquad - (3-x)^2]dx$

$\qquad = \displaystyle\int_0^3 (-6x+18+2x^2-6x-9+6x-x^2)dx$

$\qquad = \displaystyle\int_0^3 (x^2-6x+9)dx$

$\qquad = (\frac{x^3}{3}-3x^2+9x)\Big|_0^3$

$\qquad = (9-27+27)-0$

$\qquad = 9$

The volume is 9 in³.

64. $P(x,\ y) = 500x^{.2}y^{.8}$, $10 \le x \le 50$, $20 \le y \le 40$

$A = 40 \cdot 20 = 800$

Average production:

$\dfrac{1}{800}\displaystyle\int_{10}^{50}\int_{20}^{40}500x^{.2}y^{.8}\ dy\ dx$

$\qquad = \dfrac{5}{8}\displaystyle\int_{10}^{50}\dfrac{x^{.2}y^{1.8}}{1.8}\Big|_{20}^{40}\ dx$

$\qquad = \dfrac{25}{72}\displaystyle\int_{10}^{50}x^{.2}(40^{1.8}-20^{1.8})dx$

$\qquad = \dfrac{25(40^{1.8}-20^{1.8})}{72}\cdot\dfrac{x^{1.2}}{1.2}\Big|_{10}^{50}$

$\qquad = \dfrac{125}{432}(40^{1.8}-20^{1.8})(50^{1.2}-10^{1.2})$

$\qquad \approx 14,750$

66. $R = q_1p_1 + q_2p_2$ where $q_1 = 300 - 2p_1$, $q_2 = 500 - 1.2p_2$, $25 \le p_1 \le 50$, and $50 \le p_2 \le 75$.

$A = 25 \cdot 25 = 625$

$R = (300 - 2p_1)p_1 + (500 - 1.2p_2)p_2$

$R = 300p_1 - 2p_1{}^2 + 500p_2 - 1.2p_2{}^2$

Average Revenue:

$$\frac{1}{625}\int_{25}^{50}\int_{50}^{75} (300p_1 - 2p_1{}^2 + 500p_2 - 1.2p_2{}^2)\,dp_2\,dp_1$$

$$= \frac{1}{625}\int_{25}^{50} (300p_1 p_2 - 2p_1{}^2 p_2 + 250p_2{}^2$$

$$\left. - .4p_2{}^3\right)\Bigg|_{50}^{75} dp_1$$

$$= \frac{1}{625}\int_{25}^{50} (22{,}500p_1 - 150p_1{}^2 + 1{,}406{,}250$$

$$- 168{,}750 - 15{,}000p_1 + 100p_1{}^2 - 625{,}000$$

$$+ 50{,}000)\,dp_1$$

$$= \frac{1}{625}\int_{25}^{50} (662{,}500 + 7500p_1 - 50p_1{}^2)\,dp_1$$

$$= \frac{1}{625}\left(662{,}500p_1 + 3750p_1{}^2 - \frac{50p_1{}^3}{3}\right)\Bigg|_{25}^{50}$$

$$= \frac{1}{625}\left(33{,}125{,}000 + 9{,}375{,}000 - \frac{6{,}250{,}000}{3}\right.$$

$$\left. - 16{,}562{,}500 - 2{,}343{,}750 + \frac{781{,}250}{3}\right)$$

$$\approx \$34{,}833$$

Chapter 8 Review Exercises

2. $f(x, y) = 3x^2y^2 - 5x + 2y$

$f(-1, 2) = 12 + 5 + 4 = 21$

$f(6, -3) = 972 - 30 - 6 = 936$

4. $f(x, y) = \dfrac{\sqrt{x^2 + y^2}}{x - y};$

$f(-1, 2) = \dfrac{\sqrt{1 + 4}}{-1 - 2} = -\dfrac{\sqrt{5}}{3}$

$f(6, -3) = \dfrac{\sqrt{36 + 9}}{6 + 3} = \dfrac{\sqrt{45}}{9} = \dfrac{\sqrt{5}}{3}$

6. $x + y + 4z = 8$

x-intercept: $y = 0$, $z = 0$

$x = 8$

y-intercept: $x = 0$, $z = 0$

$y = 8$

z-intercept: $x = 0$, $y = 0$

$4z = 8$

$z = 2$

8. $3x + 5z = 15$

No y-intercept

x-intercept: $y = 0$, $z = 0$

$3x = 15$

$x = 5$

z-intercept: $x = 0$, $y = 0$

$5z = 15$

$z = 3$

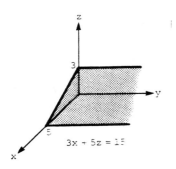

$$3x + 5z = 15$$

10. $y = 2$

No x-intercept, no z-intercept
Plane is parallel to xz-plane.

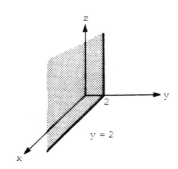

$$y = 2$$

12. $z = f(x, y) = \dfrac{x + y^2}{x - y^2}$

(a) $\dfrac{\partial z}{\partial y} =$
$$\dfrac{(x - y^2) \cdot 2y - (x + y^2)(-2y)}{(x - y^2)^2}$$

$$= \dfrac{4xy}{(x - y^2)^2}$$

(b) $\dfrac{\partial z}{\partial x} = \dfrac{(x - y^2) \cdot 1 - (x + y^2) \cdot 1}{(x - y^2)^2}$

$$= \dfrac{-2y^2}{(x - y^2)^2}$$

$$= -2y^2(x - y^2)^{-2}$$

$$\left(\dfrac{\partial z}{\partial x}\right)(0, 2) = \dfrac{-8}{(-4)^2} = -\dfrac{1}{2}$$

(c) $f_{xx} = 4y^2(x - y^2)^{-3}$

$$= \dfrac{4y^2}{(x - y^2)^3}$$

$$f_{xx}(-1, 0) = \dfrac{0}{1} = 0$$

14. $f(x, y) = 6x^5y - 8xy^9$

$f_x = 30x^4y - 8y^9$, $f_y = 6x^5 - 72xy^8$

16. $f(x, y) = \dfrac{2x + 5y^2}{3x^2 + y^2}$

$$f_x = \dfrac{(3x^2 + y^2) \cdot 2 - (2x + 5y^2) \cdot 6x}{(3x^2 + y^2)^2}$$

$$= \dfrac{2y^2 - 6x^2 - 30xy^2}{(3x^2 + y^2)^2}$$

$$f_y = \dfrac{(3x^2 + y^2) \cdot 10y - (2x + 5y^2) \cdot 2y}{(3x^2 + y^2)^2}$$

$$= \dfrac{30x^2y - 4xy}{(3x^2 + y^2)^2}$$

18. $f(x, y) = (y - 2)^2e^{x+2y}$

$f_x = (y - 2)^2e^{x+2y}$

$f_y = e^{x+2y} \cdot 2(y - 2) + (y - 2)^2 \cdot 2e^{x+2y}$

$\quad = 2(y - 2)[1 + (y - 2)]e^{x+2y}$

$\quad = 2(y - 2)(y - 1)e^{x+2y}$

20. $f(x, y) = \ln |2 - x^2y^3|$

$$f_x = \dfrac{1}{2 - x^2y^3} \cdot (-2xy^3)$$

$$= \dfrac{-2xy^3}{2 - x^2y^3}$$

$$f_y = \dfrac{1}{2 - x^2y^3} \cdot (-3x^2y^2)$$

$$= \dfrac{-3x^2y^2}{2 - x^2y^3}$$

22. $f(x, y) = -6xy^4 + x^2y$

$\quad f_x = -6y^4 + 2xy$

$\quad f_{xx} = 2y$

$\quad f_{xy} = -24y^3 + 2x$

24. $f(x, y) = \dfrac{3x + y}{x - 1}$

$f_x = \dfrac{(x - 1) \cdot 3 - (3x + y) \cdot 1}{(x - 1)^2}$

$= \dfrac{-3 - y}{(x - 1)^2} = (-3 - y)(x - 1)^{-2}$

$f_{xx} = -2(-3 - y)(x - 1)^{-3}$

$= \dfrac{2(3 + y)}{(x - 1)^3}$

$f_{xy} = \dfrac{-1}{(x - 1)^2}$

26. $f(x, y) = ye^{x^2}$

$f_x = 2xye^{x^2}$

$f_{xx} = 2xy \cdot 2xe^{x^2} + e^{x^2} \cdot 2y$

$= 2ye^{x^2}(2x^2 + 1)$

$f_{xy} = 2xe^{x^2}$

28. $f(x, y) = \ln |1 + 3xy^2|$

$f_x = \dfrac{1}{1 + 3xy^2} \cdot 3y^2$

$= \dfrac{3y^2}{1 + 3xy^2}$

$= 3y^2(1 + 3xy^2)^{-1}$

$f_{xx} = 3y^2 \cdot (-3y^2)(1 + 3xy^2)^{-2}$

$= \dfrac{-9y^4}{(1 + 3xy^2)^2}$

$f_{xy} = \dfrac{(1 + 3xy^2) \cdot 6y - 3y^2(6xy)}{(1 + 3xy^2)^2}$

$= \dfrac{6y}{(1 + 3xy^2)^2}$

30. $z = x^2 + y^2 + 9x - 8y + 1$

$z_x = 2x + 9, \quad z_y = 2y - 8$

$2x + 9 = 0$

$x = -\dfrac{9}{2}$

$2y - 8 = 0$

$y = 4$

$z_{xx} = 2, \quad z_{yy} = 2, \quad z_{xy} = 0$

$D = 2(2) - (0)^2 = 4 > 0$ and $z_{xx} > 0$.

Relative minimum at $\left(-\dfrac{9}{2}, 4\right)$

32. $z = x^3 - 8y^2 + 6xy + 4$

$z_x = 3x^2 + 6y, \quad z_y = -16y + 6x$

$3x^2 + 6y = 0$

$x^2 + 2y = 0$

$y = -\dfrac{x^2}{2}$

$-16y + 6x = 0$

$-8y + 3x = 0$

Substituting, we have

$-8\left(-\dfrac{x^2}{2}\right) + 3x = 0$

$4x^2 + 3x = 0$

$x(4x + 3) = 0$

$x = 0 \quad \text{or} \quad x = -\dfrac{3}{4}$

$y = 0 \quad \text{or} \quad y = -\dfrac{9}{32}.$

$z_{xx} = 6x, \quad z_{yy} = -16, \quad z_{xy} = 6$

$D = 6x(-16) - (6)^2 = -96x - 36$

At $(0, 0)$, $D = -36 < 0$.
Saddle point at $(0, 0)$

At $\left(-\dfrac{3}{4}, -\dfrac{9}{32}\right)$, $D = 36 > 0$ and

$z_{xx} = -\dfrac{9}{2} < 0$.

Relative maximum at $\left(-\dfrac{3}{4}, -\dfrac{9}{32}\right)$

34. $f(x, y) = 3x^2 + 2xy + 2y^2 - 3x + 2y - 9$

$f_x = 6x + 2y - 3, \quad f_y = 2x + 4y + 2$

$6x + 2y - 3 = 0$

$\underline{2x + 4y + 2 = 0}$

$$-12x - 4y + 6 = 0$$
$$\underline{2x + 4y + 2 = 0}$$
$$-10x + 8 = 0$$

$$x = \frac{4}{5}$$

$$2\left(\frac{4}{5}\right) + 4y + 2 = 0$$

$$4y = -\frac{18}{5}$$

$$y = -\frac{9}{10}$$

$f_{xx} = 6$, $f_{yy} = 4$, $f_{xy} = 2$

$D = 6(4) - (2)^2 = 2 > 0$ and $f_{xx} > 0$.

Relative minimum at $\left(\frac{4}{5}, -\frac{9}{10}\right)$

36. $f(x, y) = 7x^2 + y^2 - 3x + 6y - 5xy$

$f_x = 14x - 3 - 5y$, $f_y = 2y + 6 - 5x$

$$14x - 5y - 3 = 0$$
$$\underline{-5x + 2y + 6 = 0}$$

$$28x - 10y - 6 = 0$$
$$\underline{-25x + 10y + 30 = 0}$$
$$3x + 24 = 0$$

$$x = -8$$

$$-5(-8) + 2y + 6 = 0$$
$$2y = -46$$
$$y = -23$$

$f_{xx} = 14$, $f_{yy} = 2$, $f_{xy} = -5$

$D = 14(2) - (-5)^2 = 3 > 0$
and $f_{xx} > 0$.

Relative minimum at $(-8, -23)$

38. $f(x, y) = x^2 + y^2$, subject to
$x = y + 2$

1. $g(x, y) = x - y - 2$

2. $F(x, y, \lambda)$
$$= x^2 + y^2 + \lambda(x - y - 2)$$

3. $F_x = 2x + \lambda$
$F_y = 2y - \lambda$
$F_\lambda = x - y - 2$

4. $2x + \lambda = 0$
$2y - \lambda = 0$
$x - y - 2 = 0$

5. $\lambda = -2x$, $\lambda = 2y$
$$-2x = 2y$$
$$y = -x$$

Substituting into $x - y - 2 = 0$,
we have

$$x + x - 2 = 0.$$
$$x = 1, \ y = -1$$

So extremum is $f(1, -1) = 2$ at
$(1, -1)$.

$F_{xx} = 2$, $F_{yy} = 2$, $F_{xy} = 0$

$D = 2 \cdot 2 - (0)^2 = 4$ and $F_{xx} > 0$.

$F(1, -1) = f(1, -1) = 2$ is a
relative minimum.

40. Maximize $f(x, y) = xy^2$, subject
to $x + y = 50$

1. $g(x, y) = x + y - 50$

2. $F(x, y, \lambda)$
$$= xy^2 + \lambda(x + y - 50)$$

3. $F_x = y^2 + \lambda$
$F_y = 2xy + \lambda$
$F_\lambda = x + y - 50$

4. $y^2 + \lambda = 0$
$2xy + \lambda = 0$
$x + y - 50 = 0$

5. $\lambda = -y^2$, $\lambda = -2xy$

$$-y^2 = -2xy$$

$$y^2 - 2xy = 0$$

$$y(y - 2x) = 0$$

$y \neq 0$ since f is larger for positive x and y than for y = 0. So y = 2x. Substituting into x + y - 50 = 0, we have

$$x + 2x - 50 = 0 \text{ so } x = \frac{50}{3}, \; y = \frac{100}{3}.$$

42. Maximize f(x, y) = xy, subject to 2x + y = 400.

1. g(x, y) = 2x + y - 400

2. F(x, y, λ)

$$= xy + \lambda(2x + y - 400)$$

3. $F_x = y + 2\lambda$

$F_y = x + \lambda$

$F_\lambda = 2x + y - 400$

4. $y + 2\lambda = 0$

$x + \lambda = 0$

$2x + y - 400 = 0$

5. $\lambda = -\frac{y}{2}$, $\lambda = -x$

$$-\frac{y}{2} = -x$$

$$y = 2x$$

Substituting into 2x + y - 400, we have

$$2x + 2x - 400 = 0$$

so $\quad x = 100, \; y = 200.$

Dimensions are 100 ft by 200 ft for maximum area of 20,000 ft^2.

44. $z = 3x^2 + (x + y)^{1/2}$

$$dz = \left[6x + \frac{1}{2}(x + y)^{-1/2}\right]dx$$

$$+ \frac{1}{2}(x + y)^{-1/2} \, dy$$

46. $z = \ln |x + 4y| + y^2 \ln x$

$$dz = \left[\frac{1}{x + 4y} + \frac{y^2}{x}\right]dx$$

$$+ \left[\frac{4}{x + 4y} + 2y \ln x\right]dy$$

48. $w = \dfrac{3 + 5xy}{2 - z} = (3 + 5xy)(2 - z)^{-1}$

$$dw = \frac{5y}{2 - z} \, dx + \frac{5x}{2 - z} \, dy$$

$$+ (3 + 5xy)(2 - z)^{-2}dz$$

50. $z = \dfrac{x + 5y}{x - 2y}$, x = 1, y = -2, dx = -.04, dy = .02

$$dz = \frac{(x - 2y) \cdot 1 - (x + 5y) \cdot 1}{(x - 2y)^2} \, dx$$

$$+ \frac{(x - 2y) \cdot 5 - (x + 5y) \cdot (-2)}{(x - 2y)^2} \, dy$$

$$= \frac{-7y}{(x - 2y)^2} \, dx + \frac{7x}{(x - 2y)^2} \, dy$$

$$= \frac{-7(-2)}{(1 - 2(-2))^2}(-.04)$$

$$+ \frac{7(1)}{(1 - 2(-2))^2}(.02)$$

$$= -.0168$$

52. $\displaystyle\int_0^5 (x + 5y + y^2)dy$

$$= \left(xy + \frac{5y^2}{2} + \frac{y^3}{3}\right)\Big|_0^3$$

$$= 3x + \frac{45}{2} + 9$$

$$= 3x + \frac{63}{2}$$

54. $\int_1^3 6y^4(8x + 3y)^{1/2}\,dx$

$= \frac{y^4}{2}(8x + 3y)^{3/2}\Big|_1^3$

$= \frac{y^4}{2}[(24 + 3y)^{3/2} - (8 + 3y)^{3/2}]$

$= -\frac{1}{14}(e^{10-7y} - e^{6-7y})\Big|_1^2$

$= -\frac{1}{14}(e^{-4} - e^{-8} - e^3 + e^{-1})$

$= \frac{e^3 + e^{-8} - e^{-4} - e^{-1}}{14}$

56. $\int_3^5 e^{2x-7y}\,dx = \frac{1}{2}e^{2x-7y}\Big|_3^5$

$= \frac{1}{2}(e^{10-7y} - e^{6-7y})$

58. $\int_1^3 y^2(7x + 11y^3)^{-1/2}\,dy$

$= \frac{2}{33}(7x + 11y^3)^{1/2}\Big|_1^3$

$= \frac{2}{33}[(7x + 297)^{1/2} - (7x + 11)^{1/2}]$

60. (See Exercise 52.)

$\int_0^2 \left[\int_0^3 (x + 5y + y^2)\,dy\right]dx$

$= \int_0^2 \left(3x + \frac{63}{2}\right)dx$

$= \left(\frac{3x^2}{2} + \frac{63x}{2}\right)\Big|_0^2$

$= 6 + 63 = 69$

62. (See Exercise 56.)

$\int_1^2 \left[\int_3^5 (e^{2x-7y})\,dx\right]dy$

$= \int_1^2 \frac{1}{2}(e^{10-7y} - e^{6-7y})\,dy$

64. $\int_1^2\int_1^2 \frac{dx\,dy}{x} = \int_1^2 \ln x\Big|_1^2\,dy$

$= \int_1^2 \ln 2\,dy$

$= y \ln 2\Big|_1^2$

$= 2 \ln 2 - \ln 2$

$= \ln 2$

66. $\int_1^3\int_2^5 (2x + y)^{1/2}\,dy\,dx$

$= \int_1^3 \frac{2}{3}(2x + y)^{3/2}\Big|_2^5\,dx$

$= \int_1^3 \frac{2}{3}[(2x + 5)^{3/2} - (2x + 2)^{3/2}]\,dx$

$= \frac{2}{15}[(2x + 5)^{5/2} - (2x + 2)^{5/2}]\Big|_1^3$

$= \frac{2}{15}(11^{5/2} - 8^{5/2} - 7^{5/2} + 4^{5/2})$

$= \frac{2}{15}(11^{5/2} - 8^{5/2} - 7^{5/2} + 32)$

68. $\displaystyle\int_0^1\int_0^1 ye^{y^2+x}dy\ dx$

$\displaystyle = \int_0^1 \frac{1}{2}e^{y^2+x}\Big|_0^1\ dx$

$\displaystyle = \int_0^1 \frac{1}{2}[e^{1+x} - e^x]dx$

$\displaystyle = \frac{1}{2}[e^{1+x} - e^x]\Big|_0^1$

$\displaystyle = \frac{1}{2}[e^2 - e - e + 1]$

$\displaystyle = \frac{e^2 - 2e + 1}{2}$

70. $\displaystyle\int_3^5\int_2^4 (x^2 + y^2)dy\ dx$

$\displaystyle = \int_3^5 \left[x^2y + \frac{y^3}{3}\right]\Big|_2^4\ dx$

$\displaystyle = \int_3^5 \left[4x^2 + \frac{64}{3} - 2x^2 - \frac{8}{3}\right]dx$

$\displaystyle = \int_3^5 \left(2x^2 + \frac{56}{3}\right)dx = \left(\frac{2x^3}{3} + \frac{56x}{3}\right)\Big|_3^5$

$\displaystyle = \frac{250}{3} + \frac{280}{3} - 18 - 56$

$\displaystyle = \frac{308}{3}$

72. $\displaystyle\int_0^1\int_0^{x^3} y\ dy\ dx = \int_0^1 \frac{y^2}{2}\Big|_0^{x^3}\ dx$

$\displaystyle = \int_0^1 \frac{x^6}{2}\ dx = \frac{x^7}{14}\Big|_0^1 = \frac{1}{14}$

74. $\displaystyle\int_0^1\int_y^{\sqrt{y}} x\ dx\ dy = \int_0^1 \frac{x^2}{2}\Big|_y^{\sqrt{y}}\ dy$

$\displaystyle = \int_0^1 \frac{1}{2}(y - y^2)dy$

$\displaystyle = \frac{1}{2}\left(\frac{y^2}{2} - \frac{y^3}{3}\right)\Big|_0^1$

$\displaystyle = \frac{1}{2}\left(\frac{1}{2} - \frac{1}{3}\right) = \frac{1}{12}$

76. $\displaystyle\int_0^1\int_{x^2}^x (2 - x^2 - y^2)dy\ dx$

$\displaystyle = \int_0^1 \left(2y - x^2y - \frac{y^3}{3}\right)\Big|_{x^2}^x\ dx$

$\displaystyle = \int_0^1 \left(2x - x^3 - \frac{x^3}{3} - 2x^2 + x^4 + \frac{x^6}{3}\right)dx$

$\displaystyle = \int_0^1 \left(2x - 2x^2 - \frac{4x^3}{3} + x^4 + \frac{x^6}{3}\right)dx$

$\displaystyle = \left(x^2 - \frac{2x^3}{3} - \frac{x^4}{3} + \frac{x^5}{5} + \frac{x^7}{21}\right)\Big|_0^1$

$\displaystyle = 1 - \frac{2}{3} - \frac{1}{3} + \frac{1}{5} + \frac{1}{21} = \frac{26}{105}$

78. $c(x, y) = 2x + y^2 + 4xy + 25$

(a) $c_x = 2 + 4y$

$\quad c_x(640, 6) = 2 + 4(6)$

$\qquad\qquad\quad = 26$

For an additional 1 Mb of memory, the approximate change in cost is $26.

(b) $c_y = 2y + 4x$

$\quad c_y(640, 6) = 2(6) + 4(640)$

$\qquad\qquad\quad = 2572$

For an additional hour of labor, the approximate change in cost is $2572.

80. **(a)** Minimize $c(x, y)$

$$= x^2 + 5y^2 + 4xy - 70x - 164y + 1800$$

$$c_x = 2x + 4y - 70,$$

$$c_y = 10y + 4x - 164$$

$$2x + 4y - 70 = 0$$

$$\underline{4x + 10y - 164 = 0}$$

$$-4x - 8y + 140 = 0$$

$$\underline{4x + 10y - 164 = 0}$$

$$2y - 24 = 0$$

$$y = 12$$

$$4x + 10(12) - 164 = 0$$

$$4x = 44$$

$$x = 11$$

Extremum at $(11, 12)$

$c_{xx} = 2$, $c_{yy} = 10$, $c_{xy} = 4$

For $(11, 12)$,

$$D = (2)(10) - 16 = 4 > 0$$

$c_{xx}(11, 12) = 2 > 0$.

There is a relative minimum at $(11, 12)$.

(b) $c(11, 12)$

$$= (11)^2 + 5(12)^2 + 4(11)(12)$$

$$- 70(11) - 164(12) + 1800$$

$$= 121 + 720 + 528 - 770$$

$$- 1968 + 1800$$

$$= \$431$$

82. $C(x, y) = \ln(x^2 + y) + e^{xy/20}$

$x = 15$, $y = 9$, $dx = 1$, $dy = -1$

$$dC = \left(\frac{2x}{x^2 + y} + \frac{y}{20} e^{xy/20}\right) dx$$

$$+ \left(\frac{1}{x^2 + y} + \frac{x}{20} e^{xy/20}\right) dy$$

$dC(15, 9)$

$$= \left(\frac{2(15)}{15^2 + 9} + \frac{9}{20} e^{(15)(9)/20}\right)(1)$$

$$+ \left(\frac{1}{15^2 + 9} + \frac{15}{20} e^{(9)(15)/20}\right)(-1)$$

$$= \frac{29}{234} - \frac{3}{10} e^{27/4}$$

$$= -\$256.10$$

Costs decrease by \$256.10.

84. $V = \frac{1}{3}\pi r^2 h$

$r = 2$ cm, $h = 8$ cm,

$dr = 21$ cm, $dh = .21$ cm

$$dV = \frac{\pi}{3}(2rh\, dr + r^2\, dh)$$

$$= \frac{\pi}{3}[2(2)(8)(.21) + 4(.21)$$

$$= \frac{\pi}{3}(6.72 + .84)$$

$$= \frac{\pi}{3}(7.56)$$

$$\approx 7.92 \text{ cm}^3$$

86. $V = \frac{1}{3}\pi r^2 h$

$r = 2.9$ cm, $h = 11.4$ cm

$dr = dh = .2$ cm

$$dV = \frac{\pi}{3}(2rh\, dr + r^2\, dh)$$

$$= \frac{\pi}{3}[2(2.9)(11.4)(.2) + (2.9)^2(.2)]$$

$$= \frac{\pi}{3}[13.224 + 1.682)$$

$$= \frac{\pi}{3}(14.906)$$

$$\approx 15.6 \text{ cm}^3$$

88. (a)

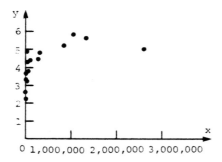

(b)

x	log x	y	(log x)²	(log x)y
341,948	5.53	4.81	30.5809	26.5993
1,092,759	6.04	5.88	36.4816	35.5152
5,491	3.74	3.31	13.9876	12.3794
49,375	4.69	4.90	21.9961	22.9810
1,340,000	6.13	5.62	37.5769	34.4506
365	2.56	2.67	6.5536	6.8352
2500	3.40	2.27	11.5600	7.7180
78,200	4.89	3.85	23.9121	18.8265
867,023	5.94	5.21	35.2836	30.9474
14,000	4.15	3.70	17.2225	15.3550
23,700	4.37	3.27	19.0969	14.2899
70,700	4.85	4.31	23.5225	20.9035
304,500	5.48	4.42	30.0304	24.2216
138,000	5.14	4.39	26.4196	22.5646
2,602,000	6.42	5.05	41.2164	32.4210
Totals	73.33	63.66	375.4407	326.0082

The data, (log x, y), is more linear than that in part (a).

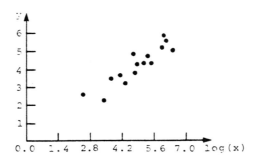

(c) $m = \dfrac{(73.33)(63.66) - 15(326.0082)}{(73.33)^2 - 15(375.4407)}$

$\quad = \dfrac{-221.9352}{-254.3216}$

$\quad \approx .873$

$b = \dfrac{63.66 - m(73.33)}{15}$

$\quad \approx -.0221$

Thus, $y' = .873 \log x - .0221$

Answers will vary depending on how $\log x$ is rounded. For example, if $\log x$ is rounded to 5 decimal places, the answer is $y' = .873 \log x - .0255$.

90. $f(a, b) = \frac{1}{4}b\sqrt{4a^2 - b^2}$

(a) $f(3, 2) = \frac{1}{4}(2)\sqrt{4(3)^2 - 2^2}$

$\quad = \frac{1}{2}\sqrt{32}$

$\quad = 2\sqrt{2}$

$\quad \approx 2.83$

The area of the bottom of the planter is approximately 2.83 ft².

(b) $A = \frac{1}{4}b\sqrt{4a^2 - b^2}$

$dA = \frac{1}{4}b \cdot \frac{1}{2}(4a^2 - b^2)^{-1/2}(8a)\,da + \frac{1}{4}\left[b \cdot \frac{1}{2}(4a^2 - b^2)^{-1/2}(-2b) + (4a^2 - b^2)^{1/2}\right]db$

$dA = \dfrac{ab}{\sqrt{4a^2 - b^2}}\,da + \frac{1}{4}\left(\dfrac{-b^2}{\sqrt{4a^2 - b^2}} + \sqrt{4a^2 - b^2}\right)db$

If $a = 3$, $b = 2$, $da = 0$ and $db = .5$,

$dA = \frac{1}{4}\left(\dfrac{-2^2}{\sqrt{4(3)^2 - 2^2}} + \sqrt{4(3)^2 - 2^2}\right)(.5)$

$dA \approx .6187$

The approximate effect on the area is an increase of .6187 ft².

CHAPTER 9 DIFFERENTIAL EQUATIONS

Section 9.1

2. $\dfrac{dy}{dx} = 3e^{-2x}$

$\quad y = \displaystyle\int 3e^{-2x}dx$

$\quad\quad = \dfrac{-3e^{-2x}}{2} + C$

4. $3x^2 - 3\dfrac{dy}{dx} = 2$

$\quad \dfrac{dy}{dx} = \dfrac{3x^2 - 2}{3} = x^2 - \dfrac{2}{3}$

$\quad y = \displaystyle\int\left(x^2 - \dfrac{2}{3}\right)dx$

$\quad\quad = \dfrac{x^3}{3} - \dfrac{2x}{3} + C$

6. $y\dfrac{dy}{dx} = x^2 - 1$

$\quad y\,dy = (x^2 - 1)dx$

$\quad \displaystyle\int y\,dy = \int(x^2 - 1)dx$

$\quad \dfrac{y^2}{2} = \dfrac{x^3}{3} - x + C$

$\quad y^2 = \dfrac{2x^3}{3} - 2x + C$

8. $\dfrac{dy}{dx} = x^2y$

$\quad \dfrac{1}{y}\,dy = x^2\,dx$

$\quad \displaystyle\int\dfrac{1}{y}\,dy = \int x^2\,dx$

$\quad \ln|y| = \dfrac{x^3}{3} + C$

$\quad\quad |y| = e^{x^3/3+C} = e^{x^3/3}\cdot e^C$

$\quad\quad\quad y = \pm e^C e^{x^3/3}$

$\quad\quad\quad y = Me^{x^3/3}$

10. $(y^2 - y)\dfrac{dy}{dx} = x$

$\quad (y^2 - y)dy = x\,dx$

$\quad \displaystyle\int(y^2 - y)dy = \int x\,dx$

$\quad \dfrac{y^3}{3} - \dfrac{y^2}{2} = \dfrac{x^2}{2} + C$

$\quad 2y^3 - 3y^2 = 3x^2 + C$

12. $\dfrac{dy}{dx} = \dfrac{y}{x^2}$

$\quad \dfrac{1}{y}\,dy = \dfrac{1}{x^2}\,dx$

$\quad \displaystyle\int\dfrac{1}{y}\,dy = \int x^{-2}dx$

$\quad \ln|y| = \dfrac{x^{-1}}{-1} + C$

$\quad\quad |y| = e^{-1/x+C} = e^{-1/x}\cdot e^C$

$\quad\quad\quad y = \pm e^C e^{-1/x}$

$\quad\quad\quad y = Me^{-1/x}$

14. $\dfrac{dy}{dx} = 3 - y$

$\quad \dfrac{1}{3 - y}\,dy = dx$

$\quad \displaystyle\int\dfrac{1}{3 - y}\,dy = \int dx$

$\quad -\ln|3 - y| = x + C$

$\quad \ln|3 - y| = -x + C$

$\quad\quad |3 - y| = e^{-x+C} = e^{-x}e^C$

$\quad\quad\quad 3 - y = \pm e^C e^{-x} = Me^{-x}$

$\quad\quad\quad\quad y = 3 - Me^{-x}$

16. $\dfrac{dy}{dx} = \dfrac{e^x}{e^y}$

$\quad e^y\,dy = e^x\,dx$

$\quad \displaystyle\int e^y\,dy = \int e^x\,dx$

$\quad e^y = e^x + C$

$\quad\quad y = \ln(e^x + C)$

18. $\dfrac{dy}{dx} = 4x^3 - 3x^2 + x$; $y = 0$ when $x = 1$.

$$y = \int (4x^3 - 3x^2 + x)\,dx$$

$$= x^4 - x^3 + \frac{x^2}{2} + C$$

Substitute.

$$0 = 1 - 1 + \frac{1}{2} + C$$

$$-\frac{1}{2} = C$$

$$y = x^4 - x^3 + \frac{x^2}{2} - \frac{1}{2}$$

20. $x\dfrac{dy}{dx} = x^2 e^{3x}$; $y = \dfrac{8}{9}$ when $x = 0$.

$$\frac{dy}{dx} = xe^{3x}$$

$$y = \int xe^{3x}\,dx$$

Let $u = x$ $dv = e^{3x}\,dx$

$du = dx$ $v = \dfrac{e^{3x}}{3}$.

$$y = \frac{x}{e}e^{3x} - \int \frac{e^{3x}}{3}\,dx$$

$$y = \frac{x}{3}e^{3x} - \frac{e^{3x}}{9} + C$$

$$\frac{8}{9} = 0 - \frac{1}{9} + C$$

$$C = 1$$

$$y = \frac{x}{3}e^{3x} - \frac{e^{3x}}{9} + 1$$

22. $x^2\dfrac{dy}{dx} = y$; $y = -1$ when $x = 1$.

$$\frac{1}{y}\,dy = \frac{1}{x^2}\,dx$$

See Exercise 12.

$$y = Me^{-1/x}$$

$$-1 = Me^{-1}$$

$$M = -e$$

$$y = -e^{1 - 1/x}$$

$$y = -e^{(-1/x)+1}$$

24. $x\dfrac{dy}{dx} - y\sqrt{x} = 0$; $y = 1$ when $x = 0$.

$$\frac{1}{y}\,dy = \frac{\sqrt{x}}{x}\,dx$$

$$\int \frac{1}{y}\,dy = \int x^{-1/2}\,dx$$

$$\ln|y| = 2x^{1/2} + C$$

$$|y| = e^{2x^{1/2}+C}$$

$$y = Me^{2x^{1/2}}$$

$$1 = Me^0$$

$$M = 1$$

$$y = e^{2x^{1/2}}$$

26. $\dfrac{dy}{dx} = x^{1/2}y^2$; $y = 12$ when $x = 4$.

$$\frac{1}{y^2}\,dy = x^{1/2}\,dx$$

$$\int y^{-2}\,dy = \int x^{1/2}\,dx$$

$$-y^{-1} = \frac{2}{3}x^{3/2} + C$$

$$-\frac{1}{12} = \frac{2}{3}(4)^{3/2} + C$$

$$C = -\frac{65}{12}$$

$$\frac{-1}{y} = \frac{2}{3}x^{3/2} - \frac{65}{12}$$

$$\frac{-1}{y} = \frac{8x^{3/2} - 65}{12}$$

$$y = \frac{-12}{8x^{3/2} - 65}$$

28. $\dfrac{dy}{dx} = \dfrac{x^2 + 5}{2y - 1}$; $y = 11$ when $x = 0$.

$$(2y - 1)\,dy = (x^2 + 5)\,dx$$

$$\int (2y - 1)\,dy = \int (x^2 + 5)\,dx$$

$$y^2 - y = \frac{x^3}{3} + 5x + C$$

$$121 - 11 = C$$

$$C = 110$$

$$y^2 - y = \frac{x^3}{3} + 5x + 110$$

30. $\dfrac{dy}{dx} = (x + 2)^2 e^y$; $y = 0$ when $x = 1$.

$$e^{-y}\, dy = (x + 2)^2\, dx$$

$$\int e^{-y}\, dx = \int (x + 2)^2\, dx$$

$$-e^{-y} = \frac{(x + 2)^3}{3} + C$$

$$-1 = 9 + C$$

$$C = -10$$

$$-e^{-y} = \frac{(x + 2)^3}{3} - 10$$

$$e^{-y} = 10 - \frac{(x + 2)^3}{3}$$

$$-y = \ln\left[10 - \frac{(x + 2)^3}{3}\right]$$

$$y = -\ln\left[10 - \frac{(x + 2)^3}{3}\right]$$

32. $\dfrac{dz}{dx} = k(1 - z)z$, $0 < z < 1$

Note $1 - z > 0$ also.

$$\frac{1}{(1 - z)z}\, dz = k\, dx$$

Observe that

$$\frac{1}{1 - z} + \frac{1}{z} = \frac{1}{(1 - z)z}$$

$$\left[\frac{1}{1 - z} + \frac{1}{z}\right] dz = k\, dx$$

$$\int\left[\frac{1}{1 - z} + \frac{1}{z}\right] dz = \int k\, dx$$

$$-\ln(1 - z) + \ln z = kx + C$$

$$\ln\left(\frac{z}{1 - z}\right) = kx + C$$

$$\frac{z}{1 - z} = e^{kx+C}$$

$$= Me^{kx} \text{ where } M = e^C$$

$z = \dfrac{1}{2}$ when $x = x_0$. Let $b = e^{kx_0}$.

$$\frac{\frac{1}{2}}{1 - \frac{1}{2}} = Me^{kx_0}.$$

$$1 = Mb$$

$$M = \frac{1}{b}.$$

Therefore,

$$\frac{z}{1 - z} = \frac{1}{b}e^{kx}$$

$$bz = e^{kx} - ze^{kx}.$$

$$(e^{kx} + b)z = e^{kx}$$

$$z = \frac{e^{kx}}{e^{kx} + b}$$

$$= \frac{1}{1 + be^{-kx}}.$$

34. $y = \dfrac{N}{1 - be^{-kx}}$ for all $x \neq \dfrac{\ln b}{k}$,

where $0 < N < y_0$ and

$$b = \frac{y_0 - N}{y_0}.$$

(a) Since $0 < N < y_0$, $0 < y_0 - N$ and $0 < y_0$, so $b > 0$. Also, $y_0 - N < y_0$ so

$$\frac{y_0 - N}{y_0} < 1 \text{ and } b < 1.$$

(b) $\lim\limits_{x \to \infty} e^{-kx} = 0$ (assuming $k > 0$), so

$$\lim\limits_{x \to \infty} \frac{N}{1 - be^{-kx}} = \frac{N}{1 - 0} = N.$$

Thus, $y = N$ is a horizontal asymptote to the curve as $x \to \infty$.

$$\lim\limits_{x \to -\infty} e^{-kx} = \infty, \text{ so}$$

$$\lim\limits_{x \to \infty} \frac{N}{1 - be^{-kx}} = 0.$$

Thus $y = 0$ is a horizontal asymptote to the curve as $x \to -\infty$.

(c) The graph has a vertical asymptote when

$$1 - be^{-kx} = 0$$

$$1 = be^{-kx}$$

$$\frac{1}{b} = e^{-kx}$$

$$b^{-1} = e^{-kx}$$

$$\ln b^{-1} = \ln e^{-kx}$$

$$-\ln b = -kx$$

$$\frac{\ln b}{k} = x.$$

(d) $y = N(1 - be^{-kx})^{-1}$, $x \neq \dfrac{\ln b}{k}$

We assume that $k > 0$.

$$\frac{dy}{dx} = -N(1 - be^{-kx})^{-2}(-be^{-kx} \cdot (-k))$$

$$= \frac{-kbNe^{-ke}}{(1 - be^{-kx})^2}$$

$e^{-kx} > 0$ for all x, $(1 - be^{-kx})^2 > 0$ for all $x \neq \dfrac{\ln b}{k}$, $k > 0$, $b > 0$, and $N > 0$.

Therefore, $\dfrac{dy}{dx} < 0$ and y is decreasing on $\left(\dfrac{\ln b}{k}, \infty\right)$ and on $\left(-\infty, \dfrac{\ln b}{k}\right)$.

(e) $y'' = -kbN\left[\dfrac{(1 - be^{-kx})^2 \cdot e^{-kx}(-k) - e^{-kx} \cdot 2(1 - be^{-kx}) \cdot (kbe^{-kx})}{(1 - be^{-kx})^4}\right]$

$$= kbN\left[\frac{-ke^{-kx}\{(1 - be^{-kx}) + 2be^{-kx}\}}{(1 - be^{-kx})^3}\right]$$

$$= \frac{k^2bNe^{-kx}(1 + be^{-kx})}{(1 - be^{-kx})^3}$$

$e^{-kx} > 0$ and $b > 0$ so $1 + be^{-kx} > 0$ for all x. $k^2 > 0$ and $N > 0$, so the numerator is always positive.

$(1 - be^{-kx})^3 > 0$, if and only if

$$1 - be^{-kx} > 0$$

$$1 > be^{-kx}$$

$$b^{-1} > e^{-kx}$$

$$\ln b^{-1} > \ln e^{-kx}$$

$$-\ln b > -kx$$

$$\frac{\ln b}{k} > x.$$

Thus y is concave upward on $\left(\frac{\ln b}{x}, \infty\right)$ and concave downward on $\left(-\infty, \frac{\ln b}{x}\right)$.

36. Let y = sales, t = time, and k = -25.

(a) $\frac{dy}{dt} = -.25y$

(b) From Example 4, $y = Me^{-.25t}$

(c) If t = 0, y = .3M.

$$.3M = Me^{-.25t}$$
$$.3 = e^{-.25t}$$
$$-.25t = \ln .3$$
$$t = \frac{\ln .3}{-.25} \approx 4.8$$

Sales will become 30% of their original value in approximately 4.8 yr.

38. Let y = GNP, t = time, and k = .02.

$\frac{dy}{dt} = .02y$, so $y = Me^{.02t}$

Let t = 0 correspond to 10 yr ago. Then $y = 10^5$ when t = 0, so $10^5 = M$. Five years from now, t = 15 and

$$y = 10^5 e^{.02(15)}$$

so $y \approx \$134,986$ or $\$1.35 \times 10^5$.

40. $y = \frac{100,000}{1 + 100e^{-x}}$

(a) x = 0

$$y = \frac{100,000}{1 + 100} \approx 990 \text{ cars}$$

(b) The maximum sales level is the numerator 100,000.

(c) $\frac{dy}{dx} = y - \frac{1}{100,000} y^2$

The maximum sales level is never achieved since $dy/dx \neq 0$ for any value of x and dy/dx exists for all x.

(d) If x = 6,

$$y = \frac{100,000}{1 + 100e^{-6}} \approx 80,136.$$
$$\frac{dy}{dx} \approx 80,136 - \frac{(80,136)^2}{100,000} \approx 15,918$$

cars per month.

Alternatively,

$$y = 100,000(1 + 100e^{-x})^{-1}$$
$$\frac{dy}{dx} = -100,000(1 + 100e^{-x})^{-2}$$
$$\cdot (-100e^{-x})$$
$$= \frac{10,000,000e^{-x}}{(1 + 100e^{-x})^2}.$$

For x = 6,

$$\frac{dy}{dx} = \frac{10^7 e^{-6}}{(1 + 100e^{-6})^2} \approx 15,918$$

cars per month.

42. $E = -\frac{p}{q} \cdot \frac{dq}{dp}$ with p > 0 and q > 0

If E = 2,

$$2 = -\frac{p}{q} \cdot \frac{dq}{dp}$$
$$\frac{2}{p} dp = -\frac{1}{q} dq$$
$$\int \frac{2}{p} dp = -\int \frac{1}{q} dq$$
$$2 \ln p = -\ln q + K$$
$$\ln p^2 + \ln q = K$$
$$\ln (p^2 q) = K$$

$$p^2q = e^K$$
$$p^2q = C$$
$$q = \frac{C}{p^2}$$

44. $\frac{dy}{dx} = 50 - y$; $y = 1000$ when $x = 0$.

$$\frac{dy}{50 - y} = dx$$

$$\int \frac{dy}{50 - y} = \int dx$$

$$-\ln (50 - y) = x + C$$

$$\ln (50 - y) = -x + C$$

$$50 - y = e^{-x+C}$$

$$= Me^{-x}$$

$$1000 = 50 - M$$

$$M = -950$$

$$y = 50 + 950e^{-x}$$

(a) If $x = 2$,

$$y = 50 + 950e^{-2} \approx 178.6.$$

About 178.6 thousand bacteria are present.

(b) If $x = 5$,

$$y = 50 + 950e^{-5} \approx 56.4.$$

About 56.4 thousand bacteria are present.

(c) If $x = 10$,

$$y = 50 + 950e^{-10} \approx 50.0.$$

About 50.0 thousand bacteria are present.

(d) If $x = 15$,

$$y = 50 + 950e^{-15} \approx 50.0.$$

About 50.0 thousand bacteria are present.

46. Let $y =$ the number of mites (in hundreds), $t =$ time, and $k = .05$.

$$\frac{dy}{dt} = .05y$$

$$y = Me^{.05t}$$

When $t = 0$,

$$y = 30$$

$$30 = M.$$

When $t = 4$,

$$y = 30e^{.05(4)} \approx 37.$$

So there were approximately 3700 mites.

48. $\frac{dy}{dx} = 7.5e^{-.3y}$, $y = 0$ when $x = 0$.

$$e^{.3y} \, dy = 7.5 \, dx$$

$$\int e^{.3y} \, dy = \int 7.5 \, dx$$

$$\frac{e^{.3y}}{.3} = 7.5x + C$$

$$e^{.3y} = 2.25x + C$$

$$1 = 0 + C = C$$

$$e^{.3y} = 2.25x + 1$$

$$.3y = \ln (2.25x + 1)$$

$$y = \frac{\ln (2.25x + 1)}{.3}$$

When $x = 8$,

$$y = \frac{\ln [2.25(8) + 1]}{.3}$$

$$\approx 10 \text{ items.}$$

50. Let $t = 0$ be the time the snow began.

If h is the height of the snow and if the rate of snowing is constant,

$\frac{dh}{dt} = k_1$ where k_1 is a constant.

$\frac{dh}{dt} = k_1$ and $h = 0$ when $t = 0$

$dh = k_1 \, dt$

$\int dh = \int k_1 \, dt$

$h = k_1 t + C_1$

Since $h = 0$ and $t = 0$, $0 = k_1(0) + C_1$. Thus, $C_1 = 0$ and $h = k_1 t$.
Since the snowplow removes a constant volume of snow per hour and the volume is proportional to the height of the snow, the rate of travel of the snowplow is inversely proportional to the height of the snow.

$\frac{dx}{dt} = \frac{k_2}{h}$ where k_2 is a constant.

When $t = T$, $x = 0$.
When $t = T + 1$, $x = 2$.
When $t = T + 2$, $x = 3$.

Since, $\frac{dy}{dt} = \frac{k_2}{h}$ and $h = k_1 t$,

$\frac{dy}{dt} = \frac{k_2}{k_1 t}$

$\frac{dx}{dt} = \frac{k_2}{k_1} \cdot \frac{1}{t}$.

Let $k_3 = \frac{k_2}{k_1}$

$\frac{dx}{dt} = k_3 \frac{1}{t}$

$dx = k_3 \frac{1}{t} \, dt$

$\int dx = \int k_3 \frac{1}{t} \, dt$

$x = k_3 \ln t + C_2$.

Since $x = 0$, when $t = T$,

$0 = k_3 \ln T + C_2$

$C_2 = -k_3 \ln T$

Thus, $x = k_3 \ln t - k_3 \ln T$

$x = k_3 (\ln t - \ln T)$

$x = k_3 \ln \left(\frac{t}{T}\right)$.

Since $x = 2$ when $t = T + 1$,

$2 = k_3 \ln \left(\frac{T + 1}{T}\right)$.   (1)

Since $x = 3$ when $t = T + 2$,

$3 = k_3 \ln \left(\frac{T + 2}{T}\right)$.   (2)

We want to solve for T, so we divide equation (1) by equation (2).

$\frac{2}{3} = \frac{k_3 \ln \left(\frac{T + 1}{T}\right)}{k_3 \ln \left(\frac{T + 2}{T}\right)}$

$\frac{2}{3} = \frac{\ln (T + 1) - \ln T}{\ln (T + 2) - \ln T}$

$2 \ln (T + 2) - 2 \ln T = 3 \ln (T + 1) - 3 \ln T$

$\ln (T + 2)^2 - \ln T^2 - \ln (T + 1)^3 + \ln T^3 = 0$

$\ln \frac{(T + 2)^2 T^3}{T^2 (T + 1)^3} = 0$

$\frac{T(T + 2)^2}{(T + 1)^3} = 1$

$T(T^2 + 4T + 4) = T^3 + 3T^2 + 3T + 1$

$T^3 + 4T^2 + 4T = T^3 + 3T^2 + 3T + 1$

$T^2 + T - 1 = 0$

$T = \frac{-1 \pm \sqrt{1 + 4}}{2}$

$T = \frac{-1 - \sqrt{5}}{2}$ is negative and is not a possible solution.

Thus, $T = \frac{-1 + \sqrt{5}}{2} \approx .618$ hr.

.618 hr $\approx$ 37 min and 5 sec
Now, 37 min and 5 sec before
8:00 A.M. is 7:22:55 A.M.
Thus, the snow began at 7:22:55 A.M.

Section 9.2

2. $y' + 4y = 10$

$$I(x) = e^{\int 4\ dx} = e^{4x}$$

$$e^{4x}y' + 4e^{4x}y = 10e^{4x}$$

$$D_x(e^{4x}y) = 10e^{4x}$$

$$e^{4x}y = \int 10e^{4x}\ dx$$

$$= \frac{5}{2}e^{4x} + C$$

$$y = \frac{5}{2} + Ce^{-4x}$$

4. $y' + 2xy = x$

$$I(x) = e^{\int 2x\ dx} = e^{x^2}$$

$$e^{x^2}y' + 2xe^{x^2}y = xe^{x^2}$$

$$D_x(e^{x^2}y) = xe^{x^2}$$

$$e^{x^2}y = \int xe^{x^2}\ dx$$

$$= \frac{1}{2}e^{x^2} + C$$

$$y = \frac{1}{2} + Ce^{-x^2}$$

6. $xy' + 2xy - x^2 = 0;\ x > 0$

$$y' + 2y = x$$

$$I(x) = e^{\int 2\ dx} = e^{2x}$$

$$e^{2x}y' + 2e^{2x}y = xe^{2x}$$

$$D_x(e^{2x}y) = xe^{2x}$$

$$e^{2x}y = \int xe^{2x}\ dx$$

Integration by parts:

Let $u = x$ $dv = e^{2x}\ dx$

     $du = dx$ $v = \dfrac{e^{2x}}{2}$.

$$e^{2x}y = \frac{xe^{2x}}{2} - \int \frac{e^{2x}}{2}\ dx$$

$$= \frac{xe^{2x}}{2} - \frac{e^{2x}}{4} + C$$

$$y = \frac{x}{2} - \frac{1}{4} + Ce^{-2x}$$

8. $3y' + 6xy + x = 0$

$$y' + 2xy = -\frac{x}{3}$$

$$I(x) = e^{\int 2x\ dx} = e^{x^2}$$

$$e^{x^2}y' + 2xe^{x^2}y = -\frac{x}{3}e^{x^2}$$

$$D_x(e^{x^2}y) = -\frac{x}{3}e^{x^2}$$

$$e^{x^2}y = \int -\frac{x}{3}e^{x^2}\ dx$$

$$= -\frac{1}{6}e^{x^2} + C$$

$$y = -\frac{1}{6} + Ce^{-x^2}$$

10. $x^2y' + xy = x^3 - 2x^2;\ x > 0$

$$y' + \frac{1}{x}y = x - 2$$

$$I(x) = e^{\int 1/x\ dx} = e^{\ln x} = x$$

$$xy' + y = x^2 - 2x$$

$$D_x(xy) = x^2 - 2x$$

$$xy = \int (x^2 - 2x)\,dx$$

$$= \frac{x^3}{3} - x^2 + C$$

$$y = \frac{x^2}{3} - x + \frac{C}{x}$$

12. $2xy + x^3 = x\dfrac{dy}{dx}$

$$x\frac{dy}{dx} - 2xy = x^3$$

$$\frac{dy}{dx} - 2y = x^2$$

$$I(x) = e^{\int -2 \ dx} = e^{-2x}$$

$$e^{-2x}\frac{dy}{dx} - 2e^{-2x}y = x^2 e^{-2x}$$

$$D_x(e^{-2x}y) = x^2 e^{-2x}$$

$$e^{-2x}y = \int x^2 e^{-2x} \ dx$$

Integration by parts:

Let $u = x^2$ $dv = e^{-2x} \ dx$

    $du = 2x \ dx$ $v = \dfrac{e^{-2x}}{-2}$.

$$e^{-2x}y = \frac{-x^2 e^{-2x}}{2} + \int x e^{-2x} \ dx$$

Let $u = x$ $dv = e^{-2x} \ dx$

    $du = dx$ $v = \dfrac{e^{-2x}}{-2}$.

$$e^{-2x}y = \frac{-x^2 e^{-2x}}{2} - \frac{x e^{-2x}}{2} + \int \frac{e^{-2x}}{2} \ dx$$

$$e^{-2x}y = \frac{-x^2 e^{-2x}}{2} - \frac{x e^{-2x}}{2} - \frac{e^{-2x}}{4} + C$$

$$y = -\frac{x^2}{2} - \frac{x}{2} - \frac{1}{4} + Ce^{2x}$$

14. $y' + 2y = e^{3x}$; $y = 50$ when $x = 0$.

$$I(x) = e^{\int 2 \ dx} = e^{2x}$$

$$e^{2x}y' + 2e^{2x}y = e^{2x}e^{3x}$$

$$D_x(e^{2x}y) = e^{5x}$$

$$e^{2x}y = \int e^{5x} dx + C$$

$$= \frac{e^{5x}}{5} + C$$

$$y = \frac{e^{3x}}{5} + Ce^{-2x}$$

$$50 = \frac{1}{5} + C$$

$$C = \frac{249}{5}$$

$$y = \frac{e^{3x}}{5} + \frac{249e^{-2x}}{5}$$

16. $x\dfrac{dy}{dx} - 3y + 2 = 0$; $y = 8$ when $x = 1$.

$$\frac{dy}{dx} - \frac{3}{x}y = -\frac{2}{x}$$

$$I(x) = e^{\int -3/x \ dx} = e^{-3 \ln x}$$

$$= e^{\ln x^{-3}} = x^{-3}$$

$$\frac{1}{x^3}\frac{dy}{dx} - \frac{3}{x^4}y = -\frac{2}{x^4}$$

$$D_x\left(\frac{1}{x^3}y\right) = -\frac{2}{x^4}$$

$$\frac{1}{x^3}y = \int -2x^{-4} \ dx$$

$$= \frac{2x^{-3}}{3} + C$$

$$y = \frac{2}{3} + Cx^3$$

$$8 = \frac{2}{3} + C$$

$$C = \frac{22}{3}$$

$$y = \frac{2}{3} + \frac{22x^3}{3}$$

18. $2\dfrac{dy}{dx} - 4xy = 5$; $y = 10$ when $x = 1$.

$$\frac{dy}{dx} - 2xy = \frac{5x}{2}$$

$$I(x) = e^{\int -2x \ dx} = e^{-x^2}$$

$$e^{-x^2}\frac{dy}{dx} - 2xe^{-x^2}y = \frac{5x}{2}e^{-x^2}$$

$$D_x(e^{-x^2}y) = \frac{5x}{2}e^{-x^2}$$

$$e^{-x^2}y = \int \frac{5x}{2}e^{-x^2} \ dx$$

$$= -\frac{5}{4}e^{-x^2} + C$$

$$y = -\frac{5}{4} + Ce^{x^2}$$

$$10 = -\frac{5}{4} + Ce$$

$$C = \frac{45}{4e}$$

$$y = -\frac{5}{4} + \frac{45}{4e}e^{x^2}$$

$$\text{or } -\frac{5}{4} + \frac{45}{4}e^{x^2-1}$$

20. $y' + 2xy = e^{-x^2}$; $y = 100$ when $x = 0$.

$$I(x) = e^{\int 2x\, dx} = e^{x^2}$$

$$e^{x^2}y' + 2xe^{x^2}y = e^{x^2} \cdot e^{-x^2}$$

$$D_x(e^{x^2}y) = 1$$

$$e^{x^2}y = \int 1\, dx = x + C$$

$$y = xe^{-x^2} + Ce^{-x^2}$$

$$100 = 0 + C = C$$

$$y = xe^{-x^2} + 100e^{-x^2}$$

22.

$$\frac{dG}{dt} = a - KG$$

$$dG = (a - KG)dt$$

$$\frac{1}{a - KG}\, dG = dt$$

$$\int \frac{1}{a - KG}\, dG = \int dt$$

$$-\frac{1}{K}\int \frac{-K}{a - KG}\, dG = \int dt$$

$$-\frac{1}{K}\ln(a - KG) = t + C_1$$

$$\ln(a - KG) = -Kt + C_2$$

$$a - KG = e^{-Kt+C_2}$$

$$a - KG = e^{C_2}e^{-Kt}$$

$$-KG = -a + e^{C_2}e^{-Kt}$$

Dividing by $-K$, we get

$$G = \frac{a}{K} + Ce^{-Kt} \text{ where } C = \frac{e^{C_2}}{-K}.$$

24. $f(t) = e^{-t}$

$$\frac{dy}{dt} = ky + f(t), \quad k = .02$$

$$\frac{dy}{dt} = .02y + e^{-t}$$

$$\frac{dy}{dt} - .02y = e^{-t}$$

$$I(t) = e^{\int -.02\, dt} = e^{-.02t}$$

$$D_t(y \cdot e^{-.02t}) = e^{-.02t}e^{-t}$$

$$ye^{-.02t} = \int e^{-1.02t}\, dt$$

$$ye^{-.02t} = -.98e^{-1.02t} + C$$

$$y = -.98e^{-t} + Ce^{.02t}$$

Since $y = 10,000$ when $t = 0$,

$$10,000 = -.98e^0 + Ce^0$$

$$10,000 = -.98 + C$$

$$C = 10,000.98.$$

Therefore,

$$y = -.98e^{-t} + 10,000.98e^{.02t}.$$

26. $f(t) = t$

$$\frac{dy}{dt} = ky + f(t)$$

$$y' = ky + t$$

$$y' - ky = t$$

$$I(t) = e^{-\int k\, dt} = e^{-kt}$$

$$e^{-kt}y' - ke^{-kt}y = te^{-kt}$$

$$D_t(e^{-kt}y) = te^{-kt}$$

$$e^{-kt}y = \int te^{-kt}\, dt$$

$$e^{-kt}y = -\left(\frac{kt+1}{k^2}\right)e^{-kt} + C$$

Use the table or integration by parts.

$$y = -\left(\frac{kt+1}{k^2}\right) + Ce^{kt}$$

At $k = .02$, $y = 10,000$, $t = 0$

$$10,000 = -\left(\frac{0 + 1}{(.02)^2}\right) + Ce^0$$

$$10,000 = -\left(\frac{1}{.0004}\right) + C(1)$$

$$12,500 = C.$$

Therefore,

$$y = -\left(\frac{.02t + 1}{.0004}\right) + 12,500e^{.02t}$$

$$= -50t - 2500 + 12,500e^{.02t}.$$

28. $\frac{dT}{dt} = -k(T - T_F)$ with $T - T_F > 0$

$$\frac{1}{T - T_F}\, dT = -k\, dt$$

$$\int \frac{1}{T - T_F}\, dT = -\int k\, dt$$

$$\ln (T - T_F) = -kt + C_1$$

$$T - T_F = e^{-kt + C_1}$$

$$T = T_F + e^{C_1} e^{-kb}$$

$$T = ce^{-kt} + T_F \text{ where } c = e^{C_1}$$

30. $\frac{dT}{dt} = -k(T - T_F)$

$$T_F = -40°F$$

(a) $\frac{dT}{dt} = -k(T - 40)$

$$\frac{dT}{T - 40} = -k\, dt$$

$$\ln |T - 40| = -kt + C$$

$$|T - 40| = e^{-kt + C}$$

$$T - 40 = ce^{-kt}$$

$$T = ce^{-kt} + 40$$

Since $T = 180°F$ when $t = 0$,

$$180 = ce^0 + 40$$

$$c = 140.$$

$$T = 140e^{-kt} + 40$$

Then, $T = 110$ when $t = \frac{1}{2}$.

$$110 = 140e^{-k/2} + 40$$

$$e^{-k/2} = \frac{1}{2}$$

$$k = -2 \ln \frac{1}{2} = -1.3863$$

Therefore,

$$T = 140e^{-1.3863t} + 40.$$

(b) $T = 140e^{-1.3863(1)} + 40$

$$T = 75°$$

(c) $T = 140e^{-1.3863(5)} + 40$

$$T = 40°$$

Section 9.3

2. $y' = xy + 2$; $f(0) = 0$, $h = .1$; find $f(.5)$.

$g(x, y) = xy + 2$

$x_0 = 0$; $y_0 = f(0) = 0$

$g(x_0, y_0) = 0 + 2 = 2$

$x_1 = .1$

By Euler's method,

$$y_{i+1} = y_i + g(x_i, y_i)h.$$

Thus, $y_1 = 0 + 2(.1) = .2$.

$g(x_1, y_1) = .1(.2) + 2 = 2.02$

$x_2 = .2$

$y_2 = .2 + 2.02(.1) = .402$

$g(x_2, y_2) = .2(.402) + 2 = 2.0804$

$x_3 = .3$

$y_3 = .402 + 2.0804(.1) = .61004$

$g(x_3, y_3) = .3(.61004) + 2$

$\qquad = 2.183012$

$x_4 = .4$

$y_4 = .61004 + 2.183012(.1)$

$\qquad = .8283412$

$g(x_4, y_4) = .4(.8283412) + 2$

$\qquad = 2.33133648$

$x_5 = .5$

$y_5 = .8283412 + 2.33133648(.1)$

$\qquad = 1.061474848$

Tabulate the results as follows.

x_i	y_i
0	0
.1	.2
.2	.402
.3	.61004
.4	.8283412
.5	1.0614748

Therefore, $f(.5) \approx 1.061$.

Use Euler's method as outlined in the solution for Exercise 2 in the following exercises. The results are tabulated.

4. $y' = x + y^2$; $f(0) = 0$, $h = .1$; find $f(.6)$.

x_i	y_i
0	0
.1	0
.2	.01
.3	.03001
.4	6.01007×10^{-2}
.5	.1004613
.6	.1514705

Therefore, $f(.6) \approx .151$.

6. $y' = 1 + \dfrac{y}{x}$; $f(1) = 0$, $h = .1$; find $f(1.4)$.

x_i	y_i
1	0
1.1	.1
1.2	.2090909
1.3	.3265152
1.4	.4516317

Therefore, $f(1.4) \approx .452$.

8. $y' = e^{-y} + x$; $f(0) = 0$; $h = .1$; find $f(.5)$.

x_i	y_i
0	0
.1	.1
.2	.2004838
.3	.3023172
.4	.4062276
.5	.5128435

Therefore, $f(.5) \approx .513$.

10. $y' = 4x + 3$; $f(1) = 0$, $h = .1$; find $f(1.5)$.

x_i	y_i
1	0
1.1	.7
1.2	1.44
1.3	2.22
1.4	3.04
1.5	3.9

Therefore, $f(1.5) \approx 3.900$.

Exact solution:

$y = 2x^2 + 3x + C$

$0 = 2(1)^2 + 3(1) + C$

$C = -5$

$y = f(x) = 2x^2 + 3x - 5$

Therefore,

$$f(1.5) = 2(1.5)^2 + 3(1.5) - 5$$
$$= 4.000$$

12. $y' = \frac{1}{x}$; $f(1) = 1$, $h = .1$, find $f(1.4)$.

x_i	y_i
1	1
1.1	1.1
1.2	1.190909
1.3	1.274243
1.4	1.351166

Therefore, $f(1.4) \approx 1.351$.

Exact solution:

$$y = \ln x + C$$
$$1 = \ln 1 + C = C$$
$$y = f(x) = \ln x + 1$$
$$f(1.4) = \ln 1.4 + 1 \approx 1.336$$

14. $y' = x^2 y$; $f(0) = 1$, $h = .1$; find $f(.6)$.

x_i	y_i
0	1
.1	1
.2	1.001
.3	1.005004
.4	1.014049
.5	1.030274
.6	1.056031

Therefore, $f(.6) \approx 1.056$.

Exact solution:

$$\frac{y'}{y} = x^2$$
$$\ln y = \frac{x^3}{3} + C$$
$$\ln 1 = 0 + C$$
$$0 = C$$

$$\ln y = \frac{x^3}{3}$$
$$y = f(x) = e^{x^3/3}$$
$$f(.6) = e^{(.6)^3/3} \approx 1.075$$

16. $y' = \frac{x}{y}$; $f(0) = 2$, $h = .1$; find $f(.3)$.

x_i	y_i
0	2
.1	2
.2	2.2005
.3	2.014975

Therefore, $f(.3) \approx 2.015$.

Exact solution:

$$yy' = x$$
$$\frac{y^2}{2} = \frac{x^2}{2} + C$$
$$2 = 0 + C = C$$
$$\frac{y^2}{2} = \frac{x^2}{2} + 2$$
$$y^2 = x^2 + 4$$

$y = f(x) = \sqrt{x^2 + 4}$, assuming $y > 0$.

$$f(.3) = \sqrt{(.3)^2 + 4} \approx 2.022$$

18. $y' = y$; $f(0) = 1$, $h = .2$; find $f(1)$.

$$y = f(x) = e^x + C$$
$$1 = 1 + C$$
$$C = 0$$

$$y = f(x) = e^x$$

x_i	y_i	$f(x_i)$	$y_i - f(x_i)$
0	1	1	0
.2	1.2	1.2214028	−.0214028
.4	1.44	1.4918247	−.0518247
.6	1.728	1.8221188	−.0941188
.8	2.0736	2.2255409	−.1519409
1.0	2.48832	2.7182818	−.2299618

20. $y' = x - xy$; $f(0) = .5$, $h = .2$; find $f(1)$.

$$y' + xy = x$$

$$I(x) = e^{\int x\,dx} = e^{x^2/2}$$

$$e^{x^2/2}y = \int xe^{x^2/2}\,dx = e^{x^2/2} + C$$

$$y = 1 + Ce^{-x^2/2}$$

$$.5 = 1 + C$$

$$C = -.5$$

$$y' = f(x) = 1 - .5e^{-x^2/2}$$

x_1	y_i	$f(x_i)$	$y_i - f(x_i)$
0	.5	.5	0
.2	.5	.5099007	−.0099007
.4	.52	.5384418	−.0184418
.6	.5584	.5823649	−.0239649
.8	.611392	.6369255	−.0255335
1.0	.6735693	.6967347	−.0231654

22. $y' = y$; $f(0) = 1$

$y = e^x$ See Exercise 18.

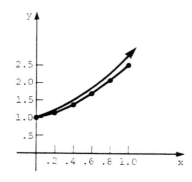

24. $y' = x - xy$; $f(0) = 5$

$y = 1 - .5e^{-x^2/2}$ See Exercise 20.

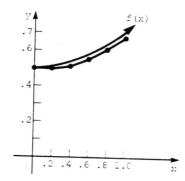

26. (a) $\dfrac{dy}{dt} = ky(150 - y)$; $k = .002$

$$\frac{dy}{dt} = .002y(150 - y)$$

$$\frac{dy}{dt} = .3y - .002y^2$$

(b) If $t_0 = 0$ corresponds to 1990, then $t_4 = 4$ corresponds to 1994.

$y_0 = 20$; $g(t, y) = .3y - .002y^2$

$g(t_0 - y_0) = .3(20) - .002(20)^2$

$= 5.2$

$t_1 = 1$; $y_1 = 20 + (5.2)(1) = 25.2$

$g(t_1, y_1) = .3(25.2) - .002(25.2)^2$

$= 6.28992$

$t_2 = 2$; $y_2 = 25.2 + (6.28992)(1)$

$= 31.48992$

$g(t_2, y_2) = .3(31.48992)$

$- .002(31.48992)$

$= 7.463745877$

$t_3 = 3$; $y_3 = 31.48992$

$+ (7.463745877)(1)$

$= 38.95366588$

$g(t_3, y_3) = .3(38.95366588)$

$- .002(38.95366588)$

$= 8.651323593$

$t_4 = 4$; $y_4 = 38.95366588$

$+ (8.651323593)$

$= 47.60498947$

About 48 firms are bankrupt in 1994.

28. $\dfrac{dy}{dt} = .02(100 - y^{1/2}) = 2 - .02\sqrt{y}$

$t_0 = 0$; $y_0 = 10$; $h = .5$; $g(t, y)$

$= 2 - .02\sqrt{y}$

$g(t_0, y_0) = 2 - .02\sqrt{10} = 1.9368$

$t_1 = .5$; $y_1 = 10 + 1.9368(.5)$

$= 10.9684$

$g(t_1, y_1) = 2 - .02\sqrt{10.9684}$
$\qquad\qquad = 1.9338$

$t_2 = 1, y_2 = 10.9684 + 1.9338(.5)$
$\qquad\qquad = 11.9353$

$g(t_2, y_2) = 2 - .02\sqrt{11.9353}$
$\qquad\qquad = 1.9309$

$t_3 = 1.5; y_3 = 11.9353 + 1.9309(.5)$
$\qquad\qquad = 12.9008$

$g(t_3, y_3) = 2 - .02\sqrt{12.9008}$
$\qquad\qquad = 1.9282$

$t_4 = 2; y_4 = 12.9008 + 1.9282(.5)$
$\qquad\qquad = 13.8649$

$g(t_4, y_4) = 2 - .02\sqrt{13.8649}$
$\qquad\qquad = 1.9255$

$t_5 = 2.5; y_5 = 13.8649 + 1.9255(.5)$
$\qquad\qquad = 14.8277$

$g(t_5, y_5) = 2 - .02\sqrt{14.8277}$
$\qquad\qquad = 1.9230$

$t_6 = 3, y_6 = 14.8277 + 1.9230(.5)$
$\qquad\qquad = 15.7892$

$g(t_6, y_6) = 2 - .02\sqrt{15.7892}$
$\qquad\qquad = 1.9205$

$t_7 = 3.5, y_7 = 15.7892 + 1.9205(.5)$
$\qquad\qquad = 16.7495$

$g(t_7, y_7) = 2 - .02\sqrt{16.7495}$
$\qquad\qquad = 1.9181$

$t_8 = 4, y_8 = 16.7495 + 1.9181(.5)$
$\qquad\qquad = 17.7086$

$g(t_8, y_8) = 2 - .02\sqrt{17.7086}$
$\qquad\qquad = 1.9158$

$t_9 = 4.5; y_9 = 17.7086 + 1.9158(.5)$
$\qquad\qquad = 18.6665$

$g(t_9, y_9) = 2 - .02\sqrt{18.6665}$
$\qquad\qquad = 1.9136$

$t_{10} = 5; y_{10} = 18.6665 + 1.9136(.5)$
$\qquad\qquad = 19.6233$

There will be about 20 species.

30. $\dfrac{dy}{dt} = -y + .02y^2 + .003y^3$; for [0, 4]

$h = 1, t_0 = 0, y_0 = 15,$

$g(t, y) = -y + .02y^2 + .003y^3$

$g(t_0, y_0) = -15 + .02(15)^2 + .003(15)^3$
$\qquad\qquad = -.375$

$t_1 = 1; y_1 = 15 + (-.375)(1)$
$\qquad\qquad = 14.625$

$g(t_1, y_1) = -14.625 + .02(14.625)^2$
$\qquad\qquad\quad + .003(14.625)^3$
$\qquad\qquad = -.963$

$t_2 = 2; y_2 = 14.625 + (-.963)(1)$
$\qquad\qquad = 13.662$

$g(t_2, y_2) = -13.662 + .02(13.662)^2$
$\qquad\qquad\quad + .003(13.662)^3$
$\qquad\qquad = -2.279$

$t_3 = 3; y_3 = 13.662 + (-2.279)(1)$
$\qquad\qquad = 11.383$

$g(t_3, y_3) = -11.383 + .02(11.383)^2$
$\qquad\qquad\quad + .003(11.383)^3$
$\qquad\qquad = -4.367$

$t_4 = 4, y_4 = 11.383 + (-4.367)(1)$
$\qquad\qquad = 7.016$ thousand

There will be about 7000 whales.

Exercises 32 and 34 are to be completed using a computer. The answers may vary depending on the computer and software used.

32. $y' = e^{.02x} + y$; $f(0) = .2$ The answer is 4.047.

34. $y' = \dfrac{x - y}{x + y}$; $f(1) = 1.5$ The answer is 1.448.

Section 9.4

2. From Exercise 1,

$$A = \frac{-2000 + 2120e^{.06t}}{.06}$$

$$20,000 = \frac{-2000 + 2120e^{.06t}}{.06}$$

$$\frac{80}{53} = e^{.06t}$$

$$\ln\left(\frac{80}{53}\right) = .06t$$

$$t = \frac{1}{.06}\ln\left(\frac{80}{53}\right) \approx 6.9 \text{ yr}$$

4.

$$\frac{dA}{dt} = .07A + D$$

$$\frac{1}{.07A + D}\, dA = dt$$

$$\frac{\ln(.07A + D)}{.07} = t + C$$

$$A = \frac{D}{.07}(-1 + e^{.07t})$$

When $t = 3$, $A = 50,000$.

$$50,000 = \frac{D}{.07}(-1 + e^{.07(3)})$$

$$= \frac{D}{.07}(-1 + e^{.21})$$

$$D = \frac{50,000(.07)}{-1 + e^{.21}} \approx \$14,977.87$$

6. $\frac{dx}{dt} = -3x + 4xy$, $\frac{dy}{dt} = -3y + xy$

$$\frac{dy}{dx} = \frac{dy/dt}{dx/dt}$$

$$= \frac{-3y + xy}{-3x + 4xy}$$

$$= \frac{y(-3 + x)}{x(-3 + 4y)}$$

$$\frac{-3 + 4y}{y}\, dy = \frac{-3 + x}{x}\, dx$$

$$\int\left(-\frac{3}{y} + 4\right) dy = \int\left(-\frac{3}{x} + 1\right) dx$$

$$-3\ln y + 4y = -3\ln x + x + C$$

(a) $y = 1$ when $x = 3$:

$$4 = -3\ln 3 + 3 + C$$

$$1 + 3\ln 3 = C$$

$$3\ln x - 3\ln y - x + 4y$$
$$= 1 + \ln 27$$

(b) $-3x + 4xy = 0$

$$x(-3 + 4y) = 0$$

$$-3y + xy = 0$$

$$y(-3 + x) = 0$$

The solution $x = 0$, $y = 0$ may be feasible. If not, $x = 3$ and $y = 3/4$.

8. Let N = population size, y = number infected.

(a) $N - y = N - \dfrac{N}{1 + (N - 1)e^{-aNt}}$

Example 4

$$= \frac{N + N(N - 1)e^{-aNt} - N}{1 + (N - 1)e^{-aNt}}$$

$$= \frac{N(N - 1)e^{-aNt}}{1 + (N - 1)e^{-aNt}}$$

$$= \frac{N(N - 1)}{e^{aNt} + (N - 1)}$$

$$= \frac{N(N - 1)}{N - 1 + e^{aNt}}$$

(b) $N = 100$, $a = .01$

$$y = \frac{100}{1 + 99e^{-t}} \text{ and } 100 - y = \frac{9900}{99 + e^{t}}$$

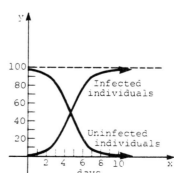

(c) $y = \dfrac{100}{1 + 99e^{-t}} = 100(1 + 99e^{-t})^{-1}$

$y' = -100(1 + 99e^{-t})^{-2}(-99e^{-t})$

$ = 9900\dfrac{e^{-t}}{(1 + 99e^{-t})^2}$

$y'' = 9900 \cdot \dfrac{(1 + 99e^{-t})^2 \cdot (-e^{-t}) - e^{-t} \cdot 2(1 + 99e^{-t}) \cdot (-99e^{-t})}{(1 + 99e^{-t})^4}$

$ = \dfrac{9900(-e^{-t})(1 - 99e^{-t})}{(1 + 99e^{-t})^3}$

Since $\dfrac{-9900e^{-t}}{(1 + 99e^{-t})^3} < 0$ for all t, y'' changes sign.

Thus, $1 - 99e^{-t}$ changes sign:

$1 - 99e^{-t} > 0$

$\phantom{1 - 99e^{-t}}\dfrac{1}{99} > \dfrac{1}{e^t}$

$\phantom{1 - 99e^{-t}}e^t > 99$

$\phantom{1 - 99e^{-t}}t > \ln 99.$

Therefore, y is concave upward if $t > \ln 99$ and concave downward if $x < \ln 99$.

If $x = \ln 99$, $y = \dfrac{100}{1 + 99\left(\frac{1}{99}\right)} = 50.$

Therefore,

$(\ln 99, 50) \approx (4.6 \text{ days}, 50 \text{ people})$ is a point of inflection.
The second derivative of $100 - y$ merely has the opposite sign as
y'' above, so $100 - y$ has the same point of inflection as y.

(d) At the point of inflection, the number of infected people is
the same as the number of uninfected people.

(e) $\displaystyle\lim_{t \to \infty} y = \lim_{t \to \infty} \dfrac{100}{1 + 99e^{-t}}$

$\phantom{\lim_{t \to \infty} y} = \dfrac{100}{1 + 99(0)}$

$\phantom{\lim_{t \to \infty} y} = 100 \text{ people}$

Therefore,

$\displaystyle\lim_{t \to \infty} (100 - y) = 100 - \lim_{t \to \infty} y$

$\phantom{\lim_{t \to \infty} (100 - y)} = 100 - 100$

$\phantom{\lim_{t \to \infty} (100 - y)} = 0 \text{ people.}$

In general,

$$\lim_{t \to \infty} y = N \text{ and } \lim_{t \to \infty} (N - y) = 0.$$

10. **(a)** $\frac{dy}{dt} = kye^{-at}$; $a = .02$ so

$\frac{dy}{dt} = kye^{-.02t}$. $y = 50$ when $t = 0$;

$y = 300$ when $t = 10$.

$$\frac{1}{y} dy = ke^{-.02t} dt$$

$$\ln y = \frac{k}{-.02}e^{-.02t} + C$$

To find k and C, solve the system

$$\ln 50 = \frac{k}{-.02} + C$$

$$\ln 300 = \frac{k}{-.02}e^{-.2} + C.$$

$$\ln 300 - \ln 50 = \frac{k}{-.02}(e^{-.2} - 1)$$

$$\ln \left(\frac{300}{50}\right) = \ln 6$$

$$= \frac{k}{.02}(1 - e^{-.2})$$

$$k = \frac{.02 \ln 6}{1 - e^{-.2}} \approx .1977$$

Therefore,

$$C = \ln 50 + \frac{k}{.02} \approx \ln 50 + \frac{.1977}{.02}$$

$$\approx 13.7970.$$

So

$$\ln y = \frac{.1977}{-.02}e^{-.02t} + 13.7970$$

$$\approx -9.885e^{-.02t} + 13.7970.$$

So

$$y \approx ^{-9.885e^{-.02t} + 13.7970}$$

$$= e^{13.7970}e^{-9.885e^{-.02t}}$$

$$\approx 981,000e^{-9.89e^{-.02t}}$$

(b) Find t when

$$y = \frac{1}{2}(10,000) = 5000.$$

$$\ln 5000 = -9.89e^{-.02t} + 13.7970$$

$$e^{-.02t} = \frac{\ln 5000 - 13.7970}{-9.89}$$

$$t = \frac{1}{-.02} \ln \left[\frac{\ln 5000 - 13.7970}{-9.89}\right]$$

$$\approx 31 \text{ days}$$

12. From equations (10) and (12) in the textbook, the solution to

$$\frac{dy}{dt} = a(N - y)y$$

is

$$y = \frac{N}{1 + be^{-aNt}},$$

where y = number of people who have heard the information and

$$b = \frac{N - y_0}{y_0}.$$

If $y_0 = 3$, $N = 500$, and $y = 50$ when $t = 2$, find y.

$$b = \frac{500 - 3}{3} = \frac{497}{3}, \text{ so}$$

$$y = \frac{500}{1 + \frac{497}{3}e^{-500at}}$$

$$50 = \frac{500}{1 + \frac{497}{3}e^{-1000a}}$$

$$1 + \frac{497}{3}e^{-1000a} = 10$$

$$e^{1000a} = \frac{27}{497}$$

$$a = -\frac{1}{1000} \ln \left(\frac{27}{497}\right) = \frac{\ln \left(\frac{497}{27}\right)}{1000}$$

$$500a \approx 1.456$$

$$y = \frac{500}{1 + \frac{497}{3}e^{-1.456t}}$$

$$= \frac{1500}{3 + 497e^{-1.456t}}$$

When $t = 5$,

$$y = \frac{1500}{3 + 497e^{-1.456(5)}}$$

$$\approx 449 \text{ people.}$$

14. $y_0 = 5$, $N = 100$, and when $t = 1$, $y = 20$.

$$b = \frac{100 - 5}{5} = 19, \text{ so}$$

$$y = \frac{100}{1 + 19e^{-100at}}$$

$$20 = \frac{100}{1 + 19e^{-100a}}$$

$$1 + 19e^{-100a} = 5$$

$$e^{-100a} = \frac{4}{19}$$

$$a = -\frac{1}{100}\ln\left(\frac{4}{19}\right) = \frac{\ln\left(\frac{19}{4}\right)}{100}$$

$$100a \approx 1.558$$

$$y = \frac{100}{1 + 19e^{-1.558t}}$$

When $t = 3$,

$$y = \frac{100}{1 + 19e^{-1.558(3)}}$$

$$\approx 85 \text{ people.}$$

16. Let y = amount (in pounds) of salt at time t. At $t = 0$, $y = 20$ lb and $V = 100$ gal.

(a) Rate of Salt In
$$= (2 \text{ gal/min}) \cdot (2 \text{ lb/gal})$$
$$= 4 \text{ lb/min.}$$

Rate of Salt Out
$$= (2 \text{ gal/min}) \cdot \left(\frac{y}{V} \text{ lb/gal}\right)$$
$$= \frac{2y}{V}(\text{lb/min})$$

Rate of Liquid In
= Rate of Liquid Out
= 2 gal/min

So $\frac{dV}{dt} = 0$ and $V = 100$ at all times t.

Therefore,

$$\frac{dy}{dt} = 4 - \frac{2y}{100} = \frac{200 - y}{50} \text{ lb/min}$$

$$\frac{dy}{200 - y} = \frac{dt}{50}$$

$$-\ln(200 - y) = \frac{t}{50} + C$$

$$-\ln 180 = C$$

$$-\ln(200 - y) = \frac{t}{50} - \ln 180$$

$$\ln(200 - y) = \ln 180 - .02t$$

$$200 - y = e^{\ln 180 - .02t}$$

$$= 180e^{-.02t}$$

$$y = 200 - 180e^{-.02t}$$

(b) One hour later, $t = 60$ min,
$$y = 200 - 180e^{-.02(60)} \approx 146 \text{ lb.}$$

(c) $\lim\limits_{t \to \infty} (200 - 180e^{-.02t})$

$$= 200 - 180(0) = 200 \text{ lb}$$

As $t \to \infty$, y increases approaching 200 lb.

18. See Exercise 16.

(a) Change Rate of Salt In to $(1 \text{ gal/min})(2 \text{ lb/gal}) = 2 \text{ lb/min}$ and Rate of Liquid In to 1 gal/min so $\frac{dV}{dt} = 1 - 2 = -1$ gal/min.

$V = -t + C$ and $V = 100$ when $t = 0$, so $V = 100 - t$.

Therefore,

$$\frac{dy}{dt} = 2 - \frac{2y}{100 - t}$$

$$\frac{dy}{dt} + \frac{2y}{100 - t} = 2$$

$$I(x) = e^{\int 2/(100-t)dt}$$

$$= e^{-2\ln(100-t)}$$

$$= \frac{1}{(100 - t)^2}$$

$$\frac{1}{(100 - t)^2} y = \int \frac{2}{(100 - t)^2} \, dt$$

$$= \int 2(100 - t)^{-2} \, dt$$

$$= 2(100 - t)^{-1} + C$$

$$y = 2(100 - t) + C(100 - t)^2$$

$$20 = 2(100) + C(100)^2$$

$$C = -.018$$

$$y = 2(100 - t) - .018(100 - t)^2$$

(b) When $t = 60$ min,

$$y = 2(100 - 60) - .018(100 - 60)^2$$

$$\approx 51 \text{ lb}$$

(c) The graph of

$$y = 2(100 - t) - .018(100 - t)^2$$

is a parabola opening downward with

vertex at $t = \frac{400}{9}$ and t-intercepts

of $-100/9$ and 100 since

$$y = 20 + 1.6t - .018t^2.$$

Thus, y increases from $t = 0$ to $t = 400/9$ and decreases from $t = 400/9$ to $t = 100$.

20. Let y = amount (in grams) of chemical at time t. At $t = 0$, $y = 5$ g and $V = 100$ liters.

(a) Rate of Chemical In = 0

Rate of Chemical Out

$\quad = (1 \text{ liter/min})(y/V \text{ g/liter})$

$\quad = y/V \text{ g/min}$

Rate of Liquid In

$\quad = 2 \text{ liters/min};$

Rate of Liquid Out

$\quad = 1 \text{ liter/min so}$

$$\frac{dV}{dt} = 1 \text{ liter/min.}$$

Therefore,

$V = t + C$ and $100 = C$ so $V = t + 100$.

$$\frac{dy}{dt} = \frac{-y}{y + 100}$$

$$\frac{dy}{y} = \frac{-dt}{t + 100}$$

$$\ln y = -\ln(t + 100) + C$$

$$\ln 5 = -\ln 100 + C$$

$$\ln 5 + \ln 100 = C$$

$$C = \ln(500)$$

$$\ln y = -\ln(t + 100) + \ln(500)$$

$$= \ln\left(\frac{500}{t + 100}\right)$$

$$y = \frac{500}{t + 100}$$

(b) When $t = 30$,

$$y = \frac{500}{130} \approx 3.8 \text{ g.}$$

22. Let y = amount (in pounds) of soap at time t. At $t = 0$, $y = 4$ lb and $V = 200$ gal.

Rate of Soap In = 0;

Rate of Soap Out

$= (8 \text{ gal/min})(y/V \text{ lb/gal})$

$= 8y/V \text{ lb/min}$

Rate of Liquid In

$= \text{Rate of Liquid Out}$

$= 8 \text{ gal/min},$

so $\dfrac{dV}{dt} = 0$ and $V = 200$ for all t.

$\dfrac{dy}{dt} = -\dfrac{8y}{200}$

$\dfrac{1}{y} \, dy = -\dfrac{1}{25}$

$\ln y = -\dfrac{t}{25} + C$

$\ln 4 = C$

$\ln y = -\dfrac{t}{25} + \ln 4$

$y = 4e^{-.04t}$

If $y = 1$,

$1 = 4e^{-.04t}$

$e^{-.04t} = \dfrac{1}{4}$

$t = -\dfrac{1}{.04} \ln \left(\dfrac{1}{4}\right)$

$= 25 \ln 4 \approx 34.7 \text{ min.}$

Chapter 9   Review Exercises

6. $\dfrac{dy}{dx} = x^2 + 5x^4$

$y = \dfrac{x^3}{3} + x^5 + C$

8. $\dfrac{dy}{dx} = \dfrac{1}{2x + 3}$

$y = \dfrac{1}{2} \ln |2x + 3| + C$

10. $\dfrac{dy}{dx} = \dfrac{e^x + x}{y - 1}$

$(y - 1) \, dy = (e^x + x)dx$

$\dfrac{y^2}{2} - y = e^x + \dfrac{x^2}{2} + C$

12. $\dfrac{dy}{dx} = \dfrac{3 - y}{e^x}$

$\dfrac{1}{3 - y} \, dy = e^{-x} \, dx$

$-\ln |3 - y| = -e^{-x} + C$

$\ln |3 - y| = e^{-x} - C$

$3 - y = ke^{e^{-x}}$

$y = 3 - ke^{e^{-x}}$

or $\qquad y = 3 + Me^{e^{-x}}$

14. $\dfrac{dy}{dx} + xy = 4z$

$y' + xy = 4x$

$I(x) = e^{\int x \, dx} = e^{x^2/2}$

$e^{x^2/2} y = \int 4xe^{x^2/2} \, dx$

$= 4e^{x^2/2} + C$

$y = 4 + Ce^{-x^2/2}$

16. $x \dfrac{dy}{dx} + y - e^x = 0$

$\dfrac{dy}{dx} + \dfrac{1}{x}y = \dfrac{1}{x}e^x$

$I(x) = e^{\int dx/x} = e^{\ln x} = x$

$xy = \int x \cdot \dfrac{1}{x}e^x \, dx$

$= \int e^x \, dx = e^x + C$

$y = \dfrac{e^x}{x} + \dfrac{C}{x}$

18. $\dfrac{dy}{dx} = 4x^3 + 2$; $y = 3$ when $x = 1$.

$y = x^4 + 2x + C$

$3 = 1 + 2 + C$

$C = 0$

$y = x^4 + 2x$

20. $\dfrac{dy}{dx} = \dfrac{x}{x^2 - 3}$; $y = 52$ when $x = 2$.

$y = \dfrac{1}{2} \ln |x^2 - 3| + C$

$52 = \dfrac{1}{2} \ln |4 - 3| + C = C$

$y = \dfrac{1}{2} \ln |x^2 - 3| + 52$

22. $\sqrt{x}\, \dfrac{dy}{dx} = xy$; $y = 4$ when $x = 1$.

$\dfrac{1}{y}\, dy = x^{1/2}\, dx$

$\ln |y| = \dfrac{2}{3} x^{3/2} + C$

$\ln 4 = \dfrac{2}{3} + C$

$C = \ln 4 - \dfrac{2}{3} \approx .720$

$\ln |y| \approx \dfrac{2}{3} x^{3/2} + .720$

$|y| = e^{2x^{3/2}/3 + .720}$

$\quad = e^{.720} e^{2x^{3/2}/3}$

$y \approx \pm 2.054 e^{2x^{3/2}/3}$

24. $\dfrac{dy}{dx} = (3x + 2)^2 e^y$; $y = 0$ when $x = 0$.

$e^{-y} dy = (3x + 2)^2\, dx$

$-e^{-y} = \dfrac{1}{9}(3x + 2)^3 + C$

$-1 = \dfrac{1}{9}(2)^3 + C$

$C = -\dfrac{17}{9}$

$e^{-y} = \dfrac{17}{9} - \dfrac{1}{9}(3x + 2)^3$

$y = -\ln \left[\dfrac{17 - (3x + 2)^3}{9} \right]$

Notice that $x < \dfrac{\sqrt[3]{17} - 2}{3}$.

26. $e^x y' - e^x y = x^2 - 1$, $y = 42$ when $x = 0$.

$y' - y = (x^2 - 1)e^{-x}$

$I(x) = e^{\int -1\, dx} = e^{-x}$

$e^{-x} y = \int (x^2 - 1)e^{-x} \cdot e^{-x}\, dx$

$\quad = \int (x^2 - 1)e^{-2x}\, dx$

Integration by parts:

Let $u = x^2 - 1 \quad dv = e^{-2x}\, dx$

$\quad du = 2x\, dx \quad\quad v = -\dfrac{1}{2}e^{-2x}$.

$e^{-x} y = -\dfrac{(x^2 - 1)}{2}e^{-2x} + \int xe^{-2x}\, dx$

Let $u = x \quad\quad dv = e^{-2x}\, dx$

$\quad du = dx \quad\quad v = -\dfrac{1}{2}e^{-2x}$

$e^{-x} y = -\dfrac{(x^2 - 1)}{2}e^{-2x} - \dfrac{x}{2}e^{-2x}$

$\quad\quad + \int \dfrac{1}{2}e^{-2x}\, dx$

$e^{-x} y = -\dfrac{(x^2 - 1)}{2}e^{-2x} - \dfrac{x}{2}e^{-2x}$

$\quad\quad - \dfrac{1}{4}e^{-2x} + C$

$y = -\dfrac{(x^2 - 1)}{2}e^{-x} - \dfrac{x}{2}e^{-x}$

$\quad\quad -\dfrac{1}{4}e^{-x} + Ce^x$

$$42 = \frac{1}{2} - 0 - \frac{1}{4} + C$$

$$C = 41.75$$

$$y = -\frac{(x^2 - 1)}{2}e^{-x} - \frac{x}{2}e^{-x}$$

$$- \frac{1}{4}e^{-x} + 41.75e^x$$

$$y = e^{-x}\left[-\frac{x^2}{2} - \frac{x}{2} + \frac{1}{4}\right] + 41.75e^x$$

$$= \frac{-x^2 e^{-x}}{2} - \frac{xe^{-x}}{2} + \frac{e^{-x}}{4} + 41.75e^x$$

28. $x^2 \frac{dy}{dx} + 4xy - e^{2x^3} = 0$, $y = e^2$

when $x = 1$.

$$\frac{dy}{dx} + \frac{4}{x}y = \frac{1}{x^2}e^{2x^3}$$

$$I(x) = e^{\int 4/x \, dx} = e^{4 \ln x} = x^4$$

$$x^4 y = \int x^4 \cdot \frac{1}{x^2}e^{2x^3} \, dx$$

$$= \int x^2 e^{2x^3} \, dx$$

$$= \frac{1}{6}e^{2x^3} + C$$

$$1 \cdot e^2 = \frac{1}{6}e^2 + C$$

$$C = \frac{5}{6}e^2$$

$$y = \frac{e^{2x^3} + 5e^2}{6x^4}$$

30. $y' = x + y^{-1}$; $f(0) = 1$; $h = .2$;

$$g(x, y) = x + \frac{1}{y}$$

$$x_0 = 0; \quad y_0 = 1$$

$$g(x_0, y_0) = 0 + \frac{1}{1} = 1$$

$$x_1 = .2; \quad y_1 = 1 + 1(.2) = 1.2$$

$$g(x_1, y_1) = .2 + \frac{1}{1.2} = 1.0333$$

$$x_2 = .4; \quad y_2 = 1.2 + 1.0333(.2)$$

$$= 1.4067$$

$$g(x_2, y_2) = .4 + \frac{1}{1.4067} = 1.1109$$

$$x_3 = .6; \quad y_3 = 1.4067 + 1.1109(.2)$$

$$= 1.6289$$

$$g(x_3, y_3) = .6 + \frac{1}{1.6289}$$

$$= 1.2139$$

$$x_4 = .8; \quad y_4 = 1.6289 + 1.2139(.2)$$

$$= 1.8719$$

$$g(x_4, y_4) = .8 + \frac{1}{1.8719} = 1.3343$$

$$x_5 = 1.0; \quad y_5 = 1.8719 + 1.3343(.2)$$

$$y_5 = 2.13876$$

$$f(1) \approx 2.138$$

32. $y' = \frac{x}{2} + 4$; $f(0) = 0$; $h = .1$,

$$g(x, y) = \frac{x}{2} + 4$$

$$x_0 = 0; \quad y_0 = 0$$

$$g(x_0, y_0) = \frac{0}{2} + 4 = 4$$

$$x_1 = .1; \quad y_1 = 0 + 4(.1) = .4$$

$$g(x_1, y_1) = \frac{.1}{2} + 4 = 4.05$$

$$x_2 = .2; \quad y_2 = .4 + 4.05(.1) = .805$$

$$g(x_2, y_2) = \frac{.2}{2} + 4 = 4.1$$

$$x_3 = .3; \quad y_3 = .805 + 4.1(.1)$$

$$= 1.215$$

Solving the differential equation gives

$$\frac{dy}{dx} = \frac{x}{2} + 4$$

$$\int dy = \int \left(\frac{x}{2} + 4\right) dx$$

$$y = \frac{x^2}{4} + 4x + C.$$

Since x = 0 when y = 0, C = 0.

$$y = \frac{x^2}{4} + 4x$$

$$f(x_3) = f(.3) = \frac{.3^2}{4} + 4(.3) = 1.223$$

$$y_3 - f(x_3) = 1.215 - 1.223 = -.008$$

36. A = 10,000 when t = 0; r = .05,
D = -1000

(a) $\frac{dA}{dt} = .05A - 1000$

(b) $\frac{1}{.05A - 1000} \, dA = dt$

$$\frac{1}{.05} \ln |.05A - 1000| = t + C$$

$$\ln |.05A - 1000| = .05t + k$$

$$\ln |.05(10,000) - 1000| = k$$

$$k = \ln |-500| = \ln 500$$

$$\ln |.05A - 1000| = .05t + \ln 500$$

$$|.05A - 1000| = 500e^{.05t}$$

Since .05A < 1000,

$$|.05A - 1000| = 1000 - .05A$$

$$1000 - .05A = 500e^{.05t}$$

$$A = \frac{1}{.05}(1000 - 500e^{.05t})$$

$$= 10,000(2 - e^{.05t}).$$

When t = 1,

A = $10,000(2 - e^{.05(1)}) \approx \$9487.29$.

38. $\frac{dy}{dt} = \frac{-10}{1 + 5t}$; y = 50 when t = 0.

y = -2 ln (1 + 5t) + C
50 = -2 ln 1 + C = C
y = 50 - 2 ln (1 + 5t)

(a) If t = 24,

y = 50 - 2 ln [1 + 5(24)]

  ≈ 40 insects.

(b) If y = 0,

$$50 = 2 \ln (1 + 5t)$$

$$1 + 5t = e^{25}$$

$$t = (e^{25} - 1)/5$$

$$\approx 1.44 \times 10^{10} \text{ hours}$$

$$\approx 6 \times 10^8 \text{ days}$$

$$\approx 1.6 \text{ million years.}$$

40. $\frac{dx}{dt} = .2x - .5xy$

$$\frac{dy}{dt} = -.3y + .4xy$$

$$\frac{dy}{dx} = \frac{dy/dt}{dx/dt}$$

$$= \frac{-.3y + .4xy}{.2x - .5xy}$$

$$= \frac{y(-.3 + .4x)}{x(.2 - .5y)}$$

$$\frac{.2 - .5y}{y} \, dy = \frac{-.3 + .4x}{x} \, dx$$

$$\left(\frac{.2}{y} - .5\right) dy = \left(\frac{-.3}{x} + .4\right) dx$$

$$.2 \ln y - .5y = -.3 \ln x + .4x + C$$

$$.3 \ln x + .2 \ln y - .4x - .5y$$
$$= C$$

Both growth rates are 0 if

.2x - .5xy = 0 and -.3y + .4xy = 0.

If x ≠ 0 and y ≠ 0, we have

.2 - .5y = 0 and -.3 + .4x = 0 so
x = 3/4 and y = 2/5.

42. Let y = the amount in parts per
million (ppm) of smoke at time t.
When t = 0, y = 20 ppm,
V = 15,000 ft³
cu ft.
Rate of Smoke In = 5 ppm,
Rate of Smoke Out
  = (1200 ft³/min)(y/V ppm/ft³)

Rate of Air In = Rate of Air out, so
V = 15,000 ft³ for all t.

$$\frac{dy}{dt} = 5 - \frac{1200y}{15,000} = 5 - \frac{2y}{25} = \frac{125 - 2y}{25}$$

$$\frac{1}{125 - 2y}\,dy = \frac{dt}{25}$$

$$-\frac{1}{2}\ln\,(125 - 2y) = \frac{t}{25} + C$$

$$-\frac{1}{2}\ln\,(125 - 2(20)) = C$$

$$C = -\frac{1}{2}\ln\,85$$

If y = 10,

$$-\frac{1}{2}\ln\,(125 - 2(10)) = \frac{t}{25} - \frac{1}{2}\ln\,85$$

$$\ln\,105 = \ln\,85 - \frac{2t}{25}$$

$$t = \frac{25}{2}[\ln\,85 - \ln\,105]$$

which is negative.
It is impossible to reduce y to
10 ppm.

44. $\frac{dy}{dx} = .2(125 - y)$; y = 20 when x = 0;
y ≤ 125.

$$\frac{1}{125 - y}\,dy = .2\,dx$$

$$-\ln\,(125 - y) = .2x + C$$

$$-\ln\,105 = C$$

$$-\ln\,(125 - y) = .2x - \ln\,105$$

$$\ln\,(125 - y) = \ln\,105 - .2x$$

$$125 - y = 105e^{-.2x}$$

$$y = 125 - 105e^{-.2x}$$

(a) If x = 10,

$$y = 125 - 105e^{-.2(10)}$$

$$\approx 111 \text{ items.}$$

(b) For large x, $e^{-2x} \approx 0$ so
y ≈ 125. For example, if x = 30,
$y = 125 - 105e^{-6} \approx 124.7$ which
rounds to 125. Mathematically,
however, y = 125 requires $e^{-.2x} = 0$
which is impossible.

46. $y = \frac{N}{1 + be^{-kx}}$; $y = y_i$ when $x = x_i$,
i = 1, 2, 3.

x_1, x_2, x_3 are equally spaced:
$x_3 = 2x_2 - x_1$, so $x_1 + x_3 = 2x_2$.

Show $N = \frac{1/y_1 + 1/y_3 - 2/y_2}{1/(y_1y_3) - 1/y_2}$.

Let

$$A = \frac{1}{y_1} + \frac{1}{y_3} - \frac{2}{y_2}$$

$$= \frac{1 + be^{-kx_1}}{N} + \frac{1 + be^{-kx_3}}{N}$$

$$- \frac{2(1 + be^{-kx_2})}{N}$$

$$= \frac{1}{N}(1 + be^{-kx_1} + be^{-kx_3} - 2 - 2be^{-kx_2})$$

$$= \frac{b}{N}[e^{-kx_1} + e^{-kx_3} - 2e^{-kx_2}]$$

Let

$$B = \frac{1}{y_1y_3} - \frac{1}{y_2{}^2}$$

$$= \frac{(1 + be^{-kx_1})(1 + be^{-kx_3})}{N^2}$$

$$- \frac{(1 + be^{-kx_2})^2}{N^2}$$

$$= \frac{1}{N^2}[1 + be^{-kx_1} + be^{-kx_3}$$

$$+ b^2e^{-k(x_1+x_3)} - 1 - 2be^{-kx_2}$$

$$- b^2e^{-2kx_2}]$$

$$= \frac{b}{N^2}[e^{kx_1} + e^{-kx_3} + be^{-k(2x_2)}$$

$$- 2e^{-kx_2} - be^{-2kx_2}]$$

$$= \frac{b}{N^2}[e^{-kx_1} + e^{-kx_3} - 2e^{-kx_2}]$$

Clearly, $\frac{A}{B} = N$.

Hence,

$$N = \frac{\dfrac{1}{y_1} + \dfrac{1}{y_3} - \dfrac{2}{y_2}}{\dfrac{1}{y_1 y_3} - \dfrac{1}{y_2{}^2}}.$$

48. From Exercise 46,

$$N = \frac{\dfrac{1}{40} + \dfrac{1}{204} - \dfrac{2}{106}}{\dfrac{1}{40(204)} - \dfrac{1}{(106)^2}} \approx 329.$$

(a) $y_0 = 40$,

$$b = \frac{N - y_0}{y_0} = \frac{329 - 40}{40}$$

$$\approx 7.23$$

If 1920 corresponds to $x = 5$ decades, then

$$106 = \frac{329}{1 + 7.23e^{-5k}}$$

$$1 + 7.23e^{-5k} = \frac{329}{106}$$

$$e^{-5k} = \frac{1}{7.23}\left(\frac{329}{106} - 1\right)$$

so

$$k = -\frac{1}{5}\ln\left[\frac{1}{7.23}\left(\frac{329}{106} - 1\right)\right]$$

$$\approx .25.$$

(b) $y = \dfrac{329}{1 + 7.23e^{-.25x}}$

In 1990, $x = 12$. If $x = 12$,

$$y = \frac{329}{1 + .7.23e^{-3}} \approx 242 \text{ million}$$

The predicted population is 242 million while the actual value is 249 million.

(c) In 2000, $x = 13$ so

$$y = \frac{329}{1 + 7.23e^{-.25(13)}}$$

$$\approx 257 \text{ million}.$$

In 2050, $x = 18$ so

$$y = \frac{329}{1 + 7.23e^{-.25(18)}}$$

$$\approx 305 \text{ million}.$$

50. $\dfrac{dT}{dt} = k(T - T_F);\ T_F = 300;\ T = 40$ when $t = 0$. $T = 150$ when $t = 1$. From Section 9.2, Exercise 27, the solution to the differential equation is

$$T = ce^{kt} + T_F$$

where c is a constant ($-k$ has been replaced by k in this exerise.)

Here, $T = ce^{kt} + 300$.

$$40 = c + 300$$

$$c = -260$$

$$T = 300 - 260e^{kt}$$

$$150 = 300 - 260e^{k}$$

$$e^{k} = \frac{15}{26}$$

$$k = \ln\left(\frac{15}{26}\right) \approx -.55$$

$$T = 300 - 260e^{-.55t}$$

$$250 = 300 - 260e^{-.55t}$$

$$e^{-.55t} = \frac{5}{26}$$

$$t = -\frac{1}{.55}\ln\left(\frac{5}{26}\right) \approx 3 \text{ hr}$$

CHAPTER 10   PROBABILITY AND CALCULUS

Section 10.1

2. $f(x) = \frac{1}{3}x - \frac{1}{6}$; [3, 4]

Show that condition 1 holds.

$$\int_{3}^{4} \left(\frac{1}{3}x - \frac{1}{6}\right) dx = \left(\frac{x^2}{6} - \frac{x}{6}\right)\Big|_{3}^{4}$$

$$= \frac{1}{6}(16 - 4 - 9 + 3)$$

$$= 1$$

Show that condition 2 holds.

Since $3 \le x \le 4$,

$$1 \le \frac{1}{3}x \le \frac{4}{3}$$

$$\frac{5}{6} \le \frac{1}{3}x - \frac{1}{6} \le \frac{7}{6}.$$

Hence, $f(x) \ge 0$ on [3, 4].
Yes, $f(x)$ is a probability density function.

4. $f(x) = \frac{3}{98}x^2$; [3, 5]

$$\int_{3}^{5} \frac{3}{98}x^2 \, dx = \frac{x^3}{98}\Big|_{3}^{5}$$

$$= \frac{1}{98}(125 - 27)$$

$$= 1$$

Since $x^2 \ge 0$, $f(x) \ge 0$ on [3, 5].
Yes, $f(x)$ is a probability density function.

6. $f(x) = \frac{x^3}{81}$; [0, 3].

$$\int_{0}^{3} \frac{x^3}{81} \, dx = \frac{x^4}{324}\Big|_{0}^{3}$$

$$= \frac{1}{4} \ne 1$$

No, $f(x)$ is not a probability density function.

8. $f(x) = 2x^2$; [-1, 1]

$$\int_{-1}^{1} 2x^2 \, dx = \frac{2}{3}x^3\Big|_{-1}^{1}$$

$$= \frac{2}{3}(1 + 1)$$

$$= \frac{4}{3} \ne 1$$

No, $f(x)$ is not a probability density function.

10. $f(x) = kx^{3/2}$; [4, 9]

$$\int_{4}^{9} kx^{3/2} \, dx = \frac{2k}{5}x^{5/2}\Big|_{4}^{9}$$

$$= \frac{2k}{5}(243 - 32)$$

$$= \frac{422k}{5}$$

If $\frac{422k}{5} = 1$, $k = \frac{5}{422}$.

Notice that $f(x) = \frac{5}{422}x^{3/2} \ge 0$ for all x in [4, 9].

12. $f(x) = kx^2$; [-1, 2]

$$\int_{-1}^{2} kx^2 \, dx = \frac{k}{3}x^3\Big|_{-1}^{2}$$

$$= \frac{k}{3}(8 + 1)$$

$$= 3k = 1$$

$$k = \frac{1}{3}$$

Notice that $f(x) = \frac{1}{3}x^2 \ge 0$ for all x in [-1, 2].

14. $f(x) = kx$; $[2, 3]$

$$\int_2^3 kx \, dx = \frac{k}{2}x^2 \bigg|_2^3 = \frac{k}{2}(9 - 4)$$

$$= \frac{5k}{2} = 1$$

$$k = \frac{2}{5}$$

Notice that $f(x) = \frac{2}{5}x \geq 0$ for all x in $[2, 3]$.

16. $f(x) = kx^3$; $[2, 4]$

$$\int_2^4 kx^3 \, dx = \frac{k}{4}x^4 \bigg|_2^4$$

$$= \frac{k}{4}(256 - 16)$$

$$= 60k = 1$$

$$k = \frac{1}{60}$$

Notice that $f(x) = \frac{1}{60}x^3 \geq 0$ for all x in $[2, 4]$.

22. $f(x) = e^{-x}$; $[0, \infty)$

$$\int_0^\infty e^{-x} \, dx = \lim_{b \to \infty} \int_0^b e^{-x} \, dx$$

$$= \lim_{b \to \infty} -e^{-x} \bigg|_0^b$$

$$= \lim_{b \to \infty} \left(1 - \frac{1}{e^b}\right) = 1$$

$f(x) \geq 0$ for all x.
$f(x)$ is a probability density function.

(a) $P(0 \leq x \leq 1) = \int_0^1 e^{-x} \, dx$

$$= -e^{-x} \bigg|_0^1$$

$$= 1 - \frac{1}{e} \approx .6321$$

(b) $P(1 \leq x \leq 2) = \int_1^2 e^{-x} \, dx$

$$= -e^{-x} \bigg|_1^2$$

$$= \frac{1}{e} - \frac{1}{e^2} \approx .2325$$

(c) $P(x \leq 2) = \int_0^2 e^{-x} \, dx$

$$= -e^{-x} \bigg|_0^2$$

$$= 1 - \frac{1}{e^2} \approx .8647$$

Notice that

$P(x \leq 2)$
$= P(0 \leq x \leq 1) + P(1 \leq x \leq 2).)$

24. $f(x) = \dfrac{20}{(x + 20)^2}$; $[0, \infty)$

$$\int_0^\infty \frac{20}{(x + 20)^2} \, dx$$

$$= \lim_{b \to \infty} \int_0^b 20(x + 20)^{-2} \, dx$$

$$= \lim_{b \to \infty} -20(x + 20)^{-1} \bigg|_0^b$$

$$= \lim_{b \to \infty} \left(1 - \frac{20}{b + 20}\right) = 1$$

f(x) ≥ 0 for all x.
Therefore f(x) is a probability density function.

(a) $P(0 \leq x \leq 1)$

$$= \int_0^1 20(x + 20)^{-2} \, dx$$

$$= -20(x + 20)^{-1} \Big|_0^1$$

$$= -20\left(\frac{1}{21} - \frac{1}{20}\right)$$

$$= \frac{1}{21} \approx .0476$$

(b) $P(1 \leq x \leq 5)$

$$= \int_1^5 20(x + 20)^{-2} \, dx$$

$$= -20(x + 20)^{-1} \Big|_1^5$$

$$= -20\left(\frac{1}{25} - \frac{1}{21}\right)$$

$$= \frac{16}{105} \approx .1524$$

(c) $P(x \geq 5)$

$$= \int_5^\infty 20(x + 20)^{-2} \, dx$$

$$= \lim_{b \to \infty} \int_5^b 20(x + 20)^{-2} \, dx$$

$$= \lim_{b \to \infty} [-20(x + 20)^{-1}] \Big|_5^b$$

$$= \lim_{b \to \infty} \left[-20\left(\frac{1}{b + 20} - \frac{1}{25}\right)\right]$$

$$= \frac{4}{5} = .8$$

Alternatively,

$$P(x \geq 5) = 1 - P(0 \leq x \leq 5)$$

$$= 1 - (.048 + .152)$$

$$= 1 - .2 = .8.$$

26. $f(x) = \frac{1}{11}\left(1 + \frac{3}{\sqrt{x}}\right); \; 4 \leq x \leq 9$

(a) $P(x \geq 6)$

$$= \int_6^9 \frac{1}{11}(1 + 3x^{-1/2}) \, dx$$

$$= \frac{1}{11}(x + 6x^{1/2}) \Big|_6^9$$

$$= \frac{1}{11}(9 + 18 - 6 - 6\sqrt{6})$$

$$= \frac{1}{11}(21 - 6\sqrt{6}) \approx .5730$$

(b) $P(x \leq 5)$

$$= \int_4^5 \frac{1}{11}(1 + 3x^{-1/2}) \, dx$$

$$= \frac{1}{11}(x + 6x^{1/2}) \Big|_4^5$$

$$= \frac{1}{11}(5 + 6\sqrt{5} - 4 - 12)$$

$$= \frac{1}{11}(6\sqrt{5} - 11) \approx .2197$$

(c) $P(4 \leq x \leq 7)$

$$= \int_4^7 \frac{1}{11}(1 + 3x^{-1/2}) \, dx$$

$$= \frac{1}{11}(x + 6x^{1/2}) \Big|_4^7$$

$$= \frac{1}{11}(7 + 6\sqrt{7} - 4 - 12)$$

$$= \frac{1}{11}(6\sqrt{7} - 9) \approx .6250$$

28. $f(x) = \dfrac{1}{(\ln 20)x}$; $[1, 20]$

    (a) $P(1 \leq x \leq 5)$

$$= \int_{1}^{5} \frac{1}{(\ln 20)x}\, dx$$

$$= \frac{1}{\ln 20} \ln x \Big|_{1}^{5}$$

$$= \frac{\ln 5}{\ln 20} \approx .5372$$

    (b) $P(x \geq 10)$

$$= \int_{10}^{20} \frac{1}{\ln 20 x}\, dx$$

$$= \frac{1}{\ln 20} \ln x \Big|_{10}^{20}$$

$$= 1 - \frac{\ln 10}{\ln 20} \approx .2314$$

30. $f(x) = \dfrac{5.5 - x}{15}$; $[0, 5]$

    (a) $P(x \geq 3)$

$$= \int_{3}^{5} \frac{5.5 - x}{15}\, dx$$

$$= \left(\frac{5.5}{15}x - \frac{1}{15} \cdot \frac{x^2}{2}\right) \Big|_{3}^{5}$$

$$= \left(\frac{5.5}{15} \cdot 5 - \frac{1}{15} \cdot \frac{5^2}{2}\right)$$

$$- \left(\frac{5.5}{15} \cdot 3 - \frac{1}{15} \cdot \frac{3^2}{2}\right)$$

$$= .2$$

    (b) $P(x \leq 2)$

$$= \int_{0}^{2} \frac{5.5 - x}{15}\, dx$$

$$= \left(\frac{5.5}{15}x - \frac{1}{15} \cdot \frac{x^2}{2}\right) \Big|_{0}^{2}$$

$$= \left(\frac{5.5}{15} \cdot 2 - \frac{1}{15} \cdot \frac{2^2}{2}\right)$$

$$- \left(\frac{5.5}{15} \cdot 0 - \frac{1}{15} \cdot \frac{0^2}{2}\right)$$

$$= .6$$

    (c) $P(1 \leq x \leq 4)$

$$= \int_{1}^{4} \frac{5.5 - x}{15}\, dx$$

$$= \left(\frac{5.5}{15}x - \frac{1}{15} \cdot \frac{x^2}{2}\right) \Big|_{1}^{4}$$

$$= \left(\frac{5.5}{15} \cdot 4 - \frac{1}{15} \cdot \frac{4^2}{2}\right)$$

$$- \left(\frac{5.5}{15} \cdot 1 - \frac{1}{15} \cdot \frac{1^2}{2}\right)$$

$$= .6$$

32. $f(x) = 3x^{-4}$; $[1, \infty)$

    (a) $P(1 \leq x \leq 2) = \displaystyle\int_{1}^{2} 3x^{-4}\, dx$

$$= -x^{-3} \Big|_{1}^{2}$$

$$= 1 - \frac{1}{8}$$

$$= \frac{7}{8} = .875$$

    (b) $P(3 \leq x \leq 5) = \displaystyle\int_{3}^{5} 3x^{-4}\, dx$

$$= -x^{-3} \Big|_{3}^{5}$$

$$= \frac{1}{27} - \frac{1}{125} \approx .029$$

(c) $P(x \geq 3) = \int_{3}^{\infty} 3x^{-4}\, dx$

$\qquad = \lim_{b \to \infty} \int_{3}^{b} 3x^{-4}\, dx$

$\qquad = \lim_{b \to \infty} (-x^{-3}) \Big|_{3}^{b}$

$\qquad = \lim_{b \to \infty} \left(\frac{1}{27} - \frac{1}{b^3}\right)$

$\qquad = \frac{1}{27} \approx .037$

Section 10.2

2. $f(x) = \frac{1}{10};\ [0, 10]$

$E(x) = \mu = \int_{0}^{10} x\left(\frac{1}{10}\right) dx$

$\qquad = \frac{x^2}{20} \Big|_{0}^{10} = 5$

$Var(x) = \int_{0}^{10} (x - 5)^2 \left(\frac{1}{10}\right) dx$

$\qquad = \frac{1}{10} \cdot \frac{(x - 5)^3}{3} \Big|_{0}^{10}$

$\qquad = \frac{25}{6} + \frac{25}{6}$

$\qquad = \frac{25}{3} \approx 8.33$

$\sigma \approx \sqrt{Var(x)} \approx 2.89$

4. $f(x) = 2(1 - x);\ [0, 1]$

$\mu = \int_{0}^{1} 2x(1 - x)\, dx$

$\quad = \int_{0}^{1} (2x - 2x^2)\, dx$

$\quad = \left(x^2 - \frac{2x^3}{3}\right) \Big|_{0}^{1}$

$\quad = 1 - \frac{2}{3}$

$\quad = \frac{1}{3} \approx .33$

Use the alternative formula to find

$Var(x) = \int_{0}^{1} 2x^2(1 - x)\, dx - \left(\frac{1}{3}\right)^2$

$\qquad = \int_{0}^{1} (2x^2 - 2x^3)\, dx - \frac{1}{9}$

$\qquad = \left(\frac{2x^3}{3} - \frac{x^4}{2}\right) \Big|_{0}^{1} - \frac{1}{9}$

$\qquad = \frac{2}{3} - \frac{1}{2} - \frac{1}{9} = \frac{1}{18} \approx .06.$

$\sigma = \sqrt{Var(x)} \approx .24$

6. $f(x) = \frac{1}{11}\left(1 + \frac{3}{\sqrt{x}}\right);\ [4, 9]$

$\mu = \int_{4}^{9} \frac{x}{11}\left(1 + \frac{3}{\sqrt{x}}\right) dx$

$\quad = \int_{4}^{9} \frac{1}{11}(x + 3x^{1/2})\, dx$

$\quad = \frac{1}{11}\left(\frac{x^2}{2} + 2x^{3/2}\right) \Big|_{4}^{9}$

$\quad = \frac{1}{11}\left(\frac{81}{2} + 54 - 8 - 16\right)$

$\quad = \frac{141}{22} \approx 6.41$

$$\text{Var}(x) = \int_4^9 \frac{x^2}{11}\left(1 + \frac{3}{\sqrt{x}}\right)dx - \mu^2$$

$$= \int_4^9 \frac{1}{11}(x^2 + 3x^{3/2})dx - \mu^2$$

$$= \frac{1}{11}\left(\frac{x^3}{3} + \frac{6}{5}x^{5/2}\right)\Big|_4^9 - \mu^2$$

$$= \frac{1}{11}\left(243 + \frac{1458}{5} - \frac{64}{3} - \frac{192}{5}\right)$$

$$- \left(\frac{141}{22}\right)^2$$

$$\approx 2.09$$

$$\sigma \approx \sqrt{\text{Var}(x)} \approx 1.45$$

8. $f(x) = 3x^{-4};\ [1, \infty)$

$$\mu = \int_1^\infty x(3x^{-4})dx$$

$$= \lim_{b\to\infty} \int_1^b 3x^{-3}\ dx$$

$$= \lim_{b\to\infty} \left(-\frac{3x^{-2}}{2}\right)\Big|_1^b$$

$$= \lim_{b\to\infty} \left(\frac{3}{2} - \frac{3}{2b^2}\right)$$

$$= \frac{3}{2} = 1.5$$

$$\text{Var}(x) = \int_1^\infty x^2(3x^{-4})dx - \left(\frac{3}{2}\right)^2$$

$$= \lim_{b\to\infty} \int_1^b 3x^{-2}\ dx - \frac{9}{4}$$

$$= \lim_{b\to\infty} (-3x^{-1})\Big|_1^b - \frac{9}{4}$$

$$= \lim_{b\to\infty} \left(3 - \frac{3}{b}\right) - \frac{9}{4}$$

$$= 3 - \frac{9}{4} = \frac{3}{4} = .75$$

$$\sigma = \sqrt{\text{Var}(x)} \approx .87$$

12. $f(x) = \frac{x^{-1/3}}{6};\ [0, 8]$

(a) $\mu = \int_0^8 x\left(\frac{x^{-1/3}}{6}\right)dx$

$$= \int_0^8 \frac{x^{2/3}}{6}\ dx$$

$$= \frac{x^{5/3}}{10}\Big|_0^8$$

$$= \frac{16}{5} = 3.2$$

(b) $\text{Var}(x) = \int_0^8 x^2\left(\frac{x^{-1/3}}{6}\right)dx - \left(\frac{16}{5}\right)^2$

$$= \int_0^8 \frac{x^{5/3}}{6}\ dx - \frac{256}{25}$$

$$= \frac{x^{8/3}}{16}\Big|_0^8 - \frac{256}{25}$$

$$= 16 - \frac{256}{25}$$

$$= \frac{144}{25} = 5.76$$

(c) $\sigma = \sqrt{\text{Var}(x)} = 2.4$

(d) $P(x > \mu) = \int_\mu^8 \frac{x^{-1/3}}{6}\ dx$

$$= \frac{x^{2/3}}{4}\Big|_{3.2}^8$$

$$= 1 - \frac{(3.2)^{2/3}}{4}$$

$$\approx .46$$

(e) $P(3.2 - 2.4 < x < 3.2 + 2.4)$

$= P(.8 < x < 5.6)$

$$= \int_{.8}^{5.6} \frac{x^{-1/3}}{6}\ dx$$

$$= \frac{x^{2/3}}{4} \Bigg|_{.6}^{5.6}$$

$$= \frac{1}{4}[(5.6)^{2/3} - (.8)^{2/3}]$$

$\approx .57$

14. $f(x) = \frac{3}{2}(1 - x^2);\ [0, 1]$

(a) $\mu = \displaystyle\int_{0}^{1} \frac{3}{2}x(1 - x^2)\,dx$

$$= \int_{0}^{1} \frac{3}{2}(x - x^3)\,dx$$

$$= \frac{3}{2}\left(\frac{x^2}{2} - \frac{x^4}{4}\right) \Bigg|_{0}^{1}$$

$$= \frac{3}{2}\left(\frac{1}{2} - \frac{1}{4}\right) = \frac{3}{8} \approx .38$$

(b) $\text{Var}(x) = \displaystyle\int_{0}^{1} \frac{3}{2}x^2(1 - x^2)\,dx - \left(\frac{3}{8}\right)^2$

$$= \int_{0}^{1} \frac{3}{2}(x^2 - x^4)\,dx - \frac{9}{64}$$

$$= \frac{3}{2}\left(\frac{x^3}{3} - \frac{x^5}{5}\right) \Bigg|_{0}^{1} - \frac{9}{64}$$

$$= \frac{3}{2}\left(\frac{1}{3} - \frac{1}{5}\right) - \frac{9}{64}$$

$$= \frac{1}{5} - \frac{9}{64}$$

$$= \frac{19}{320} \approx .06$$

(c) $\sigma \approx \sqrt{\text{Var}(x)} \approx .24$

(d) $P(x > \mu) = \displaystyle\int_{\mu}^{1} \frac{3}{2}(1 - x^2)\,dx$

$$= \frac{3}{2}\left(x - \frac{x^3}{3}\right) \Bigg|_{3/8}^{1}$$

$$= \frac{3}{2}\left(1 - \frac{1}{3} - \frac{3}{8} + \frac{9}{512}\right)$$

$\approx .46$

(e) $P(.375 - .24 < x < .375 + .24)$

$= P(.135 < x < .615)$

$$= \int_{.135}^{.615} \frac{3}{2}(1 - x^2)\,dx$$

$$= \frac{3}{2}\left(x - \frac{x^3}{3}\right) \Bigg|_{.135}^{.615}$$

$$= \frac{3}{2}\left[.615 - \frac{(.615)^3}{3}\right.$$

$$\left. - .135 + \frac{(.135)^3}{3}\right]$$

$\approx .60$

16. $f(x) = \frac{1}{10};\ [0, 10]$

(a) $\displaystyle\int_{0}^{m} \frac{1}{10}\ dx = \frac{x}{10} \Bigg|_{0}^{m} = \frac{m}{10}$

$$= \frac{1}{2} \text{ when } m = 5.$$

(b) $E(x) = \mu = 5$ (from Exercise 2)

$P(5 \le x \le 5) = P(x = 5) = 0$

18. $f(x) = 2(1 - x);\ [0, 1]$

(a) $\displaystyle\int_{0}^{m} 2(1 - x)\,dx = (2x - x^2) \Bigg|_{0}^{m}$

$$= 2m - m^2$$

$$= \frac{1}{2}$$

$2m^2 - 4m + 1 = 0$

$$m = \frac{2 - \sqrt{2}}{2} \approx .293$$

(Reject $m = \frac{2 + \sqrt{2}}{2}$, which is not in the interval $[0, 1]$.

(b) $E(x) = \mu = \frac{1}{3}$ (from Exercise 4)

$P(.29 < x < .33)$

$$= \int_{.29}^{.33} 2(1 - x)\,dx$$

$$= (2x - x^2)\Big|_{.29}^{.33}$$

$$= 2(.33) - (.33)^2$$
$$\quad - 2(.29) + (.29)^2$$

$$\approx .06$$

20. $f(x) = 3x^{-4}$; $[1, \infty)$

(a) $\int_1^m 3x^{-4}\,dx = -x^{-3}\Big|_1^m$

$$= 1 - \frac{1}{m^3} = \frac{1}{2}$$

$$m^3 = 2$$

$$m = \sqrt[3]{2} \approx 1.26$$

(b) $E(x) = \mu = 1.5$ (From Exercise 8)

$P(1.26 < x < 1.5)$

$$= \int_{1.26}^{1.5} 3x^{-4}\,dx$$

$$= -x^{-3}\Big|_{1.26}^{1.5}$$

$$= \frac{1}{(1.26)^3} - \frac{1}{(1.5)^3} \approx .204$$

22. $f(x) = \frac{1}{11}\left(1 + \frac{3}{\sqrt{x}}\right)$; $[4, 9]$

(a) See Exercise 6. $\mu \approx 6.41$ yr

(b) $\sigma \approx 1.45$ yr

(c) $P(x > 6.41)$

$$= \int_{6.41}^{9} \frac{1}{11}(1 + 3x^{-1/2})\,dx$$

$$= \frac{1}{11}(x + 6x^{1/2})\Big|_{6.41}^{9}$$

$$= \frac{1}{11}(9 + 18 - 6.41 - 6(6.41)^{1/2})$$

$$\approx .49$$

24. $f(x) = \frac{1}{(\ln 20)x}$; $1, 20]$

(a) $\mu = \int_1^{20} x \cdot \frac{1}{(\ln 20)x}\,dx$

$$= \int_1^{20} \frac{1}{\ln 20}\,dx$$

$$= \frac{x}{\ln 20}\Big|_1^{20}$$

$$= \frac{19}{\ln 20} \approx 6.34 \text{ seconds}$$

(b) $\text{Var}(x) = \int_1^{20} x^2 \cdot \frac{1}{(\ln 20)x}\,dx - \mu^2$

$$= \int_1^{20} \frac{x}{\ln 20}\,dx - \mu^2$$

$$= \frac{x^2}{2\ln 20}\Big|_1^{20} - (6.34)^2$$

$$= \frac{399}{2\ln 20} - (6.34)^2$$

$$\approx 26.40$$

$$\sigma \approx \sqrt{26.40}$$

$$\approx 5.14 \text{ sec}$$

(c) $P(6.34 - 5.14 < x < 6.34 + 5.14)$

$= P(1.2 < x < 11.48)$

$= \int_{1.2}^{11.48} \frac{1}{(\ln 20)x}\, dx$

$= \frac{\ln x}{\ln 20}\Big|_{1.2}^{11.48}$

$= \frac{1}{\ln 20}(\ln 11.48 - \ln 1.2)$

$\approx .75$

26. $f(x) = \frac{1}{2\sqrt{x}};\ [1, 4]$

(a) $\mu = \int_{1}^{4} x \cdot \frac{1}{2\sqrt{x}}\, dx$

$= \int_{1}^{4} \frac{x^{1/2}}{2}\, dx$

$= \frac{x^{3/2}}{3}\Big|_{1}^{4}$

$= \frac{1}{3}(8 - 1)$

$= \frac{7}{3} \approx 2.33$ cm

(b) $Var(x) = \int_{1}^{4} x^2 \cdot \frac{1}{2\sqrt{x}}\, dx - \left(\frac{7}{3}\right)^2$

$= \int_{1}^{4} \frac{x^{3/2}}{2}\, dx - \frac{49}{9}$

$= \frac{x^{5/2}}{5}\Big|_{1}^{4} - \frac{49}{9}$

$= \frac{1}{5}(32 - 1) - \frac{49}{9} \approx .76$

$\sigma = \sqrt{Var(x)} \approx .87$ cm

(c) $P(x > 2.33 + 2(.87))$

$= P(x > 4.07) = 0$

The probability is 0 since two standard deviations falls out of the given interval [1, 4].

28. $f(x) = \frac{105}{4x^2}$ for [15, 35]

(a) $\mu = \int_{15}^{35} x \cdot \frac{105}{4x^2}\, dx$

$= \frac{105}{4} \int_{15}^{35} \frac{1}{x}\, dx$

$= \frac{105}{4} \ln x \Big|_{15}^{35}$

$= \frac{105}{4}(\ln 35 - \ln 15)$

$= \frac{105}{4} \ln\left(\frac{35}{15}\right)$

$= \frac{105}{4} \ln\left(\frac{7}{3}\right)$

≈ 22.2

(b) $Var(x)$

$= \int_{15}^{35} x^2 \frac{105}{4x^2}\, dx - \left[\frac{105}{4} \ln\left(\frac{7}{3}\right)\right]^2$

$= \frac{105}{4} \int_{15}^{35} dx - \left[\frac{105}{4} \ln\left(\frac{7}{3}\right)\right]^2$

$= \frac{105}{4} x \Big|_{15}^{35} - \left[\frac{105}{4} \ln\left(\frac{7}{3}\right)\right]^2$

$= \frac{105}{4}(35 - 15) - \left[\frac{105}{4} \ln\left(\frac{7}{3}\right)\right]^2$

$= \frac{105}{4}(20) - \left[\frac{105}{4} \ln\left(\frac{7}{3}\right)\right]^2$

$= 525 - \left[\frac{105}{4} \ln\left(\frac{7}{3}\right)\right]^2$

$\sigma = \sqrt{525 - \left[\frac{105}{4}\ln\left(\frac{7}{3}\right)\right]^2} \approx 5.51$

(c) One standard deviation below the mean is 22.24 − 5.51 = 16.73.

$$P(x \leq 16.73) = \int_{15}^{16.73} \frac{105}{4x^2} \, dx$$

$$= \frac{105}{4}\left(-\frac{1}{x}\right)\Big|_{15}^{16.73}$$

$$= \frac{105}{4}\left(-\frac{1}{16.73} + \frac{1}{15}\right)$$

$$\approx .18$$

Section 10.3

2. f(x) = 2 for [1.25, 1.75]

This is a uniform distribution.

(a) $\mu = \frac{1}{2}(1.75 + 1.25) = \$1.50$

(b) $\sigma = \frac{1}{\sqrt{12}}(1.75 - 1.25)$

$$= \frac{.5}{\sqrt{12}} \approx \$.14$$

(c) P(1.5 < x < 1.5 + .14)

  = P(1.5 < x < 1.64)

$$= \int_{1.5}^{1.64} 2 \, dx = 2x\Big|_{1.5}^{1.64} = .28$$

4. f(t) = .05e⁻·⁰⁵ᵗ for [0, ∞)

This is an exponential distribution.

(a) $\mu = \frac{1}{.05} = 20$ yr

(b) $\sigma = \frac{1}{.05} = 20$ yr

(c) P(20 < x < 20 + 20)

  = P(20 < x < 40)

$$= \int_{20}^{40} .05e^{-.05t} \, dt$$

$$= -e^{-.05t}\Big|_{20}^{40}$$

$$= e^{-1} - e^{-2} \approx .23$$

6. f(x) = .1e⁻·¹ˣ for [0, ∞)

This is an exponential distribution.

(a) $\mu = \frac{1}{.1} = 10$ m

(b) $\sigma = \frac{1}{.1} = 10$ m

(c) P(10 < x < 10 + 10)

  = P(10 < x < 20)

$$= \int_{10}^{20} .1e^{-.1x} \, dx$$

$$= -e^{-.1x}\Big|_{10}^{20}$$

$$= e^{-1} - e^{-2} \approx .23$$

In Exercises 8–14, use the table in the appendix for areas under the normal curve.

8. z = 1.68

Area between mean z = 0 and z = 1.68 is

$$.9535 - .5000 = .4535.$$

Percent of area = 45.35%

10. Area between $z = -2.13$ and $z = -.04$ is

$$.4840 - .0166 = .4674.$$

Percent of area = 46.74%

12. Since 2% = .02, the z-score that corresponds to the area of .02 to the left of z is -2.05.

14. 22% of the total area to the right of z means $1 - .22$ of the total area to the left of z.

$$1 - .22 = .78$$

The closest z-score that corresponds to the area of .78 is .77.

18. For the uniform distribution,

$$f(x) = \frac{1}{b - a} \text{ for x in } [a, b].$$

If m is the median,

$$P(x \leq m) = \frac{1}{2}$$

$$\int_a^m \frac{1}{b - a} \, dx = \frac{1}{2}$$

$$\frac{1}{b - a} \int_a^m dx = \frac{1}{2}$$

Multiply both sides by $b - a$.

$$\int_a^m dx = \frac{1}{2}b - \frac{1}{2}a$$

$$x \Big|_a^m = \frac{1}{2}b - \frac{1}{2}a$$

$$m - a = \frac{1}{2}b - \frac{1}{2}a$$

$$m = \frac{1}{2}b - \frac{1}{2}a$$

$$m = \frac{b + a}{2}$$

20. $f(x) = ae^{-ax}$ for $[0, \infty)$ with $a > 0$.

$$\mu = \int_0^\infty xae^{-ax} \, dx$$

We first consider $\int xae^{-ax} \, dx$ using integration by parts.

Let $u = x$ and $dv = ae^{-ax} \, dx$
$\quad du = dx$ and $v = -e^{-ax}$

$$\int xae^{-ax} \, dx = -xe^{-ax} - \int (-e^{-ax}) \, dx$$

$$= -xe^{-ax} - \frac{1}{a}e^{-ax} + C$$

$$= -\frac{ax + 1}{ae^{ax}} + C$$

$$\mu = \int_0^\infty xae^{-ax} \, dx$$

$$= \lim_{b \to \infty} \int_0^b xae^{-ax} \, dx$$

$$= \lim_{b \to \infty} \left(-\frac{ax + 1}{ae^{ax}}\right) \Big|_0^b$$

$$= \lim_{b \to \infty} \left(-\frac{ab + 1}{ae^{ab}} + \frac{1}{a}\right)$$

$\mu = \frac{1}{a}$ since e^{ab} grows more rapidly than ab.

$$\text{Var}(x) = \int_0^\infty x^2ae^{-ax} \, dx - \left(\frac{1}{a}\right)^2$$

We first consider $\int x^2ae^{-ax} \, dx$ using integration by parts.

Let $u = x$ and $dv = xae^{-ax} \, dx$
$\quad du = dx$ and $v = -xe^{-ax} - \frac{1}{a}e^{-ax}$

from the previous integration by parts.

$\int x^2 a e^{-ax} \, dx$

$= x(-xe^{-ax} - \frac{1}{a}e^{-ax})$

$\quad - \int (-xe^{-ax} - \frac{1}{a}e^{-ax}) \, dx$

$= -x^2 e^{-ax} - \frac{1}{a}xe^{-ax} + \int xe^{-ax} \, dx$

$\quad + \frac{1}{a} \int e^{-ax} \, dx$

$= -x^2 e^{-ax} - \frac{1}{a}xe^{-ax}$

$\quad + \frac{1}{a}(-xe^{-ax} - \frac{1}{a}e^{-ax}) - \frac{1}{a^2}e^{-ax}$

$= -x^2 e^{-ax} - \frac{1}{a}xe^{-ax} - \frac{1}{a}xe^{-ax}$

$\quad - \frac{1}{a^2}e^{-ax} - \frac{1}{a^2}e^{-ax}$

$= -\dfrac{a^2 x^2 + 2ax + 2}{a^2 e^{ax}}$

$= -\dfrac{a^2 x^2 + 2ax + 2}{a^2 e^{ax}}$

$\text{Var}(x) = \displaystyle\int_0^\infty x^2 a e^{-ax} \, dx - \frac{1}{a^2}$

$= \displaystyle\lim_{b \to \infty} \int_0^b x^2 a e^{-ax} \, dx - \frac{1}{a^2}$

$= \displaystyle\lim_{b \to \infty} -\dfrac{a^2 x^2 + 2ax + 2}{a^2 e^{ax}} \Big|_0^b - \frac{1}{a^2}$

$= \displaystyle\lim_{b \to \infty} \left[-\dfrac{a^2 b^2 + 2ab + 2}{a^2 e^{ab}} + \frac{2}{a^2} \right] - \frac{1}{a^2}$

$= \dfrac{2}{a^2} - \dfrac{1}{a^2}$

since e^{ab} grows more rapidly than $a^2 b^2 + 2ab + 2$.

$\text{Var}(x) = \dfrac{1}{a^2}$

$\sigma = \sqrt{\dfrac{1}{a^2}} = \dfrac{1}{a}$

22. We have an exponential distribution with mean $\mu = 5$.

$$\mu = \frac{1}{a} = 5$$

$$a = .2$$

(a) $f(x) = .2e^{-.2x}$ for $[0, \infty)$

(b) $P(2 < x < 6) = \displaystyle\int_2^6 .2e^{-.2x} \, dx$

$= -e^{-.2x} \Big|_2^6$

$= e^{-.4} - e^{-1.2}$

$\approx .369$

24. We have a normal distribution with $\mu = 32.8$, $\sigma = 1.1$.

Let x = number of ounces of juice.

(a) $P(x < 32)$

$= P\left(\dfrac{x - 32.8}{1.1} < \dfrac{32 - 32.8}{1.1}\right)$

$= P(z < -.73)$

$= .2327$

(b) $P(x > 33)$

$= P\left(\dfrac{x - 32.8}{1.1} < \dfrac{33 - 32.8}{1.1}\right)$

$= P(z > .18)$

$= 1 - P(z \le .18)$

$= 1 - .5714$

$= .4286$

26. We have normal distribution, with $\mu = 54.40$, $\sigma = 13.50$

$P(-a < z < a) = \dfrac{1}{2}$

$P(z < -a) = .25$

Since the closest value to .25 is .2514, we use $z = -.67$.

$$-.67 < z < .67$$
$$-.67 < \frac{x - 54.40}{13.50} < .67$$
$$45.36 < x < 63.45$$

Therefore, $P(45.36 < x < 63.45) = \frac{1}{2}$ and the middle 50% of the customers spend between $45.36 and $63.45.

28. For an exponential distribution, $f(x) = ae^{-ax}$ for $[0, \infty)$. Since $a = 2$, $f(x) = 2e^{-2x}$ for $[0, 1]$.

(a) The expected proportion is

$$\mu = \frac{1}{2} = .5.$$

(b) $P\left(0 < x < \frac{1}{3}\right) = \int_0^{1/3} 2e^{-2x} \, dx$

$$= -e^{-2x} \Big|_0^{1/3}$$

$$= -\frac{1}{e^{2/3}} + 1$$

$$\approx .49$$

30. $\mu = 3.2$ ft, $\sigma = .2$ ft

If we wish to find the middle 50%, or .50, we want an area of

$$.50 = .75 - .25.$$

The area to the left of $z = .675$ is .75.

The area to the left of $z = -.65$ is .25.

$$z = \frac{x - 3.2}{.2}$$

$$x = .2z + 3.2$$

Largest height:

$$x = .2(.675) + 3.2 = 3.33 \text{ ft}$$

Smallest height:

$$x = .2(-.65) + 3.2 = 3.07 \text{ ft}$$

32. Uniform distribution on $[32, 44]$

$$f(x) = \frac{1}{44 - 32} = \frac{1}{12} \text{ for } [32, 44]$$

(a) $\mu = \frac{1}{2}(32 + 44) = 38$ inches

(b) $P(38 < x < 40)$

$$= \int_{38}^{40} \frac{1}{12} \, dx = \frac{x}{12} \Big|_{38}^{40}$$

$$= \frac{1}{6} \approx .17$$

34. $\int_0^{50} .5xe^{-.5x} \, dx$

This exercise is to be solved using a computer. The answer may vary depending upon the computer and software used. The answer is 1.99987.

36. From Exercises 34 and 35,

$$\int_0^{50} .5xe^{-.5x} \, dx \approx 1.99987 \text{ and}$$

$$\int_0^{50} .5x^2e^{-.5x} \, dx \approx 8.000506$$

we have the exponential distribution $f(x) = .5e^{-.5x}$ for x in $[0, \infty)$ with a = .5.

For this distribution,

$$\mu = \int_0^\infty .5xe^{.5x} \, dx \approx \int_0^{50} .5xe^{.5x} \, dx$$

$$\approx 1.99987$$

$1.99987 \approx \dfrac{1}{a}$ since $\dfrac{1}{a} = \dfrac{1}{.5} = 2$.

Also, for this distribution,

$$\text{Var}(x) = \int_0^\infty .5x^2e^{-.5x} \, dx - \mu^2$$

$$\approx \int_0^{50} .5x^2e^{-.5x} \, dx - (1.99987)^2$$

$$\approx 8.000506 - (1.99987)^2$$

$$\approx 4.00103$$

$$\sigma \approx \sqrt{4.00103} \approx 2.00026$$

$2.00026 \approx \dfrac{1}{a}$ since $\dfrac{1}{a} = \dfrac{1}{.5} = 2$

Chapter 10 Review Exercises

4. $f(x) = \dfrac{1}{27}(2x + 4)$; $[1, 4]$

$$\int_1^4 \frac{1}{27}(2x + 4)dx = \frac{1}{27}(x^2 + 4x)\Big|_1^4$$

$$= \frac{1}{27}(32 - 5)$$

$$= 1$$

Since $1 \le x \le 4$, $f(x) \ge 0$.

Therefore, f(x) is a probability density function.

6. $f(x) = .1$; $[0, 10]$

$$\int_0^{10} .1 \, dx = .1x \Big|_0^{10}$$

$$= .1(10) - 0 = 1$$

$f(x) \ge 0$ for all x in $[0, 10]$. Therefore, f(x) is a probability density function.

8. $f(x) = k\sqrt{x}$; $[1, 4]$

$$\int_1^4 k\sqrt{x} \, dx$$

$$= \int_1^4 kx^{1/2} \, dx$$

$$= \frac{2}{3}kx^{3/2} \Big|_1^4$$

$$= \frac{2}{3}k(8 - 1)$$

$$= \frac{14}{3}k$$

Since f(x) is a probability density function,

$$\frac{14}{3}k = 1$$

$$k = \frac{3}{14}.$$

10. $f(x) = 1 - \dfrac{1}{\sqrt{x - 1}}$; $[2, 5]$

    (a) $P(3 \le x \le 5)$

$$= \int_{3}^{5} [1 - (x - 1)^{-1/2}]\,dx$$

$$= [x - 2(x - 1)^{1/2}]\Big|_{3}^{5}$$

$$= 5 - 2(2) - 3 + 2\sqrt{2}$$

$$\approx .828$$

    (b) $P(2 \le x \le 4)$

$$= \int_{2}^{4} [1 - (x - 1)^{-1/2}]\,dx$$

$$= [x - 2(x - 1)^{1/2}]\Big|_{2}^{4}$$

$$= 4 - 2\sqrt{3} - 2 + 2$$

$$\approx .536$$

    (c) $P(3 \le x \le 4)$

$$= \int_{3}^{4} [1 - (x - 1)^{-1/2}]\,dx$$

$$= [x - 2(x - 1)^{1/2}]\Big|_{3}^{4}$$

$$= 4 - 2\sqrt{3} - 3 + 2\sqrt{2}$$

$$\approx .364$$

12. If we consider the probabilities as weights, the expected value or mean of a probability distribution represents the point at which the distribution is balanced.

14. $f(x) = \dfrac{1}{5}$; $[4, 9]$

    (a) $E(x) = \mu = \displaystyle\int_{4}^{9} x\left(\dfrac{1}{5}\right)dx = \dfrac{x^2}{10}\Big|_{4}^{9}$

$$= \dfrac{81}{10} - \dfrac{16}{10} = \dfrac{65}{10} = 6.5$$

    (b) $Var(x) = \displaystyle\int_{4}^{9} \dfrac{1}{5}(x - 6.5)^2\,dx$

$$= \dfrac{1}{15}(x - 6.5)^3\Big|_{4}^{9}$$

$$= \dfrac{1}{15}(2.5^3 + 2.5^3)$$

$$\approx 2.083$$

    (c) $\sigma = \sqrt{Var(x)} \approx 1.443$

16. $f(x) = \dfrac{1}{7}\left(1 + \dfrac{2}{\sqrt{x}}\right)$; $[1, 4]$

    (a) $E(x) = \mu = \displaystyle\int_{1}^{4} x\left[\dfrac{1}{7}(1 + 2x^{-1/2})\right]dx$

$$= \dfrac{1}{7}\int_{1}^{4} (x + 2x^{1/2})\,dx$$

$$= \dfrac{1}{7}\left(\dfrac{x^2}{2} + \dfrac{4}{3}x^{3/2}\right)\Big|_{1}^{4}$$

$$= \dfrac{1}{7}\left(8 + \dfrac{32}{2} - \dfrac{1}{2} - \dfrac{4}{3}\right)$$

$$\approx 2.405$$

    (b) $Var(x)$

$$\approx \int_{1}^{4} \dfrac{x^2}{7}(1 + 2x^{-1/2})\,dx - (2.405)^2$$

$$\approx \int_{1}^{4} \left(\dfrac{x^2}{7} + \dfrac{2}{7}x^{3/2}\right)dx - (2.405)^2$$

$$\approx \left(\frac{x^3}{21} + \frac{4}{35}x^{5/2}\right)\Big|_1^4 - (2.405)^2$$

$$\approx \left(\frac{64}{21} + \frac{128}{35} - \frac{1}{21} - \frac{4}{35}\right) - (2.405)^2$$

$$\approx .759$$

(c) $\sigma = \sqrt{\text{Var}(x)} \approx .871$

18. $f(x) = 4x - 3x^2$; $[0, 1]$

(a) $\mu = \displaystyle\int_0^1 x(4x - 3x^2)\,dx$

$$= \int_0^1 (4x^2 - 3x^3)\,dx$$

$$= \left(\frac{4x^3}{3} - \frac{3x^4}{4}\right)\Big|_0^1$$

$$= \frac{4}{3} - \frac{3}{4}$$

$$= \frac{7}{12} \approx .583$$

(b) $\text{Var}(x) = \displaystyle\int_0^1 x^2(4x - 3x^2)\,dx - \left(\frac{7}{12}\right)^2$

$$= \int_0^1 (4x^3 - 3x^4)\,dx - \left(\frac{7}{12}\right)^2$$

$$= \left(x^4 - \frac{3x^5}{5}\right)\Big|_0^1 - \left(\frac{7}{12}\right)^2$$

$$= 1 - \frac{3}{5} - \left(\frac{7}{12}\right)^2$$

$$\approx .0597$$

$$\sigma \approx \sqrt{\text{Var}(x)} \approx .244$$

(c) $P\left(0 \le x < \frac{7}{12}\right)$

$$= \int_0^{7/12} (4x - 3x^2)\,dx$$

$$= (2x^2 - x^3)\Big|_0^{7/12}$$

$$= 2\left(\frac{7}{12}\right)^2 - \left(\frac{7}{12}\right)^3$$

$$\approx .482$$

(d) $P(\mu - \sigma \le x \le \mu + \sigma)$

$$\approx P(.339 \le x \le .827)$$

$$= \int_{.339}^{.827} (4x - 3x^2)\,dx$$

$$= (2x^2 - x^3)\Big|_{.339}^{.827}$$

$$= 2(.827)^2 - (.827)^3$$
$$\quad - 2(.339)^2 + (.339)^3$$

$$\approx .611$$

20. $f(x) = \frac{5}{112}(1 - x^{-3/2})$; $[1, 25]$

(a) $\mu = \displaystyle\int_1^{25} \frac{5x}{112}(1 - x^{-3/2})\,dx$

$$= \frac{5}{112} \int_1^{25} (x - x^{-1/2})\,dx$$

$$= \frac{5}{112}\left(\frac{x^2}{2} - 2x^{1/2}\right)\Big|_1^{25}$$

$$= \frac{5}{112}\left(\frac{625}{2} - 10 - \frac{1}{2} + 2\right)$$

$$\approx 13.6$$

(b)

Var(x)

$$= \int_1^{25} \frac{5x^2}{112}(1 - x^{-3/2})dx - (13.6)^2$$

$$= \frac{5}{112} \int_1^{25} (x^2 - x^{1/2})dx - (13.6)^2$$

$$= \frac{5}{112}\left(\frac{x^3}{3} - \frac{2}{3}x^{3/2}\right)\Big|_1^{25} - (13.6)^2$$

$$= \frac{5}{112}\left(\frac{25^3}{3} - \frac{250}{3} - \frac{1}{3} + \frac{2}{3}\right) - (13.6)^2$$

$$\approx 43.85$$

$$\sigma \approx \sqrt{Var(x)} \approx 6.6$$

(c) $P(\mu - \sigma \leq x \leq \mu + \sigma)$

$$= P(6.9 \leq x \leq 20.3)$$

$$= \int_{6.9}^{20.3} \frac{5}{112}(1 - x^{-3/2})dx$$

$$= \frac{5}{112}(x + 2x^{-1/2})\Big|_{6.9}^{20.3}$$

$$= \frac{5}{112}\left(20.3 + \frac{2}{\sqrt{20.3}} - 6.9 - \frac{2}{6.9}\right)$$

$$\approx .58$$

For Exercises 22–28, use the table in the appendix for the areas under the normal curve.

22. Area to right of z = 1.53 is

$$1 - .9370 = .063 \quad \text{or} \quad 6.3\%.$$

24. Area to left of z = 1.03 is

.8485.

Area to left of z = −1.47 is equivalent to area to right of z = 1.47:

$$1 - .9292 = .0708.$$

Area between is

$$.8485 - .0708$$
$$= .7777 \quad \text{or} \quad 77.77\%.$$

26. $\sigma = 2.5$, $\mu = 0$, z = 0 + 2.5

Area to left of z = 2.5 is

.9938 or 99.38%.

28. We want to find the z–score for 21% of the area under the normal curve to the left of z. We note that 21% < 50% so z must be negative. The z–score for the value in the table nearest .21 is z ≈ −.81.

30. $f(x) = \frac{3}{4}(x^2 - 16x + 65)$ for [8, 9]

$P(8 \leq x < 8.50)$

$$= \int_8^{8.5} \frac{3}{4}(x^2 - 16x + 65)dx$$

$$= \frac{3}{4}\left(\frac{x^3}{3} - 8x^2 + 65x\right)\Big|_8^{8.5}$$

$$= \frac{3}{4}\Big[\frac{8.5^3}{3} - 8(8.5)^2 + 65(8.5) - \frac{8^3}{3} + 8(8)^2 - 65(8)\Big]$$

$$= .406$$

32. (a) $\mu = 8$

$\dfrac{1}{a} = 8$

$a = \dfrac{1}{8}$

$f(x) = \dfrac{1}{8}e^{-x/8}$ for $[0, \infty)$

(b) Expected number $= \mu = 8$

(c) $\sigma = \mu = 8$

(d) $P(5 < x < 10) = \displaystyle\int_5^{10} \dfrac{1}{8}e^{-x/8}\ dx$

$= -e^{-x/8}\ \Big|_5^{10}$

$= -e^{-10/8} + e^{-5/8}$

$= .249$

34. $\mu = 46.2$, $\sigma\ 15.8$, $x = 60$

$z = \dfrac{x - \mu}{\sigma} = \dfrac{60 - 46.2}{15.8}$

$\approx .8734$

.8734 is the z-score for the area of about .8078 (from the table).

$P(x \geq 60) \approx P(z \geq .8734)$

$\approx 1 - .8078$

$= .1922$

36. $f(x) = \dfrac{8}{7}x^{-2}$ for $[1, 8]$

(a) $\mu = \displaystyle\int_1^8 \dfrac{8}{7}x^{-2}(x)\,dx$

$= \displaystyle\int_1^8 \dfrac{8}{7}x^{-1}\ dx$

$= \dfrac{8}{7}\ \ln x\ \Big|_1^8$

$= \dfrac{8}{7}(\ln 8 - \ln 1) \approx 2.377$ g

(b) $\mathrm{Var}(x) = \displaystyle\int_1^8 \dfrac{8}{7}x^{-2}(x^2)\,dx - 2.377^2$

$= \dfrac{8}{7}x\ \Big|_1^8 - 2.377^2$

$= \dfrac{64}{7} - \dfrac{8}{7} - 2.377^2$

≈ 2.350

$\sigma \approx \sqrt{\mathrm{Var}(x)} \approx 1.533$ g

(c) $P(\mu - \sigma \leq x \leq \mu + \sigma)$

$= P(.844 \leq x \leq 3.91)$

$= P(1 \leq x \leq 3.91)$ since $[1, 8]$

$= \displaystyle\int_1^{3.91} \dfrac{8}{7}x^{-2}\ dx$

$= \dfrac{-8}{7}x^{-1}\ \Big|_1^{3.91}\ dx$

$= \dfrac{-8}{7}\Big(\dfrac{1}{3.91}\Big) + \dfrac{8}{7}$

$\approx .851$

38. $f(x) = \dfrac{1}{b - a}$; for $[a, b]$

$f(x) = \dfrac{1}{40 - 2} = \dfrac{1}{38}$

This is a uniform distribution for $a = 2$, $b = 40$.

(a) $E(x) = \mu = \dfrac{1}{2}(b + a)$

$= \dfrac{1}{2}(40 + 2)$

$= 21$ in

(b) $P(20 < x \leq 40) = \displaystyle\int_{20}^{40} \frac{1}{38} \, dx$

$$= \frac{1}{38}x \Big|_{20}^{40}$$

$$= \frac{40}{38} - \frac{20}{38}$$

$$= \frac{20}{38} \approx .526$$

---

40. $\mu = 7.8$ lb, $\sigma = 1.1$ lb, $x = 9$ lb

$$z = \frac{x - \mu}{\sigma} = \frac{9 - 7.8}{1.1} \approx 1.09$$

$$P(x > 9) \approx P(z > 1.09)$$

$$= 1 - .8621$$

$$\approx .1379$$

---

42. $f(x) = .05$ for $[10, 30]$

(a) This is a uniform distribution.

(b) The domain of f is $[10, 30]$
The range of f is $\{.05\}$.

(c)

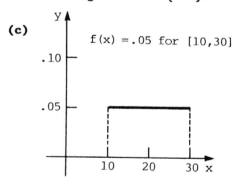

f(x) = .05 for [10,30]

(d) For a uniform distribution,

$$\mu = \frac{1}{2}(b + a) \text{ and}$$

$$Var(x) = \frac{b^2 - 2ab + a^2}{12}.$$

Thus, $\mu = \dfrac{1}{2}(30 + 10) = \dfrac{1}{2}(40) = 20$

and

$$Var(x) = \frac{30^2 - 2(10)(30) + 10^2}{12}$$

$$= \frac{400}{12}$$

$$\sigma = \sqrt{\frac{400}{12}} \approx 5.77$$

(e) $P(\mu - \sigma \leq x \leq \mu + \sigma)$

$$= P(20 - 5.77 \leq x \leq 20 + 5.77)$$

$$= P(14.23 \leq x \leq 25.77)$$

$$= \int_{14.23}^{25.77} .05 \, dx$$

$$= .05x \Big|_{14.23}^{25.77}$$

$$= .05(25.77 - 14.23)$$

$$\approx .58$$

---

44. $f(x) = \dfrac{e^{-x^2}}{\sqrt{\pi}}$ for $(-\infty, \infty)$

(a) Since the exponent of e in f(x) may be written

$$-x^2 = \frac{-(x - 0)^2}{2\left(\dfrac{1}{\sqrt{2}}\right)^2},$$

and

$$\frac{1}{\sqrt{\pi}} = \frac{1}{\dfrac{1}{\sqrt{2}}\sqrt{2\pi}},$$

f(x) is a normal distribution with
$\mu = 0$ and $\sigma = 1/\sqrt{2}$.

(b) The domain of f is $(-\infty, \infty)$.

The range of f is $(0, 1/\sqrt{\pi})$.

(c)

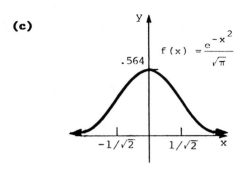

(d) For this normal distribution, $\mu = 0$ and $\sigma = 1/\sqrt{2}$.

(e) $P(\mu - \sigma \le x \le \mu + \sigma)$

$$= 2P(0 \le x \le \mu + \sigma)$$

$$= 2P\left(0 \le x \le \frac{1}{\sqrt{2}}\right)$$

If $x = \dfrac{1}{\sqrt{2}}$, $z = \dfrac{\dfrac{1}{\sqrt{2}} - 0}{\dfrac{1}{\sqrt{2}}} = 1.00$

Thus,

$P(\mu - \sigma \le x \le \mu + \sigma)$

$$= 2P(0 \le z \le 1.00)$$

$$= 2(.3413)$$

$$\approx .68.$$

CHAPTER 11 THE TRIGONOMETRIC FUNCTIONS

Section 11.1

2. $90° = 90\left(\frac{\pi}{180}\right) = \frac{\pi}{2}$

4. $135° = 135\left(\frac{\pi}{180}\right) = \frac{3\pi}{4}$

6. $300° = 300\left(\frac{\pi}{180}\right) = \frac{5\pi}{3}$

8. $480° = 480\left(\frac{\pi}{180}\right) = \frac{8\pi}{3}$

10. $\frac{2\pi}{3} = \frac{2\pi}{3}\left(\frac{180°}{\pi}\right) = 120°$

12. $-\frac{\pi}{4} = -\frac{\pi}{4}\left(\frac{180°}{\pi}\right) = -45°$

14. $\frac{7\pi}{10} = \frac{7\pi}{10}\left(\frac{180°}{\pi}\right) = 126°$

16. $5\pi = 5\pi\left(\frac{180°}{\pi}\right) = 900°$

18. Let α = the angle with terminal side through $(-12, -5)$. Then $x = -12$, $y = -5$, and

$$r = \sqrt{x^2 + y^2} = \sqrt{144 + 25}$$
$$= \sqrt{169} = 13.$$

$\sin \alpha = \frac{y}{r} = -\frac{5}{13}$ $\qquad \cot \alpha = \frac{x}{y} = \frac{12}{5}$

$\cos \alpha = \frac{x}{r} = -\frac{12}{13}$ $\qquad \sec \alpha = \frac{r}{x} = -\frac{13}{12}$

$\tan \alpha = \frac{y}{x} = \frac{5}{12}$ $\qquad \csc \alpha = \frac{r}{y} = -\frac{13}{5}$

20. Let α = the angle with terminal side through $(-7, 24)$. Then $x = -7$, $y = 24$, and

$$r = \sqrt{x^2 + y^2} = \sqrt{49 + 576}$$
$$= \sqrt{625} = 25.$$

$\sin \alpha = \frac{y}{r} = \frac{24}{25}$ $\qquad \cot \alpha = \frac{x}{y} = -\frac{7}{24}$

$\cos \alpha = \frac{x}{r} = -\frac{7}{25}$ $\qquad \sec \alpha = \frac{r}{x} = -\frac{25}{7}$

$\tan \alpha = \frac{y}{x} = -\frac{24}{7}$ $\qquad \csc \alpha = \frac{r}{y} = \frac{25}{24}$

22. In quadrant II, $x < 0$ and $y > 0$. Furthermore, $r > 0$.

$\sin \theta = \frac{y}{r} > 0$, so the sign is $+$.

$\cos \theta = \frac{x}{r} < 0$, so the sign is $-$.

$\tan \theta = \frac{y}{x} < 0$, so the sign is $-$.

$\cot \theta = \frac{x}{y} < 0$, so the sign is $-$.

$\sec \theta = \frac{r}{x} < 0$, so the sign is $-$.

$\csc \theta = \frac{r}{y} > 0$, so the sign is $+$.

24. In quadrant IV, $x > 0$ and $y < 0$. Also, $r > 0$.

$\sin \theta = \frac{y}{r} < 0$, so the sign is $-$.

$\cos \theta = \frac{x}{r} > 0$, so the sign is $+$.

$\tan \theta = \frac{y}{x} < 0$, so the sign is $-$.

$\cot \theta = \frac{x}{y} < 0$, so the sign is $-$.

$\sec \theta = \frac{r}{x} > 0$, so the sign is $+$.

$\csc \theta = \frac{r}{y} < 0$, so the sign is $-$.

26. When an angle θ of 45° is drawn in standard position, $(x, y) = (1, 1)$ is one point on its terminal side. Then

$$r = \sqrt{1 + 1} = \sqrt{2}.$$

$$\sin 45° = \frac{y}{r} = \frac{1}{\sqrt{2}} = \frac{\sqrt{2}}{2}$$

$$\cos \theta = \frac{x}{r} = \frac{1}{\sqrt{2}} = \frac{\sqrt{2}}{2}$$

$$\sec \theta = \frac{r}{x} = \sqrt{2}$$

$$\csc \theta = \frac{r}{y} = \sqrt{2}$$

28. When an angle θ of 120° is drawn in standard position, $(x, y) = (-1, \sqrt{3})$ is one point on its terminal side. Then

$$r = \sqrt{1 + 3} = 2.$$

$$\cos \theta = \frac{x}{r} = -\frac{1}{2}$$

$$\cot \theta = \frac{x}{y} = -\frac{1}{\sqrt{3}} = -\frac{\sqrt{3}}{3}$$

$$\sec \theta = \frac{r}{x} = -2$$

30. When an angle θ of 150° is drawn in standard position, $(x, y) = (-\sqrt{3}, 1)$ is one point on its terminal side. Then

$$r = \sqrt{3 + 1} = 2.$$

$$\sin \theta = \frac{y}{r} = \frac{1}{2}$$

$$\cot \theta = \frac{x}{y} = -\sqrt{3}$$

$$\sec \theta = \frac{r}{x} = -\frac{2}{\sqrt{3}} = -\frac{2\sqrt{3}}{3}$$

32. When an angle θ of 240° is drawn in standard position, $(x, y) = (-1, -\sqrt{3})$ is one point on its terminal side.

$$\tan \theta = \frac{y}{x} = \sqrt{3}$$

$$\cot \theta = \frac{x}{y} = \frac{-1}{-\sqrt{3}} = \frac{\sqrt{3}}{3}$$

34. When an angle of $\frac{\pi}{6}$ is drawn in standard position, $(x, y) = (\sqrt{3}, 1)$ is one point on it terminal side. Then

$$r = \sqrt{3 + 1} = 2.$$

$$\cos \frac{\pi}{6} = \frac{x}{r} = \frac{\sqrt{3}}{2}$$

36. When an angle of $\frac{\pi}{3}$ is drawn in standard position, $(x, y) = (1, \sqrt{3})$ is one point on its terminal side.

$$\cot \frac{\pi}{3} = \frac{x}{y} = \frac{1}{\sqrt{3}} = \frac{\sqrt{3}}{3}$$

38. When an angle of $\frac{\pi}{2}$ is drawn in standard position, $(x, y) = (0, 1)$ is one point on its terminal side. Then

$$r = \sqrt{0 + 1} = 1.$$

$$\sin \frac{\pi}{2} = \frac{1}{1} = 1$$

40. When an angle of π is drawn in standard position, $(x, y) = (-1, 0)$ is one point on its terminal side.

Then

$$r = \sqrt{1 + 0} = 1.$$
$$\sec \pi = \frac{x}{r} = -1$$

42. When an angle of $\frac{3\pi}{4}$ is drawn in standard position, $(x, y) = (-1, 1)$ is one point on it terminal side.

$$\tan \frac{3\pi}{4} = \frac{y}{x} = -1$$

44. When an angle of 5π is drawn in standard position, $(x, y) = (-1, 0)$ is one point on its terminal side. Then

$$r = \sqrt{1 + 0} = 1.$$
$$\cos 5\pi = \frac{x}{r} = -1$$

46. When an angle of $-\frac{2\pi}{3}$ is drawn in standard position, $(x, y) = (-1, -\sqrt{3})$ is one point on its terminal side.

$$\cot -\frac{2\pi}{3} = \frac{x}{y} = \frac{1}{\sqrt{3}} = \frac{\sqrt{3}}{3}$$

48. When an angle of $-\frac{\pi}{6}$ is drawn in standard position, $(x, y) = (\sqrt{3}, -1)$ is one point on its terminal side. Then

$$r = \sqrt{3 + 1} = 2.$$
$$\cos -\frac{\pi}{6} = \frac{\sqrt{3}}{2}$$

50. $\cos 58° = .5299$

52. $\tan 54° = 1.3764$

54. $\tan 1.0123 = 1.6004$

56. $\sin 1.5359 = .9994$

58. The graph of $y = 2 \cos x$ is similar to the graph of $y = \cos x$ except that it has twice the amplitude. (That is, its height is twice as great.)

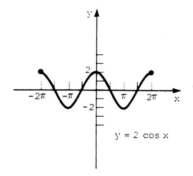

60. The graph of $y = \sin 2x$ is similar to the graph of $y = \sin x$ except that its oscillates twice as fast. Therefore, its period is π.

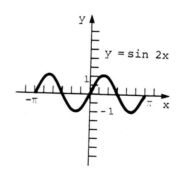

62. The graph of $y = -\frac{1}{2}\cos x$ is similar to the graph of $y = \cos x$ except that it has half the amplitude and is reflected about the x-axis.

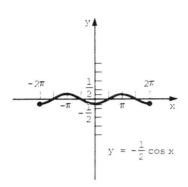

64. The graph of $y = -3\tan$ is similar to the graph of $y = \tan x$ except that it is reflected about the x-axis and each ordinate value is three times larger in absolute value. Note that the point $(-\pi/4, 3)$ and $(\pi/4, -3)$ lie on the graph.

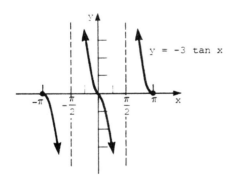

66. Solving $\dfrac{c_1}{c_2} = \dfrac{\sin \theta_1}{\sin \theta_2}$ for c_2 gives

$$c_2 = \frac{c_1 \sin \theta_2}{\sin \theta_1}.$$

When $\theta_1 = 39°$, $\theta_2 = 28°$, and $c_1 = 3 \times 10^8$

$$c_2 = \frac{(3 \times 10^8)(\sin 28°)}{\sin 39°}$$

$$\approx 2.2 \times 10^8 \text{ m/sec}.$$

68. Since each square represents 30° and the sine wave repeats itself every 8 squares, the period of the sine wave is

$$8 \times 30° = 240°.$$

70. $P(t) = 7(1 - \cos 2\pi t)(t + 10) + 100e^{.2t}$

(a) Since January 1 of the base year corresponds to $t = 0$, the pollution level is

$$P(0) = 7(1 - \cos 0)(0 + 10) + 100e^0$$
$$= 7(0)(10) + 100$$
$$= 100.$$

(b) Since July 1 of the base year corresponds to $t = .5$, the pollution level is

$$P(.5) = 7(1 - \cos \pi)(.5 + 10) + 100e^{.1}$$
$$= 7(2)(10.5) + 100e^{.1}$$
$$\approx 258.$$

(c) Since January 1 of the following year corresponds to $t = 1$, the pollution level is

$$P(1)$$
$$= 7(1 - \cos 2\pi)(1 + 10) + 100e^{.2}$$
$$\approx 122.$$

(d) Since July 1 of the following year corresponds to t = 1.5, the pollution level is

P(1.5)

= 7(1 - cos 3π)(1.5 + 10) + 100e$^{.3}$

= 7(2)(11.5) + 100e$^{.3}$

≈ 296.

72. T(x) = 37 sin $\left[\frac{2\pi}{365}(x - 101)\right]$ + 25

(a) T(60) = 37 sin$\left[\frac{2\pi}{365}(-41)\right]$ + 25

≈ 1°C

(b) T(91) = 37 sin$\left[\frac{2\pi}{365}(-10)\right]$ + 25

= 19°C

(c) T(101) = 37 sin $\left[\frac{2\pi}{365}(0)\right]$ + 25

= 25°C

(d) T(150) = 37 sin $\left[\frac{2\pi}{365}(49)\right]$ + 25

≈ 53°C

(e) The maximum and mininum values of the sine function are 1 and -1, respectively. Thus, the maximum value of T is

37(1) + 25 = 62°C

and the minimum value of T is

37(-1) + 25 = -12°C.

74. Let h = the height of the building.

$$\tan 37.4° = \frac{h}{48}$$

h = 48 tan 37.4°

h ≈ 48(.7646)

≈ 36.7

The height of the building is approximately 36.7 m.

76. This exercise is to be solved using a computer. The answer depends on the computer and software used.

(a)

P(t) = 7[1 - cos(2πt)](t + 10) + 100e$^{.2t}$

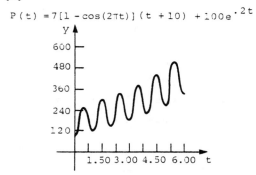

(b)

P(t) = 3.5[1 - cos(2πt)](t + 10) + 100e$^{.2t}$

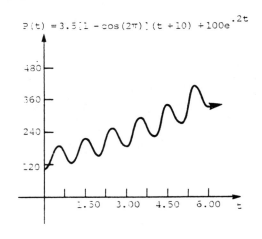

Section 11.2

2. $y = -\cos 4x$

$y' = (\sin 4x) \cdot D_x (4x)$

$ = 4 \sin 4x$

4. $y = -3 \cos (8x^2 + 2)$

$y' = [3 \sin (8x^2 + 2)] \cdot D_x (8x^2 + 2)$

$ = 16x \cdot 3 \sin (8x^2 + 2)$

$ = 48x \sin (8x^2 + 2)$

6. $y = -9 \sin^5 x$

$y' = -45(\sin x)^4 \cdot D_x(\sin x)$

$ = -45 \sin^4 x \cos x$

8. $y = 2 \cot^4 x$

$y' = 8(\cos x)^3 \cdot D_x(\cot x)$

$ = -8 \cos^3 x \csc^2 x$

10. $y = 6x \cdot \cos 3x$

$y' = 6x \cdot D_x(\cos 3x) + (\cos 3x)D_x (6x)$

$ = 6x \cdot (-\sin 3x) \cdot D_x (3x) + 6 \cos 3x$

$ = -18x \sin 3x + 6 \cos 3x$

12. $y = \dfrac{\tan x}{2x + 4}$

$y' = \dfrac{(2x + 4) \cdot D_x(\tan x) - (\tan x)D_x(2x + 3)}{(2x + 4)^2}$

$ = \dfrac{(2x + 4)\sec^2 x - 2 \tan x}{(2x + 4)^2}$

14. $y = \cos 4e^{2x}$

$y' = (-\sin 4e^{2x}) \cdot D_x(4e^{2x})$

$ = -8e^{2x} \sin 4e^{2x}$

16. $y = -8e^{\tan x}$

$y' = -8e^{\tan x} \cdot D_x(\tan x)$

$\quad = (-8 \sec^2 x)e^{\tan x}$

18. $y = \cos(\ln|2x^3|)$

$y' = [-\sin(\ln|2x^3|)] \cdot D_x(\ln|2x^3|)$

$\quad = -\sin(\ln|2x^3|) \cdot \dfrac{D_x(2x^3)}{2x^3}$

$\quad = -\dfrac{3}{x}\sin(\ln|2x^3|)$

20. $y = \ln|\tan^2 x|$

$y' = \dfrac{1}{\tan^2 x} \cdot D_x(\tan^2 x)$

$\quad = \dfrac{1}{\tan^2 x} \cdot (2\tan x) \cdot D_x(\tan x)$

$\quad = \dfrac{2\sec^2 x}{\tan x}$

22. $y = \dfrac{4\cos x}{2 - \cos x}$

$y' = \dfrac{(2 - \cos x) \cdot D_x(4\cos x) - (4\cos x) \cdot D_x(2 - \cos x)}{(2 - \cos x)^2}$

$\quad = \dfrac{(2 - \cos x)(-4\sin x) - 4\cos x \sin x}{(2 - \cos x)^2}$

$\quad = \dfrac{-8\sin x}{(2 - \cos x)^2}$

24. $y = \sqrt{\dfrac{\cos 4x}{\cos x}} = \left(\dfrac{\cos 4x}{\cos x}\right)^{1/2}$

$y' = \dfrac{1}{2}\left(\dfrac{\cos 4x}{\cos x}\right)^{-1/2} \cdot D_x\left(\dfrac{\cos 4x}{\cos x}\right)$

$\quad = \dfrac{1}{2}\left(\dfrac{\cos 4x}{\cos x}\right)^{-1/2} \cdot \left[\dfrac{(\cos x) \cdot D_x(\cos 4x) - (\cos 4x) \cdot D_x(\cos x)}{\cos^2 x}\right]$

$\quad = \dfrac{1}{2}\left(\dfrac{\cos x}{\cos 4x}\right)^{1/2} \cdot \left(\dfrac{-4\cos x \sin 4x + \cos 4x \sin x}{\cos^2 x}\right)$

$\quad = \dfrac{-4\cos x \sin 4x + \cos 4x \sin x}{2\cos^{3/2} x \cos^{1/2} 4x}$

26. $D_x(\sec x) = D_x\left(\dfrac{1}{\cos x}\right)$

$\qquad = D_x\ [(\cos x)^{-1}]$

$\qquad = -1\ (\cos x)^{-2}(-\sin x)$

$\qquad = \dfrac{\sin x}{\cos^2 x}$

$\qquad = \dfrac{1}{\cos x} \cdot \dfrac{\sin x}{\cos x}$

$\qquad = \sec x\ \tan x$

28. $R(x) = 100 \cos 2\pi x$

(a) $R'(x) = 100 \cdot (-\sin 2\pi x)(2\pi)$

$\qquad = -200\pi \sin 2\pi x$

(b) Replacing x with 1/12 (for 1/12 of a year) gives

$R'\left(\dfrac{1}{12}\right) = -200\pi \sin 2\pi\left(\dfrac{1}{12}\right)$

$\qquad = -200\pi \sin \dfrac{\pi}{6}$

$\qquad = -200\pi\left(\dfrac{1}{2}\right)$

$\qquad = -100\pi.$

(c) January 1 is 6 months, or 6/12 = 1/2 of a year from July 1. Replace x with 1/2.

$R'\left(\dfrac{1}{2}\right) = -200\pi \sin 2\pi\left(\dfrac{1}{2}\right)$

$\qquad R' = -200\pi \sin \pi$

$\qquad = -200\pi(0)$

$\qquad = 0$

(d) June 1 is 11/12 of a year from July 1.

$R'\left(\dfrac{11}{12}\right) = -200\pi \sin 2\pi\left(\dfrac{11}{12}\right)$

$\qquad = -200\pi \sin \dfrac{11\pi}{6}$

$\qquad = -200\pi\left(-\dfrac{1}{2}\right)$

$\qquad = 100\pi$

30. $y = \dfrac{\pi}{8} \cos 3\pi\left(t - \dfrac{1}{3}\right)$

(a) The graph should resemble the graph of $y = \cos x$ with the following differences. The maximum and minimum values of y are $\dfrac{\pi}{8}$ and $-\dfrac{\pi}{8}$. The period of the graph will be $\dfrac{2\pi}{3\pi} = \dfrac{2}{3}$ units. The graph will be shifted horizontally $\dfrac{1}{3}$ units to the right.

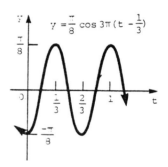

(b) velocity $= \dfrac{dy}{dt}$

Therefore,

$v = D_t\left[\dfrac{\pi}{8} \cos 3\pi\left(t - \dfrac{1}{3}\right)\right]$

$\quad = \dfrac{\pi}{8} D_t\left[\cos 3\pi\left(t - \dfrac{1}{3}\right)\right]$

$\quad = \dfrac{\pi}{8}\left[-\sin 3\pi\left(t - \dfrac{1}{3}\right)\right]D_t\ \left[3\pi\left(t - \dfrac{1}{3}\right)\right]$

$\quad = \dfrac{\pi}{8}\left[-\sin 3\pi\left(t - \dfrac{1}{3}\right)\right] \cdot 3\pi$

$\quad = \dfrac{-3\pi^2 \sin 3\pi\left(t - \dfrac{1}{3}\right)}{8}$

Acceleration $= \dfrac{d^2y}{dt^2}$

Therefore,

$$a = D_t \left[\frac{-3\pi^2 \sin 3\pi\left(t - \frac{1}{3}\right)}{8} \right]$$

$$= \frac{-3\pi^2}{8} D_t \left[\sin 3\pi\left(t - \frac{1}{3}\right) \right]$$

$$= \frac{-3\pi^2}{8} \left[\cos 3\pi\left(t - \frac{1}{3}\right) \right] D_t \left[3\pi\left(t - \frac{1}{3}\right) \right]$$

$$= \frac{-3\pi^2}{8} \left[\cos 3\pi\left(t - \frac{1}{3}\right) \right] \cdot 3\pi$$

$$= \frac{-9\pi^3 \cos 3\pi\left(t - \frac{1}{3}\right)}{8}$$

(c) $\dfrac{d^2y}{dt^2} + 9\pi^2 y$

$$= -\frac{9\pi^3}{8} \cos 3\pi\left(t - \frac{1}{3}\right)$$

$$\quad + 9\pi^2 \left[\frac{\pi}{8} \cos 3\pi\left(t - \frac{1}{3}\right) \right]$$

$$= -\frac{9\pi^3}{8} \cos 3\pi\left(t - \frac{1}{3}\right)$$

$$\quad + \frac{9\pi^3}{8} \cos 3\pi\left(t - \frac{1}{3}\right)$$

$$= 0$$

(d) $a(1) = -\dfrac{9\pi^3}{8} \cos 3\pi\left(1 - \dfrac{1}{3}\right)$

$$= -\frac{9\pi^3}{8} \cos 2\pi$$

$$= -\frac{9\pi^3}{8}$$

$$y(1) = \frac{\pi}{8} \cos 3\pi\left(1 - \frac{1}{3}\right)$$

$$= \frac{\pi}{8} \cos 2\pi$$

$$= \frac{\pi}{8}$$

Therefore, at t = 1 second, the force is clockwise and the arm makes an angle of $\pi/8$ radians forward from the vertical. The arm is moving clockwise.

$$a\left(\frac{4}{3}\right) = -\frac{9\pi^3}{8} \cos 3\pi\left(\frac{4}{3} - \frac{1}{3}\right)$$

$$= -\frac{9\pi^3}{8} \cos (3\pi)$$

$$= \frac{9\pi^3}{8}$$

$$y\left(\frac{4}{3}\right) = \frac{\pi}{8} \cos 3\pi\left(\frac{4}{3} - \frac{1}{3}\right)$$

$$= \frac{\pi}{8} \cos (3\pi)$$

$$= -\frac{\pi}{8}$$

Therefore, at t = 4/3 seconds, the force is counterclockwise and the arm makes an angle of $\pi/8$ radians backward from the vertical. The arm is moving counterclockwise.

$$a\left(\frac{5}{3}\right) = -\frac{9\pi^3}{8} \cos 3\pi\left(\frac{5}{3} - \frac{1}{3}\right)$$

$$= -\frac{9\pi^3}{8} \cos (4\pi)$$

$$= -\frac{9\pi^3}{8}$$

$$y\left(\frac{5}{3}\right) = \frac{\pi}{8} \cos 3\pi\left(\frac{5}{3} - \frac{1}{3}\right)$$

$$= \frac{\pi}{8} \cos \pi(4\pi)$$

$$= \frac{\pi}{8}$$

Therefore, at t = 5/3 second, the answer corresponds to t = 1 second. So the arm is moving clockwise.

32. **(a)** $\tan \theta = \frac{x}{40}$

Differentiate both sides with respect to time, t.

$$D_t (\tan \theta) = D_t \left(\frac{x}{40}\right)$$

$$\sec^2 \theta \cdot \frac{d\theta}{dt} = \frac{1}{40} \cdot \frac{dx}{dt}$$

Since the light rotates twice per minute, $\frac{d\theta}{dt} = \frac{2(2\pi \text{ radians})}{1 \text{ min}} = 4\pi$ radians per minute. When the light beam and shoreline are at right angles, $\theta = 0$ and $\sec \theta = 1$. Thus,

$$(1)^2 (4\pi) = \frac{1}{40} \cdot \frac{dx}{dt}$$

$$\frac{dx}{dt} = 160\pi$$

The beam is moving along the shoreline at 160π m/min.

(b) When the beam hits the shoreline 40 m from the point on the shoreline closest to the lighthouse, $\theta = \frac{\pi}{4}$ and $\sec \theta = \sqrt{2}$. Thus,

$$(\sqrt{2})^2 (4\pi) = \frac{1}{40} \cdot \frac{dx}{dt}$$

$$\frac{dx}{dt} = 320\pi.$$

The beam is moving at 320π m/min.

34. Let x be the length of the ladder, and let y be the distance from the wall to the bottom of the ladder. Then

$$\sin \theta = \frac{y + 2}{x} \quad \text{and} \quad \tan \theta = \frac{y}{9}$$

$x \sin \theta = y + 2$ and $\quad y = 9 \tan \theta.$

Thus, $x \sin \theta = 9 \tan \theta + 2$

$$x = \frac{9 \tan \theta + 2}{\sin \theta}$$

$$x = 9 \sec \theta + 2 \csc \theta$$

This expression gives the length of the ladder as a function of θ. Find the minimum value of this function.

$$\frac{dx}{d\theta} = 9 \sec \theta \tan \theta - 2 \csc \theta \cot \theta$$

$9 \sec \theta \tan \theta - 2 \csc \theta \cot \theta = 0$

$$\frac{\sec \theta \tan \theta}{\csc \theta \cot \theta} = \frac{2}{9}$$

$$\frac{\frac{1}{\cos \theta} \cdot \frac{\sin \theta}{\cos \theta}}{\frac{1}{\sin \theta} \cdot \frac{\cos \theta}{\sin \theta}} = \frac{2}{9}$$

$$\frac{\sin^3 \theta}{\cos^3 \theta} = \frac{2}{9}$$

$$\tan^3 \theta = \frac{2}{9}$$

$$\tan \theta = \sqrt[3]{\frac{2}{9}}$$

$$\theta \approx .5446 \text{ radian}$$

If $\theta < .5446$, $\frac{dx}{d\theta} < 0$.

If $\theta > .5446$, $\frac{dx}{d\theta} > 0$.

Therefore, there is a minimum when $\theta = .5446$.

If $\theta = .5446$,

$x = 9 \sec .5446 + 2 \csc .5446$

$x \approx 14.383$

The minimum length of the ladder is approximately 14.38 ft.

Section 11.3

2. $\int \sin 8x \, dx$

Let $u = 8x$, so that $du = 8 \, dx$.

$\int \sin 8x \, dx = \frac{1}{8} \int \sin 8x (8 \, dx)$

$= \frac{1}{8} \int \sin u \, du$

$= -\frac{1}{8} \cos u + C$

$= -\frac{1}{8} \cos 8x + C$

4. $\int (7 \sin x - 8 \cos x) dx$

$= 7 \int \sin x \, dx - 8 \int \cos x \, dx$

$= -7 \cos x - 8 \sin x + C$

6. $\int 2x \cos x^2 \, dx$

Let $u = x^2$, so that $du = 2x \, dx$.

$\int 2x \cos x^2 \, dx = \int \cos u \, du$

$= \sin u + C$

$= \sin x^2 + C$

8. $-\int 2 \csc^2 8x \, dx$

Let $u = 8x$, so that $du = 8 \, dx$.

$-\int 2 \csc^2 8x \, dx = -\frac{1}{4} \int \csc^2 8x (8 \, dx)$

$= \frac{1}{4} \int (-\csc^2 u) du$

$= \frac{1}{4} \cot u + C$

$= \frac{1}{4} \cot 8x + C$

10. $\int \sin^6 x \cos x \, dx$

Let $u = \sin x$, so that $du = \cos x \, dx$.

$\int \sin^6 x \cos x \, dx = \int u^6 \, du$

$= \frac{1}{7} u^7 + C$

$= \frac{1}{7} \sin^7 x + C$

12. $\int \frac{\cos x}{\sqrt{\sin x}} \, dx$

Let $u = \sin x$, so that $du = \cos x \, dx$.

$\int \frac{\cos x}{\sqrt{\sin x}} \, dx = \int \sin^{-1/2} x \cos x \, dx$

$= \int u^{-1/2} \, du$

$= 2u^{1/2} + C$

$= 2 \sin^{1/2} x + C$

or $\quad 2\sqrt{\sin x} + C$

14. $\int \frac{\cos x}{1 - \sin x} \, dx$

Let $u = 1 - \sin x$, so that $du = -\cos x \, dx$.

$\int \frac{\cos x}{1 - \sin x} \, dx$

$= -\int (1 - \sin x)^{-1} (-\cos x) dx$

$= -\int u^{-1} \, du$

$= -\ln |u| + C$

$= -\ln |1 - \sin x| + C$

16. $\int (x + 2)^4 \sin (x + 2)^5 \, dx$

Let $u = (x + 2)^5$, so that

$\qquad du = 5(x + 2)^4 \, dx.$

$\int (x + 2)^4 \sin (x + 2)^5 \, dx$

$\quad = \dfrac{1}{5} \int \sin (x + 2)^5 \cdot 5(x + 2)^4 \, dx$

$\quad = \dfrac{1}{5} \int \sin u \, du$

$\quad = -\dfrac{1}{5} \cos u + C$

$\quad = -\dfrac{1}{5} \cos (x + 2)^5 + C$

18. $\int \cot\left(-\dfrac{3}{8}x\right) dx$

Let $u = -\dfrac{3}{8}x$, so that $du = -\dfrac{3}{8} \, dx$.

Then

$\int \cot\left(-\dfrac{3}{8}x\right) dx = -\dfrac{8}{3} \int \cot\left(-\dfrac{3}{8}x\right)\left(-\dfrac{3}{8} \, dx\right)$

$\qquad = -\dfrac{8}{3} \int \cot u \, du$

$\qquad = -\dfrac{8}{3} \ln |\sin u| + C$

$\qquad = -\dfrac{8}{3} \ln \left|\sin \left(-\dfrac{3}{8}x\right)\right| + C.$

20. $\int \dfrac{x}{4} \tan \left(\dfrac{x}{4}\right)^2 dx$

Let $u = \left(\dfrac{x}{4}\right)^2$, so that

$du = 2\left(\dfrac{x}{4}\right)\left(\dfrac{1}{4}dx\right) = \dfrac{x}{8} \, dx$

$\int \dfrac{x}{4} \tan \left(\dfrac{x}{4}\right)^2 dx$

$\quad = 2 \int \dfrac{x}{8} \tan \left(\dfrac{x}{4}\right)^2 dx$

$\quad = 2 \int \tan u \, du$

$\quad = -2 \ln |\cos u| + C$

$\quad = -2 \ln \left|\cos \left(\dfrac{x}{4}\right)^2\right| + C$

22. $\int e^{-x} \tan e^{-x} \, dx$

Let $u = e^{-x}$, so that $du = -e^{-x} \, dx$.

$\int e^{-x} \tan e^{-x} \, dx$

$\quad = -\int \tan u \, du$

$\quad = \ln |\cos u| + C$

$\quad = \ln |\cos e^{-x}| + C$

24. $\int 9x \sin 2x \, dx$

Let $u = 9x$ and $dv = \sin 2x \, dx$.

Then $du = 9 \, dx$ and $v = -\dfrac{1}{2} \cos 2x$.

$\int 9x \sin 2x \, dx$

$\quad = -\dfrac{9}{2}x \cos 2x - \int \left(-\dfrac{1}{2} \cos 2x\right)(9 \, dx)$

$\quad = -\dfrac{9}{2}x \cos 2x + \dfrac{9}{2} \int \cos 2x \, dx$

$\quad = -\dfrac{9}{2}x \cos 2x + \dfrac{9}{4} \int (\cos 2x)(2 \, dx)$

$\quad = -\dfrac{9}{2}x \cos 2x + \dfrac{9}{4} \sin 2x + C$

26. $\int -11x \cos x \, dx$

Let $u = -11x$ and $dv = \cos x \, dx$.

Then $du = -11 \, dx$ and $v = \sin x$.

$\int -11x \cos x \, dx$

$\quad = -11x \sin x - \int (\sin x)(-11 \, dx)$

$\quad = -11x \sin x + 11 \int \sin x \, dx$

$\quad = -11x \sin x - 11 \cos x + C$

28. $\int 10x^2 \sin \frac{1}{2}x \; dx$

Let $u = 10x^2$ and $dv = \sin \frac{1}{2}x \; dx$

Then $du = 20x \; dx$ and $v = -2 \cos \frac{1}{2}x$.

$\int 10x^2 \sin \frac{1}{2}x \; dx$

$= (10x^2)(-2 \cos \frac{1}{2}x)$

$\quad - \int (-2 \cos \frac{1}{2}x)(20x \; dx)$

$= -20x^2 \cos \frac{1}{2}x + 40 \int x \cos \frac{1}{2}x \; dx$

Let $u = x$ and $dv = \cos \frac{1}{2}x \; dx$.
Then $du = dx$ and $v = 2 \sin \frac{1}{2}x$.

$\int 10x^2 \sin \frac{1}{2}x \; dx$

$= -20x^2 \cos \frac{1}{2}x$

$\quad + 40 \left(2x \sin \frac{1}{2}x - \int 2 \sin \frac{1}{2}x \; dx\right)$

$= -20x^2 \cos \frac{1}{2}x + 80x \sin \frac{1}{2}x$

$\quad + 160 \cos \frac{1}{2}x + C$

30. $\int_{\pi/2}^{0} \cos x \; dx = \sin x \Big|_{-\pi/2}^{0}$

$= \sin 0 - \sin \left(-\frac{\pi}{2}\right)$

$= 0 - (-1)$

$= 1$

32. $\int_{\pi/4}^{\pi/2} \cot x \; dx$

$= \ln |\sin x| \Big|_{\pi/4}^{\pi/2}$

$= \ln \left|\sin \frac{\pi}{2}\right| - \ln \left|\sin \frac{\pi}{4}\right|$

$= \ln 1 - \ln \frac{\sqrt{2}}{2}$

$= -\ln \frac{\sqrt{2}}{2}$

or $\ln \left(\frac{\sqrt{2}}{2}\right)^{-1} = \ln \sqrt{2} = \frac{1}{2} \ln 2$

34. $\int_{\pi/4}^{3\pi/4} \sin x \; dx$

$= -\cos x \Big|_{\pi/4}^{3\pi/4}$

$= -\cos \frac{3\pi}{4} - \left(-\cos \frac{\pi}{4}\right)$

$= \frac{\sqrt{2}}{2} - \left(-\frac{\sqrt{2}}{2}\right)$

$= \sqrt{2}$

36. $\int_{0}^{\infty} e^{-x} \cos x \; dx$

Use entry 48 of the table of integrals with $a = -1$, $b = 1$, and $u = x$.

$\int e^{-x} \cos x \; dx$

$= \frac{e^{-x}}{(-1)^2 + 1^2}(-\cos x + \sin x) + C$

$= \frac{e^{-x}}{2}(\sin x - \cos x) + C$

$$\int_0^\infty e^{-x} \cos x \, dx$$

$$= \lim_{b\to\infty} \int_0^b e^{-x} \cos x \, dx$$

$$= \lim_{b\to\infty} \frac{e^{-x}}{2}(\sin x - \cos x)\Big|_0^b$$

$$= \lim_{b\to\infty} \left\{ \frac{e^{-b}}{2}(\sin b - \cos b) - \left[\frac{1}{2}(0-1) \right] \right\}$$

$$= 0 + \frac{1}{2} = \frac{1}{2}$$

38. $T(t) = 50 + 50 \cos\left(\frac{\pi}{6}t\right)$

Since T is periodic, the number of animals passing the checkpoint is equal to the area under the curve for any 12-mo period. Let t vary from 0 to 12.

$$\text{Total} = \int_0^{12} \left[50 + 50 \cos\left(\frac{\pi}{6}t\right) \right] dt$$

$$= \int_0^{12} 50 \, dt + \frac{6}{\pi} \int_0^{12} 50 \cos\left(\frac{\pi}{6}t\right)\left(\frac{\pi}{6} \, dt\right)$$

$$= 50t \Big|_0^{12} + \frac{300}{\pi} \sin\left(\frac{\pi}{6}t\right)\Big|_0^{12}$$

$$= (600 - 0) + \frac{300}{\pi}(0 - 0)$$

$$= 600 \text{ (in hundreds)}$$

The total number of animals is 60,000.

Section 11.4

2. $y = \cos^{-1}(\sqrt{3}/2)$

By the definition of the inverse cosine function,

$$\cos y = \frac{\sqrt{3}}{2}.$$

Since $\cos \pi/6 = \sqrt{3}/2$ and $\pi/6$ is in $[0, \pi]$,

$$y = \cos^{-1} \frac{\sqrt{3}}{2} = \frac{\pi}{6}.$$

4. $y = \tan^{-1}(-1)$

By the definition of the inverse tangent function,

$$\tan y = -1.$$

Since $\tan(-\pi/4) = -1$ and $-\pi/4$ is in $(-\pi/2, \pi/2)$,

$$y = \tan^{-1}(-1) = -\frac{\pi}{4}.$$

6. $y = \cos^{-1}(-1)$

By the definition of the inverse cosine function,

$$\cos y = -1.$$

Since $\cos \pi = -1$ and π is in $[0, \pi]$,

$$y = \cos^{-1}(-1) = \pi.$$

8. $y = \sin^{-1}(-\sqrt{2}/2)$

By the definition of the inverse sine function,

$$\sin y = -\frac{\sqrt{2}}{2}.$$

Since $\sin(-\pi/4) = -\sqrt{2}/2$ and $-\pi/4$ is in $[-\pi/2, \pi/2]$,

$$y = \sin^{-1}\left(-\frac{\sqrt{2}}{2}\right) = -\frac{\pi}{4}.$$

10. $y = \tan^{-1}(\sqrt{3}/3)$

By the definition of the inverse tangent function,

$$\tan y = \frac{\sqrt{3}}{3}.$$

Since $\tan \pi/6 = \sqrt{3}/3$ and $\pi/6$ is in $(-\pi/2, \pi/2)$,

$$y = \tan^{-1}\frac{\sqrt{3}}{3} = \frac{\pi}{6}.$$

12. $y = \cos^{-1}(-1/2)$

By the definition of the inverse cosine function,

$$\cos y = -\frac{1}{2}.$$

Since $\cos 2\pi/3 = -1/2$ and $2\pi/3$ is in $[0, \pi]$,

$$y = \cos^{-1}\left(-\frac{1}{2}\right) = \frac{2\pi}{3}.$$

For Exercises 14–24, set calculator in degree mode.

14. $\cos^{-1}(-.1392)$

Enter .1392 $\boxed{+/-}$ $\boxed{\text{INV}}$ $\boxed{\cos}$

Display 98.00155635

$\cos^{-1}(-.1392) \approx 98°$

16. $\sin^{-1} .7880$

Enter .7880 $\boxed{\text{INV}}$ $\boxed{\sin}$

Display 51.99899924

$\sin^{-1} .7880 \approx 52°$

18. $\tan^{-1} 1.7321$

Enter 1.7321 $\boxed{\text{INV}}$ $\boxed{\tan}$

Display 60.00070461

$\tan^{-1} 1.7321 \approx 60°$

20. $\sin^{-1} .8192$

Enter .8192 $\boxed{\text{INV}}$ $\boxed{\sin}$

Display 55.00479068

$\sin^{-1} .8192 \approx 55°$

22. $\tan^{-1}(-.2867)$

Enter .2867 $\boxed{+/-}$ $\boxed{\text{INV}}$ $\boxed{\tan}$

Display -15.99759713

$\tan^{-1}(-.2867) \approx -16°$

24. $\cos^{-1} .4384$

Enter .4384 $\boxed{\text{INV}}$ $\boxed{\cos}$

Display 63.99816067

$\cos^{-1} .4384 \approx 64°$

26. $y = \cos^{-1} 10x$

$$y' = \frac{-1}{\sqrt{1 - (10x)^2}} \, D_x \, (10x)$$

$$= \frac{-10}{\sqrt{1 - 100x^2}}$$

28. $y = \sin^{-1}\left(\frac{1}{x}\right)$

$y' = \dfrac{1}{\sqrt{1 - \left(\frac{1}{x}\right)^2}}\; D_x\left(\frac{1}{x}\right)$

$ = \dfrac{1}{\sqrt{1 - \frac{1}{x^2}}} \cdot \left(-\frac{1}{x^2}\right)$

$ = \dfrac{-1}{x^2\sqrt{\frac{x^2 - 1}{x^2}}}$

$ = \dfrac{-1}{|x|\sqrt{x^2 - 1}}$

30. $y = \cos^{-1}\sqrt{x}$

$y' = \dfrac{-1}{\sqrt{1 - (\sqrt{x})^2}}\; D_x\left(\sqrt{x}\right)$

$ = \dfrac{-1}{2\sqrt{x}\sqrt{1 - x}}$

32. $y = \tan^{-1}(\ln |x + 2|)$

$y' = \dfrac{1}{1 + (\ln |x + 2|)^2}\; D_x(\ln |x + 2|)$

$ = \dfrac{1}{(x + 2)[1 + (\ln |x + 2|)^2]}$

34. $y = \ln |\tan^{-1}(3x - 5)|$

$y' = \dfrac{1}{\tan^{-1}(3x - 5)}\; D_x[\tan^{-1}(3x - 5)]$

$ = \dfrac{1}{\tan^{-1}(3x - 5)} \cdot \dfrac{1}{1 + (3x - 5)^2}D_x(3x - 5)$

$ = \dfrac{3}{[1 + (3x - 5)^2]\tan^{-1}(3x - 5)}$

38. $\displaystyle\int \dfrac{x^2}{\sqrt{1 - x^6}}\; dx$

Let $u = x^3$, so that $du = 3x^2\, dx$.

Then

$\displaystyle\int \dfrac{x^2}{\sqrt{1 - x^6}}\; dx = \dfrac{1}{3}\int \dfrac{3x^2}{\sqrt{1 - x^6}}\; dx$

$\phantom{\displaystyle\int \dfrac{x^2}{\sqrt{1 - x^6}}\; dx} = \dfrac{1}{3}\int \dfrac{1}{\sqrt{1 - u^2}}\; du$

$\phantom{\displaystyle\int \dfrac{x^2}{\sqrt{1 - x^6}}\; dx} = \dfrac{1}{3}\sin^{-1} u + C$

$\phantom{\displaystyle\int \dfrac{x^2}{\sqrt{1 - x^6}}\; dx} = \dfrac{1}{3}\sin^{-1} x^3 + C.$

40. $\displaystyle\int \dfrac{-e^{2x}}{1 + e^{4x}}\; dx$

Let $u = e^{2x}$, so that $du = 2e^{2x}\, dx$. Then

$\displaystyle\int \dfrac{-e^{2x}}{1 + e^{4x}}\; dx = -\dfrac{1}{2}\int \dfrac{2e^{2x}}{1 + (e^{2x})^2}\; dx$

$\phantom{\displaystyle\int \dfrac{-e^{2x}}{1 + e^{4x}}\; dx} = -\dfrac{1}{2}\int \dfrac{1}{1 + u^2}\; du$

$\phantom{\displaystyle\int \dfrac{-e^{2x}}{1 + e^{4x}}\; dx} = -\dfrac{1}{2}\tan^{-1} u + C$

$\phantom{\displaystyle\int \dfrac{-e^{2x}}{1 + e^{4x}}\; dx} = -\dfrac{1}{2}\tan^{-1} e^{2x} + C.$

42. $\displaystyle\int \dfrac{\cos x}{1 + \sin^2 x}\; dx$

Let $u = \sin x$, so that $du = \cos x\, dx$. Then

$\displaystyle\int \dfrac{\cos x}{1 + \sin^2 x}\; dx = \int \dfrac{1}{1 + u^2}\; du$

$\phantom{\displaystyle\int \dfrac{\cos x}{1 + \sin^2 x}\; dx} = \tan^{-1} u + C$

$\phantom{\displaystyle\int \dfrac{\cos x}{1 + \sin^2 x}\; dx} = \tan^{-1}(\sin x) + C.$

44. $\displaystyle\int \frac{1}{\sqrt{25 - x^2}}\ dx$

Let $u = \frac{x}{5}$, so that $du = \frac{1}{5}\ dx$. Then

$$\int \frac{1}{\sqrt{25 - x^2}}\ dx = \int \frac{1}{5\sqrt{1 - (x/5)^2}}\ dx$$

$$= \int \frac{1}{\sqrt{1 - u^2}}\ du$$

$$= \sin^{-1} u + C$$

$$= \sin^{-1} \frac{x}{5} + C.$$

46. $\displaystyle\int_0^{.5} \frac{1}{\sqrt{1 - x^2}}\ dx = \sin^{-1} x \Big|_0^{.5}$

$$= \sin^{-1} .5 - \sin^{-1} 0$$

$$= \frac{\pi}{6} - 0$$

$$\approx \frac{\pi}{6}$$

48. $\displaystyle\int_0^1 \frac{x^{1/3}}{1 + x^{8/3}}\ dx = \int_0^1 \frac{x^{1/3}}{1 + (x^{4/3})^2}\ dx$

Let $u = x^{4/3}$. Then $du = \frac{4}{3} x^{1/3}\ dx$.

If $x = 1$, $u = 1$. If $x = 0$, $u = 0$.

$$\int_0^1 \frac{x^{1/3}}{1 + x^{8/3}}\ dx = \frac{3}{4}\int_0^1 \frac{\frac{4}{3} x^{1/3}\ dx}{1 + (x^{4/3})^2}$$

$$= \frac{3}{4}\int_0^1 \frac{du}{1 + u^2}$$

$$= \frac{3}{4} \tan^{-1} u \Big|_0^1$$

$$= \frac{3}{4}(\tan^{-1} 1 - \tan^{-1} 0)$$

$$= \frac{3}{4}\left(\frac{\pi}{4} - 0\right)$$

$$= \frac{3\pi}{16}$$

50. Refer to the figure below.

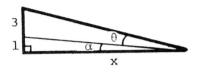

$\tan (\alpha + \theta) = \frac{4}{x}$ and $\tan \alpha = \frac{1}{x}$

$\alpha + \theta = \tan^{-1}\left(\frac{4}{x}\right)$ and $\alpha = \tan^{-1}\left(\frac{1}{x}\right)$

Thus,

$\tan^{-1}\left(\frac{1}{x}\right) + \theta = \tan^{-1}\left(\frac{4}{x}\right)$, and

$\theta = \tan^{-1}\left(\frac{4}{x}\right) - \tan^{-1}\left(\frac{1}{x}\right).$

52. $\theta = \tan^{-1}\left(\frac{4}{x}\right) - \tan^{-1}\left(\frac{1}{x}\right)$

$$\frac{d\theta}{dx} = \frac{-\frac{4}{x^2}}{1 + \left(\frac{4}{x}\right)^2} - \frac{-\frac{1}{x^2}}{1 + \left(\frac{1}{x}\right)^2}$$

$$= \frac{-4}{x^2 + 16} + \frac{1}{x^2 + 1}$$

$$= \frac{-4x^2 - 4 + x^2 + 16}{(x^2 + 16)(x^2 + 1)}$$

$$= \frac{-3x^2 + 12}{(x^2 + 16)(x^2 + 1)}$$

If $\frac{d\theta}{dx} = 0$, then

$$-3x^2 + 12 = 0$$

$$-3(x + 2)(x - 2) = 0$$

$$x = -2 \quad \text{or} \quad x = 2.$$

The value $x = -2$ is impossible in this problem.

If $x < 2$, $\dfrac{d\theta}{dx} > 0$.   If $x > 2$, $\dfrac{d\theta}{dx} < 0$.

Therefore, θ is maximum when $x = 2$.

To maximize θ, Patricia should stand 2 ft from the wall.

Section 11.5

2. Let $f(x) = \sin x$.

Then $f'(x) = \cos x$

and

$$f'\left(\frac{\pi}{4}\right) = \frac{\sqrt{2}}{2}.$$

The slope of the tangent line at $x = \pi/4$ is $\sqrt{2}/2$.

4. Let $f(x) = \cos x$.

Then $f'(x) = -\sin x$

and

$$f'\left(-\frac{\pi}{4}\right) = \frac{\sqrt{2}}{2}.$$

The slope of the tangent line at $x = -\pi/4$ is $\sqrt{2}/2$.

6. Let $f(x) = \cot x$.

Then $f'(x) = -\csc^2 x$

and

$$f'\left(\frac{\pi}{2}\right) = -\csc^2 \frac{\pi}{2}$$

$$= -\frac{1}{\sin^2 \frac{\pi}{2}}$$

$$= -\frac{1}{1} = -1.$$

The slope of the tangent line at $x = \pi/2$ is -1.

8. $f(.4) = 1000e^{2 \sin .4}$

$\approx 1000e^{2(.3894)}$

$\approx 1000(2.1789)$

≈ 2180

10. $f(.8) = 1000e^{2 \sin(.8)}$

$\approx 1000e^{2(.7174)}$

$\approx 1000(4.1988)$

≈ 4200

12. $f(1.4) = 1000e^{2 \sin(1.4)}$

$\approx 1000e^{2(.9854)}$

$\approx 1000(7.1764)$

≈ 7180

14. $f(2.3) = 1000e^{2 \sin(2.3)}$

$\approx 1000e^{2(.7457)}$

$\approx 1000(4.4433)$

≈ 4440

16. $f(3.1) = 1000e^{2 \sin(3.1)}$

$\approx 1000e^{2(.0416)}$

$\approx 1000(1.0868)$

≈ 1090

18. $f'(t) = 1000e^{2 \sin t}(2 \cos t) = 0$

when $\cos t = 0$.

Thus, critical points occur at

$$t = \frac{\pi}{2} + 2\pi n \text{ and } t = \frac{3\pi}{2} + 2\pi n$$

where n is any integer. Now

$$f\left(\frac{\pi}{2} + 2\pi n\right) = 1000e^{2(1)} \approx 7390$$

and this is the maximum value of f(t). Also

$$f\left(\frac{3\pi}{2} + 2\pi n\right) = 1000e^{2(-1)} \approx 135$$

and this is the minimum value of f(t).

20. The amplitude of $u(x, t)$ is A_0e^{-ax} where $A_0 = 11°C$ and $a = .00706$. If the amplitude is at most 1°C, then

$$11e^{-.00706x} \le 1$$

$$e^{-.00706x} \le \frac{1}{11}$$

$$-.0076x \le \ln\left(\frac{1}{11}\right)$$

$$x \ge \frac{\ln\left(\frac{1}{11}\right)}{-.00706}$$

$$x \ge 340.$$

The minimum depth is 340 cm.

22. The phase shift of $-ax$ accounts for the seasons at depth x lagging behind those at the surface. This phase shift must be π in order that it will be winter at depth x when it is summer at the surface. Therefore, $ax = \pi$ or $x = \frac{\pi}{a}$.

24. We draw θ in standard position.

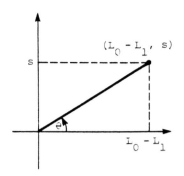

From this diagram, we see that

$$\sin\theta = \frac{s}{L_2}.$$

26. Using the sketch of θ in the solution to Exercise 24 and the definition of cotangent, we see that

$$\cot\theta = \frac{L_0 - L_1}{s}.$$

28. The length of AD is L_1, and the radius of that section of blood vessel is r_1, so the general equation $k = \frac{L}{r^4}$ is similar to $R_1 = k\frac{L_1}{r_1^4}$ for that particular segment of the blood vessel.

30. $R = R_1 + R_2$

$$= k\frac{L_1}{r_1^4} + k\frac{L_2}{r_2^4}$$

$$= k\left(\frac{L_1}{r_1^4} + \frac{L_2}{r_2^4}\right)$$

32. Since k, L_1, L_0, s, r_1, and r_2 are all constants, the only letter left as a variable is θ, so the differentiation indicated in the symbol R' must be differentiation with respect to θ.

$R' = D_\theta R$

$= D_\theta \left(k\frac{L_0}{r_1{}^4} - \frac{s}{r_1{}^4} \cot \theta + \frac{s}{r_2{}^4} \cdot \frac{1}{\sin \theta} \right)$

$= kD_\theta \left(\frac{L_0}{r_1{}^4} - \frac{s}{r_1{}^4} \cot \theta + \frac{s}{r_2{}^4} \cdot \frac{1}{\sin \theta} \right)$

$= k\left[D_\theta \left(\frac{L_0}{r_1{}^4} \right) - D_\theta \left(\frac{s}{r_1{}^4} \cot \theta \right) \right.$

$\left. \qquad + D_\theta \left(\frac{s}{r_2{}^4} \cdot \frac{1}{\sin \theta} \right) \right]$

$= k\left[0 - \frac{s}{r_1{}^4} D_\theta (\cot \theta) + \frac{s}{r_2{}^4} D_\theta \left(\frac{1}{\sin \theta} \right) \right]$

$= k\left[-\frac{s}{r_1{}^4} (-\csc^2 \theta) + \frac{s}{r_2{}^4} \left(\frac{-\cos \theta}{\sin^2 \theta} \right) \right]$

$= k\left(\frac{s}{r_1{}^4} \cdot \frac{1}{\sin^2 \theta} - \frac{s}{r_2{}^4} \cdot \frac{\cos \theta}{\sin^2 \theta} \right)$

$= \frac{ks}{\sin^2 \theta} \left(\frac{1}{r_2{}^4} - \frac{\cos \theta}{r_2{}^4} \right)$

$= \frac{ks \csc^2 \theta}{r_1{}^4} - \frac{kx \cos \theta}{r_2{}^4 \sin^2 \theta}$

34. If the last equation in the solution to Exercise 31 is multiplied by $\frac{\sin^2 \theta}{s}$, we get

$\frac{\sin^2 \theta}{s} \cdot \frac{ks}{\sin^2 \theta} \left(\frac{1}{r_1{}^4} - \frac{\cos \theta}{r_2{}^4} \right)$

$\qquad = 0 \cdot \frac{\sin^2 \theta}{s}$

$k\left(\frac{1}{r_1{}^4} - \frac{\cos \theta}{r_2{}^4} \right)$

$\qquad = 0.$

36. If $r_1 = 1$ and $r_2 = \frac{1}{4}$, then

$\cos \theta = \left(\frac{\frac{1}{4}}{1} \right)^4 = \left(\frac{1}{4} \right)^4$

$\qquad = \frac{1}{256} \approx .0039;$

from which we get

$\qquad \theta \approx 90°.$

Chapter 11   Review Exercises

4. Exact values for the trigonometric functions can be determined for any integer multiple of $\frac{\pi}{6}$ or $\frac{\pi}{4}$.

6. $120° = 120\left(\frac{\pi}{180} \right) = \frac{2\pi}{3}$

8. $270° = 270\left(\frac{\pi}{180} \right) = \frac{3\pi}{2}$

10. $420° = 420\left(\frac{\pi}{180} \right) = \frac{7\pi}{3}$

12. $\frac{3\pi}{4} = \frac{3\pi}{4}\left(\frac{180°}{\pi} \right) = 135°$

14. $\frac{7\pi}{15} = \frac{7\pi}{15}\left(\frac{180°}{\pi} \right) = 84°$

16. $\frac{11\pi}{15} = \frac{11\pi}{15}\left(\frac{180°}{\pi} \right) = 132°$

18. When an angle of 120° is drawn in standard position, $(x, y) = (-1, \sqrt{3})$ is one point on its terminal side. So

$\qquad \tan 120° = \frac{y}{x} = -\sqrt{3}.$

20. When an angle of 45° is drawn in standard position, $(x, y) = (1, 1)$ is one point on its terminal side. Then

$\qquad r = \sqrt{1 + 1} = \sqrt{2}.$

So

$\qquad \sec 45° = \frac{r}{x} = \sqrt{2}.$

22. When an angle of 300° is drawn in standard position, $(x, y) = (1, -\sqrt{3})$ is one point on it terminal side. So

$$\cot 300° = \frac{x}{y} = -\frac{1}{\sqrt{3}} = -\frac{\sqrt{3}}{3}.$$

24. When an angle of $\frac{2\pi}{3}$ is drawn in standard position, $(x, y) = (-1, \sqrt{3})$ is one point on its terminal side. Then

$$r = \sqrt{1 + 3} = 2.$$

So

$$\cos \frac{2\pi}{3} = \frac{x}{r} = -\frac{1}{2}.$$

26. When an angle of $\frac{7\pi}{3}$ is drawn in standard position, $(x, y) = (1, \sqrt{3})$ is one point on its terminal side. Then

$$r = \sqrt{1 + 3} = 2.$$

So

$$\csc \frac{7\pi}{3} = \frac{r}{y} = \frac{2}{\sqrt{3}} = \frac{2\sqrt{3}}{3}.$$

28. $\cos 59° \approx .5150$

30. $\sin (-32°) \approx -.5299$

32. $\cos .3142 \approx .9510$

34. $\tan 1.2915 \approx 3.4868$

36. Let $y = \sin^{-1}\left(-\frac{1}{2}\right)$. Then, by the definition of the inverse sine function,

$$\sin y = -\frac{1}{2}.$$

Since $\sin(-\pi/6) = -1/2$ and $-\pi/6$ is in $[-\pi/2, \pi/2]$,

$$y = \sin^{-1}\left(-\frac{1}{2}\right) = -\frac{\pi}{6}.$$

38. Let $y = \cos^{-1} 1$. Then, by definition of the inverse cosine function,

$$\cos y = 1.$$

Since $\cos 0 = 1$ and 0 is in $[0, \pi]$,

$$y = \cos^{-1} 1 = 0.$$

40. Let $y = \sin^{-1}(-1)$. Then, by the definition of the inverse sine function,

$$\sin y = -1.$$

Since $\sin(-\pi/2) = -1$ and $-\pi/2$ is in $[-\pi/2, \pi/2]$,

$$y = \sin^{-1} 1 = -\frac{\pi}{2}.$$

42. Because the derivative of $y = \sin x$ is $y' = \cos x$, the slope of $y = \sin x$ varies from -1 to 1.

44. The graph of $y = \frac{1}{2} \tan x$ is similar to the graph of $y = \tan x$ except that each ordinate value is multiplied by a factor of $1/2$. Note that the points $(\pi/4, 1/2)$ and $(-\pi/4, -1/2)$ lie on the graph.

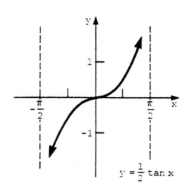

$$y = \frac{1}{2}\tan x$$

46. The graph of y = -2 sin x is similar to the graph of y = sin x except that it has twice the amplitude and is reflected about the x–axis.

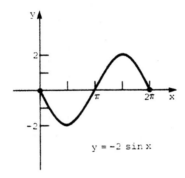

$$y = -2\sin x$$

48. $y = 6 \tan 3x$

$y' = 6 \sec^2 3x \cdot D_x(3x)$

$\quad = 18 \sec^2 3x$

50. $y = \cot(9 - x^2)$

$y' = [-\csc^2(9 - x^2)] \cdot D_x(9 - x^2)$

$\quad = 2x \csc^2(9 - x^2)$

52. $y = 2 \sin^4(4x^2)$

$y' = [8 \sin^3(4x^2)] \cdot D_x[\sin(4x^2)]$

$\quad = 8 \sin^3(4x^2) \cdot \cos(4x^2) \cdot D_x(4x^2)$

$\quad = 64x \sin^3(4x^2)\cos (4x^2)$

54. $y = \cos(1 + x^2)$

$y' = [-\sin(1 + x^2)] \cdot D_x(1 + x^2)$

$\quad = -2x \sin(1 + x^2)$

56. $y = e^{-x} \sin x$

$y' = e^{-x} \cdot D_x(\sin x) + \sin x \cdot D_x(e^{-x})$

$\quad = e^{-x} \cos x - e^{-x} \sin x$

$\quad = e^{-x}(\cos x \sin x)$

58. $y = \dfrac{\cos^2 x}{1 - \cos x}$

$y' = \dfrac{(1 - \cos x)(-2 \cos x \sin x) - (\cos^2 x)(\sin x)}{(1 - \cos x)^2}$

$\quad = \dfrac{-2 \cos x \sin x + \cos^2 x \sin x}{(1 - \cos x)^2}$

60. $y = \dfrac{\tan x}{1 + x}$

$y' = \dfrac{(1 + x)(\sec^2 x) - (\tan x)(1)}{(1 + x)^2}$

$\quad = \dfrac{\sec^2 x + x \sec^2 x - \tan x}{(1 + x)^2}$

62. $y = \ln |5 \sin x|$

$y' = \dfrac{1}{5 \sin x} \cdot D_x(5 \sin x)$

$\quad = \dfrac{\cos x}{\sin x}$

$\quad$ or $\cot x$

64. $y = \tan^{-1}(1 + x)$

$y' = \dfrac{1}{1 + (1 + x)^2} \cdot D_x(1 + x)$

$\quad = \dfrac{1}{1 + (1 + x)^2}$

$\quad = \dfrac{1}{2 + 2x + x^2}$

66. $y = \sin^{-1}(2 - x)$

$y' = \dfrac{1}{\sqrt{1 - (2 - x)^2}} \cdot D_x(2 - x)$

$= \dfrac{-1}{\sqrt{1 - (2 - x)^2}}$

$= = \dfrac{-1}{\sqrt{-3 + 4x - x^2}}$

68. $\displaystyle\int \cos 3x \; dx$

Let $u = 3x$, so that $du = 3 \; dx$.

$\displaystyle\int \cos 3x \; dx = \frac{1}{3} \int (\cos 3x)(3 \; dx)$

$= \dfrac{1}{3} \displaystyle\int \cos u \; du$

$= \dfrac{1}{3} \sin u + C$

$= \dfrac{1}{3} \sin 3x + C$

70. $\displaystyle\int \sec^2 5x \; dx$

Let $u = 5x$, so that $du = 5 \; dx$.

$\displaystyle\int \sec^2 5x \; dx = \frac{1}{5} \int (\sec^2 5x)(5 \; dx)$

$= \dfrac{1}{5} \displaystyle\int \sec^2 u \; du$

$= \dfrac{1}{5} \tan u + C$

$= \dfrac{1}{5} \tan 5x + C$

72. $\displaystyle\int 4 \csc^2 x \; dx = -4 \int -\csc^2 x \; dx$

$= -4 \cot x + C$

74. $\displaystyle\int 5x \cos 2x^2 \; dx$

Let $u = 2x^2$, so that $du = 4x \; dx$.

$\displaystyle\int 5x \cos 2x^2 \; dx = \frac{5}{4} \int \cos u \; du$

$= \dfrac{5}{4} \sin u + C$

$= \dfrac{5}{4} \sin 2x^2 + C$

76. $\displaystyle\int \sin^4 x \cos x \; dx$

Let $u = \sin x$, so that
$du = \cos x \; dx$.

$\displaystyle\int \sin^4 x \cos x \; dx = \int u^4 \; du$

$= \dfrac{1}{5} u^5 + C$

$= \dfrac{1}{5} \sin^5 x + C$

78. $\displaystyle\int x^2 \cot 8x^3 \; dx$

Let $u = 8x^3$, so that $du = 24x^2 \; dx$.

$\displaystyle\int x^2 \cot 8x^3 \; dx$

$= \dfrac{1}{24} \displaystyle\int (\cot 8x^3)(24x^2) dx$

$= \dfrac{1}{24} \displaystyle\int \cot u \; du$

$= \dfrac{1}{24} \ln |\sin u| + C$

$= \dfrac{1}{24} \ln |\sin 8x^3| + C$

80. $\int (\cos x)^{-4/3} \sin x \, dx$

Let $u = \cos x$, so that
$$du = -\sin x \, dx.$$

$\int (\cos x)^{-4/3} \sin x \, dx$

$\quad = -\int (\cos x)^{-4/3} (-\sin x) dx$

$\quad = -\int u^{-4/3} \, du$

$\quad = 3u^{-1/3} + C$

$\quad = 3(\cos x)^{-1/3} + C$

82. $\int \dfrac{4}{1 + x^2} \, dx = 4 \int \dfrac{1}{1 + x^2} \, dx$

$\qquad\qquad\qquad = 4 \tan^{-1} x + C$

84. $\int \dfrac{-12x^2}{\sqrt{1 - x^6}} \, dx$

Let $u = x^3$, so that $du = 3x^2 \, dx$.

$\int \dfrac{-12x^2}{\sqrt{1 - x^6}} \, dx$

$\quad = -4 \int \dfrac{3x^2}{\sqrt{1 - (x^3)^2}} \, dx$

$\quad = -4 \int \dfrac{1}{\sqrt{1 - x^2}} \, du$

$\quad = -4 \sin^{-1} u + C$

or $\quad 4 \cos^{-1} u + C$

$\quad = -4 \sin^{-1} x^3 + C$

or $4 \cos^{-1} x^3 + C$

86. $\int_{\pi/2}^{\pi} \sin x \, dx$

$\quad = -\cos x \Big|_{\pi/2}^{\pi}$

$\quad = -\cos \pi - \left(-\cos \dfrac{\pi}{2}\right)$

$\quad = 1 - 0 = 1$

88. $\int_{0}^{2\pi} (5 + 5 \sin x) dx$

$\quad = \int_{0}^{2\pi} 5 \, dx + \int_{0}^{2\pi} 5 \sin x \, dx$

$\quad = 5x \Big|_{0}^{2\pi} + (-5 \cos x) \Big|_{0}^{2\pi}$

$\quad = (10\pi - 0) + [-5 - (-5)]$

$\quad = 10\pi$

92. $P(x) = 90 + 15 \sin 144\pi t$

The maximum possible value of $\sin \alpha$, for any expresion α, is 1, while the minimum possible value is -1. Replacing α with $144\pi t$ gives

$$-1 \le \sin 144\pi t \le 1,$$
$$90 + 15(-1) \le P(t) \le 90 + 15(1)$$
$$75 \le P(t) \le 105.$$

Therefore the minimum value of $P(t)$ is 75 and the maximum value of $P(t)$ is 105.

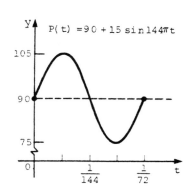

94. Let the viewing angle be θ.

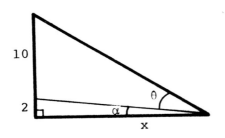

If $x < \sqrt{24} \approx 4.90$, $\dfrac{d\theta}{dx} > 0$.

If $x > \sqrt{24} \approx 4.90$, $\dfrac{d\theta}{dx} < 0$.

Therefore, θ is maximum when $x = \sqrt{24}$.

To maximize the angle, a viewer should sit $\sqrt{24}$ ft ≈ 4.90 ft from the screen.

$\tan(\theta + \alpha) = \dfrac{12}{x}$ and $\tan \alpha = \dfrac{2}{x}$

$\theta + \alpha = \tan^{-1}\left(\dfrac{12}{x}\right)$ and $\alpha \ \tan^{-1}\left(\dfrac{2}{x}\right)$

Thus,

$\theta = \tan^{-1}\left(\dfrac{12}{x}\right) - \alpha$

$\theta = \tan^{-1}\left(\dfrac{12}{x}\right) - \tan^{-1}\left(\dfrac{2}{x}\right)$

$\dfrac{d\theta}{dx} = \dfrac{-\dfrac{12}{x^2}}{1 + \left(\dfrac{12}{x}\right)^2} - \dfrac{-\dfrac{2}{x^2}}{1 + \left(\dfrac{2}{x}\right)^2}$

$= \dfrac{-12}{x^2 + 144} + \dfrac{2}{x^2 + 4}$

$= \dfrac{-12x^2 - 48 + 2x^2 + 288}{(x^2 + 144)(x^2 + 4)}$

$= \dfrac{-10x^2 + 240}{(x^2 + 144)(x^2 + 4)}$

If $\dfrac{d\theta}{dx} = 0$, then

$$-10x^2 + 240 = 0$$
$$x^2 = 24$$
$$x = \pm\sqrt{24}.$$

The value $x = -\sqrt{24}$ is impossible in this problem.

NOTES

NOTES

NOTES

NOTES